WITHDRAWN
NDSU

LONDON RECORD SOCIETY
PUBLICATIONS

VOLUME VII
FOR THE YEAR 1971

THE CARTULARY OF
HOLY TRINITY
ALDGATE

EDITED BY
GERALD A. J. HODGETT

LONDON RECORD SOCIETY
1971

© *London Record Society, 1971*
SBN 9009 5204 0

DA
676
H64
1971

THIS VOLUME IS PUBLISHED WITH THE HELP
OF A GRANT FROM THE TWENTY-SEVEN
FOUNDATION

Printed in Great Britain by
W & J MACKAY & CO LTD, CHATHAM, KENT

CONTENTS

PREFACE	vii
ABBREVIATIONS	ix
INTRODUCTION	xi
THE ILLUMINATIONS IN THE CARTULARY: A NOTE. By Professor Francis Wormald	xxii
CHRONOLOGICAL TABLE OF CONTENTS	xxiv
THE CARTULARY OF HOLY TRINITY ALDGATE	1
APPENDIX	223
GENERAL INDEX	236
NOTE ON THE LONDON RECORD SOCIETY	291

PREFACE

By publishing this calendar of the Cartulary of Holy Trinity Aldgate the London Record Society has made available a source important both for the topography and for the social and economic history of medieval London. My first duty is to acknowledge my deep debt to the University of Glasgow, the custodian of the Register, and especially to the University Librarian, Mr. R. O. MacKenna, who unhesitatingly sent the manuscript on loan to the Institute of Historical Research in London for a lengthy period and helped me on subsequent visits to Glasgow.

My thanks are also due to many scholars with whom I have discussed the problems of this edition over the years, and especially to Professor R. B. Pugh, Dr. C. J. Holdsworth, Dr. A. E. J. Hollaender of the Guildhall Library, Mr. Godfrey R. C. Davis and Mrs. A. Payne of the British Museum. Professor C. N. L. Brooke has saved me from the commission of many errors by reading through the typescript and suggesting emendations, and his research assistant Mrs. Gillian Keir from her knowledge of the original deeds has helped me with many difficulties in their cartulary copies. To Professor Francis Wormald I am doubly indebted both for his advice and for his note on the illuminations. Miss J. F. Payne helped to compile the large card catalogue upon which the index is based. Despite this help, errors for which I am alone responsible may remain. Had space and time permitted, I should like to have collated the Cartulary text with B.M. Lansdowne MS. 448, but my plea in extenuation must be that the Hunterian manuscript is a large one and that its publication has already been too long delayed.

G.A.J.H.

King's College, London

ABBREVIATIONS

B.M.	British Museum
C.A.D.	*Descriptive Catalogue of Ancient Deeds in the Public Record Office.* 6 vols. (1890–1915)
C.Ch.R.	*Calendar of Charter Rolls*
C.I.P.M.	*Calendar of Inquisitions post Mortem*
C.P.R.	*Calendar of Patent Rolls*
C. Wills	*Calendar of Wills enrolled in the Husting*, ed. R. R. Sharpe. 2 vols. (1889–90)
Cal. Letter-Bk. C	*Calendar of Letter-Book C*, ed. R. R. Sharpe (1901)
Camb. Hist. J.	*Cambridge Historical Journal*
Cart. Antiq. i, ii	*The Cartae Antiquae* [i] *Rolls 1–10*, ed. L. Landon; [ii] *Rolls 11–20*, ed. J. Conway Davis (Pipe Roll Society, new series, xvii and xxxiii, 1938–57)
Cat. Hunt. MSS.	*Catalogue of the Manuscripts in the Library of the Hunterian Museum,* by John Young and P. Henderson Aitken (1908)
def(s).	defendant(s)
Facs. Nat. MSS.	*Facsimiles of National MSS.* 4 pts. (Ordnance Survey Office, 1865–8)
H.R.	Husting Rolls (in Corporation of London Records Office)
L.M.A.S. *Trans.*	London and Middlesex Archaeological Society *Transactions*
Liber Albus	*Munimenta Gildhallae Londoniensis*, ed. H. T. Riley, i and iii, *Liber Albus* (Rolls Series, 1859–62)
London possessory assizes	*London possessory assizes*, ed. H. M. Chew (London Record Society, i, 1965)
Monasticon	*Monasticon Anglicanum*, by W. Dugdale, new edn., ed. J. Caley, H. Ellis and B. Bandinel. 6 vols. in 8 (1817–30)
P.R.O.	Public Record Office
P.R.S., x	*Ancient Charters*, ed. J. H. Round (Pipe Roll Society, x, 1888)
pl(s).	plaintiff(s)
R.H.S. *Trans.*	Royal Historical Society *Transactions*
Reg. A.-N.	*Regesta Regum Anglo-Normannorum, 1066–1154*, ed. H. W. C. Davis (and others). 4 vols. (1913–69)
Stow, *Survey*	*Survey of London*, by John Stow, ed. C. L. Kingsford. 2 vols. (1908)
V.C.H.	*Victoria History of the Counties of England*

INTRODUCTION

The Manuscript

The cartulary of the Augustinian priory of Holy Trinity (otherwise called Christ Church) has been in the custody of the University of Glasgow since 1807. It is MS. U.2.6 of the manuscripts in the Hunterian Museum Library and forms part of the collection bequeathed by Dr. William Hunter, a famous London surgeon and obstetrician, to his old university. Who acquired the cartulary upon the dissolution of the priory in 1532 is not known, but it was in the hands of Dr. Stephen Batman, an Elizabethan antiquary, who helped Archbishop Parker to collect the library now in Corpus Christi College, Cambridge, and it was used by John Stow in his *Survey of London*.[1] Batman signed his name on f. 203 and made a rather unsuccessful attempt at an Anglo-Saxon script and elsewhere wrote part of the Lord's Prayer in the same script (**341**). William Dugdale, in 1661, does not appear to have known about the manuscript, neither did Dr. Thomas Tanner in 1695, but the 1744 edition of his *Notitia Monastica* refers to it. A letter dated 27 January 1713/14 prefixed to the cartulary shows that Tanner knew that John Anstis had acquired it at least two months before that date. John Anstis, who was Garter King of Arms from 1718 until his death in 1744, was a noted collector of manuscripts, and Tanner writing to him from Norwich expressed the view in his letter that the cartulary had been written by Thomas de Axbridge, owned by Batman, much used by Stow and that it had been much enquired after in the contest between Dr. White Kennett and Dr. Richard Hollingsworth.[2] Thomas Hearne also used the cartulary when it belonged to Anstis and printed ff. 1–7 in his edition of William of Newburgh's *Historia* published in 1719.[3] Tanner, as another letter from Norwich prefixed to the manuscript shows, borrowed the cartulary in 1720–1. John Stevens, in his two volumes which appeared in 1722–3 as a supplement to Dugdale's *Monasticon*, printed in translation ff. 1–8, 149–50 and 179–96 and indicated in his preface that Garter King of Arms had 'courteously furnished a very curious Register Book of the Monastery of Regular Canons of the Holy Trinity, near Aldgate, London'. William Maitland also used the register in the preparation of the second edition of his *History of London* which appeared in 1756. On the other hand, Richard Newcourt appears to have relied upon Stow and not to have known of the cartulary's existence when he was preparing (probably in the last decade of the seventeenth century) the first volume of his *Repertorium* (1708).

The cartulary was apparently unknown and unused between 1603 when the second edition of Stow's *Survey* appeared and some time between 1708

1. Stow, *Survey*, i, 29, 120–3.
2. See G. V. Bennett, *White Kennett, 1660–1728* (1957), 178.
3. William of Newburgh, *Historia*, iii, 687, e Registro scilicet sive Rentali perveteri Anstisiano cuius in praefatione mentionem feci.

Introduction

and 1713. It seems highly improbable that its whereabouts during the seventeenth century will ever be traced, but it was also 'lost' in the nineteenth century. Caley, Ellis and Bandinel when they revised Dugdale's *Monasticon* did not find it.[1] During that century scholars relied either upon a transcript of the register made according to R. R. Sharpe about 1769,[2] but in fact probably written about 1840–1,[3] or upon copies of certain charters and narrative parts of the cartulary which appear in the City's Letter-Book C and Liber Dunthorn, the former being the more reliable. H. C. Coote[4] did not know of the cartulary, W. J. Loftie[5] recorded its existence in a footnote but did not use it, Charles Gross[6] used Letter-Book C and J. H. Round does not appear to have known of the register's existence in 1888[7] or 1892.[8] But by 1899[9] Round had discovered it in the University of Glasgow. Sharpe referred to it in his calendar of Letter-Book C in 1901 and Dr. P. Henderson Aitken completed the *Catalogue of the Manuscripts in the Library of the Hunterian Museum in the University of Glasgow* begun by Dr. John Young and saw it through the press in 1908. Only between 1892 and 1899 did the cartulary become again known to medievalists generally, despite its listing in the appendix[10] to the *Third Report* of the Historical Manuscripts Commission as early as 1872.

From its acquisition by John Anstis in or shortly before 1713 the cartulary remained the property of himself and his son until it was sold to Thomas Astle on Wednesday 14 December 1768 for £10 5s.,[11] but it must have been sold by him to Hunter before the latter's death on 30 March 1783. Hunter in fact had put in a bid of 5 guineas at the sale. In all probability he acquired it some time between the establishment of his museum in Great Windmill Street in 1769–70 and his death and he may well have owned it when Andrew Coltee Ducarel examined it in 1773 or 1779.[12] By Hunter's will the collections were left to three trustees for a period of thirty years[13] and thereafter to the University of Glasgow.

The description (item 215) in the *Catalogue of the Manuscripts in the Library of the Hunterian Museum*, supplemented by the note on the illuminations written by Professor Francis Wormald,[14] is so full that no further account of the physical characteristics of the cartulary is necessary. It was written by Thomas de Axbridge between 1425 and 1427 and he tells us that he made use of ancient books and arranged his work according to parishes and listed the property of the house held in each parish with the names of

1. *Monasticon*, vi, pt. 1, 151.
2. *Cal. Letter-Bk. C*, p. xvii n. 2.
3. Guildhall MS. 122: the watermarks in the paper are dated 1839–41.
4. L.M.A.S. *Trans.*, v (1881), 477 *et seq.*
5. *History of London*, i (1884), 163 n.
6. C. Gross, *Gild Merchant* (2 vols. 1890), i, 186 n.9.
7. P.R.S. x, 3 n.
8. *Geoffrey de Mandeville* (1892), 309.
9. *Commune of London* (1899), 97.
10. *Third Report, Appendix*, 424b.
11. *Cat. of Sale by S. Baker & G. Leigh*, B.M., S.-C.S. 7 (3).
12. *Cat. Hunt. MSS.*, 159, and A. C. Ducarel, 'History of the hospital of St. Katharine', *Bibliotheca Topographica Britannica*, ii (1790), 1.
13. *Cat. Hunt. MSS.*, p. ix (cf. *D.N.B.*).
14. See p. xxii below.

Introduction

tenants, rather than grouping all grants and concessions made by priors in chronological order (**31**). All this he did because of the demand for written evidence when disputes arose over payments of quit rent to the house. There is no evidence which leads us to believe that Thomas was negligent in his work, but concerning some matters he was ill informed. While he is reasonably accurate in his information concerning the twelfth and fourteenth centuries, he is inaccurate about the thirteenth, and his list of priors, although Caley, Ellis and Bandinel did something to revise it,[1] misled writers on Holy Trinity for five centuries. On occasions he could not read the documents which he was copying and this led him to write names which, from other sources, can be shown to be wrong. The foundation and other charters in the first seven folios are connected by pieces of narrative, which, along with the passage on the soke (ff. 149–50), provide a fairly full history of the house. These chronicles would seem to be a feature of the cartularies of Augustinian houses.[2]

The passage on the boundaries of the soke of Aldgate is an important source for the topography of twelfth-century London and it defines, at an early date, the limits of the ward of Aldgate. Folio 149 (**871**) contains an account of the English *Cnihtengild*, an institution which has been learnedly discussed by, among others, Gross,[3] F. M. Stenton[4] and F. E. Harmer[5] and upon which the present editor has no further contribution to offer. Again, great importance lies in the territorial definition of the soke for the boundaries given are those of Portsoken ward of which the prior some time after 1125 became *ex-officio* alderman. **960** illustrates the difficulties which the house had in exercising its privileges over the soke against two custodians of the Tower of London. The narrative passage (**986**) supplements the charter evidence on the relationship between the hospital of St. Katherine and Holy Trinity and demonstrates vividly the ill will between the house and Henry III's consort, Queen Eleanor. Folio 208 contains a list of early mayors and sheriffs. Thus it will be seen that the narrative passages, which form an integral part of the cartulary, are of considerable historical importance.

The foundation and importance of the priory

According to the opening narrative or *Historia*, Holy Trinity, also known as Christ Church, was founded in 1108 by Matilda, queen consort of Henry I, on a site where a certain Syredus had begun to establish a church which owed an annual rent of 30s. to the dean and chapter of Waltham Holy Cross. It was in some way subject to Waltham, for Matilda's charter (**4**) specifically exempts Holy Trinity from all subjection to any church save St. Paul's. The group of secular canons under a dean who lived at Waltham in Essex had been established there since 1060,[6] so it cannot be certainly

---

1. *Monasticon*, vi, pt. 1, 150–1.
2. e.g. Dunstable priory has a draft of the Annales in its cartulary, B. M. Harl. MS. 1885.
3. C. Gross, *Gild Merchant*, i, 186.
4. F. M. Stenton, *Norman London: an essay*, Historical Association Leaflets, 93–4 (1934).
5. F. E. Harmer, *Anglo-Saxon Writs* (1952), 231–4.
6. *V.C.H. Essex*, ii, 166.

Introduction

known when Syredus began to found his church or how far he had progressed with it when Matilda decided upon her foundation for canons regular. On Anselm's advice she gave the governance of the house to Norman, who is said to have been the first Augustinian in England.[1]

Doubtless there were many groups of secular canons in the country who were seeking some rule[2] by which to live and the Gregorian reform had introduced an element of compulsion to accept one. Such a rule was devised for secular canons on the Continent in the last quarter of the eleventh century and attributed to St. Augustine. Norman, who had studied under Anselm in France, probably at Bec, knew enough about the so-called rule of St. Augustine to inform the canons of St. Botolph's Colchester that it would be a suitable one for them to follow. Ainulf the priest of St. Botolph's asked him to find out more about the rule and Archbishop Anselm provided him with an introduction to the prior and convent of Mont-St.-Éloi, a house some six miles north-west of Arras. Although the chronicle does not mention this house further, it informs us that Norman and his brother went both to Chartres and Beauvais and perhaps it is reasonable to assume that Norman undertook this journey after Anselm's return to England in September 1106, unless he wrote to the prelate or sought him out on the Continent during his exile in order to obtain the introductory letter.[3] After his visit Norman returned to Colchester and the group of canons there accepted the Augustinian rule, Ainulf becoming prior and Norman one of the canons. Colchester readily agreed to Norman's departure, a move which may or may not argue that the house was well established[4] when he was called by the queen to preside over her new foundation in London on 5 April 1108. However, the date 5 April 1107 is also given[5] for Norman's creation: this may be a scribal error or may indicate that the foundation was a year earlier.

From the first, the house had powerful patrons; the king and queen, the archbishop of Canterbury and Richard de Belmeis I, bishop of London. Richard was elected bishop on 24 May 1108 and consecrated on 26 July of that year, so that Matilda's foundation charter (**4**) and Henry I's confirmation (**2**) of it addressed to Richard must post-date the actual establishment of the house. This was not unusual.[6] It was originally endowed with the gate of Aldgate and the soke belonging to it and with £25 *blanch* from the city of Exeter which formed part of the queen's income. Norman appears, from the beginning, to have spent lavishly on buildings, books, ornaments and vestments to such an extent that food was in short supply. But the priory immediately became popular with the citizens of London and some women decided that each of them would provide a loaf on Sundays for the canons; a practice which assured the bread supply for the rest of the week.

1. **4** and see J. C. Dickinson, *Origin of the Austin Canons and their introduction into England* (1950), 98 *et seq.*
2. For the fullest account of the history of Holy Trinity see *V.C. H. London*, i, 465–75
3 and 4. For differing views, see Dickinson, *op. cit.*
5. For a detailed discussion of the earliest Augustinian foundations, see Dickinson, *op. cit.*, especially, 109 n. 3.
6. V. H. Galbraith, 'Monastic foundation charters of the 11th and 12th centuries', *Camb. Hist. J.*, iv, no. 3 (1934), 205–22.

Introduction

After Matilda's death in May 1118, Henry I[1] continued to favour the house, allowing it to close a road between the conventual buildings and the wall of the City (**12**), but he did not give all the land which the queen had wished Holy Trinity to have (**13**). But the financial position of the priory was improving even before the grant of the soke of the English *Cnihtengild* in 1125. This grant conveyed to the priory an area later known as the ward of Portsoken. The acquisition of superiority over such a large area and of rights over the church of St. Botolph without Aldgate certainly helped towards the doubling of the priory's income which Norman achieved (**13**). The house suffered from a disastrous fire in 1132 (**13**) when one of the frequent medieval miracles occurred, on that occasion the saving of a wooden cross, and again during Ralph's priorate it was damaged by fire (**31**).

Ralph, the second prior, was on close terms with Stephen and Matilda and he acted as confessor to the queen as Norman had done to Henry I's consort. Under his sagacious rule, the rents due to the priory doubled in value, although he initiated the policy of selling land with a perpetual reserved rent in order to pay for the rebuilding after the fire. It was during his tenure of office that Queen Matilda founded the hospital of St. Katherine[2] in 1147 or 1148 on land which Holy Trinity had released to her and for which it was given compensation (**973-4**). The link with the new hospital was obviously intended to be a close one, for Holy Trinity was to have perpetual custody of it (**975**), which authority the priory maintained until 1261. Again, as in Henry I's reign, the king and queen were good friends to Holy Trinity, for they helped to secure the return of land which Geoffrey de Mandeville had seized from the house (**961**). Although Henry II did not apparently take so keen an interest in the priory, it remained within the royal circle. It can be fairly asserted that, for eighty years after its foundation and until new religious orders were attracting greater attention, the Augustinian order remained popular and the number of communities living according to its rule expanded. Holy Trinity, situated as it was in the leading English city and on the doorstep of one of the most important royal residences, remained the foremost house of regular canons and established several daughter communities.[3]

The chronicle tells us little of the work of the third prior Stephen, if indeed he merits that number, for during the vacancy from 1167 to 1170 Edmund, Osbern and William are mentioned.[4] During Stephen's priorate from 1170 to 1197 and that of his successor, Peter of Cornwall, from 1197 to 1221 a steady growth in the priory's prosperity may be assumed from the increasing number of grants made by these two priors. Peter increased the prestige of the house by his scholarship for he was one of the foremost theologians of his day (**16**). But the greatest business activity took place

---

1. R. W. Southern, 'The Place of Henry I in English History', *Proceedings of the British Academy*, xlviii (1962), 137.
2. See C. Jamison, *History of the Royal Hospital of St. Katharine* (1952), 3 *et seq.*
3. See Dickinson, *op. cit.*, for a full discussion of the communities established by Holy Trinity.
4. A full discussion of their position occurs in *Letters and Charters of Gilbert Foliot*, ed. A. Morey and C. N. L. Brooke (1967), 536.

Introduction

under Richard, prior from 1222 to 1248: 115 years after its foundation all fears of an inadequacy of daily bread had long been removed from the minds of the canons regular serving God in the eastern end of the City.

The priory and its possessions

Holy Trinity was from its inception a house which obtained much support from the citizens of London; hence it is not surprising to find that, by 1288–91,[1] the property within London (including that in Kentish Town) was valued at £125 15s. 9¼d., whereas that outside the City was worth only £71 17s. 5d. *p.a.* Spiritual income was £22 2s. 7½d.[2] The cartulary bears witness to the generosity of Londoners in granting land with or without houses and quit rents to the priory which they held in such high esteem. This cartulary contains the record of London property alone and there are few references to the convent's holdings outside the City which were mostly in Middlesex, Hertfordshire and Essex.

Roughly sixty per cent of the temporal income came from the City itself and, even if spiritual income is added to the total, over fifty-seven per cent of the house's income was drawn from London. With such a large City income, it is to be expected that Holy Trinity's interests would extend into almost every parish: it held properties or quit rents in some eighty-seven parishes. Only in the extreme western parts of the City beyond St. Paul's did the priory have few assets, although even in this quarter the parishes of St. Martin Ludgate and St. Sepulchre with St. Audoen provided incomes of 6s. and 25s. *p.a.* respectively. The priory had no property or quit rents in the parishes of All Hallows the Less, St. Antholin, St. Helen, St. Margaret Moses Friday Street, St. Mary Magdalen Milk Street, St. Michael le Quern, St. Nicholas Acon, St. Olave in the Jewry, St. Peter Paul's Wharf, St. Peter le Poor, St. Peter ad Vincula and nothing in a group of western parishes which included St. John the Evangelist, St. Anne and St. Agnes, St. Andrew by the Wardrobe, St. Nicholas Shambles and St. Olave Silver Street. The assessment of the rent and other temporal income on which the royal tenth or clerical subsidy was based (**1030**) does not contain all the rents which the house enjoyed, but it will be seen from it that Holy Trinity's main sources of revenue were in the parishes of St. Botolph without Aldgate, St. Mary Colechurch, St. Michael and St. Katherine Cree and St. Olave Hart Street. These four parishes provided the priory with £60 2s. 9½d., almost half of its temporal income from land and rents. With the exception of St. Mary Colechurch, all these parishes were in the vicinity of the conventual buildings.

The income which the house enjoyed fell into two main categories. Firstly, as has been mentioned, from the time of Prior Ralph onwards, the prior and convent sold lands while retaining to themselves fixed annual rents in perpetuity. The second source was from quit rents which pious donors had given to them either from lands which they owned or from parts of rents which were paid to the grantors. But these quit rents were not always gratuitously given to the priory, for, on occasion, the convent would

1. *Taxatio ecclesiastica auctoritate P. Nicholai IV* (Record Comm., 1802), *passim.*
2. For its income in the sixteenth century see E. J. Davis, 'The beginning of the dissolution: Christchurch, Aldgate, 1532', R.H.S. *Trans.*, 4th series, viii (1925), 131.

Introduction

enter the market to purchase quit rents. **52** shows the canons paying 8s. for the purchase of an annual quit rent of 12d., a transaction which, at eight years' purchase, was a profitable one for the house. The prices paid for quit rents varied between nine (**306**) and thirteen and a third years' (**283**) purchase; the most frequently found prices were nine or ten years. Sometimes a quit rent might be, in effect, an addition to a rent already being paid (**60**). In this instance, William Ganter (the Glover) was paid 20s. by the canons for his additional rent of 2s. *p.a.* that he added to the 5s. which he was under obligation to pay. A rough calculation shows that rather less than fifty-five per cent of the City income was provided by rents from properties which the priory still possessed and just over forty-five per cent from quit rents which had been granted to the house either gratuitously or by purchase. As Holy Trinity was dissolved in 1532, no record of its assets exists in the *Valor Ecclesiasticus*, but apparently the value of its income in the City increased between 1288–91 and the early sixteenth century.[1] It is important to distinguish between these two types of income, as, if arrears occurred, somewhat different procedures were required to recover them.[2]

Another source of income about which the cartulary provides few details derived from the churches collated to the priory. The first chapter of the document is headed 'in the parishes of Holy Trinity, St. Michael, Mary Magdalen and St. Katherine' and these apparently formed one parish. The church of St. Katherine Christ Church known as St. Katherine Cree was, at one time, a chapel served by the canons of Holy Trinity, but in the fifteenth century it became a parish church of which the prior and convent were patron.[3] All Hallows Fenchurch later called St. Gabriel Fenchurch came to the priory because it had belonged to the *Cnihtengild* (**109**) and St. Augustine Papey as part of the soke of Aldgate (**789**) while the house presented to St. Edmund King and Martyr (**358**). The gift of the *cnihts* also gave Holy Trinity the possession of the parish church of St. Botolph without Aldgate and **964** illustrates the keenness with which the house defended its right to mortuaries, while **1045** shows it maintaining its baptismal rights over the children of parishioners of this church appropriated to the priory. All Hallows London Wall was granted to the house (**779**) between 1128 and 1134 by a priest named Ranulf who gave it to the convent when he entered religion at Reading abbey. The priory encountered certain difficulties with the bishop of London, Gilbert the Universal (1127–34), but its claim was made good (**780**) and the incumbent paid 3s. *p.a.* rent to the prior and convent.

The ward of Portsoken was a valuable possession not only for the income which it brought to the priory but also for the prestige which it conferred upon the prior.[4] He was *ex-officio* alderman of the ward. A careful reading of the cartulary has not brought to light any new facts concerning the relationship between the soke of the *Cnihtengild* and the

1. See M. C. Rosenfield, 'The Disposal of the property of London monastic houses, with a special study of Holy Trinity Aldgate' (London, Ph.D. thesis, 1961), and 'Holy Trinity, Aldgate, on the eve of the Dissolution', *Guildhall Miscellany*, iii no. 3 (Oct. 1970), 159–73; and E. J. Davis, R.H.S. *Trans.*, 4th series, viii, 131.
2. *Liber Albus*, i, 181 *et seq.*
3. G. Hennessy, *Novum Repertorium* (1898), 117.
4. See E. J. Davis, R.H.S. *Trans.*, 4th series, viii, 130.

Introduction

City authorities. There is no justification for thinking that the men of the *Cnihtengild* had any special authority over the City: in fact, the soke was only exempt *de warda* and the men of the soke were subject to the Husting court, whereas those of the soke of Aldgate were free from it.[1] The fact that the successor to the *Cnihtengild*, the prior, was alderman may indicate that the gild had some special position, but on the other hand the ward of Portsoken could have been created after the soke came into the possession of Holy Trinity.[2] Neither does the cartulary say anything about the manner in which the prior exercised his aldermanic powers.[3] Holy Trinity, well endowed with property and quit rents, was a prominent London house which compared favourably in size and wealth with other London religious communities.[4]

Some aspects of the social and economic life of medieval London

Perhaps the most important reason for making the contents of the cartulary more widely available to scholars is to be found in the hope that such a work will, to quote the late Miss E. Jeffries Davis, 'throw much light on the early topography of London'.[5] Its publication should reinforce work already done on the topography of medieval London and it should also illuminate the history of the urban land market. Sopers Lane is called a new street in 1257 (**505**), St. Pancras designated a parish church in 1253–4 (**501**) and 'Brodeselde' is first mentioned in 1255–6 (**510**). Many documents bear witness to the active market that existed in quit rents: the most usual figure, as has been mentioned, for the purchase of a quit rent was nine or ten times its annual value, but evidence as to any special factors which may have influenced any particular purchase price is lacking. The figures appear over a period of nearly 300 years and it would be unwise, on the evidence available, to postulate marked changes in the market value of annual quit rents at different periods. The sale of quit rents was obviously one method of mobilizing capital for business purposes (**195, 197, 218, 369, 505, 1056** *et al.*). The priory was prepared to invest in quit rents and those selling them frequently state that they needed the money 'ad negocia mea expedienda'. The cartulary also shows an active land market to have existed in London from the twelfth century.

Holdings in London were in burgage tenure and citizens had free testamentary disposition of their property, except that they were compelled to leave one-third to their widow and one-third to their children. Traces of obligations remain, however, that may indicate tenures which, if they were not strictly feudal, were slightly less free. Such may be the rent of a silver mark to Holy Trinity as chief lords of the fee in **222**. If we knew more about the function of the prior's soke reeve (**945** *et al.*), it might be possible

1. H. W. C. Davis, 'London lands and liberties of St. Paul's, 1066–1135', *Essays presented to T. F. Tout* (1925), 48–9.
2. For a discussion of the ward of Portsoken see Stenton, *Norman London*, 13–15, and F. E. Harmer, *Anglo-Saxon Writs*, 233.
3. See A. B. Beaven, *Aldermen of the City of London* (2 vols. 1908–13), i, 179 *et seq.*
4. See W. R. Lethaby on the site of Holy Trinity, *Home Counties Magazine*, ii (1900), ii, no. 5, 45–53, and W. Besant, *Mediaeval London* (*Survey of London*), ii (1906), 241 *et seq.*
5. In Stenton, *Norman London*, 13 n. 1.

Introduction

to adjudge the degree of dependency of some tenures, but it would appear that even in the twelfth century any obligations other than those of rent were few. As the late Miss Jeffries Davis wrote, 'the seigneurial system was obsolete in the City'.[1] Citizens of London were allowed to leave property to religious houses notwithstanding the provisions of the Statute of Mortmain.[2] Leaving aside sales or gifts of quit rents, the conveyances fall into two groups, firstly those in which the prior and convent granted land and secondly those made between citizens in which Holy Trinity was in some way involved, usually as the recipient of an annual rent. The cartulary indicates that the greatest activity in the land market, judged by the volume of conveyances, took place during the tenure of Prior Richard between 1222 and 1248. The general economic trend of this period was expansionist and the second quarter of the thirteenth century, following the successful struggle for the independence of the City in the previous thirty years, probably saw considerable advances in London, but it can only be conjecture as to whether Holy Trinity was at this time enlarging or improving its buildings and needed money for such a purpose. However, during Richard's priorate the house granted away land, either with or without houses, upon which a total annual rent of £16 1s. was reserved and received in gersums £178 18s. Of these thirty-two properties a nominal rent of $\frac{1}{2}$ lb. of pepper (**555**) and 1 lb. of cumin or 1d. (**818**) was reserved upon two of them, but, of the remaining thirty, an annual rent ranging between £6 13s. 4d. and 2d. was paid. The house invariably reserved to itself the right to repurchase the property at a price below its full market value. The clause 'si A.B. etc. voluerit terram vendere etc. canonici et successores sui propriores erunt omnibus aliis de uno besancio duorum solidorum si illam voluerint habere', meaning that the prior and convent should have preference over other purchasers to the amount of a bezant of 2s., is frequently found in the deeds. There are slight variations of the formula, 'si quoque voluerit feodum suum invadiare vel vendere canonici debent esse adeo propinquiores ut aliquis alius si voluerint habere', but the general tenor of these clauses indicates that the priory was placed in a favourable position. Frequently a restrictive clause appeared in the deed preventing the grantee from leasing or selling the property to Jews or to religious houses.

Generalizations from these documents upon aspects of social and economic life may be dangerous, but there is enough evidence to show that a considerable amount of land which was not built upon existed within the City walls: both references to gardens and agreements to grant land on condition that houses were built upon it are ample testimony to these empty spaces, as, indeed, is the mention of 'le More' within the walls (**782**). The size of tenements is fully documented in most deeds in the cartulary. Although some measurements are given in feet and inches, usually holdings are measured in ells with careful notes of the frontage and depth of the tenement. In some deeds (e.g. **410**) sufficient detail is given of the abutments and the streets for the topographer to reconstruct small areas of the city. This is not the place to discuss the problem of the measures used to describe properties; whether the ells were of 45 inches or were, in fact,

1. E. J. Davis, *R.H.S. Trans.*, 4th series, viii, 130.
2. *Laws and Customs etc. of the City of London* (1765), 13, 19.

Introduction

yards,[1] is not determinable from the cartulary. Some illustration is given in **372** of the actual business methods employed in land purchase. Something is also shown of the legal process. Thomas de Axbridge's aim was not only to copy charters and lists of tenants paying rent subsequently to the initial grant or lists of those paying quit rents but also to make a record of any process that would make the priory's claims more secure: to that end he made copies of pleas in the Husting court. A number of these suits were undoubtedly collusive (e.g. **391**), brought in order to establish title. Where the rent is said to have been in arrears for many years or where the prior remitted all the arrears we can be tolerably certain that such suits were collusive. Another aspect of interest to the social historian is the remarkable longevity of some London inhabitants. Although one cannot be certain that no names have been omitted, in one list only three tenants held one property in 104 years and other instances of tenures of considerable length can be found (**454, 254 contd.**). The pressure of a growing population in the City is demonstrated by the frequent sub-division of properties. Large holdings were divided among two or three tenants and they and their heirs became responsible for portions of the rent due to Holy Trinity. Sometimes the properties originally granted were of small dimensions and **586** illustrates what may have been the size of a typical fishmonger's shop $3\frac{1}{2}$ ells 1 inch by $3\frac{3}{4}$ ells. Instances are to be found of a citizen adding one property to another (**210**), but they occur rarely in comparison with the frequent division of holdings. The historian of prices will obtain some useful data on rents, but less information on the price at which property changed hands, for it is frequently concealed in the phrase 'for a certain sum of money', although **190** may disclose the true market price of a house sold to the priory. On occasion the priory took steps actively to encourage building by beneficial rents or even by the remission of rents for a period of years (**737**). References to quays, stone houses, gardens, tenter-grounds for the racking of cloth and brewhouses illustrate aspects of commerce, building and industry in medieval London.

Notes on the edition

Calendaring rather than the printing of full text, despite some inherent disadvantages, has been the only method of making this large register available to scholars: its size, 208 folios, has until how been a serious obstacle to its publication. All essential details contained in the various types of document have been included and the full text of any doubtful or particularly significant passage has been given. Warranty clauses have, however, been omitted from calendared entries because they are common to all grants. It has also been decided not to give the full text of early charters both because so many originals exist and because most of the earliest ones are in print, but the *Historia* has been printed in the Appendix.[2] References have been given to the principal places where the deeds may be found in print, but when a full list of printed references appears in such works as *Regesta Regum Anglo-Normannorum* all these references have not

---

1. See R. E. Zupko, *Dictionary of English Weights and Measures* (1968).
2. Because it is not easily available although printed in T. Hearne's edition of William of Newburgh, *Historia*, iii, 687 *et seq*.

Introduction

been repeated. Whenever an original deed has been calendared in the *Catalogue of Ancient Deeds*, a reference is given to that source, but P.R.O. references are given only to those few deeds not included in the *Catalogue*. With a few exceptions, all charters and wills enrolled in the court of Husting have been traced on the rolls of that court or in Sharpe's *Calendar of Wills*, but no attempt has been made to trace pleas in the cartulary which appear on the Husting Common Plea Rolls.

With a document in which the entries extend in date over three centuries, the question of the treatment of surnames is a difficult one, for names which are clearly, before *c*. 1280–1300, trade or occupational names, may after that date become surnames proper. Generally the word 'the' has been placed before a trade or occupational name where it occurs before the reign of Edward I or when there is justification for believing that the man or woman may have followed that calling. Where place-names appear as surnames, 'de' rather than 'of' has been used in rendering them, unless there is reason to believe that the person named came directly from that place. The original spelling of surnames and places has been followed, but Latin place-names have usually been translated. Most of the commoner Latin forenames have been translated, but the form Matilda has been retained in preference to Maud. Suspension marks at the end of names have generally been ignored. Round brackets within words have been used to indicate doubtful readings.

Dates in both the heading and the entries have been given in days, months and years, and the years have been reckoned to begin on 1 January and not on 25 March. Dates of sheriffs have been taken from P.R.O. *Lists and Indexes*, no. 9, those of aldermen from Beaven, *Aldermen of the City of London*, and those of ecclesiastical dignitaries from the latest editions of Le Neve, *Fasti Ecclesiae Anglicanae*.[1]

The index contains entries for persons, places and subjects. Certain subjects occur too frequently in the text to make indexing profitable; these have been dealt with by a reference to the first and last item in which they are mentioned.

1. For London these are: *1066–1300*, i, *St. Paul's London*, comp. D. E. Greenway (1968); *1300–1541*, v, *St. Paul's London*, comp. J. M. Horn (1963).

THE ILLUMINATIONS IN THE ALDGATE CARTULARY: A NOTE

by

FRANCIS WORMALD

Although not as lavish as that found in contemporary liturgical manuscripts, the decoration in the Aldgate cartulary is rich when it is compared with other books of its type, and is certainly the work of professionals. Two types of illumination are to be distinguished in it. First is a series of initials painted in gold and colours with feather-like ornamental sprays growing from them. Secondly there are a large number of monochrome capitals in blue and gold with fine red and purple penwork ornaments springing from them. Within the letters the background has been filled in with colour, the same as the penwork ornaments, leaving a design in white camaieu. While these penwork initials are to be found throughout the manuscript, the richer painted capitals are confined to the opening pages of each of the three main sections of the book. First is the section with the copies of the title deeds, etc. This has painted initials on ff. 1–5. Second is the section relating to the 'Soca extra Algate', which has painted initials on ff. 149–150 r, and thirdly is the section entitled 'Carte de pluribus parochiis' with letters of this kind on f. 179 r and v.

Four separate hands may be distinguished at work on the illumination: two in the painted and two in the penwork initials. The first hand in the latter worked on ff. 1 v–147 r, and from f. 169 to the end. It is a neat formal style with blue capitals, usually taking up two lines, and red penwork ornaments. The second hand is confined to the first eighteen pages of the second section, ff. 149–66. It is a much more interesting style, being more exuberant and inventive, and is easily recognized by its use of gold for some of the letters and by the purple ink of some of the decoration. A number of grotesque human heads have also been introduced as ornament, whereas the first hand has only one rather discreet one on f. 180.

The opening page of the manuscript, f. 1, has by far the most elaborate scheme of decoration. This consists of a large initial A surmounted by a jewelled crown. Within the letter is a blue shield on which is painted in gold the well-known triangular device known as the 'Scutum Dei Triangulum' or the 'Scutum Fidei' with its inscriptions producing in diagrammatic form a statement of the doctrine of the Trinity.[1] Such shields are found on numerous medieval works of art. The Aldgate version is somewhat more elaborate than is usual. At the base of the triangle is a T-like projection. On the cross-bar is written 'Vera trinitas' and on the vertical is 'est homo'. The

---

1. For other examples with various minor differences, see F. Bond, *Dedications and Patron Saints of English Churches* (1914), 251.

The Illuminations

whole of this vertical from the middle of the shield reads now 'Deus est filius est homo'. Thus the doctrine of the Incarnation also finds a place in the scheme.[1] It would seem that this form of the 'Scutum' may have been regarded as the arms of Aldgate Priory. British Museum Harleian Charters 44.F.52 and 53, which are releases for rent given by John Bradwell, prior of Aldgate, in 1521 and 1522, are both sealed with the same small circular seal which is described as the seal which 'utimur in talibus signatis'.[2] It is not the great seal of the priory which had a different design, but must have been a signet used for less important documents. Its design consists of the 'scutum dei' of exactly the same form as the one in the initial in the cartulary.

Surrounding the text is a border of red and blue edged with gold from which grow conventional leaves and flowers. These sometimes terminate in penwork sprays decorated with small gold dots and what look like small peascods. The coloured initials on the following eight pages are in the same style and are by the same hand. The initials on f. 179 r and v are also the same. All are typical of the illumination found in English manuscripts of the first half of the fifteenth century. Rather similar leaves with sharply serrated edges and feather-like terminations are found in such books as the Admiralty Ordinances in British Museum Cotton MS. Vespasian B.XXI[3] datable about 1413–15 and the Psalter of Humphrey, Duke of Gloucester, British Museum Royal MS. 2 B.I, made between 1420 and 1430. Some of the grotesque flowers may be compared with f. 1 of British Museum Royal MS. 8 G.III, which can be dated about 1420.[4]

The second artist of the painted pages, ff. 149–50, worked in the same style as the first. His colour is a little less rich and he uses a daisy flower in either an elongated form or in the more usual shape. He also adds the spoon flower to his vocabulary. Besides this floral decoration he introduces a crown into the initial E with which the copy of the writ of Edward the Confessor begins on f. 149 and also hangs a shield of the anachronistic arms of the Confessor on the lower border.[5] On f. 150 at the foot of the page is a tinted drawing of a mitred ecclesiastic. This is probably purely decorative and cannot be regarded as representing anybody.

For the history of English illumination the decoration of the Aldgate cartulary is valuable because it can with some certainty be dated within a decade, and comparison with other English manuscripts confirms that the ornaments are contemporary with the writing of the rest of the book.

---

1. In B.M. Cotton MS. Julius D.VII, f. 3 v, there is a 13th-century drawing of the 'Scutum fidei' in which a figure of the Crucified is placed on the vertical bar running from the base to the centre of the shield. It bears the inscription 'Ihesus incarnatus'.
2. W. de G. Birch, *Catalogue of Seals in the Department of Manuscripts in the British Museum*, i (1887), nos. 3567, 3568.
3. See British Museum, *Reproductions from Illuminated Manuscripts*, Series ii (1910), pl. xvii.
4. G. F. Warner and J. P. Gilson, *British Museum, Catalogue of Western Manuscripts in the Old Royal and King's Collections*, iv, pl. 62.
5. For a discussion of the mythical arms of the Confessor, see R. H. M. Dolley and F. Elmore Jones, 'A New Suggestion concerning the so-called "Martlets" in the "Arms of St. Edward" ', *Anglo-Saxon Coins, Studies Presented to F. M. Stenton*, ed. R. H. M. Dolley (1961), 215–26.

CHRONOLOGICAL TABLE OF CONTENTS

(*a*) CHARTERS (including wills, acquittances, etc.)

Year	Entry no.	Year	Entry no.
1042–4	872	1194–5	687
1087–1100	873	1196	1024
1100–3	874	*c.* 1197–*c.* 1225	396–7
1108	2–5, 7, 9	1197–*c.* 1212	387
1108–47	624, 807	1197–1212	206, 223, 228, 1015,
1121–2	998		1051, 1061
1122	12	1197–1221	62, 64, 70, 74, 122,
1125–36	965		171, 181, 183, 185,
1126	875		204, 267, 312, 340,
c. 1127–34	780–1		353, 404, 485, 578,
1128–34	966		704, 717, 838, 848,
1135–9	1001		950, 1020
1136–54	979	1201–2	551
1140–4	962	1201–10	338
1140–6	961	1202–3	663
1147–8	973–4	1212–13	335
1147–52	975–6	1212–23	829
1147–67	232, 257, 280, 361,	1214–16	527, 545
	394, 423, 612, 644,	1214–26	546
	809, 895, 948	*c.* 1215	1011
1151–2	977–8	*c.* 1215–29	336
1151–61	980	*c.* 1215–30	325
1155–8	1002	?1216–17	701a
1157–61	78	*c.* 1217	1025–6
c. 1166	971	1217–21	620
c. 1167–70	41	*c.* 1218	1028
1170–*c.* 1185	346	1218–19	442–3, 993–4
1170–97	76, 79, 109, 136, 148,	1220–1	449, 528
	152, 157, 199, 202,	1221	372
	209, 226, 234, 236,	1222	371, 629
	241, 271, 453, 456,	1222–8	142
	471, 497, 609, 614,	1222–9	331
	666, 676, 678, 680–1,	1222–30	366, 494–5, 736, 826,
	700, 729, 747, 750,		831, 930
	776, 790, 814, 887,	1222–32	150, 161, 167
	902, 918, 931, 942,	1222–48	39, 50, 84, 86, 126,
	1054, 1058		238, 310, 316, 380–1,
1174–84	740–1		400, 406, 493, 539,
c. 1180–5	828		584, 586, 658, 714,
?*c.* 1189–93	1012		734, 800, 882, 884,
? 1190–1215	178		886, 900, 908, 910,
? before 1193	270, 273, 426, 866		923, 933, 938, 946,
1193–1212	824, 1022–3		990, 1010, 1013

xxiv

Chronological Table

Year	Entry no.	Year	Entry no.
?1222–?1248	991	1255–6	510, 893
1223–5	650	1256–7	912, 1021
1223–7	248	1257	505, 508, 985
1224	811	1258	32, 154, 512, 641
c. 1225	754, 759	1258–9	798
1225	690	1259	945, 1016
1225–6	548	before 1260	604
1225–7	283	1260	360
c. 1225–45	761–2	1261	987
1227	1004, 1014	1261–2	989
1227–9	692–3	1261–8	470, 802, 804, 880
1227–31	306	1261–78	988
1227–44	529	1262–3	124, 716, 769
1228–9	744	1263	890
1228–38	91	1263–4	535
1229–30	856	1264–5	129, 530, 785
c. 1230	314, 771	1265–80	43
1230	304	1266–8	447
c. 1231–8	222	1267–8	134
1231–2	618	1268	68, 889, 899
1234	652	1269	97, 845
1235–6	262, 549	1269–70	213, 375
1236	430–1, 1017	1270	292, 1008
? 1238–9	248	1270–1	60, 93, 369, 684, 864, 905, 916
1239–40	1018		
c. 1241	383	1271–2	173, 195, 293, 344, 1060
1241	571		
1241–2	1019	1273	197, 245, 276, 787
c. 1242–8	115	1273–4	322
c. 1243	250	1274	47
1243	299, 300, 594	1274–5	921, 928
1246	533	1275–6	37, 437
c. 1247–50	58	1276–7	307
1247–8	818	1277	378
before 1249	461	1277–8	906, 1007
1249–50	327, 720	1278	534
1249–53	462	1278–9	192
1249–60	35	1279	499
1250	218, 1056	c. 1280–9	52
1250–1	88, 329, 515	1280–1	451
1250–8	82, 139, 159, 507	1282	425
1250–60	668	1285	45, 237
1251–2	516, 616, 756	1285–6	221
1252	140, 169, 794	1286	131, 323
1252–3	189, 489, 517, 764, 792	1286–7	215, 752
		1287	144, 897
c. 1252–60	90	1288	784
1253	259	1290–1	617, 913
1253–4	190, 467, 501, 596	1292	646
1253–5	731	1293	277
1254–5	146, 476	? 1293–4	255
1255	355, 832	1294	920

Chronological Table

Year	Entry no.
1294–1302	877
1295–6	665
1296	1031
1298	72
1299	767
1300	358–9
1301	408, 711
1302	73
1302–3	631
1303	104, 955
1303–4	834
1304	537
1304–5	111
1305	112
1305–6	836
1308	732, 904, 937
1309	66, 820
1309–10	286
1310–11	95
1312	99
1314	55, 1029
1314–15	925
1315	927
1317	563
1319	165
1320	940
1325	1043
1327	532
1335	208
1338	252
1339	699, 713
1340	1047
1345	1038
?1345–6	1053
1351	410
1352	138
1354	892
1355	702
1356	959
1357	879, 1039, 1041
1359	1032
1362	1033
1363	796, 1040
1364	958
1365	415, 441
1371	956
? 1372	175
1373	1034
1374	957
1377	1035
1378	352
1379	1042

Year	Entry no.
1380	217, 588, 1005
1384	117
1385	503
1386	101
1388	324
1393	119
1397	118
1399	568
1404	374, 737
1405	773
1407	120, 1037
1410	525, 898
1412	287, 661, 727, 954
1413	398, 749
1419	581
1420	418
1423	591
1426	243, 1044

(b) PLEAS IN THE HUSTING

Year	Entry no.
1288	274, 557, 560
1292	567
1298	247
1299	542, 709
1300	49, 53, 391
1302	201
1307	432
1323	455
1328	34
1329	187, 205
1333	473
1334	54
1336	816–17
1338	269, 308, 695, 698, 721
1339	265, 438, 713
1340	520, 522, 524
1342	351
1343	57
1345	580
1346	392
1352	38
1354	478
1358	309
1359	132, 266, 660
1360	61, 156, 211, 356, 368, 543, 675, 795
1361	133, 722
1362	490
1374	188
1375	479
1422	648

Chronological Table

(*c*) OTHER DOCUMENTS

Year	Entry no.	Year	Entry no.
1161	(Papal bull) 981	1360	(Inquisition) 81
1201	(Papal letter) 876	1362–3	(Inquisition) 626
1254	(Exchequer plea) 982	1384	(Assessment) 1030
1340	(Writs) 519, 521, 523; (Inquisition) 674	1405	(Fresh force) 491
		1407	(Fresh force) 290
1343	(King's bench plea) 742	1408	(Fresh force) 480
		1425	(Fresh force) 996

THE CARTULARY OF HOLY TRINITY ALDGATE

1. [f. 1] *Chronicle*: The genealogy of Henry I and his consort is followed by a note of praise for the king's work in rebuilding churches and monasteries ruined by the Danes and in recalling Anselm. The virtues of Queen Matilda are extolled and the story of her washing of lepers' feet and her brother David's reaction to this, is narrated.
[f. 1v] On the advice of Anselm she decided to build a church in honour of the Holy Trinity and it was founded in 1108 within Aldgate in a place where Syredus had established a church from which the dean and chapter of Waltham Holy Cross had received a rent of 30s. *p.a.* The queen, so that her church might be quit of all obligation, gave a mill to Waltham in exchange for the 30s. and this was confirmed by King Henry.

>For Latin text of **1–16** see Appendix. **1–30** were printed in William of Newburgh, *Historia*, iii, 687–709.

2. [1108] *Confirmation of Henry I*: witnesses, [Roger] bishop of Salisbury, Th[omas] de Sancto Johanne, Jordan de Say, William bishop of Durham, at Dunstable.

>*Reg. A.-N.*, ii, no. 897; *Cart. Antiq.*, ii, no. 385.

3. [?1108] *Release* by the church of Waltham: addressed to Richard[1] bishop of London by Walter dean and chapter of Waltham.

>1. Richard de Belmeis I, elected 24 May 1108, consecrated 26 July 1108.

4. *Chronicle*: On the advice of Anselm, the queen gave the church to Norman, the first man to introduce the rule of the Austin canons into England and she endowed it with the gate of Aldgate and the soke pertaining to it and £25 *blanch* from the city of Exeter by the following charter:
[f. 2] [1108] *Notification* by Queen Matilda of the soke addressed to Richard bishop of London informing him that Holy Trinity is quit of subjection to any church save St. Paul's: witnesses, William bishop of Winchester, Roger bishop of Salisbury, Robert bishop of Lincoln, Randolf the chancellor and Bernard the chancellor [chaplains], Giffard Clareb', Geoffrey de Clinton, William de Ponte, Ald(uino), at Westminster.

>*Reg. A.-N.*, ii, no. 906 & p. viii.

5. [1108] *Confirmation of Henry I* of the charter in **4**; witnesses, Roger bishop of Salisbury, Robert bishop of Lincoln, at Westminster.

>*C.A.D.*, iv, A 6687; *P.R.S.*, x, no. 2; *Reg. A.-N.*, ii, no. 915; *Facs. Nat. MSS.*, i, no. 7.

6. *Chronicle*: Norman was born in the Isle of Thanet in Kent of noble stock, was educated in France [f. 2v] and returned to Colchester and found a number of priests at St. Botolph's wishing to don the religious habit. He told Ainulf, their leader, of the Austin rule and he urged him to return to the Continent and study it. Norman went to Anselm who provided him with letters of introduction to the abbot of Mont-St.-Éloi.

7. *Letter of Anselm* to John prior of the canons of Mont-St.-Éloi asking that they instruct Norman in their rule.

    Anselm, *Opera Omnia*, ed. F. S. Schmitt, iv (1949), *Epistola* 234.

8. *Chronicle*: Norman, accompanied by his brother Bernard, later prior of Dunstable, went to Chartres and Beauvais and learnt the rule and ascertained the material requirements of the canons. [f. 3] He returned to Colchester and the rule was established there but in 1108 Ainulf allowed him to leave and wrote a letter to the queen.

9. *Letter of Prior Ainulf* to Matilda in which he releases Norman upon Matilda's grant to him of the church of Holy Trinity.

10. *Chronicle*: Norman undertook the rule of Holy Trinity on 5 Apr. 1108 and daughter houses were founded at Dunstable, Launceston, Plympton, St. Frideswide's Oxford and St. Osyth. Norman and Ainulf sent to Pope Paschal that he might set his seal on their order. [f. 3v] At first the house was so poor that some pious women of the City individually undertook to bring a loaf of bread on Sundays and to persuade others to do the same. This secured the weekly supply of bread to the house until such time as its revenues were increased by, amongst other things, Matilda's grant of the gate and soke of Aldgate.

11. Boundary of the soke given by Queen Matilda:[1] From the gate of Aldgate to the gate of the bailey of the Tower called (C)ungate and all the lane called Chykenlane by Berkyngchirche [All Hallows Barking] to the cemetery except one house next to the cemetery and returning by the same road to the church of St. Olave and thence by a little lane which leads to Colemanschurch [St. Katherine Coleman] next towards Fanchirche [St. Gabriel Fenchurch] to a brewhouse which now has the sign of 'The Dove'. From there it continued as far as the house of Theo(bald) son of Ivo, alderman, in Lymstrete by a small lane which is now blocked up because it was the scene of nocturnal thieves and so it goes by the small lane against St. Michael's chapel to Lymstrete to Richard Ca(v)el's house and then by a lane next St. Andrew's church as far as the church of St. Augustine by the City Wall [St. Augustine Papey], and thence to the gate of Aldgate. Prior Norman rebuilt the gate and Geoffrey de Clynton, one of the members of the English Knyghtengild, helped him to enclose a certain road.

    1. Cf. Stow, *Survey*, i, 139, ii, 290–1, who has Tungate.

12. [f. 4] [1122] *Notification by Henry I* addressed to Richard bishop of London and Aubrey de Ver, sheriff, informing them that he has allowed

Prior Norman and the canons of Holy Trinity to enclose a road between their church and conventual buildings and the wall of the City and that the road is to run henceforth in front of their church: witnesses, Ranulf the chancellor, Geoffrey de Clynton, Ralph Basset, at Northampton.

Reg. A.-N., ii, no. 1315; *Cal. Letter-Bk. C*, 75; *Cart. Antiq.*, ii, no. 386.

13. *Chronicle*: The church had grants of land and churches in Tottenham and Walthamstow among other places, but in London, Norman acquired £20 of rents because the church was popular with the citizens. Matilda was a good friend to the house and the story is told of the scandalous way in which the monks of Westminster obtained her body after she had expressed a wish to be buried in Holy Trinity. [f. 4v] Henry did not allow them to possess some land which she had left to the house but it did obtain some of Matilda's relics including a portion of the True Cross which had been sent by the emperor in Constantinople. In 1132 the church and nearly all the conventual buildings were burnt out by a fire which started in Gilbert Beket's house in which a great part of London was destroyed. By a miracle a cross was saved. Norman, although in ailing health refused [f. 5] any additional comforts and laid it down that all his successors should share the dorter and the refectory with the canons. He died on 12 Jan. 1147.

14. *Chronicle continued*: Ralph, the second prior, was elected 17 Jan. 1147. He was a learned man, born and reared in the city of London, known and well-liked by Stephen, his queen Matilda and Archbishop Theobald. [f. 5v] Two of the royal children, Baldwin and Matilda, were buried in the church and Ralph acted as father confessor to the queen. Thomas, 'dei atleta', was a great friend of the prior and Ralph is said to have revealed the martyr's death in a dream which he had on the night of Becket's assassination.[1] He doubled the revenues of the priory. Ralph died on 14 Oct. 1167 and the house was without a prior and all was done under the name of Prior Edmund who had no letters of appointment.[2]

1. An untrustworthy account as he died over 3 years before Becket.
2. See *Letters and Charters of Gilbert Foliot*, ed. Morey and Brooke, 260, 515, 535.

15. Stephen, the third prior, was elected 17 May 1170, resigned 2 May 1197 and died 14 Aug. 1198.

16. [f. 6] Peter of Cornwall, the fourth prior, was elected 9 May 1197 and died 7 July 1221. This prior was the foremost English doctor and, after three years' argument, he converted a Jew who became a canon. He wrote many books including 'Pantheologon', 'De reparacione lapsus' and 'De duabus corigiis predestinacionis et reprobationis'. Edmund, a canon of the house, introduced the rule to Ireland where he became bishop of Limerick.[1]

1. See R. W. Hunt, 'English Learning in the late 12th century', R.H.S. *Trans.*, 4th ser., xix, 33–4, and Hunt, 'The disputation of Peter of Cornwall, against Symon the Jew', *Studies presented to F. M. Powicke* (1948), 143–56.

17. Richard, fifth prior, elected 16 July 1223,[1] died 14 Aug. 1248.

1. *Rectius* 1222, *C.P.R. 1216-25*, 342.

Chronicle

18. John de Totynge, sixth prior, elected 24 Aug. 1250,[1] died 15 June 1258.

> 1. Cf. *C.P.R. 1247–58*, 73, 75, licence to elect 26 Aug. 1250, royal assent 5 Oct. 1250.

19. Gilbert, seventh prior, elected 1260,[1] died 30 Dec. 1264.

> 1. *C.P.R. 1258–66*, 160–1, which gives the date of the licence to elect as 16 June 1261.

20. Eustace, eighth prior, elected 7 Jan. 1265,[1] died 20 Dec. 1280.[2]

> 1. *C.P.R. 1266–72*, 312, which gives the date of the writ *de intendendo* as 12 Jan. 1269.
> 2. *C.P.R. 1281–92*, 147, which gives the date upon which the news of Eustace's death reached the court as 27 Dec. 1284.

21. William Aiguel,[1] ninth prior, elected 31 Dec. 1280,[2] died 21 May 1289.

> 1. Or Aignel.
> 2. *C.P.R. 1281–92*, 147, 151–2, which gives the date of the royal assent to Aiguel's election as 10 Jan. 1285 and the restoration of temporalities as 18 Jan. 1285.

22. [f. 6v] Stephen de Watton, tenth prior, elected 1289,[1] resigned (*depositus*) 11 Mar. 1302,[2] died 5 Oct. [?1302].

> 1. *C.P.R. 1292–1301*, 70, which gives the date of licence to elect as 24 May 1294.
> 2. *C.P.R. 1301–7*, 420, gives the date of cession as 8 Mar. 1303.

23. Ralph of Canterbury, eleventh prior, elected 12 Mar. 1302,[1] died 18 June 1314.[2]

> 1. *C.P.R. 1301–7*, 120, 123, licence to elect 8 Mar. 1303, signification of royal assent, 13 Mar. 1303.
> 2. *C.P.R. 1313–17*, 480, which gives the date upon which the news of Ralph's death reached the court as 27 June 1316.

24. Richard Wymbyssh, twelfth prior, elected 25 June 1314,[1] resigned (*depositus*) 2 June 1325,[2] died 17 Mar. [?1326].

> 1. *C.P.R. 1313–17*, 478, which gives the date of the royal assent as 27 June 1316.
> 2. *C.P.R. 1324–7*, 124, 29 May 1325.

25. Roger de Poly, thirteenth prior, elected 3 June 1325,[1] resigned (*depositus*) 26 May 1331,[2] died 7 Jan. [?1332].

> 1. *C.P.R. 1324–7*, 125, royal assent 7 June 1325.
> 2. *C.P.R. 1330–4*, 120, 20 May 1331.

26. Thomas Heyron, fourteenth prior, elected 27 May 1331,[1] died 20 Feb. 1340.

> 1. *C.P.R. 1330–4*, 123, restoration of temporalities 11 June 1331.

27. [f. 7] Nicholas de Algate, fifteenth prior, elected 26 Feb. 1340,[1] died 6 July 1377.

> 1. *C.P.R. 1338–40*, 430, royal assent for Nicholas de London 29 Feb. 1340.

28. William Risyng, sixteenth prior, elected 27 July 1377,[1] died 5 Aug. 1391.[2]

    1. *C.P.R. 1377–81*, 12, royal assent 29 July 1377.
    2. *C.P.R. 1388–92*, 469, licence to elect 8 Aug. 1391.

29. Robert Execestre, seventeenth prior, elected 14 Aug. 1391,[1] died 4 Aug. 1408.[2]

    1. *C.P.R. 1388–92*, 470, signification of royal assent 17 Aug. 1391.
    2. *C.P.R. 1405–8*, 340, 347, licence to elect 19 Aug. 1408.

30. William Haradon,[1] eighteenth prior, elected 1408,[2] died 1 Sep. 1420 [f. 7v blank].

    1. Haraday in G. R. C. Davis, *Medieval Cartularies of Great Britain* (1958), 68.
    2. *C.P.R. 1405–8*, 346, restoration of temporalities 22 Sep. 1408.

[f. 8] IN THE PARISHES OF HOLY TRINITY, ST. MICHAEL, MARY MAGDALEN AND ST. KATHERINE

31. *Narrative*: Thus London was twice burnt, the first time from the house of Gilbert Bekette and secondly in the time of Prior Ralph from the house of Ailward by London Stone almost as far as Aldgate and also to the shrine of Erkenwald in St. Paul's. Because of the fire, the subsequent rebuilding and the need to make better provision for the church henceforth, the prior with the assent of the house decided to sell land with a rent reserved in perpetuity. As the world has progressed to such evil and contradicts ancient facts unless copies of charters are everywhere produced in evidence, I brother Thomas de Axebrigge called son of John de Cornwall, have made this rental not arranged under the tenure of each prior but according to the order of ancient books with the names written in them, also the tenements and the abutments, so that posterity may be better informed. O son of the most glorious Virgin urge me forward.

    For Latin text see Appendix.

32. [1258] Grant by John prior and convent to John Panyfadir (*Panyvadir*) of land and houses in the parish of Holy Trinity in the street going from Algate towards the Tower; abutments, the land of Hugh the Mason and land of the brethren of Mountjoy; rent 4s. *p.a.*; [f. 8v] the canons to have an advantage of 2s. if the grantee wishes to sell the land; gersuma 40s.; witnesses, Ralph Hardel, mayor, Matthew Bokerel, Thomas son of Thomas, sheriffs, and others.

33. [List of those paying rent]: John Panyfadir; Robert Panyfader; William Moyn; Hamo Box; Benedicta Box, 2 Ed. III, [See also after **34**] as appears by the following plea.

34. *Common plea held in the Husting, Mon. 24 Oct. 1328.*
The prior complains of arrears of rent from four shops which John Box and Benedicta Box hold of him and his church for 4s. *p.a.* Benedicta came, John

St. Katherine Cree, etc.

Box in default; the defs. were summoned and essoined three times; at a court held Mon. 17 July 1329 half the four shops were taken into the hands of the City; John to be summoned etc.; Benedicta said that she held them and that 11s. of rent were in arrears; the prior agreed.

33 contd. Stephen de Waltham, 6 and 31 Ed. III; Joan de Waltham, 36 Ed. III; Thomas Waltham, 47 Ed. III; Thomas Waltham, 8 Ric. II and the tenement is situated between the garden of Holy Trinity to the north and the tenement of the New College of St. Mary Oxford to the south, in the west part of the street from Algate towards the Tower.

35. [f. 9] [1249–60] Lease by the brothers and sisters of the hospital of St. Katherine by the Tower, with the assent of the prior and convent of Holy Trinity, to Robert de la Rocle (*de la Rokele*) of land and houses in the parish of Holy Trinity paying to Holy Trinity 4s. 6d. *p.a.* and to the brothers and sisters 2s. 6d. *p.a.*, the land formerly of Alphanus Juncarius; abutments, the land formerly of Robert Panyfadir on the west and the king's highway going to the Tower on the east: containing in length on the east 27 ells, and in length along the land formerly of Robert Panyfadir on the west 24 ells, and in breadth along the king's highway in the north $11\frac{1}{4}$ ells, and in breadth along the land formerly of Robert Panyfadir in the south $8\frac{1}{2}$ ells; gersuma 5 marks to the brothers and sisters; witnesses, Gervase the Cordwainer, alderman, Richard May, John de Cestute, Theobald the Capper.

36. [List of those paying rent]: Robert Rokele; German Crey, clerk; [See also after **38**] who paid from the same tenement 6s. 8d. *p.a.* of which the sacristan has 3s. 4d. *p.a.* as appears by the following charter.

37. [1275–6] Grant by German son of Edmund de Creya, clerk, and Alice de Marny his wife to Eustace prior and convent of 6s. 8d. of quit rent from all their tenement and houses within the parish of Holy Trinity; abutments, [f. 9v] in length between the highway on the north side and the garden of Thomas the Tailor on the south and in breadth between the king's highway to the Tower on the east and the tenement of Walter le Botere on the west; paid on condition that the sacristan has 3s. 4d. *p.a.* for the upkeep of two lamps, one at the door of the infirmary, the other in the chapter house; canons gave 4 marks and 20d.; witnesses, Gregory de Rokelle, mayor, John Horn, Ralph Blunt (*Blondus*), sheriffs, John Norhampton, alderman of this ward.[1]

1. Aldgate.

38. *Payment of 11s. 2d. by Robert Kelsey or Bery as appears in the common plea held in the Husting, Mon. 23 July 1352.*
Robert de Bery and Margaret his wife recognised that they held of the prior and convent at an annual rent of 11s. 2d. a certain tenement in the parish of St. Michael and owed four years' arrears, 44s. 8d.

36 contd. Robert Kelsey or Bery; Peter de Weston; William atte Hale,

St. Katherine Cree, etc.

31 Ed. III; Agnes atte Hale, throughout Ed. III and Ric. II; William Norton, 8 Hy. IV.

39. [1222–48] Lease by Richard prior and convent to Robert Panyfadir of land in the parish of St. Katherine; abutments, Andrew Pake and Bartholomew the Parmenter (*Parmentarius*) on one side, the said Andrew and Gervase the Capper on the other; [f. 10] in length along the main street (*secus magnum vicum*) 23¾ ells and in length along the land of Gervase 36 ells 2 poles and in breadth at the south end (*in capite australi*) 19 ells and in length along the street which goes to the Tower 13½ ells and from the aforesaid street to the land of Bartholomew 27¼ ells; rent 3s. 4d. *p.a.*; gersuma 8s.; witness, Gilbert Fulc, alderman.

40. [List of those paying rent]: Robert Panyfadir; and then the land was divided for Thomas the Parmenter paid 1s. 8d. and Walter the Potter paid 1s. 8d.: after Thomas the Parmenter; Richard Baker atte Weye or atte Basket, 1 Ed. II; Peter de Weston, 6 Ed. III; William atte Hale, 17 Ed. III; Agnes atte Hale, throughout Ric. II; William Norton, 8 Hy. IV: after Walter the Potter; Richard Bedell, 19 Ed. II; William Danyel, 32 Ed. III; and then the part of William Danyel was divided for Richard Andrew paid 8d. for a tenement which is now in the hands of Holy Trinity and Thomas Clayman paid 12d.: after Thomas Clayman; Agnes his daughter, 1 Hy. IV; John Brandeston, 13 Hy. IV.

41. [*c.* 1167–70] Lease by Edmund prior and convent to Huctredus Sted (*Stede*) of land, with reversion to Matilda his daughter, formerly of Edwar(qun); Huctredus swore fealty and gave for the grant one London sextary of wine; witnesses, Henry son of Alwin, Ralph son of Gervase.

42. [List of those paying rent]: Huctredus Stede; William Garland; William de Bristowe; Thomas Samuel; Robert Curryngham; Roger Rufus; William Cook (*Cocus*); John [f. 10v] Neubery, 1 and 19 Ed. II and 5 Ed. III; Robert Manhale, 31 Ed. III; John Bykir, 32 Ed. III; William Burdeux, throughout Ric. II and Hy. IV.

43. [1265–80] Grant in fee by Eustace prior and convent to (Hur) prior and the brethren of the hospital of Mountjoy of the land of Othulphus; rent 5s. 4d. *p.a.*; witnesses, William de Arras, Othulfus Viviano.

44. [List of those paying rent]: the brethren of Mountjoy to the time of Ric. II; now the College of the Blessed Mary at Oxford [New College] founded by the bishop of Winchester, and the two tenements are situated on the south side of the street going towards Algate; abutments, the tenement of Holy Trinity on the east and the tenement of the earl of March (*comitis de la Marche*) on the west.

45. Grant by William, prior and convent to Richard de Chyngeford, potter, of land and houses in the parish of St. Katherine in the king's highway which leads to Algate; abutments, the land of Reginald the Goldsmith on

St. Katherine Cree, etc.

the east and that of William de Suffolk (*Suthfolchia*), potter, on the west; in length along the land of Reginald $27\frac{1}{4}$ ells and in length along the land of William $32\frac{3}{4}$ ells 3 ins., and in breadth at the north end $22\frac{7}{8}$ ells and on the south side 30 ells 3 ins.; rent 40s. *p.a.*; to maintain houses in same state in which Richard received them or better; not to sell in part or in whole [f. 11] or to pledge to Jews nor to burden with annual charge except with permission of prior and convent; swore fealty; gersuma 40s.; chirograph; witnesses, Gregory de Rokesle, mayor, Robert de Rokesle, Stephen de Cornhulle, sheriffs, John de Norhampton, alderman of this ward; dated 24 June 1285.

C.A.D., ii, A 2054.

46. [List of those paying rent]: Richard Chyngeford, potter, who leased it with his wife and daughter Christine; Adam de Cobham paid 20s., 1 Ed. II and 1 and 5 Ed. III.: after Adam de Cobham; Giles Westmelle, 31 Ed. III; William de Coventre, 35 and 41 Ed. III; Nicholas Rote, 49 Ed. III; Richard Blomvylle, 8 Ric. II; Agnes at Hale, throughout Ric. II and Hy. IV; William Norton, 8 Hy.[1] and the part of Christine was divided for Richard the clerk paid 10s. and Adam Cobhambury paid 10s. which part is in the hands of Holy Trinity: after Richard the clerk; the same Richard throughout Ed. II and 1 Ed. III; John de Welles, 3 and 5 Ed. III; Richard atte Celer, 31 and 49 Ed. III; John Henkle: and these two tenements joined together are situated between the tenement of Holy Trinity on the east and another tenement on the west.

1. Probably Hy. IV.

47. Grant by Eustace prior and convent to William de Southfolk (*Suthfolchia*), citizen, of land and buildings in the parish of St. Katherine opposite (*versus*) Algate with frontage on the king's highway; abutments, Holy Trinity on the east and the land of Katherine Joie on the west: frontage on the highway 32 ells and in breadth at the lower end 37 ells and in length along the land of the canons 31 ells and on the other side along the land of said Katherine $42\frac{1}{2}$ ells; rent 40s.; [f. 11v] to maintain the houses in same state in which William received them or better; to build on the empty land 50 ft. along the king's highway at his own charges to the value of 1 mark a year, at least, within three years (*edificabunt ad valorem unius marce per annum ad minus infra triennium a confeccione presencium*); rent 6s. 8d. *p.a.* above the agreed rent of 40s.; the canons to have the preference by 6s. 8d. if the grantee wishes to sell the land; not to sell the land or houses or to pledge to Jews nor to burden with an annual charge without the assent of the canons; swore fealty; gersuma 15 marks; chirograph; witnesses, Henry le Waleys, mayor, Jurdanus Goodchep, Martin Box, sheriffs, John Norhampton, alderman of this ward; dated 12 June 1274.

48. [List of those paying rent]: William Suthfolk [See also after **49**] as appears by the following plea.

49. *Common plea held in the Husting, Mon. 13 June 1300.*
William de Suthfolk by John de Cornhull his attorney, Richard Broke-

St. Katherine Cree, etc.

sheved and Alice his wife and Bordinus atte Grene came and recognised that they were bound to pay to the prior and convent an annual rent of 40s. from the whole tenement which William de Suthfolk has by a lease; the prior impleaded them by a writ of gavelet for £4 arrears of rent.

48 contd. The tenement was divided into two parts for the abbot of Sheppeton paid 31s. 6d. and Christine daughter of William de Suthfolk paid 8s. 6d., which Christine granted her part to John de la Marche called le Potter, paying in 4 Ed. II, which John granted it to Augustine le Waleys 10 Ed. II, which Augustine acquired the tenement formerly of the abbot of Scheppeton and so paid 40s. in 1 Ed. III as appears in a plea[1] held in the Husting, Mon. 21 Feb. 1334.

    1. No details of the plea given.

50. [f. 12] [1222–48] Grant by Richard prior and convent to Clement Joie of land and houses in the parish of St. Katherine; abutment, the priory garden on the west; in breadth along the king's highway 9 ells and in breadth at the other end, towards the south, 7 ells, and in length 49 ells; rent 5s. *p.a.*; the canons to have the preference by 12d. if the grantee wishes to sell the land; Clement received the land with buildings on it (*terram hospitatam*) to the value of 40s.; if the grantee wishes to give up the land he shall leave it with buildings on it to the above value unless they have been destroyed by fire (*terram . . . quam si ipse vel heredites sui relinquere voluerunt, dimittent eam hospitatam ad valorem eiusdem precii vel de precii satisfacienti dictis canonicis inf(ra) igne alieno combusta fuerit quia tunc non tenebuntur ad predictum precium solvendum*); gersuma 4 marks; witnesses, Gilbert the alderman, Richard May.

51. [List of those paying rent]: Clement Joie, William Joie, [See also after **52**] who gave 12d. from the tenement as appears by the following charter.

52. [*c*. 1280–9] Grant by William son of Clement Joie to William prior and convent of 12d. of quit rent from land held of the canons; the canons to distrain on his house both for the 12d. and 5s.; the canons gave 8s.; witnesses, Robert Cunyngham, William Suthfolk.

51 contd. [f. 12v] Clement Joie, 6s.; Katherine Joie; Sampson Orfeur, 28 Ed. I [See also after **53**] as appears by the following plea.

53. *Common plea held in the Husting, Mon. 13 June 1300.*
Sampson Orfeur and Christine his wife came and recognised that they were bound to pay to the prior and convent an annual rent of 6s. for the tenement, once of Katherine Joie, and that they were 12s. in arrears.

51 contd. Augustine de Woxbrigge or Waleys, 1 Ed. II and 8 Ed. III, [See also after **54**] as appears by the following plea.

54. *Common plea held in the Husting,* [1334].
The prior is attached to reply to Augustine de Woxbrigge and Matilda his

St. Katherine Cree, etc.

wife in a plea of taking naam; the pls. complain that the prior has taken naam from their free tenement adjacent on the west to the tenement in which they live in the parish of St. Katherine within Aldgate on Sat. 19 Feb. 1334 to the value of 1s. and that he held it until a pledge was given to William Haversand, sheriff, that they would come into court. The prior came and said that the tenement from which naam had been taken was held of him and his church at a rent of 6s. a year of which service his predecessor Roger Pole had been seised by Augustine and Matilda the true tenants of the tenement in the right of Matilda and since 6s. was in arrears on the day on which he took the naam, he ordered the taking of the said 1s. as part of 1s. 6d. that was the first quarter's rent of that year. Augustine and Matilda came and could not deny that they held of the prior at a rent of 6s. a year and the prior held his naam and the pls. were in mercy.

51 contd. John Malwyn, 31 Ed. III; now [1425–7] the nuns of Derteford and the tenements are situated adjoining each other opposite the chapel of St. Katherine between the holdings of Holy Trinity on both sides.

55. Lease by Ralph prior and convent to John de la Marche, citizen, of land in the parish of St. Katherine towards (*versus*) Algate; abutments, the chapel of St. Michael on the north and the land of John Page on the south; in length $83\frac{7}{8}$ ells and it lies in breadth between the City wall of the said chapel on the west and the land of William Manhale on the east and contains in breadth at the north end $15\frac{1}{4}$ ells [f. 13] 3 ins. and at the south end, from the land of John Cokermuth on the east to the lane called Belleyetlane on the west $48\frac{3}{8}$ ells; rent 53s. 4d. *p.a.* for this tenement and that of John in the parish of St. Katherine; abutments of the latter, the tenement of Alice de Chyngeford on the east and that of the prior of Sippeton on the west; prior and convent to have the right to distrain him or those into whose hands the land comes if the rent is unpaid; witnesses, Nicholas de Farndon, mayor, Hugh de Garto, Robert Burdeyn, sheriffs, Anketinus de Gisors, alderman of this ward;[1] dated 7 July 1314.

    1. Aldgate.

56. [List of those paying rent]: John de la Marche who granted the land to John Clakton by charter[1] enrolled 11 Ed. II; Henry de Canterbury, 19 Ed. II; Robert Echyngham, 1 Ed. III; Richard de Kant, 17 Ed. III; [See also after **57**] as appears by the following plea.

    1. H.R. 46 (67).

57. *Common plea held in the Husting, Mon. 27 Jan. 1343.*
The prior seeks against Richard de Kent a messuage with garden and five shops with five solars as his right and that of his church as by gavelet according to the custom of the City and says that Richard holds of him and his church by a rent of 4 marks: Richard de Wymbisshe was seised by John de la March of his rent, 64 marks in arrears when writs were issued on 1 Jan. 1342 for $16\frac{1}{2}$ years preceding and the messuage could not be distrained upon for a year and a day; Richard by his attorney Christian de Bury came and

St. Katherine Cree, etc.

said that he had a lease for life of these tenements from Simon de Echynghamme, parson of the church of Hercmonnceux, with reversion to James heir to Simon son of Simon's brother Richard, by which he could not withdraw (*deducere*) the said tenement and he sought aid from James. On 5 May 1343, Richard de Kent and the prior came and James de Echynghamme did not come and it was agreed that Richard should reply alone and he said that he did not hold by the above service and that Richard de Wymbissh was not seised as the present prior said and he placed himself upon the country; the prior likewise.

56 contd. Thomas Broun, 31 Ed. III; Margery Broun; the abbot of Evesham, 4 Hy. VI.

58. [f. 13v] [*c.* 1247–50] Grant by Richard prior and convent to William le Want (*le Waunter*) of land with houses in the parish of St. Michael towards Algate; abutments, Roger de Leuesham on the east and the land of Mabel Weddes on the west; in breadth along (*iuxta*) the king's highway on the south $11\frac{3}{4}$ ells and towards the north 13 ells and in length $43\frac{1}{8}$ ells; rent 8s. *p.a.*; not to give sell or pledge to Jews or to a religious house without consent; the canons to have the preference by 2s. if the grantee wishes to sell the land; gersuma 4 marks; witnesses, Gervase Bar(n), then alderman.

59. [List of those paying rent]: William le Waunter; [See also after **60**] who gave 2s. *p.a.* to the sacristan as appears by the following charter.

60. [1270–1] Grant by William Ganter to Holy Trinity of 2s. of quit rent from land in the parish of Holy Trinity held of the canons; William Rus, sacristan, gave 20s.; witnesses, John Andrewe,[1] mayor, Henry le Waleys, Gregory Rokesle, sheriffs.

    1. *Rectius* Adrian.

59 contd. William le Gant, 10s.; William Glover; Richard Potterius, rector of Stapilford; John at Pole, 1 and 5 Ed. III; [f. 14] Thomas Savage, 20 Ed. III; who leased it to Henry his son as appears in his will[1] enrolled 23 Ed. III; Thomas Broun, 31 Ed. III; Margery Broun, 37 Ed. III; [See also after **61**] as appears by the following plea.

    1. *C. Wills*, i, 536.

61. *Common plea held in the Husting, Mon. 19 Oct. 1360.*
The prior is attached to reply to Margery widow of Thomas Broun in a plea of taking naam; Margery complained that the prior took naam from her free tenement in the parish of St. Katherine on Mon. 28 Sep. 1360 to the value of 10s. and that he held it until a pledge was given to Simon de Benyngton and John de Chichestre, sheriffs, etc. to the damage of the same Margery; the prior by Alan de Horewode his attorney said that the taking of naam was lawful because the lands, abutments, the prior and convent on the east and John de Wedford, skinner, on the west, were held of the prior and convent at a rent of 10s. a year and 5s. rent was in arrears for half a

St. Katherine Cree, etc.

year; Margery came and could not deny it; the prior retains the distress and Margery is in mercy.

59 contd. Abbot of Evesham, 4 Hy. VI.

62. [1197–1221] Grant by Peter prior and convent to Wedde de Theiden, weaver, of land and houses formerly of Roger de Chigwell; abutments, William de Algate on the east, formerly Roger de Chigwell; [f. 14v] in breadth next the path 11¾ ells and in length 44 ells and in breadth at the north end 13½ ells; rent 10s. *p.a.*; the land contains ten houses and he should retain this number of houses on it; if he should wish to sell or lease part the prior and covent to have the preference by 1s.; swore fealty; gersuma 20s.; witnesses, Gilbert the alderman, William the clerk (*clericus*), Roger de Theiden, Richard de Cestre, Simon du Bar(y), Henry the Carpenter, William de Algate, Turg(er), William Crist(e)masse, Albrico, Richard de Kent.

63. [List of those paying rent]: Wedde de Theiden; Mabel Wedde; Master Vincent; G. de la Marche; Thomas de la Marche, 1 Ed. II; Ros de Boreford, 1 and 5 Ed. III; John de Bedford, 31 Ed. III; and then the tenement was divided for John Bedeford paid 6s. 8d. and John de Cauntbrigge 6s. 8d., 47 and 49 Ed. III; and William at Nax paid 3s. 4d. for the other part, 37 Ed. III and Robert Gill 3s. 4d., 47 Ed. III and 8 Ric. II.

64. [1197–1221] Lease by Peter prior and convent to Hubert de Anesty of land in the parish of St. Michael; abutments, the land formerly of Agnes, sister of St. Thomas and the land of London Bridge; the land given to Holy Trinity by Richard de Lucy for the soul of his son Geoffrey; rent 12d. *p.a.*; gersuma 1 gold bezant; witnesses, Ralph de Rochester (*Roff.*) William de Rochester, Eustace de Rochester, Richard de Rochester, Robert Walense, Robert de Woburna, Robert de Winchester, Master Henry Lafait, Fulk de Lymstrata.

65. [f. 15] [List of those paying rent]: Hubert de Anesty; Matthew the Chandler; Joan his widow, 5 and 19 Ed. II and 1 Ed. III; John de la Bere, 5 Ed. III; William Berkyng, 31 Ed. III; William Makenheved, 34 Ed. III; Katherine Southe, 35 and 39 Ed. III; Robert Rus, 42 Ed. III and throughout Ric. II and Hy. IV and the tenement is situated in the west part of Belyetereslane, abutments, the tenement of the New Hospital of St. Mary without Bisshoppesgate on the south and the tenement [blank].

66. Grant by Ralph prior and convent to John (*de*) Sandale, clerk, of a garden in the parish of Holy Trinity; abutments, the land of the master of the monastery of Hornchurch and the tenement of Geoffrey de Fonte; in length near the king's highway which goes from Algate to the Tower by the wall of the City 88½ ells and in breadth from the house (*managium*) of John which he holds of Holy Trinity to the highway by the lands of the master of Hornchurch and William de Bristoll on the north 76¾ ells except a few inches; rent 20s. *p.a.*; the prior to have the right to distrain on lands which

St. Katherine Coleman

the lessee holds in the parish of All Hallows de Colmanchurche in case of non-payment of 20s. or 26s. 8d. for the abovementioned tenements; witnesses, Nicholas Farndon, mayor, William de Basyng, James le Botiller sheriffs; dated [f. 15v] Sun. 16 Feb. 1309.

This garden extends to the house (*hospicium*) of earl de la Marche which garden is in this parish but the house is in the parish of St. Katherine Colman.

    C.A.D., i, A 1495.

67. Total of this parish £9 16s. 6d., nevertheless it is tithed at £16 0s. 10d. as appears in the king's exemplification.

IN THE PARISH OF ALL HALLOWS OR ST. KATHERINE COLMAN

68. [1268] Grant by Gilbert prior and convent to Hawise daughter of William the Mason of land; abutments, the land of the brethren of Mountjoy on the east and land of Peter Huniteil on the west; rent 3s. *p.a.*; gersuma 10s.; witnesses, Walter Hervi, William de Dunelm, sheriffs, John de Norhampton, alderman of this ward.

    C.A.D., iv, A 7350.

69. [List of those paying rent]: Hawise; the brethren of Mountjoy; Walter the Whittawer (*Allutario*); Richard Winter; Andrew Winter.

70. [1197–1221] Grant by Peter prior and convent to Peter Honyteil, clerk, [f. 16] of land; abutment, the land of the brethren of Mountjoy; in breadth along the road $10\frac{1}{2}$ ells and in length $39\frac{1}{2}$ ells; rent 32d. *p.a.*; the canons to have the preference by 1 gold bezant if the grantee wishes to sell the land; swore fealty; gersuma 10s.; witnesses, Ralph the Porter, Moses the clerk, John de Lesn[es].

    C.A.D., ii, A 1989.

71. [List of those paying rent]: Peter Honiteil; Richard Honiteil; and then the tenement was divided for Richard Wint, sawyer, paid 2s. and Henry le Galeys 8d.: after Richard Wint; Andrew Wint and Amabilla his wife who was once the wife of Richard Wint' who granted the aforesaid lands of Hawise to William de Ste(b)eneth, chaplain of Peter the clerk, paying 5s. as appears by their charter[1] enrolled 7 Ed. I: after William de Stebeneth; John Sendal: after Henry Galeys; John Sendal; with additions which appear in the following charter.

    1. H.R. 10 (36).

72. Confirmation of a lease by Stephen prior and convent to Henry le Galeys of two pieces of land in the parish of All Hallows of Colmancherch of which one piece contains in length 9 perches and in breadth on the north and in the middle 4 perches $\frac{1}{2}$ ell and on the south 4 perches $\frac{1}{4}$ ell and it adjoins the north side of the king's highway leading towards Algate and,

St. Katherine Coleman

on the east, it adjoins the holding of Richard le Sawier and, on the west, the holding of William de Kent and, on the south, [f. 16v] the other piece of the aforesaid two pieces; which other piece contains in length, on the east side, 7 perches 2 ells and, on the west, 8 perches less a quarter ell and in breadth on the north 8 perches 1 ell and, on the south, 6 perches $3\frac{3}{4}$ ells and it lies between the garden of Holy Trinity on the east and the holding formerly of John de Vallibus on the west and the holding of Geoffrey atte Well on the south and that of Richard le Sawier and the other piece of land on the north; rent 20s. *p.a.*; dated 15 May 1298.

    C.A.D., ii, A 1994.

73. Inspeximus by Stephen prior and convent of the charter to Henry le Galeys and the confirmation of the charter of Henry le Galeys to John de Sendale, clerk, [f. 17 repeats **72**: f. 17v]; John de Sandale to pay 20s. *p.a.* to prior and convent; gersuma for the lease £100; sealed; witnesses Elya Russel, mayor, Henry de Fyngre and John Armenters, sheriffs, John le Blunt, Walter de Fynchyngfeld and the tenor of this charter we have examined in full chapter and agreed to John de Sandale holding at 20s. *p.a.*; chirograph; witnesses, John le Blount, mayor, Hugh Pourte and Simon Parys, [f. 18] sheriffs, William de Betonia, Walter de Fynchyngfeld, Nicholas de Farndon, Richard de Gloucester, in full chapter; dated 1 Nov. 1302.

74. [1197–1221] Grant by Peter prior and convent to Robert de London son of Gervase of land in the parish of All Hallows Colemanchurch; abutments, the land formerly of Gunilde Lagele and land formerly of Hamon Sprakeling; in breadth in front along the road 10 ells and on the south $17\frac{1}{4}$ ells and in the middle 11 ells and in length 46 ells; rent 2s. *p.a.*; if he should wish to pledge or lease, the prior and convent to have an advantage of 1 bezant over other buyers; swore fealty that he will keep the agreements about paying the rent without deceit, contrivance and miskenning (*et quod statutos servabit de censu bene reddende sine fraude ingenio et meskenningia*); for the lease 10s.; witnesses, Master Henry la Fai(c)ie, Nicholas Duket, Mathew Blund, alderman.

    C.A.D., ii, A 2000.

75. [List of those paying rent]: Robert de London, canon of Suthwerk; Claricia Carteys; John Sendale.

76. [1170–97] Lease by Stephen prior and convent to John Sperling (*Sprakeling*) of land formerly held by Gunilde in the parish of All Hallows; rent 12d. *p.a.*; [f. 18v] for the lease he gave to the convent a London sextary of wine and to the prior a bezant; swore fealty; tenement 130 ft. in length and in breadth at the front, 28 ft., in the middle the same and at the end next his orchard 28 ft.; witnesses, John Bucuinte, Henry son of Ailwin, Master Richard son of Reyner, Roger son of Alan.

    C.A.D., i, A 1679.

St. Katherine Coleman

77. [List of those paying rent]: John Sprakelyng; Hamon Sperling; Awyn Rufus; Nicholas his son; John le Frutrer; John Sendale, 5 Ed. II.

78. [1157–61] Lease by Ralph prior and convent to Maurice Tilteye (*de Tilteye*), sheriff, of land which Tewald the Goldsmith held by Colemanchirch.

C.A.D., ii, A 1900.

79. [1170–97] Lease by Stephen prior and convent to Geoffrey son of Maurice de Tilteye of land which his father held; rent 5s.; swore fealty; witnesses, William the chaplain, Ralph de Mandaville.

80. [List of those paying rent]: Maurice de Tilteye; the monks of Tilteye; Hamon Sperlyng; Awynus Rufus; John Sendale, 5 Ed. II who had all the tenements and paid 53s. 8d. *p.a.*; for the garden called Colmanhawe in the parish of Holy Trinity 20s. *p.a.* and for the tenements in the parish of All Hallows 43s. 8d. [*sic*]; earl of Arundell, 19 Ed. II and 1 Ed. III; Hugh de Spenser, 6 Ed. III; Giles de Batlismere, 8 Ed. III; his widow, 12 Ed. III; Bartholomew Batlismere, 20 Ed. III and then the land was divided for Lord Guy Brian paid 47s. 4d. *p.a.* 30 Ed. III [f. 19] and Lord Tiptot 6s. 4d.: after Guy de Brian; Lord Roger Mortimer, earl de la March, 32 Ed. III [See also after **81**] as appears by the following inquisition.

81. Inquisition[1] taken before Simon Dolcell (*Dolsell*), mayor of London and escheator of the same city, 10 June 1360, John Leuesham, Thomas Cok, William Daniel etc. say that Roger Mortimer, earl of March died 26 Feb. 1360 and that he was seised of a tenement, shop and garden in the parish of St. Katherine Colman worth £10 *p.a.* less 47s. 4d. of quit rent paid to the prior and convent of Holy Trinity, dated 10 June 1360.

1. C.I.P.M., x, 530.

80 contd. after Lord Tiptot; Stephen Scrope and all the aforesaid tenements are situated between the holding of the College of the Blessed Mary of Oxford [New College], once the holding of the brethren of Mountjoy on the east and the church of St. Katherine Colman on the west.

82. [1250–8] Grant by John prior and convent to John Bekham (*Bekeham*) of land etc. formerly of John de Waltham; abutments, the courtyard (*curtillagium*) of the canons of Holy Trinity, a house formerly of William Joye; [f. 19v] to assign, lease and pledge as he pleases except to Jews and religious; rent 4s. *p.a.*; lessee to maintain houses; swore fealty; the prior and convent to have the preference by a bezant of 2s. if the grantee wishes to alienate; for the lease 30s.; witness, Gervase Bran, alderman.

C.A.D., ii, A 2082.

83. [List of those paying rent]: John Bekeham; John de Waltham; William de Watteford; John the Preacher; Simon the Weaver; Robert Dewmars; Julian Houndesdych; Richard Pottar; John Boylon; Adam Cobhamb(e)ry,

Ed. I, 1 Ed. II and 1 and 5 Ed. III; Giles Westmell, 31 Ed. III; William Coventree, 35 and 41 Ed. III; Nicholas Rote, 49 Ed. III; Richard Blomvyle, 8 Ric. II; Agnes at Hale, throughout Ric. II and Hy. IV [*sic*]; William Norton, 8 Hy. IV and the tenement is situated between the tenement of Holy Trinity on the east and that of a certain Henry at Hook on the west.

84. [1222–48] Grant by Richard prior and convent to Alice daughter of Henry of land and houses; abutments, the land of Stephen Carpenter and land of John de Waltham which Richerus de Brumfeld once held; to give or assign it to whomsoever she pleases; rent 3s. 6d. *p.a.*; swore fealty; for the grant 2s.; witnesses, Richard son of Walter, Anselm the Baker.

    C.A.D., ii, A 1916.

85. [List of those paying rent]: Alice daughter of Henry; William Joye; Robert Joye, tiler; William Gyll, Ed. I, 1 and 19 Ed. II and 1 Ed. III; Thomas at Hook, 48 Ed. III; his widow, throughout Ric. II and Hy. IV and the tenement is situated between the tenement of William Norton on the east and that of Thomas Tykyl on the west.

86. [f. 20] [1222–48] Grant by Richard prior and convent to Stephen le Paumer of land with houses which Michael son of Sto(n)phardus and Ralph the Carpenter held of Holy Trinity; abutments, Richer de Bromfeld on the east and land formerly of Saie(v)e daughter [? son] of Albinus on the west; in breadth along the king's highway $12\frac{1}{2}$ ells and in length from the said highway to the land of the canons 31 ells; rent 4s. *p.a.*; swore fealty; if the grantee wishes to sell, the prior and convent to have the preference by 2s.; not to sell, pledge or lease to Jews; gersuma 1 silver mark; witness, Gilbert son of Fulc, alderman.

    C.A.D., ii, A 2058.

87. [List of those paying rent]: Stephen le Paumer, carpenter; Simon the Weaver (*Whitlok*); Robert Dewmars, 5 Ed. II; Ralph Bowstryng, 19 Ed. II and 1 Ed. III; Simon Bowstryng, 3 and 5 Ed. III; Philip Chambelyn, 48 Ed. III; Thomas at Hook, 31 Ed. III; Thomas Ottle. 8 Ric. II; Thomas Tykyl and the tenement is situated between the tenement formerly of Henry at Hook on the east and the tenement of Holy Trinity on the west.

88. [1250–1] Grant by John prior and convent to Nicholas de Ware of land; abutments, the land formerly of Stanhardus on the east and land of Ralph May; in length $34\frac{3}{4}$ ells 5 ins. and in breadth, at the south end along the king's highway, 11 ells 1 in. and in width at the north end, 10 ells 6 ins.; rent 2s. *p.a.*; the prior and convent to have the preference by 1 bezant of 2s. if the grantee wishes to sell the land; swore fealty; [f. 20v] for the grant $\frac{1}{2}$ mark of silver; witness, John Norman, mayor.

    C.A.D., ii, A 2042.

89. [List of those paying rent]: Nicholas de Ware; Ralph May; who granted

St. Katherine Coleman

this tenement to Thomas de Sartare [See also after **90**] paying ½ lb. of pepper or 4d. as appears by the following charter.

90. [c. 1252–60] Grant by Ralph May son of the late Hugh May of an annual quit rent of ½ lb. of pepper or 4d. to be paid by Thomas de Sartare from his lands which the grantor sold to the said Thomas; abutments, the land formerly of Peter son of Eustace on the west and land formerly of Albinus Ruffus on the north; to be paid to the prior and convent and their successors by Thomas his heirs and assigns at Christmas at which time the prior and convent shall give to the grantor and his heirs at the door of their buttery (*celarii*) a canon's loaf if it is asked for; for the charter and the warranty prior and convent gave 3s.; witness, Gervase Cordwaner, alderman.

89 contd. Thomas de Sartar paid 2s. 4d.; Richard Froysh; David Dullyng; Henry Proudhom, 1 Ed. II and 1 and 5 Ed. III; Thomas at Hook, 21 Ed. III; Philip Chaumberlayn, 48 Ed. III; Thomas Ottle, 8 Ric. II; John Ottle, 20 Ric. II; Thomas Tykyl throughout Hy. IV and the tenement is situated between the tenement of Holy Trinity on the east and that of Thomas Tykyl on the west.

91. [1228–38] Grant by Peter son of Eustace to Richard prior and convent of a rent of 4s. from land in the parish of All Hallows with houses which pays 20d. to the nuns of St. Helen and which Simon Hoveldere held of the grantor; abutments, the land of Robert Adhelwold on the west and land of Walter the Carter on the east; the prior and convent to hold in free alms on condition that they pay therefrom 20d. *p.a.* to the nuns of St. Helen; witness, Richard Renger.

92. [f. 21] [List of those paying rent]: Simon Hovelder; Henry the Mason (*Sementarius*); William the Mason; Henry Proudhom, 9 Ed. II; David de Dullyng, 1, 3 and 4 Ed. III; Robert Mounteux; Thomas at Hook, 30 Ed. III; Philip Chaumberleyn, 48 Ed. III; Thomas Ottle, 8 Ric. II; John Ottle, 20 Ric. II; Thomas Tykyl throughout Hy. IV; from which tenement the nuns of St. Helen received 20d. and not from Holy Trinity; and the tenement is situated between the tenement of the said Thomas on the east and that of the Countess Herford [*sic*] on the west.

93. [1270–1] Grant by William de Lunar, citizen, of an annual quit rent of 4s. to Eustace prior and convent from all the tenements and houses that he had in the parish between the land and houses of Henry the Mason on the east and lands formerly of Nicholas de Turri on the west; for the grant the prior and convent gave 40s.; if he or his heirs and assigns wish to sell, the canons have the preference by a bezant of 2s.; witness, John Adryan, mayor.

    C.A.D., i, A 1616.

94. [List of those paying quit rent]: William de Lunar who sold the tenement to Ralph Blunt who paid therefrom 4s. *p.a.* as appears in a charter[1]

St. Katherine Coleman

enrolled 26 Ed. I; Gervase Bran; William Chalfont; John Can(t); Maurice Turg, 1 Ed. II and 1 Ed. III; John Cokyrmouth who granted the tenement to Walter Dieubeye who paid therefrom 4s. *p.a.* as appears by their charters[2] enrolled 5 Ed. II; Ha(u)kynus Pepyr, 30 Ed. III; John Bortewold; Richard Herford, 49 Ed. III; and the tenement is situated between the tenement of Thomas Tykyl on the east and that of the Countess Herthford on the west.

    1. H.R. 27 (11).   2. H.R. 40 (138).

95. [1310–11] Lease by Ralph prior and convent to John Cokyrmouth, clerk, of land; abutments, the tenements of said John on the east [f. 21v] and the garden of Holy Trinity on the north; in length on the east $46\frac{1}{2}$ ells 3 ins. and on the west $53\frac{3}{8}$ ells 3 ins. and in breadth, at the north end, 24 ells and in width at the south end along the king's highway $26\frac{1}{2}$ ells 2 ins.; rent 26s. 8d. *p.a.*; the grantee authorises the prior and convent to distrain for the rent upon all the lands he holds in the said parish; John agrees for himself and his heirs to build a fence (*clausura*) and to maintain it at his and their own expense for ever; witnesses, Richer Refham, mayor, Simon Corp, Peter de Blakeney, sheriffs.

    C.A.D., ii, A 2064.

96. [List of those paying rent]: Dominus John Cokyrmouth, 4 Ed. II; Simon Symsan, 19 Ed. II and 2 Ed. III; Haukynus Pepyr, 30 Ed. III; John Dortewold; Richard Herford, 49 Ed. III; now [*c.* 1425] Countess Herford.

97. Release by Eustace prior and convent of the arrears of an annual rent of 4s. payable by John de Can(t), citizen, from a piece of land formerly of Gervase Bran; abutments, the land formerly of Nigel the chaplain on the east and land of the hospital of the infirm of St. Giles[1] on the west; released from payment of rent until Easter 1269 on condition that he builds or causes to be built property sufficient to secure payment of 4s. *p.a.*; [f. 22] John swore fealty concerning the payment; chirograph sealed; dated 17 Mar. 1269.

    1. Presumably St. Giles Holborn.
    C.A.D., ii, A 2048.

98. [List of those paying rent]: John de Kent; Roger Corbet who granted the tenement to Peter le Lane who paid 4s. *p.a.* as appears by charter enrolled 30 Ed. I; William de Chalfont, 5 Ed. II; Adam in Venella, 10 Ed. II who granted the tenement to Maurice Turgis who paid 4s. *p.a.* as appears by his charter[1] enrolled 10 Ed. II and Maurice Turgis, 1 Ed. III; Ralph Halsted, 30 Ed. III; John Halsted, 8 Ric. II; and the tenement is situated on the north side of the road which leads from Algate towards Fanchurch.

    1. H.R. 45 (115, 133).

99. Lease by Ralph prior and convent to John Page, citizen, and Agnes his wife of land; abutments, the land of Adam de la Lane on the east and the

All Hallows Staining

tenement of John de Hoddysdon on the west and extending from the king's highway which leads from Algate to Fenchurch to the garden of Holy Trinity; in breadth at the south end along the road 14½ ells 3 ins. and at the north end 9¾ ells and in length on the west side 43¼ ells and on the east side 40 ells without measuring the inches (*sine pollicibus mensuratis*); rent 26s. 8d. *p.a.*; witnesses, John de Gisors, mayor, Richard de Welford, Simon de Mereworth, sheriffs; dated 4 Jan. 1312.

100. [List of those paying rent]: John Page, 1 and 19 Ed. [II]; John Page, 1 Ed. III; Roger de Elyngham, 3 Ed. III; Roger Athelby, 6 Ed. III; William Dykeman, 30 Ed. III; Thomas Cleyman, 39 Ed. III; Thomas at Naps, 48 Ed. III and 8 Ric. II; John at Lee, 10 Ric. II as appears by indenture made between him and Holy Trinity.

101. Indenture made between William Rysing prior and convent of Holy Trinity of the one part and John at Lee and Agnes his wife of the other part witnesseth that, since Ralph, late prior, leased a certain piece of land to John Page etc. and since the land has been built upon and John at Lee and Agnes his wife occupy it by the will of Thomas at Naps and a rent of 26s. 8d. *p.a.* arises therefrom [f. 22v], the receipt of 26s. 8d. is full payment for all arrears; John and Agnes promise for themselves, their heirs and assigns that they will pay rent in perpetuity; sealed; dated 22 July 1386 and the tenement is situated on the north side of the great street leading from Fenchurch to Algate.

102. Total of this parish £6 11s. 2d., and it is tithed at this in the king's exemplification [f. 23 blank].

[ALL HALLOWS STAINING]

103. [f. 23v] Remission of 3s. 4d. from a quit rent of 6s. 8d. *p.a.* bequeathed by Matilda Flel to Eustace prior and convent from a house which she inhabited in the parish of All Hallows Stanyngchirch; abutments, the house formerly of Simon de Beverlaco on the west and the house of William Spilman on the east; Henry and William Evere afterwards tenants of the house refused to pay the aforesaid 6s. 8d.; prior and convent sued; remission of 3s. 4d. [incomplete].

[f. 24] IN THE PARISH OF ALL HALLOWS STANYNG

104. [1303] Recognisance of William de Evere, ironmonger (*ferrarius*), that he holds of the prior and convent a certain tenement for a rent of 3s. 4d. *p.a.*; abutments, William Belebouch on the east and the tenement of William de Lewes on the west; grants for himself and his heirs that the prior and convent shall distrain on all his tenements for arrears of rent; for this recognisance the prior and convent remitted another 3s. 4d. which they had had from the said tenement and all arrears up to Michaelmas 31 Ed. I; witness, John le Blunt, mayor.

C.A.D., ii, A 2569.

St. Gabriel Fenchurch

105. [List of those paying rent]: William Evere, 31 Ed. I; John Hervy, 1 Ed. II; Edmund Bernes, 5 Ed. II and 4 Ed. III; Thomas Maryns, 30 Ed. III; John Maryns, 40 Ed. III; his widow, 8 Ric. II and the tenement is situated on the north side of Fanchurch stret.

106. Grant by the abbess and convent of Berkyng to the church of Holy Trinity of 5s. of quit rent from a tenement in the parish as appears in the Charter Six[1] of several parishes.

    1. **1007.**

107. [List of those paying quit rent]: for Joce or Joseph Chapeler as appears in the account and rental of the sacristan, Walter Coke, 6 Ed. III, as appears at the end of the account of John London, sacristan, the year aforesaid; Alexander Manschipe, 15 Ed. III as appears in the account of Richard de Brik, sacristan; widow of Manschipe, 24 Ed. III; afterwards Roger Manschipe, 8 Ric. II; Robert Norton, 20 Ric. II; Robert Arnold, 2 Hy. IV; John Costyn.

    Margin: Half of 8d. received from the monastery of St. Katherine from certain tenements in the parish at Michaelmas.

108. Total of this parish 8s. 4d. 9s. [*sic*] and it is tithed at this in the king's exemplification.

[f. 24v] IN THE PARISH OF FENCHERCH

109. This church, which once belonged to the *Cnihtengild*, is in the advowson of Holy Trinity and renders to it an annual payment of 2s. since the time of the collation of the said soke to the church, which payment Ralph Stortford,[1] bishop of London, confirmed as appears in the seventh confirmation of the bishops concerning several parishes:
[?1170–97] Grant by Richard de Remi to the canons of Holy Trinity, London, in free alms, of certain land by All Hallows Fenchurch which Robert de Ponte held in fee of his father, to hold of the grantor and his heirs at a rent of 2 lbs. of cumin payable annually before Christmas; S.[2] the prior gave a gold piece for this concession; witnesses etc.; the prior granted the aforesaid land to Master Sylvester for a rent of 6s. 8d.

    1. *Rectius* Stratford, bishop of London, 1340–54.
    2. Stephen, prior, 1170–97 or Stephen de Watton, 1294–1303.
    C.A.D., ii, A 2184.

110. [List of those paying rent]: Master Silvester; John de Chesthunt; William Hardel which William divided the land between his two sons John and Thomas; to Thomas two shops [See also after **112**] as appears by the following charter.

111. *Charter*[1] *enrolled in the Husting, Mon. 21 May 1313.*
[1304–5] Grant by William Hardel, citizen, to Thomas his son of two shops with a solar built above, a garden and other appurtenances in the parish of

St. Gabriel Fenchurch

All Hallows [Fenchurch]; abutments, the tenement of Thomas de Bryddeport on the east and the grantor's tenement on the west and extending from the king's highway on the south to the tenement of the earl of Gloucester on the north; [f. 25] also a quit rent of 4d. *p.a.* payable at Easter from the tenement which William Bure holds in the parish; paying 3s. 4d. to the prior and convent of Holy Trinity and to the grantor for all his life 5 silver marks annually in equal instalments at Easter and Michaelmas; after the grantor's death, Thomas to hold free of any service to the grantor's heirs; if failure of heirs to Thomas, the reversion to John the grantor's son born of Agnes his wife; for the gift etc. John gave the grantor a sum of money beforehand; sealed; witnesses, John le Blound, mayor, John de Lincoln, Roger de Parys, sheriffs.

    1. H.R. 41 (87).

112. *Charter*[1] *enrolled as* **111**.
Grant by William Hardel to John of three shops with a solar built above; abutments, the tenement which the grantor recently gave to his son Thomas on the east and the north and the tenement of a certain Peter atte Lane on the west and the king's highway on the south; payments as in **111**; reversion to Thomas and his heirs; witnesses as in **111**; dated 8 May 1305.

    1. H.R. 41 (88).
    C.A.D., ii, A 2172.

110 contd. [f. 25v] Thomas Hardel; Robert Padegrys 3 Ric. II; the other tenement, John Hardel.

113. Memorandum: that Peter Blakeneye granted his tenement in the parish of Fenchurch to Peter atte Lane; abutments, the tenement of Master John Bussh on the north and the king's highway on the south and the tenement of William Hardell on the east and that of Katherine Bogoys on the west as appears in a charter[1] enrolled 26 Ed. I.

    1. H.R. 27 (131).

114. Note: that the prioress of Keleburn granted to William Preest a tenement on the west of that mentioned in **113** as appears by charter.

115. [*c.* 1242–8] Lease by Margery prioress of St. John Baptist Keleburn to William Preest of London, bureller, of a piece of land which the convent held in the parish; abutments, the land of Robert Hardel on the east [f. 26] and the land of Cecilia Guthlock on the west and at the lower end between the land of Robert Hardel and the said William; in depth from the king's highway to the land of Nolicia de Lymstrate; freedom to assign to all except Jews and religious; rent to Holy Trinity 4s. *p.a.*; gersuma 13s. 4d.; witnesses, Thomas de Dunholm, alderman of the ward,[1] Jordan de Coventre, then our warden, Wulonar the Baker.

    1. Langbourn.

St. Dionis Backchurch

116. Total of this parish 6s. 8d. and it is tithed at this in the king's exemplification.

IN THE PARISH OF ST. DIONIS BACCHURCH

117. Grant by Richard Estbrok, brewer, and Agnes his wife to John Fifhyde, mercer, William Creswyk, John Wakefeld, citizens, Peter Wysbech, chaplain, of 40s. of quit rent from their lands and tenements in Fanchurchstrete in the parish of St. Dionis de Bakchurch which they had as a gift and feoffment of William Bullok, citizen and tapicer; grantees to distrain if the rent is unpaid for a full year; [f. 26v] if insufficient distress taken then the grantees to take the tenements as if they were their own and hold them and occupy them and lease until the full payment is made; sealed; dated 1 Oct. 1384.

118. Release by John Wakeffeld of 40s. of quit rent to William Cresewyk which quit rent the said John had with the said William and Peter Wysebech, chaplain, by the grant of Richard Estbrok and Agnes his wife; sealed; dated 1 May 1397.

119. Release in similar terms by John Fyfhyde and Peter Wysebech of 40s. quit rent to William Cresewyk; dated 1 June 1393.

120. Bequest of 40s. quit rent by William Cresewyk to the church of Holy Trinity as appears in a will[1] enrolled in the Husting, Mon. 6 June 1407.

  1. *C. Wills*, ii, 371–3.

121. [List of those paying quit rent]: John Colvyle, 12 Hy. IV; John Sadeler, 3 Hy. V.

122. [f. 27] [1197–1221] Grant by Peter prior and convent to Godmund the Mercer of land with a stone house in Lymstrata which the said Godmundus [*sic*] previously held of them for a rent of 6s. *p.a.*; rent 3s. *p.a.*; in depth from the street to the interior 32 ells and in width along the aforesaid street 14 ells; if Godmund or his heirs wish to pledge, lease or sell fee the canons shall have an advantage of a bezant over other buyers; for lease and remission of 3s. in the rent Godmund gave 2½ marks: witnesses, Ralph the priest, Robert of Winchester.

  C.A.D., ii, A 2710.

123. [List of those paying rent]: Godmund the Mercer; William his son; Nicholas Batte; William May; Henry Grapinell; William de Basyng; John son of Symon, 19 Ed. II and 1 Ed. III; John Wodegate, 30 and 40 Ed. III; Robert Wretyl, 48 Ed. III and throughout Ric. II and Hy. IV; Thomas Gynnor, 4 Hy. V and the tenement is situated on the east side of Lymstret.

124. [1262–3] Grant by Gilbert prior and convent to William prior of Ware of land with houses build upon it formerly of John son of Bernard in

St. Olave Hart Street

Lymestrate; rent 1d. *p.a.*; if the grantees wish to lease or sell, the prior and convent to have an advantage of ½ mark over other buyers; [f. 27v] gersuma 40 marks in silver; chirograph sealed; witnesses, Thomas son of Thomas mayor, Robert Muntpelleis, Osbert de Suffolk, sheriffs.

125. [List of those paying quit rent]: Prior of Ware until 3 Hy. V; now [1425–7] the prior of Schene and the tenement is situated on the east side of Lymstret.

126. [1222–48] Grant by Richard prior and convent to William son of Godmund of land formerly held by Andrew the Goldsmith (*Orfreyfier*); abutments, the land formerly of Michael Hardel on the north and land of the hospital of St. Giles on the south; rent 1s. *p.a.*; the grantee is not to sell to Jews; if the grantee wishes to alienate, the prior and convent have the preference by 12d.; swore fealty; gersuma 5s.; witness, Thomas de Dunolm.

127. [List of those paying rent]: William son of Godmund; John Adryan; Henry Bacwell; Cecilia de Bacwell, 1 Ed. II and 1 Ed. III; Thomas de Bacwell, 30 Ed. III; Richard Dyko(n)n, 48 Ed. III and 8 Ric. II.

128. Total of this parish 44s. 1d. and it is tithed at this in the king's exemplification.

[f. 28] IN THE PARISH OF ST. OLAVE BY THE TOWER

129. [1264–5] Grant by Gilbert prior and convent to German Brid (*Bryd*), fishmonger, and Alice de Essex his wife of land with houses built upon it; abutments, the land of the canons on the east and the lane called Fulelane on the west and extending from the king's highway on the south to the land which was formerly of Richard de Hakeney on the north; in breadth along the king's highway 26¾ ells except for a few inches and in the middle 17½ ells and in length along the lane 57¼ ells and along the land of the canons on the east 46½ ells; to lease, sell or assign as they wish except to Jews and religious; rent 36s. *p.a.*; if they wish to lease or sell, the prior and convent to have the preference by a bezant of 2s.; swore fealty; gersuma 5 marks; chirograph sealed; witnesses, Thomas son of Thomas, mayor, Edward Blund, Peter son of Anger, sheriffs.

C.A.D., ii, A 2652.

130. [List of those paying rent]: German Bryd who granted part of this land to Henry Bru(n)ton and Imania his wife [See also after **131**] as appears by the following charter.

131. Grant by German Bryd, citizen and fishmonger, and Lucy his wife to Henry Bruton, tailor, and Ymania his wife of a certain messuage with appurtenances in the parish of St. Olave; abutments, the land of Holy Trinity on the east and tenement of German and Lucy in which they live on the west and extending from the king's highway on the south to the garden of the grantors on the north; in width along the king's highway 5 ells and at the north end 6¾ ells and in length from the south to the north 26¼ ells; also grant to Henry and Ymania a certain part of a sewer built on (*super*) the tenement in which the grantors live, 1¾ ells long, on condition that Henry and Imania, their heirs and assigns, shall bear yearly one third of the maintenance, repair and renewal (*emendacionem*) of the sewer; [f. 28v] to lease as they wish except to Jews and religious; rent 8s. *p.a.*; gersuma 6s. 8d.; duplicate charter sealed; witnesses, Ralph de Sandwich, kt., warden of London, Walter le Wythe, John Wade, sheriffs, William de Herford, alderman of this ward,[1] Richard de Derby, clerk; dated 24 Aug. 1286.

1. Aldgate.

130 contd. German Bryd paid 28s. and Henry Bruton paid 8s.: after German, those paying 28s.; Edmund Marney, 1 Ed. II; William de Hertyng, 1 Ed. III; John Kyngiston, 30 Ed. III from whom Prior Nicholas recovered the tenement [See also after **133**] as appears by the following plea.

132. *Common plea held in the Husting, Mon. 4 Nov. 1359.*
The prior of Holy Trinity complains that John de Kyngeston owes him 56s. being two years in arrears with his rent of 28s. *p.a.* before the day of the suing out of the writ, 18 Feb. 1359; the messuage could not be distrained upon for a year and a day as gavelet according to the custom of the City; John summoned three times, essoined once and still he did not come; messuage with its appurtenances seized etc. John summoned to be at the next court of Common pleas, Mon. 18 Nov. 1359; the prior, by Alan Horwode his attorney, present against John; John de Chichestre one of the sheriffs by Robert Cone, his clerk, testifies that on Thurs. 14 Nov. he seized the messuage by the view of J. Ha(u)ekyn, Walter Strangray, William Wordon [f. 29] and John atte Wall, capper; John de Kyngeston summoned by J. Ferthyng and J. Cobbe to be at the next court but he did not come; the prior recovered the messuage against John de Kyngeston to hold for a year and a day as gavelet.

133. *Common plea held in the Husting, Mon. 1 Feb. 1361.*
At the Husting of Common pleas held 34 Ed. III Walter de Berneye, one of the sheriffs, was ordered to warn John de Kyngeston to be present this day to say why judgment of shartford[1] should not be passed against him concerning a messuage which he ought to return to the prior of Holy Trinity; which prior had recovered it by a writ of gavelet on 18 Nov. 1359; the sheriff by Robert Cone, his clerk, testifies that John was warned by J. atte Wall, capper, and William de Wymondyswold to be here at this day; the def. did not come; the prior recovers the messuage etc. to hold as shartford; John in mercy.

1. Process for the recovery of a tenement, a year and a day after the issue of a writ of gavelet; see *Liber Albus*, i, 186.

130 contd. After Henry Bruton those paying 8s.; Emma his widow, 1 Ed. II who granted the tenement to Ralph Henteston, as appears in their charter[1] enrolled 10 Ed. II; William Breklesworth, 14 Ed. III; William Wymonyswold, 32 Ed. III; wardens of the church of St. Olave, 34 Ed. III; Ralph Burwell, 8 Ric. II.

    1. H.R. 45 (161).

134. [1267–8] Grant by Gilbert prior and convent to John le Waffrer of land with houses built upon it; abutments, the land and houses formerly of Richard Hakeney on the east, on those of the prior and convent, formerly [f. 29v] of Stacius de Gardino, clerk, on the west and extending from the king's highway to the former garden of Richard Hakeney; rent 9s. *p.a.*; the grantee is not to destroy the houses but to repair and maintain them; if John or his heirs wish to lease or sell, the prior and convent to have the preference by a bezant of 2s.; swore fealty; gersuma 10s.; chirograph sealed; witnesses, John Adrian, Luke de Batingcourt, sheriffs.

    C.A.D., ii, A 2674.

135. [List of those paying rent]: John Waffrer; John de Stratteford, 1 and 5 Ed. II; afterwards the Crutched Friars (*fratres sancte Crucis*).

136. [1170–97] Lease by Stephen prior and convent to Edward son of Robert the Cook of land which his father held of them for 2s. 8d. *p.a.*; rent 2s. *p.a.*; swore fealty; gersuma 1s.; witnesses, Gregory the chaplain, Alexander the deacon, Ailward the Baker, Richerus de Sartino, Hugh the clerk, Gilbert the Cook, Gilbert Foliot, cook, Richard de Bemtona, William de Infirmorio and others.

137. [List of those paying rent]: Edward son of Robert the Cook, then the land was divided for Goetha wife of Robert paid 1s. for her part and Brian Bagger paid 1s. for the other part: [f. 30] after Goetha; Thomas Black (*Niger*) alias Jurdan: after Brian Bagger; John son of Goodhier; Richard Murer after whose death the tenement came to Thomas Jurdan: after Thomas Jurdan paying 2s.; Geoffrey de Fonte; Reginald de Cobham, 1 and 19 Ed. II and 1 Ed. III; William Stanford, 14 Ed. III[1] and the tenement is situated between the garden of the earl of March, which was once of John Sendale, clerk, on the north and the land belonging to the church of St. Dunstan on the east by the bequest of John Maykyn which was once of Richard Carleton, on the west.

    1. *Margin:* See in the parish of Holy Trinity.

138. Grant by John Colvell to Richard Carleton of a tenement in the parish of St. Olave; abutments, the tenement and garden once of William de Staneford on the north and the tenement of the New Hospital of St. Mary without Bisshopisgate as appears in their charter[1] enrolled 15 Oct. 1352.

    1. H.R. 80 (?156).

139. [1250–8] Grant by John Renger son of Richard Renger to John prior and convent of a quit rent of 20d. from a house which was of Godfrey le Wanter.

St. Olave Hart Street

140. Grant by John Renger of other quit rents; a rent of 15s. 4d. *p.a.* made up as follows: 40d. from the tenement with houses of Gervase le Capeler, 20d. from the house that was of Godfrey le Wanter, 20d. from the house of Roger le Pes(c)ur and 8s. 8d. of rent which the canons were accustomed to pay him from a tenement which they held of John; [f. 30v] canons to pay for him and his heirs 6d. at the king's socage on the vigil of Easter; gersuma 11 marks; sealed Aug. 1252, Adam de Basing then mayor.

    C.A.D., ii, A 2400.

141. [List of those paying rent]: for the house of Godfrey le Wanter, Richard the Saddler (*Cellarius*).

142. [1222–8] Grant of Richard prior and convent to Agnes daughter of William of all land which Robert Cristemasse her husband held; abutments, the land of Richard the Saddler (*Sellarius*) on the south and the land of John Cheke on the north, in breadth along the king's highway 11¼ ells and at the south end 57½ ells; rent 1s. 4d.; not to pledge to Jews or to another religious house, if she wishes to sell, the prior and convent to have the preference by 1s.; swore fealty; gersuma 2s.; witnesses, John de St. George, Constantinus, chaplains, John Travers.

    C.A.D., ii, A 2395.

143. [List of those paying rent]: Agnes daughter of William; Robert Coringham who bequeathed the said tenement to Adam his *famulus* as appears in his testament[1] enrolled 14 Ed. I.

    1. *C. Wills*, i, 78.

144. Bequest of quit rents: Gilbert de la March, Ralph le Tanner and German the clerk, executors of the testament of Robert de Coringham, citizen, by authority of the testament[1] legally proved in full Husting Mon. 25 Mar. 1286, assigned to William prior and convent 2s *p.a.* quit rents [f. 31] which Robert bequeathed as a pittance for the canons, from land and houses built thereon held in a place which is called Cristemasselond; sealed; witnesses, Ralph de Sandwich, warden of the City, Thomas Cros, Walter Hawteyn, sheriffs, William de Hereford, alderman of the ward, William de Suffolchia, Richard le Poter, ?Humphrey le Poter, Thomas the Tailor (*Cissor*), Michael Unctor; dated 11 Apr. 1287.

    1. *C. Wills*, i, 78.
    C.A.D., ii, A 2403.

145. [List of those paying rent of 3s. 4d.]: Adam; William Coryngeham son of Robert who granted the tenement to William Bernerd,[1] as appears in a charter of 20 Ed. I and who paid 1 and 5 Ed. II; John Colwell.

    1. Cf. *C.A.D.*, ii, A 2399.

146. [1254–5] Grant of John prior and convent to Robert (*de*) Coringham of land, viz. a piece of land being the corner (*angulum*) which lies between

St. Olave Hart Street

London Wall on the east and the king's highway on the west; rent 1s. *p.a.*; gersuma ½ mark; swore fealty; chirograph sealed; witnesses, Ralph Hardel, mayor, Henry de Walerunt, Stephen de Ostregate, sheriffs.

    C.A.D., ii, A 2401.

147. [List of those paying rent]: as in **145**.

148. [1170–97] Lease of Stephen prior and convent to Bryan the Merchant (*Mercator*) of a tenement which Thomas the Saddler held of them; rent 1s. 4d. *p.a.*; [f. 31v] swore fealty; gersuma 3s.; witnesses, William the chaplain of the Bailey (*de balio*), Robert [   ],[1] chaplain, Roger the chaplain of St. Edmund.

    1. Illegible.

149. [List of those paying rent]: Brian; afterwards Thomas the Saddler; Robert Christemasse; Robert Coryngeham; Agnes Coryngeham; John Colewell.

150. [1222–32] Grant of Richard prior and convent of land to Ralph the Capper (*Capellarius*); abutments, the land of Holy Trinity on the south and land of Richard the Saddler on the north; in width at the south end 47 ells and at the north end 41½ ells and in the middle 44¼ ells and in length 62 ells; rent 8s. *p.a.*; not to sell to Jews; the prior and convent to have the preference by a bezant of 2s.; swore fealty; gersuma 20s.; witnesses, Gilbert son of Fulk, alderman, and others.

    C.A.D., ii, A 2651.

151. [List of those paying rent]: Ralph the Capper; Geoffrey de Santon or Shanketon; Richard de Shanketon, barber, who granted the said tenement with part of the land leased to Brian the Merchant, to William Bernard paying therefrom to Holy Trinity, 8s. 6½d. as appears in their charter made 18 Ed. I, Ralph de Sandwich then warden of London;[1] William Bernard, 1 and 5 Ed. II; John Colewell, paid 15s. 4d., 18 Ed. II as appears by the poundage viz. 8s. for land leased to Ralph the Capper and 1s. 4d. for land granted to Brian the Merchant and 1s. 8d. from the gift of John Renger, 1s. 4d. for the land granted to Agnes daughter of William, 1s. for the land leased to Robert Corngeham [*sic*] and 2s. for the same lands by the will[2] of the said Robert; John Colwell, 1 Ed. III; William Bristowe, 30 Ed. III; Robert Salesby, 35 Ed. III; Idonea Salesby, 44 Ed. III; Geoffrey Puppe, 4 Ric. II; John Gravesend, 10 Hy. IV; now [1425–7] William Cro(m)er.

    1. Cf. *C.A.D.*, ii, A 2402.   2. See **143**.

152. [f. 32] [1170–97] Lease of Stephen prior and convent to Robert the Saddler and Alice his wife of land which Thomas the Saddler bought of Adam the clerk; rent 4d. *p.a.*; and to the king, ½d.; to pay rent without miskenning; swore fealty; gersuma 1s.; witnesses, Benet the deacon, Ralph the deacon, Theobald the alderman.

St. Olave Hart Street

153. [List of those paying rent]: Robert the Saddler; Richard the Saddler; John Gilberd; Richard le Barber; Roger le Barber; Thomas Sely, 5 and 9 Ed. II and 1 Ed. III; Nicholas Bole, 30 Ed. III; John Sely, 44 Ed. III and 8 Ric. II; Henry Talbot, 10 Hy. IV and 4 Hy. V.

154. [1258] Grant by Nicholas de Gippeswich, clerk, to John prior and convent of a quit rent of 1s. 6d. *p.a.* which Ingolf (*Ingulphus*) the Baker was accustomed to pay to him from land and houses which he held of him in Wondero(v)elane; the canons to pay to grantor and his heirs ½d. or 1 lb. of cumin; [f. 32v] the canons gave 1 silver mark; witnesses, William son of Richard, mayor, Henry de Coventre, Adam Brounyng.

    C.A.D., ii, A 2656.

155. [List of those paying quit rent]: Ingolf the Baker; Geoffrey Santon; Henry Bockyng, carpenter; Agnes Boton(er); William Wysset who granted this tenement to Richard Glouceter paying 1s. 6d. as appears by their charter[1] enrolled 35 Ed. I; the abbot of Lyleshull as appears by the following plea.

    1. H.R. 35 (45).

156. *Common plea held in the Husting, Mon. 16 Nov. 1360.*
The abbot of Lilleshull complained that on Mon. 2 Nov. 1360 the prior of Holy Trinity took naam from his free tenement in the parish of St. Olave in Tower ward to the value of 10s. etc. until a pledge had been given to Walter de Bernere, sheriff etc. The prior by Alan de Horewode attorney came and said the distresses were lawful etc. 12s. due to the prior for the rent eight years in arrears; the abbot by Thomas Newport attorney came and could not deny it; the prior held his naam and the abbot in mercy.

157. [1170–97] Lease by Stephen prior and convent to Edulf brother of Walter the Hosier of land which Ralph his brother held before him; rent 5s. *p.a.*; to pay rent duly (*sine male ingenio et calumpnia*); to have the aforesaid land with a lodging house upon it (*terram herbergatum per convencionem*); gersuma 1 lb. of pepper; witnesses, Jordan son of Seth, Geoffrey Glov(eru)s, Richard de Averhill, Ralph the Capper, Henry the Tanner.

    C.A.D., iv, A 7274.

158. [f. 33] [List of those paying rent]: Edulf Hosier;[1] William Sabern;[1] Robert de Turri; afterwards the Crutched Friars.

    1. Founders of the Crutched Friars, Hart Street by the Tower, *Monasticon*, vi, 1586.

159. [1250–8] Grant by John Renger to John prior and convent of a quit rent of 1s. 8d. *p.a.* from the gift of Roger le Pestur.

160. [List of those paying rent]: Roger le Pestur; Adam de Mallyng; afterwards the Crutched Friars.

St. Olave Hart Street

161. [1222–32] Grant by Reginald de Mallyng to Richard prior and convent of a quit rent of 10s. *p.a.* from three tenements which Richard Swetenote, Constantine the Capper and William Cristemasse held of him; attorns the same tenants to pay 10*s. p.a.* to the prior and convent paying therefrom to Richard son of William son of Renger 15s. 8d.; Richard and his heirs warrant the rent in perpetuity to the prior and convent according to the law of the City; the prior and convent gave for the sale etc. 24s. sterling; witness, Gilbert son of Fulk, alderman.

    C.A.D., ii, A 2673.

162. Remission by John son of Richard Renger of 15s. 8d. and thus the rent was divided and R. Swetenote paid 3s. *p.a.*, Constantine the Capper 4s. *p.a.* and William Cristemasse 3s. *p.a.*

163. [List of those paying quit rent]: after Richard Swetenote; William the Carpenter; afterwards the Crutched Friars: after Constantine the Capper; Stephen de Eldyng; afterwards the Crutched Friars.

164. Note that the Crutched Friars paid 5s. *p.a.* for a tenement once of Robert de Turry; 1s. 8d. *p.a.* for a tenement once of Adam de Mallyng; 3s. *p.a.* for the tenement of William the Carpenter and 3s. *p.a.* for a tenement of Stephen de Eldyng and this total sum appears in a composition made between them and Holy Trinity.

165. Composition made between Richard de Wymbisch, prior, and convent of Holy Trinity of the one party and Adam, prior, and the brethren of the Crutched Friars of the other party, that since the Crutched Friars hold a tenement in the parish of St. Olave by the Tower by rent service of 13s. 8d. *p.a.* within which the friars' church is to stand and also a cemetery, the which tenement extends along the king's highway on the north from the tenement [f. 33v] of John Priour to that of Constance de Stratford and on the south from the tenement of the abbot of Lilleshall to that of Roger Frowyk and at the east and west ends from the highway to the same abbot's holding, which church as yet undedicated measured in length, $26\frac{1}{4}$ ells and in width $9\frac{1}{4}$ ells and the cemetery, as yet unconsecrated 25 ells in length on the south and 18 ells on the north and 16 ells in width on the east and 14 ells on the west. As the Crutched Friars intend to have the church dedicated and the cemetery consecrated, they will and grant expressly that no prejudice shall be caused to Holy Trinity in respect of the rent which they agree to pay and that Holy Trinity shall be allowed to distrain for the same, if it is in arrears. Moreover the Crutched Friars grant that they will cause no obstruction to the path or means of entry and exit to prevent the prior and convent from freely entering to obtain the rent notwithstanding any legal pleas. Because Holy Trinity might be impeded by the dedication of the church and the consecration of the cemetery, the Crutched Friars grant that if this is so, then the official of the archdeacon of London for the time being to whom they willingly submit, faith having been pledged on the foregoing, shall, upon the oath of the proctor of Holy Trinity alone, compel them to pay the 13s. 8d. as often as it is in arrears by pronouncing sentence of major excommunication against the prior and of interdict against the church. Chirograph sealed; dated 1 Mar. 1319.

> For Latin text, see Appendix.
> *C.A.D.*, ii, A 2666.

166. [List of those paying rent]: 3s. for William Cristemasse; his widow; Jordan de Capella; John de Stratteford; Constance de Stratteford; afterwards the Crutched Friars.

167. [f. 34] [1222–32] Grant by Reginald de Mallying to Richard prior and convent of a quit rent of 3s. *p.a.* which William Asseford (*de Asseford*) paid him from certain land with houses in the parish next the land of William Cristemasse on the east; payment to Richard son of William son of Renger, the chief lord or his successors 2s. *p.a.*; gersuma ½ mark of silver; witness, Gilbert son of Fulk, alderman.

168. [List of those paying rent]: William de Asshford; his widow; William de Burgundia; Adam le Messager and Zarilda his wife, daughter and heir of William Burgoyn, who granted the tenement to Adam Hutman, as appears by their charter[1] enrolled 27 Ed. I; afterwards the Crutched Friars, 18 Ed. II.

> 1. H.R. 28 (33).

169. [1252] Grant by John son of Richard Renger to John prior and convent of a quit rent of 3s. 4d. *p.a.* from the house of Gervase le Capeler in the same parish as appears in the twelfth charter.[1]

> 1. **140** (i.e. ? 12th 'charter' of this parish).

170. [List of those paying rent]: Gervase le Capeler; Geoffrey de Sanctona; Henry de Bockyng; Agnes le Botoner; Ralph Brumle and afterwards the Crutched Friars.

171. [1197–1221] Grant of Peter prior and convent to Alfred Bochere (*le Bochier*) of land held immediately before him by John Herliyn; rent 1s. *p.a.*; swore fealty; width in front along the street 6½ ells and in depth 30½ ells; if the grantee wishes to pledge or sell, the prior and convent to have the preference by a bezant; gersuma 1s.; witnesses, John de Ballio, heob' [?haberdasher], alderman, Geoffrey Blundus, Geoffrey, junior (*Iuvenis*), Hamon Capell, Peter Capell, Roger Chose, Robert Capell, Alexander Bald, Ralph Carpenter, Ralph de Mend, Richard de Beni(t) and Helia, cooks, ?Hugh and Gervase, 'pistoribus', Gervase Cordwainer, Turg(und), servant and many others.

> *C.A.D.*, iv, A 7840.

172. [f. 34v] [List of those paying rent]: appearing in an ancient rental with the letter 'B' and in all following rentals: Alfred Bosier; Ralph Burel and then the land was divided for John Burel paid 6d. and Peter paid 6d.; and these paid 6d. after Peter Coffyn; Geoffrey Boys; John Chykewelle, 1 Ed. II: and these paid 6d. after John Burel; Henry Orpedeman; Roger Marchall, smith, 1 Ed. II; Henry Wymund, 1 and 6 Ed. III; his sister, 30 Ed. III; Richard Kyng, 35 Ed. III; Alan Russell, 8 Ric. II and afterwards the Crutched Friars, and the tenement is situated on the south side of the street between the tenement of the canons of the New Hospital outside Bishopsgate on the east and the tenement of the nuns of St. Helen on the west.

173. [1271–2] Grant by Richard Capeler and Sibyl his wife to Eustace prior and convent of 8s. *p.a.* of quit rent from the tenement which Henry[1] between that tenement and Marthelane next the land of Benet de Hakeneye; if the rent is not paid the canons and their successors to be able to distrain; for the lease the canons gave 6 marks; witnesses, Walter Hervi, mayor, Richard de Paris and John de Bodele, sheriffs.

    1. Presumably 'Henry . . . held': the phrase is incomplete.
    C.A.D., ii, A 2655.

174. [List of those paying quit rent]: Richard le Capelere, 45 Hy. III; Martin Box who divided the tenement between his two daughters, Elena, paying 4s. *p.a.* for four shops and [blank] his daughter, wife of Nicholas de Bononia, the other part of the tenement, as appears in the will[1] of the said Martin enrolled 29 Ed. I: and these paid 4s. after Elena; John Reneshale, 1 Ed. III; Henry Wymond, 6 Ed. III; Henry Pykard, 30 Ed. III; his widow, 36 Ed. III; John Pykard, 8 Ric. II: and these paid 4s. [f. 35] after [blank] the other daughter, wife of Nicholas de Bononia; Richard Colle, 1 Ed. III; Richard Horwode, 6 and 49 Ed. III and throughout Ric. II until 5 Hy. IV; Thomas Colshill, 1 and 5 Hy. V; his widow, 7 Hy. V.

    1. *C. Wills*, i, 154.

175. Bequest by William Hynelond, rector of St. Olave, to Eustace Glaston(bury) and other parishioners and their successors for ever of all his tenements and appurtenances once of Benet Hakeneye which he had by gift of Henry Petipas, 'stokfisshmongere', that they and their successors shall hold the day of his anniversary in the church of Holy Trinity where his body lies buried,[1] as appears in the testament which follows, proved in the Husting[2] Mon. 22 Nov. 1372, bequeathing to Eustace, William Whetele and John atte Walle, the tenements for the object above-stated and to cause fifteen masses to be celebrated on the day of his anniversary for his soul, to distribute 2s. 6d. to the poor on that day, to spend 6d. on a peal of bells (*pro clasico*), 1s. for the dirge, 1s. in lights and 11d. for the saying of the psalter and all profits from the tenements, beyond the amount necessary for the reasonable maintenance of the property and above charges, to be devoted to the use of the nave (*usui corporis*) of St. Olave and to the improvement and maintenance of the books and ornaments of the said church and if the legatees or their successors fail in fulfilling the above-mentioned duties or cease to observe the testator's anniversary for one whole year then the tenements to revert to the prior and convent of Holy

All Hallows Barking

Trinity to celebrate masses for his soul and under the terms of this will the parishioners pay 2s. 6d. *p.a.* dated 24 Dec. [?1372].

    1. *Margin.* Buried in front of the garden (*sepelitur ante ortolanum*).
    2. *C. Wills*, ii, 151–2.

176. [List of those paying for legatees]: John Curteis, 20 Ric. II; Thomas Colshill, 1 Hy. V; his widow, 6 Hy. V.

177. Note: William Hynelond was admitted to the freedom of the city of London in the time of Richard Lac, mayor, and Thomas de Maryns, chamberlain, and it is enrolled in a green book (*in viridi papiro*) of payments for freedom, Mon. 25 Sep. 1346.

178. [f. 35v] [?1190–1215] Grant by Juliana formerly wife of Alan Balon (*de Balon*) for the salvation of the soul of Alan and of her own soul, to the canons of Holy Trinity of 1s. *p.a.* of quit rent which Ralph Burel was accustomed to pay from a certain piece of land with houses in Marthelane; abutments, the land of Turb(er)nus Arcon(er)us on the north and land of Peter the Tiler (*Coopertoris*); for the gift the canons gave 6s.; witnesses, Peter Blundus, alderman, Robert de Turry.

    C.A.D., iv, A 7354.

179. [List of those paying quit rent]: Ralph Burel; William Burel; Benet de Hakeneye; Cecily de la More, 5 Ed. II; Walter the Capper (*le Hurere*), 19 Ed. II and 5 Ed. III; his widow, 6 Ed. III; John atte Harpe, 20 Ed. III; his widow, 30 Ed. III; Thomas Cressingham, 40 Ed. III and 8 Ric. II; Edmund Olivere, 19 Ric. II and 1 Hy. IV; his widow, 12 Hy. IV; Robert Arnold, 3 Hy. V and the tenement is situated on the west side of Martlane between the tenement of Robert Arnold on the north and [blank].

180. Total of this parish £3 9s. 4d. and yet it is tithed at £5 1s. 10½d. in the king's exemplification.

[f. 36] IN THE PARISH OF ALL HALLOWS BERKYNGGECHIRCHE

181. [1197–1221] Grant of Peter prior and convent to Ralph the Capper (*Capellarius*) of land which was held immediately before him by William the Carpenter; width in front along (*super*) the lane 13¼ ells and depth from the lane to the west end 30 ells; abutments, the land formerly of Susanna Trentemarse and land which William the Carpenter held of the canons of Southwark (*Suwerka*); rent 4s. *p.a.*; if the grantee or his heirs wish to pledge or sell the land, the canons to have the preference by a bezant; swore fealty; to pay rent duly; gersuma 6s.; witnesses, Peter the Cutler (*Cutellarius*), Robert Goy, Ralph de Coventr'.

    Original deed, P.R.O. E40/14313.

182. [List of those paying rent]: Ralph the Capper who gave this land to the prior and brethren of St. John of Jersualem as appears by the charter made between Holy Trinity and St. John of Jerusalem.

All Hallows Barking

183. [1197–1221] Confirmation by Peter prior and convent to the prior and friars of the hospital of St. John of Jerusalem of the land and houses granted to them by Ralph Freure, capper, in free alms which he held of Holy Trinity; abutments, the land of the canons of Southwark and land formerly of Susanna Trentemars; rent 4s. *p.a.*; brother Richard, their vice-gerent, swore fealty; witnesses, Thomas de Haverill; Solomon de Basinge.

Original deed, P.R.O. E40/14312.

184. [List of those paying rent]: the prior of the hospital of Jerusalem; John May; Simon le Mesagere, 5 Ed. II; Richard Gray, 19 Ed. II and 1 and 6 Ed. III; Thomas Ireland or Brandon, 30 Ed. III and 1 Ric. II.

185. [f. 36v] [1197–1221] Grant of Peter prior and convent to Henry son of Epi son of Goderic Murte and his mother of a dwelling (*mansio*) with land once of Goderic Murte; paying 1s. *p.a.* as a recognition (*de recognicione*) to the canons and their heirs as did Goderic and Epi his son; witnesses, Baldwin the priest, Haldenus, Geoffrey minister of the sheriff, Ordgarus Fince, Martin B(ani)sshere, Gunter (*Guntro*) de Arraz, Wulgarus, Adam, William son of Haldenus, L(iuin)gus the alderman.

Original deed, P.R.O. E40/14311.

186. [List of those paying rent]: Henry son of Epi; Peter Blund or Feltriere; Jordan de Turri; Robert de Turri; Ralph Beamond; John de Kyngeston, 1 and 5 Ed. II; Walter Cle(v)hand, 3 Ed. III [See also after **187**] as appears by the following plea.

187. *Common plea held in the Husting, Mon. 12 June 1329.*
Walter Clevehand and Matilda his wife summoned three times, essoined once and a second time on Mon. 25 July [1328] and again on Mon. 16 Jan., the prior sought that they should perform their right service from the free tenement which they held of him and they had until this day in which to pay and they did not come and the tenement was seized into the hands of the City authorities and Walter was summoned to reply on Mon. 24 Sep. 1330; the prior said that Walter and Matilda held the tenement of him at a rent of 1s. and that Richard Wymbisch, once prior, was so seised and it was not distrainable for a year and a day and he sought gavelet according to the custom of the City and Walter and Matilda acknowledged this and paid the rent and arrears.

186 contd. Thomas Perle, 30 Ed. III; Reginald Lofe, [f. 37] [See also after **188**] as appears by the following plea.

188. *Common plea held in the Husting, Mon. 20 Feb. 1374.*
On Mon. 6 Feb. 1374 the prior by John Aschwell his attorney appeared against Reginald Love that he should do him right service for a tenement in Ce(v)e(t)henlane; rent 1s.; in arrears five years before the day of the suing out of the writ, viz. 12 Oct. 1373 and the tenement is not distrainable for a year and a day and the prior seeks gavelet; Reginald was given a day

All Hallows Barking

and did not come; the sheriffs, John Fipbod[1] and Awbrei seized the property into the hands of the City authorities on Sat. 18 Feb. by the view of John atte Wall, Richard Kyngs, Roger Hinton and Richard atte Celer(er); the said Reginald summoned by John Wakefeld and John Asshewelle to be here at this day; Reginald came and by Gilbert Meldeborne his attorney recognised that he held the tenement of the prior at a rent of 1s. *p.a.* and that he owes 5s. for five years in arrears; the prior recovers the rent and arrears and Reginald is in mercy; and for security it was conceded that if Reginald ceased to pay for one whole year then the sheriffs should levy double the rent and pay it to the prior; and Reginald by his attorney agreed to this and paid 5s. arrears into court and thus the prior was satisfied.

    1. *Rectius* Fifhyde.

186 contd. [f. 37v] Reginald Lofe, 49 Ed. III; Thomas Yrlond or Brandon, 1 Ric. II who granted the two tenements to Robert Knollys, kt., paying 5s. *p.a.* as appears in their charter[1] enrolled 3 Ric. II; now [1425–7] the college of Pon(ne)frert; and the tenement is situated between the cemetery of St. Olave on the north and the tenement formerly of John le Hurere on the south.

    1. H.R. 108 (43).

189. [1252–3] Grant by Philip de Belvaco to John prior and convent of 4s. *p.a.* of quit rent which Roger de la Ture paid the grantor from a certain house in the parish; abutments, the land of Master William de Turri on the south and another house of the grantor's between the land of Alan le Hurere on the north; rent to the grantor and his heirs, a rose on 24 June; gersuma $2\frac{1}{2}$ marks of silver; witnesses, John de Tulesan, mayor, Thomas de Wymburn, William de Dunolm, sheriffs, John Gisors, Michael Tovy, Roger son of Roger, Nicholas Batte.

190. [1253–4] Grant by Philip de Belvaco to John prior and convent of certain land with houses; abutments, the house which Robert de Turri holds of the canons on the south and land of Alan the Capper (*le Hurere*) on the north; rent to the grantor and his heirs, a rose on 24 June; [f. 38] gersuma 21s. in silver; witnesses, Nicholas Batte, mayor, John de Norhamtona, Richard Picard, sheriffs, Roger son of Roger, Thomas Dunolm, Gervase Bran, William son of Richard, Adrian the alderman, Robert de Curryngham, William de Turri, Hugh de Eldyng.

191. [List of those paying quit rent under **189**]: Roger de la Turre; Alan the Capper which Alan had also the land in the charter next written for 2s. *p.a.* and so Alan paid 6s.: after Alan; Roger Poete; Stephen Eldyng; John de Stratford, 5 Ed. II; Constance de Stratford, 19 Ed. II and 1 Ed. III whose executor granted the tenement to John le Hurere as appears in a charter[1] enrolled Mon. 22 May 1329 whose wife Isabel bequeathed the tenement to the church of All Hallows Barking as appears in a will[2] enrolled before 25 Mar. 1349 and the wardens (*custodes*) paid as appears by

St. Dunstan in the East

indentures made between them and the tenement is situated between the land of the college of Pontefract on the north and [incomplete].

 1. H.R. 57 (61).   2. C. *Wills*, i, 532–3.

192. *Charter*[1] *enrolled in the Husting, Mon. 4 May 1271.*[2] [1278–9] Stephen de Eldyng, capper, citizen of London, for the salvation of the grantor's soul etc., has given etc. 8s. of quit rent in free alms out of his whole tenement in Chikinelane and in the cemetery of All Hallows which is of the fee of the canons of Waltham Holy Cross which 8s. he has by the gift of Peter Maltmetere and Agnes his wife, free from all services; sealed; witnesses, Gregory Rokesle, mayor, William Mazerere, Robert de Basynges, sheriffs.

 1. H.R. 4 (101).
 2. The heading refers to the feoffment of Stephen de Eldyng read and enrolled in the Husting on that day.
 C.A.D., i, A 1648.

193. [List of those paying quit rent]: Solomon le Cofferere who granted the tenement to John Broun who paid 8s. to Holy Trinity as appears in a charter[1] enrolled 12 Ed. II; John Bedeford, 14 and 33 Ed. III; afterwards the abbot of Waltham; William Parker, 8 Ric. II.

 1. H.R. 47 (51).

194. [f. 38v][1] Total of this parish 19s. and it is tithed as appears in the king's exemplification.

 1. This f. is blank except for the total.

[f. 39] IN THE PARISH OF ST. DUNSTAN IN THE EST

195. [1271–2] Grant by William Cron (*de la Cron*), citizen, to Eustace prior and convent of 8s. *p.a.* of quit rent, for the salvation etc., from certain land in the street opposite Wyvelaston with a house containing an oven (*cum forno*) and shops adjacent; abutments, the tenement with tentergrounds (*cum tentoriis*) formerly of Matthew Bokerel on one side and the tenement of Roger de Grasch(ur)ch on the other; grant in free alms; if the canons or their successors are unable to distrain for the rent on account of lack of maintenance or fire (*et si contigerit quod absit quia dicti canonici et successores sui per defectum sustentacionis vel combustionis pro dicto redditu in prefato tenemento competenter distringere non possint*), then the canons are to distrain on all the grantor's rents in the city of London to their full satisfaction; for the gift the canons gave 60s. and 12s. to expedite the grantor's business (*ad negocia mea expedienda*); sealed; witnesses, Walter Hervy, then mayor, Richard de Parys, John de Buttele, sheriffs.

196. [List of those paying quit rent]: William Cron.[1]

 1. About half f. 39 is blank.

197. [f. 39v] Grant by John de Suffolk (*Suffolchia*) and Agnes his wife, daughter and heir of Peter son of Roger, to Eustace prior and convent of 1 mark *p.a.* of quit rent from a wharf (*cayo*) and houses and shops (*sopis*) built thereon; abutments, from the king's road to the Thames and from the corner of the lane called Aubrees Wat(er)gate which is on the east side of this tenement to the wharf of Wlmer(us) son of Ed(ward) de Essex on the west; rent to the grantor and their heirs, a clove-gillyflower on Michaelmas day; for this gift the canons gave $8\frac{1}{2}$ marks to expedite the grantor's business; if rent in arrears, the prior and convent may distrain on any of the houses or shops to the full value of the rent; sealed; witnesses, Walter Hervy, mayor, Walter le Pot(er), John Horn, sheriffs, Herman le Estreys, William le Corner; dated Sun. 21 May 1273.

    C.A.D., iv, A 7283.

198. [List of those paying rent]: Ralph Crepyn, clerk, otherwise called Algate.

199. [1170–97] Lease of Stephen prior and convent to Jordan de Turri, clerk, of all the messuage that Edwin the Felter (*Feltrarius*) held of them and all land which is in front of that house (*managium*) extending to the main street (*magnum vicum*) which Edwin held and after him Terricus, his son and all the land once of Robert Burrell near (*prope*) Wifladeston; rent 8s. *p.a.*; Jordan swore fealty; gersuma 1 mark; witnesses, Walter the alderman, Godard his brother.

200. [List of those paying rent]: Jordan de Turri who had two sons Robert and John and the land was divided for John de Turri paid 2s. and Robert de Turri 6s. [f. 40] and these names paid 2s. after John de Turri; John de Camera, 1 Ed. I; afterwards the rector of St. Dunstan's: and these paid 6s. after Robert de Turri; Matthew Bokerel; Fulk de St. Edmund; Walter Crepyn otherwise called de Glovernia [See also after **201**] as appears by the following plea.

201. *Common plea held in the Husting, Mon. 19 Feb. 1302.*
Walter de Glovernia son of Ralph de Algate, clerk, complained that on Mon. 12 Feb. 1302 the prior of Holy Trinity came and took naam from his tenement; abutments, the tenement of the rector of St. Dunstan on the east and the tenement of Matilda le Wolf on the west; to the value of 1s. until a pledge had been given to the sheriff etc. The prior came and said that the seizure was just, as the pl. owed 10s. in arrears. The parties agreed by licence of the court; Walter recognised the rent as owing to the prior and his successors for ever whereupon the prior remitted arrears; Walter in mercy.

200 contd. Nicholas de Jernemouth, 6 and 31 Ed. III; his widow, 48 Ed. III and 8 Ric. II; Henry Edes;[1] Edward Salle; John Croke during Hy. VI and Ed. IV.[2]

    1. Inserted above the line.   2. Inserted in a later hand.

St. Dunstan in the East

202. [1170–97] Lease of Stephen prior and convent to Alfred the Tiler (*Coopertor*) of land for houses (*terram domorum*) which Pain the Fishmonger (*Piscator*) his brother had held; rent 1s. 8d. *p.a.*; to hold duly (*sine calumpnia et omni malo ingenio*); swore fealty; the grantee gave a London sextary of wine; witnesses, Walter the chaplain, Adam the chaplain, Adam the Chamberlain (*Camerarius*).

    C.A.D., i, A 1711.

203. [List of those paying rent]: Alfred the Tiler; Humphrey Rufus; Edeua daughter of Walter to whom Peter prior and convent granted land at a rent of 4s. *p.a.* [See also after **204**] as appears by the following.

204. [1197–1221] Grant of Peter prior and convent to Edeua daughter of Walter of land that Walter Brown (*Brunus*), mercer, held of them; in length $25\frac{1}{4}$ ells and in width $8\frac{1}{2}$ ells; abutments, the land of Robert Hardel and the land of Humphrey Rufus near (*iuxta*) Ma(nun)lane; leases all that it has in wood and stone; rent 4s. *p.a.*; Edeua undertook for herself and her heirs to keep houses on the land and the houses roofed at a cost of 40s. if she or they wished to lease the fee 40s. *p.a.* rent to be paid unless the land had been wasted by fire in which event the payment would not be levied; if the grantee wishes to pledge or sell, the prior and convent to have the preference by a gold bezant; swore fealty; [f. 40v] gersuma 2 marks of silver; witnesses, Gilbert the alderman, Ralph Stepranc, Ralph Chaloner, Reimundus.

    C.A.D., i, A 1710.

203 contd. Edeua paid 5s. 8d. and after her Robert Coch; Gylminus Fraunces; Martin le Wolf; William Basyng; Simon Symean, 1 Ed. II; John Cokirmouth, 19 Ed. II and 3 Ed. III [See also after **205**] as appears by the following plea.

205. *Common plea held in the Husting, Mon. 23 Oct. 1329.*
John Cokermouth summoned to reply to the prior of Holy Trinity concerning his free tenement held of the prior at a rent of 5s. 8d.; John said he was not the tenant and had not been on the day of the suing out of the writ and places himself on the country and the prior likewise, and a jury is summoned for the next court; John essoined Mon. 4 Dec. 1329; his messuage seized; Mon. 12 Mar. 1330 John summoned to answer concerning a plea that he should do right service to the prior from his free tenement of which Richard Wymbysh, the prior's predecessor, was seised etc. and because 24s. were in arrears on the day of the suing out of the writ on 23 Feb. 1329 and the messuage could not be distrained upon for a year and a day the prior sought the messuage as gavelet and John came and acknowledged that he held of the prior and the prior received the messuage.

203 contd. Thomas Walden, 31 Ed. III; William de Stanys, 36 and 47 Ed. III; Lord de Gray, 48 Ed. III and 8 Ric. II; William Parker, 18 Ric. II;

Thomas Wylford; [17 lines blank] and the tenement is situated on the east side of Mynchynlane.

    C.A.D., i, A 1713.

206. [f. 41] [1197–1212] Grant of Peter prior and convent to Elias son of Godard of land which Spirling the Moneyer (*monetarius*) held; abutments, the land of Ralph Flael and other land of Elias which he holds of the king; rent 1s. 6d. *p.a.*; and from the land which he holds of the Crown he gave a quit rent of 2s. *p.a.* to the canons; if the rent is unpaid, the canons to have the right to take naam in all his lands which he holds of the king as far as Mangunelane if they do not find sufficient naam in the land which Spirling gave them; Elias for himself and his heirs placed the canons in security (*in contraplegium*) in all the land he held of the Crown in perpetuity; swore fealty and to pay rent without miskenning; sealed chirograph; witnesses, Henry mayor of London, Roger son of Alan.

207. [List of those paying rent]: Elias son of Godard; William Brown (*Brunus*); New Hospital without Bishopisgate until 9 Ed. III when the hospital granted the land to Reginald de Conductu [See also after **208**] as appears by the following.

208. Release of the prior and chapter of the New Hospital of St. Mary in the above-mentioned tenement [**206**] saving certain rents to themselves and to the prior and convent of Holy Trinity; indenture, John de Habiton(ne), prior of the New Hospital of St. Mary without Bishopisgate in the suburb of London, greeting etc. when William de Horton, prior, and chapter, leased a certain messuage in Maionelane to Reginald de Conductu, citizen and alderman, for a term of 100 years at a rent of 14s. 6d. *p.a.* for the true value (*pro vero valore dicti tenementi*) and a quit rent of 1s. 6d. *p.a.* to Holy Trinity; abutments, another tenement of Reginald on the north and the tenement once of William Flori on the south; in length from Ma(n)ionelane on the east to the tenement of Reginald on the west; and the holding was in such bad repair (*debile et ruinosum*) that it could not be maintained unless it was completely (*de novo*) rebuilt and Reginald wished to lease the property and rebuild in default of repairing the houses (*pro defaltu reparacionis domuum*) for the rebuilding the prior and chapter quitclaim their right and that of their successors in the property, reserving to themselves a rent of 12s. 6d. and to Holy Trinity 1s. 6d. *p.a.*; the prior of the hospital to have powers to distrain for arrears; dated 6 Mar. 1335.

207 contd. [f. 41v] Afterwards Thomas Appilby was constituted tenant (*reddituarius*) of Reginald by the king and paid 1s. 6d. as appears by Holy Trinity's acquittance;[1] Thomas Peerle, 34 Ed. III.

    1. **1040.**

209. [1170–97] Grant of Stephen prior and convent to James the chaplain of that land not built on (*illam terram nudam*), which the grantors had of the Lady Roais who was wife of Robert Mantel, in Manionelane to hold to him and his heirs in fee for 5s. 6d.; James swore fealty; gersuma 2s.; witnesses, Robert the chaplain, Master Robert the chaplain of St. Olave, John de St. Michael.

210. [List of those paying rent]: from which 5s. 6d. James paid 1s. 6d. to the hospital of St. Katherine which sum Ralph prior and convent had granted to the hospital and James paid another 1s. 6d. to the hospital which Peter prior and convent conceded to the hospital as appears by a chirograph made between Holy Trinity and the hospital and thus James paid the hospital of St. Katherine 3s. *p.a.* and Holy Trinity 2s. 6d.: and after James; his widow; Walter the Goldsmith (*Aurifaber*); Ralph the priest (*presbiter*); Stephen Casuen; John Casuen; then the tenement was divided and Michael Unctor paid 1s. and Edmund Combe 1s. and John Bussh or Boys 6d.: and after Michael; William de Wynton; Reginald de Conductu, 19 Ed. II: and after Edmund; Hugh Hereford, 5 Ed. II; Reginald de Combe, 19 Ed. II: and after John; Reginald de Conductu paid the total 2s. 6d., 19 Ed. II and 1 Ed. III. Thomas Peerle paid 4s. for the properties in **208** and **209** as appears by the following plea.

211. *Common plea held in the Husting, Mon. 26 Jan. 1360.*
Thomas Peerle complained that on Wed. 6 Nov. 1359 the prior of Holy Trinity came to the pl.'s free tenement and took naam etc. to the value of 13s. 4d. etc. until a pledge was given to Simon de Bedyngton one of the sheriffs etc. The prior came by his attorney Alan de Horwode and said that the taking of naam was just etc. because the prior should receive a rent charge of 8s. *p.a.* which he had had from Reginald de Conductu and that 40s. was due for five years' arrears etc. and Thomas Peerle said that the rent was 4s. and that he was prepared to satisfy the prior and they were given until the next court and the matter was then delayed, because the parties were conferring, until the court held on Mon. 18 May 1360; the prior recognised that the rent was 4s. *p.a.* and the pl. paid the arrears, and 4s. in future.

210 contd. [f. 42] John Fysymon, 48 Ed. III; Philip Burton [13 lines blank].

Margin: Charter[1] of Hugh Sprot through the guardians (*per custodes*) of the heirs of Thomas Perle enrolled after 12 Mar. 1395.
1. H.R. 123 (99).

212. Note: that the tenement of John Cory, clerk, in the parish of St. Dunstan is situated in Mynchinlane between the tenement of John Covert, kt., and Margery de Chissebech his wife which was once of Thomas de Kent (*Cancia*) on the south and the tenement of Reginald de Conductu on the north and it extends from Mynchinlane on the east to the tenement of Isabel at Vyne on the west as appears in a charter[1] of John Cory, enrolled after 1 Nov. 1346.

1. H.R. 73 (124).

213. [1269–70] Grant by Thomas de Oxford (*Oxon*), bureller (*burelarius*),

St. Dunstan in the East

and Alice his wife to Master John Rosamund of 20s. *p.a.* of quit rent from rents which they had in the parish of St. Dunstan by the Tower opposite the church in a lane which goes by the Tower; rent to the grantors and their heirs ½ lb. of cumin or three grains of pepper; the grantor and his heirs free to distrain (*namiare seu distringere*) and may distrain on the grantees' land in the parish of St. Mary Bothaw which is between the land of John le Minor on the west and land formerly of Robert de Wrotham on the east and extends from the king's road in Candelwykstrate to the land of Michael To(v)i; John gave 15 marks of silver; sealed; witnesses, Hugh son of Hocton (*fitz Hoctonis*) then constable of the Tower, Robert de Cornhill, Thomas de Basing, sheriffs; Master John Rosamund gave this quit rent of 20s. to the church of Holy Trinity as appears by Charter Seven[1] of several parishes.

1. See **1008**.

214. [List of those paying quit rent]: Thomas de Oxford; Roger Hattefeld who granted the tenement to William de Ham(m)e who paid 20s. to Holy Trinity [See also after **215**] [f. 42v] as appears by the following charter.

215. [1286–7] Charter of Roger de Hattefeld, citizen of London, granting to William de Hamme, citizen and wool merchant (*lanarius*), land with houses built thereon; abutments, the tenement of Simon Boys and that once of Andrew Essex on the east and the king's road on the west and the cemetery of St. Dunstan on the south and a road called Tourstrate on the north together with 10s. *p.a.* of quit rent which the grantor has received from the tenement of Thomas Porter which he had by the lease of Thomas de Cap(oes)hors and 8s. *p.a.* of quit rent received from the tenement of Laurence de Hocton which he had of the lease of the said Thomas de Capon(er) and 10s. and 8s. *p.a.* of quit rent received there from a certain piece (*placea*) of land which Henry the Carpenter had of the same land by the lease of the grantor; all in land, buildings, wood and stone in length breadth and height leased in fee in perpetuity; rent to the grantor and his heirs one clove-gillyflower at Easter, to the heirs of Henry de Frowyk 50s. of silver, to the heirs of John de la Tour 4s., to the canons of St. Mary of Southwork 4s., to the king ¾d. of socage on Palm Sunday, to the prior of Lewisham and his successors 7d. at Michaelmas and to the canons of Christchurch (Holy Trinity) 20s.; gersuma £20 sterling; witnesses, Ralph de Sandwich, warden of London, Thomas Cros, Walter Hautein, sheriffs.

216. [List of those paying rent]: William de Hamme or Woolchirchehawe who granted the tenement to Walter Mon(e)n(er) or Me(lu)arad as appears by their charter enrolled 5 Ed. II, who paid 18 Ed. II as appears by poundage (*pondagium*); Edward Sannford, 1 and 6 Ed. III and then the land was divided as follows; John Morton paid for his part 10s.; Adam Changour paid for his part 2s.; Matthew Broun for another part paid 2s.; Agnes Berners paid for another part 2s.; Robert atte Hyll paid for another part 2s.; Richard Causton paid for another part 2s.; total 20s.; and John Morton paid as appears by the following acquittance [See also after **217**].

St. Dunstan in the East

217. Acquittance by William Risyng, prior, for 50s. of arrears of rent from Robert Morton, dated Easter 1380.

    C.A.D., i, A 1715.

216 contd. After John Morton; Thomas Evesham, 11 Ric. II; Nicholas Potyn, 20 Ric. II; now [1425–7] the church of St. Dunstan; [f. 43] 2s. after Adam Changour; John Hay, 47 Ed. III; William Lenn: 2s. after Matthew Broun; his widow, 48 Ed. III; John Broun: 2s. after Agnes Berners; John Blokely, 49 Ed. III; Richard Rothyng: 2s. after Robert at Hill; John Prisket, 48 Ed. III; Walter de Kent who bequeathed it to the rector and parishioners of the church of St. Peter Paul's Wharf (*iuxta cayam Sancti Pauli*) as appears by his will[1] enrolled after 25 Apr. 1361: 2s. after Richard Causton; his widow, 41 Ed. III; Richard Baret, 49 Ed. III; Richard Rothyng, 4 Ric. II [f. 43v blank].

    1. *C. Wills*, ii, 18.

218. [f. 44] Grant of Peter fitz Roger otherwise called Mayresmay son of William to Richard prior and convent of 4s. *p.a.* of quit rent; 2s. from land and houses with a wharf (*kaio*) which Benet Stocfysch held of the grantor; abutments, the land of Robert Panifader on the west and land of John de St. Dunstan on the east and extending from the king's highway to the Thames (*usque in Tamisiam*) and 2s. from land with houses which William Dela(m)e held of the grantor; abutments, the land of Nicholas Bat on the west and land of John de St. Dunstan on the east; declaration that the grantor has these annual rents from these lands; grant in free alms; the canons and their successors to pay 1½d. socage to the Crown on Palm Sunday and to the grantor and his heirs ½d.; the prior and canons gave for the grant 40s. to expedite the grantor's business; dated Fri. 11 Mar. 1250; witnesses, Roger fitz Roger, mayor, John Tulsan(us), Ralph Hardel, sheriffs.

    Margin: Nota quod continetur in libro de socagio qui in officino camere monachorum Westmonasterii habetur inter cetera sic Hoc socagium colligetur in ramis Palmarum ad ecclesiam Sancti Dunstani est De tenemento Benedicti Stocfish post Heres Roberti Gresch(ir)ch modo Sancta Trinitas jd. ob. per tenementum quod fuit Johannis de Sancto Dunstano.
    C.A.D., ii, A 2407.

219. [List of those paying quit rent]: after Benet Stocfysch or Trenchem(er) who granted the tenement to Robert de Greschirch whose wife afterwards was married to David de Halliwell and they released all their right in the tenement to John de Canterbury whose own tenement is between that of William Monek on the west and the tenement of Pentecost le Ferun on the east and extends from the king's highway on the north to the Thames (*ad aquam Thamisie*) on the south as appears in their charter[1] enrolled before 12 Mar. 1274; afterwards, Clemence, widow of the above-mentioned Peter de Maresmay who released all her right in a tenement called Stokfishwharf to John de Canterbury as appears in their charter[2] enrolled after 6 Feb. 1278; afterwards John Cant[erbury] who bequeathed the aforesaid tenement to Margery his daughter situated between the tenement of John

Stertford on the west and that of Roger de Rokesle on the east as appears in his will[3] enrolled 32 Ed. I; afterwards Margaret his wife[4] paid 18 Ed. II as appears in a subsidy roll (*in rotulo taxacionis regi concesse viz. 12d. de nobili*); afterwards Henry Commarty, 1 Ed. III; afterwards Henry Staunton: [f. 44v] after William Lambeth (previously Dela(me)e); Richard Bonaventur(e); William Box, 1 Ed. II; Thomas Cros, 5 Ed. II; William Box, 1 and 6 Ed. III; Andrew Turk, 30 Ed. III and 4 Ric. II; Peter atte Very for the heirs of Andrew, 11 Ric. II; Henry Hirton; Hugh Battysford.

 1. H.R. 6 (48). 2. H.R. 9 (26). 3. *C. Wills*, i, 162–3.
 4. Presumably wife of John Canterbury *rectius* Margery.

220. Note: that the monks of Westminster have 20s. *p.a.* from the tenement of William Moigne or Monek which house (*domus*) is situated by the Thames (*super Tamisiam*); abutments, the house of John de Hertford, glover, on the west and the house of John de Canterbury on the east as appears in an old rental 'A' and afterwards the executors of William granted the tenement to John de Storteford who paid 20s. to the monks as appears by the following charter.

221. [1285–6] Sale by Benet Hakeney, William de Combe and John de Caunterbury, citizens, executors of the will[1] of William le Moygne, formerly woolmonger, to John de Stortford, citizen and glover (*cirotecarius*), all that whole tenement which the deceased had in the parish of St. Dunstan; abutments, the tenement of John de Caunterbury on the east and that of John de Hertford on the west and extending in length from the king's highway on the north to the Thames on the south; which tenement he left to be sold to pay his debts as is contained more fully in the letter of probate; quit rent therefrom to the abbot and convent of Westminster 20s. *p.a.*; witnesses, Ralph de Sandwich, warden of London, Walter le Blount, John Wade, sheriffs; dated 14 Ed. I.

 1. *C. Wills*, i, 50.

222. [f. 45 inset][1] [*c.* 1231–8] Grant by Roger Duke to the prior and canons of Legh of land and a residence (*capitale managium*) with house and 'kays' formerly of Roger de Blakesapelton; abutments, land formerly of Goda the Usurer (*fen(er)atricis*) on the east and the gate of the Thames at the bridge of Wulsun (*ad pontem Wulsuni*) on the west; all in length and breadth, in wood and stone etc. conveyed; rent to the grantor and his heirs ½ lb. of cumin or 1d. at Michaelmas; excepting the services therefrom to the chief lords of the fee, Holy Trinity, 1 mark of silver; for the grant the prior and canons gave 35 marks; sealed; witness, Richard Reinger.

 Margin: Hec carta sigillata remanet in prioratu de Lyes in Essex.
 1. A piece of parchment 9 ins. wide by 5⅜ ins. long inserted between f. 44v and f. 45.

223. [f. 45] [1197–1212] Grant of Peter prior and convent to Roger de Blakesappilton of all the land with a stone house and wharf (*hwervum*) formerly of Master James in the parish of St. Dunstan in the soke of the archbishop of Canterbury; rent 13s. 4d. *p.a.*; swore fealty; to pay rent

St. Dunstan in the East

without fail; if the grantee wishes to pledge or sell, reversion to the prior and convent if they wish; length from the upper end (*superiori parte*) 39 ells to the public street (*ad stratam pubplicam*) by (*versus*) the Thames and in width 11½ ells and from the outer part by the public street 13 ells; the wharf is 13 ells in width; gersuma 8 marks and 3s. for pittances (*ad pitanciam*); witnesses, Ralph the priest of St. Mary at Hill, John de Ball, priest of St. Dionis, Henry, mayor of London, Peter his son.

224. [List of those paying rent]: Roger Blakesappilton; William his son who granted the tenement to Roger le Duke, weaver, who granted it to the prior of Leighs [See also after **225**].

225. Recognisance of Walter Auberkyn for himself, his heirs and assigns that he owes a rent of 13s. 4d. *p.a.* to the prior and convent of Holy Trinity from his house which was once leased by Roger de Blakesappilton from them; abutments, the lane which leads to the house (*managium*) of Matilda de Sandwich on the west and the tenement of Hamon de Pariis on the east and the public street on the south and the house once of Brandus on the north; for this recognisance the prior and convent remitted to Walter and his heirs etc. arrears of rent; witnesses, [not named].

224 contd. William Bristowe whose executors granted the tenement to W. Brewer who paid 13s. 4d. as appears in their charter[1] enrolled 33 Ed. I; Richard Ko(u)ncedieu, 1 and 19 Ed. II and 6 Ed. III; John Mandeville, 30 Ed. III; John Malewayn, 36 Ed. III as appears by an inquisition[2] taken in the time of John Pechche, mayor of London, 36 Ed. III and the jury said that he died seised of one tenement in parish of St. Dunstan which was valued at 10 marks a year if it might be located from which an annual rent of 1 mark was paid; Helmyngus Leget, 39 Ed. III; William Walworth, 10 Ric. II; William Ascham.

1. H.R. 33 (72).   2. *C.I.P.M.*, xi, 131.

226. [f. 45v] [1170–97] Grant of Stephen prior and convent of land to Hugh Polested (*de Polested*) of land near the Thames which William the priest held at an annual rent of 2s.; the same William, with the assent of the prior and convent, sold land to Hugh for 10 marks and 9 marks [£12 13s. 4d.] and gave 2s. and a London sextary of wine to the prior and convent; Hugh swore fealty; witnesses, Roger de G(in)ges, Henry and Robert, his brothers.

C.A.D., iv, A 7292.

227. [List of those paying rent]: Hugh Polested; Richard Blundus; Edmund the Baker; Adam Rokesle, 1 Ed. II who granted the tenement to Peter de Blakeney as appears in Peter's will[1] enrolled 5 Ed. II; Godwin Turk who granted the tenement to Robert Wodhous as appears by their charter[2] enrolled 19 Ed. II; Thomas Broun, 11 Ed. III; his widow, 31 Ed. III as appears by the Acquittance Two[3] of several parishes; abbot of Evesham, 4 Hy. VI as appears by the Acquittance Seven[4] [26 lines blank].

1. *C. Wills*, i, 223.   3. **1039.**
2. H.R. 54 (14–16).   4. **1044.**

St. Mary at Hill

228. [f. 46] [1197–1212] Grant of Peter prior and convent to Ralph the Usurer (*Fenarius*) and Goda his wife of land which Stephen the Dyer (*tinctor*) held; rent 6s. *p.a.*; to hold as long as rent is paid without fraud or miskenning; gersuma 20s. sterling; witnesses, Henry mayor, Matthew the alderman, Robert Bat.

C.A.D., i, A 1775.

229. [List of those paying rent]: Ralph and his wife; Robert Bat; Lyedulfus; William de la Corner; Christine Box who granted the tenement to Matilda de la Barre who paid 6s. as appears by charter, 25 Ed. I; Adam Lutekyn, 5 and 19 Ed. II and 1 Ed. III; William Hansard, 6 Ed. III; William Stroder, 34 and 49 Ed. III; William Yngs paid 3s. for his part; Alice Hertwell 3s. for Thomas Hertwell formerly her husband [26 lines blank] and this site is on the south side of Thames Street.

230. [f. 46v] Total of this parish 63s. and it is tithed as it appears in the king's exemplification.

[f. 47] IN THE PARISH OF ST. MARY ATTE HULLE

231. Charter of William son of Alulf granting to the prior [*sic*] and convent of St. Peter Westminster land with a wharf (*cay*); abutments, land formerly of Richard son of Oswant and the lane which is by (*contra*) Billyngsgate; in length along the lane $18\frac{1}{4}$ ells and in breadth along the Thames $13\frac{1}{8}$ ells.

232. [1147–67] Grant of Ralph prior and convent to Richard son of Edwin son of Oswant of land in Byllyngsgate; rent 3s. *p.a.*; to hold as long as they pay the rent and are faithful to the church; width 55 ft. and the lower edge is on the Thames in width 47 ft. and the tenement is 103 ft. in length; gersuma a thousand herrings (*millenar* (*ium*) *de haringis*); witnesses, Eilward the priest (*presbiter*), Geoffrey Taun.

C.A.D., ii, A 2419.

233. [List of those paying rent]: Richard son of Oswant; John Sperlyng; Bricus the Ropemaker (*cordarius*); Martin Sperlyng; Philip le Taillour; Martin le Furner; John Laurence, 1 and 5 Ed. II; John Cros or de St. Edmund, 18 Ed. II; as appears by a subsidy granted to the king in that year; Gilbert Cros, 1 and 5 Ed. III; John Londonstone, 6 and 30 Ed. III; Roger at Ston, 33 Ed. III; Adam Changour, 39 and 49 Ed. III; Robert Knoll, 8 Ric. II; now [1425–7] the college of Pontefract: Knolles College.

234. [1170–97] Grant of Stephen prior and convent to Matthew of land which Ketellus held; rent 2s. *p.a.*; gersuma 2s.; the land has 42 ft. in [length] and 54 ft. in depth; witnesses, Robert de Hereford, Ketel, Nicholas the priest (*sacerdos*), Robert the clerk, Robert Ruhaued, Richard son of Oswant, William de Camera, Laurence Blund, Alberic of Billingesgate, Robert de Schop(pe), Diringus.

C.A.D., ii, A 2442.

St. Mary at Hill

235. [List of those paying rent]: Matthew, Alexander Sperlyng; William Veisin to whom a certain piece of land adjacent was granted [See also after **236**] as appears by the following charter.

236. [f. 47v] [1170–97] Lease of Stephen prior and convent to William Veisin of a curtilage which Alexander son of Sperling leased to Holy Trinity; rent 1s.; to hold as long as rent is duly paid; William swore fealty; gersuma 1s; witnesses, Ralph the priest, John son of Alexander Sperlyng, Gilbert Feutrier, Wilbertus.

    C.A.D., ii, A 2441.

235 contd. the abbot of Waltham who granted the tenement to William Carpenter paying to the abbot 38s. and to Holy Trinity 3s. *p.a.* as appears in their charter; J. Garland; Thomas Garland; John Hardel; J. Maydston, 13 Ed. I [See also after **237**] as appears by the following acquittance.

237. Release by William prior and convent to John de Maidenestan, clerk of the illustrious king of England, of 16s. sterling of arrears of rent from land once of John Hardel, citizen; John promises henceforth to pay 3s. *p.a.*; chirograph sealed in the presence of Robert Giffard, kt., John Hardel, John Gillingham, brothers Richard Wymbysch and Walter Buruch, canons; dated Wed. 27 June 1285.

    C.A.D., ii, A 2418.

235 contd. John Romeney, 1 and 5 Ed. II; John de Wrotham, 19 Ed. II and 1, 5 and 6 Ed. III; his widow, 30 Ed. III; William Bys, 37 and 49 Ed. III and 8 Ric. II; John Walworth, vintner, 20 Ric. II; John Weston, throughout Hy. IV and the tenement is on the west side of the lane leading from Billingesgate and the church of St. Mary de la Hulle.

238. [1222–48] Grant by Hamon son of Constantine to Richard prior and convent of a quit rent of 4s. 4d. *p.a.* which Michael the clerk was accustomed to give the grantor from land and houses which he held of the grantor near the land of the abbot of Waltham [f. 48] on the south; rent ½ lb. of cumin or 1d. annually to the grantor and his heirs at the election of each canon (*ad electionem eorundem prioris et canonicorum infra quindecim dies Pasche apud Sanctam Trinitatis sine omni occasione*); gersuma 40s. in silver; witness, Ralph Sperling.

    C.A.D., ii, A 2446.

239. [List of those paying quit rent]: Hamon added 6s. 8d. which he owed to the canons of Southwark, so Holy Trinity received 11s. but paid 6s. 8d. to Southwark; 4s. 4d. paid by Michael Clerk; Alexander Bysshop or Knyght; the abbot of Waltham; Peter Knyght; John Middleton who granted the tenement to Godwin Philypper, who paid to the canons of Waltham 25s. 8d. and to the canons of Southwark 6s. 8d. and to the *conversi* of the Temple 4s., making no mention of the rent to Holy Trinity

St. Andrew Hubbard

as appears from their charter[1] enrolled after the feast of St. Margaret 35 Ed. I; Alan Gyll; John le Hoder(e).

   1. H.R. 35 (94) enrolled 18 July 1306.

240. Total of this parish 10s. 4d. and it is tithed as it appears in the king's exemplification.

[f. 48v] IN THE PARISHES OF ST. MARGARET PATYNS AND ST. ANDREW ESTCHEP OR HUBERT

241. [1170–97] Lease of Stephen prior and convent to Richard Comper(e), baker, of land that was once of Saleda Smith (*Faber*); rent 2s. *p.a.*; to hold as long as rent is paid without any fraud and detraction; swore fealty; gersuma 1 bezant to the prior and a London sextary of wine to the canons; witnesses, Master Cyprian, Odo the chaplain (*capellanus*) of St. Andrew, Jordan the alderman son of Jordan Sperlyng, William son of Reyngarus.

242. [List of those paying rent]: Richard Compere, baker; John Garland; Richard Renger; Roger Dux; Stephen de Oxford; Stephen Iuvenus [*sic*]; Robert Wandelworth, 5 Ed. II and 6 Ed. III; then the tenement was divided for Adam Canoun paid 1s. and John Boshenham paid 1s., 30 Ed. III: after Adam Canoun; John Denyver, 8 Ric. II: after John Boshenham; Thomas Hovyle, 40 Ed. III; Katherine Hovyle, 8 Ric. II; William Turnour paid all,[1] 10 Hy. IV; Clement Mylius taking as wife Margaret widow of W. Turnour as appears by the following.

   1. Presumably 2s.

243. Indenture made between William prior and convent and Clement Mylius and Margaret his wife, citizens of London, witnesseth that at Easter 1426 Clement and Margaret owed rent for seven whole years at 2s. *p.a.* for the tenement formerly of William Turnour; abutments, the tenement of William Halle on the south and that of the Bridge of London on the north and the king's road on the east and the garden of the Guildhall[1] (*collegii Guyhalde*) on the west and agreeth that Clement and Margaret shall pay off the arrears at 2s. *p.a.* together with the 2s. *p.a.* rent; sealed; dated 10 May 1426.

   1. ? Possibly the guildhall of the men of Cologne (Steelyard).

244. Total of this parish 2s. and nevertheless it is tithed at 3s. 6d. as appears in the king's exemplification.

[ST. ANDREW HUBBARD]

245. Agreement made between Eustace prior and convent and Simon Wynchestre (*Wirencestre*), baker, that Simon undertook to go bail that he shall make sufficient and distrainable that piece which he holds of the fee of the prior and convent next the messuage of John Noth in the parish this side the bounds (*citra finem*) of St. Michael, rent 3s. *p.a.*; for this promise and agreement the prior and convent remitted to Simon 30s. of arrears except (*usque ad*) 10s. which he has paid them from the said land; if Simon and his heirs shall default, he grants that the prior [f. 49] and convent shall enter and retain all the aforesaid land until they are satisfied in the 20s. arrears; chirograph sealed; dated Thurs. 27 Apr. 1273.

246. [List of those paying rent]: Simon de Wynchestre; Robert the Smith (*Faber*); Benet Bowier(e); John Noth; John Fowliner, 26 Ed. I [See also after **247**] as appears in the following plea.

247. *Common plea held in the Husting, Mon. 5 May 1298.*
Recognisance of J. de Fouliner that he held of the prior and convent of Holy Trinity and was 40s. in arrears of rent at 3s. *p.a.* from a tenement formerly of John Noth and he paid to brother Geoffrey, rent-collector (*rentario*), 20s. on 24 June and 10s. on 1 Aug. and for his recognisance the remainder of the arrears remitted.

246 contd. Richard Wolmer(e), 5 Ed. II; Hamon Godchep, 19 Ed. II and 1 and 5 Ed. III; his widow, 6 Ed. III; Richard Dowble, 30 Ed. III; Richard Croydon, 34, 48 and 49 Ed. III; John Philpot.

248. [1223–7 or 1238–9] Sale by Reginald Dang(er) and quitclaim for himself and his heirs to Richard prior and convent of 8s. 4d. of quit rent from all the grantor's lands and houses in the parish of the fee of the canons: abutments, the land of John Eu on the south and land of Walter de Sudflete on the north; 8s. 4d. quit rent which Roger the Baker was accustomed to pay the grantor from a stone house there and in addition a rent of 5s. *p.a.* which the canons had from the same house; sale of ½ lb. of cumin or 2d. which Ralph Sperlenc paid the grantor annually from land with houses contiguous to the same stone house saving to the canons a rent of 2s. 4d. which they received from the said land; to hold in perpetuity [f. 49v] 8s. 4d. *p.a.* of quit rent and ½ lb. of cumin or 2d.; for this sale the canons gave 5 marks of silver; witness, Richard Renger, mayor.

Cf. *C.A.D.*, ii, A 2117.

249. [List of those paying quit rent of 13s. 4d.]: Reginald Danger, baker; R. de Sabrygelworth; Simon Sturry, 'catteler' [? cutler]; then the land was divided for Katherine Cotteler(e) paid 6s. 8d. for her part and William Storry 6s. 8d. for the other part: after K. Cotteler, William son of Nicholas Beawneys to whom she granted her part as appears by charter[1] enrolled 31 Ed. I; John Faukoner, 1 Ed. II; Hamo Godchop, 19 Ed. II and 5 Ed. III; his widow, 6 Ed. III; Richard Double, 30 Ed. III; Richard Croydon, 34 and 49 Ed. III; John Philpotts: after William Storrey, Robert Fuller to whom he granted his part by charter[2] enrolled 1 Ed. II; Adam Hunteman, 19 Ed. II and 5 Ed. III; William Dyry, 6 Ed. III; Robert Chaundos, 30 Ed. III; John Cok, 35 Ed. III; John Beufront, 48 Ed. III and 8 Ric. II; Richard Spark; John Dalby and these three tenements are situated joined

St. Andrew Hubbard

together on the west of the lane between the great gate once of John Philpotts on the north and [incomplete].

1. H.R. 31 (67). 2. H.R. 36 (107).

250. [*c.* 1243] Grant of Richard son of Benet the Goldsmith to Richard prior and convent of 1s. 10d. *p.a.* of quit rent from the land which John Suffolke held of the grantor; abutments, the land of Pentecost Wodemongere on the south and land of Richard May on the north; to hold in free alms; sealed; witness, Ralph Sperlyng, then alderman.

C.A.D., i, A 1696.

251. [f. 50] [List of those paying quit rent]: John Suffolk; Richard Curteys, 5 Ed. II; Hamo Goodchep, 19 Ed. II and 1 and 5 Ed. III; his widow, 12 Ed. III [See also after **252**] as appears by the following acquittance.

252. Acquittance of brother Thomas prior and convent of Holy Trinity for the arrears of 1s. 10d. annual quit rent received from the lady Isabel widow of Hamo Godchep from her tenement once of John de Suffolk; abutments, the land of Gerard, guardian (*custos*) of the queen's wardrobe, and the tenement of Robert le Maydour and situated opposite Isabel's yellow house (*jaune mansionis*); sealed by both parties; witnesses, William de Wrotham, Richard de Lo(m)huth, Richard atte Gate, John de Bromhil, Arnold le Chaundeler; dated 24 Dec. 1338.

251 contd. Richard Double, 30 Ed. III; Richard Croydon, 34 and 49 Ed. III; John Philepot and the tenement is situated on the east side of a lane called Philpott lane.

253. Declaration by John Sperlyng that he holds of the prior and convent of Holy Trinity in 1s. 6d. *p.a.* from certain land in the parish as appears in Charter Eight[1] of several parishes.

1. **1009**.

254. [List of those paying rent]: John Sperlyng; Luke le Aylere; Walter son of Luke who granted the land to Robert de Kynggeston, clerk [See also after **255**] as appears by the following charter.

255. [?1293–4] Conveyance by Walter son of Luke the Stockfishmonger, once citizen of London, to Robert de Kynggeston, clerk, of all the tenement which the grantor had of his father in the parishes of St. Andrew Hubbard, St. Mary at Hill and St. Margaret Pattens with houses built thereon; abutments, the capital messuage of John Spirlyng on the south and the king's road which leads to the Tower on the north extending from the king's street which leads to the gate of Billynggesgate on the east to the tenement once of Miles de Winchester on the west; rent to Holy Trinity 1s. 6d. *p.a.* and to the grantor and his heirs a clove-gillyflower at Christmas; [f. 50v] gersuma 55 marks in silver; witnesses, John le Breton, kt., warden of London, Robert de Rokeslee, Martin de Aumbesbury, sheriffs, Thomas

St. Botolph Billingsgate

Cros, alderman of the ward,[1] William, the king's baker, Wlmar de Essexia, Robert le Trayer, Peter de Co(rnu)b', Semmanus, clerk then serving in the said ward.

1. Billingsgate.

254 contd. Robert Dycton [*sic*], 22 Ed. 1 and 19 Ed. II and 5 Ed. III; Richard Croydon, 30 and 49 Ed. III; John Gysors, 8 Ric. II; James Gysors, throughout Hy. IV; Edward Gysors, 6 Hy. V and this tenement is situated on the south side of the street.

256. Total of this parish 19s. 8d. and it is tithed as it appears in the king's exemplification.

[f. 51] IN THE PARISH OF ST. BOTOLPH BILLYNGYSGATE

257. [1147–67] Grant by Ralph prior and convent to Brounlocus of two wharves (*wervos*) with adjacent land in Roderesgate; rent 22s. *p.a.*; if the grantee or any of his heirs seek damage to the church, they shall lose the fee unless they obtain the mercy of the prior and brethren; witnesses, Robert the Priest, Robert de St. Alphege.

C.A.D., iv, A 7361.

258. [List of those paying rent]: Brounlocus; John Abraham; Gregory Abraham; Turold de Kyneli; William Frosh(er); Geoffrey Frosh(er) from whom the land got the name Froyssh(er) werf; John Bourne, 5 Ed. II; afterwards in the king's hands; Simon Levelyf, 33 Ed. III; now [1425–7] the abbey of St. Mary Graces.

Margin: Nota quod anno regni regis Edwardi quarti vj° fuit quedam controversia inter abbatem de Tothill et priorem ecclesie Sancte Trinitatis pro xxijs. predictis et pro xixs.vjd. in parochia Sancti Botolphi extra Algate. Tandem concordati sunt per arbitrium Whattenow et Jacobi Braddeman lege peritorum viz. quod dictus prior pardoneret dicto abbati vijli.ixs. et quod dictus abbas solveret dicto priori Cs. pro arreragiis et sic factum est ut patet per acquietanciam (ponentem) in quadam pixide ubi cetere composiciones inter dominum abbatem et priorem ponuntur etc.

259. Grant of John prior and convent to Baudricus the Fishmonger (*pis(c)arius*) of land with houses once held by Ralph the priest of the church of St. Magnus; abutments, the house once of Edward Sare on the south and the house of Thomas Wateman on the north, extending from the lane by Redersgate to the tenement of Walter de Chesewyk; rent 1 mark of silver *p.a.*; declaration that the houses built on the land are valued (*appreciate*) at 10 marks; if the grantee or his heirs etc. wish to relinquish the holding, the prior and convent to have the preference by a bezant of 2s.; [f. 51v] gersuma 5 marks in silver; chirograph sealed; Feb. 1253; witnesses, John de Tulesan, mayor, Thomas de Wymburn, William de Dunolm, sheriffs.

C.A.D., ii, A 1912.

St. George Botolph Lane

260. [List of those paying rent]: B. the Fishmonger; John de Waltham; Robert Yo(u), 19 Ed. II; his widow, 1 Ed. III; John Yo(u), 6 Ed. III; Robert Hwyte, 30 Ed. III; Nicholas Holborne, 49 Ed. III; Geoffrey Mawfeld, 8 Ric. II.

261. Total of this parish 35s. 4d. and it is tithed as it appears in the king's exemplification.

[f. 52] IN THE PARISH OF ST. GEORGE ESTCHEPP

262. [1235–6] Sale by Walter Joye son of Benet Joye, butcher, to Josceus Junior of 8s. of quit rent which Roger de Benedisse, butcher, paid the grantor annually for a certain shop which he holds of the grantor in the Shambles (*macello*) of Eastcheap; abutments, the land and shop once of Derekinus the Spicer (*speciarius*) on the south and the shop of St. Margaret of Southwark on the north; for the sale and renunciation (*forisaffidacione*) Josceus gave 100s.; witnesses, Andrew Bokerell, mayor, Gerard Batte, Robert Hardell, sheriffs.

263. Note: that Felicia wife of Josceus granted to Richard prior and convent 8s. from the shop mentioned in **262** as appears in Charter Nine[1] of several parishes.

    1. **1010**.

264. [List of those paying quit rent]: Roger Benedisse; Robert Blund; Alan Draper; Thomas de Estchep; Edmund son and heir of Thomas granted the said tenement situated on the north side of the tenement of Robert Robilard to Gregory Rokesle as appears in their charter[1] enrolled 14 Ed. I; Thomas Bakwell, 1 Ed. II; Thomas Bacwell his son, 13 Ed. III [See also after **266**] as appears by the following plea.

    1. H.R. 16 (134).

265. *Common plea held in the Husting, Mon. 15 Feb. 1339.*
Thomas son of Thomas de Bacwell summoned to reply to the prior concerning a plea that he should do his lawful service for his free tenement which he holds of the church of Holy Trinity of which Richard Wymbissh, once prior, was seised in his demesne as of fee by Thomas de Bacwelle, father, and this Thomas whose heir he is, is £6 in arrears on the day of suing out the writ, 12 Mar. 1338 for fifteen years past; the tenement not distrainable for a year and a day and the prior sought the messuage as gavelet; Thomas through his guardian Thomas de Bury said that Thomas was a minor and sought that the action be deferred until he came of age.

266. *Common plea held in the Husting, Mon. 2 Dec. 1359.*
Thomas de Bacwell summoned to answer (as in **265**); [f. 52v] the prior by his attorney, Alan Horewode, said Thomas held of him and his church and 24s. owing for arrears of three years past before the day of suing out etc. 18 Mar. 1359; and not distrainable etc.; Thomas by John Dauncere his

St. George Botolph Lane

attorney could not deny he held of the prior and paid the arrears; decided that the prior had seisin and Thomas is in mercy.

264 contd. William Bacwell, 49 Ed. III and 8 Ric. II; John Squyrry and this tenement is situated on the east side of a lane called Puddynglane or Retherlane between the tenement once of Robert Tropinell, afterwards of Walter Dogett on the south and a tenement of St. Paul's on the north.

267. [1197–1221] Grant of Peter prior and convent to Robert Tropinell of land next to the land of Alan the Draper on the west and containing in width besides (*secus*) Alan's land $9\frac{1}{2}$ ells 8 ins. and in width on the west [*sic*] 12 ells 3 ins. and in length from Alan's land towards the corner (*corneriam*) $20\frac{1}{4}$ ells 3 ins.; rent 5s. *p.a.*; swore fealty; [f. 53] canons never to be able to dispossess the grantee and his heirs (*de hospitari R. et heredes suos causa aliquem hominem vel feminam ibidem hospitandi*) as long as rent is paid; gersuma 5s.; witnesses, Ralph Sperlyng, Alan the Draper.

    C.A.D., i, A 1806.

268. [List of those paying rent]: Robert Tropinell; Robert Robilard; Denise Robilard who granted the tenement to Gemma Oyledebef as appears by their charter[1] enrolled 18 Ed. I; Thomas de Canefeld, 1 and 19 Ed. II and 1 Ed. III; Adam Pikeman, 12 Ed. III [See also after **269**] as appears by the following plea.

    1. H.R. 19 (36).

269. *Common plea held in the Husting, Mon. 23 Nov. 1338.*
The prior of Holy Trinity seeks against Adam Pikeman a messuage as gavelet; Adam holds a messuage of him at a rent of 5s. *p.a.* and is 10s. in arrears on the day of the suing out of the writ, 12 Mar. 1338; tenement undistrainable etc.; the defendant came and recognised that he held of the prior etc.; the prior recovered the messuage for one year unless in the meantime Adam satisfied the prior; for that cause the execution of judgment of shartford will cease after a year and a day (*ideo cesset execucio iudicii de sharthford post diem et annum*).

268 contd. Walter Dogett(s), 39 Ed. III and 8 Ric. II; Alice his widow, throughout Hy. IV and Hy. V and the tenement is situated on the east side of Puddynglane between the tenement of William Bacwelle on the north and the king's road on the south.

270. [? before 1193] Grant of Jordan, alderman, son of Jordan Sperling to Holy Trinity of the land which William son [f. 53v] of Nicholas held of the grantor's father and of the grantor in free and perpetual alms for the salvation of his soul etc.; witnesses, Nicholas the deacon, John de Paris, deacon, Geoffrey, Hugh de Celario, Sigerus, Edward the Cook, John de Mereton, Alexander the clerk, Bartholomew the clerk, Moses the clerk, Ralph White (*Albo*), Ralph the Carpenter, German the Parmenter, Ailward the Baker, Rigero Warino, *et de nobilibus huius civitatis testibus*, Henry

St. George Botolph Lane

son of Alwin, Richard son of Ren(er)n,[1] Robert the Chamberlain (*Camberario*), John son of Herlicon.

   1. *Rectius* Reyner.
   C.A.D., ii, A 2103.

271. [1170–97] Grant of Stephen prior and convent to Ralph the Butcher (*avunculo machecrario*) also called Ralph 'Machechrier', of land which Edric the Butcher held of Holy Trinity in Eastcheap; rent 1s. *p.a.*; in length on the south $19\frac{3}{4}$ ells and in breadth towards the north $17\frac{1}{2}$ ells and on the north the land of Wicera, on the west the land of St. Saviour, on the east the land of Holy Trinity which Bernard the Baker holds and on the south, land of Holy Trinity which Edric holds, to which this land used to pertain; swore fealty and pledged himself to the canons in their chapterhouse and that his heirs would pledge themselves (*securitatem faciens*) on the four gospels that the divisions of the land should remain as they were at the time of the grant; gersuma a London sextary of wine, Ralph and his heirs gave to the canons a stall in Eastcheap for 2s. paid by them; witnesses, Helius the priest, Luke the priest, Stephen son of Toki, Godard the Merchant, Fulcred, Nicholas the Butcher, William son of Nicholas.

   C.A.D., i, A 1687.

272. [List of those paying rent]: Ralph the Butcher; William the Butcher; German the Mercer to whom William Facetus granted certain land at a rent of 2s. *p.a.* [See also after **273**] as appears from the following charter.

273. [? before 1193] Grant by William son of Ralph la Faiciet to German the Mercer of land which Robert le Chachepoll held and land which William Stalke held next the church of St. George in Eastcheap on the west; rent 2s. *p.a.* except 2d. that the grantor grants that German gives from the socage to the abbot of Chertsey (*de socagio abbati Certesie*); and the grantor and his heirs to have no claim to the land beyond the 2s. rent; [f. 54] gersuma 1 bezant; witnesses, Ralph Buccel, Andrew Bucherel, Richard son of Ranus [? Ranulf], Henry son of Ailwyn, William de Haverhull, John son of Nigel.
William Facetus granted this 2s. to Holy Trinity and handed over the above charter to the church when he became a canon of Holy Trinity and so German the Mercer paid 4s. *p.a.*

272 contd. after German; Rose his daughter; Hugh de Estchep; Thomas de Estchep; Richard Persted; William Fisshbourn, holders of the tenement once of Thomas de Estchep [See also after **274**] recognised this.

   C.A.D., i, A 1686.

274. *In the Husting, Mon. 1 Feb. 1288.*
The prior impleaded Richard de Persted and William de Fisshbourn by a writ of gavelet; the defs. recognised that they were 12s. in arrears of rent at 4s. *p.a.*; Ralph de Sandwich, warden of London at that time, William de Hereford, Thomas Stanys, sheriffs.

St. Magnus the Martyr

272 contd. Ralph de Stortford, 5 Ed. II who granted the tenement to John Traynell as appears in their charter[1] enrolled 11 Ed. II; John Traynell, brewer, 1 Ed. III; Richard Smeltts, 30 Ed. III; Richard Croydon, 49 Ed. III; Thomas Cornwaleys, 8 Ric. II; John Cornwaleys.

    1. *C.A.D.*, ii, A 2089; H.R. 46 (47, 69).

275. Total of this parish 17s. and it is tithed as it appears in the king's exemplification.

[f. 54v] IN THE PARISH OF ST. MARGARET SOUTHWERK

276. Grant by Adam le Trehur and Alice his wife, daughter of Henry Martyn, in free alms of a quit rent of 6s. *p.a.* from land and houses built thereon once of Matilda daughter of Benet son of Luke and mother of Alice; sealed; witnesses, Geoffrey Northman, bailiff of Suwerk, Reginald the Forester; dated June 1273.

277. Quitclaim of Alice widow of Adam le Trehur releasing all her right in the above rent to William prior and convent which the prior received from a tenement which Stephen Abbot held in the parish which rent he had by the gift of Adam le Trehur; for this quitclaim prior and convent gave 2 marks sterling; sealed; witnesses, William Wynnok, John Moun(er); dated at Suthwark 28 June 1293.

278. [List of those paying quit rent]: Adam le Trehur; Stephen Abbot; John Milward, 1 and 19 Ed. II and 1 Ed. III; Robert de Staunford, 13 Ed. III;[1] John Plumer, 31 Ed. III; John Thoursway, 39 Ed. III; Robert Ryffyn, 46 Ed. III; his widow, 1 and 3 Ric. II; now [1425–7] St. Thomas's Hospital.

    Margin: Nota quod istud tenementum est modo hospicium et habet pro signo leonem.
    1. Inserted above the line: "as appears in a little book (*quaternum*) with letter 'A' f. 29 *Kalendari primi*."

279. Total of this parish 6s.

[f. 55] IN THE PARISH OF ST. MAGNUS THE MARTYR

280. [1147–67] Grant by Ralph prior and convent to Roesia daughter of Richard de Barsham of land formerly held by Ralph the chaplain from Robert Helebuc; rent 2s. 6d.; to hold to Roesia and her heirs lawfully begotten; if she dies without lawful heirs, the land to revert to the canons of Holy Trinity; gersuma 1 gold bezant; witnesses, Richard Renger, alderman, Joce son of Peter, James de Haverhill, John Blund, Richard de Lefstanech(er), Benet Linendraper, Walter de Fullham.

    C.A.D., ii, A 2440.

St. Margaret Fish Street Hill

281. [List of those paying rent]: Roesia; Walter Hoggles; Walter the Carter.

282. Total of this parish 2s. 6d.

[f. 55v] IN THE PARISH OF ST. MARGARET PONTIS

283. [1225–7] Sale and quitclaim by Pain Bouchere (*Bustcher*) to Joce Junior of 20s. of quit rent from the grantor's three shops in Brygestrate near the Bridge (*versus Pontem*); of the fee of the hospital of St. Giles without London; abutments, land and shop that was of Wygot the Mercer on the south and the land and shop of Richard Blund, fishmonger, of the same fee on the north and between the king's road on the east and the land and house (*managium*) of Geoffrey Sopper of the same fee on the west; and 12s. of the quit rent to come from that shop which Alexander Ruffus, fishmonger, holds of the grantor and 8s. of quit rent to come from the other two shops; if the shop of Alexander Ruffus does not suffice for the payment of 12s. the grantee and his heirs to distrain on the whole tenement until they have received 20s.; for the sale Joce gave 20 marks of silver; witnesses, Richard Reynger, alderman and then mayor, Roger Duc, Martin son of William, sheriffs.

284. Grant by Felicia wife of Joce of the above quit rent of 20s. to Holy Trinity as appears in Charter Nine[1] of several parishes.

    1. **1010**.

285. [List of those paying quit rent]: 12s. for the shop of Alexander Rufus, Geoffrey Rufus or Badecok(s); Ralph Pykenia; John Mockyng, 1 Ed. II; John Sterr(y), 5 and 19 Ed. II; John Mockyng, 1 and 6 Ed. III; Nicholas Mockyng, 30 Ed. III; as appears by inquisition[1] held before John Wroth(am), mayor and escheator, Mon. 16 Nov. 1360 when Reginald le Fuller swore that Nicholas had two tenements with three shops and two solars in Briggestret worth £6 1s. *p.a.* from which he was accustomed to pay 12s. *p.a.* to Holy Trinity; Roger Shipbrok, 49 Ed. III; the prior of the Charterhouse, 8 Ric. II; 8s. for two shops of John Ramsden which Laurence son of Pain confirmed to Holy Trinity; afterwards the holding was divided for Thomas Cros granted one of the shops to Henry Lambyn paying to Holy Trinity 4s. [See also after **286**] as appears by the following charter.

    1. *C.I.P.M.*, x, 506–7.

286. [f. 56] [1309–10] Grant of Thomas Cros, citizen, to Henry Lambyn, fishmonger, of a shop with two solars in Bridge Street; abutments, the shop once of Geoffrey Batecocks on the south and the shop once of Richard Knotte on the north and extending from the street on the east to the tenement once of Edmund le Trayere; rent to Holy Trinity 4s. *p.a.* and a rose on 24 June to the grantor and his heirs; gersuma a certain sum of money (*quandam summam pecunie*); sealed; witnesses, Thomas Romeyn, James de St. Edmund, Roger le Palmere, sheriffs.

    C.A.D., i, A 1615.

St. Margaret Fish Street Hill

285 contd. Henry Lambyn, 1 Ed. III; Edmund Lambyn, 6 Ed. III; William Tathyngbury, 30 Ed. III; John Horn(er), 49 Ed. III; John Rous: 4s. for the third shop, John Ramesden; Gilbert Cheswyk; John Lambyn, 1 Ed. II; Richard Knot, 19 Ed. II; Ancelinus Knot, 2 Ed. III; William Ancett, 5 Ed. III; William Hastyng, 20 Ed. III; John Kytell, 30 and 49 Ed. III; John Rous, 1 Ric. II who bequeathed the two shops to the church of St. Margaret Bridge Street as appears in his will[1] enrolled after 25 July 1381; wardens of the church, 13 Hy. IV as appears by an acquittance made between Holy Trinity and the wardens.

    1. *C. Wills*, ii, 224–5.

287. This indenture witnesseth that Thomas Axbrigg, rent collector and canon of Holy Trinity received of John Philip, rector of St. Margaret in Bridge Street, Robert Whaplode and Geoffrey Clerk, churchwardens, 2s. in full payment of the arrears of rent of 8s. *p.a.* from two shops which John Rous bequeathed to the rector and parishioners of the church for the maintenance of a perpetual chaplain for the quarter day of St. John Baptist last past; [f. 56v] sealed; dated 16 Aug. 1412 and the three shops are adjacent on the west side of Bridge Street.

288. Grant by Alan son of Peter to Holy Trinity of a quit rent of 13s. 4d. *p.a.* from a tenement formerly of Jordan Sperlyng as appears in Charter Ten[1] of several parishes.

    1. **1011**.

289. [List of those paying quit rent]: Walter de Becham; Nicholas Tryp, girdler; Richard Chnotte; John Lambyn, 1 Ed. II and 1 Ed. III; John Croydon, 3 and 5 Ed. III; John Torks, 12 Ed. III; John Malwyn, 30 Ed. III; Robert Ramesey, 49 Ed. III and throughout Ric. II and 7 Hy. IV as appears by the following plea.

    Margin: Carta[1] Ricardi Knotte per Nicholaum Trippe irrotulatur in festo Augustini archiepiscopi anno regni regis Henrici III 44º.
    1. H.R. 4 (64) *rectius* 54 Hy. III.

290. *Plea of assize held at the Guildhall, Sat. 12 Feb. 1407.*
Before Geoffrey Brook and Nicholas Wotton, sheriffs, the presence of the coroner not expected; the assize came to recognise if Robert Ramesey and William Derhant had unlawfully disseised Robert prior of Holy Trinity of his free tenement in Briggestrete and therein the prior by his attorney Richard Foster complained that they had disseised him of 13s. 4d. of rent; Robert Rameseye and William were summoned and did not come, therefore the assize is taken against them in default; the prior ordered to show title and cause of the disseisin, declares that it is an annual quit rent arising from a tenement in sight of the Bridge (*in visu Pontis*) of which he and all his predecessors had been seised from time out of mind and that he sought the rent and the defs. refused to pay; jurors charged, William Braibroke, John Double, John Appulby, Robert Coks, Thomas Peron(e), John More, William Bryan, Robert Mersk, John Elyngham, Henry Preston, John

St. Michael Crooked Lane

Parnes, John Borham; tested and sworn to say whether the said prior etc. seised etc.; they assess damages to the prior by occasion of the disseisin apart from arrears of rent at 10s.; [f. 57] jurors also asked to enquire how long the rent has been in arrears and they find one and a half years; whether disseisin was by force of arms, they find not by force of arms; whether any fraud or collusion contrary to the statute against mortmain, find none but that the prior has the greater right to the rent as he alleged; which predecessor of the present prior held seisin in the reign of Henry III, they find prior Richard; therefore it is acknowledged by the view of the jurors that the prior should recover the arrears amounting to 20s. and damages which the prior has sustained taxed by the jurors at 10s.; total 30s.; defs. in mercy.

C.A.D., ii, A 1859; *London possessory assizes*, no. 220.

291. Total of this parish 33s. 4d. and it is tithed as in the copy of King Richard [f. 57v blank].

[f. 58] IN THE PARISH OF ST. MICHAEL OF CANDILWYKSTRETE

292. Grant by Martin Horn and Alice, daughter of the late Stephen Nicholas, his wife, to Thomas Jordan, citizen, and Alice his wife of 1 mark *p.a.* of quit rent from the whole capital messuage with two shops in front (*anterioribus*) once of Edmund the Smith; abutments, the grantor's tenement leased to John le Barbour on the east and the tenement of Matthew le Chandeler, which he holds of the nuns of St. John de Haliwell, on the west and extending from the king's road on the north to the tenter-grounds (*ad tentas*) of Matthew Bokerell on the south; rent to the grantors and their heirs four clove-gillyflowers, one at each quarter day; the grantees have full powers to enter and distrain; the grantees paid 9 marks sterling; sealed; witnesses, John Adrian, mayor, Gregory de Rokesle, Henry le Waleys, sheriffs; charter[1] enrolled in full Husting, Mon. 1 Dec. 1270.

1. H.R. 4 (77).

293. [f. 58v] [1271–2] Grant by Thomas Jordan and Alice his wife to Eustace prior and convent of 1 mark *p.a.* of quit rent from the property named in **292**; canons gave for the gift 10 marks; sealed; for greater security the grantors have deposited the charter of Martin and Alice Horn with the canons; witnesses, Walter Hervi, mayor, Richard de Parys, John de Buddele, sheriffs.

C.A.D., ii, A 2045.

294. [List of those paying quit rent]: Martin Horn; Ralph le Tapisser who granted the tenement to William le Ne(v)e paying 13s. 4d. as appears by charter[1] enrolled 10 Ed. I; John de Harwe, 1 and 19 Ed. II and 1 Ed. III; John Lovekyn; now the church itself (*ipsa ecclesia*) [12 lines blank].

1. H.R. 13 (56).

295. Memorandum: that the prioress of Kylebourne has 11s. from the

St. Leonard Eastcheap

tenement of the late John Barnet in the parish of St. Leonard Estcheap which tenement is situated between the tenement of William Neve on the west and that of John Cros on the east as appears in a charter of John Que [incomplete].

296. Total of this parish 13s. 4d.

[f. 59] IN THE PARISH OF ST. LEONARD ESTCHEP OR MILKECHIRCHE

297. Alan son of Peter gave to Holy Trinity 8s. *p.a.* from a certain stall as appears in Charter Ten[1] of several parishes.

    1. **1011.**

298. [List of those paying rent]: Benet son of Turkyll; Benet Long; Robert Rippyle; Richard Sharp who granted the tenement to William de Cray paying therefrom 8s. to Holy Trinity as appears in their charter[1] enrolled after 12 Mar. 1310 and he paid 19 Ed. II; William Bray, 1 Ed. III; Nicholas Bray, 6 Ed. III; Andrew Turk, 30 Ed. III; John Spaldyng, 34 Ed. III; his widow, 37 Ed. III; Robert Spaldyng 47 and 49 Ed. III; William I(u)ory, 8 Ric. II who bequeathed the tenement to the church of St. Clement as appears in his will[2] enrolled after 13 Jan. 1391 and this tenement is on the north side of Candelweykstrete.

    1. H.R. 38 (101).   2. *C. Wills*, ii, 282-3.

299. Grant by Ralph [*rectius* Richard] prior and convent to William Melkere of land; abutments, the land of Hugh de Estchep on the north and the land of Stephen son of Nicholas on the south; the canons have discharged (*disgacionaverunt*) shartford in the Husting; rent 6s. *p.a.*; if grantee wishes to lease or sell, the canons to have the preference by a bezant of 2s.; gersuma 7 marks; done in the year 1243; witnesses, Ralph Sperlyng, alderman, Reynger de Bungay and the grantee undertook to build on the land as appears by the following charter.

    C.A.D., i, A 1743.

300. [1243] Charter of William le Melkere, citizen, announcing his obligation for himself and his heirs to the prior and convent to build on a piece of empty land which he holds of the canons next to the messuage of Hugh de Estchep within this present year in such a way as they or their attorney shall approve as he is bound to do by the terms of **299** by the 6s. rent from the aforesaid shop and by 4s. from another shop currently in our hands [? Holy Trinity] by the will[1] of Hugh Robiry; he concedes that he shall distrain in all his capital messuage as appears from a plea [f. 59v] that the prior and convent impleaded William in the Husting by royal writ concerning 6s. of annual rent and also concerning rent of 4s. *p.a.*

    1. *C. Wills*, i, 641-2.
    C.A.D., i, A 1736.

301. [List of those paying rent]: William Melkere; Thomas Estcheap;

St. Leonard Eastcheap

Christine Box; Henry Gyldeford, 1 Ed. II who granted the tenement to St. Paul's as appears in a composition[1] of the executor of the same (*in composicione executoris eiusdem*) enrolled 7 Ed. II.

1. H.R. 42 (111).

302. Geoffrey son of Stephen granted to Peter prior and convent a quit rent of 6s. in the west corner opposite (*in occidentali cornerio versus*) London Bridge as appears in Charter Eleven[1] of several parishes.

1. **1012.**

303. [List of those paying the quit rent]: Reginald the Butcher; Reginald Scaldour; Osbert Scaldur; William Prensse; William Tresse; Richard Curteys; afterwards Thomas Derby, prior of the New Hospital without Bishopsgate.

304. Grant by Roger the Butcher to Richard prior and convent of 1 mark of quit rent from land and houses; abutments, the land that was of Robert Bruscus and the land that was of Goda the Usurer (*Feneratricis*); rent to the grantor and his heirs 1d. *p.a.*; prior and convent to have the right to distrain on the premises (*managium*) and to take naam and also to plead gavelet until they have received 1 mark *p.a.*; [f. 60] gersuma 10 marks of silver; dated 1230; witnesses, Roger Duc, mayor, Richard Renger, alderman, John Hanin, deputy alderman (*subaldermanno*).

305. [List of those paying quit rent]: Roger the Butcher; Roger Sweyft who granted 3s. *p.a.* to Holy Trinity [See also after **306**] as appears by the following charter.

306. [1227–31] Grant by Roger Swyft, butcher, to Richard prior and convent of a quit rent of 3s. *p.a.* from a certain shop in Eastcheap which is situated between two shops of Walter Goye; right to the prior and convent to distrain both on his capital messuage and on the shop until satisfied as to arrears of rent; for this grant the canons paid 2 marks; witnesses, Roger le Duc, mayor, Roger Renger, alderman, John Hanin, deputy alderman.

305 contd. Roger paid 16s. 4d. and after him; John Dogett; Stephen Aswy who granted 14s. from the same tenement [See also after **307**] as appears by the following charter.

307. [1276–7] Grant by Stephen Aswy son of Ralph Aswy, citizen, to Eustace prior and convent of a quit rent of 14s. *p.a.* from the whole tenement which John Doget held of the grantor; abutments, the land and house of Richard Densouth on the north and the house of Richard le Kyng on the south extending from the king's road on the east to the land and house of Adam Mullyng on the west; to hold in free alms; [f. 60v] sealed; witnesses, Gregory de Rokesle, mayor, Ralph le Fevre, Robert de Arras, sheriffs.

305 contd. John Doget paid 30s. 4d. *p.a.* and after him; Boidewinus de

St. Leonard Eastcheap

Grene who granted the tenement to John Sterr(e) as appears in their charter[1] enrolled 3 Ed. II; John Sterr(e), 5 Ed. II; John de Mockyngg, 19 Ed. II and 5 Ed. III; William Knyght, 6 Ed. III; then the land was divided for Thomas de Bury, 10 Ed. III paid 15s. 2d. [See also after **308**] as appears by the following plea.

1. H.R. 38 (94).

308. [1338] Plea [no heading]; the prior of Holy Trinity seeks against Thomas Bury, butcher, a messuage as gavelet; asserts that Thomas holds of him and his church for a rent of 15s. 2d. *p.a.* of which rent Roger Poly, once prior, was seised by Boidinus atte Grene; 30s. 4d. in arrears on the day of the suing out of the writ, 12 Mar. 1338, for two years; messuage not distrainable for a year and a day; sought as gavelet etc.; Thomas came and recognised that he was tenant; the prior recovers against Thomas de Bury for a year and a day as gavelet unless meanwhile Thomas satisfies the prior as to arrears etc.; afterwards he satisfied him etc.

305 contd. Robert Furneux, 34 Ed. III; John Leman and Andrew Pekeham, 48 Ed. III; John Dogett, 8 Ric. II and Nicholas Mockyng paid 15s. 2d. [See also after **309**] as appears in the following.

309. [French] May it please the mayor and alderman that the prior has a fee etc. to which fee he had access to distrain through the edge of the tenement of Nicholas son and heir of John de Mockyngg, [f. 61] late citizen and fishmonger, but that the said Nicholas has stopped up the entry through which he was accustomed to distrain so that he cannot enter his fee to distrain for his services whereby the prior seeks a remedy and that you shall make an entry according to the usages of the City as has been done to others time out of mind.
[Latin] By virtue of which bill the sheriffs are ordered to summon Nicholas to be at the next Husting of Common Pleas to reply to the prior etc.; Alan de Horew[ode] attorney for the prior; afterwards at the Husting of Common Pleas held Mon. 28 May 1358 the prior came by his attorney, the sheriff testified that Nicholas was summoned by William atte Walle and William Lemman etc. and Nicholas was not present; the sheriffs to distrain on Nicholas etc.; at the Husting held Mon. 11 June 1358 the prior came and Nicholas in person sought the hearing of the bill etc. and Nicholas says that he is in the wardship of John Malewayn who has in his custody all his muniments concerning the rent of this tenement and without these he cannot answer and he seeks aid from the aforesaid John and this is granted; then at the Husting held Mon. 23 July 1358 the prior came by his attorney, Nicholas did not come and thereupon the prior etc. sought an enquiry through the oath of lawful men of the neighbourhood as to whether the prior and his predecessors had been accustomed to have free entry and egress to distrain for his services as appears in the bill and the mayor and aldermen agree that it seems to them that this is the ancient custom in the City and the sheriff ordered to summon twenty-four proven and lawful men of the neighbourhood to enquire etc.; [f. 61v] the truth of the articles of the bill; then at the Husting held Mon. 22 Oct. 1358 the prior came by

his attorney, Nicholas did not come and the jury came, John Vannere, Henry atte Beth, Robert Boyden, John Lemman, Nicholas Sahipp, Robert Lodewyk, Philip Page, John Musard, Adam Kylinworth, Walter Vannere, John de Ware, John Herlawe who say on oath that John de Mockyng father of Nicholas whose heir he is had a tavern in the parish called Poulestaverne which tavern Paul le Taverne now holds on lease of Nicholas and they say that the prior had free entry through the door of the tavern to distrain in a certain house of John de Bury, butcher, which house Robert Fourneaux, John Fraunceys and Margery who was the wife of Richard Lemman, butcher, now hold and they say that John Mockyng for fourteen years last past made obstructions (*quedam de meremio terra plastrata*) on the north side in the tavern in the place where the prior was accustomed to have free entry and exit to distrain and so the place is maliciously stopped up so that the prior cannot distrain; the prior sought judgement; granted by the mayor and alderman that this place etc. should be unstopped so that the prior shall have entry etc.; the sheriffs ordered to go to the place and both by view of the jurors and other men of the neighbourhood of Eastcheap cause the wall to be unstopped; this done, the sheriffs to certify the mayor and alderman at the next Husting; at the Husting held Mon. 5 Nov. 1358 the prior by his attorney and the sheriffs by Thomas Listyngston their chief clerk (*capitalem clericum*) reported that it had been done so that the prior could distrain; and Nicholas paid well as appears by an inquisition[1] taken before John Wroth, mayor and escheator, [f. 62] on Mon. 16 Nov. 1360; Reginald le Fuller and others, jurors, say that Nicholas had a great tenement with one shop worth £13 6s. 8d. *p.a.* from which he paid a quit rent of 15s. 2d. to the prior of Holy Trinity.

1. *C.I.P.M.*, x, 506–7.

305 contd. Elmyngus Leget, 48 Ed. III and 8 Ric. II; Adam Bamme, 20 Ric. II; his widow throughout Hy. IV, V and VI; John Phillipot, 10 Hy. VI and these two tenements are situated adjacent on the west side of Briggestrete.

310. [1222–48] Grant by Ralph de Gardino and Roesia his wife to Richard prior and convent of a quit rent of 1s. *p.a.* out of 4s. which Robinellus the Butcher was accustomed to give the grantors annually for half of a certain shop which he holds of them in the Shambles of Estcheap; to hold in free alms; sealed; witness, Gilbert son of Fulc, alderman.

C.A.D., ii, A 2099.

311. [List of those paying quit rent]: Robinellus the Butcher; Denise Robinel; Reginald Ca(n)efeld; Richard Sharpp; Nigel de Hakenay; Richard de Hakeney, 1 and 19 Ed. II and 1 Ed. III who bequeathed the shop to the church of St. Mary atte Hill as appears in his will[1] enrolled; now [1425–7] the churchwardens.

1. *C. Wills*, i, 467–8.

312. [1197–1221] Lease by Peter prior and convent to Richard the Butcher (*Mascecario*) son of Siwat of a shop in Estcheap; rent 6s. *p.a.*; swore fealty;

St. Benet Gracechurch

[f. 62v] on the south side it is contiguous to the land of the hospital of St. Giles and in depth it is 4 ells 4 ins. and in width 3 ells 2 ins.; gersuma ½ mark; witnesses, John de Balleo, Alan son of Peter, Nicholas the Butcher.

C.A.D., i, A 1692.

313. [List of those paying rent]: Richard Blandecute or Macererier; Matilda daughter of Richard granted the tenement to Robinel [See also after 314] as appears in the following charter.

314. [*c.* 1230] Grant by Elias the Mercer and Matilda, daughter of Richard, his wife, to Robinel the Butcher of a shop; abutments, the shop of Robert Long on the north and the shop of Benet Long on the south; paying to the canons of Holy Trinity 6s. *p.a.* and to the grantors and their heirs 1d. at Easter; gersuma 40s. sterling; witnesses, Richard Renger, Ralph Sperlyng, alderman, Alan the Draper.

C.A.D., i, A 1691.

313 contd. Robinel; Denise Robinel; Boidewinus Grene, butcher, 1 Ed. II; Alice, his wife, 1 Ed. III; Nicholas Bray, 6 Ed. III; Andrew Turk, 30 Ed. III; Robert Spaldyng, 48 Ed. III; John Brounesby; William Yvory bequeathed the tenement to the church of St. Clement as appears in his will[1] enrolled after 13 Jan. 1391.

1. *C. Wills*, ii, 282.

315. Total of this parish 57s. 2d. and it is tithed as appears in the king's exemplification.

[f. 63] IN THE PARISH OF ST. BENET GRASCHIRCH

316. [1222–48] Grant by Laurence Draper to Richard prior and convent of 6s. *p.a.* of quit rent which Joce de Cornhelle, draper, was accustomed to pay the grantor for certain land with houses which he held of the grantor; abutments, the land of William son of Benet on the north and of Richard Sharpp on the south; rent to the grantor and his heirs 8d. *p.a.*; for the grant the prior and convent have remitted to the grantor and his heirs 5s. 4d. *p.a.* of quit rent which he was accustomed to pay them from the land which Richard Blandekete once held next to the land of Peter Feli(m) on the east 4s. and from a certain garden next the aforesaid land on the north which Ralph E(ui) once held 1s. and a certain part of the garden which Hugh Sotebrok(s) once held next to the land that was once of Reginald Danger on the west 4d.; chirograph sealed, witnesses, John Hanyn, Robert Long.

C.A.D., ii, A 2217.

317. [List of those paying quit rent]: Joce de Cornhill; Geoffrey Druy; William Fynk(s); Adam Broun; Lucy Broun who granted the tenement to John atte Hill paying 6s. as appears by their charter[1] enrolled 16 Ed. II; his widow, 5 Ed. III; John Hatfeld, chandler, 30 Ed. III; Richard Claveryng, 48 Ed. III; Richard Hatfeld, 8 Ric. II; John Olney throughout Hy. IV;

St. Benet Gracechurch

Thomas Hatfeld, 7 Hy. V, who died 5 Oct. 1422 and who bequeathed the tenement to the masters of London Bridge and it is situated on the west side of Graschirchstete [*sic*].

1. H.R. 51 (4).

318. Note: that Amice daughter of William Wilkyn gave to Richard prior and convent 21d. from land which the hospital of Sandon held in the parish as appears in Charter Twelve[1] of several parishes and the master of Sandon conveyed the right he had in this land to the master of London Bridge as appears in the muniments (*evidenciis*) of the same Bridge.

1. **1013**.

319. [f. 63v] [List of those paying rent to the hospital of Sandon by (*iuxta*) Kyngeston]: Richard Seriant; John de Stepynght, 1 Ed. II; Gregory de Stepynght; John Hornn, 19 Ed. II and 1 Ed. III; Richard Patrik, 5 and 30 Ed. III; his widow, 48 Ed. III; John Cotland, 49 Ed. III; William Olyver, 8 Ric. II and the tenement is situated on the west side of Graschirchstrete.

320. Note: that Amice daughter of William Wilekin gave to Richard prior and convent, 21d. from land which William Burser held of the hospital of St. Katherine by the Tower as appears in Charter Twelve[1] of several parishes.

1. **1013**.

321. [List of those paying quit rent]: William Burser; Robert Burser who granted a quit rent of 13s. 4d. *p.a.* to Holy Trinity [See also after **323**] as appears by the following grant.

322. [1273–4] Grant by Robert le Burser to Eustace prior and convent of 1 mark *p.a.* of quit rent from his whole tenement in the parish; abutments, the house of John le Tailur and John de Stebenhethe; the canons to have right to enter and take distresses for arrears; gersuma 9 marks; witnesses, Henry Walesis, mayor, Henry de Coventre, Nicholas de Wynton, sheriffs.

323. [f. 64] Exchange between the master, brethren and sisters of the hospital of St. Katherine by the Tower and William prior and canons of Holy Trinity. As a result of disagreements over arrears of certain rents and lesser tithes, by agreement the prior and convent remitted to the master etc. all exactions and demands which they had to 4s. 8d. of annual rents in the tenement between the house of Alexander le Treyere and the house of John Cross (*de Cruce*) in the soke without Algate and all the tithes of these lands which were of William Leman and John le Lymbernere and Simon le Vannere in the parish of St. Botolph saving the right of the parish church; for this release the master gave to the prior ½ mark *p.a.* of quit rent received from a rent which the hospital was accustomed to have from a tenement that was of Robert le Burser in Graschurchstrete; now [1423–4] held by John Sadelere, vintner, who has completely rebuilt the tenement; chiro-

St. Benet Gracechurch

graph sealed; witnesses, Ralph de Sandwich, warden of London, John Soudan, canon of St. Paul's; dated 11 June [1286].

321 contd. Robert Burser paid 21s. 9d., 15 Ed. I and 1 Ed. II; John Cotekyn, 19 Ed. II; Egidia Hornn, 6 and 30 Ed. III; Richard Toky, 48 Ed. III and 11 Ric. II; [See also after **324**] as appears by the following acquittance.

324. Acquittance given by William prior to Richard Toky for receipt of 43s. 6d. for the two past years in full payment of arrears due to Holy Trinity from a rent of 21s. 9d. *p.a.* from a tenement situated between the tenement of William Oliver once of John Stebenhethe on the south and one of Richard Toky once of John Horn on the north;[1] [f. 64v] sealed; dated Whitsuntide 1388.

> 1. Inserted above the line: 'now Bernard'.
> *C.A.D.*, ii, A 2222.

321 contd. John Spencer, 1 Hy. IV; Richard Baynard, 1 Hy. V; John Sadeler, 6 Hy. V and 2 Hy. VI and the tenement is situated on the west side of Graschirchstrete between the tenement of William Olyver on the south and Richard Beynard on the north.

325. [*c*. 1215–30] Grant by Alice widow of Master Roger the Doctor to Holy Trinity of 10s. *p.a.* of quit rent from a tenement held by Roger Long; to hold in free alms; moreover Roger gave the grantor 4s. to give to the monks of Reading (*Radyng*); sealed; witnesses, Richard fitz Reggi, alderman, William Wilekyn.

> *C.A.D.*, i, A 1643.

326. [List of those paying quit rent]: Robert Long; James son of Robert Long who granted 3s. 4d. from the same tenement to Holy Trinity [See also after **327**] as appears by the following charter.

327. [1249–50] Grant by James son of Robert Long to Richard prior and convent of 3s. 4d. *p.a.* of quit rent from his capital messuage from which James had paid 10s. *p.a.* after his father's death; canons to be allowed to distrain both for the 3s. 4d. and for 10s.; [f. 65] if the grantor or his heirs wish to sell or lease in fee (*in feodum dimittere*) the canons to have the preference by a bezant of 2s. to obtain the land if they wish to have it; for the gift the canons gave 40s. sterling; sealed; witnesses, Roger son of Roger, mayor, John Tuselan, Ralph Hardel, sheriffs.

> *C.A.D.*, ii, A 2227.

326 contd. James son of Robert Long; Geoffrey Fairchyld who granted the land to Robert Chaumpeneys paying to Holy Trinity 13s. 4d. as appears by their charter enrolled 5 Ed. I; Simon de Kydemynstre, 1 and 19 Ed. II and 1 Ed. III; Arnold Chaundeler, 6 Ed. III; Adam Boseworth, 30 Ed. III; Roger de Leycestre, 40 Ed. III; the nuns of Clerkenwell, 46 Ed. III.

All Hallows Lombard Street

328. Total of this parish 42s. 10d. and it is tithed as appears in the king's exemplification.

[f. 65v] IN THE PARISH OF ALL HALLOWS GRASCHIRCH

329. [1250–1] Grant by Ives le Gwayt and Matilda his wife to John prior and convent of ½ mark of quit rent together with 20s. *p.a.* which the canons already had from the tenement with houses built thereon; abutments, land of Aurifilia, daughter of Alan Oyldelaru(m) on the north and land that was of William Wylekyn on the south; 20s. was by gift and confirmation of Augustine the Mercer; the canons can take naam and distrain both for 6s. 8d. and 20s. until satisfied; gersuma 60s.; Ives and Matilda in full Husting; for greater security the sale was enrolled there (*ad maiorem securitatem dictam vendicionem ibidem irrotulari fecimus*); sealed; done in Lent 1251; witnesses, John Norman, mayor, Humphrey le Fevre, William son of Richard, sheriffs.

    C.A.D., ii, A 2226.

330. [List of those paying quit rent]: Ives le Gwayt, 35 Hy. III; Henry de Eure; Berthus de Rudham; Christine Gorges; Roger de Frowyk, 1 Ed. III; Arnold Chaundeler,[1] 19 Ed. II and 1 Ed. III; Richard de Berkyng, 5 and 30 Ed. III; Walter Berneye, 40 and 49 Ed. III; John Heylisdon, 6 Ric. II; John Seyton, 10 Ric. II; Henry Pomifreyt, 4 Hy. IV and throughout the said King Henry; William Tristour; John Coventre, 3 Hy. VI; John Cornewayle; now the fraternity of the fishmongers (*fratres pissinariorum*)[2] and the tenement is situated on the west side of Graschirchstrete with the tenement of Humphrey Poumfreyt on the south.

    1. Above the line: 'pon'. *Margin:* pondagium.
    2. In a later hand.

331. [f. 66] [1222–9] Grant by Richard prior and convent to Geoffrey de Frowyk, goldsmith, of land of the canons' fee on the west and the street next to the cemetery of All Hallows on the east; abutments, the king's highway on the south and the land that was of William Wilekyn, alderman, on the north and the land of Geoffrey Delabore on the east and Thomas de D(un)ol(mi)a on the west; rent ½ mark *p.a.*; if the grantee or his heirs wish to sell etc. the canons to have the preference by 2s.; Geoffrey, his heirs and assigns to be allowed to lease the fee to whomsoever they wish, except Jews, saving the right of the canons; Geoffrey swore fealty; gersuma 20s.; witnesses, John Travers, alderman, Henry de Colchirch.

332. [List of those paying rent]: Geoffrey de Frowyk; Geoffrey de Essex; Robert son of John; Robert de Lincoln; Richard Palmer; William A(rn)yze, 1 Ed. II; John atte Rye, 19 Ed. II and 6 Ed. III; Richard Carleton, 11 Ed. III; Katherine his wife, 34 Ed. III; then the land was divided for Roger Bernard paid 3s. 4d. for his part, 48 Ed. III and Nicholas Exton 3s. 4d. the same year: after Roger Bernard; the dean of Westminster chapel: after Nicholas Exton; John Curteys, 8 Ric. II and 5 Hy. IV and the ? issues (*euntes*) are openly enough demonstrated in the charter.

All Hallows Lombard Street

333. [f. 66v] Grant by the convent of Christchurch to Daniel of certain land which it had by the gift of Ralph son of Herl; witness, Ralph Aurfice.

C.A.D., ii, A 2214.

334. [List of those paying rent]: Daniel; John his son to whom the prior and convent granted the aforementioned land at a rent of 8s. [See also after **335**] as appears by the following charter.

335. [1212–13] Grant by the prior [unnamed] and convent to John son of Daniel of all that messuage (*managium*); abutments, the land which is of the fee of the monks of St. Saviour of Bermondsey and the land of the nuns of St. Helen; containing in width along the street 16 ells less 1 in. and in width against the ? courtyard (*versus curtim*) 8½ ells and in length from the king's highway to the land that was of Ralph Cucu, 54 ells less 1 in.; all in wood and stone etc.; rent 8s. *p.a.*; swore fealty; for the grant, lease and confirmation the grantee increased the rent by 4s. *p.a.* on this tenement; witnesses, Roger son of Alan, mayor, Gervase de Aldermaunebury, Richard son of John, John son of James, Robert Blund, William de Parisius [*sic*], Master Roger the Doctor, John de Liesn', William de Waltham, then chamberlain, German Parmen(ter), Hugh de Sartrino, Richard the Priest (*?presbitero*), Richard de Beninton.

C.A.D., ii, A 2215.

334 contd. John son of Daniel which John had other land beside the aforesaid land for which he paid to the church of St. Helen 4s. *p.a.* which 4s. the prioress and convent of St. Helen granted to Matilda [See also after **337**] as appears by the following quitclaim.

336. [*c.* 1215–29] Grant by Matilda prioress of the church of St. Helen to Matilda wife of Robert the son of Alice and her heirs of 4s. *p.a.* of quit rent which John son of Daniel [f. 67] was accustomed to pay the grantor from land in the parish; abutments, the land of John son of Daniel and the land of Geoffrey Marshal; quitclaim; 40s. for the grant; witnesses, William son of Alice Marshall daughter of Alice, John Travers.

337. Note: the above-mentioned Matilda granted to the prior and convent of Holy Trinity the aforesaid 4s. for the salvation of the soul of her late husband Robert son of Alice and handed to Holy Trinity charter **336**, and so John son of Daniel paid 12s. *p.a.*

334 contd. Osbern de Stapilford; John Wylymyn, 'ferrour', 1 Ed. II as appears by the poundage (*pondagium*) Cambin Fulberti, 6 Ed. III; his widow viz Christine Cambyn, 30 Ed. III; Henry Pykard, 39 Ed. III; Margery Pykard, 48 Ed. III and 8 Ric. II; John Pykard throughout Hy. IV and 7 Hy. V and this tenement is situated on the east side of Graschirchstrete.

338. [1201–10] Grant by Hugh prior of St. Saviour in Bermundeseye to

St. Michael Cornhill

John son of Daniel of land; abutments, land of the said John and land of John son of James, goldsmith, rent 7s. *p.a.*; sealed; no witnesses.

> *Margin:* Nota quod haberemus vs. in eadem parochia de terra Walteri filii Jacobi aurifabri iuxta terram predicti Johanis filii Daniel ut patet in carta xi[a] de pluribus parochiis.[1]
> 1. **1012.**

339. [f. 67v: 34 lines blank] Total of this parish 45s. 4d. and nevertheless it is tithed at 53s. 10d. in the king's exemplification.

[f. 68] IN THE PARISH OF ST. PETER CORNHILL

340. [1197–1221] Heading of a grant by Peter prior and convent to Simon Blound of 12s. *p.a.* of quit rent from certain land in the parish; rent 1 lb. of cumin or 1d. as appears in the following charter [no charter has been copied].

341. Three lines of the Lord's Prayer written in Old English script.[1]

> 1. Probably in the hand of Stephen Batman.

342. [List of those paying rent]: Simon Blound; now [1425–7] the prior of the New Hospital without Bisshoppysgate.

343. Total of this parish 1d. and nevertheless it is tithed at 20s. 4d. as appears in the king's exemplification.

[f. 68v] IN THE PARISH OF ST. MICHAEL CORNHILL

344. [1271–2] Grant by Eustace prior and convent to John (*de*) Evere, citizen, of all that Stephen de Giseborne held of the grantors; abutments, the land of Peter de St. Paul, chaplain on the west and the land of Henry de Cornhull on the east containing in width along the king's highway, $11\frac{1}{2}$ ells and at the lower end (*in inferiore capite*) 11 ells and in length it extends from the king's highway on the south to the land of Margaret Sibeling on the north, $21\frac{1}{4}$ ells; to hold in perpetuity; rent 3s. *p.a.*; chirograph; witnesses, Walter Hervy, mayor, Richard Parys, John de Wodeleye, sheriffs, Walter Pot(er), alderman.

> *C.A.D.*, ii, A 2337.

345. [List of those paying rent]: John Evere; Roger de Evere; John Hauteyn or Hakeneye, 1 and 19 Ed. II and I Ed. III; Henry Hardyngham, 6 Ed. III; his widow, 30 and 48 Ed. III and 8 Ric. II; Roger Stokton throughout Hy. IV and 6 Hy. V.

346. [1170–*c.* 1185] Grant by Stephen prior and convent to John son of Serlo of land [f. 69] which Serlo himself held; rent 3s.; to hold in fee as long as he pays the rent duly; gersuma 1s. 4d. for pittances; witnesses, Geoffrey

St. Michael Cornhill

the alderman, Henry de Chesewyke, Fulk the Baker, Alfred the Baker, William de Suthfolch, Ralph de Northfol, Nicholas the Bedell.

C.A.D., ii, A 1997.

347. [List of those paying rent]: John Serle; Simon Ni-(n)ler, the widow of Ni-(n)ler; then the land was divided for Robert Hardel paid 1s. 6d. and James Coteler 1s. 6d.; afterwards John Bacon paid the whole sum and granted the tenement to Peter de Halstede paying 3s. as appears in their charter enrolled 3 Ed. I and Peter de Halstede otherwise called de St. Paul paid; the nuns of Halliwell; Hugh de Waltham, 1 Ed. II; Nicholas Pykott, 5 Ed. II and 1 Ed. III; John Pykott, 5 and 6 Ed. III; John Rokell, 30 Ed. III; Thomas Pykott, 48 Ed. III and 8 Ric. II; Thomas atte Swanne, 18 Ric. II; widow of the same, 8 Hy. IV and these two tenements are situated one after another adjacent on the north side of the great street of Cornhull.

348. Note: that Richard Dokesworth granted two tenements adjacent to Thomas Orpedman paying therefrom to Holy Trinity 6s. *p.a.* as appears by their charter[1] of 15 Ed. I.

1. H.R. 17 (48).

349. Memorandum: William de Belmonte gave to the prior and convent 15s. *p.a.* which John Blond, clerk, was accustomed to pay him from certain land as appears by Charter Thirteen[1] of several parishes.

1. **1014**.

350. [List of those paying rent]: John Blond; Paulinus Mercer; Gilbert Ferrinier; Ralph Lupus, 1 Ed. II; Walter Wolffe, 19 Ed. II and 1 Ed. III; James Gorney otherwise called Scherman, 16 Ed. III [See also after **351**] as appears by the following plea.

351. *Common plea held in the Husting, Mon. 4 Nov. 1342.*
[f. 69v] James de Gourneye complained that on Mon. 1 May 1340 the prior came to the pl.'s free tenement and took naam to the value of 40s. etc. until by gage and pledge of William de Thorneye, one of the sheriffs, a date was given etc.; the prior by his attorney Alan Gilyngham came and said the taking of naam was lawful because Thomas Heroun, his predecessor, was seised by the aforesaid James and John Leflyf as true tenants and because the rent was 45s. in arrears on the day of taking the naam; the pl. said he had nothing in the land except by the right of his wife Joan and he was not able to answer for the said tenement (*onerare vel exonerare*); at a court held Mon. 15 July 1342 the prior, James and Joan present, the pls., said they did not hold of the prior and placed themselves on their country; jury summoned; at a court held Mon. 21 Oct. 1342 the pls. essoined. The prior was attached to reply to James le Shereman concerning the plea etc.; on Mon. 15 July 1342 the prior came to his free tenement and took naam that was valued at 30s. until by gage and pledge of John de Rokelee, one of

St. Michael Cornhill

the sheriffs, a day was given etc.; the prior by his attorney Alan de Gillyngham came and said that it was lawful as the rent was 37s. 6d. in arrears [incomplete].

350 contd. Afterwards the land was divided for John Leflyf paid 3s. 4d. for his part and James Gourneye, shereman, 11s. 8d. for the other part: 3s. 4d. after John Leflye; Thomas Yrland, 35 Ed. III and 1 Ric. II; [f. 70] the churchwardens of St. Michael Cornhull; 11s. 8d. after James Gourneye; Geoffrey Stuuecle 48 Ed. III and 1 Ric. II which part was divided [See also after **352**] as appears by charter[1] enrolled 18 Oct. 1378.

    1. H.R. 107 (40).

352. Indenture made between Geoffrey Stu(u)ecle and William Wodehous, citizen and skinner, witnesseth that, since William and Alice his wife have a tenement and two shops with a solar built thereon by the enfeoffment of Geoffrey and since Geoffrey has two shops and since Thomas Ireland, citizen and skinner, has another tenement and one shop, all which lands and tenements are liable to pay 15s. *p.a.* to Holy Trinity of quit rent of which rent Thomas paid 3s. 4d. *p.a.* and the rest of the rent of 11s. 8d. *p.a.* is divided between Geoffrey and William as they wish, Geoffrey and William agree that the tenement, shops and solar of William and Alice shall be charged with 3s. 4d. *p.a.* and the two shops of Geoffrey shall pay 8s. 4d. *p.a.*; and if William and Alice, their heirs and assigns are asked for more than 3s. 4d. they may distrain on the property of Geoffrey his heirs and assigns and vice-versa; [f. 70v] sealed; dated 4 Aug. 1378.

350 contd. 8s. 4d.: Geoffrey Stu(u)ecle; 3s. 4d.: Thomas Irland; 3s. 4d.: William Woudhous, 6 Ric. II: after Geoffrey Stu(u)ecle; his widow, 8 and 19 Ric. II; Richard Boteler, 1 Hy. IV: after William Wodhous; Thomas Wodhous, 16 Ric. II and 4 Hy. IV: after Thomas Irland; the churchwardens of St. Michael Cornhull to the present day [1425–7] and these tenements are situated one after the other adjacent to the west to the street of Cornhull between the tenement once of Robert Burell now of John Weston [incomplete].

353. [1197–1221] Heading of a grant by Peter prior and convent to Matthew the Baker of land at a rent of 4s. 2d. *p.a.*

354. [List of those paying rent]: Matthew the Baker; Stephen Bokerell who granted the tenement to Thomas le Batur [See also after **355**] as appears by the following charter.

355. [1255] Lease by Stephen Bukerell to Thomas le Batur of certain land with houses built thereon containing in width along the street leading towards Cornhull from the corner of Bersker(u)ereslane up to the grantor's land on the east, 10 ells 15 ins. and [f. 71] in length from this corner up to the grantor's land on the south along the lane of Bersker(u)ereslane $17\frac{1}{2}$ ells and in depth from the king's highway up to the half of the private room

St. Edmund King and Martyr

(*usque ad medietatem camere private*) on the south 24¾ ells; the grantee to hold all in wood and stone etc.; rent to Holy Trinity 4s. 2d. and to the grantor and his heirs 23s. 10d. *p.a.*; chirograph sealed; witnesses, Ralph Hardell, mayor, Stephen de Oystergate, Henry de Valen(ern) [*sic*], sheriffs, Roger son of Roger, alderman, Thomas de Dunolm, Nicholas son of Joce.

354 contd. Thomas le Batur; John le Batur; Roger le Pessoner, 1 and 19 Ed. II and 1 Ed. III; his widow, 6 Ed. III; John Tripyl, 30 and 34 Ed. III [See also after **356**] as appears by the following plea.

356. *Common plea held in the Husting, Mon. 23 Feb. 1360.*
John Triple, citizen and fishmonger, complained that on Thurs. 29 Jan. 1360 the prior came to his tenement and took naam etc. to the value of 4s. 2d. etc. until by gage and pledge of Simon de Benyngton, sheriff, etc.; the prior by his attorney Alan Horwode said naam just etc., the tenement situated in the parish of St. Michael in the corner of Berche(u)erislane next the church between the tenement of John [f. 71v] Bertelot, carpenter, on the south and that of Andrew le Pyebakere on the east and the prior was seised of the tenement and the tenant John de Triple was in arrears to 4s. 2d. for one whole year before the taking of naam and John could not deny this; the prior has the return of the naam which is not subject to replevin and John de Triple in mercy.

354 contd. Simon de Sudbury, bishop of London, 48 Ed. III; the abbot of Westminster, 8 Ric. II; the college of Sudbury, 1 and 5 Hy. IV.

357. Total of this parish 25s. 2d. and it is tithed at this in the king's exemplification.

[f. 72] IN THE PARISH OF ST. EDMUND GRASCHIRCH

358. Composition between the dean and chapter of St. Paul's and Holy Trinity whereby the rector of the parish church pays 13s. 4d. *p.a.* to Holy Trinity; agreement between the two parties on the right of advowson to the church of St. Edmund the King near Graschirch, a disagreement having arisen when the living was vacant and reference being made to a decree[1] (*ordinacio*) of Gilbert Foliot, former bishop of London; it was agreed that the prior and convent should continue to have a pension of 1 mark annually stated in this decree but that they should pay to the dean and chapter ½ mark annually on 22 Nov. and that as often as the church falls vacant, without contradiction or hindrance from the dean and chapter, the prior and convent shall present to the said church; sealed chirograph; dated 27 Oct. 1300.

    1. See *Early Charters of St. Paul's*, ed. M. Gibbs (Camden 3rd series, lviii, 1939), no. 246.

359. Confirmation of Richard[1] bishop of London of **358**; ratification and approval; sealed; dated at Foleham 8 Nov. 1300.

    1. Richard de Gravesend, bishop of London, 1280–1303.

St. Edmund King and Martyr

360. Recognition of Martin rector of St. Edmund of the pension mentioned in **358** [f. 72v] after a disagreement concerning the payment, the prior and convent remitted arrears to Martin who promised to pay the pension in full from that time forward and if he failed to pay he was to become liable for the payment of the arrears in full; sealed; dated 28 Oct. 1260.

361. [1147–67] Lease by Ralph prior and convent to David son of Ralph de Cornhull of land which was of Suething Be(n)ercher(u)er in Bersker(u)ereslane; rent 6s. *p.a.*; witnesses, [not named].

362. [List of those paying rent]: David de Cornhull; William his son who granted the tenement to William Nied [See also after **363**] as appears in the following charter.

363. Grant of William son of David de Cornhulla to William Nied of certain land in Benerche(u)erelane; abutments, the land of Benet the Goldsmith and land which was of John Scot, containing in length $9\frac{1}{2}$ ells and in width along the king's highway $7\frac{1}{2}$ ells.

362 contd. Benet Gelusdi, goldsmith; Richard son of Benet who granted the land with other lands annexed to the nuns of Haliwell and the sealed charter of Holy Trinity remains with the nuns in a book of the nuns called 'Domesday' folio 52 and the nuns paid the rent as long as the land was in their hands.

363a. Inquisition by which the jurors swear that Robert Motone was seised of one brewhouse in the parish of St. Edmund and of three shops in Birchenlane in the same parish from which he paid 6s. *p.a.* to Holy Trinity.

364. [List of those paying rent]: Alice Rous; Adam Rous, 48 Ed. III; the prior of St. Bartholomew, 8 Ric. II; John Pays, 20 Ric. II; John Chircheman, 1 Hy. IV; Robert Wedyngdon, 1 Hy. V; Stephen Forster, Hy. VI; Agnes his wife, Ed. IV; now[1] Thomas Wellys, draper.

    1. Date uncertain.

365. [f. 73] Note: that in a charter[1] of John Schaftysbury enrolled 18 Ed. I mention is made of a tenement situated between the tenement of Alice atte Vyne on the east and north and the king's highway on the south and west owing to the nuns of Haliwell 9s. *p.a.*

    1. H.R. 19 (15).

366. [1222–30] Lease of Richard prior and convent to Ede(u)a Bel(ere)ce wife of Estmundus Cap(er)e of land with houses in the parish of St. Edmund; abutments, the land of Ralph Flael on the west and the land of Geoffrey Frowic on the east; in width along the king's highway at the south end $9\frac{1}{2}$ ells, in the middle 8 ells 15 ins. and at the north end $5\frac{3}{4}$ ells and in length from the king's highway to the court of the said Ralph on the north 28 ells; rent 5s. *p.a.*; not permitted to pledge the land with houses to the

St. Edmund King and Martyr

Jews or to transfer the house without the consent of the canons; if the tenement is burnt by a fire of Ede(u)a's own making and she or her heirs do not wish to leave it they shall pay to the canons ½ mark of silver; [f. 73v] gersuma 2 marks of silver; swore fealty; witnesses, John Travers, Walter de Insula, aldermen.

C.A.D., i, A 1808.

367. [List of those paying rent]: E. Bel(ere)ce; Henry Bole; Gilbert Marescall who granted the land to Richard Marescall who paid 5s. as appears from a charter enrolled 19 Ed. II; Richard Marescall, 1 Ed. III; Roger Lapyn, 6 Ed. III; John Warner, 30 and 34 Ed. III [See also after **368**] as appears by the following plea.

368. *Common plea held in the Husting, Mon. 9 Mar. 1360.*
John Warner complained that on Wed. 4 Feb. 1360 the prior came to his free tenement in the parish of St. Edmund in Lumbardstrete and took naam worth 13s. 4d. etc. until by gage and pledge of Simon de Bedyngton, one of the sheriffs, etc.; the prior by his attorney Alan de Horwode said that the taking of the naam was lawful because the tenement owed a rent of 5s. *p.a.* to the prior and convent and 30s. was in arrears for six years and the prior claims naam for two and a half of the six years and the prior retains the naam of 13s. 4d. which is not subject to replevin (*habeat retornum namiorum predictorum irripleg'*) John Warner is in mercy.

367 contd. Walter Leycestre, 48 Ed. III and 8 Ric. II and this tenement is situated on the north side of Lumbardstrete.

369. [f. 74] [1270-1] Grant by William le Cornere, citizen, to Eustace prior and convent of a quit rent of ½ mark which the grantor was accustomed to receive from land and houses which Master Adam de Cantebrigg' holds in the parish of St. Edmund the King and Martyr; if the tenement fails through lack of maintenance or through fire, the grantor obliges himself and his heirs that the canons may distrain on his whole tenement which he has in the parish of St. Dunstan, formerly of Ledulf, for the rent up to 60s. or until such time as he and his heirs provide another ½ mark of quit rent; the canons gave 60s. to expedite the grantor's business; sealed; witnesses, John Adrian, mayor, Gregory de Rokesle, Henry Valensi, sheriffs, Matthew Bokerell, alderman of this ward.[1]

1. Langbourn.
C.A.D., i, A 1800.

370. [List of those paying quit rent]: Master Adam de Cantebrigg'; Elias le Hodere; Gilbert Marshall (*Marescallus*), 1 and 5 Ed. II; Robert atte Folde, 19 Ed. II and 1 Ed. III; Matilda atte Vyne, 6 and 30 Ed. III; Richard Toky, 33 and 49 Ed. III and 8 Ric. II and the tenement is situated on the south side of Lumbardstrete.

371. Grant by John Bekeounte[1] son of Geoffrey Bekeounte[1] to Holy

St. Edmund King and Martyr

Trinity of a quit rent of 4s. *p.a.* from certain land which Gilbert de Schelford held of the grantor in the parish of St. Edmund next the land of William Chamberlain (*Camerarii*) [f. 74v] on the west; to hold in free alms; 2s. of this quit rent are to be spent on the refection of the canons on the grantor's anniversary; the canons are to have the same liberty to compel the tenants of the fee as the grantor; in the event of non-payment the canons have the right of entry upon the capital messuage; dated 2 Feb. 1222; witnesses, John Travers, Gilbert son of Fulk, aldermen.

    1. *Rectius* Buccuinte.
    C.A.D., ii, A 2113.

372. [1221] Agreement between John Bokeount son of Geoffrey Bokeount and Nigra wife of Master Henry de Waltham that John had sold and quitclaimed to Master Henry and Nigra his wife all the lands and rents which he had in the parish of St. Edmund; abutments, the land that was of Walter the Shoemaker (*Calcearii*) and the land of Gilbert de Seluorde; all is conveyed except a rent of 4s. *p.a.* which Gilbert was accustomed to pay to Holy Trinity; to hold to Master Henry and Nigra his wife for a payment of 17 marks of silver; John received 5 marks beforehand and the remaining 12 marks are payable to the said John or his assigns in the octave of St. Martin after the consecration of lord E. de Fawkenberge as bishop of London, 6 marks, and on the morrow of St. Andrew, 6 marks; these 12 marks to be handed over to John by E. the sub-prior of Holy Trinity (*tradi ad opus prefati Johannis in manibus E. supprioris*) who received the seisin of the land and rents on the part (*ad opus*) of Master Henry and Nigra by such an agreement that if the first term for the payment of the 6 marks was disregarded then Henry and Nigra lose the 5 marks agreed upon and the charter placed in the hands of the sub-prior at the time of this sale shall be delivered (*liberabitur*) to the said John; if the last term for the payment of the [second] 6 marks be disregarded then the first 5 marks shall be forfeited and the said John shall refund 6 marks to Henry and Nigra on the feast of St. Nicholas [6 Dec.]; on the return of the 6 marks the charter of sale shall be handed over to John; and John [f. 75] shall be free to do as he pleases with the seisin of the land and rents without any impediment; this agreement was sworn to hold to Henry and Nigra; and because Nigra had no seal, the part remaining with John Bokeount at her request is sealed with the seal of John Travers, alderman; witnesses, John Travers, alderman, Simon Blundus, Thomas son of William Wilkyn.

    C.A.D., iii, A 6080.

373. [List of those paying quit rent]: Gilbert de Schelford; Elias le Hoder; E. Pheleper; Gilbert Marshall, 1 and 5 Ed. II; Robert atte Folde, 19 Ed. II and 1 Ed. III; Matilda atte Vyne, 6 and 30 Ed. III; Richard Toky, 33 and 49 Ed. III and 8 Ric. II; John Sandherst; then the land was divided for Richard Baynard paid 2s. for half the tenement and the perpetual chaplain of the chantry of Matilda atte Vyne 2s. for the other half; and Richard Baynard in addition to 2s. paid 6s. 8d. *p.a.* for a tenement once of Adam de Cantebrigg and thus he paid 8s. 8d. *p.a.* 10 Hy. IV and 7 Hy. V as appears

St. Edmund King and Martyr

by the following agreement, and the tenement is situated on the south side of Lumbardstrete.

374. [f. 75 inset][1] Charter of Robert prior and convent of Holy Trinity; since John Rosamund for the salvation of his soul etc. had granted, before the statute of mortmain, to Holy Trinity and to brother Eustace its prior ½ mark of quit rent which he had of the gift of Adam de Gysseborne and Marcella his wife from all his lands with houses which Adam and Marcella held of Gilbert de Selford in the parish of St. Edmund to hold to the prior and convent in free alms; and since the king by letters patent granted and ratified to the rector and parishioners of St. Michael in Cornhull for the maintenance of a certain fraternity in honour of St. Anne founded in the said church; and since a controversy arose between the prior on the one side and Thomas Whythed, rector of St. Michael, John Whytby, rector of St. Mary Abchirch in Candelwykstrete, Robin Lardener and Thomas Baldok, masters of the fraternity on the other side; and since the prior pleaded through the assize against the afore-mentioned; it was settled in this way that they paid 20s. to the prior for all costs, damages and arrears of quit rent and agreed for themselves and for all the brothers of the fraternity to pay ½ mark *p.a.* to the prior and his successors; sealed by all five; witnesses, Thomas Kent, Roger Stocton, Robert Rus; dated 25 June 1404.

1. A piece of parchment $7\frac{9}{10}$ ins. wide by $4\frac{3}{10}$ ins. long is inserted between f. 74 and f. 75, f. 75 inset, the verso of which is also written upon.
C.A.D., ii, A 2225.

375. [f. 75 inset v] [1269–70] Grant by Adam de Gyesburne to Master John Rosamund of ½ mark of quit rent from the grantor's land with houses built thereon in the parish of St. Edmund which he has by the grant of Gilbert de Selford whose entrance is between the house of Henry le Paumer on the east on (*iuxta*) the king's highway and the house of Henry called le Bole on the west; to hold to Master John, his heirs and assigns for ever; gersuma 5 marks; sealed; witnesses, Hugh son of Otto, warden of London, Robert de Kornelle, Thomas de Basyng, sheriffs, Matthew Bokerel, alderman, Nicholas the rector of the place (*rector loci*).

376. [f. 75] Note: that Master John Rosamund granted the 6s. 8d. [conveyed in **375**] to the church of Holy Trinity as appears by Charter Seven[1] of several parishes.

1. **1008**.

377. [List of those paying quit rent]: Master John de Bedford; Henry de Fornham who granted the tenement to Reginald de Subiria [See also after **378**] as appears by the following charter written in the register of the rectors of London.

378. [1277] Grant by Henry de Fornham, clerk, to Reginald de Subiria, a friend, of all that tenement with houses once of John de Bedford, vicar of

St. Clement Eastcheap

the church of Westham?, London diocese, which the grantor bought of the said John; the tenement is situated in the parish of St. Edmund near Greschirch; abutments, the tenement of Ralph de Cestre on the west and the tenement of Ydonia widow of Geoffrey de Trye on the east extending in length from the king's highway on the south side to the tenement of the said Idonea on the north; to hold in fee in perpetuity; rent one rose on 24 June and to the chief lords of the fee the services due, to the nuns of Halliwell 12s. to the canons of Holy Trinity ½ mark and to the chaplains of the parish churches of London 3s. 4d. for pittances and to Idonea daughter of the late Roger de Scadeburgh, citizen of London, one clove-gillyflower at Easter; gersuma 30 marks; sealed; witnesses, Gregory Rokesle, mayor, John Adrian, Walter le Engleis [*sic*], sheriffs, Nicholas de Wynton, alderman of the ward.

377 contd. John de Totenham; William le Furbur, 1, 5 and 19 Ed. II and 1 Ed. III; Gilbert de Mordone, 6 Ed. III; Robert Scherwode, 30 Ed. III; Richard Rothyng, 49 Ed. III; Robert Andrewe junior, Thomas Andrewe, 8 Ric. II; now [1425–7] the fraternity of St. Anne of St. Michael's church Cornhull as appears at the following sign[1] and the tenement is situated on the north side of Lumbardstrete.

    1. *Margin:* The sign of a hand with the words 'superius in cedula presenti'.

379. Total of this parish 28s. 4d. and it is tithed as it appears in the king's exemplification.

[f. 75v] IN THE PARISH OF ST. CLEMENT CANDELWYK

380. [1222–48] Grant by Ernald son of Simon the Chaloner to Richard prior and convent of certain land with a house in St. Clement street by Candelwykstrete; abutments, the land with a house which the grantor gave to his brother on the north and land that was of Michael le Tulusan on the south; to hold to the priory in free alms paying to the lords of the fee for all services, to John son of Bernard and his heirs 9s. 4d. *p.a.* and to the heirs of Ernald the Bowmaker (*Arcenarii*) 2d. *p.a.* and to Margaret the daughter of Ernald and her heirs 2d. *p.a.*; the canons to have ½ mark *p.a.* for pittances on the morrow of St. Edmund the King and Martyr [21 Nov.] and ½ mark *p.a.* for pittances on the day of the grantor's death and as long as grantor lives, he wishes that these pittances shall be on the day of St. Leodegarius [2 Oct.]; also ½ mark to find wax candles for (*coram*) the canons at supper and drinking as often as is necessary; sealed; witnesses, Thomas de Dunolm, alderman, Robert de Suthflite.

    C.A.D., ii, A 2271.

381. [1222–48] Lease by Richard prior and convent to Robert de Catelon (*Katelon*) of certain land with houses built upon it in the parish of St. Clement; abutments, the land of Anselm on the south and the land of the canons on the north containing in width along the king's highway 13¼ ells 1 in. and from the king's highway on the east to the land of the said Robert

St. Martin Orgar

on the west 20⅜ ells and from the king's highway to the land of Simon Abindon and Robert de Basingg on the west 7⅜ ells 2 ins.; rent ½ mark *p.a.*; swore fealty; but the tenement and houses were destroyed;[1] [f. 76] gersuma 12 marks; witnesses, Thomas de Duranlino, Robert Blund, aldermen.

    1. In the text 'as above', but there is no previous mention of any destruction.
    C.A.D., ii, A 2014.

382. [List of those paying rent]: Robert Catelon; Walter Camail; Peter Micham [See also after **383**] to whom another part of the aforesaid land was granted as appears by the following charter.

383. [*c.* 1241] Grant by Richard prior and convent to Peter de Michham of land with houses in the parish of St. Clement by (*iuxta*) Candelwykstrete; abutments, the land of Robert Katelone on the south and the land that was of Walter son of Simon on the north containing in length from the king's highway to the land of Robert de Katelonie on the west 20½ ells and in breadth along the king's highway 7½ ells 4 ins. and from the west side 6½ ells; also a grant of another piece of land next the aforesaid land on the north which extends from the house of Walter son of Simon to the land of Robert de Plass[ey] and contains in length 12½ ells and in width 2¾ ells; rent 3s. 4d. *p.a.*; the prior and his successors to have the preference by a gold bezant if the grantee wishes to sell the land; swore fealty; Peter and his heirs not to allow the houses to deteriorate; gersuma 7 marks sterling; chirograph sealed; witness, Thomas de Dunolm, alderman.

    C.A.D., ii, A 2044.

382 contd. Peter de Michham paid 10s.; to Holy Trinity 1s. and to a certain chantry in St. Paul's 9s., which Peter granted the tenement to Michael de Brakley [f. 76v] paying 1s. as appears by charter[1] enrolled 9 Ed. I; afterwards, John Wortham; John's widow, 1 Ed. II; Simon atte Grene, 48 Ed. III; John Po[u]der, 8 Ric. II; Richard Storme, Hy. IV and the tenement is situated on the west side of St. Clement's lane and it has for a sign Oitheram and it is now a brewhouse (*bracinea domus*).

    1. H.R. 12 (118, 126).

384. Total of this parish 1s. and it is tithed as it appears in the king's exemplification.

[f. 77] IN THE PARISH OF ST. MARTIN ORGAR

385. Grant by Benet abbot and convent of Stratteford to Peter prior and convent of 7s. of land which Ralph Long held of them in the parish of St. Martin as appears in Charter Fourteen[1] of several parishes.

    1. **1015**.

386. [List of those paying rent]: Ralph Long; Joce Junior; Stephen Casuen; the canons of Merton; John Casewem; Simon de Merworth, 1 and 19 Ed.

St. Martin Orgar

II and 1 Ed. III; William Hamelamstede, 6 Ed. III; John Aubre, 36 Ed. III; Thomas Hanamstede, 49 Ed. III; Richard Odiam, 8 Ric. II and this tenement is situated on the north side of Candelwykstrete.

387. [1197–c. 1212] Grant by Peter prior and convent to Henry son of Rennerus son of Berengarius of a tenement in Candelwrithestrete in the parish of St. Martin in Candelwithestrate formerly held by Gilbert the clerk, nephew of Malger; rent ½ mark; to hold as long as the rent is paid without miskenning; swore fealty; land, in length 94 ft. and in breadth 25 ft.; gersuma 15s.; witnesses, James the alderman, Matthew the alderman, Maurice de Russie.

    C.A.D., ii, A 2025.

388. [List of those paying rent]: Henry son of Rennery; Godewin Marshal; Richard Sabrigtesworth; John Ferebras; John Fa(n)eneri; Walter Papworth, 1 and 19 Ed. II and 1 Ed. III; John le Clerk, 6 Ed. III; the nuns of Stratteford, 30 Ed. III and thereafter, and the tenement is situated on the north side of Candelwykstrete.

389. Grant by William son of Roger to John prior and convent of a quit rent of 24s. *p.a.* which Henry Dunolm and Agnes widow of Adrian Aschwy were accustomed to pay the grantor from two adjacent tenements in the parish of St. Martin from which sum 10s. went to the abbey of Bermundesey as appears by Charter Fifteen[1] of several parishes.

    1. **1016.**

390. [List of those paying quit rent]: Henry Dorham then the two tenements were divided for Alice wife of Henry paid 12s. *p.a.* for one tenement and Margery daughter of Henry paid 2s. *p.a.* for the other, which Margery granted the tenement to Firminus the chaplain who paid 2s. to Holy Trinity and 10s. to the monks of Bermundesey as appears in their charter[1] enrolled [f. 77v] 2 Ed. I; afterwards Agnes Aswy paid all; Richard Abyndon; Adam the Tailor (*Cissor*) [See also after **391**] as appears by the following plea.

    1. H.R. 5 (60).

391. *Common plea held in the Husting, Mon. 14 Nov. 1300.*
Adam Tailor and Denise his wife complained that the prior came to their free tenement in the parish of St. Martin Orgar and took naam to the value of 1s. etc. until through the gage and pledge of John Armenters etc.; and the prior came and it was agreed and Adam and Denise recognised that a rent of 14s. *p.a.* was payable and the prior remitted all arrears.

390 contd. Stephen de Abyndon, 1 and 19 Ed. II and 1 Ed. III; Richard Bacon, 6 and 20 Ed. III [See also after **392**] as appears by the following plea.

392. *Common plea held in the Husting, Mon. 6 Feb. 1346.*
Richard Bacon complained that on Wed. 1 Feb. 1346 the prior came to his

St. Lawrence Pountney

free tenement in the parish and took naam to the value of 7s. etc. until by gage and pledge of Edmund de Hemenhale etc.; the prior came and claimed that the taking of naam was just because the tenement was held of Holy Trinity by a rent of 24s. *p.a.* and that the rent was 12s. in arrears; Richard could not deny this; the prior has return of the naam of 7s. and Richard is in mercy.

390 contd. Walter Sebily, 48 Ed. III; William Bacon, 8 Ric. II.

393. Total of this parish 27s. 8d. and yet it is tithed at 28s. as appears in the king's exemplification.

[f. 78] IN THE PARISH OF ST. LAWRENCE CANDELWYKSTRETE

394. [1147–67] Lease by Ralph prior and convent to Brithmar, son-in-law of Godwin Brothesouche of land in the parish which Roger the nephew of Hubert and Brithmar himself and also David Da(c)er held; rent 10s. *p.a.*; the land is in Ebbegate, London; witnesses, Ralph the clerk, Godwin the alderman, Estmundus the alderman, John the bedel, Stephen the convert (*Conversus*), David Dac(us).

395. [List of those paying rent]: Brithmar; Eudo the Cutler; William de Wroth; Henry de Staundon who had two daughters[1] Christine and Wimark who granted the tenement to Serlo the Mercer [See also after **396**] as appears by the following charter.

    1. *Rectius* grand-daughters.

396. [*c.* 1197–*c.* 1225] Grant by Christine and Wymark daughters of Agnes daughter of Henry de Staunton to Serlo the Mercer of all the land in the parish of St. Lawrence by (*versus*) the Thames which lies between the land of Serlo on the east and the land that was of Adrian de Winchester (*Wynton*) on the west, containing in breadth along the front to the king's highway 8¾ ells and in length 36¾ ells and in frontage along St. Martin's lane 12 ells; rent to the grantors and their heirs ½ lb. of cumin or 1d. at Michaelmas to each saving the service to the chief lord which Serlo must do; Christine and Wymark and their heirs not able to dispossess the grantee and his heirs.

Margin: Iste carte sigillate habentur in Novo Hospitali extra Bisshopsgate.

395 contd. The New Hospital without Bisshopesgate which paid 10s. *p.a.* to Holy Trinity [See also after **397**] as appears by the following charter.

397. [*c.* 1197–*c.* 1225] Grant by Serlo the Mercer for the safety of his soul and that of Isabel his wife etc. to the New Hospital without Bisshopesgate for the maintenance [f. 78v] of the poor; to hold in free alms; of all the grantor's lands in the parish of St. Lawrence; all the land he had of Geoffrey son of Henry de Tanton; abutments, the land that was of Adrian de Winchester and the lane of St. Martin Orgar extending along this lane from

St. Lawrence Pountney

the king's highway on the south to the land that was of Arnold Moyne on the north; the grantees to pay the service due to the chief lords of the fee, namely for the land held of Geoffrey to Geoffrey and his heirs 1 lb. of cumin or 2d. and from the same land to the canons of Merton 5s. *p.a.* and from the land held of Christine and Wymark to them and their heirs 1 lb. of cumin or 2d. and from the same land to the canons of Holy Trinity 10s. *p.a.*

395 contd. The New Hospital which leased the land to Thomas son of Adrian but the hospital continued to pay 10s. *p.a.* to Holy Trinity; William de Stanford who recognised himself to be bound to pay to the Hospital without Bishoppesgate 22s. *p.a.* from one of the two tenements which he held and from which a rent of 10s. was due to Holy Trinity as appears by their charter[1] enrolled 25 July 1344; John Leycestre, 43 Ed. III; John Walkote, 8 Ric. II; John Tetesbury, 12 Hy. IV as appears by the following acquittance.

    1. H.R. 71 (92).

398. Indenture witnessing that William prior and convent received of John Tetesbury, citizen and skinner (*pelliparius*), 5s. for the term of Christmas last in payment of all arrears due on the payment of 10s. *p.a.* from a tenement once of Stephen Stamford and afterwards of William Stamford in the parish of St. Lawrence; abutments, the land of the said John on the west and a tenement of the prior and convent which is next Ebgate on the east; 5s. to cover the arrears except for £3 which John, his heirs or executors are to pay on 26 Dec. next; sealed by both parties; dated 29 Dec. 1413, and the tenement is situated on the north side of Tamesestrete.

399. Note: that Thomas the priest, son of Alwin Sherehog, gave to Holy Trinity, when he was made a canon, land adjacent to the wall of the cemetery of St. Lawrence which afterwards the prior and convent leased to Ralph Sumer.

400. [f. 79] [1222–48] Lease by Richard prior and convent to Ralph Sumer of land which William Locwrichte held; rent 4s. *p.a.*; witnesses, William the priest of Scherehog, Andrew the priest, Richard the priest, Jordan the priest, Roger Hat, Robert de Chent, William Russo and Gregory his brother.

    C.A.D., iv, A 7360.

401. [List of those paying rent]: Ralph de Sumeri; Emma his daughter who granted the tenement to Joce the Weigher (*Ponderator*) [See also after **402**] as appears by the following charter.

402. Grant by Emma daughter of Ralph de Sumeri to Joce the Weigher of all the land of the grantor's father in the parish of St. Lawrence; abutments, the cemetery of that church on the south and the land that was of Matthew Blund, alderman, on the north containing in frontage on the east of the king's highway 11½ ells and at the west end 12 ells and in length at both

St. Mary Abchurch

sides 27 ells; rent to the grantor 6d. *p.a.* and to Holy Trinity 4s. *p.a.*; [no witnesses].

401 contd. Bola daughter of Joce granted the land to William de Cheyndeduit, rector of St. Lawrence, and he gave it to St. Peter Westminster and the monks of Westminster duly paid; now [1425–7] the hall and the chamber (*aula et camera*) of the master of the college of St. Laurence founded by Sir John Pulteney, kt.

403. Total of this parish 14s.

[f. 79v] IN THE PARISH OF ABBECHIRCH

404. [1197–1221] Grant by Peter prior and convent to Ralph son of Osbert of land in the parish of St. Mary Abbechirch; abutments, the land which was of Robert Bat on the east; rent 12s. *p.a.*; the land $3\frac{1}{4}$ ells in width and $8\frac{1}{2}$ ells in length; the prior and convent to have the preference by a bezant if the grantor wishes to sell the land; swore fealty; rent to be paid without miskenning; gersuma 2s.; witnesses, Solomon Vnbarrio, William Winter.

405. [List of those paying rent]: Ralph son of Osbert; Goda Gabliere; John Junior; John Norman; Fulk de Sancto Edmundo; Edmund the Tailor who granted the tenement to William de Morton who paid 12s. *p.a.* as appears by their charter enrolled 1 Ed. I; Richard Mereworth, 1 and 19 Ed. II and 1 and 6 Ed. III; Denise Virly, 30 Ed. III; Richard Chessham, 36 Ed. III; Edward Wodirton, 48 Ed. III and 8 Ric. II; John Halle; Robert Axstone, 1 Hy. IV and 1 Hy. V; John Sadeler and the tenement is situated on the north side of Candelwykestrete.

406. [1222–48] Grant by Richard prior and convent to Geoffrey Brokeshevede (*de Brokesheved*) of land with houses; abutments, the land of Amice daughter of William on the east and the land of Henry the Girdler (*Corigiarius*) on the west in Candelwykstrete, extending from the king's street to the cemetery of St. Lawrence the Martyr; rent 54s. *p.a.* [f. 80] declared that the value of the houses built on the land was 25 marks of silver; if Geoffrey or his heirs wish to leave the fee they shall leave the land fully built upon to the value of the above estimate unless it shall have been burnt by someone else's fire (*nisi igne alieno combusta fuerit*); the grantee and his heirs shall not destroy the houses or deteriorate the property nor lease it to Jews or religious houses; if they wish to sell or lease, the prior and convent to have an advantage of a bezant over other buyers; swore fealty; gersuma 100s.; witnesses, Joce Junior, alderman, Geoffrey de Essex, Simon de Stanes.

C.A.D., ii, A 1932.

407. [List of those paying rent]: G. de Brokesheved and then the tenement was divided for Nicholas de Weston paid 27s. *p.a.* and John de Plumstede 27s. *p.a.*; Thomas de Winchester paid the whole sum, 1 and 19 Ed. II and 1 and 6 Ed. III; Robert Cor(um); William Olyver, 8 Ric. II and these two

St. Mary Abchurch

tenements are situated at length adjacent on the south side of Candylwykstrete.

408. [1301] Grant by Henry called Juvenis, bureller (*borelarius*), to the prior and convent of Holy Trinity of 1 mark of quit rent in pure and perpetual alms for the augmentation of the vestments of the religious there; to be paid from a tenement in the parish of St. Mary Abbechirch in Candelwykstrete; abutments, the house in which the grantor lives on the west and the tenement of Stephen Ferbras on the east and north and the king's street of Candelwykstrete on the south; the grantor concedes for himself and his heirs that the prior and convent may take naam and distrain in all the tenement both for the mark and for arrears; sealed; witnesses, John Blount, mayor, Peter Bosenham, Robert.[1]

> 1. le Caller, P.R.O. *Lists & Indexes*, ix, 201.
> *C.A.D.*, ii, A 1964.

409. [f. 80v] [List of those paying quit rent]: Henry the Bureller (*Borelarius*); John de Winchester, 1 and 19 Ed. II and 1 and 5 Ed. III; Robert Kersteven, 30 Ed. III; New Hospital; Katherine Plom(m)er, 36 Ed. III; Richard atte Dyche, 48 and 49 Ed. III; Simon Mereworth and this tenement is situated on the south side of Candelwykstrete.

410. Grant by Thomas son of Thomas son of Robert Denxmas, former citizen and ropemaker, to John Malewayn, citizen and merchant, and Margery his wife of 60s. *p.a.* of quit rent of which 40s. came to the grantor after the death of Robert his grandfather by inheritance from all those tenements formerly of John Sterre in the parish of St. Mary Abbechirch situated on the corner (*super cornerium*) between St. Lawrence street on the east and the tenement of the late William de Stanford on the west and Candelwykstrete on the north and the close of the college of St. Lawrence on the south; and 20s. *p.a.* of quit rent which the grantor received from Bartholomew Denxmars, citizen and ropemaker, from the same land; to hold to the grantees paying the services to the chief lords; sealed; witnesses, Richard Kisselynbury, mayor, John Notte, William de Wircestre, sheriffs; dated Sat. 9 July 1351.

411. Note: John Malewayn bequeathed to Holy Trinity the above-mentioned 60s. *p.a.* as appears by his will[1] enrolled in the Husting of Common Pleas, Mon. 26 July 1361.

> *Margin:* Johannes Malwayn vinetarius admissus fuit in libertate civitatis Lond' et iuratus tempore Symonis Fraunces maioris et Thome Maryns camerarii et introitur in viridi papiro de empcione libertatum et apparuit viz. die jovis proxime post festum Epiphanie anno r.r. Edwardi tercii post conquestum xvj°.
> 1. C. *Wills*, ii, 38.

412. [List of those paying quit rent]: El(mun)dus Legett, 36 Ed. III and 8 Ric. II; now [1425–7] the prior of the Carthusians.

413. Note: that Richard Renger granted to Richard prior and convent 14d.

St. Swithin

of quit rent from a certain tenement in the same parish as appears in Charter Sixteen[1] of several parishes.

1. **1017**.

414. [List of those paying quit rent]: Adam le Taillour; Awreda Pelham whose executor granted the tenement to William Jordan who paid 14d. to Holy Trinity as appears by their charter[1] enrolled 14 Ed. I; William Jordan granted the tenement to John Hatfeld as appears in their charter; Peter Hatfeld, 1 Ed. II; John Hatfeld, 19 Ed. II; John Yonge, 1 Ed. III; Thomas Yonge, 39 Ed. III [See also after **415**] as appears by the following acquittance.

1. H.R. 16 (46).
Cf. *C.A.D.*, ii, A 1945.

415. Indenture which witnesseth that Thomas Yonge son of John Yonge is liable to pay 14d. *p.a.* to the prior of Holy Trinity from the tenement of the said Thomas in the parish of St. Mary; know that John Ha(u)ekyn, rent collector of the prior and convent, has received 14d. for the whole year and that Thomas is quit by these presents; [f. 81] sealed by the two parties; dated Easter Week 1365.

Cf. *C.A.D.*, ii, A 1944.

414 contd. John Prentys, 8 Ric. II.

416. Total of this parish £7 0s. 6d. and it is tithed as it appears in the king's exemplification.

IN THE PARISH OF ST. SWITHIN

417. Note: Elias Gofair, citizen, was seised of 10s. of rent from a certain tenement in the parish of St. Swithin which Ralph the Baker held which same Elias in his will[1] proved, proclaimed and enrolled in the Husting of Common Pleas held Mon. 6 Feb. 1329 left the 10s. of rent to be sold by his executors as appears in the same will and James de Sancto Edmundo and John de Daunehurst, executors, granted 10s. to the rector of St. Swithin as appears by the following charter; the aforementioned [*sic*] William granted the said 10s. to Warin Myngy as appears by the following charter; Margaret wife and executor of Warin granted it to Henry Preston and Isabel de Preston daughter and heir of Henry granted all her rights in the 10s. to John Wiltshyr and John Ryder and others and John Ryder granted the aforesaid rent to Richard Wyltshyr and Richard Gyn as appears by charter.

1. *C. Wills*, i, 209.

418. Grant by Richard Wiltshyr of Haydon, co. Essex, to Richard Whytinton, mention being made of all the above-mentioned charters,[1] enrolled in the Husting of Common Pleas Mon. 20 Jan. 1421; since Elias Gofair by will[2] bequeathed 10s. rent and James de St. Edmund and John de Daunehurst sold it to the rector of St. Swithin's on Sun. 4 Oct. 1310, and since

St. Swithin

William granted it to Warin Myngy, bureller and citizen, on Sun. 8 Jan. 1318, and since Margaret, Warin's widow and Richard Pageman, executors, proved his will³ [f. 81v] on Mon. 17 Oct. 1328 and sold the rent to Henry Preston, ropemaker and citizen, on Mon. 16 Oct. 1329 and Isabel de Preston daughter and heir of Henry on Mon. 15 Mar. 1378 granted to John Wiltshir, citizen and pepperer (*pipario*), and Alice his wife, John Chesterford, Nicholas son of Hugh Parys, and John Ryder, clerk, all her right in the land, rents and services in the Ropery (*in le Ropereye*) and in Heiwharflane in the parishes of All Hallows ad Fenum [the Great], St. Swithin Candelwykstrete and St. Nicholas Oldfyshstrete which John Rider by charter dated 2 June 1404 with the aforesaid John Wiltshir etc., Hugh Parys being dead, granted all the land to Richard Wiltshir and to a certain Richard Gyn, citizen and grocer, now dead; declaration that Richard Wiltshir granted to Richard Whytington, citizen and alderman, William Shepton and William Grove the 10s. rent from that tenement which Robert Coton, citizen and draper, now holds and lives in in the parish of St. Swithin in Candelwykstrete; abutments, the tenement of John Suthcote, esquire, on the east and south and the king's highway on the north and the tenement of John Kirkeby on the west; if the rent is in arrears all the grantees shall enter and distrain; sealed; witnesses, R. Whitington, mayor, Robert Whitingham, John Boteler, sheriffs, John Pen(n)e, alderman of this ward,⁴ John Botelere [*sic*], Robert Coton, John Brockele, John Saikye, Peter Wymundham; dated 10 July 1420.

1. H.R. 148 (47).
2. *C. Wills*, i, 209.
3. *C. Wills*, i, 337.
4. Walbrook.

419. Note: that R. Whitington and the other grantees mentioned in **418** granted the 10s. rent to William Est as appears by their charter¹ enrolled after the feast of St. Bartholomew [24 Aug.] 1421 which William bequeathed the rent to Holy Trinity as appears by his will² enrolled Mon. 20 July 1422.

1. H.R. 149 (26). 2. *C. Wills*, ii, 430.

420. Note: William Est was admitted to the freedom and sworn when Baldwin Radington was warden of the City and Stephen Speleman chamberlain and entered in a paper book (*papiro*) with the letter 'B' viz. 28 Sep. 1392.

421. Memorandum: that the mayor and commonalty of the city of London have in the right of the said city an annual rent of 8s. issuing from a tenement of the prior and convent situated in the parish of St. Mary Colechirch and the prior and convent have in the right of the house and church of Holy Trinity an annual rent of 10s. issuing from the tenement of the mayor and commonalty in the parish of St. Swithin Candelwykstrete; and Peter then prior and the convent on Wed. 13 [*sic*] Oct. 9 Hy. V [1421] came to the common council before William Cauntbrigge, mayor, alderman and commonalty and sought from the mayor and commonalty that they themselves might, in place of a certain collapsed stone wall (*prostrato quodam obliquo muro lapidum*) which the prior and convent have, situated along the king's

St. Mary Bothaw

street in the parish of St. Katherine near the house and church of Holy Trinity enclosing the cemetery of the house containing in length from the east end of the church of St. Katherine to the tenement of the prior and convent on which William Wakefeld once lived on the east 40 ft., rebuild another wall on the same line direct from the east end of the church to the corner of the said free tenement by taking about half of the same wall from the common ground (*de communi solo*) of the City for the rebuilding, thus making 4 ft. 4 ins. in width along a length of 20 ft.; and the prior and convent offered that their successors henceforth would demand none of the rent of 10s. from the mayor and commonalty or their successors; the mayor allowed the prior and convent and their successors to rebuild the new wall peacefully along the line (*linealiter*) and to possess it and they [i.e. the mayor and commonalty] demanded nothing of the 8s. of rent from the prior and convent or their successors; and on this, the mayor, aldermen and commonalty considering the crooked (*obliquus*) wall, as it is now set up, unsightly (*indecens*) and disgraceful (*indecorus*) to the City and exceedingly dangerous, unanimously granted that the prior and convent should rebuild the overthrown (*prosternatum*) wall as requested and it was agreed that both the aforesaid rents should be placed in suspense and remain not leviable (*illevabiles*) as long as the prior and convent have (*gaudeant*) their aforesaid wall which they rebuilt.

422. No total for this parish [because the 10s. has been remitted by **421**].

[f. 82] IN THE PARISH OF ST. MARY BOTHAWE

423. [1147–67] Grant of Ralph prior and convent to Peter de Buurges and his heirs male of Bothaw (*Bothaga*); rent 7s. *p.a.*; to hold as long as the rent is paid; to have this land, from the entrance (*introitu*) to the other end, in length 123 ft. and in width at the entrance end (*in capite introitus*) 18 ft. and at the other end also between the stone house of his sister O. 8d. [*sic*] which is on one side and the land which Ernulf holds which is on the south side, they have in breadth 75 ft. but in the middle from the north extremity (*cornu*) of the monastery next the land of Ernulf they have 61 ft. but the right line of this land on the north is from the stone house of sister O. up to the northern extremity of the monastery and is contiguous on the east and south to the wall of the church up to the entrance of the said land and on the south side it is joined to the land which Ernulf holds and this is his boundary; witnesses to this agreement, Osbert Beche, William Paien, Robert Brito, William de Cobeham, William Armiger, Bartholomew Stephen, Peter the priest, Ernulf.

C.A.D., ii, A 3022.

424. [List of those paying rent]: Peter Buurges; William son of Reynery to whom Stephen prior and convent remitted 4d. and thus William paid 6s. 8d.; John Exsport; Humphrey Dockett; William Marchall; John de Suffolk (*Southfolchia*) who granted the land to Stephen de Cornhull who paid 6s. 8d. *p.a.* as appears in their charter enrolled 5 Ed. I and Stephen gave part of the tenement to the abbot and convent of Oseney who paid 6s. 8d. as

St. Mary Bothaw

appears in the following charter and this tenement is situated on the south side of Candelwykstrete.

425. [f. 82 inset][1] Grant by Stephen de Cornhull, for the salvation of his soul and the souls of his father and mother and of his brother Roger, to William, abbot, and the church of St. Mary of Osneye, co. Oxford, and the convent and their successors of a certain messuage in London once of Humphrey Dockett; abutments, the grantor's messuage on the north and the church of St. Mary of Bothaw on the other part and extending on the east above the grantor's messuage and on the west above the king's street; rent to grantor and his heirs a clove-gillyflower at Easter and to the king's socage 6d. at Martinmas and to the prior and convent of Holy Trinity 6s. 8d. and to the heirs of John de Betonia 9s.; witnesses, Henry le Waleys, mayor, William le Maseren(er), Richard Chykewell, sheriffs; dated 26 Mar. 1282. Now [1425–7] the New Hospital.

1. A piece of parchment $8\frac{4}{5}$ ins. wide by $4\frac{1}{2}$ ins. long is inserted between f. 81 and f. 82.

426. [f. 82] [? before 1193] Grant by Henry son of Ailwin, for the salvation of the souls of King Henry and of the grantor, to God and the church of Holy Trinity, in pure and perpetual alms, 5s. of quit rent from land which Henry Toltrich held of the grantor; abutments, the land which Ailwin Dubbur held on the east and land which Laurence the Plumber (*Plumbarius*) held on the west; to hold by doing service for the soul of King Henry on the anniversary of the grantor's death when it shall have come; sealed with the grantor's seal.

C.A.D., iv, A 7351.

427. [List of those paying quit rent]: Henry Toltrich, dubber; his widow; Robert Scotte; Gilbert Wolfe, 44 Hy. III; John Kemesyng, baker, 1 and 5 Ed. II; his widow, 19 Ed. II; Henry Aumener, 1 Ed. III; John Kemesyng, goldsmith, who granted to John Hamond the tenement in the parish of St. Mary Bothaw in width between [f. 82v] the tenement of the late William Reyner on the east and the tenement of Thomas de Sarum which was once of William de Londonstone on the west extending from the king's street of Kandelwykstrete on the south to the garden of the prior of Tortyngtone on the north as appears in their charter[1] enrolled Mon. 29 Apr. 1336; John Hamond, 11 Ed. III; his widow, 30 Ed. III; Thomas Salesbury, 35 Ed. III; Paul Salesbury, 8 and 11 Ric. II; now [1425–7] the fraternity of Drapers and thus the masters of this art viz. William Crowmer, John Gedeney, William Weston, John Hyham and Richard atte Lee, having seen the above-written charter, with the consent of all the art gathered in their hall, paid well whence a quittance was received dated 30 Sep. 1428 and they had a copy of the said charter and caused it to be inscribed in their book (*papiro*).

1. H.R. 63 (186).

428. Note: In a charter[1] of William Waleran made by William de Londonstone enrolled 35 Ed. I concerning a tenement which is situated between the tenement of John de Kemesyng on the east and that of Augustine le Gaunt

All Hallows the Great

on the west and the king's street on the south and the tenement of the prior of Tortyngton on the north; the prior of the New Hospital has 5s. *p.a.* as appears by charter and also from the same the abbot of Westminster has 5s. *p.a.* and the abbot of Bermundesey 5s. *p.a.*

1. H.R. 35 (2).

429. Total of this parish 11s. 8d. and nevertheless it is tithed at 23s. 2d. as appears in the king's exemplification.

[f. 83] IN THE PARISH OF ALL HALLOWS HEYWARFE

430. Grant of Master Alexander rector of St. Swithin, Richard Reniger and John de Augo, executors of William Whyte, who had bequeathed a quit rent of 60s. from his tenement in the parish of All Hallows to the canons of Holy Trinity, of two shops situated in front of the stone house on the north next Dowgate which house was William Whyte's, with a cellar under the same house with free access to light (*visu*) to the cellar towards the south by an iron-barred window (*per fenestram ferratam*) without any exclusion (*opturacione*) or impediment to the light; also 40d. of quit rent from four shops adjacent to the said cellar and the shops on the west from (*per manus*) the canons of Southwark; the executors wish and ordain that the tenants shall load and unload the cellar itself (*tenentes ipsum cellarium karkient et diskarkient*) and unload their wines free from carriage on the wharf (*vina sua sine karagio super kaynum*) which belongs to John de Augo; to hold in perpetuity for the 60s. quit rent which the executors had assigned to the canons from all the tenement that was William Whyte's in the parish of All Hallows Heywarf so that the canons were contented with this assignment and the said carriage (*kariacio*) without damage to John or his heirs that the canons would not claim more fully therefrom by reason of the rent first assigned to them; quitclaim by John de Augo; prior and convent to have the power of taking naam in all the executors' tenements; done 13 Feb. 1236; sealed; witnesses, Master Walter de London, Robert Hardel.

C.A.D., i, A 1716.

431. [1236] Release by Master Alexander rector of St. Swithin to the prior and convent of Holy Trinity of all his right and claim in the tenement of William Whyte, late citizen of London, in Dowgate in the parish of All Hallows, by occasion of his will; Alexander has obliged himself, in the presence of the official of the archdeacon of London, that neither he nor anyone for him shall demand anything from the canons in the said fee by reason of the will; sealed; witnesses, Roger vicar of St. Mary Abbchirch Gilbert de St. Nicholas, chaplain, William rector of St. Lawrence: and afterwards the prior[1] paid well as appears in a charter made for the same prior which is written in his old book, folio 109; and Richard Barbour paid for the prior as appears by the following plea.

1. Inserted over the word prior 'Overy'.

St. Michael Paternoster

432. *Common plea held in the Husting, Mon. 22 May 1307.*
[f. 83v] The prior defended himself in a plea of taking naam and Richard le Barbour, pl., agreed by licence of the court that he is liable to pay 3s. 4d. *p.a.* from a tenement of the prior and convent of St. Mary de Southwark next Dowgate and that he is 20s. in arrears: afterwards the prior of St. Mary Southwark paid and the said shops are situated on the south side of le Vyntery with a tenement of Holy Trinity on the east [incomplete].

433. Total of this parish 3s. 4d. and nevertheless it is tithed as 47s. 4d. as appears in the king's exemplification.

[f. 84] IN THE PARISH OF PATERNOSTER CHIRCH

434. Grant of William the Chamberlain (*Camerarius*) to Ralph le Justice of 42s. *p.a.* of quit rent as dowry (*in librum maritagium*) on the occasion of the marriage of Denise his daughter, from several tenements on condition that if he did not have legitimate heirs then the prior and convent of Holy Trinity should receive the 42s. as appears in Charter Seventeen[1] of several parishes.

1. **1018**.

435. Note: that Ralph le Justice confirmed to Richard prior and convent 6s. 8d. *p.a.* from the house of Peter de Trie because he did not have legitimate heirs, as appears in Charter Eighteen[1] of several parishes.

1. **1019**.

436. [List of those paying rent]: Peter de Trie; Jeremiah de Trie; Robert de Suthfolk, 4 Ed. I who granted the tenement to Walter de Forda [See also after **437**] as appears by the following charter.

437. [1275–6] Grant by Robert de Suthfolk, citizen of London, to Walter de Forda, citizen, and Christine his wife of all the tenement which he had of the lease of Jeremiah de Trie in a lane called les Arches in the parish of St. Michael de Paternosterchirch; abutments, the wall of the seld called Wynchestreselde on the east and the said lane on the west and the tenement of the grantor on the south and that of Reginald de Samewelle on the north and containing in breadth along the lane $19\frac{3}{4}$ ells and in the middle $17\frac{1}{2}$ ells 2 ins. and in length on the north 13 ells and on the south $15\frac{3}{8}$ ells; all conveyed except a room on the outside (*camera forinseca*) with a solar built over it between the wall of the grantor's tenement and the house of Walter; to Walter and his wife and to whomsoever they wish to sell, bequeath, mortgage; rent to the grantor and his heirs 1 silver penny on 24 June and to the chief lords of the fee service viz. to Holy Trinity $\frac{1}{2}$ mark, to St. Mary's Suthwerk 4s., to St. Bartholomew de Smethfeld, 3s. 4d., to the nuns of Kelebourne 3s. 4d. and to lady Joan de Sancto Benedicto, a nun of Kelebourne 2s.; gersuma £20; [f. 84v] sealed; witnesses, Gregory de Rokesle, mayor and alderman of this ward,[1] John Horn, Ralph Blund, sheriffs.

1. Vintry.
C.A.D., iv, A 7823.

St. Michael Paternoster

436 contd. Richard de Wihal, 1 Ed. II; John de Fridaiestrete, 5 Ed. II; Henry le Palmer, 19 Ed. II [See also after **438**] as appears by the following plea.

438. *Common plea held in the Husting, Mon. 15 Nov. 1339.*
Henry le Palmer summoned to reply to the prior of Holy Trinity that he should do right service for his free tenement which he holds of him; the prior says that Henry holds a messuage of him at a rent of 6s. 8d. *p.a.* of which rent Roger Poley, later prior, was seised and that the rent was £4 in arrears on the day of the suing out of the writ, 12 Mar. 1338; he seeks the messuage as gavelet and Henry came and recognised that he held of the prior and his church and acknowledged the arrears; the prior recovers the messuage for a year and a day unless in the meantime Henry satisfies him as to the arrears; Henry in mercy and he came into full court and paid the arrears.

436 contd. Matthew Palmer, 30 Ed. III; Roger Torold, 36 Ed. III; Robert Fanner, 48 Ed. III; Agnes atte Hale, 8 Ric. II; William Norton, 8 Hy. IV and 7 Hy. V and the tenement is situated on the east side of Bowelane.

439. Note: William the Chamberlain (*Camerarius*) gave to Holy Trinity 8s. *p.a.* of quit rent from the house of Nicholas Dokett in the parish as appears in Charter Seventeen[1] of several parishes.

   1. **1018**.

440. [List of those paying quit rent]: Nicholas Dokett; Reyner de Bungey; Hugh de Donyngton; [f. 85] Walter Waldesshef, 1 Ed. II and 6 Ed. III; Richard Lac(er), 30 Ed. III, who had two daughters Alice and Katherine, Alice was married to Robert Mar[n]i and Katherine to John atte Pole, between whom all the possessions of their deceased father were divided and then there was assigned to Katherine the whole tenement and she paid 8s. *p.a.* [See also after **441**] as appears by the following indenture.

441. [French] Indenture made at London, Sat. 18 Oct. 1365, between Robert Marny, kt., and Alice his wife, daughter and one of the heirs of Richard Lacer senior, her father, late citizen, and sister and heir of Richard Lacer junior, Robert de Bourton, formerly guardian of the chantry of the church of Leyre Marny, John Mareys of Salcote Virly, chaplain, and Philip atte Brygge of the one part and Katherine, who was the wife of John atte Pole of Shordich, the other daughter and heir of Richard Lacer senior and sister and heir of Richard Lacer junior, of the other part, witnesseth that, since Katherine sued out a writ in the Husting against Robert and Alice to secure a sharing out of all the tenements held by the late Richard and his father upon the which writ it was awarded that the partition should take place according to the laws and usages of the City, on the day above-written there being assembled Adam de Bury, mayor, William de Halden, recorder, John de Brikelesworth and Thomas de Irland, sheriffs, Thomas Spigurnel and John de Romeseye etc. an agreement was made between

St. Michael Paternoster

Robert and Alice and Robert de Bourton, John Marreys and Philip who claimed an estate in the aforesaid tenements which should have belonged to Alice of her purparty by enfeoffment made to them by Alice before her marriage and Katherine in the following manner: declaration that Robert, John and Philip have for their purparty all the tenements between the church of St. Michael Paternosterchirch and Bowelane on the south side and the tenement held by Domengo de Espayne on the north and between the highway called le Reole on the west and Walbrok and a long stable of Domengo's tenement on the east together with the stone walls etc. belonging to the tenement and with access to light for the four windows in the said tenements on the north side, one window in the wall of the room, another in the wall of the solar at the end of the said room, one in the wall of the kitchen and the fourth in the stone wall of a cellar, in length and breadth as they are at present, with the gutters and other water courses descending from the same tenements already built or to be built in the future and that Katherine has for her purparty all the tenements held by Domengo with the stable and one solar over it extending to the north $13\frac{1}{2}$ ells in length and in breadth on the west $7\frac{1}{4}$ ells and on the east $7\frac{1}{8}$ ells which tenements extend [f. 85v] along Walbrok and adjoin the tenements of Nicholas Bremble on the east and along the king's highway called la Roial on the west and between the aforementioned tenements assigned to the other purparty on the south and the tenement of Nicholas Bremble on the north with the gutters and water courses descending from the roof of the said solar on the south side towards the said stable; and it was agreed between the two parties that respecting the payment of 11 marks devised in the testament[1] of Walter Waldeschef the purparty of the first party should be charged at 7 marks a year and the purparty of Katherine at 4 marks a year plus 29s. to the prior and convent of Seinte Maire Overee de Suthwerk and 8s. to Cristeschirche; also agreed that each of the parties shall pay these rents according to their portion and acquit the other of that portion of the rent assessed on their purparty and if any part of the rent be levied on the wrong purparty then either party shall have the right within a fortnight to distrain on the purparty of the other and take a sum equivalent to the sum that has been unjustly levied by the other party, if other charges are determined in the future, they shall be equally apportioned; each party shall hold themselves and their heirs and assigns to perform these covenants; sealed by the parties.

 1. *C. Wills*, i, 395.
 C.A.D., ii, A 2387.

440 contd. Katherine Pole, 3 Ric. II as appears by Acquittance Five[1] of several parishes; Drugo Barentyne, 8 Hy. IV; Richard Broun, baker, 9 Hy. IV who granted the tenement to the church of St. Michael and the tenement is situated on the east side of le Roial between the church of St. Michael recently (*de novo*) founded on the south and the tenement of Richard Whytyngton on the north.

 1. **1042.**

442. [f. 86] [1218–19] Grant of Agnes daughter of Robert the Chamberlain to William her brother of 6s. 8d. *p.a.* of quit rent from land and a house;

St. Michael Paternoster

abutments, the land that was of Nicholas Duket on the south and land that was of Peter the clerk on the north; gersuma 4 marks; witnesses, Serlo the Mercer, mayor, John Viell, Joce, sheriffs, Thomas de Haverhill, Martin son of Alic', aldermen, Constantine son of Alulf.

443. [1218–19] Quitclaim of Robert de Bedford and Alexander his brother, sons of Agnes, to their uncle of property mentioned in **442**; William Chamberlain gave $\frac{1}{2}$ mark to each of them; witnesses, Serlo le Mercer, John Viell, Joce, T. de Haverhill, Constantine son of Alulf, Arnulf his brother.

444. Note: William the Chamberlain granted to Ralph le Justice 6s. 8d. *p.a.* of quit rent as dowry on the occasion of the marriage of Denise his daughter on condition that if he did not have legitimate heirs then the prior and convent of Holy Trinity should receive the 6s. 8d. as appears in Charter Seventeen of several parishes. [See **434**].

445. Note: Ralph le Justice confirmed to the prior and convent 6s. 8d. of quit rent from the house of the countess of Oxford and because his wife and son were dead, the house had all, as appears in Charter Eighteen[1] of several parishes.

    1. **1019**.

446. [List of those paying quit rent]: Countess of Oxford; Peter de Gysors who granted the tenement to Richard de Wylehale [See also after **447**] as appears by the following charter.

447. [1266–8] Grant of Peter de Gysorco, citizen, to Richard de Wylehale as dowry on the occasion of his marriage with Joan the grantor's daughter of all that tenement in the parish of St. Michael; abutments, the grantor's tenement formerly held by Nicholas Duket on the south and his other tenement formerly held by Alan le Weyder on the north and above the highway on the west and Walbroke on the east; and 20s. of quit rent from the houses [f. 86v] which were once of William de Staundon in the parish of St. Michael Candelwystrate; 7s. of quit rent from land and houses once of the late Robert de Lenn in the parish of St. Andrew Estchep; all the grantor's houses with a garden and quay and meadow in Southwark and the marshes; 2 acres of meadow which lies in le Hale in the town of Stanes between the meadow of John de Laston and that of John the Reeve of Laleham; to hold to Richard and Joan and their heirs born of Joan; annual rents, to the king's socage 4d., to St. Bartholomew's hospital 20s., to Holy Trinity 6s. 8d., to the earl of Oxford 6d. or a pair of gilt spurs at Easter, for the said 20s. and for an old quit rent, to the nuns of Clerkenwell 8s., to the heir of John Norman 6d., for the 7s. of annual quit rent to the chief lord of the fee 1d. in the middle of Quadragesima, for the houses and garden in the town of Suthwerch and for the 2 acres in Stanes, to the chief lords of the fee, 2 clove-gillyflowers on 25 Mar.; sealed; witnesses, John Adrian, Luke de Batancort, sheriffs, John de Gisors, alderman of this ward, Reginald de Suffouk, Philip le Tailour, Henry le Waleis.

    Margin: Hec Carta sigillatur cum cera viridi in pressa signo cuiusdam capitis habita in custodia executorum Ricardi Whytyndon.

St. Martin Vintry

446 contd. Richard Wyrehall who bequeathed the tenement to his son Richard as appears in his will[1] enrolled 14 Oct. 1331; John Talbot, 13 Ed. III; John Stodey, 30 Ed. III; Nicholas Brembyl, 42 Ed. III and 8 Ric. II; Richard Whytendon, throughout Hy. IV and Hy. V.

1. *C. Wills*, ii, 117.

448. Total of this parish 21s. 4d. and it is tithed at this in the king's exemplification.

IN THE PARISHES OF ST. MARTIN VINTRYE AND ST. JOHN DE WALBROK

449. [1220–1] Grant by Simon son of Robert Blund to the church of Holy Trinity of 14s. 8d. of quit rent from land which Simon de Kokham held of the grantor in the parish of St. Martin of Beremaneschirch at the kitchens of the Vintry; to hold in free alms; 1 mark to be spent on pittances on the anniversary of Robert, the grantor's father and 16d. in wax for the lights (*ad luminare in cereis*) and the residue of the wax to be collected (*et quod residuum fuerit de cereis in crastino dicti aniversarii ante altare domine super candelabrum collocetur percipiendum*); sealed; witnesses, Henry[1] archbishop of Dublin, Serlo the mayor, Joce son of William, Richard Renger [sheriffs].

1. Henry de Loundres, archbishop of Dublin, 1213–28.
C.A.D., i, A 1647.

450. [List of those paying quit rent]: Simon de Kokham; Robert de Suthfolk; Robert Hardel; Thomas de Conductu who refused to pay whereupon Prior Eustace impleaded him in the Guildhall [See also after **451**] when it was agreed as follows.

451. [f. 87] [1280–1] Release by Eustace prior and convent to Thomas de Conductu, vintner and citizen, his heirs and assigns of 5s. *p.a.* of quit rent and all arrears of the 10s. *p.a.* which the prior sought from Robert Hardel from land of the late Simon de Cokham between two lanes by Walebrok in the parish of St. Martin's by (*versus*) the Thames whereon there was a plea in Guildhall; Thomas and his heirs undertake to build on the land and to maintain buildings so that it will always yield sufficient to pay the annual rent; chirograph sealed; witnesses, Gregory de Rokesle, mayor, William de Frandon, Nicholas de Winchester (*Wynton*), sheriffs.

C.A.D., ii, A 2487.

450 contd. Thomas de Conductu, 9 Ed. I; John de Lincoln, 1 and 19 Ed. II and 1 Ed. III; William Stodey, 30 and 48 Ed. III; Henry Fa(n)nere, 8 Ric. II; Gilbert Merssh; his widow, 1 Hy. IV; John Wenne, 5 Hy. IV; and the limits of this tenement are clearly enough shown in the aforesaid charter.

452. Total of this parish 5s. and nevertheless it is tithed at 15s. 4d. in the king's exemplification.

[ST. JOHN THE BAPTIST WALBROOK]

453. [1170–97] Grant by Stephen prior and convent to Nicholas son of Ranulf Dokett of half a stone house which was of Hugh de Roland[1] in the parish of St. John which David de Cornhull leased and granted to the house in free alms which gift Ralph brother of Joce the Vintner confirmed; rent 22s. *p.a.*; [f.87v] to hold without any 'causa' or miskenning; Nicholas swore fealty; gersuma 20s.; witnesses, Ralph, brother of Joce, Matthew Blund.

    1. *Rectius* Bocland.
    C.A.D., ii, A 2500.

454. [List of those paying rent]: Nicholas Dokett; Mary Dokett; Peter Gesors; Richard de Wilihale who granted the tenement to Roger Drayton, as appears in a charter[1] enrolled 16 Ed. I; Margery Weluby, 1 Ed. II; Simon de Kinardisle, 16 Ed. II; [See also after **455**] as appears by the following plea.

    1. H.R. 18 (6).

455. *Common plea held in the Husting, Mon. 30 May 1323.*
Simon de Kinardisle complained that on Wed. 23 Feb. 1323 the prior came to his free tenement and took naam worth 20s. until by gage and pledge of Roger de Ely, one of the sheriffs, etc.; and the prior came and defended his action because the tenement was held of him by a rent of 22s. *p.a.* of which Ralph de Caunterbury, prior, was seised by Roger de Thunderle, his tenant, and £14 11s. was in arrears; Simon said that he had no interest in the tenement except that his wife Margery had it for her life; Simon and Margaret [*sic*] did not prosecute; they and their pledge in mercy and the prior retains the naam.

454 contd. Simon, 1 Ed. III; William Venour, 48 Ed. III; Robert Wymburne, 8 Ric. II; John Hende, 20 Ric. II; now [1425–7] the fraternity of Skinners.

456. [1170–97] Grant by Stephen prior and convent to Michael son of William Fulbert of that land which Ernaldus Furbur held in fee; rent 3s. 6d. *p.a.*; swore fealty; [f. 88] Michael gave 1 bezant to the prior and half a London sextary of wine to the canons; witnesses, Walter the priest, William Fulbert, William son of the same William [Brun].

    C.A.D., ii, A 2492.

457. [List of those paying rent]: Michael Fulbert; Thomas Black (*Niger*); Walter de Wretele; Roger de Hadestoke who granted the land to John le Blund as appears by their charter[1] enrolled 9 Ed. I; John, 1 and 19 Ed. II and 1, 5 and 6 Ed. III; Edward Blund, 30 Ed. III; Walter Blund, 48 Ed. III and 8 Ric. II.

    1. H.R. 12 (82).

458. Note: Thomas son of Jurdan granted to the lady Felicia widow of

St. John the Baptist Walbrook

Joce Junior certain land in the same parish as appears by charter[1] and Felicia gave to Richard prior and convent 14s. *p.a.* of quit rent as appears by Charter Nine[2] of several parishes.

1. Charter 'ad tale signum' but the margin has no sign.
2. **1010**.

458a. [List of those paying quit rent]: Gilbert de Norfolk; Avice wife of Walter the Cordwainer; Walter Taillour; James le Boteler; Agnes his widow, 1 and 19 Ed. II and 1 Ed. III; now [1425–7] the New Hospital, and this tenement is situated on the south side of Candelwykstrete between the tenement of Holy Trinity on the east and of Walter the Glover (*Gantorum*) on the west.

459. Note: Adam Bedell granted to Holy Trinity some land in the same parish as appears in a book (*?ocanta*) with the letter 'A' at folio 21 according to which the prior and convent granted to Peter Bukerel [land] for 6d. *p.a.* as appears in an old rental with the letter 'B' and in all subsequent rentals.

460. [List of those paying rent]: Peter Bokerell; Osbert dean of the Arches who gave the land to the monks of Bermundeseye [See also after **462**] as appears by the following charter.

461. [before 1249] Grant by Osbert, chaplain (*capellanus*) and rector of the church of St. Mary de Bothaghe, for the salvation of his soul, to the church of St. Saviour Bermundsey of half of the land with a house built on it which Walter Bokerel leased in fee; abutments, the land that was of Thomas the Tailor on the east and the other half of the land which the grantor gave to the hospital of St. John of Jerusalem on the west; to hold in free alms; grantees to do the services due to the lords of the fee viz, to Walter Buk(erel) and his heirs $\frac{1}{4}$ lb. of cumin or a silver $\frac{1}{2}$d. and to William son of Reinner and his heirs 7d. [f. 88v] and to the canons of Holy Trinity 12s. *p.a.*; witnesses, Simon son of Mary, alderman, John Gouayr, Michael Corry, Walter son of Baldewun, Alexander Ferre, John Wodcok.

462. [1249–53] Grant by Humbert prior of the church of St. Saviour Bermondsey to Alexander Marescall of land and a house which Osbert the chaplain gave and bequeathed to the house in the parish of St. John Walbrok; abutments, the land that was of Thomas Gysors on the east and the house of St. John of Jerusalem on the west; rent 10s. *p.a.*; Alexander and his heirs to be responsible for the service of the lords of the fee viz. to the canons of Holy Trinity 6d. *p.a.*; gersuma 1 mark of silver; witnesses, Alexander le Ferru[n], alderman, John his son, Jordan le Coteler.

460 contd. Ralph Marchall; Robert de Multon, 20 Ed. I who granted the tenement to James le Boteler who paid to Holy Trinity 6d. and to the monks of Bermundeseye 10s. as appears in their charter[1] enrolled 32 Ed. I, which James bequeathed the tenement to the prior and convent of the hospital of

St. Mary Woolchurch

St. Mary without Bisshypisgate as appears in his will[2] enrolled 19 Ed. II and the tenement is situated on the south side of Candelykstrete.

    1. H.R. 32(70).   2. *C. Wills*, i, 276 enrolled 11 Ed. II.

463. Total of this parish 38s. and it is tithed at this in the king's exemplification.

[f. 89] IN THE PARISHES OF ST. STEPHEN WALBROK AND ST. MARY NEWCHIRCH OTHERWISE WOLCHIRCH

464. Note: the prioress and nuns of Stratford granted to Holy Trinity 22d. of quit rent which John the Parmenter was accustomed to pay from land in the parish of St. Stephen as appears in Charter Nineteen[1] of several parishes.

    1. **1020**.

465. [List of those paying quit rent]: John the Parmenter; Robert de Clapwell, 5 and 6 Ed. III; his widow, 30 Ed. III; Robert Makesey, 38 Ed. III; John Sely, 8 Ric. II; Robert Markele and the tenement is situated on the west side of Walbrok.

466. Total of this parish 22d. and it is tithed at this in the king's exemplification.

NEWCHIRCH OTHERWISE WOLCHIRCH

467. [1253–4] Grant of Eustace son of David de Stanford to John Scharp, woolmonger, and Alice his wife of land with houses built thereon in the parish of St. Mary Newchirch; abutments, the land that was of Solomon de Basing on the west and other land and houses of the grantor on the east containing in breadth along the king's street $11\frac{1}{4}$ ells 3 ins. and in breadth alongside the land of John son of Adrian 19 ells 6 ins. with half a privy (*camere necessarie*) and in length against the church of St. Mary Wolmarichirch $22\frac{1}{4}$ ells 5 ins.; all in buildings etc. with half the chamber to hold freely in fee; rent 26s. 8d. *p.a.*; grantees and their heirs are not to pull down or to allow the houses to deteriorate but to repair (*emendare*) them; [f. 89v] warranty against the lords of the fee; gersuma 2 marks; witnesses, John Tolosan, mayor, John Northampton, Richard Pycard, sheriffs, Alexander Ferrum, alderman of the ward.[1]

    1. Walbrook.

468. Note: Eustace de Staunford gave to Holy Trinity the 26s. 8d. *p.a.* as appears in Charter Twenty[1] of several parishes.

    1. **1021**.

469. [List of those paying quit rent]: John Sharp; his widow; Richard Sharp who conceded that the prior was allowed to distrain both in the

St. Mary Woolchurch

house and in two houses which he had in the parish of St. Leonard Estchep [See also after **470**] as appears in the following charter.

470. [1261–8] Grant of Richard son of Thomas Sharp of 18s. of quit rent to Gilbert prior and convent of Holy Trinity.

469 contd. John Page, 1 Ed. II and 6 Ed. III; Stephen Caundych, 30 Ed. III; John Frensch, 44 Ed. III; John Mortymer, 45 Ed. III who bequeathed the tenement to the church of Wolchirch as appears in his will[1] enrolled 6 Nov. 1368 and the churchwardens paid until 5 Hy. IV; Stephen Sewale, 7 Hy. IV; John He(n)ore as appears by indenture made between him and Holy Trinity and the tenement is situated on the south side of Berbynderyslane.

1. *C. Wills*, ii, 117.

471. [1170–97] Grant of Stephen prior and convent to Gilbert the clerk of land which immediately before him was held by his uncle Malgerus, namely a forge and land belonging thereto; rent ½ mark of silver *p.a.*; swore fealty; gersuma ½ mark and 3s. for pittances; witnesses, John the chaplain of the Bailey (*de ballio*), John our [Holy Trinity] chaplain of St. Michael.

C.A.D., iv, A 7298.

472. [List of those paying rent]: Gilbert the clerk; Walter the Woolmonger who had two sons Simon and Gilbert and thus the land was divided and each paid 3s. 4d. *p.a.*; Emma Sibilyn; John Shippe; Godwin Phelipper; Thomas Godewyn, 1 and 19 Ed. II; Nicholas [f. 90] Godewyn, 1 and 7 Ed. III [See also after **473**] as the following plea shows.

473. *Common plea held in the Husting, Mon. 22 Feb. 1333.*
Nicholas Godwyne, skinner, complained that on Mon. 8 June 1332 the prior came to his free tenement and took naam worth 72s. until by gage and pledge of Andrew Aubrey, one of the sheriffs, etc.; and the prior came and said the naam was taken from two tenements made into one shop and that it was lawful because it was held of him at a rent of 6s. 8d. *p.a.* and that it was 10s. in arrears, ½ mark for one year and 40d. for a half year; Nicholas said he had no interest except by reason of his custody of Stephen son of Thomas Godwyne and that nothing was in arrears of the ½ mark from the shop and as to the other tenement he has a free tenement in the same and he asks that it should be enquired into by jury; in 11 Ed. III Nicholas Godwyne in the chamber of the Guildhall recognised that he owed to Thomas Heron, prior, 72s. and that he ought to pay the arrears as appears in an inquisition taken before Gregory atte Shire, alderman, and Thomas de Maryns, chamberlain, Fri. 23 May 1337.

472 contd. Then the tenement was divided for Walter Foster paid 3s. 4d. for one part and Stephen Godwyne 3s. 4d., 23 Ed. III; and these paid 3s. 4d. after Walter Foster; the prior of the Carthusians, 49 Ed. III until the writing of the cartulary: and these paid 3s. 4d. after Stephen Godwyne

St. Mary Woolchurch

which Stephen granted the tenement to William Bakere who paid 3s. 4d. as appears in their charter[1] enrolled 27 Ed. III; William Ferbourne, 49 Ed. III; John Donyngton, 8 and 16 Ric. II; Lettice Caundissh, 1 Hy. IV; John Megre, 1 Hy. V; John Trenowthe, 37 Hy. VI;[2] Richard Da(n)ers, 5 Hy. VII,[2] and these two tenements are adjacent between Lumbardstrete on the south and Cornhull on the north and the king's way on the west and the tenement of John Shipp, now [1425-7] of the prior of the Carthusians on the east.

    1. H.R. 81(69).   2. These entries are in a later hand.

474. [f. 90v] Note: Ralph Blount bequeathed to the prior and convent 4 marks of quit rent from a tenement of the late John Shipp as appears in a will[1] enrolled Mon. 12 Feb. 1296 and contained in the First Will[2] of several parishes.

    1. *C. Wills*, i, 126.   2. **1031**.

475. [List of those paying quit rent]: John Shipp; Godwin Phelipper; Thomas Godwyn, 1 Ed. II; John Yweyn, 6 and 30 Ed. III; Walter Forster, 34 Ed. III; the prior of the Charterhouse, 49 Ed. III; and the tenement is situated on the south side of the great street of Cornhull between the tenement of the prior in which Holy Trinity has a rent of 3s. 4d. on the west [incomplete].

476. [1254-5] Grant of John prior and convent to Alan de Wodekot of land with houses which Eustace son of David gave to Holy Trinity; abutments, the house of John Sharpp on the west and the house of Roger Goueyre on the east; rent 20s.; the grantee not to deteriorate the houses but to repair and maintain them; if he wishes to sell, the prior and canons to have an advantage of a bezant of 2s. over other buyers; swore fealty; gersuma ½ mark; chirograph sealed; witnesses, Ralph Hardel, mayor, William Eswy, Richard de Ewelle, sheriffs.

477. [List of those paying rent]: Alan de Wodekot; Roger de Cumbe; Walter le Hore, 1 and 19 Ed. II and 1 Ed. III; John de Wrestelyngworth [See also after **478**] as appears by the following plea.

478. *Common plea held in the Husting, Mon. 16 June 1354.*
The sheriff is ordered to inform John de Wrestlyngworth and Juliana his wife [f. 91] to be at the next court of Common Pleas to say why judgment of scharford against them should not be returned for the prior of Holy Trinity concerning a messuage which the prior recovered against them at a court held Mon. 12 Mar. 1352, by writ, and by custom held for a year and a day as gavelet according to the custom of the City. At a court held Mon. 28 July 1354 the prior by his attorney Alan de Horewode appeared against John and Juliana and they did not come and they were declared by the sheriff to have been summoned by John Botiller, draper, and Thomas Nolyf, draper, and the prior holds the messuage in perpetuity as (*tanquam*) scharford and John and Juliana in mercy.

St. Mary Woolchurch

477 contd. John Longe, 49 Ed. III [See also after **479**] as appears by the following plea.

479. *Common plea held in the Husting, Mon. 21 May 1375.*
John Longe, fishmonger, in person sought against Nicholas prior and convent three messuages and one shop of which a certain William Ostage, citizen and fishmonger, was seised as appears in his will[1] proved in the Husting Mon. 4 May 1349, which tenement he and his wife Matilda had acquired from Walter le Hore and Berta his wife in Berebynderslane and which he left to Juliana his daughter and her lawful heirs by virtue of which Juliana was lawfully seised; John Longe as her son and heir seeks that after the death of Juliana the shops and land should descend to him; and the prior through John Aschewell said that this was only one messuage and that the rent was in arrears and that he had brought a writ of gavelet and recovered it [as in **478**] [f. 91v] and that as the arrears had not been paid he had recovered the messuage as sharford; judgment is sought whether John Longe can have an action therein against the above-named recovery; and John Longe says that because the prior does not deny that William Ostage bequeathed the messuage to Juliana his daughter and heir nor that John Longe is the son and heir of Juliana in which case the prior cannot recover finally to the exclusion of the issue of Juliana and he seeks judgment and seisin of the land and it is judged that John Longe should recover against the prior his seisin of the three messuages and one shop and the prior is in mercy and John Longe recovered the tenement paying therefrom 20s. *p.a.*

1. *C. Wills*, i, 565.

477 contd. Thomas Restwolde, 8 Ric. II and 1 Hy. IV; James Coke, 9 Hy. IV as appears by the following plea.

480. *Pleas of assize held at the Guildhall, Sat. 5 May 1408, before Henry Halton and Henry Pountfreit, sheriffs, the presence of the coroner not expected.*
The assize comes to recognise whether William Hert, citizen and cutler, William Parker, John Whytebred, William Thirlewell, James Cok, cutler and Joan his wife unjustly disseised William prior of Holy Trinity of his free tenement in the parish of St. Mary Woolchirch; the prior by Richard Foster his attorney complains that he is disseised of 20s. of rent and William Hert and the others were summoned but did not come; therefore the assize is taken against them by default; the prior shows that the rent is a quit rent of which he and all his predecessors were seised and the above refused to pay the rent; recognitors summoned, Adam Smalstrete, Robert Marchall, Stephen Herdy, William Fynch, John [f. 92] Lemman, William Weston, John Gedeney, Robert Markele, John Megre, Robert Twyer, Richard Storme, Richard Coroner and elected triers (*triatores*) and they swore that the prior and his predecessors were so seised and assessed damages beyond the payment of arrears at 6s. 8d. and the rent was $1\frac{1}{2}$ years in arrears; the defs. did not resist by force and arms (*vi et armis*) but refused to pay; no fraud or collusion between the parties under the statute of mortmain be-

St. Mary Woolnoth

cause the priors had been seised of the tenement since the time of Henry III for Prior Richard was so seised; and the prior to recover his seisin of the rent and the arrears of 30s. and 6d. 8d. damages; William Hert and the others in mercy and afterwards the prior released all except 22s. and this tenement is situated on the south side of Berbyndereslane.

London possessory assizes, no. 225.

481. [f. 92v] Note: William de Blemonte to Richard prior and convent of 20s. *p.a.* of quit rent from certain land in the said parish as appears by Charter Thirteen[1] of several parishes.

    1. **1014**.

482. [List of those paying quit rent]: Robert son of Bartholomew; Simon Blund; Andrew Blund and then the land was divided for Thomas Box paid 12s. and Richard Cook 8s.: after Thomas Box; Richard Lymbrennere; Richard Hoddesdon, 1 Ed. II; his widow, 19 Ed. II: after Richard Cook; John de Ware or de Woodford who granted this tenement to Adam Broun who paid 8s. to Holy Trinity as appears in their charter[1] enrolled 18 Oct. 1316: afterwards Richard Hoddesdon son of Richard above paid the whole sum of 20s., 30 Ed. III; John Marys, 49 Ed. III; Stephen atte Halle, 8 Ric. II; Edmund Hoddesdon *alias* Barnet, throughout Hy. IV.

    1. H.R. 45 (55).

483. Total of this parish £6 6s. 8d. and it is tithed at this as appears in the king's exemplification.

[f. 93] WOLNOTH [ST. MARY WOOLNOTH]

484. Note: Robert son of John Cherenbur(c)er gave to Holy Trinity a certain stone house as appears in Charter Twenty-one[1] of several parishes.

    1. **1022**.

485. [1197–1221] Grant by Peter prior and convent to Adrian the Mercer of a stone house [**484**] in the parish of Wolnothemariechirch; abutments, the house of William Whyte on the north; to hold to Adrian and his heirs in fee; rent a silver mark; no obligation on Holy Trinity to the chief lords of the fee; swore fealty and to pay the rent without miskenning; gersuma 100s.; witnesses, Robert de Winchester, Richard de Wenton, Joce the Weigher (*ponderatore*).

    C.A.D., ii, A 2461.

486. [List of those paying rent]: Adrian the Mercer; his widow; Thomas Adrian; John de St. Osyth; John Pyne who granted the tenement to William de Hame who paid 13s. 4d. *p.a.* as appears by their charter[1] enrolled 18 Ed. I; Warin Myngy, 1 and 19 Ed. II and 1 and 6 Ed. III; Nicholas Hotot, 30 Ed. III; Thomas Albon, 49 Ed. III; Nicholas Hotot, 8 Ric. II who granted the tenement to John Godyn as appears in a charter[2] enrolled

St. Mary Woolnoth

after 25 June 1425 and the tenement is situated on the east side of St. Swithin's lane.

    1. H.R. 19 (72).   2. H.R. 153 (59).

487. Note: William de Blemonte gave to Richard, prior and convent 2s. of quit rent from certain land as appears in Charter Thirteen[1] of several parishes.

    1. **1014**.

488. [List of those paying quit rent]: Robert Burel; Laurence Wastel; Richard Derekyn who granted the land to the abbot and convent of Messenden and they sold the land to Geoffrey Godard who paid 2s. *p.a.* to Holy Trinity [See also after **489**] as appears by the following charter.

489. [1252–3] Grant and sale by Roger abbot of Messendone [f. 93v] to Geoffrey Godard, merchant, of two messuages in London in Longebordstrete towards Graschirch in the parish of St. Mary Wolnoth; abutments, the land and houses that were of Henry le Burser on the east and the land and houses that were of John le Frounceys, goldsmith, on the west extending from the said street to the great street of Cornhull on the north; to hold in fee in perpetuity; rent to the grantors and their successors 1d. or ½ lb. of cumin at Michaelmas; to the bishop 1½d. for socage; to the chapter of St. Paul's 12d. *p.a.* and to Holy Trinity 2s. *p.a.*; witnesses, John Tolosan, mayor, Thomas de Wymborne, William de Durham, sheriffs.

488 contd. Geoffrey who granted the tenement to William Hor(er)med called Aras who paid 2s. as appears in a charter written at this sign;[1] John Bond, 1 Ed. II; Richard de Wirhale, 19 Ed. II; John Bond, 1 Ed. III; Henry Pykard, 30 Ed. III; Thomas atte Noke and Thomas Ware, 36 Ed. III [See also after **490**] as appears by the following plea.

    1. The sign is an orb with a cross on it but it does not recur in the MS.

490. *Common plea held in the Husting, Mon. 12 Dec. 1362.*
Thomas atte Noke and Thomas Ware complained that on Sat. 10 Dec. 1362 the prior came to their free tenement in the parishes of St. Mary Wolnoth in Lumbardstrete and St. Michael de Cornhull and took naam worth 12d. until by gage and pledge of John de St. Albans, one of the sheriffs, etc; and the prior by John Asshewell his attorney came and said that the place where the naam was taken was a certain tavern called the Cardinalishatt with three shops adjacent on both sides of the tavern viz. two on the east side and one on the west which tavern and two shops are situated between the tenement of John Pecche which was once of Nicholas Whyte and two shops are situated between the tenement of Robert Rus on the east and the tenement of Simon atte Grene on the west in the parish of St. Michael and an end (*caput*) of the same tavern and shops abuts on (*versus*) Cornhull on the south side and the other end on the north and that this tenement owes a rent of 2s. *p.a.* to Holy Trinity [f. 94] and 12d. was in

St. Benet Sherehog

arrears; Thomas atte Noke and Thomas de Ware could not deny this and they are in mercy.

488 contd. John Bisshopyston, 48 Ed. III and 8 Ric. II; Master John Coumbe, 1 Hy. IV; John Coumbe son of John, 6 Hy. IV as appears by the following plea.

491. *Pleas of assize held at the Guildhall, Sat. 21 Feb. 1405, before Stephen Spelman and William Louthe, sheriffs, the presence of the coroner not expected.*
The assize comes to recognise whether John Coumbe senior and John Coumbe junior and Joan his wife unjustly disseised Robert prior of Holy Trinity of 2s. of his free tenement in the parish; the prior by Richard Foster his attorney complained that he is disseised of 2s. of rent and the defs. summoned did not come but Nicholas Symcok, their bailiff, replied for them and they placed themselves upon the assize and the prior likewise; John Coumbe senior by Nicholas Symcok his attorney said that he was the tenant of one messuage and that the messuage was outside the fee and demesne of the prior and the prior by his attorney said that he and all his predecessors were seised in demesne as of fee and that Prior Richard was seised in the time of King Henry and the present prior was seised in the time of King Richard [f. 94v]; the assize said that the prior was so seised and that the rent was in arrears for eight years and assessed damages for expenses at 6s. 8d.; declared that Joan did not disseise the prior, that the disseisin was not by force and arms (*vi et armis*); no fraud or collusion between the parties against the statute of mortmain; the prior to recover his seisin and rent and damages, in all, 22s. 8d.; both Johns are in mercy for a false claim; William Treynell, an officer of the sheriff is to distrain on the goods and chattels of both Johns so that he shall have the money at the next assize on Sat. and William Traynyll did execution [f. 95] and this tenement is situated on the north side of Lumbardstrete.

London possessory assizes, no. 213.

492. Total of this parish 15s. 4d. viz. in the parish of St. Swithin 13s. 4d. and in St. Mary Wolnoth 2s. and it is tithed at this in the king's exemplification.

IN THE PARISH OF ST. BENET SCHORHOG

493. [1222–48] Grant and sale by Clemence widow of Richard de Hispania daughter of Robert Blund to Richard prior and convent of 20s. *p.a.* of quit rent which Richard her husband assigned in dower from a stone house with a solar and a messuage (*managium*) which Edmund the Mercer held; to hold as long as Richard [her husband] or his heirs satisfy the grantor concerning 50 marks of gold [*sic*] with which he endowed her at the door of the monastery and also 2d. rent from the said messuage; the canons to hold freely paying the grantor and her heirs 1d. at Christmas; the canons gave 6 marks of silver; witnesses, William son of Benet the alderman, Philip de Winchester, John Wa(u)ch.

C.A.D., i, A 1660, which has 50 silver or 5 gold marks.

St. Benet Sherehog

494. [1222–30] Quitclaim by Peter son of Richard de Hispania in favour of Richard prior and convent of a rent of 20s. which Edmund the Mercer was accustomed to pay to his mother Clemence as part of her dower from Richard, Peter's father, from a certain messuage in the parish of St. Benet Sherehog; abutments, the land that was of James Illefoster and the land of Guy of Flanders (*Flandrensis*) paying to Peter and his heirs $\frac{1}{2}$ lb of cumin or 1d. at Christmas at the option of the canons; warranted for 10 marks of silver as gersuma; witnesses, William son of Benet, Philip de Winchester.

    C.A.D., ii, A 1890 and A 2571 and cf. *C.A.D.*, i, A 1621.

495. [f. 95v] [1222–30] Quitclaim by Clemence in terms similar to **494** the canons gave 6 marks of silver; witnesses, as in **494**.

    C.A.D., i, A 1621.

496. [List of those paying quit rent]: Edmund the Mercer; Ralph the Smith (*Faber*); Gilbert; William Mazerere; Henry Palmer, 1 and 19 Ed. II and 1 Ed. III; John Coggishale, 6 Ed. III; John Boteler, 30 Ed. III; John Walkote, 38 Ed. III and 8 Ric. II; his widow throughout Hy. IV and this tenement is situated on the south side of Bokelerisbury.

497. [1170–97] Grant by Stephen to Geoffrey the Vintner of a messuage to hold by hereditary right (*hereditario iure*); rent 2s. *p.a.* and a messuage which Edward son of Alfward gave to Holy Trinity with Richer his son when he was made a canon, at the end on the east side of the land which the same Edward has; this land has in width along the street in frontage 9 ells, at the other end $7\frac{1}{2}$ ells and in length $53\frac{1}{2}$ ells; gersuma 1 London sextary of wine; swore fealty; witnesses, Bartholomew Blund, Robert de Cornhull, Ralph the Vintner, Ralph Brand, John de Cresburt, Gozo son of Ralph the Vintner, William his brother.

    C.A.D., ii, A 2575.

498. [List of those paying rent]: Geoffrey the Vintner; Ralph de Cornhull; Peter son of Eustace; John Viel who granted the tenement with Isabel his daughter to Nicholas Basynges who granted the tenement to William le Maseliner [See also after **499**] as appears by the following charter.

499. [1279] Grant by Isabel widow of Nicholas de Basynges, citizen daughter of John Viel junior [f. 96] to William Mazeliner, citizen, and Roisia his wife of the tenement which she had in the parish of St. Benet Schorhog opposite the church between the tenement of the late Edward le Blund on the south and the king's street on the north and the tenements of Robert de Aras and John de Eu on the west and the king's street on the east, all that came to the grantor by heredity through the death of her late father; to hold to William and his heirs and assigns and also to Roisia for her life if she survives her husband; rent to Isabel and her heirs 10 marks *p.a.*; to the abbot of Glastonbury 20 lbs. of pepper; to Holy Trinity 2s.; to the nuns of Berkingg 22d.; the grantees to pay the king's socage; declaration that the grantees shall maintain the houses and buildings; the tenement is to be distrained

St. Pancras Soper Lane

upon if the payments are in arrears and if this is insufficient, all the grantees' lands and goods are to be distrained upon; the grantees concede that if the payments shall be in arrears for two terms by default then Isabel and her heirs shall enter the tenement and recover and retain it and the grantee renounces for himself and his heirs and Roisia the limitation of the custom of the City in the suing out of writs [f. 96v] through which this charter may by any process of time be weakened; this charter to be firm notwithstanding any custom until now used in the City; gersuma 2 marks; chirograph sealed; witnesses, Gregory de Rokesle, mayor, Ralph de Mora, sheriff.

C.A.D., ii, A 2574.

498 contd. Henry Palmere, 1 Ed. II and 1 Ed. III; Thomas de Garton, 5 Ed. III as appears by poundage; Hugh de Garton, 6 Ed. III; Adam Fraunceys, 30 Ed. III; John Twyford, 33 Ed. III; James Andrew, 37 Ed. III; Nicholas Twyford, 48 Ed. III and 8 Ric. II [23 lines blank].

500. Total of this parish 32s. and it is tithed at this in the king's exemplification.

[f. 97] IN THE PARISH OF ST. PANCRAS

501. [1253-4] Grant of William Wylehale (*Wilehale*), citizen, for the salvation of his soul etc. to John prior and convent of 10s. 4d. of quit rent which Gilbert le Bas was accustomed to pay him from certain lands with houses which he held in the parish of St. Pancras next Sopereslane; abutments, the church on the east and the tenement once of Richard son of Walter on the west; to hold in free alms; witnesses, Nicholas Batte, mayor, John de Norhampthon, Richard Pykard, sheriffs, Adam de Basinges, Roger son of Roger, Michael Tovy, John de Gysorz, John Adryan, William son of Richard, Ralph le Fevre.

C.A.D., ii, A 2697.

502. [List of those paying quit rent]: Gilbert le Bas; Thomas Heyroun; Richard Vantot, 1 Ed. II; William Hervy, 5 and 19 Ed. II; Richard Vantot, 1 Ed. III; John Stanhoppe, 30 Ed. III; Adam Stable, 48 Ed. III; John Hadlee, 9 Ric. II to whom William prior and convent remitted 3s. 8d. for a term of twenty years [See also after **503**] as appears in the following charter.

503. Release by William prior and convent to John Hadele, who has built a house on part of the land consecrated as a cemetery for the church of St. Pancras, of all arrears of rent for all time preceding [f. 97v] and he shall pay only 6s. 8d. *p.a.* for twenty years from Michaelmas next coming; prior and convent have the right to enter and distrain for the 6s. 8d. and at the end of twenty years the present concession shall be null and void and thereafter the rent of 10s. 4d. *p.a.* shall be paid; counterpart indenture; dated 24 June 1385.

C.A.D., v, A 11640.

St. Pancras Soper Lane

502 contd. The rector and churchwardens as appears by the following acquittance [no acquittance follows].

504. Note: Laurence de St. Michael gave to J.,[1] prior and convent 14s. 8d. which William Totham was accustomed to pay him as appears by Charter Five.[2]

    1. Presumably Prior John, 1250–61.   2. **512**.

505. Grant by William de Totham and Margery, daughter of Walter de Essex, his wife, of ½ mark of quit rent from two shops at the corner (*in cornera*) of a new street (*novi vici*) called Soperislane by Cheap (*iuxta forum London'*) on the east which shops contain in length 3 ells and in breadth 1⅓ ells; the canons gave 4 marks of silver to further the grantors' most urgent business (*ad urgentissima negocia nostra utiliter expedienda*); the sale was made in the presence of the grantors' daughter Christine being of lawful age and with her agreement and she sealed the charter together with the seals of the grantors; [f. 98] and if Christine wishes to sell or lease the shops or part thereof then the canons have the first claim to receive ½ mark of silver; dated St. Laurence's day [? 10 Aug.] 1257; witnesses, Ralph Hardel, mayor, Richard de Ewelle, William Aswy, sheriffs.

    C.A.D., ii, A 2609.

506. [List of those paying quit rent]: William Totham paid 13s. 4d. for his obligations under **504** and **505** and afterwards the land was divided for Katherine Totham paid 6s. 8d. and Helewisa paid 6s. 8d.; and these paid 6s. 8d. after Katherine; Alan Norhamton who granted the tenement to John le Botoner who paid 6s. 8d. to Holy Trinity as appears by their charter[1] enrolled 23 Ed. I; John le Boteler or Botoner, 1, 5 and 19 Ed. II and 1 Ed. III; John Botonere, 6 and 30 Ed. III; Thomas Everand, 33 and 49 Ed. III; Walter Doget, 8 Ric. II: and these paid 6s. 8d. after Helewisa; Richer Refham, 1 and 19 Ed. II; John Refham, 1 and 49 Ed. III and 8 Ric. II.

    1. H.R. 24 (33).

507. [1250–8] Grant of Laurence de St. Michael son of William to John prior and convent of 60s. *p.a.* of quit rent which the grantor received from three shops in Sopereslane which shops are next to the corner of Cheap (*proximas in cornera versus magnum forum London'*) out of which one shop pays 28s. *p.a.*, the other shop 20s. *p.a.* and the third shop 12s. *p.a.*; rent to the grantee and his heirs 20s. *p.a.*; the canons gave 30 marks of silver as gersuma (*in liberam gersumam*); sealed; witnesses, Peter son of Alan, Nicholas son of Joce, John Adrian, draper.

    Margin: pro magistro Pakyngton in foro Lond'.
    C.A.D., ii, A 2560.

508. [1257] Release by Laurence de St. Michael of 20s. which [f. 98v] the prior and convent ought to pay him out of the 60s. which they ought to receive from three shops in Sopereslane; the canons to pay to Michael and

St. Pancras Soper Lane

his heirs 2s. *p.a.* or 1 lb. of cumin at the option of the canons on 2 July; the canons gave 15 marks of silver as gersuma; witnesses, Ralph Hardel, mayor, Thomas son of Thomas, Robert Cateluyne, sheriffs, Peter son of Alan, Roger son of Roger.

509. [List of those paying quit rent]: the dean and chapter of St. Martin's; now [1425–7] in the hands of the abbot of Westminster, and these three shops are situated adjacent in the west corner of a street called Sopereslane which abuts on the market.

510. [1255–6] Grant of Richard Essex (*de Essex*), shop-keeper, to John prior and convent of 6s. *p.a.* of quit rent from the grantor's two shops with a solar built above which are near the gate of the 'Brodeselde' which was once of Walter le Brun on the east; abutments, the gate of the seld itself on the west and the land which was of Walter le Waunt(er) on the east with free access to and exit from the solar by the outer door of the seld; the canons to have the right to enter and distrain until arrears of rent are paid in full; the canons gave 4 marks of silver; sealed; witnesses, Ralph Hardel, mayor, John le Minur, Matthew Bukerel, sheriffs.

C.A.D., iv, A 9656.

511. [f. 99] [List of those paying quit rent]: Richard Chivaler and then this rent was divided for Walter Norwich paid 3s. and John Marchaunt paid 3s.; and these paid 3s. after Walter Norwich; Roger de Cau(n)dyche, 1 Ed. II and 1 Ed. III; Roger Donkele, 5 Ed. III; William Causton, 30 Ed. III; John de Enfeld, 36 Ed. III; Richard Northbiry, 48 Ed. III; note the same Richard and Robert Godistold paid 3s. for two shops, 1, 8 and 14 Ric. II: and these paid 3s. after John Marchaunt, 1 Ed. II and 1 Ed. III; Nicholas Marchaunt, 30 Ed. III; Robert Godistold, 48 Ed. III; note John Garton paid 3s. for the solar above the two shops, 1 Ric. II; John Prentys, 8 Ric. II; John Garton, 14 Ric. II and these shops are situated on the south side of Cheap in front of the seld called Brodeselde.

512. [See **504**] [1258] Grant by Laurence de St. Michael son of William to John prior and convent of 14s. 8d. *p.a.* of quit rent which William de Totham was accustomed to pay the grantor from a certain shop in Sopers-lane; to be held of the grantor and his heirs at a rent of 8s. *p.a.* to be paid without any fraud or quibbling (*cavillatione*); the canons gave 5 marks in gersuma; sealed; witnesses, William son of Richard, mayor, Thomas son of Thomas, William Grapefige, sheriffs, Adam Rasyng, alderman; and thus there remains to Holy Trinity 6s. 8d. of the 14s. 8d.

C.A.D., ii, A 2565.

513. [List of those paying quit rent]: William de Totham; Helewisa; Richer Refham, 5 and 19 Ed. II; John Refham, 1, 5 and 38 Ed. III and 8 Ric. II [f. 99v: 38 lines blank].

514. Total of this parish £4 9s. 8d. and it is tithed at this in the king's exemplification.

St. Mary Le Bow

[f. 100] IN THE PARISH OF ST. MARY DE ARCUBUS

515. [1250–1] Grant by John le Lunge to John prior and convent of 9s. *p.a.* of quit rent that Ralph son of Thomas was accustomed to pay from shops, with solars built over them, in Cheap; abutments, the seld of Roger son of Roger and that of Emma Sibeling; the canons to pay the grantor and his heirs ½ lb. of cumin at Michaelmas; the canons gave 6 marks of silver as gersuma; witnesses, John Norman, mayor, Humphrey le Fevre, William son of Richard, sheriffs.

    C.A.D., ii, A 2483.

516. [1251–2] Grant by Ralph the Goldsmith to John prior and convent of 6s. *p.a.* of quit rent which Ralph son of Thomas was accustomed to pay from a certain shop in Westchepe next the seld of Roger son of Roger; the canons to pay the grantor and his heirs ½ lb. of cumin or ½d. at Easter; the canons gave 60s. as gersuma; witnesses, Adam de Rasing,[1] mayor and alderman of this ward,[2] Nicholas Bat, Laurence Frowyk, sheriffs.

    1. *Rectius* Basing.   2. Cheap.
    C.A.D., ii, A 2482.

517. [1252–3] Grant by Emma widow of Thomas Sybelyng to John prior and convent [f. 100v] of 4s. *p.a.* of quit rent which Ralph son of Thomas was accustomed to pay from two solars in Westchepe between the grantor's seld and that of Roger son of Roger with free access to and exit from the solar through the porch (*atrium*) of the grantor's seld; the canons gave 30s. as gersuma; witnesses, John Tulsan, mayor, Thomas de B(un)burne [*sic*], sheriff.

    C.A.D., ii, A 2463.

518. [List of those paying quit rent]: the whole sum of 19s.; Ralph son of Thomas; Nicholas son of Ralph; Robert de Kelysseye, 1 and 19 Ed. II and 1 Ed. III; Nicholas Armerer, 6 Ed. III; Thomas Kelysseye, 15 Ed. III [See also after **524**] as appears by the following royal writ and plea held Mon. 5 Nov. 1341.

519. Writ to the mayor and sheriffs ordering them to see justice done to the prior of Holy Trinity in the matter of the withholding of just service to him by Thomas, clerk; witnessed by Edward, duke of Cornwall and earl of Chester, guardian of England, at Schottele, 22 June 1340.

520. The prior seeks against Thomas de Keleseye, clerk, a shop which for some time was two shops and a solar as gavelet because the said Thomas holds from him at a rent of 9s. *p.a.* which rent his predecessor Prior Roger de Poulay was seised of by his tenant Robert de Kelesey, father of the said Thomas, and on the day of the suing out of the writ, the rent was £6 15s. in arrears for fifteen years and the tenement cannot be distrained upon for a year and a day; the def. in person could not deny this but he did not pay the arrears and the prior recovers for a year and a day as gavelet.

St. Mary Colechurch

521. [1340] Another writ as **519** with Thomas son of Robert de Kelesey for Thomas a clerk.

522. [f. 101] Another plea as **520** with another shop at a rent of 6s. *p.a.* and £4 10s. in arrears.

523. [1340] Another writ as **519** with Thomas de Kelesey parson of the church of Uherst.

524. Another plea as **520** with a solar at a rent of 4s. *p.a.* and 60s. in arrears.

518 contd. The rector of St. Stephen Walbrok, 30 Ed. III; John Gyrdelere, 37 and 49 Ed. III; John Hailesdon, 1 Ric. II; John Wodecok, 21 Ric. II; the executors of the same 11 Hy. IV as appears by the following acquittance.

525. Acquittance of brother Thomas Axbrygge, rent-collector (*reddituarius*) of the house of Holy Trinity, acknowledging receipt from the heirs and executors of John Wodecok, formerly citizen and mercer, by Simon Flete, mercer, of 4s. 9d. of an annual quit rent of 19s. paid from the front [part] of a certain shop called 'le Crowne' situated in Chepe in the parish of St. Mary-le-Bow between the shop formerly of Sir Robert Knoll called 'le legge' on the east and one of the prior and convent of St. Bartholomew de Smethfeld called 'le Threleggs' on the west 4s. 9d. due for the quarter day of 24 June last; [f. 101v] sealed by both parties; dated 25 June 1410, and the tenement is situated on the south side of the market.

    C.A.D., ii, A 2509.

526. Total of this parish 19s. and nevertheless it is tithed at 25s. as appears in the king's exemplification.

[f. 102] IN THE PARISH OF ST. MARY COLECHIRCH

527. [1214–16] Grant by Geoffrey de Maundevilla (*Maundevyle*), earl of Essex and Gloucester to Gilbert de Walecune (*Waketone*) for his homage and service of all the grantor's land with houses in the parish of St. Mary de Colechirch between the land and houses of John Walensis on the west which is of the fee of Hugh de Nevile on the north which land lies at the corner of a lane called Ysmongerslane; to hold in perpetuity; the grantee and his heirs to pay the grantor and his heirs a tercel (*tercellium*) or 4 bezants on St. Margaret's day; the grantee to perform the service to the chief lords of the fee, to the monks of St. Albans 7s. *p.a.* and to the monks of Christchurch Canterbury 11s. *p.a.*; the grantor and his heirs to demand nothing from the land except the tercel; Gilbert to pay any tallage or aid; gersuma 20 marks of silver; witnesses, William de Mandavilla, Hugh de Byblesword, then steward, Serlo, then mayor of London and many others.

528. [1220–1] Grant and sale by Gilbert de Waleton to Master Alexander de Dorchester of all the land and houses which the grantor had from Geoffrey de Mandavilla [in **527**] at the corner of Ysmongerislane; gersuma 20 marks

St. Mary Colechurch

of silver; witnesses, Serlo the Mercer, mayor, William son of Benet, alderman, Richard Renger, Joce Junior, sheriffs.

529. [f. 102v] [1227–44] Will of Master Alexander de Dorchester; his body to be buried in the church of Holy Trinity and all his rents in the market and in the parish of St. Mary Colechirch between the land of John Walensis on the west and the fee of Hugh de Nevill on the north to Holy Trinity; all his debts to be paid from his movables viz. to the king £300; any defaults to churches are to be made good by his executors (*Item defectus ecclesiarum mearum volo ut rationabiliter et modeste suppleantur secundum provisionem executorum meorum*); to Holy Trinity ½ mark for pittances on the testator's anniversary day for ever and this ½ mark is to be obtained from his money by the provision of his executors; to Simon the Cook, the house which William the Baker used to hold of the hospital without Bisshopsgate; to Grun the house which Edward the Vintner used to hold [and] 20s.; to Jordan 100s.; the custody of the land which the testator has at (*de*) Wintellesbury until his term (*usque ad terminum meum*) to Walter Reyn his nephew so that Robert his ward (*alumpnus*) shall have half until the aforesaid term and to the same Robert 40s.; to Nicholas the chaplain 20s.; to the chaplains of London 40s.; 10s. to the poor and also 40s. to be distributed on the day of burial; to the three hospitals, namely, St. Bartholomew, St. James and St. Thomas ½ mark *p.a.* each to be taken from his house in the parish of St. Peter Bradestrat; to each hospital round London ½ mark, namely to the nuns of Halywell, the nuns of Clerkenwell and the nuns of St. Helen; all the testator's mentioned and unmentioned movables and immovables and all his goods and his debts he hands over completely to the ordering of his executors; appointed as executors of the will, the bishop of Chichester, chancellor of the king, the bishop of Bath and Wells, Richard prior of Holy Trinity, Richard the chaplain of the church of St. Peter Bradestrat, Robin [*sic*] the testator's clerk.

C.A.D., ii, A 1915.

530. [1264–5] Grant by Gilbert prior and convent to William de Wilyhale (*Wylihale*) son of Robert de Eston, citizen, of certain land with three shops, a seld and houses built thereon in Chepeward in the parish of Colechirch; abutments, the land and houses of Peter son of Alan on the west and the land and houses of Roger le Seriaunt on the east extending in length from the king's street to the messuage of the Fratres de Penetencia Jewry on the north; rent 10 marks *p.a.*; quitclaim against the lords of the fee; if the grantee wishes to sell, the prior and convent to have the preference by ½ mark; the grantee is not to pull down the houses [f. 103] or let them decay but to maintain them; swore fealty; chirograph sealed; witnesses, Thomas son of Thomas, mayor and alderman of this ward, Peter Augier, Edward Blund, sheriffs.

C.A.D., i, A 1673.

531. [List of those paying rent]: William de Wilyhale; John Lok; William de Burgo, 1 and 19 Ed. II and 1 Ed. III [See also after **532**] as appears by the following indenture.

St. Mary Colechurch

532. Indenture made between Roger prior of Holy Trinity of the one part and William de Burgo, clerk, and Margery his wife of the other part concerning a rent of 10 marks *p.a.* which William and Margery now hold of the gift and enfeoffment of John Lok of the prior and convent; because of certain disagreements William and Margery declare that they hold of the prior and concede for themselves and their heirs that they hold by this service and that the prior may distrain; sealed counterpart; dated London 19 Apr. 1327.

C.A.D., i, A 1672.

531 contd. William de Burgo, 3 Ed. III; Thomas Cavendych, 6 Ed. III; Thomas Broun, 30 Ed. III; his widow, 31 Ed. III as appears by Acquittance Two[1] of several parishes; Thomas Broun, 8 Ric. II; his widow, 1 Hy. V.

1. **1039.**

533. [1246] Grant by Richard prior and convent to William Wylihale (*de Wylihale*) of certain land with shops, selds and solars built thereon in the parish of Colechirch between Ysmongereslane on the east and the land of Peter son of Alan on the west extending from the king's highway of Cheap to the land of Peytevin the Jew on the north; rent 10 marks *p.a.*; William and his heirs are not to deteriorate the tenement nor to sell or pledge it to Jews or to other religious [f. 103v]; if the grantee wishes to lease it to others, the prior and convent to have the preference by a bezant of 2s.; swore fealty; gersuma 100 marks of silver; witnesses, John de Gysors, mayor, Robert de Cornhell, Adam de Bentleghe, sheriffs.

C.A.D., i, A 1646.

534. Quitclaim by John son and heir of William Wylihale senior, once citizen of London, to Eustace prior and convent of three houses, shops, solars and cellars; abutments, [as in **533**] which rent the canons had by the grant of William at Ston, Robert son of Hervi and Master Thomas Aelwy, canon of St. Paul's, executors of the will; the grant is for the maintenance of three chaplains, canons or seculars, to celebrate for the soul of William etc., in Holy Trinity for ever; quitclaim; the grantor and his heirs not to proceed in any court civil or ecclesiastical against the canons; sworn before the official of the archdeacon of London; sealed; witnesses, Gregory de Rokeslee, mayor, William le Mazerer, Robert de Basing, sheriffs; dated Christmas 1278.

C.A.D., ii, A 2236.

535. [1263–4] Grant by Gilbert prior and convent to Roger le Seriaunt of certain land with houses built thereon in Chep Ward which land contains in length between the house of the Fratres de Penetencia Jewry on the north and the house of the canons held by Eymerycus Bruning on the south, 15 ells and in width along Ysmongerslane and the selds of the canons $8\frac{1}{2}$ ells; rent 57s. 4d. *p.a.*; gersuma 2 marks sterling; if the grantee wishes to sell, the prior and convent to have the preference by $\frac{1}{2}$ mark of silver; Roger and his heirs [f. 104] shall not pull down the houses or let houses built thereon

All Hallows Honey Lane

decay nor allow stone walls to be thrown down but shall maintain them at his own cost; the canons may distrain on the grantee's tenements in the parish of St. Matthew Friday Street; swore fealty; chirograph sealed; witnesses, Thomas son of Thomas son of Richard, mayor, Thomas de Forda, Gregory de Rokeslee, sheriffs.

 C.A.D., ii, A 2072.

536. [List of those paying rent]: Roger le Seriaunt; William de Wylihale who bequeathed all the rent which he had in Cheap of the fee of the prior and convent as appears in his will[1] [See also after **537**] and afterwards Ralph prior and convent granted the same land to Richar de Refham[2] for £7 p.a. except the shop on the corner.

 1. C. Wills, i, 43. 2. Cf. C.A.D., iv, A 7373.

537. Agreement between Ralph prior and convent and Richer de Refham, citizen and mercer, over the exaction of a certain rent; concluded that the prior with the assent of the convent granted that Richer held of the prior the following tenements; that which Roger le Seriaunt once held at a rent of 57s. 4d. p.a. situated between Ysmongerslane and the tenement once of Adam de St. Albans, farrier, in the parish of St. Mary Colechirch and that solar on the corner of the lane between the lane itself and the solar once of Adam de St. Albans 'next chepe' from which solar the prior and convent received 33s. p.a. and also three shops next Chepe street of which, Richer has two shops by the lease of the prior and convent for 40s. p.a. and the third shop by the lease of Peter de Hildresham for 24s. p.a.; for a rent of £7 p.a. paid to the prior and convent; prior and convent release and quitclaim to Richer and his heirs all right and claim to the title of the aforesaid shops and solars beyond £7 p.a. in rent and remit all arrears before Michaelmas 1304; Richer gave 1 mark p.a. of quit rent from the tenement at the corner of Ysemongerlane which mark he had by the lease of John de Chelse, chandler (*unctarius*); the prior and convent and their successors to have the right of distraint; [f. 104v] counterpart sealed; witnesses, John le Blunt, mayor, Roger de Pareys, John de Lyncoln, sheriffs; dated London Fri. 30 Oct. 1304.

536 contd. Richer de Refham, 32 Ed. I, 1 and 19 Ed. II and 1 Ed. III; John Refham, 6 Ed. III; his widow, 30 Ed. III; Adam Fraunces, 48 Ed. III and throughout Ric. II and Hy. IV; Thomas Charleton, throughout Hy. V and the tenement is situated on the north side of Cheap (*fori London*') between Ir(en)mongerslane on the east and the tenement of the late Thomas Broun on the west [26 lines blank].

538. Total of this parish £13 13s. 4d. and it is tithed at this in the king's exemplification.

[f. 105] IN THE PARISH OF ALL HALLOWS HONYLANE

539. [1222–48] Grant by Geoffrey Frowyk (*de Frowyk*) to Richard prior and convent of 20d. p.a. out of 8s. 4d. p.a. which the canons of St. Mary

St. Mary Aldermary

Suthwerk were accustomed to pay the grantor from a seld which they hold of him in the market, which 20d. *p.a.* of rent Geoffrey bought of John son of Terricus; to hold in free alms; sealed; witnesses, Robert son of John, William Fokes, William Berkyng and others.

    C.A.D., iv, A 7302.

540. Note: Geoffrey de Frowyk bequeathed to the prior and convent all the rent, 8s. 4d. *p.a.*, as appears in his will [17 lines blank].

541. [List of those paying quit rent]: the canons of Southwerk; John Moton, 27 Ed. I [See also after **542**] as appears by the following plea.

542. *Common plea held in the Husting, Mon. 19 Oct. 1299.*
The prior, def., in a plea of taking naam and John Moton, pl., agree by licence of the court; John recognises that he owes 9s. arrears in an annual rent of 8s. 4d. whereupon the prior remits the arrears.

541 contd. John Poyntel; Thomas Leggey, 30 Ed. III whose executors satisfied the arrears as appears by Acquittance Four[1] of several parishes; William Brangwayn [f. 105v] as appears by the following plea.

    1. **1041**.

543. *Common plea held in the Husting, Mon. 14 Dec. 1360.*
William Brangwayn complains that the prior took naam on Mon. 26 Jan. 1360 worth 40s. [incomplete] and the tenement is situated on the north side of the great street called Chepe.

544. Total of this parish 8s. 4d. and nevertheless it is tithed at 48s. 4d. as appears in the king's exemplification.

[f. 106] IN THE PARISH OF ALDERMARYCHYRCH

545. [1214–16] Grant of William Cal(m)erar (*Ca(m)er*), son of Jordan Camer to John Ta(u)ers[1] of land in the parish of St. Mary Aldermarychirch between the land of William Sputyng on the east and Cordwainer street (*vicus de corueria*) on the west and between the street on the south and the land which is of the fee of the hospital of St. Giles on the north; to hold in fee; rent 1 mark *p.a.*; William and his heirs in no way to deprive (*dehospitari*) John of the said land; gersuma 12 marks; witnesses, Serlo the Mercer, Henry de St. Albans.

    1. *Rectius* Travers.

546. [1214–26] Grant by William the Chamberlain (*Camerarius*) son of Jordan to Holy Trinity in free alms of 1 mark of rent which John Ta(u)ers pays to the grantor from a tenement; [the abutments as in **545**]; to hold in perpetuity for pittances on the anniversary of the grantor's death; sealed; witnesses, Reginald and W. chaplains of Henry de Castell, Eustace the Mercer.

    C.A.D., ii, A 1877.

St. Thomas the Apostle

547. [List of those paying quit rent]: John Tra(v)ers to whom Richard prior and convent remitted 6s. 8d. [See also after **549**].

548. [1225–6] Release by Richard prior and convent to John T(r)avers of 1 mark of rent which William son of Jordan Cam(er) gave to Holy Trinity in the parish of St. Mary Aldermarie of the fee of Hamon the Butler (*Pincerne*); rent ½ mark *p.a.*; gersuma 2 marks; witnesses, Richard Renger, mayor, Roger le Duc, Martin son of William.

549. [1235–6] Recognisance of Margery daughter of John Travers that she owes to Richard prior and convent ½ mark *p.a.* of rent from land; [abutments as in **545**]; [f. 106v] if Margery and her heirs do not pay the rent, they shall give by way of penalty ½ mark; this convention to last as long as the land shall be built upon (*hospitata*) and the canons shall have the right of distraint; sealed; witnesses, Andrew Bokerel, mayor, Gerard Bat, Robert Hardel, sheriffs.

547 contd. Margery Travers; Nicholas de Winchester (*Wynton*), 1 Ed. II; Richard Constantyn, 19 Ed. II and 1 Ed. III; John Constantyn, 30 Ed. III; John Pech(am), 48 Ed. III; John Costantyn, 8 Ric. II [33 lines blank].

550. Total of this parish 6s. 8d. and it is tithed at this in the king's exemplification.

[f. 107] IN THE PARISH OF ST. THOMAS THE APOSTLE

551. [1201–2] Grant by David son of Ralph the Vintner to Holy Trinity of 20s. *p.a.* of quit rent from certain land which Robert de Basingge held of the grantor beside the cemetery of the same church on the east; the canons to pay a rent of 10s. *p.a.* to the grantor and his heirs; the canons gave 10 marks of silver as gersuma; witnesses, Henry mayor of London, Norman Blundus, John de Cayo, sheriffs.

    C.A.D., ii, A 1936.

552. [List of those paying quit rent]: Robert de Basyng; then the land was divided for Aldstanus paid 6s. 8d. *p.a.* and John son of Godfrey (*Godefridi*) 13s. 4d.: after Adelstanus; Peter Gysors; Robert le Cytoler; Elias de Honilane; Robert Hod, 1 and 19 Ed. II and 1 Ed. III; Katherine his daughter, 6 Ed. III who granted the tenement to William Chaumpeneys who paid 6s. 8d. as appears by their charter[1] enrolled in the Husting Mon. 25 July 1345 and William bequeathed the tenement to the church as appears in his will[2] enrolled after 14 Feb. 1351 and William paid 22 Ed. III; then the tenement was divided for Matthew Pecok paid 3s. 4d. and John Mychel 3s. 4d., 39 Ed. III: after Matthew Pecok; his widow, 47 Ed. III; and the church[3] (*ecclesia ipsa*), 10 Ric. II: after John Mychel; John Stodey, 49 Ed. III; Thomas Goodlak, 10 Ric. II: [f. 107v] and after John Godard [*sic*]; his widow Christine; Richard Reyner; John the clerk; Richard Poterell; Robert the clerk; Roger de Vinea, 1 and 19 Ed. II and 1 Ed. III; William Burdon 20 Ed. III; Thomas Barnet, 20 Ed. III who bequeathed

St. Thomas the Apostle

the tenement to the master and church of St. Thomas [de Acon] as appears in his will[4] enrolled after 2 Feb. 1350 and the master paid until now [1425–7].

    1. H.R. 72 (79).   3. Presumably the church of St. Thomas.
    2. *C. Wills*, ii, 13–14.   4. *C. Wills*, i, 624.

553. Note: Ralph le Justice quitted to Richard prior and convent 4s. *p.a.* which William the Chamberlain gave to him when he married Denise daughter of William from land with houses which were held by the prior of Lewys in the parish of St. Thomas as appears by Charter Eighteen[1] of several parishes.

    1. **1019**.

554. [List of those paying quit rent]: the prior of Lewys; Thomas Romayn, 1 and 19 Ed. II; Juliana Romayn, 1 Ed. III; Andrew Aubry, 6, 30 and 49 Ed. III and 3 Ric. II and this tenement is situated on the south side of a street called [name missing] between the tenement of the late John Deverose on the west and the king's street on the east.

555. Note: William the Chamberlain gave to Richard prior and convent 5s. *p.a.* and ½ lb. of pepper from land with houses that was held by Robert son of Symon in the same parish as appears in Charter Seventeen[1] of several parishes.

    1. **1018**.

556. [List of those paying quit rent]: Robert son of Symon; Godmund Taylour, 16 Ed. I as appears by the following recognisance.

557. *Plea held Mon. 1 Feb. 1288.*
Godman le Taylour and Helen his wife, tenants of a certain tenement; abutments, the tenement of John de Norhamtone on the west and that of the prior of Lewes on the east, acknowledge in full Husting that they hold of the prior of Holy Trinity for 5s. *p.a.* and ½ lb. of pepper for the above tenement and the recognisance was enrolled the same day: by licence of the court it was agreed for the defs. by Richard Gladewyn, their attorney, that they held at the above rent and thereon the prior remitted all arrears up to this day; Ralph de Sandwich, warden of London, William de Hereford, Thomas de Stanes, sheriffs; and Godman granted the tenement to John de Norhamtone paying to Holy Trinity as appears by their charter[1] enrolled 16 Ed. I.

    1. H.R. 18 (2).

558. Note: William the Chamberlain gave to the prior and convent 5s. *p.a.* and ½ lb. of pepper from a tenement adjacent, [to that mentioned in **555**] once of William le Taylour as appears in Charter Sixteen[1] of several parishes.

    1. **1017**.

St. Thomas the Apostle

559. [List of those paying quit rent]: William le Taylour; John de Norhamtone [See also after **560**] as appears by the following plea.

560. [f. 108] *Common plea held in the Husting, Mon. 1 Feb. 1288.*
John de Norhamtone, clerk, recognises that he holds of William prior and convent for 5s. *p.a.* and 1 lb. of pepper from a certain tenement which Godman le Taylour and Helen his wife held of the prior and convent and upon this the prior remitted all arrears of rent before Michaelmas 1287.

559 contd. Robert Callere.

561. Note: William the Chamberlain gave 1 lb. of pepper from land with houses adjacent to the prior's tenement held by Andrew Blund, the pepper payable at Michaelmas, as appears by Charter Seventeen[1] of several parishes.

    1. **1018.**

562. [List of those paying quit rent]: Andrew Blund; John Horewode; Edward Blund; Robert le Callere, 1 Ed. II [See also after **563**] as appears by the following charter.

563. Indenture made between Robert le Callere and the prior of Holy Trinity wherein Robert recognises that he holds of the prior by a rent of 10s. *p.a.* and 2 lbs. of pepper or 12d. from three tenements which he holds in the parish of St. Thomas the Apostle situated between the tenement of the prior of Lewys on the east and Cordewanestret on the west viz. from the tenement with houses which were once of Godman the Tailor on the side of the prior of Lewis 5s. and ½ lb of pepper or 3d., and from the adjacent tenement with houses on the west side which were once of John de Norhamtone 5s. and ½ lb. of pepper or 3d., and from the tenement with houses which was once of Edward Blund on the west side 1 lb. of pepper or 6d.; Robert concedes for himself and his heirs that the prior shall take naam and distrain in all the aforesaid tenements; the prior for this recognisance and concession remitted all arrears owed to him before Easter 1317; sealed; witnesses, John de Wengave, mayor, William de Causton, Ralph le Balanc(er), sheriffs; dated London 30 Apr. 1317.

    C.A.D., ii, A 2279.

562 contd. Robert Callere paid 11s., 19 Ed. II and 6 Ed. III; and afterwards the land was divided for Simon Salle paid 5s. *p.a.* and ½ lb. of pepper or 3d., and Walter Maune 5s. and ½ lb. of pepper or 3d., and Adam Brabeson 1 lb. of pepper or 6d., 33 Ed. III: after Simon Salle his tenement was again divided for Benet Zakarye paid 2s. 6d. *p.a.* and 1½d. for ¼ lb. of pepper and Robert Westmyll similarly: after B. Zakere; John Ypr(e), 48 Ed. III and 8 Ric. II; John Deverose, 15 Ric. II: [f. 108v] after Robert Westmell; Henry Norhamtone, 36 Ed. III; William Herlowe, 49 Ed. III; his widow, 5 Ric. II; Isabel Norhamtone, 8 Ric. II; Henry Gerard, 15 Ric. II; John Gav(er), 4 Hy. IV: after Walter Maune; Benet Zakarye, 41 Ed. III; John

St. James Garlickhithe

Ypr(e), 48 Ed. III; John Deverose, 15 Ric. II: and after Adam Brabason; John Horerwode, 36 Ed. III; John Scorfeyn, 49 Ed. III; Thomas Freton, 'browderer', 5 and 15 Ric. II and these tenements are situated adjacent between the tenement which Henry Subseye holds of the prior of Lewes on the east and Cordwanestret on the west [20 lines blank].

564. Total of this parish 35s. and it is tithed at this in the king's exemplification.

[f. 109] IN THE PARISH OF ST. JAMES GARLYKHYTHE

565. Note: William the Chamberlain gave to Richard prior and convent 15s. *p.a.* of land with houses upon it which Ralph Ely once held in the parish of St. James as appears in Charter Seventeen[1] of several parishes.

    1. **1018.**

566. [List of those paying quit rent]: Ralph de Ely and then the land was divided for Stephen Crasser paid 5s. *p.a.* for the part which abutted on Cordweynstret and John Tavers 10s. for that part which abutted on Kyronlane: after Stephen Crasser, Ralph le Justice confirmed this grant to the church of Holy Trinity as appears in Charter Eighteen[1] of several parishes and from this tenement abutting on Cordweynstret 5s. *p.a.* was paid by Adam le Tailour; Stephen de Upton; John de Oxford, 1 Ed. II; Henry at Swan, 19 Ed. II; Stephen Upton, 1 Ed. III; Michael Mynot, 3 and 6 Ed. III; Richard Mallyng, 30 Ed. III; Walter Neel, 31 Ed. III; the bishop of Rochester, 34 Ed. III; John Mychel, 36 Ed. III; Gilbert Bonet, 48 Ed. III and 8 Ric. II; Robert Newton who granted the tenement to John Crouche and Isabel his wife who paid 5s. to Holy Trinity as appears by their charter[2] enrolled 3 Hy. IV: after John T(r)avers from the tenement abutting on Kyronlane 10s. was paid by William Haddstok, 20 Ed. I [See also after **567**] as appears by the following plea.

    1. **1019.**   2. H.R. 130 (109).

567. *Common plea held in the Husting, Mon. before St. Peter 1292.*
William de Haddestok came and recognised that 10s. *p.a.* of quit rent was due to Holy Trinity from his messuage in the parish of St. James Garlekheth and that 40s. of arrears was payable to the prior on Tues. 15 Apr. 1292; Henry Waleys, then mayor [*sic*] of London; the recognisance was enrolled.

566 contd. John de St. Albans who granted the tenement to Bartholomew Vyndi(n)es who paid 10s. to Holy Trinity as appears by their charter[1] enrolled 7 Ed. II; Gauselinus Pagan, 1 Ed. III; Michael Mynot, 3 Ed. III; Richard Mallyng, 30 Ed. III; John Middleton, 33 Ed. III; Gilbert Bonet, 37 Ed. III; Adam Chongonur, 40 Ed. III; Peter Lacy, 46 Ed. III; Richard Lyons, 49 Ed. III and 3 Ric. II; William More, 1 Hy. IV as appears by the following acquittance.

    1. H.R. 42 (67).

Holy Trinity the Less

568. Indenture between Robert prior and convent and William More, citizen and vintner, witnesseth that on this day the prior received 5s. in full payment of all arrears of a quit rent of 10s. due from a tenement once held by Richard Lyouns in Kyrunlane; sealed by both parties; dated London 6 Oct. 1399.

569. Total of this parish 15s. and it is tithed at this in the king's exemplification.

[f. 109v] IN THE PARISH OF HOLY TRINITY THE LESS

570. Note: William the Chamberlain gave to Richard prior and convent all his capital messuage (*managium*) in the parish of Holy Trinity as appears by Charter Seventeen[1] of several parishes.

    1. **1018**.

571. [1241] Grant of Richard prior and convent to John son of Norman, citizen, of all the capital messuage which was of William the Chamberlain in the parish of Holy Trinity; abutments, the land that was of Richard Renger on the east and the street on the west going towards the church of St. James and it extends from the street on the north to the land that was of Stephen Crasser on the south; to hold in fee; rent ½ lb. of pepper or 3d. within the quindene of Easter for all services except the king's socage, 21d. which John and his heirs should pay on Palm Sunday; quitclaim for the canons and their successors for every claim except ½ lb. of pepper; gersuma 100 marks; witnesses, Ralph Eswy, mayor, John son of John son of Viel, Thomas de Durham, sheriffs.

572. [List of those paying quit rent]: John Norman; Ydonia; William de Haddestok, 1 and 5 Ed. II; John Pulsham, 1 Ed. III; John Aubrer, 32 Ed. III; Thomas Hanhamsted, 48 Ed. III; Richard Lyons, 1 and 3 Ric. II and the tenement is situated on the east side of Cordwaynstret between the tenement of John Crouch on the south and the king's street on the north.

573. Total of this parish 3d. and it is tithed at this in the king's exemplification.

[f. 110] IN THE PARISH OF ST. OLAVE BREDSTRET

574. Note: Benet abbot of Stratford and convent granted to Peter prior and convent 5s. *p.a.* quit rent from certain land which Walter Pappekertel 'le Tailiator' held of them as appears by Charter Fourteen[1] of several parishes.

    1. **1015**.

575. [List of those paying quit rent]: Walter Puppekertel; Richard Puppekertel; Robert Furmage; Walter Blund; Roger de Overe; Henry de Waldegrave who granted the tenement to John de Norhamtone who paid 5s. as appears by their charter[1] enrolled 13 Ed. I; Peter de Newcastle (*de novo castro*), 1 and 19 Ed. II and 1 Ed. III; Roger Payable, 6 Ed. III; Thomas Kendale, 30 Ed. III and the tenement is situated on the west side of Bredstrete.

1. H.R. 15 (38).

576. Note: Time out of mind the priory has had 1 lb. of cumin at Michaelmas from a tenement once of Henry Kyngisson in the parish of St. Olave as appears in a rental with the letter 'G' and after Henry; Laurence de Hereford; John de Norhamtone, 1 Ed. II; William de Norhamtone, 19 Ed. II. [20 lines blank].

577. Total of this parish 5s. and it is tithed at this in the king's exemplification.

[f. 110v] IN THE PARISH OF ST. NICHOLAS COLDABBEY

578. [1197–1221] Grant of Peter prior and convent to Alan Kyng of a certain shop in the parish of St. Nicholas in the West Fish Market (*apud Westpiscaria*) which is next on the east to a shop which Richard de Hese holds of the canons; in width at the front along the street and everywhere (*ubique*) $2\frac{1}{4}$ ells and in depth from the street to the house of Consaldus $3\frac{5}{8}$ ells; rent 7s. *p.a.*; if the grantee or his heirs wish to sell then the prior and convent to have the preference by 12d.; swore fealty; to hold without ill intent and miskenning; gersuma $\frac{1}{2}$ mark; witnesses, John Burg(um), Walter Blund, Walter Black (*Nigro*).

C.A.D., i, A 1695, and ii, A 2510.

579. [List of those paying rent]: Alan Kyng; Alan But; Walter de Belch; Richard Palmer; Richard Flynthard who granted the land to William Prodehom who paid 7s. as appears by their charter[1] enrolled 9 Ed. II; William Prodehom, 19 Ed. II and 1 Ed. III; John Tryple, 19 Ed. III [See also after **580**] as appears by the following plea.

1. H.R. 44 (75).

580. *Common plea held in the Husting, Mon. 7 Mar. 1345.*
The prior seeks against John Tryple and Katherine his wife a shop and a solar as gavelet according to the custom of the City and says that they hold of him and Holy Trinity at a rent of 7s. *p.a.* of which William[1] Poley, once prior, was seised by William Prodehomme; the rent was 119s. in arrears on the day of the suing out of the writ on 29 Nov. 1343 for seventeen years past; the tenement could not be distrained for a year and a day and he seeks it etc; John and Katherine by their attorney recognise that they hold of the prior at a rent of 7s. and the prior recovers for a year and a day unless the defs. pay the arrears whereupon the prior by his attorney Alan de Horewode remits the arrears.

1. *Rectius* Roger.

St. Nicholas Cole Abbey

579 contd. John Tryple until 8 Ric. II; the churchwardens of St. Nicholas as appears by the following acquittance.

581. Acquittance from William Haradone, prior, and convent noting receipt from Reginald Darkyngton and John Neweton, citizens and fishmongers, and wardens of the goods of the church of St. Nicholas Coldabbey, 20s. sterling in full payment of all arrears of rent; sealed counterparts; dated London 30 Sep. 1419 [f. 111] and this shop is situated on the north side of Oldfyschstret.

582. Grant by Richard Hese of 12d. of quit rent from his messuage (*managium*) in the parish of St. Nicholas at West Fishmarket; abutments, the land of Ralph Carbunel and the land of Walter Blund; if the rent is unpaid, the canons are allowed to enter the grantor's shop and take naam until they are satisfied both as to the rent of the shop and this quit rent; the canons gave 10s. sterling; witnesses, Walter Bruning, Stephen the Fishmonger (*Piscar*), Eudo the Fishmonger.

    C.A.D., ii, A 2480.

583. [List of those paying quit rent]: Richard Hese; Walter Belegh.

584. [1222–48] Grant of Richard prior and convent to Ralph de Bixile of a shop at West Fishmarket which Ralph Trey formerly held; abutments, the shop of Henry Kyngeston and the shop of Hugh de Newton and it has in width on the front along the street, $2\frac{1}{4}$ ells and in depth from the street to the land of Denise la Vileine, $3\frac{5}{8}$ ells; rent 5s. *p.a.*; the grantee is not to sell or pledge to Jews nor to lease to anyone else without the permission of the canons; if he wishes to lease or sell the fee, the canons are to have an advantage of a bezant of 2s. over other buyers; swore fealty; gersuma 40s.; witnesses, John Vyel, alderman, Henry Kyngsone.

    C.A.D., ii, A 2725.

585. [List of those paying rent]: Ralph de Bixile; John le Kyng; John Kyng who granted the shop to Robert Ely and Thomas Edmund who paid 5s. to Holy Trinity as appears by their charter[1] enrolled 15 Ed. II; T. Edmund, William Edmund, 19 Ed. II and 1 and 6 Ed. III; John Cambrygge, 30 and 48 Ed. III; John Poynant, 49 Ed. III and 8 Ric. II; William Chambere throughout Hy. IV.

    1. H.R. 50 (112).

586. [f. 111v] [1222–48] Grant by Richard prior and convent to Hugh Upchurch, fishmonger, of a certain shop in the Fishmarket in the parish of St. Nicholas, abutments, the shop of Adam de Passeto on the west and the shop of Ranulf le Treyer on the east in width along the street $3\frac{1}{2}$ ells and 1 in. and in length $3\frac{3}{4}$ ells; the grantee may assign to whomsoever he wishes except Jews and religious; rent 6s. 8d. *p.a.*; swore fealty; gersuma 20s;

St. Nicholas Cole Abbey

sealed; witnesses, John Viel, alderman of this ward.[1] Henry Kyngston, Adam de Plesseto.

1. Bread Street ward (? or Queenhithe).
C.A.D., ii, A 2496.

587. [List of those paying rent]: Hugh Upchurch; John de Crey; Robert Hakeney who granted the shop to Roger de Ely who paid 6s. 8d. as appears in their charter[1] enrolled 15 Ed. II; Roger de Ely, 19 Ed. II and 1 Ed. III; Adam Brabason, 6 and 30 Ed. III; William Newport, 49 Ed. III and 4 Ric. II [See also after **588**] as appears by the following charter.

1. H.R. 50 (56).

588. Charter of William Newport, citizen and fishmonger, since he has inspected the principal charters and muniments of Holy Trinity, he has noted that his shop which he acquired (*perquisivi*) from Robert Brabason is held by an annual rent of 6s. 8d. payable to Holy Trinity; the shop is in a lane called West Fishmarket between the shop of John Poyaunt on the east and that of William Tryple, belonging to the chantry of William Prudhom, on the west, both of which are of the fee of Holy Trinity of which it has been seised time out of mind; William concedes that the prior and convent shall be allowed to enter into the shop and distrain on all his goods and chattels until the rent is paid together with damages; sealed by William and with the seal of the convent; dated London 30 Sep. 1380; witnesses, John Hadle, mayor, Walter Doget, William Knightecote, sheriffs.

C.A.D., ii, A 2488.

587 contd. Thomas Hougate throughout Henry IV [f. 112] and this tenement is situated on the north side of the line called Oldfyschstret.

589. Note: Ralph le Justice granted to Richard prior and convent 3s. *p.a.* of quit rent from a shop once of John Schonk as appears in Charter Eighteen[1] of several parishes.

1. **1019**.

590. [List of those paying quit rent]: John Schonk; Matilda Lo(v)ekyn; Nicholas S(um)d; Richard de Hakeney; Roger de Ely, 1 Ed. II; William Stoulard, 5 Ed. II; Walter de Reynham, 6 and 30 Ed. III; John Lac, 32 Ed. III; Agnes Lac, 48 Ed. III and 8 Ric. II; William Kelcyll or Chaumbrer or Con(u)errs, throughout Hy. IV and Hy. V and 1 Hy. VI as appears by the following indentured acquittance.

591. Acquittance of William prior and convent declaring that they have received of William Convers or Kelshill, citizen and fishmonger, 18s. in full payment of arrears from his shop in Oldfyschstret; abutments, the shop of John Ardern(ne), esquire, on the east and the shop of John Ascheton, citizen and fishmonger, on the west and the king's street on the south and north; in full payment of arrears of 3s. *p.a.* of quit rent; sealed by William Convers and the prior and in further evidence and witness the seal of the venerable and discreet man William Sevenok, alderman, is placed on these indentured acquittances; dated London 5 Apr. 1423.

    C.A.D., iv, A 7326.

592. Total of this parish 21s. 8d. and it is tithed at this in the king's exemplification.

[f. 112v] IN THE PARISH OF ST. MILDRETHE BREDSTRET

593. Note: William the Chamberlain granted to Richard prior and convent 12s. of quit rent from certain land in the parish of St. Mildred as appears by Charter Seventeen[1] of several parishes.

    1. **1018**.

594. Recognisance of Roger son of Richard son of John that he owes 12s. *p.a.* of quit rent which William the Chamberlain formerly gave as dower (*maritagium*) to Margaret his daughter given in marriage to Gilbert de Podyngden, from certain of Roger's land with stone houses built thereon in the parish of St. Mildred Virgin at the corner of Bredstret paying to the canons for ever 12s. *p.a.*; sealed; for this recognisance and confirmation the canons gave the grantor 2 marks of silver; done at London 4 Apr. 1243; witnesses, John Viel, John de Codres, Laurence Corner.

595. [List of those paying quit rent]: Roger son of Roger; William le Cornur; William le Sta(u)ndon; Roger Palmer, 1 and 19 Ed. II and 1 and 5 Ed. III who bequeathed all the aforesaid to Beatrice his wife, as appears by his testament[1] enrolled 5 Ed. III and then the land was divided for Nicholas Tamworth paid 6s. *p.a.* and John Horwode 6s. *p.a.*, 33 Ed. III: after N. Tamworth; James Cok, 49 Ed. III; Arnold Pykeneye, 3 and 8 Ric. II; John Langhorne, 6 Hy. IV; Alice Langhorne, 2 Hy. V; Thomas Frowyk or Shadword, Hy. VI[2] [no year stated]: after John Horwode; William de Walcli(v)e as appears by charter enrolled 34 Ed. III; Robert Rois, 48 Ed. III; Isabel Newport, 3 and 8 Ric. II; Adam Walcreth, 11 Hy. IV; Alan Everhard, 12 Hy. IV; Sayerus Acres, 11 Hy. VI;[2] John Acres 33 Hy. VI[2] and these tenements are situated adjacent on the north side of Knyghtryderlane.

    1. *C. Wills*, i, 363.
    2. In a later hand.

596. [1253–4] Exchange between John prior and convent and William Viel, citizen, by which Holy Trinity quitclaimed to William 7s. *p.a.* of quit rent which he was accustomed to pay from a tenement once of Elias le Kant(er) in the parish of St. Augustine by St. Paul's churchyard; for which quitclaim William gave to the canons 5s. *p.a.* of quit rent from two shops in the parish of St. Mildred between the tenement that was of Nicholas le Juvene and the lane through which there is a way (*per quam itur*) opposite the church of St. Margaret; if the rent falls into arrears, the canons are allowed to take naam without any impediment and to distrain on the tenement [f. 113] in

St. Michael Queenhithe

the parish of St. Augustine until they are satisfied; chirograph sealed; witnesses, Nicholas Bat, mayor, Richard Picard, John Norhamtone, sheriffs.

    C.A.D., i, A 1605.

597. [List of those paying rent]: William Viel; Martin Cup(gher); John Viel, 1 and 5 Ed. II and 1 Ed. III; John Wodgate, 30 Ed. III; Richard Chatisle, 48 Ed. III; Isabel Norable, 49 Ed. III and 8 Ric. II; William Rasyn, 22 Ric. II, 6 Hy. IV and 2 Hy. V; Thomas Lovett and the limits of this tenement are shown in the charter.

598. Total of this parish 17s. and it is tithed at this in the king's exemplification.

[f. 113v] IN THE PARISH OF ALL HALLOWS BREDSTRET

599. Note: Ralph Blound bequeathed to the prior and convent 2 marks of quit rent from a tenement of John Gysors on the corner of Bredstret as appears in Testament One[1] of several parishes enrolled Mon. 12 Feb. 1296.

    1. See **1031**.

600. [List of those paying quit rent]: John Gysors; his widow; Elias de Suthfolk, 1 Ed. II; John de Hynton, 30 Ed. III; his widow, 32 Ed. III; Henry Hynton, 37 Ed. III; Margery Pykard and Francus [*sic*] Gysors, 49 and 3 Ric. II; John Vynent, 12 Ric. II and the tenement is situated on the west corner of Bredstret opposite Cheap.

601. Total of this parish 26s. 8d.

[f. 114] IN THE PARISH OF ST. MICHAEL AD RIPAM

602. Note: William the Chamberlain gave to Holy Trinity 20s. of quit rent from land with houses which was of John Colem(an) as appears in Charter Seventeen[1] of several parishes.

    1. **1018**.

603. [List of those paying quit rent]: John Colem(an) [See also after **604**] as appears by the following recognisance.

604. [before 1260] Recognisance of John Colem(an) that he owes a quit rent of 20s. *p.a.* for all his tenement in Tymbheth as far as the Thames near Batoneslane and that this is binding upon himself and his heirs; sealed; witnesses, Thomas son of Thomas, alderman of this ward,[1] Alan Bal(an), Baldwin le Greyner.

    1. Queenhithe; he was alderman for Cheap, 1260–5.

603 contd. The abbot of Lesnes, and the tenement is situated on (*super*) the Thames.

St. Benet Paul's Wharf

605. Total of this parish 20s. and it is tithed at this as appears in the exemplification of King Richard.

[f. 114v] IN THE PARISH OF ST. MARY SOMERSET

606. Note: In the year of grace 1236 in the 15th year of the priorate of Richard, Richard Renger the executor of Roger Ducis gave to Holy Trinity for the soul of Roger 2s. *p.a.* from a house in the parish of St. Mary which William de Stanys held, as appears by Charter Sixteen[1] of several parishes and also by the king's exemplification.

   1. **1017**.

607. [List of those paying quit rent]: William de Stanis; Adam Meremearer; Richard Meremearer; Richard Gladewyn; John de Bloxham, 1 and 19 Ed. II and 1 Ed. III; John Bole, 30 Ed. III; Walter Flynt, 40 Ed. III; his widow, 49 Ed. III; John Maynard, 8 Ric. II.

608. Total of this parish 2s. and it is tithed at this in the exemplification of King Richard.

[f. 115] IN THE PARISH OF ST. MARY MAGDALEN IN WEST FISHMARKET

609. [1170–97] Grant of Stephen prior and convent to William Basset[1] and his heirs by the law of inheritance to hold land in the Fishmarket in the parish of St. Mary; rent 30d. *p.a.*; this land the canons had of the gift of Osbert Torneis and it is of the soke of G(or)aleng; in depth 108 ft. and in width 24 ft.; William swore fealty; gersuma one gold piece (*aureum*) and 2 'barsos'; witnesses, Richard the priest of the chapel, Richard the priest of St. Mary Magdalen, Ernald the priest of St. Mary Somerset.

   1. William *genero* Basset; ? the son-in-law of Basset.
   C.A.D., ii, A 2423.

610. [List of those paying rent]: William Basset; William Rufus; Laurence Rufus; his widow; John de Algate, 1 and 3 Ed. II who granted the tenement to John de Montague (*Monte Acuto*) who paid 2s. 6d. as appears by their charter[1] enrolled 3 Ed. II; Adam de Montague; Ralph de Lynne, tailor, who bequeathed the tenement to London Bridge as appears in his will enrolled 12 Mar. 1359.

   1. H.R. 38 (20).

611. Total of this parish 2s. 6d. and it is tithed at this in the exemplification of King Richard.

[f. 115v] IN THE PARISH OF ST. BENET WEST

612. [1147–67] Grant by Ralph prior and convent to Hugh the Palmer of land which Algar held in fee; rent 8s. *p.a.*; to hold as long as he pays this rent and is faithful to the church; swore fealty and gave 1 lb. of pepper and

St. Benet Paul's Wharf

1 lb. of cumin as gersuma; witnesses, Algar the priest, Hugh the priest, Ralph the deacon[1] or rather (*vel potius*) the abbot and convent of Stratford gave Holy Trinity 8s. from certain land in the same parish as appears by Charter Fourteen[2] of several parishes.

    1. Inserted.   2. **1015**.
    C.A.D., ii, 2173 (ii).

613. [List of those paying rent]: Hugh Palmer; Stephen Crass[us]; Richard Potell; John Potell, 1 and 19 Ed. II and 1 Ed. III; Richard Lac who had two daughters married viz. Alice to Robert Marny and Katherine to John at Pole between whom all the possessions of the dead father were divided and thus the above-mentioned tenement was assigned to Katherine who paid 8s. as appears in a charter[1] enrolled 39 Ed. III and Katherine was paying, 3 Ric. II, as appears in an acquittance[2] of the quittances of several parishes; Richard Forster, 20 Ric. II; Henry Haltone, 1 Hy. IV.

    1. H.R. 93 (49–52).   2. **1042**.

614. [1170–97] Grant by Stephen prior and convent to Richard Rufus in fee of all the land which Geoffrey Constable, canon of St. Paul's, once held of Holy Trinity which was in front of the yard (*ante curtem*) which belonged once to two brothers, Archdeacons Richard Ruffus and Richard de Belmeis; the land extended on the west to the street on the east (*versus west usque ad vicum versus east*) paying to Holy Trinity 4½d. *p.a.*; rent 3s. 6d. *p.a.*; Richard swore fealty; gersuma one London sextary of wine; witnesses etc.

    C.A.D., i, A 1485.

615. [List of those paying rent]: Richard Rufus who paid 1d. for the adjacent tenement formerly of Robert son of Walter as appears in a charter written on the following folio at this sign;[1] William de Turri [See also after **616**] who granted Holy Trinity 3s. from the same tenement as appears by the following charter.

    1. The sign is a trefoil.

616. [1251–2] Grant by William de Turri, citizen, to John prior and convent of 3s. *p.a.* of quit rent in the parish of St. Benet out of that mark of annual rent which William le Viel was accustomed to pay the grantor from the tenement which he held of him, together with 43d. which the grantor already pays to Holy Trinity; for this grant, the canons remitted to the grantor 4s. *p.a.*, with arrears which are owed to them from empty land in the parish of St. Mary Magdalen by West Fishmarket for which the grantor had been impleaded in the Husting; chirograph sealed; witnesses, Adam de Basing, mayor, Nicholas Bat, Laurence de Frowyk, sheriffs.

    C.A.D., i, A 1487.

615 contd. William Viel; Robert de Turri; Hamon Perarys paying 6s. 7d. [See also after **617**] as appears by the following recognisance.

St. Gregory

617. [1290–1] Recognisance of Hamo Perariis, clerk, in which he binds himself and his heirs to pay 6s. 7d. *p.a.* to Holy Trinity which he had as a gift from William de Turri, late citizen, as appears in a charter of gift which he has inspected; [f. 116] if the rent is in arrears the canons shall take naam and distrain in all the tenement; for this recognisance, the prior and convent remitted all arrears up to Easter 1291; chirograph sealed; witnesses, Ralph de Sandwich, warden, Thomas Romayn, William le Leyr, sheriffs, Richard Aswy, alderman of this ward.

    C.A.D., i, A 1486.

615 contd. Thomas Peryere, 29 Ed. I, who sold the tenement to William de Bristol who paid 6s. 7d. as appears by their charter[1] enrolled 36 Ed. I; John de Niewbery, 1 and 19 Ed. II and 1 Ed. III; John Darcy, 6 Ed. III; Simon Kegworth, 30 Ed. III; Thomas Morlee who bequeathed the tenement to the maintenance of a chapel in the church of St. Benet as appears in his will[2] enrolled 42 Ed. III; the churchwardens of St. Benet and the tenement is situated on the east side of a street which goes from Poulisheyn to Pouliswharf between the tenement of Henry Halton on the north and [incomplete].

    1. H.R. 30 (64) *rectius* 29 Ed. I.   2. *C. Wills*, ii, 111.

618. [1231–2][1] Grant by Richard prior and convent to Robert son of Walter and his heirs of 8s. *p.a.* of quit rent which Holy Trinity has from the messuage and houses which were of Osbert de Camera of its fee; rent 1d. *p.a.*; sealed (*munimine roboravimus*); witnesses, Andrew Bukerel, mayor, Richard Reigner, Roger le Duc, Henry de St. Albans, Walter le Bufle, Michael de St. Helens, sheriffs.

    1. The trefoil sign referred to in **615** is here inserted.
    C.A.D., i, A 1485.

619. Total of this parish 14s. 7d. and it is tithed at this in the king's exemplification.

[f. 116v] IN THE PARISH OF ST. GREGORY

620. [1217–21] Grant by Peter prior and convent to Ralph Haryng, 'our chosen friend' and his heirs, of land with houses which Master Brand, once canon of St. Paul's, gave to Holy Trinity; rent 20s. *p.a.*; Ralph swore fealty and to pay his dues without miskenning and fraud; sealed; witnesses, William de Sancte Marie Ecclesia, bishop of London, Master Robert de Watford, dean of St. Paul's, P.[1] treasurer of St. Paul's.

    1. Peter de Ste.-Mère-Eglise.

621. Note: From this 20s. the prior of St. Mary Overy had 6s. 8d., the chapels of the City 10s. and the anchorites (*anachorite*) of the same city 3s. 4d.

622. [List of those paying rent]: Ralph Haryng; Henry de Oxford; John de

St. Faith the Virgin

Dureyn; Thomas Everard; James de Montibus who sold the land to Thomas de Kyngsbery who paid 20s. *p.a.* as in their charter[1] enrolled 3 Ed. I; John Harwe; Master William Melford, 1 and 19 Ed. II and 1 Ed. III; John Mareys who alienated (*forisfidavit*) it to the king; and all the goods are in the king's hand and so until now [1425–7] nothing has come from the property.

    1. H.R. 7 (70).

623. Total of this parish 20s.

[f. 117] IN THE PARISH OF ST. FAITH THE VIRGIN

624. [1108–47] Grant of Norman prior and convent to Theodoric and his heirs of land which was of Brihtmar the priest (*presbiteri*); rent 10s. *p.a.*; to hold as long as the rent is paid; the agreement made before all the canons; witnesses, Te(u)redus the priest, Aluricus the priest, Richard the priest, Bra(n)dus, Godacus Murta, Henry son of Turgisius, Theodoric the Moneyer who entered upon this land gave ½ mark of silver as gersuma to the canons.

625. [List of those paying rent]: Theodoric (*Teodoricus*); Geoffrey Bu[ciunc]te; Gilbert Festigart; William Ely, sacristan of St. Paul's; John Carpenter; Robert Osekyn; William Melford, 1 Ed. II; Alan Brancestre, 19 Ed. II and 1 Ed. III; Alan Brancestere, 6 Ed. III; Christine Salman, 30 Ed. III; Nicholas de Chaddesden and Geoffrey de Chaddesden appropriated this tenement for the chantry of Master Henry de Chaddesden, former archdeacon of Leicester, as appears by inquisition taken before Stephen de Caundysch, escheator, 36 Ed. III.

626. [1362–3] Inquisition declares that it is not to the damage etc. of the king to concede to Master Nicholas, clerk, and Geoffrey de Chaddesden, parson of the church of Longwatton, executors of the will of Master Henry de Chaddesden, former archdeacon of Leicester, that they may give and assign a messuage in Brisstret and one in Paternosterstret which are worth 53s. 4d. from which is paid to St. Paul's 5s. *p.a.* and to Holy Trinity 10s. *p.a.* paid at present by the occupants of the said tenements; and this tenement is situated on the north side of Paternoster street.

627. Note: Benet abbot of Stratford granted to Peter prior and convent 8s. *p.a.* of quit rent from certain land which was of John Marny which Godfrey the Chamberlain held of the same monks in the parish of St. Faith as appears in Charter Fourteen[1] of several parishes.

    1. **1015**.

628. [List of those paying quit rent]: Godfrey the Chamberlain; Laurence the Scot (*Scotus*); Geoffrey the Chamberlain [See also after **629**] who recognised the annual rent as follows.

629. Final concord made between Richard prior and convent and Geoffrey the Chamberlain concerning a tenement which Laurence Scot, goldsmith, held in the parish of St. Faith and concerning which the prior had impleaded Geoffrey as gavelet; Geoffrey recognises in full Husting that he owes 8s. *p.a.* for the tenement which is of the fee of Holy Trinity and concedes for himself and his heirs that the canons may enter, take naam and distrain until the rent is paid; sealed by Geoffrey; done Mon. 21 [*sic*] Aug. 1222, the 1st year of Richard's priorate; acting for the mayor (*agente vices maioris*), Richard Renger, sheriff, William Jonner, Thomas Lambert; witnesses, Serlo Crassus, John Viel.

C.A.D., ii, A 2185.

628 contd. John Carpenter; Roger de Chichester (*Cicestria*); John de London; John Teveresham, 1 and 19 Ed. II and 1 and 6 Ed. III; William Teveresham, 30 Ed. III; Reginald Irchestre, 49 Ed. III; David Mort, 8 Ric. II.

630. Total of this parish 18s. and thus it is tithed by the king as it appears in the king's exemplification.

[f. 117v] IN THE PARISH OF ST. MATTHEW FRYDAYSTRETE

631. [1302–3] Grant of Theobald de Conyngsby, clerk, Walter de Legh, Adam Hallyngby and Stephen de Schefhanger, executors of the will of Henry le Galeis, late citizen, the will read and enrolled in the Husting Mon. 16 July 1302, of 3s. *p.a.* of quit rent from the tenement with houses built thereon that Thomas Brancestre holds in the parish of St. Matthew; abutments, the tenement of William de Causton late of Walter le Galeys on the east and that of Adam de Halyngby on the west; for this grant the prior and convent gave 3s. *p.a.* which they were accustomed to receive from the Friars Minor for a certain 'ar(er)a'; Holy Trinity quitclaims the 3s. for themselves and their successors for ever; the part of the chirograph remaining with Holy Trinity is sealed with the seal of the house and with the common seal of the Friars Minor and the other part remaining with the Friars Minor is sealed with the seal of Holy Trinity; witnesses, John le Blund, mayor, Simon de Parys, Hugh Pout, sheriffs, Nicholas de Farndon, alderman.

C.A.D., ii, A 2179.

632. [List of those paying quit rent]: Thomas de Brancester; John Dallyng, 1 and 19 Ed. II and 1 Ed. III; Alice de Lesueur, 6 Ed. III; John Heldest, 30 and 49 Ed. III; Stephen Kendal, 8 Ric. II and this tenement is situated on the south side of Cheap.

Margin: Nota quod moniales de Clerkenwell habent de eodem tenemento xvs. ijd.

633. Total of this parish 3s.

[f. 118] IN THE PARISH OF ST. AUGUSTINE IUXTA PORTAM

634. Grant by Thomas the Chamberlain son of Robert the Chamberlain to

St. Augustine by St. Paul's

John de Balio of 2s. *p.a.* of quit rent which Andrew the chaplain of St. Augustine next the gate of St. Paul's was accustomed to pay to Thomas from land next to the said church on the north next the street on the west; for this 2s. John de Ballio shall pay to the grantor and his heirs 12d. *p.a.* without fail or miskenning; John gave 1 lb. of pepper as gersuma; witnesses, Ralph de Hakrege, John Alwell.

635. Confirmation by Thomas the Chamberlain of the gift of 12d. *p.a.* of quit rent made by John de Baillio which he had from the 2s. rent which Andrew the chaplain used to pay Thomas; also Thomas granted to Holy Trinity, for the salvation of his soul and those of his father and mother, the remaining 12d. which Andrew paid him in free alms; sealed; witnesses, John son of Daniel, William Gyspo, Richard de Aras.

C.A.D., i, A 1510.

636. [List of those paying quit rent]: Andrew the chaplain who granted the tenement to the canons of Messeden who paid 2s. [See also after **637**] as appears by the following charter.

637. [f. 118 inset][1] Grant by Andrew the chaplain, once of St. Paul's, to the canons of Messenden all that tenement held by him in the Old Fishmarket (*in Veteri Piscaria*); to hold in free alms; the canons to pay 2s. *p.a.* to Holy Trinity and 12d. *p.a.* to Alan son of Peter for all rents and services saving the procession of the church of St. Augustine on solemn days; sealed; witness, Roger the chaplain.

1. A piece of parchment 9 ins. wide and 5⅔ ins. long is inserted between f. 117 and f. 118.

636 contd. [f. 118] Master Andrew Con(v)ers as appears by a plea held in the Husting, Mon. 20 Oct. 1242; the land was adjudged to Holy Trinity with the houses which were held by Master Andrew Conversus, Reinerus de Bungeye gave judgment in full Husting, Ralph Eswy, then mayor, Adam de Rasing [*sic*], Hugh White (*Albo*), sheriffs; Alexander the Whittawer (*Allutarius*); Stephen de Cornhull; Alan Chaundeler; his widow, 1 and 19 Ed. II and 1 Ed. III; Sibyl at Cok, 6 and 30 Ed. III; John Blanket, 46 Ed. III and 8 Ric. II; William Frenyngham, 10 Ric. II; Robert Forster, 4 Hy. IV; John Wydmere, 12 Hy. IV; now the church itself,[1] and this tenement is situated on the east side of Old Chaunge and half this tenement is by the north aisle of the church.

1. Presumably the church of St. Augustine.

638. Note: William the Chamberlain gave to Richard prior and convent 1 lb. of cumin from the land with houses which was of John de Wylehale in the same parish as appears by Charter Seventeen[1] of several parishes.

1. **1018**.

639. [List of those paying quit rent]: John de Wylehale; Joan de Wylehale, 1 Ed. II; Richard de Wylehale, 1 Ed. III; Adam Haket, 35 and 49 Ed. III;

St. Vedast

Roger Shyry(v)e, 8 Ric. II [f. 118v] and this tenement is situated on the south side of Watlyngstret between the tenement of the monks of Tyltey on the west as appears in their charter[1] enrolled 6 Ed. I and that of the late Ingelinerus the Goldsmith from which the prior of the New Hospital has 7s. *p.a.*

1. H.R. 9 (48).

640. Total of this parish 2s. and it is tithed at this in the king's exemplification.

IN THE PARISH OF ST. VEDAST

641. [1258] Grant by John de Wylihale (*Wylehale*), citizen, for the salvation of his soul etc., to John prior and convent of 33s. *p.a.* of quit rent and 1 lb. of cumin or 2d. without the soke of St. Martin's in the Fields (*sine soka sancti Martini in campis et sine secta et sine libertatibus predicte secte pertinentibus*); out of that 32s. 6d. which Alan Godard holds of the grantor in Cheap between Godrunlane and the house which was of Henry Waleys; and also 6d. and 1 lb. of cumin from land which is next to the land of John Travers on the east and the land which Alan Godard holds of the grantor on the west; the canons to hold all the 33s. and 1 lb. of cumin in free alms; rent to the heirs of the grantor's brother William 1 lb. of cumin or 2d. in the octave of Michaelmas; sealed; witnesses, John de Gysors, mayor, Robert de Cornhull, John Adryan, sheriffs.

642. [List of those paying quit rent]: Alan Godard; Katherine Godard; Roger de Lyntona, 5 Ed. II; Henry de Pipehurst, 19 Ed. II then the tenement was divided for William Horwod paid 24s. 8d., Walter Louthe 8s. and William de Wylehale 12d.: after William Horwod; John Ysle, 37 Ed. III; John Isele junior who granted the two tenements to Robert Payn who paid from one tenement 24s. 8d. and from the other which Walter Lowthe held, 8s. to Holy Trinity as appears in a charter[1] enrolled Mon. 29 Feb. 1372; Robert Payn, 49 Ed. III; Richard Betele, 16 Ric. II and 4 Hy. IV; William Tristur: [f. 119] after Walter Louthe; Robert Payn; John Isele junior who granted the tenement to William Lyncoln who paid 8s. as appears by charter[2] enrolled after the feast of St. Margaret 1372 and who paid 16 Ric. II; Stephen Spylnia, 4 Hy. IV; Simon Sewale: and after William Wylehale; his son William to whom his father had bequeathed all the rents he had in Cheap towards (*versus*) the church of St. Michael; William de Assendon; Katherine Assendon; Robert de Wyndesor, 1 and 5 Ed. II; Robert Lyghtfot, 19 Ed. 11; now [1425–7] the master of the Saddlers and the said tenements are situated adjacent between Gutturlane on the east and the tenements of the master of the Saddlers on the west. Note: in the charter[3] of Thomas Hardy enrolled 10 Ed. II on the limits of the above tenement which is situated in breadth between the tenement of Robert Lyghtfoot on the east and extends in length from the tenement of R. Lynton on the north to the king's street of West Chep on the south.

1. H.R. 100 (10). 2. H.R. 100 (88–90). 3. H.R. 45 (67).

St. John Zachary

643. Total of this parish 33s. 8d. and it is tithed at this in the king's exemplification.

[f. 119v] IN THE PARISH OF ST. JOHN ZAKARIE

644. [1147–67] Grant by Ralph prior and convent to Godfrey de Wyndlesores of land in the parish of St. John which Osbert Tornes held; rent 3s. 4d. *p.a.*; the grant to last as long as Godfrey pays the rent and remains faithful to the church; witnesses, L(unn)gus, alderman, Ilgirus.

645. [List of those paying rent]: Godfrey de Wyndlesores or Draper; Walter the Goldsmith or Black (*Niger*); John de Woburne; the hospital of St. Bartholomew; Nicholas de Woburne; William de Aqua who granted the land to Richard de Wylehale, 1 and 19 Ed. II and 1 Ed. III; John Wyrhale, 6 Ed. III; Hugh de Zadelyngstanes, 30 Ed. III; his widow, 42 Ed. III; Nicholas Twyford, 46 Ed. III; William Cresswyk, 20 Ric. II; the hospital of St. Bartholomew.

646. Grant by William prior and convent to Adam de Allyngebery (*Alyngbery*), citizen, of all the empty land in the parish of St. John between Godrunlane and Hoggenlane between that tenement which John de Morpat, lorimer, holds of Holy Trinity; the tenement will remain to the canons entirely (*integraliter*) and contains in length from Godrunlane towards the east $18\frac{3}{4}$ ells and in width at the west end along Godrunlane and in the middle next the gate of the Old Fishmarket $10\frac{1}{2}$ ells and at the east end against the latrine 8 ells 3 ins. and the empty land lies between the tenement of Thomas de Lychfeld on the north and that of John de Sonner; also granted to Adam and his heirs, as an easement, half their aforesaid latrine on condition that Adam and his assigns shall clean (*mundare*) all the latrine at their own charge and on their own land as often as necessary and that they shall find the cost of half the repairs of the latrine; also granted free entry to and exit from Godrunlane to the gate of the old bakehouse (*pistrina*) and Adam and his heirs grant to the prior and convent and their successors free access to and from the bakehouse directly to the lane called Hoggen and to others who may wish to go through, for ever; the grantee and his heirs undertake not to build or to do anything to the detriment of the holding; rent 28s. *p.a.*; if the rent is in arrears Adam concedes for himself etc. that the prior shall take naam and distrain on his tenements both that which he holds on the corner opposite the church of St. Michael of Hoggenlane as well as in the aforesaid land until he is satisfied; warranty except that tenement which John de Morpat holds of the prior and convent; gersuma 20s.; [f. 120] two charters chirographed sealed; one remaining with the prior and convent sealed with the seal of Adam and the other remaining with Adam sealed with the seal of Holy Trinity; witnesses, Ralph de Sandwich, warden, Elias Russel, Henry le Bole, sheriffs; dated 21 Sep. 1292.

647. [List of those paying rent]: Adam de Alyngbery, linendraper (*langiarius*), 1 and 19 Ed. II and 1 Ed. III; Margery Alyngbery, 6 Ed. III; John

St. Mary Staining

Hatfeld, 36 Ed. III; Thomas Hatfeld throughout Ric. II and Hy. IV which Thomas died 5 Oct. 1422 without lawful heirs by whose death the tenement with the bakehouse annexed and two shops in Gutterlane came to William Tretheck by a charter made in his favour by Thomas against the will[1] of his father which was enrolled in the Husting Mon. 16 Oct. 1363 on account of which Holy Trinity sought a writ *ex gravi querela* against William as appears in the following plea.

1. *C. Wills*, ii, 79.

648. *Common plea held in the Husting, Mon. 26 Oct. 1422.*
It is ordered that the sheriff warn William Trethek to be at the next Husting to reply to the prior of Holy Trinity in a plea concerning the execution of the testament of John de Hatfeld senior, late citizen and chandler. Mon. 9 Nov. 1422: William Trethek against the prior of Holy Trinity in the above plea represented by John Good; the prior names in his place John Hethingham against William Trethek. Mon. 30 Nov. 1422: the prior by his attorney offers himself against William Trethek in a plea that according to the custom of the City, it is allowed to each and every citizen to leave his tenements as chattels in his last will to whomsoever he wishes and that John de Hatfeld senior left two shops etc. in Gothernlane to Thomas his son to hold to the said Thomas and his lawfully begotten heirs, so that when Thomas died without heirs the tenement should have remained to Denise the daughter of John and to her lawful heirs and if she died without heirs the tenement should remain in perpetuity to the prior and convent; and William Trethek, after the death of Thomas and Denise without heirs, entered the said tenement and detained it illegally from the prior and the charge is that it is against the wish of the aforesaid testator; William did not come and has a day to essoin etc.; judgment is that the tenement and shops be seized into the hands of the City etc. and that William be summoned to be at the next Husting. Mon. 18 Jan. 1423: it is ordered that the sheriff take into the hands of the City the bakehouse and two shops opposite in Hoggenlane and two shops in Gothernlane [no further record].

649. Total of this parish 31s. 4d. and nevertheless it is tithed at 51s. 4d. as appears in the king's exemplification.

[f. 120v] IN THE PARISH OF ST. MARY DE STANYNGLANE

650. [1223–5] Grant by Richard prior and convent to Peter son of Daniel certain land in the parish of St. Mary; abutments, the land of Peter himself on the south and a little street which leads to Wood street on the north; rent 12d. *p.a.*; sealed witnesses, Richard son of William, mayor, Andrew Bukerel, John T[r]avers, sheriffs.

651. [List of those paying rent]: Peter son of Daniel who recognised the rent [See also after **652**] as appears by the following charter.

652. Recognisance of Peter son of Daniel that he owes a rent of 12d. *p.a.* from certain land which is between his messuage (*managium*) on the north

St. Michael Wood Street

and a little street leading to Wodestret and if the prior and convent cannot take naam he concedes for himself and his heirs that they can take naam and distrain in all his messuage; sealed; given in Jan. 1234; witnesses [as in **650**].

651 contd. Peter Daniel [*sic*]; Philip Goodchep; Master Richard de Staford; John de Norwic; Ralph Basset, 1 and 19 Ed. II and 1 Ed. III; John Schardlowe, 30 Ed. III; Thomas Schardlowe, 48 Ed. III; Richard Tiryton, 3 Ric. II; Robert Ascomb, 12 Ric. II [14 lines blank].

653. Total of this parish 12d.

[f. 121] IN THE PARISH OF ST. PETER WODSTRET

654. Note: the master of the hospital of St. Bartholomew granted to William son of Isabel a certain seld in the parish of St. Peter in Cheap; rent 20s. *p.a.*; and William granted to John Blund a shop next the gate of this seld at a rent of 16s. *p.a.* as appears by the following.

655. Grant by William son of Isabel to John the Goldsmith, son of Bartholomew Blund, all that shop next to the grantor's seld in Cheap towards the west which he holds of the fee of [the hospital of] St. Bartholomew; rent 16s. *p.a.*; John gave 4 gold bezants as gersuma and to Denise, the grantor's wife, 2 gold bezants; witnesses, Ralph de Barra, Nigel the Goldsmith, Bartholomew Blund.

656. Note: John Blund bequeathed to Holy Trinity 4s. *p.a.* of quit rent from the shop [in **655**]; Holy Trinity does not have [? the record of] the will because it was not necessary.

657. [List of those paying quit rent]: Roger the Goldsmith; Thomas de Stanes; Peter de Staundon, 1 Ed. II; John his son, 19 Ed. II; Robert Bret, 8 Ed. III [incomplete] and this tenement is situated on the south side of Cheap between the tenement of the late Thomas Bacwell, once a master goldsmith on the east and that of the nuns of Halywell on the west and Holy Trinity pays tenths to the king for the above 4s. as appears by the exemplification.

[f. 121v] IN THE PARISH OF ST. MICHAEL IN WODESTRET

658. [1222–48] Grant by Richard prior and convent to Geoffrey de Essex, goldsmith, of land next the land of Thomas de A(u)deville on the east containing in length 23 ells and in width on the north side $10\frac{1}{4}$ ells and on the south $10\frac{1}{4}$ ells; rent 5s. *p.a.*; if the grantee or his heirs wish to sell or lease the fee, the canons to have the preference by one gold bezant; swore fealty; gersuma 20s.; witnesses, Norman Blund, draper, Walter Travers, goldsmith.

C.A.D., ii, A 2718.

St. Alban Wood Street

659. [List of those paying rent]: Geoffrey the Goldsmith; Stephen Wa(n)delworth; Geoffrey Frowyk; John Eylond; Edmund Blak who granted the land to Walter Fynchyngfeld who paid 5s. as appears by charter[1] enrolled 10 Ed. I; he granted the land to Robert Burchayn as appears by charter[2] enrolled 1 Ed. II; Robert Burchayn, 19 Ed. II and 1 Ed. III; Thomas Pypehurst, 33 Ed. III [See also after **660**] as appears by the following plea.

    1. H.R. 13 (44).   2. H.R. 36 (106).

660. *Common plea held in the Husting, Mon. 4 Nov. 1359.*
Thomas Pipehurst complained that on Wed. 31 July 1359 the prior came to the pl.'s free tenement in the parish of St. Michael Hoggenlane and took naam worth 6s. 8d. until by gage and pledge of John Burys and John de Bernes, former sheriffs, etc. and the prior defending his action said that the tenement was held of him at a rent of 5s. *p.a.* and that it was 35s. in arrears for seven years past and that 5s. was taken for one year and 20d. for part of another year; Thomas said that he had no interest except *iure uxoris* Joan; he was ordered to have his wife at the next Husting; plea continued Mon. 16 Nov. 1360 when the prior by his attorney, Alan de Horewod, and Thomas by his attorney, John Dauncere, and Joan by her guardian were present and they could not deny that they held of the prior and convent and that the rent was in arrears; the prior retains his naam; Thomas was in mercy; the prior remitted the arrears to Joan and Thomas.

659 contd. Henry Frowyk, 48 Ed. III and 8 Ric. II; John Wyssingshed as appears by the following acquittance.

661. Acquittance of Robert Percy, rent collector of Holy Trinity, that he has received from J. Wyssyngshede 30s. from a tenement in the parish of St. Michael Wodestret; abutments, the tenement of John himself on [f. 122] the north and the lane of Ingestret on the south and the king's highway of Wodestret on the east, in full payment of all arrears of a quit rent of 5s. *p.a.*; seal of the office of the rent-collector and of John attached; dated, 4 Apr. 1412, and the tenement is situated on the west side of Wodestret [27 lines blank].

    C.A.D., ii, A 2460.

662. Total of this parish 5s.

[f. 122v] IN THE PARISH OF ST. ALBAN IN WOODSTRET

663. [1202–3] Grant by Richard Ca(v)el to Holy Trinity of 8s. *p.a.* of quit rent from certain land which Baldwin the Parmenter (*Permentarius*) holds of the grantor on Wood Street in the parish of St. Alban; abutments, the land of Turold the Shoemaker (*sutoris*) which he had of Robert Scrip on the north and the land of Baldwin which he holds of Thomas de Haverhull on the south containing in width along the street 19 ells and in the middle and at the back at the end against the court of Geoffrey Manekyn, 16 ells; the length is from the street to the court of Geoffrey which length contains

St. Alban Wood Street

on the north side from the road to the court 26¾ ells and on the south 21⅞ ells; rent to grantor and his heirs 6d. *p.a.* at Easter and to the heirs of Geoffrey Manekin 6d. *p.a.*; the prior and convent gave 6 marks in silver as gersuma; witnesses, Henry son of Alwin, mayor, Walter Brun, William the Chamberlain (*Camerarius*), sheriffs, William de Haverhull, alderman.

  C.A.D., ii, A 2502.

664. [List of those paying quit rent]: Baldwin the Parmenter then the land was divided for Richard son of Baldwin paid 4s. and Richard Gowell paid 4s.: after Richard Baldwin; Alan Wympler; Beatrice widow of Alan granted the tenement to the nuns of Clerkenwell who paid 4s. as appears in a charter made in favour of the nuns, Gregory Rokesle, mayor, Ralph Blound, John Horn, sheriffs [1275] and the nuns granted the tenement to William Kent [See also after **665**] as appears by the following charter.

665. [1295–6] Lease by Agnes de Marcy, prioress of Clerkenwell to William de Kent, tailor (*cissor*) and citizen, all that tenement which the house has in the parish of St. Alban near Crepilgate by the lease of Beatrice widow of Alan Wympler; abutments, the land of Baldwin the Parmenter on the south and the land of Corold [*sic*] the Shoemaker on the north containing 27¾ ells and in width along the street 9½ ells and at the west end 10¾ ells; rent 24s. *p.a.*; witnesses, John le Breton, warden, Adam de Alyngbery, John de Dunstapel, sheriffs.

664 contd. The nuns of Clerkenwell: after Richard Gowell who granted the tenement to Robert le Marescall as appears in a charter enrolled 23 Ed. I; Thomas de Derby who bequeathed the tenement to Robert le Ca(n)s who granted it to John Pelham; John de Winchester (*Wynton*), 1 and 30 Ed. III; John de Carswell, 34 Ed. III; John Mayn, 49 Ed. III; Gilbert Lyrp(er) or Baker, 3 Ric. II; William Walworth, 8 Ric. II; William Ascham, 1 Hy. IV and these two tenements are adjacent on the west side of Wodestret.

666. [1170–97] Note: that Stephen prior and convent granted to Alban the Tailor land in the parish of St. Alban which was held [f. 123] immediately before him by Ralph the Doctor; rent 2s. *p.a.* to hold as long as the grantee pays the rent without fraud; swore fealty; frontage along the street 21 ft. and in depth 24 ft.; gersuma 2s.; witnesses, Geoffrey Blund, William de Cu(ni)ghope, Hugh Pa(n)chemer.

  C.A.D., ii, A 2719.

667. [List of those paying rent]: Alban the Tailor; Nicholas S(um)d; Richard son of the same Nicholas who granted to John prior and convent 2s. *p.a.* from the said land which Robert de Haketon held.

668. [1250–60] Grant by Richard son of Nicholas Sumd to John prior and convent of 2s. of quit rent from a certain house which Robert de Aketon holds of the canons in the parish of St. Alban; rent to grantor and his heirs

St. Alphege

½d. at Easter; canons gave 18s. in gersuma; witnesses, Stephen Bukerel, alderman of this ward,[1] Thomas de Harang.

> 1. Cripplegate.
> C.A.D., ii, A 2720.

669. Note: Robert Aketon paid 4s. *p.a.* and afterwards Bartholomew de Castro who gave the tenement to the New Hospital of St. Mary outside Byshopisgate as appears by the following charter.

670. Grant by Bartholomew de Castro to the New Hospital of all the land with houses built thereon in the parish of St. Alban; abutments, the tenement of William Bokerell on the north and that of David de Enefeld on the south and the tenement of Isabel Bokerell on the east and the king's street on the west; the grantees are free to sell or lease; the hospital to pay a clove-gillyflower to the grantor and his heirs at Easter and 10s. to the chief lords of the fee viz. to Holy Trinity 4s., to G. le B[r] and his heirs 2s., to the nuns of Klerkenwell 2s. and to the prior of St. Mary Suthwerk 2s.

671. Total of this parish 12s. and it is tithed at this in the king's exemplification.

[f. 123v] IN THE PARISH OF ST. ALPHEGE MARTYR

672. Grant by the convent of Holy Trinity to William the Goldsmith, brother of Godard, of certain land at Crepilgate which Swethmanus held; rent 4s. *p.a.* to hold in fee as long as the rent is paid; swore fealty; gersuma 2 bezants; witnesses, Geoffrey the priest, Algar the priest.

> C.A.D., ii, A 2011.

673. [List of those paying rent]: Geoffrey the Goldsmith; Zakary the Goldsmith; Serlo the Mercer; the nuns of Halliwell; John Lesthild; Robert Burden, 1 Ed. II; Walter Burden, 1 Ed. III who died 13 Ed. III as appears by an inquisition taken before Andrew Aubry, mayor, Roger de Depam, alderman, and Thomas de Maryns, chamberlain.

674. Inquisition taken Thurs. 26 July 1340 to enquire what lands and tenements etc. have descended to John son of Walter Borden, if he is of age, the value of the lands etc. by the oath of Peter at Corn(er), William de Hoo and others who say that John son of Walter has a tenement in the parish of St. Alphege within Cripelgate which Joan widow of John le Hore holds; worth 4 marks *p.a.*; on which John owes 12s. *p.a.* quit rent to the prioress of Haliwell and 4s. *p.a.* to Holy Trinity.

675. Note: the prior was attached to reply to William Borden in a plea of taking naam; William complained that the prior on Fri. 16 Jan. 1360 came to his free tenement in the ward of Crepilgate and took naam worth 6s. 8d. until by gage and pledge of John Chichestre, one of the sheriffs, etc.; the prior by his attorney, Alan de Horerwod, came and defended his action because the tenement was held of him at a rent of 4s. and 2s. was in arrears

St. Alphege

for half a year past and William could not deny this; the prior retained his naam; William Bordeyn in mercy. And afterwards John Bernes.

676. [1170–97] Grant of Stephen prior and convent to Warin the chaplain of land in Philipeslane where Geoffrey the Baker, Pascharius and Richard the Cordwainer (*Corvesarius*) formerly lived; rent 3s. *p.a.*; to hold as long as the grantee pays the rent; swore fealty; [f. 124] gersuma 2s.; witnesses, Geoffrey the chaplain, son of the aforesaid Warin, William the Baker.

    C.A.D., iv, A 7927.

677. [List of those paying rent]: Warin the priest (*presbyter*); Philip his nephew; then the land was divided for Geoffrey Curreour paid 18d. and Nicholas Cambrygge the other 18d.: after Geoffrey Correour; Gunilda his wife; Agnes Westmylle who granted the tenement to Geoffrey de Botham; Simon de Munden; Bartholomew de Castro, 5 Ed. II; William Elsyng, 6 Ed. III; the prior of Elsyngspitel: after Nicholas Cambrygge; Agnes his wife; Robert Derby; John Thorp who granted part of this land to Peter Knut who paid 12d. to Holy Trinity as appears in their charter[1] enrolled 17 Ed. II; afterwards the full sum of 3s. was paid by Matilda Munden, 19 Ed. II; William Elsyng, 6 Ed. III; the prior of Elsyngspitel.

    1. H.R. 52 (67).

678. [1170–97] Grant by Stephen prior and convent to Robert the Cook (*cocus*), whom Ralph Diuinus fostered (*nutrivit*), of that land which Geoffrey the Baker held in the parish of St. Alphege; rent 3s. *p.a.*; swore fealty; gersuma 15d.; witnesses, Walter the chaplain of St. Alphege, Benet de Hull.

    C.A.D., v, A 11858.

679. [List of those paying rent]: Robert the Cook; Nicholas de Cambrige; Robert de Derby; Juliana de Berkyng; John Hayron, 1 and 5 Ed. II; John Payn, brewer, 19 Ed. II and 1 Ed. III; William de Elsyng, 6 Ed. III; the prior of Elsyngspitell.

680. [1170–97] Grant of Stephen prior and convent to Ralph de Wincestre of land built upon which, immediately before, Robert le Parux had in Philipplane; rent 4s. *p.a.*; to hold as long as the rent is paid without ill intent and fraud; swore fealty; gersuma 1 bezant and to the convent one London sextary of wine; witnesses, Geoffrey the chaplain of St. Alphege, Laurence the chaplain, his son.

    C.A.D., iv, A 7926.

681. [1170–97] Grant of Stephen of the same land [in **680**] to William the Baker; rent 3s. *p.a.*

    C.A.D., iv, A 7933.

682. [List of those paying rent]: William the Cook, son of Jordan the Chamberlain; John his son; Nicholas de Cambryge; Robert de Derby;

St. Mary Aldermanbury

Bartholomew de Castro; John de Thorp; Peter the Painter (*Pictor*), 1 and 19 Ed. II and 1 and 6 Ed. III; John Walden, 32 Ed. III; John Bryan, 34 Ed. III; his widow, 37 Ed. III; the prior of Elsyngspitell, 48 Ed. III.

683. Total of this parish 11s. 6d. and it is tithed at this in the king's exemplification.

[f. 124v] IN THE PARISH OF ST. GILES WITHOUT CREPELGATE

684. [1270–1] Grant of Alice widow of Michael de Westmeln' to Eustace prior and convent of 4s. 9d. of quit rent in the parish of St. Giles from land with houses which John de Hailee holds of the grantor; abutments, the grantor's capital messuage on the west and the land and houses of Geoffrey de Katenham, once of Richard de Mora, painter; for the work of the canons for the sick in the infirmary of the priory; if the payment is in arrears, the grantor concedes that the canons shall take naam in the capital messuage aforesaid until they are satisfied; sealed; witnesses, John Adryan, mayor, Henry Wales, Gregory de Rokesle, sheriffs, Bartholomew de Castell, alderman of this ward.[1]

    1. Cripplegate.
    C.A.D., v, A 11864.

685. [List of those paying rent]: John Hayle; Robert le Sacker; John Sacker who granted the tenement to Henry Denicomb as appears by their charter[1] enrolled 5 Ed. III and Henry also bequeathed 1 mark *p.a.* from the same tenement to the church of St. Thomas de Acon as in his will[2] enrolled 22 Ed. III; Alice widow of H. Denicomb, 24 Ed. III; Gilbert Lyrpp(er) who granted the garden belonging to this tenement to Gilbert Prynce as appears in their charter[3] enrolled 6 Ric. II; John Multon, skinner.

    1. H.R. 59 (85).   2. *C. Wills*, i, 504.   3. H.R. 111 (158).

686. Total of this parish 4s. 9d. and yet it is tithed at 28s. as appears in the king's exemplification.

[f. 125] IN THE PARISH OF ST. MARY ALDERMANBERY

687. [1194–5] Grant by Atheliza Holebagge to Gilbert de Reding, spurrier, of all that land in the parish of St. Mary between the land that was of Andrew Senis and the land which Geoffrey Skyrwyt holds; to hold to the grantee and his heirs by hereditary right paying to the lords (*seignuragiis*) of the fee viz. Alfred the Mercer and his heirs 2s. *p.a.*; Gilbert gave the grantor one gold brooch (*firnaculum*); witnesses, Henry son of Ailwin, Roger son of Alan, Robert Bisant, Jukell, then sheriffs.

688. Note: Richard de Flytt and Alice daughter of Alfred granted to the prior and convent of Holy Trinity 6s. *p.a.* of quit rent from two pieces of land, one in Aldermanbery and the other in Bassyngshawe; from the land

St. Mary Aldermanbury

in Aldermanbery 2s. *p.a.* as appears by Charter Twenty-two[1] of several parishes.

    1. **1023**.

689. [List of those paying quit rent]: Richard Blund; Ralph Cant(er); Roger Cant(er); Alice daughter of Ralph Cant(er) who granted to Richard prior and convent 18d. *p.a.* which Roger Cant(er) was accustomed to pay her from the aforesaid tenement as appears by the following quitclaim.

690. [1225] Sale and quitclaim by Alice daughter of Ralph for herself and her heirs to Richard prior and convent of a rent of 18d. *p.a.* which Roger Cant(er) and Marsilia his widow paid the grantor; the prior and convent gave 10s.; witnesses, [Richard] Renger, mayor, Roger Duce, sheriff, Andrew Bukerel, alderman.

    C.A.D., ii, A 1881.

691. [List of those paying quit rent]: at 3s. 6d.; Roger; Stephen le Coteler; Gunote Fererbras; Bartholomew de Castro; Ingellard; John de Schirburne, 1 and 19 Ed. II and 1 and 6 Ed. III who bequeathed the tenement to Margery his widow as appears in his will[1] enrolled 28 Ed. III; his widow, 32 Ed. III; John de Toure, 51 Ed. III and 8 Ric. II; the churchwardens of St. Mary Aldermanbery.

    1. *C. Wills*, i, 680.

692. [1227–9] Grant by Richard prior and convent to Robert de Gypewych, goldsmith, of certain land with houses which is between the land of Matthew Bukerel both on the south and on the north containing in length along the king's street 26 ells and at the south end $17\frac{1}{2}$ ells and at the north end $18\frac{3}{8}$ ells; rent 4s. of quit rent from the tenement that was of William Wyte and 2 marks *p.a.*; the grantee not to destroy the property nor to pledge it to Jews or religious houses; if he wishes to sell, the prior and convent to have the preference by 1 gold bezant; swore fealty; gersuma 6s. 8d.; sealed; witnesses, Roger Duce, mayor, Richard Reinger, Stephen Bukerel, Henry de Cokam, sheriffs.

    C.A.D., i, A 1489.

693. [f. 125v] [1227–9] Recognisance of Robert de Gypwich that he owes 2 marks *p.a.* of rent to Holy Trinity and that this sum shall be paid from his seld in Cheap; abutments, the land of the canons of St. Mary Suthwerk and that of Robert Bassyng on the east; this may be done until the rent from the tenement in Aldermanbery is sufficient to pay the canons; sealed; witnesses, Roger le Duc, mayor, Richard Reinger, Stephen Bukerel, Henry Cokam, sheriffs.

    C.A.D., i, A 1490.

694. [List of those paying rent]: Robert de Gypwich; Ralph Aswy, 1 and 18 Ed. II and 1 Ed. III as appears by Acquittance Six[1] of several parishes and

St. Mary Aldermanbury

then the land was divided for Richard Lac paid 13s. 4d. as appears by the following plea.

    1. **1043**.

695. *Common plea held in the Husting, Mon. 20 July 1338.*
Richard le Lac complains that on Fri. 15 May [1338] the prior came to his free tenement in Aldermanbery and took naam worth 13s. 4d. until by gage and pledge of Nicholas Crane, one of the sheriffs, etc.; the prior said that a piece of land between Richard's gate and the tenement of John Colwell was the place which was held of him at a rent of 13s. 4d. *p.a.* and that he had been seised of the rent by Stephen de Aschwy, kt., his tenant and that the rent was 26s. 8d. in arrears for two years and Stephen could not deny this and the prior retained his naam; Richard in mercy.

696. Note: [partly on f. 126] Richard paid 30 Ed. III and had two daughters, Alice married to Robert Marny and Katherine married to John at Pole between whom the whole possessions of the father were divided and the above tenement [in **695**] was assigned to Alice who paid 13s. 4d. *p.a.* to Holy Trinity as appears in a charter of 39 Ed. III and so Robert Marny paid throughout Ric. II.

697. Note [f. 125v] John de Colwell paid 3s. 4d. *p.a.* [*sic*] for his part as appears by the following plea [See also after **699**].

698. Plea [no heading] John de Colwell summoned to reply to the prior in a plea that he shall do right service for his free tenement which he holds of Holy Trinity, viz. a rent of 13s. 4d. *p.a.* which is 10s. in arrears for three years past[1] on 12 Mar. 1338; the tenement is not distrainable for a year and a day and the prior sought as gavelet etc.; John recognises this and the prior recovered for a year and a day; John in mercy; John satisfied the prior as to the arrears.

    1. Some confusion as to the rent, probably 13s. 4d.

699. Acquittance of Thomas prior and convent acknowledging the receipt from John de Colwell, citizen and mercer, of 40d. sterling in payment of all arrears of a rent of 40d.; indentured acquittance sealed counterparts; dated London Wed. 27 Oct. 1339.

697 contd. [f. 126] John de Colwell, 30 Ed. III; William Bristowe, 32 Ed. III; Simon de Bristowe, 42 Ed. III; the prior of Elsyngspitell, 49 Ed. III and from then on.

700. [1170–97] Grant by Stephen prior and convent to Roger the Bursar of that land which immediately before, Mabel de Tresgoz held of Holy Trinity; rent 4s. *p.a.*; swore fealty; gersuma 5s.; witnesses, John the chaplain of St. Michael, Robert the chaplain who was clerk of Holy Trinity.

    C.A.D., ii, A 1976.

St. Lawrence Jewry

701. [List of those paying rent]: Roger the Burser; Richard Dererkyng; Stephen Bukerel from whom Holy Trinity received a bakehouse or land for a bakehouse which was later called 'Pistrina Bokerel'; John de Osberne who granted the tenement to John de Bockyng who paid 4s. as appears by their charter[1] enrolled 13 Ed. II and John de Bockyng granted it to William le Lac who paid 4s. as a charter of Richard Lac, goldsmith, enrolled 29 Ed. III shows, from which Richard prior Nicholas [*sic*] claimed to have 34s. more from the said tenement. [See also after **702**].

    1. H.R. 17 (22).

701a. [? 1216–17][1] Grant[2] by William de Mandavill for the repose of his soul and for the souls of his father and mother and Geoffrey his brother of a quit rent of 40s. *p.a.* in the parish of St. Mary Aldermanbury; 36s. from lands and tenements which Edward de Cestrehunt, whittawer, held and 4s. from a stone house next the above on the south; if 4s. is not there obtainable, the canons may take this sum from other of the grantee's rents; to hold in free alms; 20s. to be devoted to pittances on the anniversaries of the grantee's father and brother; witnesses, William Dunston, Ralph de Sendon, Henry de Furnell.

    Margin: Vacatur.
    1. If this is a charter of William, 6th earl of Essex (1216–27), it may have been granted before he took seisin in 1217: possibly though not probably a charter of William, 3rd earl (1166–89).
    2. A diagonal line has been drawn through this entry but the reason for its cancellation is not stated.

702. Release from Prior Nicholas of 34s. *p.a.* to Richard Lac; the rent issuing from Richard's holding in the parish of St. Mary between the tenement of William de Bristowe on the north and that of John de Enefeld on the south; saving 4s. *p.a.* of rent which Holy Trinity has received from the tenement; sealed by the conventual seal [f. 126v] and by the seal of Richard Lac; dated London Thurs. 15 Dec. 1355.

    C.A.D., ii, A 1885 and A 1975.

701 contd. John Salesby, 42 Ed. III; John Tours, 49 Ed. III who bequeathed the tenement to the church of Aldermanbury as in his will[1] enrolled after 18 Oct. 1386; the churchwardens of St. Mary Aldermanbury [26 lines blank].

    1. *C. Wills*, ii, 259.

703. Total of this parish 34s. 2d. and it is tithed at this in the king's exemplification.

[f. 127] IN THE PARISH OF ST. LAWRENCE IN JURY

704. [1197–1221] grant by Peter prior and convent to Robert le Curteis (*Curteys*) son of Robert and Margaret his wife daughter of Robert de Bensted of land in the parish and street of St. Lawrence Jewry (*apud*

St. Martin Pomary

Judaismum), which land was given to Holy Trinity by William son of Sabeline, in free alms, and the land next to the land of Robert le Curteis on the north, containing in depth 18½ ells and in width along the street 6¼ ells 2 digits and in width towards the west 6¼ ells 2 digits; rent 4s. *p.a.*; if the grantees wish to sell the land, the canons to have the preference by 1 gold bezant; swore fealty; gersuma 2 gold bezants; witnesses, Walter Gulle, William Bonvalet.

    C.A.D., i, A 1787.

705. [List of those paying rent]: Robert Curteis; Bartholomew Curteis; Thomas de Fowest; Stephen de (F)olond; Robert de Colebrok; Richard Godesname, 1 and 19 Ed. II and 1 Ed. III; Nicholas de Reygate, 6 Ed. III and the tenement was divided for Thomas Legg paid 2s. and Nicholas de Reygate paid 2s.: after Thomas Legg; Ralph de Cambrygge and Walter Forster, executors of Thomas, 31 Ed. III as appears in Acquittance Four[1] of several parishes; William Kyng, 32 Ed. III; Stephen Kyng, 42 Ed. III; his widow, 8 Ric. II: after Nicholas Reigate; Nicholas his son, 32 and 42 Ed. III; John Bosheham, 8 Ric. II.

    1. **1041**.

706. Total of this parish 4s. and it is tithed at this in the king's exemplification.

[f. 127v] IN THE PARISH OF ST. MARTIN POMORUM

707. Note: In the year of grace 1233 Master Alexander de Dorset gave to Holy Trinity with his body two selds and five shops in Cheap next Ismongereslane towards the west and a stone house in the same lane and, next to it, certain land with houses on the north which Holy Trinity leased to Benet Pete(v)yn, a Jew, for a gersuma of 40 marks and a rent of 6s. 8d. *p.a.* as appears by a charter written in Hebrew (*per cartam iudaice scriptam*) and, for that reason, not written here [14 lines blank].

708. [List of those paying rent]: Benet Petevyn; Seymoth, a Jewess; Elias, a Jew; Isabel de St. Albans, 27 Ed. I [See also after **709**] as appears by the following plea.

709. *Common plea held in the Husting, Mon. 9 Mar. 1299.*
Prior Stephen summoned to reply to Isabel de St. Albans in a plea of taking naam; the prior defended his action; it was agreed by licence of the court that Isabel recognises that she holds by a rent of ½ mark and that she is 20d. in arrears; for this recognisance, the prior remitted the arrears.

708 contd. Ralph Balls, 1 Ed. II who granted the tenement to John Redyng who paid 6s. 8d. as appears by charter[1] enrolled 3 Ed. II and John paid 1 Ed. III; John Horerwod, 20 Ed. III; Adam Stable, 30 Ed. III; the executors of the duke of Lancaster gave the tenement to St. Paul's for a chantry in the

St. Michael Bassishaw

church for the duke; the dean and chapter of St. Paul's and the tenement is situated on the west side of Ysmongereslan.

    1. H.R. 38 (21).

710. Total of this parish 6s. 8d. and it is tithed at this in the king's exemplification.

[f. 128] IN THE PARISH OF ST. MICHAEL IN BASSYNGESHAWE

711. [1301] Grant by Stephen prior and convent to John Dode, citizen, of land; abutments, the land of John Dode himself, late of William Sprot on the north and the tenement of Margery la Fo(u)ndur on the south and extending in length from the street on the east side to the curtilage of the Guildhall on the west side; rent 1 silver mark *p.a.* and to Joan, daughter and heir of the late William de Hodestok, and her heirs in the name of Holy Trinity 20s. *p.a.*; gersuma 10 marks sterling; the grantee and his heirs to maintain all buildings and houses in repair at their own costs for ever; if the rent is in arrears, the prior and convent are allowed to enter the grantee's tenement, late of John Sprot, and distrain until they are fully satisfied; sealed counterparts; witnesses, John le Blound, mayor, Peter de Bosenham, Robert le Callere, sheriffs; dated London Wed. 20 Dec. 1301.

    C.A.D., ii, A 1860.

712. [List of those paying rent]: John Dode; John de Steynton, 1 Ed. II; John Berdfeld, 19 Ed. II and 1 Ed. III; Robert Hanham, 13 Ed. III [See also after **713**] as appears by the following plea.

713. *Common plea held in the Husting* [1339].
Robert de Hanham complains that on Fri. 1 Oct. 1339 the prior came etc. and took naam worth 20s. etc. until by gage and pledge of William de Thorney, one of the sheriffs, etc.; the prior came and defended his action because the tenement was held of him at a rent of 13s. 4d. and was 40s. in arrears for three years past and he took 20s. for one and a half years; Robert said that he had no interest in the tenement except *iure uxoris* [no further details].

712 contd. William Thodyngton called Dodenham, 30 and 48 Ed. III; Henry Forster; Adam Fraunceys, 8 Ric. II and the tenement is situated on the west side of Bassingshawe.

714. [1222–48] Grant of Richard prior and convent to Wiganus de Arcubus of land in Bassieshawe; abutments, the land of Wiganus himself and the land of Sabina widow of Alan son of Peter containing in width along the front next the street [f. 128v] on the east $25\frac{1}{4}$ ells and in length, on the north side $10\frac{3}{4}$ ells and on the south side $8\frac{1}{2}$ ells and at the west end $27\frac{3}{4}$ ells; rent 2s. *p.a.*; if the grantee or his heirs wish to pledge or sell the fee, the canons to have the preference by 12d.; swore fealty; if the grantee or his heirs fail to pay the rent for one whole year, the prior and convent shall take into

St. Michael Bassishaw

their own hands the land with houses, if there are any houses, or other fixtures, without compensation (*sine recuperacione*) to the grantee etc. unless the prior and convent wish to show any favour to them in these matters (*nisi prior et conventus eis super hiis aliquam graciam facere voluerint*), gersuma 4s.; witness, Hugh Tabur, alderman.

    C.A.D., ii, A 1923.

715. [List of those paying rent]: Wiganus de Arcubus; the daughter of Wiganus; Martin de Oxford otherwise Preaty who gave the tenement to William Manhale [See also after **716**] to whom Gilbert prior and convent confirmed the gift as follows.

716. [1262–3] Confirmation of Gilbert prior and convent to William Manhale, citizen, of land which he had of the gift of Martin Prea(t)y and Matilda his wife; abutments, the land of William Manhale on the south and the land of the late Richard Queyntel on the north extending from the street on the east side to the land of John le Minour on the west; rent 2s. *p.a.* to Holy Trinity; William gave 1 silver mark for this confirmation and a bezant worth 2s. for pittances; chirograph sealed; witnesses, Thomas son of Thomas, mayor, Robert de Muntpeller, Osbert de Suthfolk, sheriffs, Richard de Walbrok, alderman.

    C.A.D., i, A 1637.

715 contd. Roger Miles, 4 Ed. III; Robert Burton, 6 Ed. III; Thomas Burton, 30 Ed. III; the earl of Oxford, 32 Ed. III; John Frowyk, 34 Ed. III; John de Stowe, 40 Ed. III; John Chapman, 48 Ed. III; the church of St. Mary Magdalen for the chantry of John Ofham and this tenement is on the west side of Bassyngshawe.

717. [1197–1221] Grant of Peter prior and convent to Warin (*Warinerius*) le Sa(vun)er of land which was of Jordan Saet containing in width throughout 23 ells and in length from the street to the east side from the south end (*parte*) $27\frac{1}{2}$ ells and from the north end 26 ells; rent 15s. *p.a.*; if the grantee and his heirs wish to sell or pledge the fee, the prior and convent to have the preference by 1 gold bezant; swore fealty; [f. 129] gersuma 3 marks for pittances; witness, William Wilkyn, woolmonger (*lanarius*).

    Original deed P.R.O. E 42/440.

718. [List of those paying rent]: Warin Soppier; Aldwin Hume; his wife Alice who sold the tenement to John Travers [See also after **719**] who paid Holy Trinity 15s. *p.a.* as appears by the following charter.

719. Grant by Alice daughter [*sic*] of Aldwin Hume, in her widowhood, to John Travers land with houses in the parish of St. Michael; abutments, the land of Hugh Tabur on the south and the land that was of Adam de Ware on the north; [measurements as in **717**]; John is allowed to lease it to

St. Michael Bassishaw

whomsoever he wishes; rent to the grantor and her heirs, ½ lb. of cumin or 1d. within the octave of Easter and to Holy Trinity 15s. *p.a.*; John gave to Alice 40s. gersuma; witness, Hugh Tabur.

    C.A.D., iii, A 6054.

718 contd. Richard de Parys; Edward de Littlinton [See also after **720**] as appears by the following recognisance.

720. [1249–50] Recognisance of Edward de Littlinton, whittawer (*allutarius*), that he holds a tenement which he has bought from John Travers at a rent of 15s. *p.a.* to Holy Trinity; sealed; witnesses, Roger son of Roger, mayor, John de Tolesane, Ralph Hardel, sheriffs.

718 contd. Robert de Araz; Walranius de Recheford, 1 and 19 Ed. II and 1 Ed. III; Thomas Chamberlayn, 6 Ed. III; Henry Chamberlayn, 11 Ed. III [See also after **721**] as appears by the following plea.

721. *Common plea held in the Husting, Mon. 19 Jan. 1338.*
The prior offers himself against Walter de Ca(v)ewediss concerning a plea about one piece (*placea*) of land containing 27 ells in length and 23 ells in width which the prior seeks against Walter as gavelet; this plea was decided otherwise in court, namely at a court held on Mon. 26 Jan. 1360 when it was considered that the prior should recover seisin of the land by default which Walter had made after the land was in the hand of the City on account of Walter's default after he had been summoned three times and essoined; the prior held for a year and a day and still Walter did not come and the prior recovered the piece of land as sharford and Walter was in mercy.

718 contd. Walter Ca(v)ewedisch, 35 Ed. III [See also after **722**] as appears by the following plea.

722. *Common plea held in the Husting, Mon. 24 May 1361.*[1]
The prior seeks against Henry Chamberlayn a messuage as gavelet and says that Henry holds of him at a rent of 15s. and that the late prior Richard de Wymbyssh was seised by Walranus de Rocheford of which £9 was in arrears on the day of the suing out of the writ, 10 May 1336, for twelve years past and the tenement was not distrainable for a year and a day and he sought as gavelet; Henry said that the messuage was in the seisin of John at Re of Aspeden which messuage he gave out of his seisin to Waleranus de Rocheford, kt., to hold for life so that after the death of Waleran the tenement reverted to H. Chamberlayn and Parnel his wife for the term of the lives of Henry and Parnel and their son Thomas and his heirs in perpetuity and Henry has a charter enrolled in the Husting testifying this; [f. 129v] and Henry says that W[aleran] and P[arnel] are dead and he holds for the term of his life with a reversion to Thomas; a process between the parties at a court held Mon. 16 Mar. 1338, and Thomas son of Henry came and he could not deny that the messuage is held of Holy Trinity; the prior to

St. Michael Bassishaw

hold for a year and a day unless he is satisfied; Henry and Thomas in mercy and later they satisfy the prior as to the arrears.

Margin: Placitum precedens deberet hic poni placitum.
1. **722** should precede **721**.

718 contd. The widow of William Carwe, 35 Ed. III; William Calesby, 48 Ed. III; widow of John Middilton, 8 Ric. II and this tenement is situated on the east side of the street of Bassingshawe.

723. Note: Richard Flitt and Alice his wife sold to Holy Trinity 4s. *p.a.* of quit rent as appears in Charter Twenty-two[1] of several parishes.

1. **1023**.

724. Note: William de Haverhill tenant of the said tenement recognised the rent to be due to the prior as appears by Charter Twenty-three[1] of several parishes.

1. **1024**.

725. [List of those paying quit rent]: William de Haverhull then the land was divided for Simon the Carpenter paid 2s. and Martin Smith (*Faber*) paid 2s.: after Martin Smith; his widow; the nuns of Halliwell until now [1425–7]: after Simon the Carpenter; Torald the Carpenter to whom Simon had granted the tenement [See also after **726**] as appears by the following charter.

726. Grant of Simon the Carpenter to Torald the Carpenter of certain land; abutments, the land of Richard Sten(n)batur on the south and the land that was of Martin Smith on the north containing in width along the street $6\frac{1}{2}$ ells and in length from the street to the land of Roger Bat 30 ells, in width at the back 8 ells; to hold in fee paying 2s. *p.a.* to Holy Trinity; gersuma one gold bezant; witnesses, Robert the chaplain, William the Saltmonger.

C.A.D., ii, A 1919.

725 contd. Richard Tynbeter; John Barher; John Enefeld; Thomas Romayn. 1 and 5 Ed. II; Juliana Romayn, 19 Ed. II and 1 Ed. III; William Hanasted, 6 Ed. III; John Aubrey, 30 Ed. III; Hugh Fastolf, 40 Ed. III; John Bryan, 13 Hy. IV as appears by the following acquittance.

727. [1412] Acquittance of William Haradon prior and convent that they have received from John Bryan, citizen, 2s. in payment of arrears from the tenement between that of the prioress of Halliwell on the north and that of John Horer, brewer, and Alice his wife on the south; sealed by both parties; dated London 25 June 1412 [f. 130] and these tenements are adjacent on the east side of Bassyngeshawe.

C.A.D., iv, A 10369.

728. Total of this parish 34s. 4d.

St. Stephen Coleman Street

IN THE PARISH OF ST. STEPHEN IN COLMANSTRETE

729. [1170–97] Grant of Stephen prior and convent to Reimund de Gipeswich, moneyer, that messuage (*managium*) which immediately before him a certain old woman Edith widow of Estmund held 'ad aquam currentem'; rent 2s. 3d. *p.a.*; swore fealty; gersuma 4s.; witnesses, Hubert the chaplain, Roger son of Alan, Walter the deacon.

C.A.D., i, A 1669 and A 1676.

730. [List of those paying rent]: Reimund the moneyer; Gerard Gorgurer; Henry de Oxford; Adam de Basyng; Gilbert Stebheth [See also after **731**] to whom John prior and convent granted more land adjacent at a rent of 3d. *p.a.*

731. [1253–5] Grant of John prior and convent to Gilbert de Stebheth, clerk, of land; abutments, the land of Roger son of Roger and the tenement of Gilbert himself extending towards the wall of the city of London; Gilbert to have the right to lease it to whomsoever he pleases except to Jews and religious houses; rent 3d. *p.a.*; gersuma ½ mark of silver; chirograph; witnesses, Nicholas Bat, mayor, John de Norhamtone, Richard Picard, sheriffs.

C.A.D., i, A 1664.

730 contd. paying 2s. 6d; Gilbert; Eustace de Dertford; Henry de Bydyk, 1 Ed. II who granted the tenement to Richard 'Whytawiere' [See also after **732**] as appears by the following charter.

732. [1308] Grant of Henry de Bydik to Richard le Whitawier of the parish of All Hallows by the Wall of the grantor's messuage and curtilage adjacent; abutments, the tenement of Richard de Lincoln, skinner, and Roger le Purser on the west and the tenement of Richard le Whitawier himself and John son of the late Peter on the east, the northern end of which extends to the king's street and the southern end as far as the land of the aforesaid John son of Peter; to hold the messuage with the garden adjacent; rent 16s. *p.a.* to the grantor and his heirs and 2s. 6d. *p.a.* to Holy Trinity; the grantee obligates himself and his heirs to allow Henry and his heirs to enter a tenement which Richard has next this one with the tenement of Simon Franks on the east and the end of which extends towards London Wall on the north and the garden of John son of Peter and to take naam; sealed counterparts; [f. 130v] witnesses, John le Blount, kt., mayor, William de Basyng, James le Botiler, sheriffs; dated London Wed. 2 Oct. 1308.

C.A.D., iv, A 9808.

730 contd. Richard Witawier, 19 Ed. II and 1 Ed. III; Richard de Staundon, 6 Ed. III; John Denys, 30 and 44 Ed. III; Nicholas Brembir, 46 Ed. III and 8 Ric. II [36 lines blank].

St. Margaret Lothbury

733. Total of this parish 2s. 6d. and nevertheless it is tithed at 10s. 6d. in the king's exemplification.

[f. 131] IN THE PARISH OF ST. MARGARET LOTHBERY

734. [1222–48] Grant by Nigel de Rouen (*Rotomag'*) to Richard prior and convent, for the salvation of his soul etc., of 1 mark *p.a.* of quit rent from land in the parish of St. Margaret; abutments, the land of Laurence Pottar on the west and the land of Walter de Essex on the east; to hold in free alms; the prior and convent to be allowed to distrain and, if necessary, to implead the tenants by gavelet; sealed; witnesses, 'lord' James, 'lord' Gilbert son of Fulk the alderman.

C.A.D., iv, A 10392.

735. [List of those paying quit rent]: Nigel de Rouen; William de Rouen. [See also after **736**].

736. [1222–30] Grant by Walter son of Simon to Richard prior and convent of 5d. *p.a.* of quit rent which William de Rouen was accustomed to pay the grantor from a messuage which is in the fee of the canons; the canons gave the grantor 5s. sterling; witnesses, James the alderman, Walter de Essex.

C.A.D., iv, A 10391.

735 contd. Paying 13s. 9d.; William de Rouen; John Westwode; John de Essex, 1 and 19 Ed. II and 1 Ed. III; William Yfford, 6 Ed. III; William de Yford, 30 Ed. III; John Organ, 48 Ed. III; the rector of the church[1] itself, 8 Ric. II; Edmund Hoddisdon, 6 Hy. IV as appears by the following release.

1. Presumably the church of St. Margaret.

737. [1404] Release by Robert prior and convent to Edmund Hoddisdon of all arrears of rent if he builds upon the land; recites the gift of Nigel of Rouen before the statute of mortmain and describes the holding; if Edmund Hoddisdon, citizen and mercer, builds within ten years, he is relieved of all arrears and the rent for him and his heirs is reduced to 8s. 5d. *p.a.* for forty years from the making of these presents; the prior and convent may distrain and take naam for this 8s. 5d.; at the end of forty years this concession will terminate and the tenants shall pay 13s. 9d. *p.a.*; Edmund Hoddisdon to pay 10 marks sterling at Christmas next following the date of this agreement as is contained in the aforesaid bond (*scriptum obligatorium*) but if he builds within ten years this obligation [f. 131v] shall not be enforced (*sit ullius*[1] *valoris*); dated 30 Sep. 1404.

1. *Rectius* nullius.
C.A.D., iv, A 10390.

738. Total of this parish 13s. 9d.

St. Mildred Poultry

[f. 132] IN THE PARISH OF ST. MILDRETHE

739. Note: Sprakelingus the priest (*sacerdos*) of the church of St. Mildred was made a canon of Holy Trinity in the time of Prior Norman, which Sprakelingus gave with himself the church of St. Mildred with the chapel of St. Mary in Poultry (*Pultrie*); Holy Trinity later granted these to Herbert, afterwards bishop of Avranches (*Abricen'*) for 12d. *p.a.* and afterwards to Alan nephew of the said Herbert for the same rent; Alan granted his 'patrimonium' in London to Richard[1] bishop of Winchester by reason of which the church and chapel remained in the hands of the bishop of Winchester as appears in a book (*quanta*) with the letter 'A' folio 26 and at length, at the instance of friends, Bishop Richard granted the church with the chapel to the canons of Southwark and to Holy Trinity a pension of 10s. *p.a.* therefrom as appears by the following charter.

    1. Richard of Ilchester, bishop of Winchester, 1174–88.

740. [1174–84] Charter of Richard bishop of Winchester granting that the canons of Holy Trinity shall have 10s. *p.a.* from the church of St. Mildreth and the chapel of St. Mary from which they formerly received 12d. *p.a.* and that the canons of St. Mary Suthwerca, to whom he has given these churches, shall hold of Holy Trinity paying to it 10s. *p.a.* but nothing more; present, Bartholomew bishop of Exeter,[1] Master John de Sarum,[2] treasurer of Exeter, Robert[3] archdeacon of Surrey, John Cumin.

    1. Bishop of Exeter, 1161–84.
    2. Treasurer in 1174.
    3. Archdeacon in 1171.

741. [1174–84] Grant and confirmation by the prior and convent of St. Mary Southwek of the 10s. *p.a.* [mentioned in **740**]; witnesses, Bartholomew bishop of Exeter, Master John de Sarum and others.

742. *Plea held at Westminster before John de Stonor and his fellow justices of king's bench, the quindene of Easter 1343.*
The prior of St. Mary Southwerk is in mercy for several defaults and he was summoned to reply to the prior of Holy Trinity that he owed him £10 of arrears of a rent of 10s. *p.a.*; the prior of Holy Trinity said that Prior Richard de Wymbysh was seised of the rent and that it was twenty years in arrears on the day of the suing out of the writ, viz. 28 Sep. 1341; and the prior of St. Mary refused and refuses to pay and says that he is impoverished (*deterioratus*) and that he has loss (*dampnum*) to the value of 100s.; and the prior of St. Mary by his attorney, Richard le Frye, says that he is an ecclesiastical person and seeks judgment whether the court wishes to recognise in this case anything but a spiritual burden (*si curia hic vellet cognoscere in loquela ista nisi aliquid spirituale*) in the way in which the annual rent originally remains (*supersit*); the prior of Holy Trinity offers a chirograph which contains the disposition of Richard bishop of Winchester etc. [**740**]; the prior of St. Mary says that he ought not to be burdened because neither the prior of Holy Trinity nor his predecessors were seised time out of mind of the annual rent and he places himself on the country;

St. Bartholomew by the Exchange

and because the property is in London, a writ is sent to the sheriff that he should come on the quindene of Trinity; on that day, a respite was given to the octave of Michaelmas by R. de Kellhull at St. Martin le Grand; [f. 132v] afterwards, before R. de Kellhull, the jury says that the prior of Holy Trinity and all his predecessors until ten years ago were seised of the annual rent and the prior of St. Mary refused to pay to the damage of 100s. to Holy Trinity; the prior recovers the rent and arrears to the value of 125s.; the prior of Holy Trinity chose to free all the goods and chattels of the prior of St. Mary except the oxen and half of the lands and tenements [which he retains] up to the value of 125s. to hold against the arrears and he had a writ according to statute returnable in the octave of Hilary.

743. Total of this parish 10s.

[f. 133] IN THE PARISH OF ST. CHRISTOPHER

744. [1228–9] Grant and confirmation by Richard prior and convent of the grant which Nicholas and Walter sons of Edmund son of Gerard made to John Travers, citizen, of certain lands and houses which are of the fee of the canons in the parish of St. Christopher next Cornhull from which a rent of 16s. *p.a.* is paid to Holy Trinity; John swore fealty to the canons to pay this rent; sealed; witnesses, Martin de Patishill, dean of London, Roger Duce, mayor, [Richard] Renger, Stephen Bukerel, Henry Cokam, sheriffs.

    C.A.D., i, A 1682.

745. [List of those paying rent]: John Travers; Geoffrey de Winchester (*Wintonia*); Walter le Potter; Richard de Gloucester (*Glovernia*), 1 Ed. II; Walter Waldeschef, 19 Ed. II; Ralph de Cauntebrig, 6 Ed. III who bequeathed the tenement to Henry his son as appears by his will[1] enrolled 39 Ed. III; John Sely, 48 Ed. III; Nicholas Exton, 8 Ric. II and under Hy. IV; Thomas Lancastre; John Gravisend; John Erith, 10 Hy. IV; John Gedney, 2 Hy. V and 3 Hy. VI; Richard Stacy; John Erith aforesaid, 31 Hy. VI; Mary Erith [?10 Hy. VII].

    1. *C. Wills*, ii, 91.

746. Total of this parish 16s. and it is tithed at this in the king's exemplification.

[f. 133v] IN THE PARISH OF ST. BARTHOLOMEW THE LESS[1]

747. [1170–97] Grant of Stephen prior and convent to Richard Walensis of all the land which Robert Pa(n)chier held; rent 3s. *p.a.*; swore fealty; witnesses, Richard the priest (*presbiter*) of St. Christopher, Robert Blund, Alolin.

    1. i.e. St. Bartholomew by the Exchange and not the parish later known as St. Bartholomew the Less within the precincts of St. Bartholomew's Hospital.

748. [List of those paying rent]: Richard Walensis; Geoffrey de Barra; John Gofair(er); Matilda Gofair(er); Giles Oault; Walter Eur(e), 1 and

St. Bartholomew by the Exchange

19 Ed. II and 1 and 6 Ed. III; Thomas Legge, 30 Ed. III whose executors paid the arrears as appears in Acquittance Four[1] of several parishes; John at Harp, 1 Ric. II; John Gille, 1 Hy. V as appears by the following acquittance.

> 1. **1041**.

749. [1413] Acquittance of William Haradon, prior, and convent acknowledging the receipt of 3s. of quit rent from Richard Gylle from his tenement situated between the tenement of the prior of Christchurch Canterbury on the east and that of John Erith on the west and south and Bradestrete on the north; dated London 24 Apr. 1413.

750. [1170–97] Grant of Stephen prior and convent to Richard de Donewich of land which Elias the Moneyer held immediately before him; rent 4s. *p.a.*; to hold as long as he pays the rent without fraud and ill intent; swore fealty; gersuma 1 bezant and to the convent one London sextary of wine; witnesses, Nicholas the chaplain, Roger son of Renus senior.

> *C.A.D.*, ii, A 1905.

751. [List of those paying rent]: Richard de Donewich; Elias the Moneyer; Richard de Bruhull; Osbert Noreys; the New Hospital; Peter Daniel; John Tywe; Michael To(n)y(l);[1] Margery Sybillyng; Roger Sybillyng who granted the tenement to John Bocton who paid 4s. [See also after **752**] as appears by the following charter.

> 1. *Margin*: Tonyl custos pontis Lond' concessit dictum tenementum Thome Sybilyng redditus inde Ponti vs. et ecclesie Christi Lond' iiijs. ut patet in carta que habetur in custodia magistri pontis predicti postea.

752. [1286–7] Grant of Roger Sibillyng son of Thomas Sibillyng, citizen, to John de Bocton, citizen and 'coffrar', of all his land in the parish of St. Bartholomew called 'le Petyt'; abutments, the tenement of Matthew le Paumer on the east and that of John Gofair(er) on the west and the tenement of Walter Hauteyn, William Spinythiot and Richard Lu(m)bour on the south and the king's street on the north; all that the grantor has since the death of his father and Margaret, his mother, to hold to John and to whomsoever he may wish to sell or lease except religious or Jews; rent to the grantor and his heirs, 6d. *p.a.*, to the Bridge 5s. *p.a.*, to Holy Trinity 4s. *p.a.*, to the hospital of St. Giles without London 3s. 6d. *p.a.*, to the heirs of Peter Daniel 1d. at Michaelmas and to Henry de St. Albans and his heirs ½ lb. of cumin at Easter; gersuma [f. 134] £100 sterling; sealed; witnesses, Ralph de Sandwich, warden, Walter Hauteyn, Thomas Cros, sheriffs, Robert de Arraz, then alderman of this ward.[1]

> 1. Broad Street Ward.
> *C.A.D.*, i, A 1625.

751 contd. Robert Patryk; William Sta(u)nford, 1 and 19 Ed. II and 1 Ed. III; John Lyttille, 6 Ed. III who bequeathed the tenement to the prior and convent of Christchurch Canterbury and the tenement is situated on the

St. Martin Outwich

south side of Bradestrete between the tenement of the late Richard Walensis, later of John Gylle on the west [incomplete].

753. Total of this parish 7s.

IN THE PARISH OF ST. BENET FYNK

754. [*c*.1225] Grant by Richard prior and convent to Roger de Mendeham of land in the parish of St. Benet next Cornhull; abutments, the land that was of Hugh Belebarb(er) and the land that was of Aspo(n)is containing in width next the road 14 ells less some inches and at the other end next the garden of James Blund, 11 ells and in length from the said road (*cheminum*) to the said garden 26 ells; rent 3s. *p.a.*; if the grantee wishes to sell or pledge, the canons to have the preference by 12d.; swore fealty; gersuma 2s.; witnesses, James Blund, then alderman, Master Benet de Mandeham.

C.A.D., ii, A 2139.

755. [List of those paying rent]: Roger de Mendeham; Henry le Wympler, 1 Ed. II; John Berden, 19 Ed. II and 1 and 6 Ed. III; Thomas Walden, 30 Ed. III; Henry Fysch, 32 Ed. III; Walter Walden, 36 Ed. III and 8 Ric. II; Walter Strete.

756. [1251–2] Release by John prior and convent to William Aswy, citizen, of 20s. of quit rent which the grantee was accustomed to render from a certain tenement in the same parish; rent 1 lb. of cumin or 1d.; gersuma 15 marks; chirograph; witnesses, Adam de Basyng, mayor, Nicholas Bat, Laurence de Frowyk, sheriffs, Michael To(v)i, John de Gysors, Robert Hardel and other aldermen.

C.A.D., ii, A 1922.

757. [List of those paying quit rent]: William Aswy; the abbot of St. Albans.

758. Total of this parish 3s. 1d. and it is tithed at this in the king's exemplification.

[f. 134v] IN THE PARISH OF ST. MARTIN OTESWYCH

759. [*c*.1225] Grant by William de Brokedych son of Walter to Holy Trinity of 2s. 6d. of quit rent, in free alms, which William de Berkyng, baker, was accustomed to pay the grantor from land between the land that was of James Fynk on the west and land that was of Henry de St. Helen on the east; also William the Baker and his heirs will quit the fee (*acquietabunt finaliter*) against Martin son of William son of Isabel and his heirs of all services which they owe to the fee; William warrants the prior and convent against all; witnesses, James Blund, alderman, Adam de St. Helen, Martin de Oteswych.

C.A.D., ii, A 2668.

St. Martin Outwich

760. [List of those paying quit rent]: William de Berkyng; Andrew Ferron who granted the tenement to Stephen Palmer as appears by the following charter.

761. [*c.*1225–45] Grant of Andrew Ferron and Wymarca his wife to Stephen Palmer and Eufemia his wife of all his land in the parish of St. Martin; abutments, the land late of Henry de St. Helen on the east of the fee of the nuns of Godestowe and the land which James Fink held on the west which land the grantors bought from William de Berkyng, baker, and Matilda his wife containing in length from the road to the land that was of Philip the Cook (*Cocus*) 45 ells and in width along the road 23¾ ells and at the end of the court it contains in width 12½ ells; to hold to the grantees and their heirs and to whomsoever they may wish to assign it; rent to the ancient lords of the fee 5s. 1d., to Martin son of William 15½d., to Holy Trinity 15d. at Michaelmas, and to William son of William 15½d., and to Holy Trinity 15d. at the same term, and to the grantees and their heirs ½ lb. of cumin or 1d. without fail or miskenning; gersuma 16 marks; sealed; witnesses, James Blund, alderman, Ralph the chaplain, writer of this deed, (*compositor huius scripti*), Serlo the Mercer.

762. [*c.*1225–45] Grant by Stephen Palmer and Eufemia his wife to Jordan de Coventre of land [described as in **761** above] which the grantors bought from Andrew Ferron etc.; [f. 135] to hold [as above with the same outgoings as above] to Holy Trinity 15d. at Easter and 15d. at Michaelmas; gersuma 16 marks; witnesses, Robert rector of St. Martin Oteswych, James Blund, mayor.[1]

    1. James Blund was alderman but never mayor.

763. Note: Jordan de Coventre and William Bray paid the rent mentioned in **762**.

764. [1252–3] Grant by John de Coventre to John prior and convent of 10s. 11d. of quit rent which William Bray had been accustomed to pay the grantor from a tenement in the parish of St. Martin which Stephen le Paumier sold to Jordan, the grantor's brother; the canons gave 8½ marks sterling as gersuma; the grantor gave the canons all the muniments he had concerning the aforesaid rent together with his sealed charter; witnesses, John de Tolosan, mayor, William de Dunolm, Thomas de Wimburn, sheriffs.

    C.A.D., ii, A 2258.

765. Note: William son of Roger gave to John prior and convent 23d. *p.a.* of quit rent which William Bray paid to him as appears in Charter Fifteen[1] of several parishes.

    1. **1016**.

766. Note: William Bray paid 15s. 4d. and afterwards Henry the Cofferer and Joan his wife who granted the same tenement to William de Otiswich as appears by the following charter.

767. [1299] Grant of Joan 'le Coffrere' de St. Edmund in her widowhood to Master William de Oteswich, surgeon (*sirugicus*), of London of all that tenement with two shops which John de St. Edmund, once her husband had with the grantor in the parish of St. Martin; abutments, the tenement of the abbey of St. Albans and that of Master William on the west and the houses and tenement once of Thomas de Louekenore and Thomas Brangweyn on the east and extending from the king's street on the south to the garden of the late Gilbert le Kyssere on the north; to hold of the grantee and her heirs begotten by John de St. Edmund; rent 40s. *p.a.* to the grantee and her heirs and to St. Mary Somerset 8d. *p.a.*; Master William to maintain the houses and shops [f. 135v] so that they do not deteriorate; if the rent is not paid Joan and her heirs have the right to enter and take naam and Master William allows entry on all his tenements in this parish; two charters chirographed; witnesses, Elias Russel, mayor, John de Armentieres, Henry de Fingre, sheriffs.

    C.A.D., ii, A 2667.

768. [List of those paying quit rent]: William de Oteswich, 28 Ed. I and 1 and 19 Ed. II; John Brystowe, 6 Ed. III; John Clo(u)e, 20 Ed. III; the lady Alice ?Regina, 32 Ed. III; William Hervi, 46 Ed. III; Richard Olyons, 48 Ed. III and 3 Ric. II; John Wakle.

769. [1262–3] Grant by William Bray to Gilbert prior and convent of 4s. *p.a.* of quit rent from the grantor's land and houses next the parish church of St. Martin opposite the grantor's capital messuage (*managium*) next the land and houses of Richard the Carpenter; if the canons cannot obtain 4s. therefrom he pledges his whole messuage which he holds of their fee so that they can take naam there both for the 4s. and for the rent he previously owed them; the canons gave 40s.; sealed; witnesses, Thomas son of Thomas son of Richard, mayor, Osbert de Suffolc, Robert de Muntpell(ier), sheriffs, Peter Armiger, alderman.

    C.A.D., ii, A 2394.

770. [List of those paying rent]: William Bray; Robert Stere; his widow; Edmund de Hamundesham who granted the tenement to Walter de Leycestre as appears in their charter enrolled 29 Ed. I; Master William Oteswich, 1 and 5 Ed. II and 1 Ed. III; John Broun, 20 Ed. III; Adam Carpenter, 30 Ed. III; Alice Regina, 49 Ed. III and 8 Ric. II; John Chirchman, 6 Hy. IV.

771. [c.1230] Grant by Martin the Baker of Cornhull to Holy Trinity, for the salvation of his soul and that of Eugenia, his wife, of 3s. *p.a.* of quit rent out of 19s. *p.a.* which Isabel widow of Richard Radyng was accustomed to pay the grantor from land which she holds of him in the parish of St. Martin saving to himself and his heirs 16s.; the canons to hold in free alms;

St. Olave Broad Street

if the rent is in arrears the canons are allowed to take naam until 3s. is paid; witnesses, Walter de Insula, alderman, John son of Daniel.

C.A.D., ii, A 2665.

772. [f. 136] [List of those paying quit rent]: Isabel Radyng; Hugh Maresch(all); Ralph Mersch; Henry Merk; the canons of Sothwark; Peter le Hodere; Ralph Crepi(n), 1 and 19 Ed. II and 1 and 6 Ed. III; John Totenham, 30 Ed. III; Walter Tudenham, 48 Ed. III; John Chirchman, 8 Ric. II and 6 Hy. IV which John had two tenements and paid 7s. as appears by the following acquittance [See also after **773**].

773. Acquittance of Robert prior and convent which acknowledges the receipt from John Chirchman, citizen and grocer, of 7s. of arrears of an annual quit rent and another 7s. at Michaelmas from a certain tenement with gardens and shops situated in Bradestrete between the church of St. Martin on the east and the tenement of the Carthusians on the west and 3s. comes, time out of mind, from the tenement and shops between the tenement of the Carthusians on the east and the tenement of the Tailors' hall (del Taillourshalle) on the west; sealed by both parties; dated London 30 June 1405.

772 contd. The Tailors' gild by the gift of John Chirchman who paid until the writing of the cartulary [1425–7].

774. Total of this parish 22s. 4d. and it is tithed at this in the king's exemplification.

IN THE PARISH OF ST. OLAVE BRADESTRETE

775. Note: In the parish of St. Olave Bradestrete[1] was once the church of St. Olave but now the Austin Friars have destroyed the church and made their own church there; but there is another church there namely St. Peter [le Poor].

1. Broad Street.

776. [1170–97] Grant of Stephen prior and convent to Master Gregory the Doctor (*medicus*), of land which Edwin Asse held in the parish of St. Olave; rent 42d. *p.a.*; this land is not built on (*nudata et non edificata*); frontage 34 ft., in the middle 60 ft. and at the end (*in fine*) $66\frac{1}{2}$ ft. and in length 225 ft.; swore fealty; gersuma a repast (*refeccionem dedit*) to the brothers; witnesses, Adam Lac, Laurence the clerk.

777. [List of those paying rent]: Gregory the Doctor; Roger Hereloc; Henry Wal[e]; Fulk de Oily or de Oyry; now the Austin Friars for their place occupies the aforesaid land.

778. Total of this parish 3s.

All Hallows London Wall

[f. 136v] IN THE PARISH OF ALL HALLOWS SUPER MURUM

779. Note: In the time of Prior Norman and of Gilbert the Universal, bishop of London,[1] Henry I being king, a certain priest Ranulf putting off the secular habit to become a monk at Reading, gave to Holy Trinity in free alms the church of All Hallows London Wall and certain land outside the wall and sustained the fraternity of Holy Trinity and afterwards King Henry wrote to Bishop Gilbert who had seized the same church into his hands, as follows.

    1. Bishop of London, *c.* 1127–34.

780. [*c*.1127–34] Writ of Henry I to the bishop of London ordering him to restore seisin to Holy Trinity of its church of All Hallows and its land in his soke which Ranulf the clerk gave to it in free alms, for Holy Trinity has been disseised without judgment; the canons should hold it peacefully as they are able to justify by legal witnesses that they hold it in free alms.

    Cf. *C.A.D.*, iii, A 6682 and *P.R.S.*, x, no. 16.

781. [*c*.1127–34] Letter of the abbot of Reading to Gilbert bishop of London presenting evidence about the church of All Hallows and urging that the canons of Holy Trinity should not be disturbed because a brother of Reading, Ranulf, granted the church to them. The canons allowed Osbern nephew of Ranulf to hold the church from them at a rent of 3s. He begs the bishop to carry out Ranulf's gift.

782. Note: From the time of Henry I, Holy Trinity had land in 'le More' within the wall of the City near 'le Brook' which Jordan Saet and his sisters held at a rent of 2s. *p.a.* plus 4½d. paid on Palm Sunday as appears in a book with the letter 'A' folio 27 and Jordan so paid, then the land was divided for Ida the widow of T. Hauerhyll paid 8d. at Christmas and 1½d. on Palm Sunday and William Vileyn paid 16d. and 1½d. part of which was divided for Richard Longe paid 9½d. and Roger Fraunceis paid 9½d.

783. [List of those paying rent]: after Richard le Lunge; Richard Tailhast who recognised on Mon. [*sic*] 23 Feb. 1288 that he held of the prior at a rent of 8d. plus 1½d. of the soke for certain tenements which he held in the parish of All Hallows London Wall, which tenement lies next to that once of Alexander de Leycestre and the recognisance was registered the same day [See also after **784**].

784. [1288] Note of the recognisance: Richard Tailhast agreed by licence of the court that he held by a rent of 8d. plus 1½d. for socage and for this the prior and convent remitted all arrears of rent, Ralph de Sandwich, warden, William de Hereford, Thomas de Stanes, sheriffs, and the prior had impleaded him by writ of gavelet.

783 contd. John Hore *alias* Heyham, 5 Ed. II and 1 Ed. III; John Baldewyn, 33 Ed. III; Geoffrey at Feld; William Belhume, 48 Ed. III and 5 Ric. II:

St. Ethelburga

after Roger Fraunceys; Alice, his widow, who bequeathed the tenement to the canons of St. Bartholomew; Peter le Hoder who paid to the canon, warden of the refectory of St. Bartholomew, 3s. *p.a.* and to Holy Trinity 8d. plus 1½d. [See also after **785**].

785. [f. 137] [1264–5] Grant by John prior and convent of St. Bartholomew to Peter le Hoder, skinner (*feliparius*) of all the land in 'la More' opposite London Wall between the land that was of Richard le Lunge, gate-keeper, (*janitor*) on the west and the land that was of Geoffrey le Vyleyn on the east extending in length from the street towards the north to the ditch (*fossatum*) of Walbrok towards the south, which land was of Alice widow of Roger le Fraunceis and which Holy Trinity has, in free alms, by the gift of Alice; to hold to the grantee, his heirs and assigns, except religious and Jews; rent 3s. *p.a.* to the warden of the refectory of St. Bartholomew, to the heirs of Walter le Fust(er) ½d. at Easter and to Holy Trinity 8d. plus 1½d.; the warden of the refectory is to be allowed to enter and take naam; gersuma 40s.; chirograph sealed; witnesses, Thomas son of Thomas, mayor, Edward Blund, Peter Aunger, sheriffs, Peter, alderman of this ward.[1]

1. Broad Street Ward.

783 contd. Alexander de Leycestre; Peter le Batur, 5 Ed. II; Nicholas Rumbold, 19 Ed. II; Master Thomas de Pontisbury: after Ida Haverhill; Geoffrey Vileyn; Geoffrey de Rothyng who recognised that he held of Holy Trinity when Gregory de Rokesle was mayor at the beginning of his third year, which recognisance was enrolled 17 Nov. 1277 after he had come into the Husting and recognised his tenure and rent because he had been impleaded there by writ; Alexander de Leycestre; Herman de Walden, clerk; Arnold le Brother, 5 and 19 Ed. II; Master Thomas de Pontesbury, 19 Ed. II and 1 Ed. III for two tenements; John David, 48 Ed. III; John Beverle, 49 Ed. III; Robert Bardolf, 16 Ric. II; Amice his widow.

786. Total of this parish 2s. 4½d. and it is tithed at this in the king's exemplification.

[f. 137v] IN THE PARISH OF ST. ETHELBURGA

787. Grant by Isabel widow of Nicholas de Bisshopsgate, John Wilemy of Graschirch, Osbert the Woolmonger and William le Meguzer, executors of the will of Nicholas, of 5s. *p.a.* of quit rent to Eustace prior and convent from land and houses which Bartholomew the Cook holds in the parish of St. Ethelburga Virgin within Bischopsgate; sealed; witnesses, Walter Hervi, mayor, Walter Potter, John Horn, sheriffs; dated 1 July [1273] and this tenement is on the west side of Bischopsgatstret [26 lines blank].

C.A.D., i, A 1620.

788. Total of this parish 5s. and nevertheless it is tithed at 7s. as appears in the king's exemplification.

St. Augustine Papey

[f. 138] IN THE PARISHES OF ST. AUGUSTINE PAPIENSIS AND ST. MARY AX.

789. Note: This church [St. Augustine Papey] is of the collation of Holy Trinity, pertaining to that soke which Queen Matilda granted to the foundation of this church and it was accustomed to pay 12d. by way of a pension at Michaelmas as appears in ancient books with the letters 'B' and 'C'.

790. [1170–97] Grant of Stephen prior and convent to William Palmer son of Osmund, vintner, of land which lies in front of St. Augustine which Peter son of Le(u)egarius held immediately before him; rent 2s. *p.a.*; swore fealty; the tenement has a frontage along the wall of the City of 31 ells and in depth towards the land of Al(u)ena Mitegolde 23 ells; gersuma 1 bezant and to the convent one London sextary of wine; witnesses, Osbert the chaplain of St. Augustine, Alan the deacon.

791. [List of those paying rent]: William Palmer; Ricarius; Matilda Herberti after whose death the land came into the hands of Holy Trinity [See also after **794**] and was granted to Richard Hadestok

792. [1252–3] Grant by John prior and convent to Richard de Hadestok, chaplain, son of William, of a certain piece of land in the parish of St. Augustine; abutments, the land of the nuns of St. Helen and the land that was of Richard Barun and which abuts on the king's street towards London Wall; rent 2s. *p.a.*; if the grantee wishes to sell, the canons to have the preference by a bezant of 2s.; swore fealty; chirograph sealed; witnesses, John de Tholusan, mayor, Thomas de Wynburne, William de Duream, sheriffs.

C.A.D., ii, A 1974.

793. Total of this parish 2s.

[ST. MARY AXE]

794. Grant of John prior and convent to Richard Hadestok, chaplain, of land with two houses in the parish of St. Mary del Ax; abutments, the land of the nuns of St. Helen on the south and on the north and the land of William Som(er) on the west and the king's street on the east containing in length 29 ells and in width along the land of William Somer $12\frac{1}{2}$ ells 2 ins. and at the east end 13 ells; to hold to Richard and to whomsoever he wishes to assign it; rent 2s. 6d. *p.a.*; gersuma 50s.; [f. 138v] sealed counterparts; done in June 1252; witnesses, Adam de Basyng, mayor, Nicholas Bat, Laurence Frowyk, sheriffs.

791 contd. Richard de Hadestok; the prior of Wenlok who had from Emma la Ruse two lands adjacent in the parish of St. Augustine and St. Mary Axe at a rent of 4s. 6d. as appears by the following plea.

St. Mary Axe

795. *Plea held in the Husting, Mon. 10 Feb. 1360.*
The prior by his attorney, Alan de Horewode, sought against the prior of Wenlok a garden and says that the prior holds of him in the parishes of St. Augustine and St. Mary Axe at a rent of 4s. 6d. *p.a.* and that the rent was 22s. 6d. in arrears on the day of the suing out of the writ, 18 Feb. 1359, for five years past and the garden was not distrainable for a year and a day and he seeks as gavelet; the prior of Wenlok by his attorney, John de Morton, does not recognise that the garden is held of Holy Trinity and says that John, a former prior of Holy Trinity, granted it to him by charter [incomplete].

796. Indenture which witnesseth that Henry prior of Wenlok leased at farm to Richard de Putford and Margaret his wife a certain garden in the parishes of St. Mary at Ax and St. Augustine Paphay within Bisshopsgate; to hold the garden from 2 Feb. 1363 for the term of their lives and to the survivor; rent 10s. *p.a.* and 4s. 6d. *p.a.* to the prior of Crystchurch [Holy Trinity]; the lessees to repair the walls of the garden and maintain them at their own cost; if the rent of 14s. 6d. is unpaid one month after either term of payment, the prior of Wenlok is allowed to enter and distrain until the rent is paid and to repossess the holding; given in the chapel of Wenlok on the above date.

797. [f. 139] Note: John le Brevetur son of William de Chyngelford, bequeathed to Auger son of Henry Godhewe 2s. *p.a.* of quit rent during his lifetime after the death of Auger, he bequeathed it to Holy Trinity as appears in John's will[1] enrolled 11 Ed. I and the executors of John granted the tenement itself to William de Haddon who paid 2s. as appears by a charter[2] enrolled 11 Ed. I.

    1. *C. Wills*, i, 64.   2. H.R. 14 (78).

798. [1258–9] Grant of John prior and convent to Thomas de St. Edmund of land with houses; abutments, the land of John Portar on one side and the land of Katherine widow of Moses on the other extending from the land of William Bray to the king's street called Seyntmaristrete and containing in length 25 ells and 1 in. and in width 13 ells less 3 ins.; rent 6s. *p.a.*; warranty not to pull down or deteriorate the houses but to maintain them; if the grantee or his heirs wish to sell, the prior and convent to have the preference by a bezant of 2s.; gersuma 20s. and 2s. for pittances; chirograph sealed; witnesses, William son of Richard, mayor, Henry de Coventre, Adam Bruning, sheriffs.

    C.A.D., ii, A 2663.

799. [List of those paying rent]: Thomas de St. Edmund who granted the tenement to William de Haddam who paid 6s. as appears by charter[1] enrolled 9 Ed. I and so William paid 8s. *p.a.* for the two tenements which were adjacent; Thomas Coberd called de Leycestria; Henry I(s)lelane, 1 and 19 Ed. II and 1 Ed. III; Peter de Weston, 6 Ed. III as appears by Acquittance One[2] of several parishes; John Trompton, 30 Ed. III; Alice

St. Mary Axe

Trompton, 48 Ed. III; Thomas David, 8 Ric. II; Walter Gautrun, 11 Hy. IV and the two tenements are situated adjacent on the east side of Seyntmarystrete between the tenement of the late Moses de Waltham and now of John Howham on the south and the king's street on the north and the west.

    1. H.R. 12 (12).   2. **1038**.

800. [1222–48] Grant of Richard prior and convent to Moses de Waltham and Katherine his wife of land in the parish of St. Mary; abutments, the land of the canons themselves on the south and that of Oliva, daughter of Robert de Dacia on the north; rent 2s. 6d. *p.a.*; [f. 139v] the grantees not to pledge to Jews or religious; the prior and convent to have the preference by a bezant of 2s.; gersuma 30s.; witnesses, Norman 'le Meguser', Nicholas 'le Meguser', John de Wares, Clement de Joye, John de Waltham.

    C.A.D., ii, A 2662.

801. [List of those paying rent]: Moses de Waltham; Katherine his widow who was later married to Henry Goodhewe who granted the tenement to Auger their son who paid 2s. 6d. as appears in a charter[1] enrolled 15 Ed. I; Henry Godhewe, 1 Ed. III; Denise Plomer or Virly, 6 and 30 Ed. III; John Frytmonger, 33 Ed. III; John Helpiston, 48 Ed. III; his widow, 8 Ric. II; William Man, 1 and 6 Hy. IV; John Hooham, 10 Hy. IV and this tenement is situated on the east side of Seyntmaristrete between the tenement once of Thomas de St. Albans now of Walter Gautrun on the north and the tenement belonging to the sacristan of Holy Trinity on the south.

    1. H.R. 17 (22).

802. [1261–8] Grant by Gilbert prior and convent to Asketin de Halsted, 'meguzer' [whittawer] of land with houses; abutments, the land formerly of the prior of Ware on the north and the land of Edmund Epping on the south containing in length $31\frac{1}{2}$ ells 6 ins. and in width along the road at the west end $10\frac{3}{4}$ ells 2 ins. and at the east end $9\frac{3}{4}$ ells 3 ins.; rent 6s. *p.a.*; the grantee not to deteriorate but to maintain the houses; the prior and convent to have the preference by a bezant of 2s.; swore fealty; gersuma 15s. and 2s. for pittances; chirograph sealed; witnesses, John de Norhamtone, alderman of this ward,[1] Robert Coryngham.

    1. Lime Street Ward.
    C.A.D., ii, A 2431.

803. [List of those paying rent]: Asketin de Halsted; Peter Chyld.

804. [1261–8] Grant by Gilbert prior and convent to Edmund Spyng called del Ax [f. 140] of land in the parish of St. Mary; abutments, the land of Asketin de Halsted on the north and that of John the clerk on the south [measurements, warranty, rent and witnesses as in **802**].

    C.A.D., ii, A 2432.

805. [List of those paying rent]: Edmund Epping or de Ax; Peter Chyld

St. Andrew Cornhill

who paid 12s.; William Skynner, 1 Ed. II; William Wedon, 1 and 6 Ed. III; John Fysch, 30 and 48 Ed. III; Thomas Exton, 8 Ric. II; Thomas Oxbrygge, 1 Hy. IV [21 lines blank].

806. Total of this parish 24s. 6d. and it is tithed at this in the king's exemplification.

[f. 140v] IN THE PARISH OF ST. ANDREW ON CORNHULL OR AT KNAP

807. [1108–47] Grant by Norman prior and convent to Wolfinus Grand of land next to the church of St. Andrew; rent 5s. 4d. *p.a.*; and for *landceape* the grantee gave 12d. to the canons; witnesses, Leowinus the priest (*presbiter*), William son of Wolfwinus, Richard brother of William.

    C.A.D., ii, A 2338.

808. [List of those paying rent]: W. Grand; Huthredus Stede; Edmund Stede; Heluisa de Whytsand; Robert de Coryngham; William Hadham; Henry in le Lane, 1 and 19 Ed. II and 1 Ed. III; John Hadham, 6 Ed. III; Robert Bro(o)m, 30 Ed. III; Robert de la More, 48 Ed. III; Geoffrey Newton, 8 Ric. II; William Reynwell and the tenement is situated on the east side of Sentmaristrete with the cemetery of St. Andrew's church on the south.

809. [1147–67] Grant by Ralph prior and convent to William Facetus of land which his uncle gave to Holy Trinity; to hold in fee; rent ½ mark *p.a.*; witnesses, Robert son of Le(f)tanus, Edmund the alderman.

    C.A.D., iv, A 7285.

810. [List of those paying rent]: William Facetus; Master Henry Facet; William Fulbert, his sister's husband (*sororius*), who had another tenement next to the aforesaid tenements on the east from which the prioress of Halliwell was accustomed to receive 2s. 8d. *p.a.* [See also after **811**] which prioress granted the tenement by an exchange made as follows.

811. Note: in the year of our Lord 1224 an exchange was made between Richard prior and convent and Matilda prioress and the nuns of Halliwell whereby the prioress granted to Holy Trinity 32d. *p.a.* of quit rent which William Folbert gave them from lands and houses to the east of land which William held of them in the parish of St. Andrew towards Algate, paying therefrom 3d. to the socage of the bishop of London, and 9 acres of land in Bracking, 3 acres lying next the messuage of Richard Walensis, 2 acres next the croft of Richard son of David on the north, 3 acres of land in Kingshohell in two places and 1 acre of land lies in Gatisbifeld; and in exchange the prior granted to Halywell 29d. of quit rent from land which John Serlo holds of them in the suburbs of London in the parish of St. Botolph without Bischopgate below the Bar and 9 acres in Bracking in Wodcroft enclosed on every side; chirograph; sealed counterparts; witnesses, John de Solio, Gilbert Fulc.

St. Andrew Cornhill

810 contd. Paying 9s. 4d.; William Fulbert; William le Fayth by whose will[1] enrolled 14 Ed. I, his executors gave to Clement le Stetter one piece of land [f. 141] separate from the chief tenement which lies between the tenement of Gilbert de la Marche on the east and north and the king's street on the south and the tenement of Walter le Blond on the west as appears in a charter enrolled 19 Ed. I; Robert de Parys, potter; Gilbert de la Marche, 28 Ed. I.

    1. ? *C. Wills*, i, 72: William Facet, enrolled 13 Ed. I.

812. Grant by Walter Blundus (*le Blond*) to Holy Trinity, for the salvation of the grantor's soul and that of Matilda his wife etc., of 2s. 6d. of quit rent from land which Philip the chaplain holds of the grantor which land is of the fee of Margaret widow of Gladwin for 20d. and from land which the grantor holds of John the Spicer (*Speciarius*) for 10d.; the quit rent is given for pittances to be given to the canons on the day of the grantor's anniversary; sealed; witnesses, Simon the Merchant, William the Bell-ringer (*Campanarius*), Turgisius, Hugh de Sartrino.

    C.A.D., ii, A 1982.

813. [List of those paying rent]: Walter le Blond, potter; his widow; William le Faith; Robert le Parys, potter; Gilbert de la Marche, potter, 28 Ed. I; William de la Marche, 30 Ed. I; Robert Frekeberewere and N. his wife, mother of the aforesaid William, gave 100s. for the term of her life from the tenement which was situated between the tenement of Thomas brother of William on the east and that of William Peyntour on the west and in width between the street on the south and the garden of the prioress of St. Helen on the north as appears in their charter[1] enrolled 33 Ed. I; Thomas de la Marche.

    1. H.R. 32 (17, 18).

814. [1170–97] Grant by Stephen prior and convent to Odelina widow of William Gant of 2 'mansure' of land adjacent in the parish of St. Andrew next Holy Trinity which Gunter and Lefsi held; rent 3s. *p.a.*; and Odelina put in her place as security for her Ralph the Goldsmith and John Facetus her nephew by touching the holy gospels in the chapter-house of Holy Trinity; she gave one London sextary of wine to the convent and 2s. as gersuma; the land had a frontage on the street of $21\frac{1}{4}$ ells and at the other end on the inside (*introrsus*) a width of 15 ells and in length $34\frac{1}{2}$ ells; witnesses, William Facetus, John his son.

    C.A.D., iv, A 7284.

815. [List of those paying rent]: Odelina; Henry Facet; Gilbert de la Marche, 20 Ed. I who bequeathed all the above tenements to William and Thomas his sons by his will[1] enrolled 28 Ed. I; Thomas de la Marche paid all the rent above-noted, 14s. 10d., except 8d. to Holy Trinity as appears by an assessment (*taxacio concessa*) of the king made 18 Ed. II and Thomas bequeathed the tenements to John Toppesfeld as in his will[2] enrolled 20

St. Andrew Cornhill

July 1332; then they were divided for Walter Chelmesford paid 5s., Henry de Cofford paid 3s. 4d. and John Toppesfeld 5s. 8d: after Walter Chelmesford; Agnes, his widow, 6 Ed. III; Walter Chelmesford, 10 Ed. III [See also after **816**] as appears by the following plea.

    1. *C. Wills*, i, 151.   2. *C. Wills*, i, 375.

816. *Common plea held in the Husting, Mon. 3 Mar. 1336.*
Walter de Chelmesford complains that on Tues. 4 Feb. 1336 the prior came to his free tenement and took naam worth 15s. until by gage and pledge of Walter de Mordon, one of the sheriffs, etc.; the prior defended his action because the tenement was held of the prior at a rent of 5s. *p.a.* [f. 141v] and that it was 10s. [*sic*] in arrears from four years past and Walter did not deny this; the prior retained the naam and Walter is in mercy.

815 contd. Augustine Waleis from the executors of Walter de Chelmesford by charter[1] enrolled 3 May 1343; Robert Broun who granted the tenement to Richard Dunmowe by charter[2] enrolled 6 May 1357; William Chyvele, 46 Ed. III; Edmund son of Simon, 8 Ric. II: after Henry Cofford; John Horwood, 10 Ed. III [See also after **817**] as appears by the following plea.

    1. H.R. 71 (55).   2. H.R. 85 (40).

817. *Common plea held in the Husting, Mon. 3 Feb. 1336.*
John Horwood and Matilda his wife complained that on Tues. 4 Feb. 1336[1] the prior came to their free tenement and took naam worth 10d. etc. until by gage and pledge of W. de Mordon, one of the sheriffs, etc.; to their damage 20s.; the prior said that the rent of 3s. 4d. was 10d. in arrears for the Michaelmas term [as **816** above].

    1. Some error here in the dating.

815 contd. Augustine Waleis and Robert Broun by the charter of John Horwod as by their charter[1] enrolled 19 Ed. III and the tenement contains in width along the road 7 ells 2 ins.; Robert Broun gave the tenement to John Plotte as appears by charter[2] enrolled 31 Ed. III; John bequeathed it to the abbess of St. Clare without Algate as appears in his will[3] enrolled 10 Hy. IV: and after John Toppisfeld this holding was divided for Robert Broun paid 3s. 6d. *p.a.* to Holy Trinity, 32 Ed. III and the hospital of Dortford paid 14d. the same year and the same Robert paid 14d.: after Robert Broun; Roger Rose or de Bury, 43 Ed. III; John Langhorn, brazier; John Chapsheth and John Writele in mercy because they did not pursue their plaint against William prior and convent and William Brole, confrater of the prior, in a plea of taking naam and the prior had return of the naam worth 5s. and replevin: and after the hospital of Dertford; John Clapsheth, 48 Ed. III: and after Robert Broun; Master John Turk, 37 Ed. III.

    1. H.R. 72 (7).   2. H.R. 85 (41).   3. *C. Wills*, ii, 382.

818. [f. 142] [1247–8] Grant of Richard prior and convent to William de

St. Sepulchre Newgate

Kylkenny (*Kilkenny*) of land and gardens with a chapel situated there which were held by Gilbert son of Fulk in Lymstrate; to hold by hereditary right; rent 1 lb. of cumin or 1d. at Michaelmas; gersuma 20 marks; sealed; witnesses, William de Haverhull the king's treasurer, Michael To(v)y, mayor, Nicholas Bat, William Vyel, sheriffs.

C.A.D., i, A 1470.

819. [List of those paying quit rent]: Master William de Kylkeny who bequeathed the tenement to Richard son of Robert, his nephew, which Richard granted it to Philip Lovel as appears by charter enrolled Mon. 5 Nov. 1257.

820. [f. 142v] [1309] Grant by Robert de Kampeden, skinner (*phelliparius*), to William Bonsergaunt (*Bonseriaunt*), moneyer (*minetarius*), of a quit rent of 6s. 8d. from a tenement with shops; abutments, the tenement of James de Lamburne, kt., on the west and the tenement of Thomas son of Gilbert de Marchia on the east and the king's street on the south and the garden of the said James on the north; the grantee gave a certain sum of money as gersuma; sealed; witnesses, Thomas Romeyn, mayor, James de Saint Edmund, Roger le Palmer, sheriffs.

821. Note: Thomas Bonseriaunt called de Algate, son and heir of William, bequeathed 6s. 8d. *p.a.* to Holy Trinity as appears in Will Two[1] of several parishes enrolled 33 Ed. III.

1. **1032.**

822. [List of those paying quit rent]: John Aschford then the tenement was divided and the portion which Thomas Bellhows holds on the west which contains on the street 4 ells 11 ins. pays 22d. and the other portion which Robert Gille holds on the east which contains 11 ells 6½ ins. pays 4s. 10d. [no name of subsequent tenants] and these two tenements are situated adjacent on the north side of Algatestret.

823. Total of this parish 26s. 11d. and it is tithed at this in the king's exemplification.

[f. 143] IN THE PARISHES OF ST. SEPULCHRE WITHOUT NEWGATE AND ST. AUDOENUS

824. [1193–1212] Grant and sale by Ralph son of Robert the Chamberlain to William his brother of 14s. *p.a.* of quit rent which the nuns of Haliwell used to pay the grantor, viz. 10s. from the messuage (*managium*) which the bishop of Chester holds of the nuns along London Wall on the south at Newgate and 4s. from the other side of the street on the north from certain land which Ralph de Lanham holds of the same nuns; abutments, the land that was of Ralph Blund and the land that was of Henry Mansel; William and his heirs to acquit that rent to William Martel of 1 lb. of pepper; William gave Ralph 12 marks sterling; witnesses, Henry mayor of London, Roger son of Alan, Alan son of Peter.

St. Sepulchre Newgate

825. Note: William the Chamberlain gave to Holy Trinity 14s. *p.a.* of quit rent as appears in Charter Sixteen[1] of several parishes; and these names paying 10s.; the nuns of Haliwell; William de Brumtune; now [1425–7] the earl of Warwick and this garden is situated within the walls of the City and the nuns of Haliwell pay the other 4s.

    1. **1017**.

826. [1222–*c*. 1230] Grant of Richard prior and convent to Christine daughter of Ralph the Smith (*Faber*) of Newgate in the parish of St. Sepulchre without the Walls of land which H. le Frances held; abutments, the land of Roger de Beverle on the west and the land of Peter de Bures on the east; rent 2d. *p.a.*; the grantee is not to sell or pledge to Jews; swore fealty; gersuma 1 mark; [f. 143v] witnesses, Joce son of Peter, alderman, John de Woburne.

827. [List of those paying rent]: Christine Smith; Agnes de Hulla; Thomas the chaplain of the hospital of St. Bartholomew.

828. [*c*.1180–5] Grant by William de Newham (*de Niweham*) of the Knights Templar (*minister milicie Templi*) to Ives the chaplain of St. Sepulchre of his land which Gilbert Maillard held of him; rent 20d. *p.a.*; sealed; witnesses, William the preceptor, brother Warin (*Garinus*).

829. [1212–23] Grant by John Testard, clerk, for the salvation of his soul and that of his uncle Ives and of his father and mother, 1 mark *p.a.* of quit rent which William Taillefer, marshal, paid from a tenement in the parish of St. Sepulchre [the tenement in **828**] and is in the fee of the Templars; the canons to hold in free alms of the Templars and paying to them 20d. *p.a.*; sealed; witnesses, Hugh master of the hospital of St. Bartholomew, Gerard master of the hospital of St. Giles.

830. [List of those paying quit rent]: William Taillefer [See also after **831**] to whom Richard prior and convent remitted 16d. of rent.

831. [1222–*c*. 1230] Release by Richard prior and convent of 16d. of rent to W. Tailfer out of a rent of 1 mark from the tenement between that of William Cupere and the land of Roger Palmer; so that the rent is 12s.; sealed; witness, Joce son of Peter, alderman.

830 contd. Richard Merlan; William Sta(m)mer; Robert de Manifeld, 1 and 19 Ed. II and 1 Ed. III; his widow, 6 Ed. III; Richard de Weseby, 30 Ed. III; John Slory, 8 Ric. II and throughout Hy. IV and Hy. V and this tenement is situated on the south side of the street which leads from Newgate towards Holbourne Brygge between the street on the east and north.

832. [f. 144] [1255] Grant of Richard de Hereford, tailor, and Isabel, daughter of Hugh Blund, his wife, to John prior and convent of 7s. *p.a.* of quit rent from certain land with houses which Isabel Ridelestrete held in

St. Sepulchre Newgate

the Bailey in the parish of St. Sepulchre in the suburb of London which John the Cook once held in fee of Adam de Aluerma without Luthgat in the Old Bailey; the canons to hold freely without secular service, tallage and similar exactions; the canons gave 60s.; sealed by Isabel and her husband; witnesses, Ralph Hardel, mayor, Stephen de Ostregate, Henry Walemunt, sheriffs.

833. [List of those paying quit rent]: Isabel Ridelstrete; Roger Convers who granted the tenement to Hamo the Moneyer who paid 7s. as appears by their charter[1] enrolled 6 Ed. I and Hamo granted it to Simon son of Oliver de Carleton as appears by charter[2] enrolled 24 Ed. I; Robert Marny; Thomas Topusfeld, 6 Ed. III; Richard Wylughby, 30 Ed. III; Simon Hosteler, 48 Ed. III; John Slory, 8 Ric. II.

Margin: De eodem, ecclesie sancte Brigide xviijd. et monachis sancti Albani vs. vjd.
1. H.R. 9 (22).   2. H.R. 25 (6).

834. [1303–4] Grant by Thomas le Kyng, butcher, and Alice, daughter of Walter de Holherst, his wife, to Adam de Brachyng, clerk, of ½ mark *p.a.* of quit rent in the parish of St. Sepulchre in 'le Bail' from a tenement which is between that of William Castell on the south and that of John Montagu, fishmonger, on the north and west and the king's street on the east; the rent to be paid in perpetuity on condition that he and his heirs find five wax candles, in memory and honour of the five wounds of Jesus Christ for the salvation of the whole world by his passion and crucifixion, before the Holy Cross in the conventual church of Holy Trinity; Adam and his heirs are allowed to enter and take naam if the rent is in arrears; gersuma 4 marks of good and lawful money; sealed; witnesses, John le Blond, mayor, [f. 144v] William de Combemartin, John de Boreford, sheriffs.

835. [List of those paying quit rent]: Thomas Kyng; Nicholas Burnel.

836. [f. 144] [1305–6] Grant by John de Montagu, citizen and fishmonger, to Master James de Bohun of all that tenement in 'le Bail' situated between the tenement once of Reginald son of Peter on the north and that once of William de Castello called le Armener on the south extending from the street called 'le Bail' on the east to the tenement of the aforesaid Reginald on the west; dated 34 Ed. I.

Margin: Hec carta habetur in Prioratu Sancti Bartholmei.

837. [f. 144v] Note: that Adam de Brachyng granted a quit rent of 6s. 8d. *p.a.* [conveyed to him in **834**] to Ralph prior and convent as appears in Charter Twenty-eight[1] of several parishes.

1. **1029.**
Cf. *C.A.D.*, ii, A 1965.

838. [1197–1221] Grant by Peter prior and convent to Alexander the Mercer of land in Kockeslane in the parish of St. Sepulchre; abutments, the land of William Westmyll and that of Alexander himself containing in frontage 11½

St. Martin Ludgate

ells and in depth 19 ells; rent 12d. *p.a.*; if the grantee wishes to sell, the canons to have the preference by 12d.; swore fealty; gersuma 10s.; witnesses [blank]. This sealed charter is in the house of the nuns of Haliwell and written in their book called 'Domesday' at folio ix.

839. [List of those paying rent]: Alexander Mercer; John Lyndraper; Ralph Clare; Robert le Cordwaner, 36 Hy. III; Arnold the Cook (*cocus*), 15 Ed. I; Hugh le Chandeler, 1 Ed. II; Matilda le Chandeler, 7 Ed. II; Hugh Chandeler, 1 Ed. III; William at Wyle, 30 Ed. III; his widow, 35 Ed. III; John Squyer, 49 Ed. III and 14 Ric. II.

> *Margin:* Patet per pondagium sic monialibus de Kelbourne de eodem tenemento: iijs. Item de eodem Priori ecclesie Christi xijd.

840. [f. 145] Note: that Eustace son of David gave to Holy Trinity 3s. *p.a.* of quit rent from land in Cockislane which was of William the Glazier (*Vitrii*) as appears by Charter Twenty[1] of several parishes.

1. **1021.**

841. [List of those paying quit rent]: Alexander de Godrunelane who granted the tenement to the nuns of Haliwell who pay 3s. *p.a.* as appears in the charter by which it was conveyed to them and which is in their 'Domesday'.

842. Grant by William de Clerkenwell, for the salvation of his soul, to Holy Trinity of 3s. *p.a.* of quit rent which the grantor was accustomed to receive from land with houses built thereon outside the Bar of Smithfield (*extra barram*); abutments, the land once held by Roger Mortimer on the south and that held once by Roger de Wuburne on the north; to hold in free alms on condition that a candle is maintained in memory of William de Colchester and Emma his wife for ever in the chapel of St. Mary; rent to the lord of the fee, certain gloves (*cirotecas*) or ½d. within the octave of Easter; sealed; witnesses, John Balistarius, Stephen son of Andrew, Hugh le Yreis.

843. [List of those paying quit rent]: Ralph the Coalman (*Carbonarius*); Peter at Gate, 33 Ed. III; William Porter, 37 Ed. III; Robert Stowe, 6 Ric. II; William Stowe, 10 Ric. II; now [1425–7] the prior of the Carthusians.

844. Total of this parish 47s. 6d. and it is tithed at this in the king's exemplification.

[f. 145v] IN THE PARISH OF ST. MARTIN LUDGATE

845. [1269] Grant by Ralph the Goldsmith, son of John, to Holy Trinity of ½ mark of quit rent in the suburb of London in the Old Bailey towards Newgate from which tenement Robert de Brackele (*Bracle*) paid the grantor 6s. *p.a.* from a house held of the grantor and 8d. *p.a.* of quit rent from the grantor's capital messuage (*managium*) which is of the canons' fee; to hold to the sacristan; the canons are allowed to enter and take naam in the house

St. Botolph Bishopsgate

of R. de Brackele and in the capital messuage; the canons gave 60s. for this gift; sealed; witnesses, Hugh son of Otto, warden, Robert de Cornhell, Thomas de Basyng, sheriffs.

846. [List of those paying quit rent]: Robert de Brackele 6s. and after him; William Pasfeld, 18 Ed. II as appears by the poundage (*pondagium*) and also 27 Ed. III; Nicholas Sporier and Thomas atte Crouche, 'sporryer', as is evidenced by a plea in the Husting, Mon. 1 Feb. 1361; Thomas Boturwyke, 6 Ric. II: Ralph the Goldsmith 8d. and after him; Roger Convers; Hamon the Moneyer; Simon Carleton; Robert Marney; Thomas Toppusfeld, 6 Ed. III; Richard Wiluby, 30 Ed. III; Simon Hosteler, 48 Ed. III; John Slory, 8 Ric. II.

Margin: St. Sepulchre.

847. Total of this parish 6s. and it is tithed at this in the king's exemplification.

[f. 146] IN THE PARISH OF ST. BOTOLPH EXTRA BYSCHOPSGATE

848. [1197–1221] Grant by Elias son of Richard de Cornhull to Peter prior and convent of 11s. *p.a.* of quit rent in the parish of St. Botolph of which Walter son of Ailred pays 5s. from land alongside that of the nuns of Haliwell on the south and William son of Geoffrey Cras pays 6s. from land which lies against that of the nuns of Keneburne [*sic*] on the south; the canons to hold for ever in exchange for a capital messuage[1] (*managium*) which was of Roger the Tailor in the parish of St. Peter Wodestrete paying therefrom for all services of socage to the bishop of London 4d.; sealed; witnesses, Henry de St. Helena, alderman, Roger Goodcheep, William Basset.

1. Cf. *C.A.D.*, ii, A 1851.
C.A.D., i, A 1663.

849. [List of those paying quit rent]: 5s.: Walter son of Ailred; John Serle; Nicholas Bat; Thomas de Mora; Walter de Lodeby; Richard de Lodeby called More; the New Hospital and the tenement is situated on the east side of Bisshopsgatestret between the tenement of the late John de Haveryng on the south and the tenement of the New Hospital on the north; 6s.: William Goodcheep called Crassus who granted the tenement to the New Hospital of St. Mary without Bishopsgate by charter[1] enrolled 9 Ed. I and this tenement is situated on the west side of Bishopsgate between the tenement that was of St. Thomas de Acris [*sic*] on the north and the tenement belonging to the church of St. Dionis.

1. H.R. 12 (14).

850. Note: that a certain Wulnardus gave to Holy Trinity land in the parish of St. Botolph which the prior and convent granted to Solomon de Stebee at a rent of 8d. *p.a.* as appears in a book with the letter 'A' at folio 29.

St. Botolph Bishopsgate

851. [List of those paying rent]: Solomon de Stebee; Aliena his wife; the nuns of Kelbourne; Richard de Lodeby called More; the New Hospital.

852. [f. 146v] Note: that Richard Renger granted to Richard prior and convent 6d. *p.a.* of quit rent as appears in Charter Sixteen[1] of several parishes.

    1. **1017**.

853. [List of those paying quit rent]: Nicholas Batte; John Cakyer; the New Hospital without Bishopsgate.

854. Note: that the hospital of St. Thomas in Suthwerk has 20d. from the land of the late Nicholas Bat which lies between the land of Nicholas himself on the north and the land of London Bridge on the south as appears in a charter of the said hospital.

855. Sale and quitclaim of William Blund to Serlo Mercer and William Alman for the wardens of London Bridge of all the land with a garden which the vendor has in the parish of St. Botolph between the land of Richard the Cheesemaker (*Casiarii*) on the north and the land of Robert Cuspy on the south and the street called Berwardyslane on the east.

856. [1229–30] Grant by William Agulus to Roger Duke (*Duci*), citizen, of 4s. 6d. *p.a.* of quit rent which Geoffrey the Baker was accustomed to pay the grantor from land and buildings; abutments, the lands of the nuns of Cestrehunt and the lands that were of Robert de la Ford and 3s. *p.a.* of quit rent which Simon le Cureur pays from land; abutments, the land of William son of the priest and that of Walter Lymbarner; rent $\frac{1}{2}$ lb. of cumin or 1d. excepting the service to the chief lords of the fee which Roger must perform; sealed; witnesses, Richard Renger, Robert son of John, Walter de Winchester (*Winton*), sheriffs.

857. Note: Richard Renger granted to Richard prior and convent the 4s. 6d. [in **856**] for the soul of Roger Duc as appears in Charter Sixteen[1] of several parishes.

    1. **1017**.

858. [List of those paying quit rent]: Jordan de Mora; John de Anesty, his son J. Anesty who granted the tenement to the New Hospital of St. Mary who paid 4s. 6d. as appears by their charter, William son of Richard being mayor; and this tenement is situated on the east side of Bishopsgate.

859. [f. 147] Grant by Robert the Saddler (*Sellarius*) to Holy Trinity of 7s. *p.a.* of quit rent from land which Henry Tannar held of the grantor which is of the fee of Henry de Cornhell and adjacent to the grantor's capital messuage (*managium*) which is of the same fee, both of which the grantor holds of Benet Wandegos; rent 3s. *p.a.*; the canons are allowed to take naam in the grantor's messuage; the prior and convent gave 33s. 8d. in

St. Botolph Bishopsgate

gersuma and 2s. to Cecily, the grantor's wife; witnesses, John de Ball, Gilbert the Moneyer (*Monetarius*) then 'socner' of the bishop of London.

860. Release of Peter the Clerk son of Benet Cokelin heir of Robert the Saddler to the prior and convent of the 3s. rent [in **859**] for the salvation of his soul; sealed; witnesses, Osbert dean of the Arches, Walter the Saddler, William the chaplain of St. Botolph.

C.A.D., ii, A 1854.

861. [List of those paying quit rent]: Henry Blond, tanner; his widow; William Blund; Simon de Parys; the New Hospital as appears by the poundage (*pondagium*), and the tenement is situated on the west side of Bishopsgate between the tenement of the church of St. Dionis Bacchirch on the north and the tenement of William Mower on the south.

862. Note: William Agulus gave to Roger Duc 3s. *p.a.* [in **856**] and Richard Renger gave it, for the soul of Roger Duc, to Richard, prior and convent as appears by Charter Sixteen[1] of several parishes.

1. **1017.**

863. [List of those paying quit rent]: Simon Bungey, currier (*le coreour*); Thomas Bungey who granted the tenement to Richard Parys [See also after **864**] as appears by the following charter.

864. [1270–1] Grant by Thomas de Bungeye, currier (*le coreour, coureyur*) and citizen, to Richard de Parys of a tenement in the parish of St. Botolph; abutments, the tenement of Sabina de Salle on the south and that of Hugh le Cornmeter on the north, the street on the west and the garden of the New Hospital on the east containing in width along the king's street $9\frac{3}{4}$ ells 6 ins. and in the middle $11\frac{3}{8}$ ells 2 ins. and at the lower end 15 ells and in length from the street to the said garden 63 ells; [f. 147v] rent to the grantor and his heirs two clove-gillyflowers at Christmas and 3s. *p.a.* to Holy Trinity, to the nuns of St. Helen 15d., to the nuns of Halliwell 15d.; gersuma 10 marks in silver; sealed; witnesses, John Adryan, mayor, Henry le Waleys, Gregory de Rokeslee, sheriffs.

C.A.D., i, A 1680.

863 contd. Stephen Nycol; Thomas Juvenis; John Geryn, 1 and 19 Ed. II and 1 and 30 Ed. III; John Popil, 32 Ed. III; Richard Lambe, 41 Ed. III; Gilbert Champeneys, 44 Ed. III; John Curteys, 47 Ed. III and 11 Ric. II and this tenement is situated on the east side of Bischopsgatstret between the tenement once of Hugh Cornmonger or Cornmeter which now is held by the heir of William Parker on the north, from which the prioress of Kylborne has 7s. 6d. *p.a.* as appears in a charter[1] which Hugh made with Stephen the Spurrier (*Calciatori*) enrolled 10 Ed. I, and the tenement once of Sabina Salle now of the master of Bedlehem on the south.

1. H.R. 21 (25) *rectius* 20 Ed. I.

St. Botolph Aldgate

865. Note: The tenement of Walter Bedfunt of which the prioress of Kelebourne has 7s. 6d. is situated between the tenement once of William Acton on the north and that of John Geryn on the south as appears in a charter[1] of Walter enrolled 29 Ed. I.

    1. H.R. 30 (12).

866. [? before 1193] Grant by Henry son of Alwin to the nuns of Godestowe for the salvation of the soul of King Henry and the grantor's ancestors and predecessors, 5s. *p.a.* of quit rent; to hold in free alms; the rent to be paid from land which Robert the Baker holds of the grantor; sealed.

867. Total of this parish 26s. 8d. and it is tithed at this in the king's exemplification [f. 148 is blank].

[ST. BOTOLPH ALDGATE]

868. [f. 148v] Summary of the statute[1] by which rents may be recovered in the city of London.

    1. *Statutes of the Realm*, i (1810), 222; *Liber Albus*, i, 468.

869. Form of the writ[1] to be issued to the mayor and sheriffs in a case of non-payment of arrears of rent.

    1. *Liber Albus*, i, 62, 186.

870. Note: the form (*natura*) of this writ appears in a plea held in the Husting on the Mon. after or before 6 Dec. 19 Ed. II between the abbot of Waltham and Adam le Treyer concerning a wharf called Holyrodewharf.

871. [f. 149][1] In the time of King Edgar [959–75] thirteen knights 'satis amabiles' obtained from the king derelict land in the eastern part of London. It was granted on condition that each of them should fight three duels, one on land, one below [ground] and one in the water and this was done on one day on what is now called Estsmethfeld. On that day the king named the body the 'knyghtegilda' and defined its limits: from Aldgate to the place where the bars (*barre*) now are, towards the east on both sides of the lane towards the gate now known as Bishoppesgate to the house of William the priest, afterwards of Geoffrey the Tanner then of the heirs of Coluere and then of John Esby now 'de Bursere' and to the south to the Thames as far as a horseman riding into the river at low tide can throw a lance. So all Estsmethfeld with part of the lane on the right going to Doddyngpond in the Thames and the land which now has the hospital of St. Katherine with the mills and the outer wall and the new ditch (*fossatum*) of the Tower stand part of the fee. The wall and the ditch were built by the bishop of Ely as justiciar during Richard's absence in Jerusalem and by this Holy Trinity lost ½ mark of rent and the mill was removed because it was in the way and the greater part of a garden destroyed but Edward I gave them 5½ marks *p.a.*

St. Botolph Aldgate

The knights had no further charter from Edgar, Aethelred or Cnut but their heirs obtained one from Edward the Confessor [See also after **872**].

> 1. Cf. *Cal. Letter-Bk. C*, 216 *et seq.*

872. [1042–4] King Edward to Bishop Aelfweard and Wulfgar, portreeve, declares that his men of the gild of English 'cnihtas' are to have their sake and soke within borough and without over their lands and over their men and as good laws as they had in the days of King Edgar and of the king's father and of Cnut.[1]

> 1. For the original text, translation and commentary, see F. E. Harmer, *Anglo-Saxon Writs* (1952), 231–5, and *British Borough Charters, 1042–1216*, ed. A. Ballard (1913), 126–7, 257.

871 contd. [f. 149v] William son of William the Conqueror granted a charter [See also after **874**].

873. [1087–1100] Notification by William II addressed to M[aurice] bishop [of London], Geoffrey de Mandaville and R. Delpare confirming to the men of the 'Cnihtengild' their land and customs; witness, H[ugh] de Boch[land] at Reading.

> *Reg. A.–N.*, i, no. 444; *Cal. Letter-Bk. C*, 218; *L.M.A.S. Trans.*, v, 488; *British Borough Charters, 1042–1216*, 127.

874. [1100–3] Confirmation of Henry I of **873**; witnesses N.[1] de Mountford, H[ugh] de Boch[land], R. Bigot, at Westminster.

> *Reg. A.–N.*, ii, no. 663; *Cal. Letter-Bk. C*, 219; *L.M.A.S. Trans.*, v, 489.
> 1. *Rectius* R[obert].

871 contd. The priory was founded in 1108. In 1125 certain burgesses of London, descendants of the noble English knights, namely Ralph son of Algod, Wlunard le Douerisshe, Orgar le Prude, Edward Hupcornhille, Blakstan, Alwin his relative, Alwin and Robert his brother sons of Leofstan, Leofstan the Goldsmith and Wizo his son, Hugh son of Wlgar, Algar Secusne, Orgar son of Deremann, Osbert Drinchepyn, Adelard Hornepitesune came to the chapter house and gave to the priory the land and the soke of the 'Anglisshe cnihtegild'. And to establish this they laid Edward the Confessor's charter on the altar and formally offered the church of St. Botolph without Aldgate; witnesses, Bernard prior of Dunstable, John prior of Launde, Geoffrey chamberlain de Clynton, Peter and Nicholas Ci(m)and, [f. 150] William the clerk, Edward son of Alfward, Hugh son of Ralph, his dapifer and chaplain, Edward de Southwark and William his son, Leuegar the priest, Eilwin son of Syredus, Haco the deacon, Algar the priest, Aschellus and many others. The donors sent Orgar le Prude to Henry to obtain his confirmation [See after **875**].

875. [1126] Notification by Henry I addressed to Richard bishop of London and to the sheriff and reeve and all of London and Middlesex confirming the grant by the cnihtegild of the land and of the church of St. Botolph to

St. Botolph Aldgate

Holy Trinity; witnesses, Adeliza the queen, Geoffrey the chancellor, Geoffrey de Clinton, William de Clinton; at Woodstock. Enrolled in Memoranda Book 'C'[1] at the Guildhall.

Margin: Hec carta scripta est in rotulo Regis Ricardi anno regni eius viij°.
1. *Cal. Letter-Bk. C*, 220-1; L.M.A.S. *Trans.*, v, 479; *Reg. A.-N.*, ii, no. 1467.

871 contd. Henry sent Alberic de Ver and Roger the nephew of Hubert to invest the church with its possession. After the collation of the church of St. Botolph, Holy Trinity had the church and its large garden and a canon was appointed to supervise the property and to administer the sacraments to the parishioners. This was in accordance with a letter of Innocent III.

876. Letter of Innocent III permitting Holy Trinity to serve the churches of St. Botolph, St. Katherine and St. Michael [f. 150v] by two of their canons: at the Lateran 18 May 1201.

Letters of Pope Innocent III, ed. C. R. and M. G. Cheney (1967), no. 319 and p. 224.

871 contd. Before the acquisition of the soke Laurence Houndsditch paid 6s. 8d. *p.a.* to the Knyghtgylde and Prior Norman became seised of this rent from a tenement from which Robert de Retherhethe and Agnes his wife, daughter of Laurence Salamon son of Laurence Houdesditch, gave [a further] 3s. rent.

877. [1294–1302] Agreement between Stephen prior and convent and John de Cambio of Canterbury, clerk, that the prior and convent have granted to John a piece (*placea*) of land; abutments, the tenement of Agnes de la More on the east, a tenement of the aforesaid John on the west, the tenement of John le Cofferer on the south and between the great garden of the priory on the north; the grantee, his heirs and assigns to cause to be made their own fence (*propriam clausuram*) and maintain it; the piece contains 12 perches in length and 10 perches in width; rent 9s. 3d. *p.a.*; the said John ex Cambio [f. 151] granted to the prior and convent a certain piece (*quandam particulam*) of the above-mentioned tenement lying between the great garden on the east and the new garden of the priory on the west and between the land of the said John on the south and that of the bishop of London on the north, containing in length $30\frac{1}{2}$ perches and in width 5 perches; exchange sealed by both parties; witnesses, Edmund Trentmars, Peter Berneval, John Pottere.

878. [List of those paying rent]: John of Canterbury (*de Cantuaria*), 1 and 5 Ed. II; Roger Horold, 19 Ed. II and 1 Ed. III; Richard Preston, 31 Ed. III [See also after **879**] as appears by the following indentured quittance.

879. Indenture witnessing that Nicholas prior and convent received from Richard de Preston, citizen, 13s. 4d. in payment of arrears of rent of 9s. 3d. *p.a.*; sealed; dated London 12 Mar. 1357.

878 contd. Simon Haverhull; William Taillour, 35 Ed. III; William Dawe,

St. Botolph Aldgate

49 Ed. III; Simon his son throughout Ric. II and Hy. IV; this tenement is situated on (*super*) Houndesdyche between the land of the priory on the west and that of William Belhome which was once of Roger the Gardener on the east.

880. [1261–8] Grant by Gilbert prior and convent to Roger the Gardener (*Gardinerius*) of Waltham and Alice his wife of a messuage with houses built thereon in the parish of St. Botolph without Aldgate extending from the king's highway of Houndesdyche to the wall of the prior's garden; abutments, the land and houses of Simon son of William Chyngeford on the east [f. 151v] and the land and houses of Richard the Tanner (*Tannator*) on the west; rent 6s. *p.a.*; the grantees are not to destroy or allow the houses to deteriorate but to maintain them and not to build against (*super*) the garden wall; swore fealty; if the grantees wish to sell, the canons to have the preference by a bezant of 2s.; chirograph sealed; the grantees gave a pittance of 2s.; witnesses, Thomas de Wymborne, then 'sockener' of this soke, Robert de Hakeneye, Walter Trentmars.

881. [List of those paying rent]: Roger Gardiner; John le Turnour; Robert his son; widow of the same Robert, 1 and 19 Ed. II and 1 Ed. III; John Gate, 33 Ed. III; Adam Canon, 35 Ed. III; Thomas Saham, 1 Ric. II; his widow, 8 Ric. II; this tenement is situated on Houndesdyche between the tenement of Simon Dawe which was once of John de Cambio on the west and on the east [incomplete].

882. [1222–48] Grant by Richard prior and convent to Stephen Tannar of land; abutments, the grantee's own land on the west; containing in width along the lane (*chiminum*) and 'ubique' 14 ells less a few inches and extending from the lane to the ditch (*fossatum*) of the priory garden; to hold to the grantee's heirs in fee; [f. 152] rent 3s. *p.a.*; if the grantee wishes to sell or pledge the fee, the canons to have an advantage of a bezant of 2s. over other buyers; swore fealty; gersuma 40s.; witnesses, William de Algate, Terricus, Adam, Bartholomew, brothers of the same.

883. [List of those paying rent]: Stephen Tanner; his widow; John le Coferer then the land was divided for Adam de Buctone paid 2s. 6d. and William Wastell paid 2s. 6d.: after Adam de Buctone; William Revell, 31 Ed. III; William Cory, 40 Ed. III; Hauekyn, 46 Ed. III; Stephen Daubeney, 8 Ric. II: after William Wastell; his widow, 1 Ed. II and 1 Ed. III; Richard Rislingbury, 32 Ed. III; Robert Risby, 49 Ed. III and 8 Ric. II and these two tenements are situated adjacent on (*super*) Houndesdyche between a tenement of the priory on the west and the tenement once of Stephen Tanner now of Richard Hammes on the east.

884. [1222–48] Grant of Richard prior and convent to Stephen Tannar of land lying between his own land on the west [in all particulars as **882** except for the insertion of Ralph in the list of witnesses].

885. [f. 152v] [List of those paying rent]: Stephen Tannour; Robert Baddyng [See also after **886**] as appears by the following charter.

St. Botolph Aldgate

886. [1222–48] Exchange between Richard prior and convent and Robert Baddyng by which Holy Trinity quitclaimed to Robert 18d. *p.a.* of the annual rent of 3s.; for which quitclaim Robert gave to the canons all the land which he holds of them between the land once of Roger Bigge and the land of the canons themselves; sealed; witnesses, Solomon son of Laurence, Stephen the Tanner (*Tannatore*), William de Algate, Terricus, Ralph, Bartholomew, brothers.

885 contd. R. Baddyng 1s. 6d.; Henry de Barra; Thomas de Balsham, 1 and 19 Ed. II; Matilda his widow, 32 Ed. III; John Hauekyn, 49 Ed. III; Thomas Morhaunt, 1 Ric. II; Hauekyn 'Brouderer', 8 Ric. II; this tenement is situated on Houndesdych.

887. [1170–97] Grant of Stephen prior and convent to Edric the Merchant (*Mercator*) of land which Richard the chaplain (*capellanus*) bought from Norman son of Alfred Horeh; to hold in fee; rent 4s. *p.a.*; swore fealty; gersuma to the prior 1 bezant and to the convent, a London sextary of wine; witnesses, Robert the chaplain, Ralph the clerk of Stebeheth, Adam his brother.

    C.A.D., iv, A 7353.

888. [List of those paying rent]: Edric; Robert Lambard; his son whose wife Albreda granted the tenement to William son of Stephen de Sharnbrok [See also after **889**] as appears by the following charter.

889. Grant by Albreda widow of Robert Lambert to William son of Stephen de Sharnbrok of a messuage with a curtilage which the grantor had in the suburb of London without Algate in [f. 153] the parish of St. Botolph; abutments, the cemetery of St. Botolph on the west and the land of Mundekinus Trentmars on the east extending from the king's highway on the south to the priory garden on the north; the grantee is free to sell or assign as he pleases; rent to the grantor and her heirs ½d. at Easter, to Holy Trinity 4s. *p.a.*; gersuma 20 marks; sealed; witnesses, Alan la Suche, warden, John Adrian, Luke de Batencuit, bailiffs, Roger de Leuesham; made 10 Jan. 1268.

888 contd. William de Sharnbrok or de Algate who granted the tenement to William de Wellis as appears in a charter[1] enrolled 27 Ed. I; Thomas Bidell, 1 Ed. II; Nicholas Derman, 19 Ed. II and 1 Ed. III; William Cosyn, 30 Ed. III; William Barford, 49 Ed. III; Robert Burford throughout Hy. IV.

    1. H.R. 28 (53).

890. Grant of Gilbert prior and convent to Edmund son of Walter Trentmars of land with houses built thereon which Walter holds of the fee of the priory; abutments, the land of Robert Lambert and the land of Laurence of Ipswich (*de Gipewiz*) extending from the king's street without Algate to the wall of the priory garden; rent 4s. 10d. *p.a.*; 15s. paid for the grant and for arrears; chirograph sealed; [f. 153v] witnesses, Thomas son of Thomas

St. Botolph Aldgate

fitzRichard, mayor, Robert de Mundepelles, Osbert de Suthfolk, sheriffs; done 4 Mar. 1263.

891. [List of those paying rent]: Edmund Trentmars; John the chaplain then the land was divided for Joan Goldcorn paid 4s. 4d. and Geoffrey Hakeseye paid 6d.: after Joan Goldcorn; Robert Barbour or Youn; his widow, 1 Ed. II and 1 Ed. III; Thomas Copyn, 30 Ed. III; Alice Perers, 44 Ed. III; William Burford, 47 Ed. III; Robert his son throughout Ric. II and Hy. IV: after Geoffrey Hakeseye; his widow; John Digge or Gigge, 1 Ed. II and 1 Ed. III; John Norton, 20 Ed. III; [See also after **892**] to whom prior Nicholas granted a piece (*particula*) of the priory garden to increase the tenement as appears by the following indenture.

892. Indenture made between the prior and convent and John de Norton, citizen, and Alice his wife witnesseth that the prior and convent has granted to them a certain piece of the priory garden; abutments, the tenement of the said John on the west and the said garden on the east; in width 2½ ells and in length extending to the fountain which is between the two tenements on the south and the great garden of the prior and convent on the north, which length is 46½ ells; rent 2s. *p.a.*; the easement to the spring being protected in perpetuity (*aisiamento fontis . . . salvo imperpetuum*) so that the costs and repairs shall be, in perpetuity, shared between the two parties to the indenture, their heirs and assigns; whoever defaults in this respect shall lose the easement; John and Alice pledge for themselves and their successors all their built-up tenement next to this plot that the prior may distrain therein for the rent of 2s. [f. 154] if in arrears, as for the rent of 6d.; sealed by both parties; dated London 1 Apr. 1354.

891 contd. John de Norton paid 2s. 6d., 28 Ed. III; Adam Stable, 48 Ed. III; his widow, 8 Ric. II; afterwards the executors of John duke of Lancaster appropriated the tenement to the church of St. Paul for the maintenance of a certain chantry for the duke's soul; the dean and chapter of St. Paul's; and the three tenements are situated at length adjacent on the north of the great street of Algatestrete between the tenement of the priory on the east and the cemetery of the church of St. Botolph on the west.

893. [1255–6] Grant of John prior and convent to Warin de Hakeney of land in the parish of St. Botolph with houses built thereon; abutments, the messuage which John Cust held of the priory and the land of Matilda Junior; in width along the street 11¼ ells and in the middle 7 ells less 4 ins., extending from the king's street to the priory garden; rent 7s. *p.a.*; the grantee not to destroy or allow the houses to deteriorate but to maintain them; if the grantee wishes to sell, the canons to have an advantage of 2s. over other buyers; gersuma 20s.; swore fealty; chirograph sealed; [f. 154v] witnesses, Ralph Hardell, mayor, Matthew Bukerell, John Mynur, sheriffs.

894. [List of those paying rent]: W. de Hakeney then the land was divided for Geoffrey de Haneke 'seise' paid 3s. 6d. for his part which part is now in the hands of the priory: and Robert Turnour paid 3s. 6d. for the other part:

St. Botolph Aldgate

after Robert Turnour; his widow, 1 Ed. II and 1 Ed. III; John Longe, 6 Ed. III; Nicholas Longe, 30 Ed. III and 8 Ric. II; his widow, 9 Hy. IV; John Shawe, 11 Hy. IV; and the tenement is situated on the north side of Algatestrete between the tenement of the priory on the west and the tenement once of Matilda Juvenis, now of John Raulyn on the east.

Margin: Longitudo istius tenementi continet xl ulnas regis ut patet in testamento[1] Roberti Turnour quod irrotulatur post festum Mathei apostoli anno Edwardi filii Edwardi xij°.
1. *C. Wills*, i, 282.

895. [1147–67] Grant of Ralph prior and convent to Goditha wife of Solomon de Stebbehetha of a tenement (*managium*) which was the bishop's; rent ½ mark *p.a.*; swore fealty; witnesses, Herman, canon of Suwer(c), Robert Hus(c)ardus.

896. [List of those paying rent]: Goditha; Solomon her son, then the land was divided for 8d. was paid from the tenement once of Matilda Juvenis, and for that once of Simon Marchall 18d., and for that once of William Buxford 12d.; Juliana daughter of Ralph Crepyn or Algate, clerk, paid for his house and another adjacent 2s.; the widow of William Haveryng paid for the house in which Roger Underwode lives 9d.; Robert de Hakenay paid for the house of the late Richard Heved 9d.; and thus the total sum of 6s. 8d. [as in **895**]: after Matilda Juvenis; Godfrey Marchal who granted the tenement to William Horsham as appears in their charter 22 Ed. I, John Breton being warden of London; William Manhale, 1 Ed. III; Robert Brom, 30 Ed. III; Richard Cotyngham, 32 Ed. III; John Chaltone, 36 Ed. III; Nicholas Longe, 48 Ed. III and 8 Ric. II; John Rawlyn throughout Hy. IV and Hy. V: 18d. for the tenement of Simon Marshal who granted 2s. 6d. *p.a.* of quit rent [See also after **897**] as appears by the following charter.

897. Grant by Simon Marshal (*Marescallus*) and Roysia, daughter of the late Richard de Depedene, his wife to William prior and convent of Holy Trinity of 30d. *p.a.* of quit rent; the canons to hold in free alms; the quit rent issuing from a certain [f. 155] tenement which Richard de Depedene held of the fee of the said canons; the grantors concede that the canons shall distrain and take naam in the aforesaid tenement both for the 30d. and the 18d.; Simon and Roesia will not pull down the houses or increase the rent without the assent of the canons; sealed; witnesses, Ralph de Sandwich, warden, Walter Hauteyn, Thomas Cros, sheriffs; dated 20 Apr. 1287.

C.A.D., ii, A 1972.

896 contd. Simon Marshal paid 4s. who granted the tenement to William de Haveryng as appears by their charter[1] enrolled 20 Ed. I; William Manhale, 1 Ed. II and 1 Ed. III; Robert Brome, 30 Ed. III; Nicholas Longe, 32 Ed. III; William Webbe, 37 Ed. III; John Horleus, or Pyioun, 3 Ric. II; Robert Bussheye, 8 Ric. II: after William Buxford who granted the tenement to William de Haveryng as in their charter[2] enrolled 23 Ed. I; his

St. Botolph Aldgate

widow, Agnes Crepyn, 1 Ed. II; Richard Bryccheford, 36 Ed. III; William Webbe, 48 Ed. III; John Horleus or Pyioun, 3 Ric. II; Robert Bussheye, 8 Ric. II, who bequeathed the aforesaid two tenements to the church of St. Michael de Bassyeshawe; the wardens of that church [See also after **898**] as appears by the following quittance.

    1. H.R. 21 (58).   2. H.R. 24 (12).

898. Quittance of William Haradon prior and convent of Holy Trinity upon the receipt of 25s. of quit rent from Richard Osbarn and Henry Hert, citizens, from a certain tenement in the parish of St. Botolph; abutments, the tenement of John Raulyn on the west and that of Isabel Furneys on the east, extending from the king's street on the south to the garden of the abbot and convent of St. Mary Graces beside the Tower on the north; [f. 155v] payment in full of all arrears of a quit rent of 5s. *p.a.*; sealed counterparts; dated 22 Mar. 1410.

896 contd. After Juliana, daughter of Ralph Crepyn, clerk, otherwise called Algate; Roger Undurwode: afterwards for the tenement which Ralph Crepyn had of the late William Haveryng paying 2s. 9d. *p.a.*; Julia daughter of Ralph who granted the tenements to Hamundus de Coptone, moneyer, as appears in their charter[1] enrolled 35 Ed. I; Hamo Coptone until 5 Ed. II when he granted the tenement of the late William Haveryng to John de Welco(m)stowe,[2] rent to Hamo and his heirs, 20s. *p.a.* and to Holy Trinity 9d. *p.a.*: after H. de Coptone, 6 Ed. III paying 2s.; John Chaucer, 20 Ed. III; William Furneux, 31 Ed. III; his widow, 36 Ed. III; the abbot of St. Mary Graces by the Tower, from 42 Ed. III: after John Wolcomstowe; William Rodyng, 6 Ed. III; Robert Ecclesale, 30 Ed. III; his widow, 36 Ed. III; Richard Chadisle, 41 Ed. III; Alice Perers, 47 Ed. III; Thomas Clerk, 8 Ric. II: after Richard Heved paying 9d.; Robert Hakenay [See also after **899**] who granted 13s. 4d. *p.a.* to the prior and sacristan of Holy Trinity as appears by the following charter.

    1. H.R. 35 (41).   2. See **925**.

899. [1268] Grant by Robert de Hakeney, woolmonger, to the priory of Holy Trinity of 1 mark *p.a.* of quit rent in the suburb of London from a messuage which the grantor had in the soke without Alegate of the fee of the canons; to hold to the said canons and the sacristan for the time being; the canons to have the right to distrain; the canons gave 9 marks; sealed; witnesses, Stephen de Edesworth, warden, William de Dunelm, Walter Hervy, bailiffs, Walter Tovi, Edmund Trentmars, John le Rus.

896 contd. After Robert paying 14s. 1d.; Richard de Algate who granted the tenement to William Wastel as by their charter[1] enrolled 33 Ed. I; John de Enefeld, 1 Ed. II and 1 Ed. III; John Stowe, 4 Ed. III; William Rodyng, 6 Ed. III; Robert Ecclesale, 30 Ed. III; his widow, 36 Ed. III; Richard Chadisle, 41 Ed. III; Alice Perers, 47 Ed. III; Thomas Clerk, 8 Ric. II and all these tenements are situated at length adjacent [f. 156] on the north side of Algatestrete between the tenement once of Robert

St. Botolph Aldgate

Turnour now of John Shawe on the west and the tenement of Henry at Hoke on the east.

    1. H.R. 33 (31, 32).

900. [1222–48] Grant by Richard prior and convent to Ralph Marescall of a certain construction (*fabrica*) which John Cylbryght, marshal (*marescallus*), held of the canons; rent 4s. *p.a.*; the grantee not to sell to Jews or to pledge to anyone nor to grant it to religious; if the grantee wishes to sell, the prior and convent to have an advantage upon payment of a bezant of 2s. over other buyers; swore fealty; gersuma 1 mark of silver; witnesses, William de Alegate, Ralph his brother, Stephen Tanner, Alfred the Butcher.

901. [List of those paying rent]: R. Marchall; John Mabun and then the construction was divided for William Tannour paid 12d. and John Krau(er) 3s.: after William Tannour; William Lewes, 1 Ed. II; Nicholas Derman, 1 Ed. III; Thomas Croucheman, 33 Ed. III; Robert Caxton, 38 Ed. III; John at Water, 48 Ed. III; Henry at Hok, 8 Ric. II: after John Krau(er); Simon de Chigewell; John Horn(er); William Bonseriaunt; John le Lunge; Nicholas Derman, 1 Ed. II; John Romeney, 10 Ed. III; Thomas Croucheman, executor of John, 30 Ed. III; now [1425–8] the wardens of St. Botolph.

902. [1170–97] Grant of Stephen prior and convent to William nephew of Keneward and to his sister Estrilda of two adjacent lands to hold for a rent of 3s. 8d. *p.a.* and 16d. *p.a.* respectively saving the customs which belong to the soke; swore fealty; gersuma 1 mark and a London sextary of wine; witnesses, William, Facetus, Turbertus, Roger, William, armiger.

903. [156v] [List of those paying rent]: Keneward paying 3s. 8d.; Simon de Chigwell; John Horn(er); William Bonseriaunt; Nicholas Derman, 5 Ed. II who bequeathed the tenement to John Romney as in his will[1] enrolled after 30 Nov. 1335 and the same John bequeathed the two tenements to the church of St. Botolph for the maintenance of a perpetual chapel (*capella*) by his will[2] enrolled 33 Ed. III; the executor of the will, Thomas Croucheman: Estrilda paying 16d.; William Hippynke; Agnes daughter of William Buriler; Geoffrey Horn(er); John Ace; Martin Dulyngham; Agnes his wife who granted the tenement to Gregory Norton [See also after **904**] as appears by the following charter.

    1. *C. Wills*, i, 408–9.   2. *C. Wills*, i, 555, enrolled 23 Ed. III.

904. Grant by Agnes once wife of Martin de Dolyngham to Gregory de Norton, citizen, of a plot (*placea*) of land with houses built thereon in the parish of St. Botolph; abutments, the land of William Bonseriaunt once of John Horner on the west and Spitelelane on the east, the tenement of John le Lung on the north and the king's street on the south; rent to the chief lords of the fee, viz. to Holy Trinity 16d. *p.a.* and to St. Botolph 4s. *p.a.*; gersuma a sum of money [unspecified]; sealed; witnesses, John le Blount, mayor, Nicholas Picot, Nigel Drury, sheriffs, Ralph prior of Holy Trinity,

St. Botolph Aldgate

then alderman of that ward, Peter Berneval, John le Lung, Edmund Trentmars, John le Poter, Alan le Poter, Nicholas Dereman, Hamon le Poter, Jordan de Alegate, butcher, John de Billirica, Simon the sergeant (*seriuiente*) of that ward, Henry the clerk and many others; dated London 27 Aug. 1308.

903 contd. Then the tenement was divided for Stephen Talp(er) paid 8d. and William Pisere 8d.: after Stephen Talp(er); [f. 157] John Romeneye who bequeathed the shop to the fabric (*operi*) of the church of St. Botulph by his will[1] enrolled 23 Ed. III which shop the wardens of the fabric of the church granted to John Hamerton: after William Pisere; John Romeneye who bequeathed the shop to Agnes his daughter by will mentioned above, which shop Agnes gave to the wardens of the above church.

1. *C. Wills*, i, 555.

905. [1270–1] Grant of Eustace prior and convent to Benet de Hakeneye, citizen, and Emma his wife of a garden which the priory had in the corner (*in cornera*) between the messuage of John le Poter on the south and that of John son of the late Richard Rusy on the east in the parish of St. Botolph in the suburb of London; to hold in fee; the grantees not to sell to religious or Jews; quit rent of 1 mark *p.a.*; if the garden decays so that the rent cannot be paid, then the grantors may distrain upon it and upon a tenement which the grantees have in the parish between the field of Stebenhethe by Smethefeld on the east and the messuage of Walter Daniel on the west but when the garden and the houses built thereon [f. 157v] are sufficient for distraint then the grantors or anyone on their behalf shall no longer have any rights in the aforementioned tenement; if the grantees wish to sell the garden in whole or in part, the prior and convent to have an advantage upon payment of 2s. over other buyers; swore fealty; sealed chirograph; witnesses, John Adrian, mayor, Gregory de Rokesle, Henry le Waleis, sheriffs, Thomas de Wymburne, Ralph de la More, Hervy de Martelane, John le Rus, Ralph Crepyn, Robert de Hakeneye, Richard de Hundesdich, Robert de Coryngham, Henry Deubeneye, Walter le Poter, William Tanner, Ralph the Marshal (*Marescallo*), John the clerk (*clerico*).

906. [1277–8] Grant of a quit rent of 2s. 8d. *p.a.* by Benet de Hakeneye, and Emma his wife to Eustace prior and convent from a tenement which the grantors hold of the canons; [described as in **905**] the canons to hold in free alms; sealed; witnesses, Gregory de Rokesle, mayor, John Brian,[1] Walter le Engleis, sheriffs, John de Norhamtone, John de Enefeld, Henry Deubeneye, Robert de Coryngham, Reginald the Goldsmith, Thomas the chaplain, German the clerk, Thomas the Tailor, William de Alegate, Norman the clerk.

1. John son of John Adrian.

907. [List of those paying rent of 16s.]: Benet de Hakeneye; Margery Lyncolne; John de Billirica, 19 Ed. II; William of the Wardrobe (*de Gardroba*) or de Ragton, 1 and 30 Ed. III; Peter Taillour, 32 Ed. III; his widow, 35 Ed. III; the abbot of St. Mary Graces from 44 Ed. III.

St. Botolph Aldgate

908. [f. 158] [1222–48] Grant of Gilbert son of Benet to Richard prior and convent of 3s. 6d. *p.a.* of quit rent which Walter son of Walter de Porta was accustomed to pay the grantor from certain land with houses; abutments, the garden of the canons on the north and the land of Robert Blondy on the south; the canons to hold in free alms; the prior and canons gave 20s. sterling; witnesses, William de Alegate, Ralph de Alegate, Stephen the Tanner (*Tannatore*).

909. [List of those paying quit rent]: Walter de Porta; John le Potter; Robert Raughton, potter, 1 and 19 Ed. II and 1 Ed. III; Peter de Weston, 6 Ed. III as appears by the First Acquittance[1] of several parishes; Alice Trumpton, 35 Ed. III; John Lawe, 49 Ed. III then the tenement was divided for Alice Trumpynton paid 21d. and Philip Chamberleyn 21d., 1 Ric. II: after Alice Trumpynton; Thomas Clerk, 4 Ric. II: after Philip Chamberleyn; Roger Ryot, 14 Ric. II; William Wodeward, 'foundour'.

1. **1038.**

910. [1222–48] Grant and sale by Martin son of Benet to Richard prior and convent of 3s. *p.a.* of quit rent which Alfred the Butcher paid from land with houses of the fee of the prior and convent; if the land is insufficient to pay the quit rent, payment is to be made from all the grantor's lands and tenements which he holds in the parish of St. Botolph of the grantees; the prior and convent gave 20s.; witnesses, William de Alegate, Ralph [f. 158v] Alegate, Solomon son of Laurence, Stephen the Tanner.

911. [List of those paying quit rent]: Alfred the Butcher; Ralph Marchall who granted the tenement to Stephen Wenden(e) [See also after **912**] as appears in the following charter.

912. [1256–7] Grant by Ralph Marshall (*Marescallus*) and Matilda his wife to Stephen de Wenden(e), clerk, of certain land with a house built thereon in the parish of St. Botolph; abutments, the land of the grantee on the north and the land of Holy Trinity on the south, containing in width at the end along the street $8\frac{1}{2}$ ells 7 ins. and in depth from the street to the land of Roger de Leuesham 30 ells and in width along the land of the said Roger $5\frac{3}{4}$ ells 4 ins.; all the land as the grantors bought it from the late Richard le Pater; to hold to Stephen and his heirs in perpetuity; rent to Ralph and his heirs 2d. *p.a.* and 3s. *p.a.* to Holy Trinity; gersuma 24s.; sealed; witnesses, Ralph Hardel, mayor, William Eswy, Richard de Ewelle, sheriffs, Thomas de Wymburne, alderman, William de Hakeneye, goldsmith, Walter Trentmars, Gilbert de Wymburne, William Katel.

911 contd. S. Wenden[e]; John de Sancta Ositha whose daughter granted the tenement to John de Alegate as appears by their charter[1] enrolled 19 Ed. I from which tenement Ralph le Marchall granted to Richard prior and convent 2d. *p.a.* in addition to the 3s. [See also after **913**].

1. H.R. 20 (94).

913. [1290–1] Grant of Ralph le Mareschal to the prior and convent of Holy Trinity of 2d. *p.a.* of quit rent which John de Sancta Ositha paid from land which he had on lease from the grantor which land was of the canons' fee; abutments, the messuage of the late William le Waleis on the south and that of Cecily de Distavelane on the north; the canons to hold with the 3s. *p.a.* in free alms; sealed; witnesses, Edmund Trentmars, [f. 159] Stephen de Houndesdich, William le Tannour, William Lambert.

911 contd. Hamo Copton, moneyer, 1 and 19 Ed. II and 1 Ed. III; William de Rothyng, 6 Ed. III; William Underwode, 30 Ed. III; his widow, 8 Ric. II.

914. Memorandum: that the priory has had 14d. *p.a.* from a tenement which once belonged to William Wallensis as appears in an old rental with the letter 'H' and in subsequent rentals.

915. [List of those paying quit rent]: William Walleys; Hamo de Copton; John Algate who sold the tenement to Alan le Potter who bequeathed the tenement to Agnes his daughter by his first wife as appears in his will[1] enrolled 1 Ed. II; Agnes le Potter who married William le Clerk who paid 1 and 19 Ed. II; his widow, 1 Ed. III; John Romeney, 6 and 20 Ed. III from which tenement John Chaucer and Agnes his wife granted to William at Hale 13s. 4d. *p.a.* of quit rent as appears by their charter[2] enrolled 39 Ed. III which same William bequeathed 13s. 4d. to Thomas his son, the canon, and after the death of Agnes his wife and the said Thomas to the prior of Holy Trinity, as appears in the will[3] of William enrolled 42 Ed. III.

    1. *C. Wills*, i, 196.   2. H.R. 93 (154).   3. *C. Wills*, ii, 118–19.

916. [1270–1] Grant by Eustace prior and convent to Walter son of Robert (*le*) Flemyng of Bixhill of a messuage which Stephen Quernebeter held of the grantors; abutments, the messuage of the late William Walensis on the north and that of Richard de Houndesdiche on the south containing in width along the street $7\frac{1}{2}$ ells and at the end beside the land once of Roger de Leuesham on the east $5\frac{3}{4}$ ells and in length 31 ells; to hold in perpetuity to Walter, his heirs and assigns except other religious and Jews; rent 14d. *p.a.*; if the grantee wishes to sell, the canons to have the first claim upon payment of 2s.; chirograph sealed; [f. 159v] witnesses, John Adrian, mayor, Henry Walensi, Gregory Rokesle, sheriffs.

    C.A.D., ii, A 1868.

917. [List of those paying rent]: Walter le Flemyng, gate-keeper (*ianitor*) who granted the tenement to John de Algate, potter, which John granted it to Alan de Suthfolk which Alan bequeathed it to Agnes his wife as appears by his will[1] enrolled 1 Ed. II.

    1. *C. Wills*, i, 196.

918. Note: [1170–97] that Stephen prior and convent granted land to Fulchered at a rent of $6\frac{1}{2}$d. *p.a.*

    C.A.D., ii, A 1949.

St. Botolph Aldgate

919. [List of those paying rent]: Fulchered; Ralph the priest (*sacerdos*); Simon fitz Rauf; William the priest (*sacerdos*); Roger Eppyng; Richard Algate who granted the tenement to Alan Suthfolk as appears by their charter[1] enrolled 29 Ed. I which Alan bequeathed the tenement to Agnes his wife as appeared by his will[2] enrolled 1 Ed. II; Agnes; William Clerk; his widow, 1 Ed. III; John Romeney, 6 Ed. III which John bequeathed the aforesaid three tenements at length adjacent to the church of St. Botolph for the maintenance of a perpetual chapel by his will[3] enrolled 23 Ed. III and these three tenements are situated adjacent between the tenement of John at Lee formerly of William Underwode on the north and a tenement of Holy Trinity on the south and the sum of the quit rents of these premises is 16s. 2d. *p.a.*

1. H.R. 30 (87).   2. C. *Wills*, i, 196.   3. C. *Wills*, i, 555.

920. [1294] Grant of Stephen prior and convent to Lord Edmund [brother of Edward, king of England] son of the Lord Henry once illustrious king of England, so that he can assign it to the Minoresses of London without Algate in free alms, of a tenement which is of the canons' fee, notwithstanding the statute of mortmain; the tenements were of Master Thomas of Bredstrete, William the Shoemaker (*Sutoris*), Alexander son of Geoffrey 'le Coureour' and Hodierna his wife, William de Wautham and Ellen his wife, Adam le Wyndrawere and Alice his wife and Thomas de la More; the Minoresses paying a rent to Holy Trinity of 16s. $9\frac{1}{2}$d. *p.a.*; free access reserved to the canons and their successors to the fee [f. 160] to distrain on the goods and chattels therein without the contradiction of the sisters; saving also all temporal and spiritual rights belonging to Holy Trinity and to its church of St. Botolph without Allegate in the above tenements and also those of Solomon le Teuler and John Goldcorn so that all indemnity should be preserved (*conservatur*) to Holy Trinity for ever; chirograph; sealed counterparts; dated London 23 Aug. 1294.

921. [1274–5] Grant by Walter son of Robert le Flemyng of Bixle to Eustace prior and convent of Holy Trinity of 2s. *p.a.* of quit rent which the grantor had from the whole tenement of Osbert son of Richard le Chapman of Hakeneye formerly of Stephen le Gardiner and Florence his wife beside Estsmethefeld; abutments, the land of Edmund the Bedell on the south and the land of Nicholas the clerk on the north and containing throughout its length the same width of $9\frac{1}{4}$ ells and extending from the street to the land of Edmund Trentmars on the east; free entry and exit to distrain is granted; if this tenement is not distrainable, the grantor grants that the canons may enter all the lands which he has of their gift once of Stephen le Quernbetere in the parish of St. Botolph and take naam therein; [f. 160v] the canons gave 18s.; sealed; witnesses, Gregory de Rokesle, mayor, Henry de Frowyk, Luke de Batincourt, sheriffs, Edmund Trentmars, William Tanner, John Hervey.

922. [List of those paying quit rent]: Osbert the Chapman (*carectarius*) then the tenement was divided for John de Billirica paid 12d. *p.a.* and Osbert paid 12d. *p.a.*: after John de Billirica; John his son, 1 Ed. II and 1 Ed. III;

St. Botolph Aldgate

William atte Wyke, 30 Ed. III; Eustace Westwode, 48 Ed. III and 2 Ric. II; Nicholas Longe, 8 Ric. II: after Osbert; Walter Cobbe, 1 Ed. II and 1 Ed. III; Robert Greylond, 30 Ed. III; his widow, 2 Ric. II.

923. [1222–48] Grant by Richard prior and convent to Ralph son of Adam de Benyton of land with a house built thereon in the parish of St. Botolph; abutments, the land formerly of John Basse and the land of the late Roger le Gardiner extending on the west along the street and containing at the end (*caput*) in width $5\frac{1}{2}$ ells 2 ins. and on the east it extends along (*super*) the land of Walter Trentmars and contains at that end $5\frac{1}{2}$ ells 3 ins. and in the middle, $5\frac{1}{4}$ ells 4 ins.; rent 18d. *p.a.* and to Bartholomew de Alegate $\frac{1}{4}$d. at Michaelmas; [f. 162] the grantee is not to pledge to Jews nor to sell to any religious without the assent of the prior and convent; if the grantee wishes to sell, the prior and convent to have an advantage upon payment of a bezant of 2s. over other buyers; swore fealty; gersuma 20s.; witnesses. Adam de Alegate, Walter Trentmars, John le Vinor.

924. [List of those paying rent]: Ralph the Gate-keeper (*Portarius*); Edmund the Bedel then the land was divided for William Daniell paid 12d. *p.a.* and John de Billirica 6d. *p.a.*: after William Daniell; Agnes Bosham, 19 Ed. II and 6 Ed. III; William Daniell, 30 Ed. III; John Chalton, 48 Ed. III and 2 Ric. II: after John de Billirica; John Payn to whom John de Billirica granted the tenement;[1] John Payn, 19 Ed. II whose wife Margery granted the tenement to Alexander Cobbe as appears by their charter[2] enrolled after 25 Mar. 1335 which Alexander paid 30 Ed. III; Nicholas Cobbe, 48 Ed. III; Richard Morecok, 2 Ric. II.

    1. See **927**.   2. H.R. 63 (25, 26).

925. [f. 161][1] [1314–15] Grant by Hamo de Coptone, moneyer and citizen, to John de Wolcomstowe, potter (*ollarius*), of London and Constance his wife of a certain tenement with a garden; abutments, the tenement of William Godefray on the east and the tenement of the grantor on the west containing in width at the foremost part along the street 6 ells 2 ins., in the middle $6\frac{3}{4}$ ells, in the part following (*sequente*) $12\frac{1}{2}$ ells and at the back (*posteriore*) part $18\frac{1}{4}$ ells and in length from the street on the south to the garden of Holy Trinity; rent to Holy Trinity 9d. *p.a.* and to the grantor and his heirs 20s. *p.a.*; allowance to the grantor and his heirs to distrain if the rent falls into arrears; gersuma a certain [unspecified] sum of money; sealed counterparts; witnesses, John de Gesors, mayor, Stephen de Abyndon, Hamo de Chigwell, sheriffs, Ralph [prior of Holy Trinity] alderman of that ward, Nicholas Derman, William le Potter, clerk, Robert le Tournour, William Wastel, Thomas le Bedel, 8 Ed. II.

    1. f. 161 is an inserted leaf of full width but $1\frac{1}{2}$ ins. short in length.

926. Note: that Hamo de Coptone died without heirs and after his death Agnes as next-of-kin (*consanguinea*) and heir, namely the daughter of John Hamo's brother, received this rent of 20s. and was seised of the messuage and married (*cepit in virum*) a certain John Chaucer which John and Agnes,

St. Botolph Aldgate

by a charter[1] enrolled in the Husting 19 Jan. 1366, granted to William at Hale, citizen of London, the quit rent of 20s. *p.a.* and William bequeathed the 20s. if his heirs died; half to the prior and convent of Holy Trinity and half to the abbess and sisters of St. Clare without Algate as appears in his will[2] enrolled 20 Nov. 1368.

1. H.R. 93 (154). 2. *C. Wills*, ii, 118–19.

927. [f. 161v] Grant by John de Billerika, carter (*carectarius*) of London, to John called Payn le Brewere and Margery his wife of all that part of the land with houses built thereon which the grantor had of the gift and enfeoffment of Stephen de Retherhethe and Juliana his wife in the parish of St. Botolph without Algate against the Tower of London; abutments, in width $3\frac{7}{8}$ ells from the street on the south to the land of Walter Trentemars on the north between the tenement of John Page on the south and that of William Daniel on the north; and all that land which the grantor had of the gift and enfeoffment of Laurence son of Edmund le Bedel towards (*versus*) the Tower in the same parish stretching (*pretendentem*) in width from the king's street towards the west as far as the land of Walter Trentemars on the east containing 3 ells and in the middle between the tenement of William Daniel on the north and that of John de Billerika on the south $3\frac{1}{4}$ ells 1 in. and along the street between the two aforesaid tenements $2\frac{3}{4}$ ells and in length from the street towards the west as far as the land of W. Trentemars on the east 129 ells; to hold to the grantees and their heirs together with the reversion of a certain house which William de Leddrede and Margery his wife hold for the term of their lives when the lease falls in; rent a clove-gillyflower at Christmas and to Stephen de Retherhethe and Juliana his wife and their heirs 1d. at Michaelmas, to the New Hospital of St. Mary 16d. *p.a.*, to Edmund Trentemars and his heirs 16d. *p.a.* and to Holy Trinity 6d. *p.a.*; gersuma a certain [unspecified] sum of money; sealed; witnesses, John de Gesorcis, mayor, Stephen de Abyndon, Hamon de Chiggewell, sheriffs, Walter Trentemars, Nicholas Dereman; dated London 11 June 1315.

928. [f. 162] [1274–5] Grant by Walter son of Robert (*le*) Flemyng of Bixle to Eustace prior and convent of 2s. *p.a.* of quit rent which the grantor received from land with houses from Matilda widow of Nicholas de Ipswich (*Yepeswych, Gypeswico*), clerk; abutments, Matilda's land on the north and the land of William Somer towards Estsmethefeld; [f. 162v] with free entry and exit for the canons to distrain upon the houses if the quit rent is in arrears; if the land is not distrainable, the canons are to enter the grantor's lands which he holds in the parish and which were once of Stephen de Quernbeter; the canons gave 18s. sterling; sealed; witnesses, Gregory de Rokesle, mayor, Henry de Frowyk, Luke de Batincourt, sheriffs, Edmund Trentmars.

C.A.D., ii, A 1933.

929. [List of those paying quit rent]: Matilda Gepiswych; William the Whittawer (*Alutarius*); his widow; William Wastell; his widow, 1 Ed. II and 1 Ed. III; Peter de Weston, 6 and 30 Ed. III; Thomas Cornewaleys, 36 and 49 Ed. III.

930. [1222–*c*.1230] Grant by Richard prior and convent to Bartholomew de Algate son of Edricus of land with houses in the parish of St. Botolph; abutments, the land of Robert Baddyng and the land of Norman fitz Alwin, containing along the street $20\frac{1}{4}$ ells and extending from the street to the land of Geoffrey son of Susan on the east; rent 6s. *p.a.*; if the rent falls into arrears and no naam can be found on the said land, the canons may distrain on the capital messuage (*managium*) of Bartholomew in the soke; Bartholomew and his heirs to maintain the houses which they find on this land or [f. 163] elsewhere constructed so that men of the ward may dwell in them and they shall be responsible for other things which pertain to the soke (*ut in eis homines manere possent qui de warda et aliis que ad soccam pertinent respondeant*); if the grantees wish to sell, the canons to have an advantage on the payment of a gold bezant over other buyers; swore fealty; gersuma $2\frac{1}{2}$ marks; witnesses, Stephen Crassus, alderman, William, Terricus, Adam, Ralph de Alegate, brothers, Keneward Turnour, Stephen Tanor.

931. [1170–97] Grant by Stephen prior and convent to Reginald Tannur of land in the soke which Edmund the Gate-keeper (*Portarius*) held, namely half the land which Hecstan held in fee; rent 3s. *p.a.*; swore fealty; gersuma 1 bezant to the prior and one London sextary of wine; witness, Robert the subprior.

932. [List of those paying rent]: Reginald; Hervy the Shoemaker (*Sutor*) and then the land was divided for John son of Hervy paid 18d. and Kenewardus 18d. [See also after **933**].

933. [1222–48] Grant by Richard prior and convent to Simon de Neweport and Florietta his wife of certain land with houses in the soke; abutments, the land of John Keneward on the south and of Terricus de Alegate on the north extending from the street to the field (*campus*) of Geoffrey Trentmars; to hold to Simon and his heirs by Florietta; rent 3s. *p.a.*; swore fealty; gersuma 15s.; witnesses, William de Alegate, Terricus, Bartholomew, brothers, Richard May, Hugh the Gate-keeper (*Janitor*), John son of Robert, Turgisius, Stanhardus.

934. [List of those paying rent]: S. de Neweport; John Hervy paid 6s. *p.a.*[1] and after John Hervy; Agnes Bosham, 1 Ed. II and 6 Ed. III; William Daniel, 32 Ed. III; Adam Canon, 42 Ed. III; Richard Rothyng, 49 Ed. III; the brothers of the Holy Cross,[2] 8 Ric. II.

  1. Possibly a reference to **932** although the rent from the two tenements would appear to be 4s. 6d.   2. The Crutched Friars.

935. [f. 163v] Note: that Osbert Trentmars rendered to the knights of the 'Knyghtgyld' 7s. 5d. *p.a.* from his principal tenement in the parish of St.

St. Botolph Aldgate

Botolph and that the knights gave this rent to the canons when they granted the whole soke.

936. [List of those paying quit rent]: Osbert; Susan Trentmars; Geoffrey son of Susan; Walter Trentmars; Edmund Trentmars, 1 Ed. II [See also after **937**] as appears by the following indenture.

937. Indenture of Edmund Trentmars by which he acknowledged that he owed the prior and convent of Holy Trinity 44s. 6d. of arrears of a certain rent of 7s. 5d. *p.a.* issuing from his principal tenement and granted the prior and convent or their rent-collector (*rentarius*) 8s. 11d. *p.a.* in part payment of the aforesaid arrears for five years from the making of the indenture, namely 2s. 7d. *p.a.* from that 10s. *p.a.* which Roger de Sart(er)ino and Agnes his wife owe to Edmund from their tenement which was once of Geoffrey Haukeseye in Alegatestrete and 6s. 4d. *p.a.* from a tenement which William de Basyng holds of Edmund in Estsmethefeld by the Tower of London and Holy Trinity shall take the remaining 7s. 5d. out of the 10s. by which Roger and Agnes hold for the 7s. 5d. due from Edmund's principal tenement for five years so that the prior and convent shall demand nothing from Edmund's principal tenement and if they are not able to obtain the arrears he grants that they may distrain on his principal tenement; indenture sealed by Edmund and the prior of Holy Trinity; dated London 25 Mar. 1308.

936 contd. Edmund Trentmars, 6 Ed. III; Henry Fanner, 16 Ed. III; his widow, 30 Ed. III; Thomas Cornwaleys, 33 Ed. III as appears by a plea held in the Husting, Mon. 7 Dec. 1359.

938. [f. 164] [1222–48] Grant by Richard prior and convent to Ernald 'Horsdrivere' of land with houses which the grantee and Robert Hottere once held of William Basset; abutments, the land of Kenewardus the Turner (*Tornator*) on the south and the land of Geoffrey Waterladere on the north; rent 7s. *p.a.*; swore fealty; if the grantee wishes to sell, the prior and convent upon the payment of a gold bezant or 2s. sterling shall have an advantage over other buyers; the grantee is not to pledge to Jews or other religious except to Holy Trinity; gersuma 10s.; witnesses, William de Alegate, Terricus, Ralph, Bartholomew, brothers, Geoffrey son of Susan, Geoffrey the Ewerer (*Aquarius*).

939. [List of those paying rent]: Ernald; his widow then the land was divided for Norman the clerk paid 12d. for one part and Alexander le Tryer paid 6s.: after Norman; John Lorchon, son of the same Norman, 1 Ed. II and 1 and 6 Ed. III; John Cobeler, 30 Ed. III; Richard Paxton, 35 and 49 Ed. III; John Stokynbury, 8 Ric. II: after Alexander this part was divided for William Bullok paid 5s. for his part and after W. Bullok; John de Caustone; Walter Bardeneye otherwise called Papworth; Matilda Aubyn 1 and 19 Ed. II; Thomas Langedon, 30 Ed. III; the prioress of St. Helen: and the third part which is in the middle of the two parts aforesaid from which Holy Trinity had 12d. came into the hands of the priory by gavelet which was afterwards leased to Henry Gamene for 3s. *p.a.* as appears by the following.

940. Lease of Richard prior and convent to Henry Gamene, carter (*carectarius*), of a plot of land in the parish of St. Botolph in Portsoken; abutments, the tenement of Walter de Bardeneye on the south and the tenement of John Lorchon on the north and extending from the street which leads from Alegate to the Tower as far as the garden of John Lorchon, containing in length from the tenement of Walter to that of John along the street $5\frac{3}{8}$ ells 1 in. and in length below (*infra*) the said tenements along the garden of the said John $5\frac{1}{4}$ ells 1 in. and in [f. 164v] depth from the street to the said garden of the south next to the tenement of Walter de Bardeneye $6\frac{3}{8}$ ells 2 ins. and in width at the north end against the tenement of the said John $6\frac{1}{2}$ ells 3 ins.; rent 3s. *p.a.*; indenture sealed by both parties; witnesses, Hamon de Chigwelle, mayor, John de Prestone, Simon de Abyndone, sheriffs, Nicholas Derman, Robert de Raughton, John de Billirica, William Clerk, potter, John Eliot, Simon le Hoder, bedel; dated London 21 Dec. 1320.

941. [List of those paying rent]: Henry Gamene; John de Notyngham, 1 Ed. II [*sic*]; Richard Clerk, 19 Ed. II; John de Notyngham, 1 and 6 Ed. III; John Cobeler, 30 Ed. III; Richard Paxton, 35 and 49 Ed. III; John Stokynbury, 8 Ric. II and these tenements are situated at length adjacent between the tenement of the hospital of St. Katherine, from which Holy Trinity once had a rent of 4s. 8d. which they remitted[1] to the brothers and sisters, on the south and the tenement of John Cornwaleys on the north.

    1. See **323**.

942. [1170–97] Grant by Stephen prior and convent to Lambert the Glover (*Wanterius*) of land which Godwin son of Firminus and his wife held before him; rent 2s. *p.a.*; to hold as long as the grantee pays the rent without fraud (*calumpnia*); swore fealty; the grantee received it for a lodging (*herbergacio*) and he holds it by custom (*et per convencionem illam herbergacionem tenere debet*); he who lives in this land or Lambert ought to attend the halimote (*ille qui in illa terra per Lambertum manebit debet sequi hallimotum vel ipse Lambertus*); gersuma 12d. and 12d. to the convent for pittances; witnesses, Fulchred the Limeburner (*Limbernarius*), James, Peter, Richer de Sarterino.

943. [List of those paying rent]: Lambert the Glover; John Trauaill; William Trauaill who granted the land to Nicholas Cross (*de Cruce*) who paid 2s. *p.a.* to Holy Trinity and [f. 165] 3s. *p.a.* to the grantor [See also after **945**] which 3s. was remitted to Nicholas as appears by the following.

944. Agreement between William Trauaill of Pullokeshill and Nicholas Cross that William remitted and quitclaimed to Nicholas 3s. *p.a.* of rent from a tenement in the parish of St. Botolph; abutments, the land of John Yhope and the land of Walter Daniel; quitclaim of the rent with all things

St. Botolph Aldgate

and 'ecchatris' belonging thereto; Nicholas gave 30s. sterling; sealed; witnesses, Thomas de Sorcwod, Richard Wiskard, Walter Blaunchard, Stephen Albano.

945. Recognisance of Nicholas Cross by which he binds himself and his heirs to pay 3s. *p.a.* of quit rent to Holy Trinity from the tenement which he holds in Estsmethefeld together with 2s. *p.a.* which the house was formerly due to receive; sealed, Christmas 1259; witnesses, Thomas de Wymburne, then sokereeve (*sokenreve*) of the prior, Walter Trentmars, Walter Daniel, Simon le Hosteler, Roger the Tiler (*Tegulario*), John the Gate-keeper (*Janitore*), Alexander de Rerdon.

943 contd. Nicholas Cross; the abbot of Coggeshale.

946. [1222–48] Grant by Richard prior and convent to Robert le [f. 165v] Wateraldere, son of Goldyng, of land in the parish of St. Botolph lying next to Estsmethefeld; abutments, the land of John Trauail on the west and the land of Richard the Spurrier (*Calcerius*) on the east extending from the path (*chimino*) to the land of the hospital of St. Katherine; rent 2s. *p.a.*; the grantee not to sell or pledge to Jews or to lease it in any way (*vel aliquo alio modo dimittere*); if the grantee wishes to sell or lease then the prior and convent shall have a preference by 12d.; swore fealty; ½ mark gersuma; witnesses, William de Alegate, Terricus, Adam, Ralph, brothers, Solomon son of Laurence, Stephen the Tanner, Ralph the Tanner, Theobald the Capper (*Capillario*), Richard de Westmeln', Alkelinus the Baker (*Pistore*), John de Halewyk, William Haket.

947. [List of those paying rent]: Robert Wateraldere; John Gardyner then the land was divided for William Chese paid 4½d. and William Danyel 6d.; Alexander de Chynggeford 4½d. and John Hakeneye 9d., 1 and 5 Ed. II: after William Chese; Peter de Staunton and Alexander de Chynggeford paid 9d., 1 Ed. II and Emma de Hakeney paid 9d. and Agnes de Boseham paid 6d. the same year; the abbot of Coggeshale 6d. and Robert Greylond 18d., 30 Ed. III; the tenement is to the west of that of the abbot of Coggeshale.

948. [1147–67] Grant by Ralph prior and convent to Turbertus of land which Kingus held at a rent of 18d. *p.a.* during his lifetime; rent 2s. *p.a.* after the death of Kingus; witnesses, William the priest (*presbiter*), Geoffrey the clerk, Geoffrey Tannur, Raginaldus cum botis, Hereward Palmer, Algar Basse, Siward son of Herebricht.

949. [List of those paying rent]: Turbertus; Geoffrey (*Galfridus*) his son otherwise called Wateraldere.

950. [1197–1221] Grant by Peter prior and convent to Geoffrey le Wateraldere [f. 166] of land next to Estsmehtefeld on the east held by the late Hereward Ruffus; to hold to Geoffrey and his heirs in fee; rent 6d. *p.a.*; if the grantee wishes to sell or lease the land then the prior and convent shall have the preference by 1 gold bezant; swore fealty; 12s. gersuma and one salmon of the value of 2s. for pittances; witnesses, Laurence Lindraper, Richard son of Gocelinus, Edward his brother, [Ig]hanne Thiep, Geoffrey Trentmars, Wurthing the Carpenter (*Carpentarius*). Geoffrey le Waterladere paid 2s. 6d. *p.a.*

951. [List of those paying rent]: Robert Waterledere; John Gardyner; Jordan de St. Paul; Walter in le Herne, 1 and 19 Ed. II and 1 Ed. III; Roger atte Ponde, 6 Ed. III; John Cory, 23 Ed. III in which year the pestilence first began; John Lovekyn now[1] mayor of the City.

    1. Mayor, 1348–9, 1358–9 and 1366–7.

952. Note: that John Cory at the instigation (*excitione*) of substantial men of the City with the agreement of Prior Nicholas asked Michael Northburgh, bishop of London, to consecrate a toft at the rear of the said land (*unum toftum aretro dictam terram*) as a burial ground so that this field is called the cemetery of Holy Trinity. In which place Edward III with the consent of the prior and convent founded the abbey of St. Mary Graces A.D. 1359[1] and so the rent of 2s. 6d. [mentioned in **951**] was paid by the abbot.

    1. Probably in error for 1349.

953. Total of this parish £8 6s. 8½d. and yet it is tithed at £14 10s. 1d. as appears in the king's exemplification.

954. [f. 166v] Agreement made in 1412 between William Wodeward, founder, John Kokyr, incumbent (*ico*[*nim*]*os*) of the church of St. Botolph without Algate, John Cornwaleys, Robert Borford, John Byrd, John Edward, John Bray, Thomas Brygth and other parishioners and William Haradon, prior of Holy Trinity and rector of St. Botolph by the mediation (*medianter*) of Thomas Axbrygg, canon, concerning a chantry in the church for the soul of John Romeney, once citizen and potter (*ollarii*), of London, whose executors had left the custody of it to the prior, which custody was in fact exercised by the parishioners. The prior conceded the custody to the parishioners reserving to himself and to Holy Trinity an annual quit rent. The parties chose two men, John Cornwaleys for the parishioners and Richard Osberne, clerk of the Chamber at the Guildhall, for the prior and convent, to examine the evidences and they found that the prior and convent were seised by John Romeney of an annual quit rent of 6s. 8d. from one of his houses now inhabited by John Haverill; abutments, the tenement of Henry atte Hook on the west and that once of John Romeney now of John Hamerton on the east; and also of 8d. *p.a.* from two shops once belonging to John Romeney situated between the tenement of John Hamerton on the west and Spytillane on the east; and also of 2s. 10d. *p.a.* from three other tenements of John Romeney which Nicolas Taillour and John Wiryng had by a lease of the prior and convent situated between the tenement of John atte Lee on the north and those of the prior and convent and of the abbess of the Poor Clares (*Sancte Clare*) on the south; and also of 13s. 4d. *p.a.*

St. Botolph Aldgate

from the same tenements which William atte Hale bequeathed to the prior and convent as appears in his will[1] enrolled in the Husting of Common Pleas, Mon. 20 Nov. 1368. The parishioners promised to pay the total annual rent of 23s. 6d. [f. 167] For this agreement the prior and convent agreed to pay to John Dalby the chantry priest and his successors 26s. 8d. *p.a.*, to be paid by Thomas [Axbridge] and his successors from the profits of the church of St. Botolph except at any time when the said church be let to farm by the prior and convent. The prior and convent grant all the brewhouse equipment (*omnia utensilia et vasa sua bracine*) in the tenement which John Haverill holds to the parishioners on condition that all the aforementioned obligations are performed and, if they are not, the prior and convent have the power to enter the house and remove the equipment; witnesses, William Norton, alderman and others.

1. *C. Wills*, ii, 118–19.

955. Licence was granted to Edmund son of Henry III to assign certain tenements held of Holy Trinity to the abbey of the Poor Clares. Release to Juliana abbess of St. Mary without Alegate of the order of St. Clare, of all claims for the priory or for the church of St. Botolph which the prior had, saving to Holy Trinity the canonical portion according to the papal statute if any of the parishioners of Holy Trinity dwelling outside the bounds of St. Mary's seek burial in that abbey and a rent of 16s. 9½d. *p.a.* The tenements, which Edmund made over to the abbess were held of Holy Trinity at the above-mentioned rent and were once held by Master Thomas de Bredstre, William the Shoemaker (*Sutor*), Alexander son of Geoffrey le Coureur and Hodierna his wife, William de Waltham, Helen his wife, Adam le Windraker[1] and Alice his wife, and Thomas de la More and also those of Solomon le Tuler and John Golcorn. The prior and convent granted tithes to the abbey as it had obtained exemption of all such payments from Boniface VIII. [f. 167v] Holy Trinity freed all their men who lived within the ambit of the abbey. The limits of abbey contained in length on the west side from the tenement formerly of Gilbert de Thotenham, potter, to that of Simon the Tiler, 15 perches 7 ft. and within the limits (*distantibus*) 5 perches 3 ft. from the outer door of the sisters on the west side from the south side of the tenement which was formerly Solomon's as far as the tenement once of Peter Berneval near (*sub*) the tenements of Ranulf Alan and Nicholas John, potters, and John Goldcorn, 14 perches 6 ft. Also on the east side next the field of Eadmund Trentemars from the tenement of Peter Breneval [*sic*] as far as the tenement formerly of Gilbert the Potter (*Potater*) 27 perches and in width on the south side from the said field to the king's street 24 perches and on the north side next the tenement of P. Breneval from the aforesaid field to the tenements of John Goldcorn and John Poter 20 perches. Indenture sealed by the prior and convent and by the abbess of the monastery of the order of St. Clare, dated Easter 1303.

1. *Rectius* Winedrawer.

956. [f. 168] Release by Katherine abbess of St. Mary of the order of St. Clare, after a lawsuit, of rights in a certain plot and to a rent of 2s. *p.a.* therefrom; dated Easter Sunday 1371.

St. Botolph Aldgate

957. Release by Katherine abbess of the monastery of St. Clare, after a lawsuit, of rights in a certain plot with a little house built upon it and to a rent of 12d. *p.a.* therefrom; abutments, the tenement formerly of Robert de Gadesby on the north and the enclosed field? (*ceptum*) of St. Mary's on the south and its tenement situated next to the outer gate of the monastery on the west and the earth wall (*murum terrenum*) lying next to the little garden of St. Mary opposite the gate leading to the dwelling in which the lady de Clare (*domina de Clara*) lived a short time ago, on the east, containing in length 20 ells and in width 10 ells; the prior and convent to have the right to enter and distrain; [f. 168v] sealed; dated London 16 Nov. 1374.

 Margin: Concordia inter priorem et conventum ecclesie Christi Lond' et Minorissas pro quadem placea situata inter tenementum quondam R. Gadesby modo elemosinari nostri et portam predictarum minorissarum.

958. [f. 169] Composition made between Nicholas prior and convent and the abbey and convent of St. Mary Graces; starts with a memorandum as to how the abbey was founded by Edward III at the time of the pestilence and records the inadequacy of space for the burial of the victims and the consequent consecration of a new cemetery near the Tower of London; the establishment of this Cistercian house within the parish of St. Botolph without Algate, led, as this church was annexed to Holy Trinity, to a conflict between the two houses on oblations and tithes upon which Simon bishop of London adjudicated; it was decided that 100s. *p.a.* should be paid to Holy Trinity in compensation, to be paid by the sheriff out of the farm of London and Middlesex; in return, all the tithes and oblations from certain tenements should not be paid to the parish church but to the abbey; [f. 169v] namely, a toft lying on the east next to a common field between Hoggestrete on the north and the garden of St. Mary Graces on the south containing 147 ells in length and in length on the west side extending from Hoggestrete to the garden of John de Cory, clerk, and across a certain plot also for the cemetery up to the holding of the abbot on the south, 123 ells 2 ft. with the thickness of the earth wall in Hoggestrete and the north end of the plot contains 93 ells and the south end contains 65 ells; the lands and tenements formerly of Helen Cros and Nicholas de Dedynton where the monks were living on the 'buttancia' on 'le Tourhill' containing in width 24 ells upon which a gateway opening on to Tower Hill had been built; also the tenements formerly of John de Basyng and Geoffrey de Henewade situated between those of Helen and Nicholas on the north and that of John de Parys on the south containing along Tower Hill $26\frac{1}{4}$ ells; also a tenement formerly of John Brawstok abutting on the south on (*super*) the street which leads from Tower Hill towards Duddyngespond situated between the tenement once of Richard de Parys on the east and the west and containing in width $24\frac{1}{2}$ ells 2 ins.; also a tenement once of Peter atte Vyne abutting on the same street situated between the tenement of Richard de Parys on the west and that of William de Box on the east and containing in width $12\frac{7}{8}$ ells; also a tenement once of Henry de Sutton, William Baconn and Alice his wife, of Richard le Porter and Lucy his wife and Matilda Sewtyng sister of Lucy and Geoffrey Waterleder abutting on the same street situated between the tenement of William Box on the west and that of

St. Botolph Aldgate

William Game on the east containing in width 70⅜ ells 7 ins.; and also a tenement of William Game situated between tenements of the said William on the west, east and north containing [f. 170] in width 3¾ ells; all these tenements are in the county of Middlesex and extend from Tower Hill on the west and from the said street on the south towards the cemetery and garden of the abbot and convent of St. Mary Graces except one piece of a tenement once of Geoffrey Waterlader which extends above the common field on the north. Cession by Holy Trinity of all tithes, oblations and other spiritual obventions from burials etc. and the bishop decreed that if St. Mary Graces should acquire more lands etc. in the parish all parochial rights were to be reserved to Holy Trinity; sealed by the bishop and chapter of St. Paul's and by Holy Trinity; dated 20 Mar. 1364.

959. Charter of Edward III granting 100s. *p.a.* to Holy Trinity to be paid out of the farm of the city of London and the county of Middlesex; [ff. 170v–171][1] Westminster, 1 Dec. 1356.

Margin: Enrolled in Michaelmas Term 5 Ric. II, roll 28.[2]
1. The charter repeats all the tenements mentioned in **958**.
2. See *C.P.R. 1354–58*, 487–8.

960. Note: Othwerus once custodian of the Tower of London and his successor Aschuillus disputed control over part of the soke of the Englyschkynztengyld with Holy Trinity. Prior Norman asked King Henry that justice be done to which the king agreed but the matter was not settled before his death. In the second year of King Stephen's reign the prior aided by Matilda, Stephen's wife, Algar bishop of Coutances, Roger then chancellor, Arnulf archdeacon of Sées (*Sagiensi*), William Martel dapifer, Robert de Curcy, Alberic de Ver, Geoffrey de Mandeville, Hugh le Bigot, Adam de Balnai, Andrew Buch(iun)te and many others, citizens of London, approached the king who agreed that a day be appointed to settle the matter. It was shown that the part of the soke in dispute belonged to the rest of the soke and had so belonged since the time of Edward the Confessor and this was proved by the oaths of twenty-one men; Orgar the monk surnamed le Prude, Ailwin son of Rad(uin)fi, Estmund, Alfric Cheic, Brictred Cuherd, Wlfred, Semar, Batun, Alsius, Berman, Wlpsus the Smith (*Faber*), Alfwin Halle(n), Leues(in)e the Smith, Wlwinus Abbot, Ailwin the clerk, Algar brother of Geraldus, Wlfric the Butcher (*Carnifex*), Elfiet Cugel, Wlfric, Edric Modlieuesune, Godwin Balle and many others were ready to testify but this number was judged sufficient.

Reg. A.–N., iii, no. 506 and Round, *Commune of London*, 99.

961. [f. 171v] [1140–6] Confirmation of the land [in dispute in **960**][1] by Stephen to Holy Trinity; the land of Smethfeld which Earl Geoffrey had taken possession of for a vineyard; witnesses, Queen Matilda, Thomas the chaplain, William de Ypres, Richard de Luci.

1. See *Reg. A.–N.*, iii, no. 506 f.n.
Reg. A.–N., iii, no. 507; Round, *Commune of London*, 100; P.R.S., x, no. 28; *Cal. Letter-Bk. C*, 221; *C.A.D.*, iv, A 6683.

St. Botolph Aldgate

962. [1140–4] Release by Geoffrey earl of Essex to Holy Trinity, addressed to the bishop of London, of their mill by the Tower and all the land outside the Tower which belonged to the Engliscecnithtengilda with Smethefeld with all their men and with all things belonging thereto and half a hide in Brembelega with all liberties and customs as William son of Wido had granted it to the house when he took the habit of a canon; to hold in free alms of the grantor and his heirs; witnesses, Countess Rohesa, the grantor's wife, Gregory the dapifer, Warin son of Gerold, Ralph de Crichcote, Geoffrey de Querendun, Ernulf the doctor (*medico*), Iwodus the doctor; also a grant of 1 mark of silver from the rent (*servicio*) of Edward de Selegeford; by the testimony of the above-written witnesses plus William archdeacon of London.

Round, *Commune of London*, 101; *Cal. Letter-Bk. C*, 222.

963. List of the witnesses of all the acts [mentioned in **960**, **961** and **962**] done in the second year of Stephen's reign: Ralph son of Algadus, Randulf, canon of St. Paul's, Haconus a deacon, William Travers, Gilbert the priest, Lungus, Wimundus, Joseph, Godefrey, John, Hubert, Leofwine, Godard, Aluric, Richard, Alwardus, all priests, James, Gervase, William, all clerks, Andrew Buchiunte, Stephen Bukerel, William the chamberlain (*camerario*), Ralph son of Andrew, Laurence Buchiunt, Theodoric son of Deremanus, John Buchiunt, Stephen Bukerel [*sic*], Gilbert Beket, Gervase son of Agnes, Hugh son of Wlgarus, Eustace nephew of Fulcred, Walkelinus, Robert son of Ralph, and his brothers Richard and David, Ailward the Forger (*fabricio*), Edmund Warde alderman, Edward son of Si(mu)us, Edgar Fuloc, Edward, Robert son of But, Alfegus, Ailwinus, Godwin, Ralph Godesune and Algar his son and Edmund his brother, Huneman Suethinus, [Si]ward Here, Godwin Brodhers, Hereward, Gerald, Sexi Forfot, Godwin Oxefot, John son of Edwin, Sawardus, Siredus and many others.

Round, *Commune of London*, 101–2.

964. Record of a disagreement between Holy Trinity and Ailward priest of St. Peter in the bailiwick of the Tower in the third year of Henry II's reign 1157, when Ralph was prior and Hugh de Mateni[1] archdeacon, the cause of which was that Ailward took off for burial the body of Godlune wife of Eilricus 'rusticus' of Smethefeld claiming her as his parishioner when Witthulfus the priest of St. Botolph had performed the last rites. Holy Trinity went to the archdeacon but Ailward appealed to him without the knowledge of the convent and the official was persuaded to allow the burial in the cemetery of St. Peter. [f. 172] The dispute as to parochial boundaries was settled and all Smethefeld and all the street and all the ponds of Dudyngspond were adjudged to be in the parish of St. Botolph as it had been in the time when Robert had been priest of St. Botolph and Derman(n)us priest of St. Peter to which Archbishop William had testified as appears in the following.

1. *Rectius* Mareni.

965. [1125–36] Letter from William[1] archbishop of Canterbury to W.[2] the

St. Botolph Aldgate

dean, the archdeacon and the chapter of St. Paul's ordering that the parish of St. Botolph be vested in Prior Norman which parish has been adjudged his in the chapter before the archbishop.

    1. William de Corbeil, archbishop, 1123–36.
    2. William de Mareni, dean, 1111–38.

966. [1128–34] Letter from Gilbert bishop of London to William and Haco (*Hacone*) the dean ordering them to do justice to the canons of Holy Trinity concerning the parish of St. Botolph of which Derm(m)anus the priest of the Tower (*sacerdos de Turre*) has unjustly deprived (*aufert*) them; also the entire chapter of St. Paul's is admonished to help them to recover the parish as quickly as possible.

967. List of those present in the chapter when the record was made; Randulf the dean, Algar the priest of St. Benet, Hurricus, Robert de St. Nicholas of Cole Abbey, Richard the priest of St. Margaret, Ailnodus 'presbiter scriba', Master Maurice, Tiulfus canon of St. Martin, and many other great men.

968. Note: that the day following the chapter which had been held on Wed. in the 4th week of Lent 1157 the 'rusticus' came into the church of Berkyngchirch and divided the oblation, as had been ordered, and gave to Withulfus, in the presence of Prior Ralph and Walter and Elias, canons, and Ralph the dean and Master James, a cloak (*pallium*), a roe-buck? (*che(v)sam*) and six sheep.

969. Note: that in 1166 Robert the Philosopher brought Holy Trinity again into the case of the parish of Smethefeld, having obtained a royal writ, saying that his church had been unjustly deprived of three sheep while he was absent in the king's service in the army of Toulouse (*Tologe*). Many times the prior was called before Archdeacon Nicholas also before Gilbert bishop of London, when it denied the claim and produced witnesses to show that the deceased woman was a parishioner of St. Botolph and Robert was induced to renounce his claim and this was done at Westminster on 9 May on the same day that a plea was heard between Earl Alberic and his wife which went on appeal to the pope.

970. List of those present at Westminster in the chapel of the sick (*capella infirmorum*): Prior Ralph, Walter the sub-prior, Gilbert and Robert, canons, Hui(n)gus a monk, Nicholas the archdeacon, Richard the archdeacon, Godfrey the treasurer, Richard the brother of Archdeacon Nicholas who confirmed the verdict by the following.

971. [*c*. 1166] Letter of Nicholas archdeacon of London to all faithful reciting the cause of dissension as to whether Smithfield was in the parish of St. Peter in the Tower (*in pedeplanis Turris*) or in the parish of St. Botolph and that Robert had renounced his claims and that it was in the parish of St. Botolph without Algate.

Hospital of St. Katherine

972. Note: that King Stephen and Matilda his wife gave to Ralph prior and convent of Christchurch London 6 librates in the manor of Braching in exchange for a mill of the convent and for that part of land which Earl Geoffrey occupied to make a vineyard in which place Queen Matilda founded the hospital of the poor.

[f. 172v] HOSPITAL OF ST. KATHERINE

973. [1147–8] Charter of Stephen by which he granted 100s. of land in Brackyng in Hertfordshire to hold to Holy Trinity in free alms for ever for the repose of the souls of Baldwin his son and Matilda his daughter who lie in the church of Holy Trinity; and also 6 librates of land [as above in **972**] which is in the part of the manor which will remain in the royal demesne after a partition and in which the church is, to which church the market belongs; to hold in free alms with sac and soc and toll and theam and infangenetheof; witnesses, Theobald archbishop of Canterbury, Robert bishop of London, Robert bishop of Hereford, Robert bishop of Exeter, Hilary bishop of Chichester, William bishop of Norwich, Queen Matilda, Earl E[ustace] the king's son, William de Ypres, Robert de Ver, William Martel, Henry de Essex, Richard de Lucy.

Reg. A.–N., iii, no. 511; *Cart. Antiq.*, ii, no. 405; *Cal. Letter-Bk. C*, 222.

974. [1147–8] Confirmation of Matilda of the grant of 100s. of land in the manor of Bracching to Holy Trinity and also of 6 librates of land in exchange for what they have granted to Matilda next the Tower where she has erected a hospital; witnesses as in **973** at London.

Reg. A.–N., iii, no. 152; *Cart. Antiq.*, ii, no. 406; *Cal. Letter-Bk. C*, 223.

975. [1147–52] Confirmation by Stephen of the perpetual custody of the hospital of St. Katherine to the prior and convent of Holy Trinity; the canons to hold the hospital with the mill together with a payment of £20 *p.a.* out of the rent of Edredeshede as the queen has granted them so that they may move it where it can be more conveniently placed (*ita quod transponant illud ubi oportunius sisti potuerit*); witnesses, Earl E[ustace] the king's son, Henry de Essex, Richard de Lucy, Warner de Lusor(e); at Hayngham.

Original deed P.R.O. E 40/4897; *Reg. A.–N.*, iii, no. 504.

976. [1147–52] Grant by Queen Matilda of the hospital of St. Katherine by the Tower to the prior and canons of Holy Trinity; the canons are to place the mill in a more suitable place and to maintain thirteen poor people in the hospital for ever for the salvation of the souls of the queen, King Stephen and their two children Constance and William; a grant of £20 *p.a.* from the rent of Edredeshede in free alms; King Stephen agreeing; witnesses, Henry de Essex, the king's constable, Richard de Ca(nv)ill, Warner de Lusor(e), A. the chancellor, Thomas the chaplain, Richard Montague (*de Monte Acuto*); at Hayngham.

Reg. A.–N., iii, no. 503; *Sir Christopher Hatton's Book of Seals*, ed. L. C. Lloyd and D. M. Stenton (1950), no. 424; C. Jamison, *History of the Royal Hospital of St. Katharine* (1952), App. 1.

Hospital of St. Katherine

977. [1151–2] Charter of William de Ypres addressed to Theobald archbishop of Canterbury and legate and to the bishop of London [f. 173] granting to God and to the prior and canons of Holy Trinity in free alms Edredeshetha (*Edredeshede*) now called *Ripa Regine anglice Quenhyth* on condition that they give from the rent of this hythe £20 *p.a.* for the maintenance of the hospital which is in their custody; and they shall give 100s. *p.a.* to the monks of St. Saviour (*Bermundesheia*) and 60s. to the infirm brethren of the hospital of St. Giles and what remains of the rent[1] the canons shall have for clothing (*vestitura*) and other necessities; the grant has been made with the agreement of King Stephen for the souls of the king and queen and for the souls of their children Baldwin and Matilda buried in the church of Holy Trinity and for the remission of the sins of the donor and for the salvation of his soul and the souls of all his ancestors, relations and friends; witnesses, Roger archdeacon of Canterbury, Odo the clerk, Ralph the chaplain, John the clerk, Richard de Lucy, Ralph Picot, Warner de Lusores, Erchebald Pas(c)e, Roger Waleis and others.

1. *Margin*: Ecclesie Christi Lond' Cs.

978. [1151–2] Confirmation of **977** by King Stephen, addressed to the bishop of London etc.; confirms the grant of 100s. to Holy Trinity made by William de Ypres out of the farm of Edredeshetha which the king had granted to him; witnesses, Queen Matilda, E[ustace] the king's son, William Martel, Richard de Lucy; at London.

Reg. A.–N., iii, no. 501.

979. [1136–54] Confirmation by Stephen, addressed to the justiciar, the sheriff and citizens of London, to Holy Trinity of Edredeshetham as it had been granted to them by Matilda, wife of his uncle King Henry; witness, Roger de Fraxine(n)t; at Norham'.

Reg. A.–N., iii, no. 502.

980. [1151–61] Confirmation by Archbishop Theobald of the gift which William de Ypres gave to the canons of Holy Trinity from Edredeshida as King Stephen had confirmed it [**978**]; also confirms to Holy Trinity the custody of the hospital with a mill near the Tower of London as confirmed by the king and granted by Queen Matilda.

J. Nichols, *Bibliotheca Topographica Britannica*, ii, sec. i, 101; P.R.S., x, no. 32; A. Saltman, *Theobald* (1956), no. 162; *C.A.D.*, iv, A 6684.

981. [1161] Confirmation by Pope Alexander [III] to the prior and convent of Holy Trinity of the order of St. Augustine having received a petition from the house showing that the canons had been granted the perpetual custody of the hospital of St. Katherine the Virgin within the parish of St. Botolph without Algate, this is confirmed; dated Viterbo 30 Oct. the 3rd year of his pontificate.

982. [f. 173v] *Plea held at Westminster, Thurs. 3 Dec. 1254.* John prior of

Hospital of St. Katherine

Holy Trinity, at Westminster before William de Kylkeni, chancellor, Philip Lovel, treasurer, John Franceis, Peter de Orival, Edward of Westminster and other barons of the exchequer against Stephen once a clerk, the prior being accused by the writ of Queen Eleanor[1] concerning (*super*) the custody of the hospital; on that day there was enrolled in the plea roll of the exchequer the charters of Stephen, Matilda and Henry III and the prior showed a writing to the barons about a certain composition made between Holy Trinity and the hospital about the commutation of a certain rent which writing had been made at the instance of the brethren and sisters of the hospital; the prior was protested if he wished to renounce the composition and on the same day the perpetual custody of the hospital was adjudged to the prior and his successors for ever.

> 1. Regent in Henry III's absence, see Jamison, *History of the Hospital of St. Katharine*, 11.

983. Note: that the same year [1254] when Ralph Hardel was mayor an inquisition about the hospital was made; all the aldermen of London replied with one voice that the prior and convent of Holy Trinity had continuously the custody and lordship (*dominium*) of that hospital from the time of King Stephen.

984. Note: that Queen Eleanor inspired by the malevolent suggestions of Stephen one of the brothers of the hospital, wrote in the following threatening terms to Fulk Basset, bishop of London, to use his powers to say that Holy Trinity's claims to the hospital were not valid.

985. [before 3 May 1257] Letter of Eleanor to Fulk bishop of London recalling that, as the hospital was founded by her predecessor Queen Matilda, she has the patronage of it and accusing Holy Trinity of failing to support the hospital adequately; Stephen the bearer of the letter is to explain the position more fully to the bishop and to ask him to enquire into his accusations of detention of charters and of the seal of the hospital by the prior and convent; he enquired not only of the brethren and sisters but also from citizens of London, both lay and ecclesiastical.

> See Jamison, *History of the Hospital of St. Katharine*, 13.

986. [f. 174] Note: that the bishop, on the orders of the queen, called together some great men and came to Holy Trinity on 1 Sep. 1257 to enquire what spiritual right (*ius spirituale*) they had in the hospital and they replied that they had the same rights over the brethren and sisters as they had over their brothers at Corney, Berkeden, Brachyng, Totenham, Welcomstowe and Lyesnes since all received their habit in the chapterhouse of Holy Trinity and swore before the prior and convent; they enjoyed this right because the hospital was situated in the parish of St. Botolph which formed part of Holy Trinity's endowment of the Englischknythtengild and that whatever spiritual right they had in the hospital they had by grant and by the confirmation of the bishop of London; asked why they had put a certain canon Rusus over the hospital they replied that the brethren had been contentious and given to getting drunk (*ebriosi*) and that he was to restore them to religion, sobriety and devotion; the bishop, moved by a desire to please the queen rather than God, removed this canon, forbidding Holy Trinity to meddle in the affairs of the hospital and handed the custody of the hospital to a certain Gilbert, chaplain of the hospital; he permitted that the oath taken by the brothers and sisters should no longer be taken to the prior and convent and thus matters stood until the death of that bishop[1] which occurred soon afterwards whereupon Henry de Wyngeham succeeded him; he also was influenced by the suggestions of the queen so that in 1261 he, assisted by R[obert][2] bishop of Carlisle and E[gidius][3] bishop of Salisbury, sent for prior John and some of the canons and compelled them to agree to the following.

1. Fulk Basset, d. May 1259. 2. Robert de Chause, bishop of Carlisle, 1258–78. 3. Giles de Bridport, bishop of Salisbury, 1256–62.

987. Letter of H[enry] de Wyngeham, bishop of London addressed to all, declaring that on Mon. before the feast of St. Margaret 1261 the prior of Holy Trinity and the steward of the place (*yconomus*) released to Queen Eleanor all right which they had, both spiritual and temporal, in the hospital of St. Katherine by the Tower; in testimony whereof the bishop affixed his seal; given at London, Wed. after the feast of SS. Simon and Jude in the year of his bishopric etc.[1]

1. Presumably 2 Nov. 1261.

988. [1261–78] Inspection by R.,[1] bishop of Carlisle of **987** repeating it in similar terms.

1. Robert de Chause, 1258–78.

989. [1261–2] Inspection by E.,[1] bishop of Salisbury of **987** repeating it in similar terms.

1. Giles de Bridport, 1256–62.

990. [1222–48] Grant and confirmation by Richard prior and convent to the brethren and sisters of the hospital of St. Katherine of the cemetery, saving to the grantors and their successors the custody and the custom (*ordinacio*) which they have and 2 lbs. of wax by way of parochial rights and that henceforth [f. 174v] any doubt may be removed on these matters (*super hiis tollatur ambiguum*); chirograph sealed with the seal of Holy Trinity on the part remaining with the hospital and with the seal of the dean and the archdeacon of London on the part kept by Holy Trinity because the brethren and sisters did not have a seal.

991. [?1222–?1248] Exchange made between Holy Trinity and the hospital of St. Katherine whereby Holy Trinity released to the hospital an annual rent of 5s. which they owed to the canons as 'Schaldflet' and also the exaction of tithes on the mill and the gardens (*ortorum et gardinorum*)

Hospital of St. Katherine

which the canons received since the hospital, mill and gardens were all within the limits of the parish of St. Botolph, appropriated to Holy Trinity; in return the brethren and sisters granted to the canons a rent of 15s. 4d. *p.a.* in Edelmeton and 2½ acres of meadow there and they handed over all the relevant muniments; chirograph sealed with the seal of Holy Trinity on the part remaining with the hospital and with the seal of the dean and archdeacon of London [as in **990**]; witnesses, John Blund, Gilbert de Thotech, William de Forda and others.

992. Note: to seek another composition made between Prior William and Brother Thomas master of the hospital of St. Katherine in the parish of St. Benet Graschyrch when Ralph Sandwich was warden of London.

993. [1218–19] Grant by R. [*sic*] prior and convent and confirmation to the brethren and sisters of the hospital of St. Katherine of 34s. 4d. *p.a.*, i.e. 3s. *p.a.* which Angodus son of Odo was accustomed to pay from land next to land formerly of Robert the Mercer on the north in the parish of St. Mary Aldermanbury; 18d. *p.a.* from land which Lambert the Glover (*Wanterius*) held next the land of Richard de Arras on the west in the parish of Holy Trinity by (*versus*) Algate; 2s. *p.a.* from land which Robert Norensis held in the parish of All Hallows Stanenechirch next the cemetery of the church on the south; 4d. *p.a.* from land which Walter Brown (*Brunus*) held in the same parish next Craddokeslane on the west; 5s. *p.a.* from land which Bartholomew son of Philip held in the same parish next the land of Walter Brown on the west; 5s. *p.a.* which Simon Chaloner paid from land next to that of Ralph Chaloner on the west; 4s. *p.a.* from land which Robert de Beuerlac held in the same parish next the land of the aforesaid Simon on the west; 4s. *p.a.* from land which Thomas de Wileby held next the land of the aforesaid Robert on the west in the parish of All Hallows Fanchirch; 18d. *p.a.* from land which James the priest held in the parish of St. Dunstan; 12d. *p.a.* from land which William Vicinus held next the land of Joce the Weigher (*Ponderator*) on the south in the parish of St. Mary at Hill (*de Hylla*); 3s. *p.a.* from land which Robert Basse held next the land of Robert Cincur on the west in the parish of St. Botolph; 12d. *p.a.* which Ralph the Bureller (*Burel*) held in the parish of St. Olave by the Tower; 3s. *p.a.* from land which Semmanus held in the same parish next to the land of the aforesaid Ralph on the south; to hold to the hospital in perpetuity; rent to Holy Trinity 4d. *p.a.* to be paid within the octave of Easter without 'occasio' and miskenning; warranty against all persons; gersuma 29 marks; witnesses, Serlo Mercer, mayor, John Viel, Joce the Weigher, sheriffs and others.

994. [f. 175] [1218–19] Grant and confirmation[1] of P[eter of Cornwall], prior and convent to the hospital of St. Katherine of rents of 31s. 4d. *p.a.* [rents repeated as in **992** with the exception of 3s. *p.a.* which Angodus was accustomed to pay; warranty as in **993**]; gersuma 26 marks; witnesses, [as in **993**].

994 appears to be a correction of **993**.

Soke of Aldgate

[f. 175v] THE SOKE

995. Note: that John Dalby, chaplain of the aforesaid chantry[1] ministered to the parishioners in the absence of Thomas as long as he held the chantry; and after John Dalby; John Worthyn; William Matheu; John Tauntoft and they all took from Thomas Axbrygge 26s. 8d. *p.a.* according to the concord written 10 folios back [**954**] until 1420 when T. Axbryg withdrew and went to study in Oxford; the same year Richard Lythum, one of the executors of William Wodward, the founder, enfeoffed (*fecit feoffarise*) Thomas Bryght, John Edward, Alexander Sprott and John Croft with all the lands and tenements formerly of John Romeney and the chantry to a certain chaplain John Skelton; which being done, Richard Lythum resigned the church of Reynis in Essex and removed John Tauntoft from the chantry so that he might serve the chantry himself but he did not minister to the parishioners according to the above-written agreement [**954**]; whereupon William Clerk, prior of Holy Trinity, at the request of the parishioners, leased the church to John Tauntoft for £10 *p.a.* and so he served from Michaelmas to St. John the Baptist next following when he withdrew and the prior appointed Richard Malmesbury who celebrated daily until the visitation of John Kempe, bishop of London; 1 July 1424, at the visitation in St. Andrew Cornhill, Richard Lucas, the warden and other parishioners, Richard Lythum being dead and John Tauntoft absent, accused the prior that he did not have a chaplain present at night; whereupon the prior was summoned to appear before the bishop and he acknowledged that he was in default, being in breach of the agreement [**954**] but his opponents denied that any agreement had been made; the bishop asked who had drawn up the agreement and was told that he was in Oxford and he advised that the truth should be ascertained from him; Sat. 12 Aug. 1424 Thomas [Axbridge] came from Oxford (*a scola*) and since Richard Malmesbury had come, Richard Lucas and other malicious persons of the parish ordered the chaplains to pay no attention to R. Malmesbury and they removed books, vestments and church ornaments so that he could not celebrate, in defiance of the prior and against the decree of the bishop who was in Essex on a visitation; by the advice of Master David Prys he bore this patiently and sent Thomas Axbrygge to Colne in Essex where the bishop examined him about the agreement; the bishop returned on 13 Oct. [1424] and the next day all the most important of the parishioners met in the church of St. Botolph where it was decided that the next day Louis Jon who was the greatest man in the parish and who lived in the eastern part of the cemetery of the abbey of St. Mary Graces with his wife, who was the sister of the earl of Oxford, should go to the bishop, which Louis was to say that all the parishioners wished to have a vicar; in the presence of the prior the bishop received the parishioners and told them that the priory was privileged and that he could not grant them their request nor did he wish to do so; [f. 176] John Edward added that no parishioner ought to confess to a canon but the bishop ruled that the prior should enjoy his privilege and that the parishioners were actuated by malice and he threatened with excommunication any who had removed the ornaments of the high altar; Richard Lucas admitted that, as warden, he had received oblations and he was excommunicated and then absolved at the instance of the prior on condition that he and his associates came to an agreement with the prior; John Crofte one of the executors of the founder of the chantry negotiated with the prior and the bishop ordered that all things taken from the high altar should be returned before vespers on 31 Oct. and absolved them but then he was translated to the archbishopric of York; he thereby ceased to act and the heart of the parishioners was hardened so that they did not prevent the chaplain from ministering but they stopped the payment of a quit rent so that the prior impleaded them by a plea of the assize of fresh force as follows.

1. See **954**.

996. *Plea of the assize of fresh force held in the Guildhall in the parish of St. Lawrence Jewry before William Milreth and John Brokle, sheriffs, and Adam May, coroner, Sat. 24 Nov. 1425.*
The assize of fresh force came to recognise if Thomas Bryght, John Edward, Alexander Sprott, John Crofte, John Mathew and Geoffrey Brydde unjustly etc. disseised William, prior and convent of Holy Trinity concerning a free tenement in the parish of St. Botolph etc. *post primam* etc. and within forty days etc. whereupon the prior through John Hethingham, attorney, stated that they had disseised him of 23s. 2d. of rent within forty days of the levying of the bill of assize namely on Mon. 29 Oct. 1425; the assize was taken in the absence of the defs.; the prior said that the rent came from four messuages and one shop once of John de Romoney, citizen and potter, viz. 13s. 4d. *p.a.* from a messuage of which William Potter was once seised who held of Hamon Copton, citizen and moneyer, for a rent of 13s. 4d. which was later paid to Agnes daughter of John, Hamon's brother, and she married John Chaucer, citizen and vintner, and they, by charter[1] enrolled Mon. 19 Jan. 1366 but granted 16 Jan. 1356, gave this rent to William atte Hale, citizen and taverner, and Agnes, his wife, and by his will[2] enrolled in the Husting of Common Pleas held Mon. 21 Nov. 1368 he bequeathed the rent to his son Thomas canon of the priory of Crichirch for his life [f. 176v] and the life of Agnes and then to Holy Trinity; the prior stated that Nicholas de Algate, prior, was to have received it in free alms after the death of Agnes and the aforesaid Thomas and William Haradon was seised of the rent by the hands of William Wodeward, founder, and John Bridde then tenants of the messuage and that by the custom of the City citizens are allowed to bequeath tenements and rents within the city to the Church (*ad manum mortuam*) and the rest of the rent up to 23s. 2d. the prior and his successors have always had; and the prior has always distrained for arrears on each property separately and he stated that the rent was six and three quarter years in arrears and he wished to distrain 40s. by his collector (*redditarius*) Richard Waterden but the defs. would not allow him to distrain and therefore he sought the assize etc.; after forty days the jury asked what right the present prior had in the rent and which of his predecessors was seised of it and what damage the prior had sustained and whether the disseisin was by force and arms (*vi et armis*) and if there was any fraud or collusion against the statute of mortmain to which it was replied that prior Ralph was seised in the time of Edward I and all his successors had been

seised and that [f. 177] the arrears amounted to £7 16s. 4d.; the jury assessed the damages at 20s. above the arrears and found that the disseisin was not by force and arms and that there was no fraud or collusion and the total was assessed at £8 16s. 4d. and Thomas etc. in mercy. [Most of f. 177 and ff. 177v–178v are blank.]

    1. H.R. 93 (154).   2. *C. Wills*, ii, 118.

[f. 179] CHARTERS OF SEVERAL PARISHES

997. Memorandum: that Queen Matilda being dead and, as we have said above,[1] buried, contrary to her last wishes, at Westminster, King Henry hastened to London from the Continent and Prior Norman came to him. The king when he learnt that the last wish of the queen had not been carried out was exceedingly angry and gave nothing to the monks who had hoped for a gift. Following bad counsel he did not allow the land which the queen had bequeathed to Holy Trinity to be granted but he was well disposed because of his love for the queen and granted a foundation charter (*et cartam fundacionis nostre perfectam quam antea non habuimus suo prudentissimo consilio nobis in hec verba dedit*).

    1. **13.**

998. [1121–2] Notification by Henry I that the canons of Holy Trinity shall be free from subjection to other churches; that the canons may close the road between their church and the wall of the City; the king grants them £25 *p.a. blanch* from the farm of Exeter in free alms, also Alegate with the soke; grant of the English Cnithenegild with all lands and liberties both within the City and without; the canons and their men to hold with all liberties and free customs with sac and soc and toll and team and infaganethief, quit of all gelds, scots, wites, assizes, sheriffs' aids, suits of shires and hundreds [f. 179v] and leets and hustings and of pleas and plaints; hidages and tallages, military service and riding service (*de excercitibus et equitacionibus*), journeys (*de oneribus expedicionum*), keeping watch, work on castles, parks, bridges, stews, walls, enclosures, toll on carts, obligation to provide carrying service (*summagio*) and shipping service, the building of royal residences and of all secular service and exactions, all toll in any market or fair and of all tolls on journeys by road, bridge or sea throughout the kingdom; and the canons' men shall plead only in the canons' court and they shall not be impleaded for any tenement except before the king or his chief justice (*capituli justiciario meo*); the canons and their men are in the king's special protection; witnesses, Ranulf the chancellor, G. de Clinton, Ralph Basset, at Northampton.

    Facs. Nat. MSS., i, no. 6; *Reg. A.–N.*, ii, no. 1316 and f.n.

999. Note: that this charter [**998**] is enrolled in the Memoranda Rolls of the exchequer between the recorda of Trinity Term 8 Ed. II.

    Margin: Carta prima de pluribus parochiis.

1000. Note: it [**998**] is enrolled in the Guildhall in the great Memoranda book with the letter 'C' folio 48.

Cal. Letter-Bk. C, 73–4.

1001. [1135–9] Confirmation by Stephen of the grant made by Matilda wife of King Henry [as confirmed in **998**], witnesses, bishop of Winchester and William de Ponte Arc' [Pont de l'Arche] at Westminster.

Margin: Carta ij^a.
Facs. Nat. MSS., i, no. 8; *Reg. A.–N.*, iii, no. 499.

1002. [1155–8] Confirmation by Henry II [f. 180] of **998** mentioning specifically that the canons are to be free from subjection to any church except St. Paul's; witnesses, Queen Eleanor, Hubert Albrinc[1] bishop, Thomas chancellor, Richard de Lucy, Humphrey de Bohon dapifer, Ralph de Hastings, at London.

Margin: Carta iij^a.
1. Bishop of Avranches. See *C.Ch.R.*, v, 268, no. 8 where it is dated 1155–8.

1003. Memorandum: that St. Thomas archbishop of Canterbury was the king's chancellor at the time of the granting of the above-mentioned charter.

1004. Inspeximus and confirmation by Henry III of **998** mentioning specifically that Holy Trinity is free from subjection to the church of Waltham and confirming especially the gift of Algate with the soke and £25 *blanch* from the city of Exeter payable at the exchequer by the sheriff of Devon, their land at Leyton and the custody of the hospital next the Tower [f. 180v] and their lands in Bracking granted by King Stephen and Queen Matilda and other lands of the honour of Boulogne (*Bolon(ie)*), namely the land of Berkeden(e) of the gift of Richard de Anesteye and the land of Corneye and the church of Lefstanechirch of the gift of Hugh Triket and the chapel of Alsiswyk of the gift of Richard son of William; confirmation of their lands and rents in Bekeham and Clayherst of the gift of Picotus Empascorat with the liberties there granted by the Empress Matilda, daughter of Henry I; confirmation of the following gifts; of Roger son of Brian and Matilda his wife, 2 carrucates of land in Hoddenho and Trockyng; of Robert de Gatton, his land in Hamstede as Gilbert de Bradele held it of him at fee-farm; of Hubert the queen's chamberlain 4 librates in the manor of Brackyng; of Richard Wallensis 81½ acres of land and 4 acres of meadow in Brackyng with the services of Augustine the son of Wlwardus, Edith the widow and Richard Cruyland; of Ralph Hareng 25½ acres of land in the field of Heston and the meadow belonging to this tenement and the service which Robert the Smith (*faber*) of Heston was accustomed to pay annually; of William Blemund all his wood with the heath (*bruera*) as are enclosed by trenches (*fossatis*) in the parish of St. Pancras in Kentissetune next the plot (*partum*) of the bishop of London on the south and of William Uggel and his heirs and their services; of Ralph Triket a croft called Hogue or Hocus and a small piece (*morcellum*) of land next his barn (*horreum*) in

Charters of Several Parishes

Brambeleg and Nortmado 'et Spareweham et wildam et Wigewikam' and land formerly of Eadmund and Hugh son of Baldwyn, Hugh's house (*managium*) with an adjacent field; of Richard son of Osbert a certain place in which a mill was situated in Brambeleg which mill was one of four mills next to that of the nuns of Stratford on the east; of Robert Burell 10s. rent in Brambeleg; of William de Pyrho 16s. rent from a mill called the Monks' Mill in Brambeleg; of Ralph de Heyrun and William Thrisse and William de Berkyng 42 acres of land and 1 acre of meadow and an annual rent of 15s. 6d. and ½ lb. of pepper in Edelmeton; of William, earl of Esscx and earl Geoffrey his father his land of Selegeford and 1½ hides in Brambeleg; of Richard de Lucy 20s. rent in Newton and all the land which Godfrey Beifuin his servant (*serviens*) held a day and a night (*una die et una notte*) in the manor of Leesnes; of Henry de Furnell and Theobald de Brackyng the mill of Brackyng; of Henry de Corneya land and meadow and a rent of 37d. which he had in Corneya and Widihale; of [f. 181] Peter de Bendeng 10s. of quit rent from land in Bilesherse; of Hubert de Anestie and Denise his wife 9s. of quit rent from the mill of Kaldecote; of Nicholas de Catesber[y] and Katherine his wife 11 acres in Catesbiry; of Thomas de Bordesdon 9 acres of land in Bordesden; of Hugh de Marines 17 acres 1 rood of land and the service of Stephen le Wayte and his heirs in Westmel(n)e; of Richard son of Robert 1¼ virgates of land with pasture in Westmelne and the service of Geoffrey his brother from half the land of the donor's father; of Henry de Scalar(us) and Joan his daughter 9½ acres of land in Widihal; by the permission and confirmation of Earl William de Mandavill forty cartloads of brushwood from the wood of Enefeld; of Walter de Mandevill the church of Brumfeld with its lands and all tithes; and of the same Walter the church of Nuteleg and its lands and all tithes; witnesses, E[ustace] bishop of London, J[ocelin] bishop of Bath and Glastonbury, R[ichard] bishop of Salisbury, Hubert de Burgh justiciar, Ranulf earl of Chester and Lincoln, William de Eynesford, Richard de Argent(an) the king's steward, Stephen [f. 181v] de Beg(ne), Henry de Capella and others, given under the hand of R[alph] bishop of Chichester, chancellor, at Westminster 8 Feb. 1227.

Margin: Carta iiij[a].
C.Ch.R., i, 3; *Monasticon*, vi, 153–4.

1005. Inspeximus and confirmation of Richard II of **998**; **973**; [f. 182] **1001**; and another charter of Stephen[1] granting to Holy Trinity the men and the land of the Cnithenegelda as they had held in the time of the king's grandfather William I and in the time of both his uncles William II and Henry I and in the time of Liovestanus[2] and to be quit of watch (*warda*) and forfeiture, witnessed by Queen Matilda and W. de Lusore at Bermondsey; of **961**; [182v] and of another charter of Stephen[3] granting 2 hides of land in Leytona which Simon the Miller (*de Molendino*) and Adelina his wife and after them Robert de Ver gave in free alms to hold with full liberties, witnessed by Robert Caus, William Marc and Fulk de Dilli at Westminster; and another charter of Stephen[4] granting his special peace to all those who attend the canons' market at Bracching and that any who disturb them are liable to a forfeiture of £10, witnessed by W. Marc at

Charters of Several Parishes

Bermondsey; of a charter of Henry I[5] that the canons shall hold the land and the men of the Cnithenegilda [f. 183] witnessed by R[obert] de Ver at Westminster; of a charter of Henry III granting free warren in all the priory's demesne lands in Hertfordshire, Kent and Middlesex as long as they are not within the limits of royal forest, no one is to enter without the permission of the prior and canons upon pain of forfeiture of £10 and the grant of a market at Corneye weekly on Tuesdays and a fair for eight days from 23 Aug. provided they do not damage neighbouring fairs and markets, witnessed by Master William of Kilkenny archdeacon of Coventry, John de Grey, Henry de Peyte(v)in, given at Ha(v)ering 4 Apr. 1253, [ff. 183v, 184, 184v]; of **1004**; of a charter of Edward II to hold £10 of land or rents notwithstanding the statute of mortmain, letters patent[6] 3 Nov. 1317; of a charter of Edward III relieving Holy Trinity from the obligation to maintain corrodians after the death of those to whom they owe an obligation, letters patent,[7] at York, 6 June 1335; [f. 185] and a grant that Holy Trinity enjoy a messuage, toft and wharf in the parish of St. Mary at Hill which Thomas Richeer left in his will and a messuage and a shop in the parish of St. Botolph without Algate which William de Thormeston bequeathed all of which were held of the Crown in burgage tenure and which the canons had not received because of litigation under the statute of mortmain and also £7 17s. 4d. *p.a.* being the residue of an annual rent of £10, witnesses, S[imon] archbishop of Canterbury, chancellor, Thomas bishop of Exeter, treasurer, John duke of Lancaster, Edmund earl of Cambridge, Thomas of Woodstock earl of Buckingham, [f. 185v] our most dear uncles, Richard Arundell, Thomas Beauchamp of Warwick, earls, William Beauchamp, chamberlain, Hugh de Segrave, steward of the household, John de Fordam, keeper of the privy seal and others, given at Westminster 31 May 1380.[8]

    Margin: Carta v[a].
    1. *Reg. A.–N.*, iii, no. 505.
    2. *Margin*: Nota quod iste Leouestanus erat pater Alwini patris Henrici maioris London' primi cuius carta habetur in Prioratu de Tortyngton.
    3. *Reg. A.–N.*, iii, no. 520.   6. *C.P.R. 1317–21*, 48.
    4. *Reg. A.–N.*, iii, no. 514.   7. *C.P.R. 1334–8*, 117.
    5. *Margin*: H. secundus.   8. *C.Ch.R.*, v, 265–8.

1006. *Interpretation of 'soke' and of other words contained in the above-written charters.*
[The following words are defined]: Soke, Sake, Tol, Theam, Infagenethef, Hutfagenethef, Hamsokene,* Grythebriche, Blodwyte, Philtwyte, Phlythwyte, [f. 186] Fordwyche,* Flemenesfrith, Lecherwite, Chyldwite, Forstall, Schot, Gelde like Hornhilde, Hitage or Carrcage, Danegelde, Horngelde, Wapentall,* Lestage, Stallage, Stenger or Hedwyng* (quieti de attachiamentis in aliqua curia et coram quibuscumque de querelis ostensis et non advocatis), Misheryng,* Burgbriche, Wardewite,* Auerpays [Averpenny], Hundredata, Bordalpany, Burgbote, Brigebote,* Thethepeny, Mundebrych.*

    English translation in J. Stevens, *History of ancient abbeys*, ii (1723), 94.
    * These terms are not in Rastell, *Les Termes de la Ley* (1629); the other terms are in Rastell, often defined in the same or almost the same words.

1007. [1277–8] Grant by Alice de Merton abbess of St. Athelburge of Berkyng and the convent to Holy Trinity of a quit rent of 13s. 8d. *p.a.* namely 8s. 8d. [f. 186v] from land and houses built thereupon once of Edmund the Cordwainer in the parish of St. Michael by Algate; abutments, the tenement of the late Roger de Leuesham on the west and that of the late Thomas le Breton on the east; and 5s. *p.a.* from land and houses once of Joce the Barber (*Capillarius*) in Marthlane in the parish of All Hallows Stanyngcherch by the Tower; abutments, the tenement of Alice de Portesmuthe on the south and that of Henry le Lung on the north; to hold on condition that half of all the rent shall be used for the church and half for the infirm in the infirmary; rent a clove-gillyflower at Easter; the canons to have the right to enter and take naam if the rent is in arrears; the canons gave 10 marks; sealed; witnesses, Gregory de Rokesle, mayor, John Adrian, Walter le Engleis, sheriffs, John de Norhamtone, William de Hadestoke, aldermen of these wards, Ralph de la More, John Cok, clerk.

Margin: Carta vi^a.

1008. [1270] Grant by John Rosamund to brother Eustace and the canons of Holy Trinity 40s. *p.a.* of quit rent; 20s. which the grantor has as a gift from Thomas de Oxonia, bureller, and Alice his wife from their rent in the parish of St. Dunstan opposite the church in the street which leads to the Tower; 13s. 4d. from Godfrey de Essex and Lettice his wife from a certain messuage with a shop in the parish of St. Mary Abeycherch in Candelwikstrate; 6s. 8d. of quit rent which the grantor had of Adam de Gyseburne and Marsilla his wife [f. 187] which they have of Gilbert de Felford in the parish of St. Edmund by Garscherch; to hold in free alms; rent to Thomas de Oxonia and his wife ½ lb. of cumin or 3 grains of pepper and the same to G. de Essex and his wife; sealed; witnesses, John Adrian, mayor, Philip le Tailur, Walter le Poter, sheriffs, Matthew Bokerell, Thomas and Aluard, aldermen.

Margin: Carta vij^a.

1009. Recognisance of John Sperlenc that he owes 18d. *p.a.* of quit rent from certain land near the gate (*ianua*) of his capital messuage (*managium*) along the street in the parish of St. Andrew Estchep and another 8d. *p.a.* of quit rent from certain land in the parish of St. Botolph without Alegate between the cemetery of the church on the south and the land of Ralph the chaplain on the north; permission to the canons to take naam in the donor's capital messuage in the parish of St. Mary de la Helle if they do not find sufficient to cover the rent in the above-mentioned lands; the canons remitted 9s. 6d. rent and all claims to arrears; witnesses, Roger Duce, Augustine Mercer.

Margin: Carta viij^a.

1010. [1222–48] Grant by Felicia widow of Joce Juvenis to Richard prior and convent in free alms a quit rent of 40s. *p.a.* from land and three shops which are of the fee of St. Giles' hospital [f. 187v] in Bridge St. (*in vico*

Pontis London'); abutments, the land and shop of Wygod the Mercer on the south and the shop formerly of Richard Blund of the same fee on the north and the land and messuage which was of Geoffrey the Shopkeeper (*Schopparii*) on the west 20s. *p.a.* of quit rent; also from a certain shop which is Roger the Butcher's; abutments, the shop formerly of Derekinus the Spicer (*speciarii*) on the south and the shop of St. Mary of Suthwerke on the north 8s. *p.a.* of quit rent; also from certain land with houses and shops in the parish of St. John de Walbrok; abutments, the land formerly of Geoffrey de Frowyk on the east and the land formerly of Alan Weyder on the west 14s. *p.a.* rent from which 2s. *p.a.* has to be paid to the lords of the fee (*dominis fundi*); the grantor has handed over all charters and muniments to the canons; sealed with the grantor's seal and the seal of her husband's executors; witnesses, Ralph Sperleng, Robert Hardel, Robert de Cornhill, Alexander Ferrun, John Prian.

Margin: Carta ix^a.
C.A.D., iv, A 7296.

1011. [*c.* 1215] Grant by Alan son of Peter to the canons of Holy Trinity of 26s. 4d. *p.a.* of quit rent; namely 13s. 4d. which William Becham paid the grantor from lands formerly of Jordan Sperleng in the parish of St. Margaret versus Pontem next the cemetery of the church on the south; 5s. rent which Roger the Fishmonger paid the grantor from his messuage (*managium*) in the parish of St. Clement which belonged to Paul the parson of the church; 8s. rent which Benet son of Turkill paid the grantor from a certain stall in the Shambles (*macellum*) of Estchep between the stall formerly of Richard Blandekete and the stall of Robert Asse; rent to the grantor and his heirs 4d. *p.a.* within the octave of Easter; gersuma 20 marks of silver; [f. 188] witnesses, William Hardell, mayor, John Bucci(u)nte, Thomas de Haverhill.

Margin: Carta x^a.

1012. [?*c.* 1189–93] Grant by Geoffrey son of Stephen to the canons of Holy Trinity of 6s. *p.a.* of quit rent from a certain shop which Reginald the Butcher son of Nicholas holds of the grantor in the Shambles of Estchep in the corner by the bridge (*in corneria versus pontem*); 5s. of rent from certain land next the house of John son of Daniel which Walter son of James the Goldsmith holds of the grantor in the parish of All Hallows by Garscherch; 10s. 8d. rent from certain land next the land of the same Robert on the east which Andrew de Herghes, parmenter, holds of the grantor; 18d. of rent from certain land formerly of Kenutus the Tanner (*Tannarius*) which Alan son of Peter holds in Colemannestrata in the parish of St. Stephen; 3s.[1] rent from land which Daniel the Draper (*Draperius*) holds of the grantor in Staningelana viz. between the land of the said Daniel and the small lane (*venula*) which is between that land and the church of St. Mary de Staningelane; 7s.[2] rent from land containing in length 66 ft. of the feet of St. Paul's (*de pedibus sancti Pauli*) and in width 40 ft. which Stephen de Wendleswurth, goldsmith, holds of the grantor which land is alongside land which was formerly of Thomas de Aude(v)ill on the east in the parish of St.

Charters of Several Parishes

Michael at Wudestret; to hold in free alms doing service to the lords of the lands (*fundorum*) which the aforesaid lands owe; and 2s. *p.a.* quit rent out of 7s. rent which Gilbert the Whittawer (*Allutarius*) holds of the grantor in the parish of St. Alban Wood Street along the street between the land of Geoffrey Bone(ch) and that of the canons of St. Bartholomew which Henry son of Alfred held and in the middle between the land of Norman Blund and that of Daniel the Draper which land is of the fee of the monks of St. Alban's and extends from Wood Street to Staningelane to hold for ever 7s. *p.a.* of which 5s. *p.a.* goes to the monks of St. Albans; sealed; witnesses, Henry son of Alwin, mayor, Roger fitzAlan, William son of Sabeline, William de Haverhill.

Margin: Carta xj^a.
1. *Margin*: Hoc tenementum combustum et post recuperatum per Ricardum priorem dimissum fuit Petro filio Daniel pro xiid.
2 *Margin*: Hoc tenementum combustum et post recuperatum per Ricardum priorem dimissum fuit Galfrido de Essex pro vs.

1013. [f. 188v] [1222–48] Grant by Avice daughter of William Wilekin, alderman, for the salvation of her soul and that of Richard her former husband, to Richard prior and the canons of Holy Trinity of 7s. *p.a.* of quit rent which the grantor's father gave her and from which 7s. Gervase de Garscherch owes 42d. *p.a.* from the land and house in which he lives in the parish of All Hallows de Garscherch and the hospital of St. Katherine by the Tower owes 21d. *p.a.* for the land and house which William Bursier holds of the said hospital in the parish of St. Benet de Garscherch and the hospital of Sandun by Kingeston owes 21d. *p.a.* for the land and house which Alditha holds of the said hospital in the parish of St. Benet; to hold in free alms on condition that half the rent shall be used for pittances for the canons on the anniversary of Richard the grantor's husband and the other half on the grantor's anniversary; sealed; witnesses, Ralph Sperling, John de Solio, aldermen, Robert Long.

Margin: Carta xij^a.

1014. [1227] Grant of William de Blemonte to Richard prior and convent of 20s. *p.a.* quit rent which Robert son of Bartholomew, alderman, was accustomed to pay the grantor from certain land and houses in the parish of St. Mary de Newcherch between the land of Michael Tolosanus on the west and a lane next the cemetery of Newcherch which goes towards Bokelesby on the east; to hold in free alms; and also 17s. *p.a.* viz. 15s. which John Blund, clerk, used to pay to the grantor from land and houses which Paulinus the Mercer, brother of the said John, in Cornhill and John Frauncois held of the same John the clerk in the parish of St. Mary Wulnodmaricherch between the land of Gilbert the Woolmonger (*Lanarius*) on the west and the stone house of Robert Burell which is of the grantor's fee and adjacent to the said land on the east and 2s. which Robert Burell paid from the said stone house; to hold in free alms paying therefor 3d. to the soc of the bishop of London so that the canons shall have power to [f. 189] take naam and distrain and, if necessary, to plead gavelet concerning

Charters of Several Parishes

all the 37s. of rent; sealed; witnesses, Richard Renger, mayor, Stephen Bukerell, Henry de Cokham, sheriffs.

Margin: Carta xiij[a].

1015. [1197–1212] Agreement between Benet abbot of Stratford and convent and Peter prior of Holy Trinity and convent acknowledging that the abbot of Stratford has given to Holy Trinity 60 marks of silver and 40s. *p.a.* of secure quit rent (*de securo et quieto redditu*) in London in exchange for two pieces of land, one called Luymudhe which Robert the clerk of Westhame held of the canons lying next to Luiam on the east and the other called Holec(u)hame lying near the monks' mill called Pikeshoc to hold to the abbot and monks for ever; the 40s. *p.a.* of quit rent in exchange comes from the following places, 8s. in the parish of St. Faith from the land of John de Mareni which Godfrey the Chamberlain held of the monks, 8s. in the parish of St. Benet from lands which Alfred Finatat held, 5s. in the parish of St. Nicholas [Cole Abbey] in the ward of Alan Baalun[1] which Walter Talliator, who was married to the daughter of Michael son of John, held, 7s. in the parish of St. Martin in Candelwrichestrate from land which Ralph Long held, 12s. in the parish of St. Peter Cornhill from land which Osbert Rufus held; if the abbey of Stratford cannot warrant either all or part of these payments it will make the sum good from other rents in London up to the amount of 40s. *p.a.*; [f. 189v] Holy Trinity to hold these quit of all services to the lords of the land and Holy Trinity will warrant the above lands; the agreement was read and agreed in full chapter of both houses; witnesses, Henry son of Ailwin, Roger son of Alan, Alan son of Peter.

Margin: Carta xiiij[a].
1. Queenhithe.
C.A.D., iv, A 7294.

1016. [1259] Grant by William son of Roger, citizen of London, to John prior and convent of 24s. *p.a.* of quit rent which Henry de Dunolm and Agnes, widow of Adrian Aswy, paid to the grantor from houses which they held of him in St. Martin's Lane by Kandelwrihtestrate; also 23d. *p.a.* of quit rent which William Bray paid the grantor from his houses in the parish of St. Martin Oteswych; to hold in free alms paying for the grantor and his heirs to the monks of St. Saviour Bermundeseye 10s. *p.a.*; the canons gave 12 marks, sealed; witnesses, William fitzRichard, mayor, Adam Bruning, Henry de Coventre, sheriffs, Geoffrey de Winton, alderman, John de Gysors.

Margin: Carta xv[a].

1017. [f. 190] Grant by Richard Renger, citizen of London, to Richard prior and convent for the salvation of the soul of Roger Duc once mayor of London 2s. *p.a.* of free quit rent from a certain stone house which William de Stanes holds in the parish of St. Mary de Somersete; also 14d. in the parish of St. Swithin in Candelwikstret from the house of Solomon le Dubhour; also 3s. in the parish of St. Botolph without Bisschopsgate from

Charters of Several Parishes

the house of Simon le Coureour; also 4s. 6d. in the same parish from the land and houses of Jordan de Mora; also 6d. in the same parish from the land of Nicholas Bat; warranty for the donor and his heirs; dated 1236; sealed; witnesses, Master Alexander rector of St. Swithin, Robert Hardell, Peter Bacon.

Margin: Carta xvj^a.

1018. [1239–40] Grant by William the Chamberlain son of Robert the Chamberlain to Richard prior and convent of his capital messuage (*managium*) in the parish of Holy Trinity the Less; also 5s. *p.a.* of quit rent and ½ lb. of pepper from land with houses formerly of Robert son of Simon; also 5s. of quit rent and ½ lb. of pepper from land with houses which William Taillur held; also 1 lb. of pepper from land with houses formerly of Andrew Blund in the parish of St. Thomas; also 8s. in the parish of Paternoster church from land with houses formerly of Nicholas Duket; also 12s. of rent in the parish of St. Mildred Bredestrete from land etc. formerly of Helen daughter of Walter Blund which 20s.[1] the grantor had as a gift from his sister Margaret; also 15s. of rent from land with houses which Ralph de Ely held and 20s. from the land with houses which Ralph Frany(er) held in the parish of St. James [Garlickhithe] (*super Tamisiam*); also 20s. in the parish of St. Michael [Queenhithe] (*super ripam*) from land etc. formerly of John de Kolemere; also 8s. in the parish of St. Nicholas Olave from land etc. formerly of Thomas son of Thomas son of Richard; also 1 lb. of cumin in the parish of St. Augustine by St. Paul's from land etc. formerly of John de Wylenhale; also 4s. of rent which the nuns of Haliwell owe from certain land with houses which is below Newegate on the north side and on the south side of the same street from certain land and a garden adjacent to the City [f. 190v] wall; 10s. in the parish of St. Audoen which the said nuns owe; to hold in free alms; and if William son of Ralph the Justiciar and Denise, the grantor's daughter dies before coming of age, 40s. which the grantor gave in dower (*maritagium*) to the said Ralph with his daughter; sealed; witnesses, Gerard Bat, mayor, Reyner de Bungeye, Ralph Eswy, sheriffs, Henry de Chobham, Henry de St. Albans.

Margin: Carta xvij^a.
1. Refers presumably to the two previous items of 8s. and 12s.

1019. [1241–2] Grant by Ralph le Justice to Richard prior and convent of 42s. *p.a.* of quit rent which William the Chamberlain gave to him in free dower with Denise his daughter viz. from the lands and houses of the countess of Oxford in the parish of Paternoster church 6s. 8d.; from the lands and house of Peter de Trye in the same parish 6s. 8d.; from the house of Stephen Crassus in the parish of St. James 5s.; from the house and land of the prior of Lewes in the parish of St. Thomas the Apostle 4s.; from the house and land of William Crassus in the same parish 10s.; from the shop of John Sonke in West Fishmarket in the parish of St. Nicholas 3s.; from the house and land of Richard Foliot in the parish of St. Faith 6s. 8d.; to hold to the canons in perpetuity; the prior and canons gave 10 marks in

Charters of Several Parishes

silver; witnesses, Ralph Aswy, mayor, John son of John Viel, Thomas de Dunholm, sheriffs.

Margin: Carta xviij^a.

1020. [1197–1221] Letter of Peter prior and convent [f. 191] that they have granted to the nuns of St. Leonard's Stratford that they will at their own costs cause to be mown all the tithes which belong to the nuns from the priory's demesne in Brackyng and that the 'famuli' of the nuns with their carts (*bigis et carris*) shall enter freely into the grantor's fields and follow the priory's carts to collect their tithes and carry them away; for this concession and as a recompense for Holy Trinity's expenses the nuns have given 40d. *p.a.* of rent in the city of London viz. 18d. which Lambert the Glover (*Wanterius*) holds of the nuns in the parish of Holy Trinity and to this rent Lambert assigned to Holy Trinity 22d. *p.a.* which John the Parmenter paid the nuns from certain land which is next the land of Simon Blund on the south, in the parish of St. Stephen Walbrok; warranty of the 40d. by the nuns and of the costs of reaping by Holy Trinity; sealed; witnesses, Roger Hus(c)aill, William his son, William Cole, William de Piro, German the Parmenter.

Margin: Carta xix^a.

1021. [1256–7] Grant by Eustace son of David de Staunford to John prior and convent of 2 marks *p.a.* of rent which John Sharp used to pay from certain land with houses in the parish of St. Mary de Newchurch; also 22s. 4d. *p.a.* of rent from the next house in the same parish from which the service due to the lords of the fee, Robert de Agulun and his heirs is 9s. *p.a.*; also 3s. *p.a.* of quit rent which the grantor used to receive from all the land and houses formerly of William the Glazier (*Vitrius*) in Colkeslane; also all the land with a garden which the grantor had in the parish of St. Olave by the Tower paying thereon 2d. *p.a.* to the king's socage in the middle of Quadragesima; to hold in free alms; [f. 191v] during the lifetime of the grantor the canons gave him 6 marks of silver *p.a.* from their chamber (*camera*); sealed; witnesses, Ralph Hardell, mayor, Richard de Ewell, William Aswy, sheriffs, Matthew Bokerel, alderman, John de Gisors.

Margin: Carta xx^a.

1022. [1193–1212] Grant of Robert son of John Cherunburt to Holy Trinity, in free alms, of a certain stone house in the parish of St. Mary Wulnothmariecherch next to the house of William White on the north paying 1d. to the king for soke and 2s. to the monks of Moroton [?Merton]; also certain land in the parish of St. Mary Abbechirch alongside the land formerly of William Tailiator on the west which land is of the fee of Holy Trinity; also 8s. *p.a.* of rent from land which Alexander de Linton holds of the grantor in the parish of St. Mary de Newcherch, the grantees paying 2s. *p.a.* to Henry son of Ailwyn and his heirs; sealed; witnesses, Henry son of Ailwin, mayor, Alan son of Peter, Thomas de Haverhill and Richard his brother.

Margin: Carta xxj^a.

Charters of Several Parishes

1023. [1193–1212] Sale and quit claim by Richard de Flit and Alice daughter of Alfred the Mercer to the prior and convent of Holy Trinity of 6s. *p.a.* of quit rent from two lands which Henry and Richard sons of Henry Blund held of the donors; [f. 192] one is in Bassinghahe between the land that Andrew Neuel(im) held of the canons and the land of the canons of Merton and the other is in Aldermanneb(ur)ia and lies between land that was formerly of Andrew the Old (*Senis*) and that of Michael the Cordwainer (*Cordwanerius*);[1] the prior and convent gave 50s.; witnesses, Henry mayor of London, Roger fitzAlan, John de Cay, sheriffs.

Margin: Carta xxij^a.
1. *Margin*: Bassinghawe 4s., Aldermanbury 2s.
C.A.D., i, A 1502.

1024. [1196] Grant by William son of Brithmar of Haverhull to Holy Trinity, in free alms, of 3s. *p.a.* of rent in the parish of St. Nicholas de Westmacekaria in the [street] which runs from the church of St. Nicholas to the wall of the City from land which Alice daughter of Thomas the priest (*sacerdos*) holds of the grantor in fee for 6s. *p.a.* which land lies next on the south to the land which William Yreis holds of the grantor; the gift is made by the concession of Alice, the grantor's wife and Thomas his son and heir and in return the canons have released the grantor from all arrears, namely 40s. of arrears of rent for five years from two lands which he holds of them for 8s. *p.a.*, one in the parish of St. Mary Magdalene in the Fishmarket by St. Paul's at 4s. *p.a.* which lies between land which he holds of Roger Too(ni) and the land of Alfred de Windeleshores and the other in the parish of St. Michael de Bassishaghe against the wall of the City at 4s. *p.a.* which lies between land which he holds of the sick girls (*puellis infirmis*) of St. James and the land formerly of Serlo the Saddler (*sellarius*); and the canons granted that they would remember the grantor and his relatives when they celebrated on the grantor's anniversary; made in the year 1196; witnesses, Anselm the priest of St. Nicholas, [f. 192v] John the priest of St. Peter Wodestrete, Henry son of Ailwin son of Leofstan, mayor, William son of Sabelina.

Margin: Carta xxiij^a.
C.A.D., ii, A 2507.

1025. [*c.* 1217] Confirmation by Sabina daughter of David Cordiwisse of the sale and quitclaim which her son William Piedefer made to Holy Trinity of 7s. *p.a.* of quit rent which she had in the parish of St. George and St. Leonard in (*apud*) Estchep which quit rent Robert Bat and Robert Blund, butcher, used to pay Sabina and William which Osbert Piedefer, once her husband, gave her in dower; to hold to the said canons freely, which grant Sabina made after the death of Richard Bacun her husband; the canons gave her $\frac{1}{2}$ mark of silver; witnesses, John Sperling, alderman, John Abraham, William Versin.

Margin: Carta xxv^a. [*sic*].

1026. [*c.* 1217] Sale and quitclaim by William son of Osbert Piedefer as in **1025**; abutments of the land from which the quit rent is paid, the land of

Charters of Several Parishes

William the Cook and the land of William Ruffus; the canons gave to the grantor 5 marks of silver; witnesses, John Sperling, John Abbraham, William Versin, Geoffrey Verhierde.

Margin: Carta xxiiij{a}.

1027. Grant by Ralph son of Roger the Palmer to Holy Trinity of his capital messuage (*managium*) in the parish of St. Peter Wood Street with two shops which he has by his father's will; to hold in free alms, [f. 193] the grantee to pay to the lords of the land 2½ marks for all services; also 18d. *p.a.* which William, Henry and Nicholas his brothers used to pay the grantor; also one shop which the grantor had at St. Ives (*apud Sanctum Ivonem*); sealed; witnesses, William the chaplain of Wood Street, Richard the Goldsmith, William de Berkyng.

Margin: Carta xxvj{a}.
C.A.D., ii, A 2704.

1028. [*c.* 1218] Grant by Thomas de Hauerhill to Holy Trinity in free alms of 3s. *p.a.* of quit rent from land which Hamo Brand holds of the grantor outside the Bar of the New Temple in the parish of St. Clement and 3s. from land in Cockeslane which the grantor holds of Holy Trinity from which the canons owe 2s. *p.a.* to Roger de Turri and all the land Thomas bought from Constantine Nimore and Joan his wife which William Flael left them which land is next to the forge on the east of the capital messuage (*managium*) in the parish of St. Edmund which the grantor bought of John de Angulo which land is next to the land of the canons; on condition that from these rents ½ mark may be taken for pittances to the canons on the grantor's anniversary; sealed; witnesses, Peter prior of Holy Trinity, Martin prior of St. Mary of Suthwerk, Godfrey prior of the New Hospital outside Bischopsgate, Serlo the Mercer.

Margin: Carta xxvij{a}.
C.A.D., i, A 1661.

1029. [f. 193 inset][1] [1314] Quitclaim of Adam de Braunhingg, clerk, to Ralph prior and the sacred convent of Holy Trinity of all right in two tenements which he acquired from Geoffrey de Hakeneye and Agnes his wife in the parish of St. Botolph without Algate; also 6s. 8d. *p.a.* of quit rent which he has of the gift of Thomas de Kyng and Alice from a tenement in the parish of St. Sepulchre without Newgate; the two tenements and the rent leased to the prior and convent for a term of twenty years for a certain sum of money paid to Adam; sealed; witnesses, John de Gysors, mayor, Hamon de Chiggewell, Stephen de Habyndon, sheriffs.

Margin: Carta xxviij{a}.
1. Here is inserted a piece of parchment 8½ ins. wide by 8⅜ ins. long.
C.A.D., ii, A 1865.

1030. [f. 193 contd.] *Exemplification of all the rents pertaining to the church of Holy Trinity assessed to the royal tenth.*
Richard etc. king of England and France etc. Know that, having inspected the roll concerning the particulars of the taxation of the temporalities of the

clergy of the city of London in the diocese of London, in the same it is accounted, among other things, as follows, that the assets (*bona*) of the priory of Holy Trinity in the various parishes are:
St. Mary de Wolch[ir]chawe 72s. 4d.; St. Christopher 16s.; All Hallows Colemanchurch 55s. 4½d.; St. Olave ad Turrim [Hart Street] 200s. 10½d.; St. Peter Wood Street 4s.; St. Michael Cornhill 25s. 4d.; All Hallows ad Fenum [the Great] 47s. 4d.; St. Giles without Cripplegate 28s.; St. Martin Ludgate 6s.; St. George 17s.; St. Mary le Bow 25s. 8d.; St. Michael Paternoster 15s.; St. John Walbrok 24s.; St. Ethelburga 7s.; St. Botolph Billingsgate 35s. 4d.; St. Martin Outwich 21s.; St. Sepulchre 25s.; St. Mary del Ax 23s. 2d.; [f. 193v] All Hallows de Berkyng 11s.; St. Andrew Cornhill [Undershaft] 18s.; St. Peter Cornhill 20s. 4d.; St. Alphege 5s. 5d.; St. Michael ad Ripam [Queenhithe] 20s.; St. Clement Candlewick Street 12d.; St. Benet Fink 3s.; St. Margaret Pattens 3s. 6d.; St. Benet Sherehog 22s.; St. Pancras in London 66s. 8d.; de Althermarich [St. Mary Aldermary] 6s. 8d.; All Hallows Greschirch [Lombard Street] 25s. 8d.; Holy Trinity the Less 3d.; St. Martin Candlewick Street [Orgar] 28s.; All Hallows London Wall 2s. 4½d.; St. Nicholas Olave 5s.; St. Augustine ad Portam 2s.; St. Lawrence Jewry 4s.; St. Swithin 13s. 4d.; St. Faith 18s.; St. Mary Aldermanbury 34s. 2d.; St. Botolph without Bishopsgate 24s. 8d.; St. Mary Woolnoth 2s.; All Hallows Staining 8s. 4d.; All Hallows Fenchurch 6s. 8d.; St. Margaret ad Pontem [Fish Street Hill] 33s. 4d.; St. Mary Magdalene in Piscaria [Old Fish Street] 2s. 6d.; St. Vedast 5s.; St. Mary Somerset 2s.; St. Mary at Hill 3s.; St. Benet Gracechurch 42s. 2d.; St. Alban Wood Street 10s.; St. Thomas Apostle 30s.; St. James Garlickhithe 15s.; St. Martin Vintry 15s. 7d.; All Hallows Honey Lane 48s. 4d.; St. Stephen in the Jewry [Coleman Street] 10s. 6d.; St. Stephen Walbrok 22d.; St. Mildred Bread Street 17s.; St. Dionis [Backchurch] 3s.; St. Michael Bassishaw 32s. 6d.; St. Mary Abchurch 67s. 2d.; St. Michael and St. Katherine within Alegate [St. Katherine Cree] £16 0s. 13d.; St. Benet Wodewarf [Paul's Wharf] 12s.; St. Botolph without Algate £14 10s. 1d.; St. Mary Bothaw 23s. 2d.; St. Dunstan East 62s.; St. Martin Pomary 6s. 8d.; St. John Zachary 51s. 4d.; St. Nicholas Coldabbey 21s. 8d.; St. Andrew Hubbard 16s. 4d.; St. Leonard 5½ marks; St. Mary Colechurch £13 6s. 8d.: all the foregoing, at the application of the prior of Holy Trinity, have been exemplified under the seal of the exchequer, in witness whereof our letters have been made patent, R. de Plesyngton at Westminster 26 Jan. 1384, by the said detailed roll in the treasury and by the barons: total of the abovewritten £121 16s. 6½d. of which the tenth is £12 3s. 7¾d. and the half tenth £6 0s. 22d.; the church of St. Botolph without Algate 10 marks of which the tenth is 13s. 4d. and the half tenth 6s. 8d. the church or chapel (*sive capella*) of St. Katherine 1 mark of which the tenth is 16d. and the half tenth 8d.

C.A.D., ii, A 2529.

[f. 194] WILLS CONCERNING SEVERAL PARISHES

1031. *Will of Ralph Blunt proved and enrolled in the Husting, Mon. 12 Feb. 1296,* in which he bequeathed, after the death of Matilda his wife, 6 marks of quit rent viz. from a tenement once of John Skip in the parish of St. Mary Woolchurch, 4 marks; from a tenement of John Gisors on the corner of Bread Street in the parish of All Hallows Bread Street, 2 marks for a mass for his soul and his wife's; his executors are enjoined to give security for the quit rent; brother Alan, a canon, is to celebrate the mass; no one is to impede the canons.

Margin: Testamentum primum.
C. *Wills*, i, 126.

1032. *Will of Thomas de Algate proved and enrolled in the Husting of pleas of land, Mon. 14 Oct. 1359*, in which Thomas rector of the church of Schering in the diocese of London, will made Sat. 2 Feb. 1359, left his body to be buried beside his father and mother in the church of Holy Trinity, a tenement in the parish of St. Katherine within Algate to his brother Nicholas prior of Holy Trinity and to the canons of Holy Trinity a quit rent of 6s. 8d. *p.a.* from a certain plot (*placea*) in the parish of St. Andrew Cornhill; also all his tenement in the parish of St. Botolph without Algate to the alms office (*officio elemosinarie*) of Holy Trinity for the perpetual increment [f. 194v] of the sustentation of the choir boys together with 10s. *p.a.* of quit rent from the same tenement which his father acquired of Simon le Hoodere, his mother previously had the tenement; also to Hugh son of the late John le Skynner £10 sterling payable to him after the completion of his apprenticeship if he survives and if he dies before the completion, the said £10 to Holy Trinity to pray for his and his parents' souls and for the souls of the testator's parents; the residue of all his goods movable and immovable to his brother Nicholas that he will do what shall seem fit for his soul and his parents' souls; John Hauekyn and John Crowhurst appointed executors and his brother is appointed supervisor.

Margin: Testamentum ij^m.
C. *Wills*, ii, 10.

1033. *Will of Thomas Richer, chaplain, proved and enrolled in the Husting, Mon. 14 Mar. 1362*, in which he, will made Wed. 13 Jan. 1361, left to the work of the fabric of Holy Trinity 20s.; to each canon 3s. 4d.; to John Richer his kinsman (*cognato*) 3s. 4d.; to Margery and Lorissa Richer, 13s. 4d.; to Mabel and Matilda Richer 40s.; and to the prior and convent of Holy Trinity all the tenement with a wharf and an empty plot adjacent in the parish of St. Mary at Hill[1] which he acquired from Robert Hwite, executor of John Warefeld by virtue of John's will; also to Holy Trinity all the lands and tenements which he acquired from Nicholas de Chikewell in the parish of Great Holy Trinity [f. 195]; also to Holy Trinity a certain tenement with a garden which he acquired from Margery widow of John Hoder, late citizen and skinner, and Joan the daughter of the said Margery in the parish of St. Botolph without Algate; also to the Friars Preachers of London 5s.; to the Friars of Mount Carmel 5s.; to the Friars Minor 5s.; to the Austin Friars 5s.; to the Crutched Friars 5s.; to Master John de Cantebregg 6s. 8d.; to William de Wardon 6s. 8d.; to Robert de Ramesdon 6s. 8d.; the residue for masses and to the poor of the hospitals of London and other necessitous persons dwelling in that city, the distribution to be where his executors think will be to the best advantage of the testator's soul; William de Wardon and Robert de Ramesdon appointed executors and Master John de Cantebregg to be supervisor.

Margin: Testamentum iij^m.
1. See **1005**.
C.A.D., i, A 1604; *C. Wills*, ii, 67.

1034. *Will of Simon Hatfeld proved [and enrolled Mon. 17 Oct. 1373]*,[1] in which he left to Holy Trinity all that tenement which he acquired from Roger Rook called 'atte Basket' situated in the parish of St. Katherine in the cemetery of Holy Trinity viz. between the tenement of Richard Andrew formerly William Daniel on the east and that of the prior and convent, formerly of Thomas Bonesergant, on the west and extending in length from the street on the north to the garden of the late Stephen Waltham on the south, for the use of the sacristan for the repair and maintenance of the church, on condition that on the day of the testator's death and on each anniversary thereof the sub-prior shall say mass for his soul and on the same day[s] the sacristan shall give to each canon who ministers 6d. [f. 195v] and if the sacristan fails to pay, he wished the tenement to remain with the prior and convent to the augmentation of their treasury (*camera*) as a supplementation to each canon except the sacristan, but if the profit is converted to other uses then the whole tenement shall go to the chapel of the Guildhall on condition that the chaplain celebrates for his soul; also to Holy Trinity 20s. *p.a.* of quit rent which he acquired from John Baas and Emma his wife from a tenement of the said canons once of Walter in which Simon the Baker (*Pistor*) then lived in the parish of St. Katherine; also to Holy Trinity 12d. *p.a.* of quit rent which he acquired from Simon Hauerill from a tenement of the said religious in the parish of St. Botolph once of J. Bonsergant; also to Holy Trinity 11s. *p.a.* of quit rent acquired from Roger Segrave and William Norwysch, executors of Thomas de Marlee, clerk, from a tenement of the said religious in the parish of St. Botolph.

Margin: Testamentum iiij^m.
1. *C. Wills*, ii, 155–6.

1035. *Will of John de Cantebregg proved and enrolled in the Husting, Mon. 30 Nov. 1377*, in which John, citizen and fishmonger, will made Sat. 9 Aug. [1376], left his body to be buried in St. Mary de Cricherch where Master John de Cantebregg his son and Elizabeth and Agnes his late wives lie buried; to Holy Trinity all the tenements which he acquired from Robert Denton, chaplain [f. 196] at Ebbegate in the parish of St. Lawrence Candlewyk Street together with the reversion of a certain tenement in the parish of St. Giles without Cripplegate which tenement Felicia wife of John de Waltham has and holds of him for the term of her life; also to Holy Trinity all the tenements which he once had of the gift and feoffment of William Baldewyne, citizen and saddler (*cellarius*), and Emmota his wife, situated in the parish of St. Katherine to hold to Holy Trinity after the death of Felicia on condition that they pray for his soul; also to his wife Katherine all that tenement which Henry Godchep and Agnes his wife holds for him for the term of their lives in survivorship in the parish of

St. Sepulchre without Newgate called Bacunnysyn paying to him 5 marks and doing to the lord of the fee the service due and also his wife shall have the 5 marks after his death for the term of her life with the reversion after the death of Henry and Agnes; also to the abbot and convent of Burton, co. Staff., the tenement of Bacunnysyn after the death of Katherine his wife on condition that they pray for his soul; also to William Kelhull, citizen and fishmonger, and Agnes his wife or to the surviving one all that tenement with a great gate and cellar adjacent in the parish of St. Nicholas atte Coldabbey for the term of their lives in survivorship and after their death it shall remain to William son of Thomas Con(v)ers and his legitimate heirs doing to the lord of the fee the service due; [f. 196v] also all the tenements he acquired from Thomas Convers and Isabel his wife shall remain to the aforesaid William after the death of Thomas and Isabel except that half house which he bought of Agnes daughter of the late Roger de Ely otherwise called Agnes Rayham in the parish of Holy Trinity the Less which he bequeaths to Katherine his wife and if the aforesaid William [Convers] die without legitimate heirs, then all the tenements left to him shall be divided equally between the abbot and convent of Westminster, the prior and convent of Holy Trinity and St. Mary Overe in Suthwerk; also to St. Mary Overy to say 'placebo' and 'dirige' and celebrate mass on his anniversary, all that shop which he acquired from John Ecclesale, clerk, in the Goldsmithery (*Aurifabria*) in the parish of St. Matthew the Apostle in Friday Street between the shops of the prioress and convent of St. Helen on the east and west and extending at the rear along the king's street of Westchep on the north and the tenement of Alan de Conductu on the south, St. Mary Overy to perform the services due to the capital lord of the fee; Katherine his wife and John de Kynggeston his former apprentice appointed executors; witnesses Robert his chaplain, Thomas de Estwyk, citizen and fishmonger, John Leuere his apprentice, Henry de Middleton, clerk, and others.

Margin: Testamentum v^m.
C. *Wills*, ii, 197–8.

1036. Note: that Thomas Convers was chamberlain (*camerarius*) to lord Bartholomew Borwasch and was therefore called Thomas Chaumbyr and his son William was apprentice to William Kelshull and therefore called William Kelshull and he lived in the parish of St. Michael Crokydlane in 12 Hy. IV.

1037. *Will of William Creswyk proved and enrolled in the Husting, Mon. 13 June 1407.*
Testamentum vj^m. [The will has not been copied, f. 197 is blank].

C. *Wills*, ii, 371–3.

[f. 198] ACQUITTANCES OF SEVERAL PARISHES

1038. First Acquittance: this indenture witnesseth that, since Peter de Weston, potter and citizen, owes to Holy Trinity 34s. 4d. *p.a.* viz. for a

Acquittances of Several Parishes

tenement which Robert de Raughtone held in the parish of St. Botolph without Algate 3s. 6d.; for a tenement which Peter himself held in the same parish of the prior and convent for a term of years 10s.; for a tenement formerly of Robert de Kelseye within Alegate in the parish of Holy Trinity the Great 11s. 2d.; for part of a tenement leased to Robert Panifader afterwards to Richard atte Waye in the same parish 20d.; and for part of a tenement once leased to Henry in le Lane in the parish of St. Mary atte Ax opposite the church of St. Augustine Papie namely in the corner there 8s.; the prior has been fully satisfied of all arrears outstanding on the day of the making of this document viz. £17 13s. 9d. by the melting down of a certain bell (*infusione cuiusdam campane*) together with the rent due to Michaelmas 1353; sealed by both parties; witnesses, John de Romeneye, John de Stowe, potter, John de Neul(i)n, Walter de Constentyn, William Daniel, Thomas Savage, clerk, Simon de Thotenhale; given at London 1 Aug. 1345.

C.A.D., i, A 1517.

1039. Second Acquittance: this indenture witnesseth that Nicholas prior and convent on the day of the making of this document have received from Margery widow of Thomas Broun £3 17s. 2d. in payment of all arrears from three tenements of an annual rent of 10 marks coming from the tenement of the late Thomas Cavendisch in the parish of St. Mary Colechurch and a rent of 53s. 4d. [f. 198v] from the tenement of the late John de Enefeld in the parish of Holy Trinity the Great and a rent of 2s. from a tenement of the late Adam Rokesle in the parish of St. Dunstan; and that all the arrears are cleared to Michaelmas last past; sealed counterparts; given at London 28 Oct. 1357.

1040. Third Acquittance: this indenture witnesseth that Nicholas prior and convent received on 26 Dec. 1363 the sum of 18d. of a certain annual rent from a tenement then empty from John son of Symon formerly held by Reginald de Conductu situated in the parish of St. Dunstan in the East in Menchunlane between the tenement of John Cory on the south and that of Peter Sterre on the north and also 2s. of a certain annual rent from a tenement of the said John son of Symon called Weuel atte Stone in the parish of All Hallows Barking, by the hands of Thomas de Appulby, rector of St. Olave, collector of the aforesaid rents deputed by the king, which tenements were formerly of Reginald de Conductu and which at present are in the king's hands for wool carried to Durdraght in Reginald's name; sealed counterparts; given at London the year abovesaid.

1041. Fourth Acquittance: this indenture witnesseth that Nicholas prior and convent received of Ralph de Cantebregg and Walter Forster, executors of the late Thomas Legg, late citizen and alderman of London, £10 10s. 10d. in payment of all [f. 199] arrears from four tenements once of the said Thomas viz. from a certain annual rent of 20s. 4d. and from his tenement newly built in the parish of St. Peter Cornhill;[1] 3s. *p.a.* from his tenement formerly of Walter Euere in the parish of St. Bartholomew the Less; 8s. 4d. *p.a.* from a tenement in the market called le Goot in the parish of All Hallows Honey Lane; 2s. *p.a.* from his tenement once of Nicholas

Reygate in the parish of St. Lawrence Jewry; and that all arrears are cleared to Michaelmas last past; sealed counterparts; 28 Oct. 1357.

1. *C.A.D.*, ii, A 1985.

1042. Fifth Acquittance: this indenture witnesseth that William prior and convent received of Katherine atte Pole 40s. in payment of all arrears from two tenements; 8s. *p.a.* for a certain rent from her tenement which she holds of the priory in the parish of St. Michael de Paternostercherch in la Riole; 8s. *p.a.* from her tenement in the parish of St. Benet Paul's Wharf; and that all arrears are cleared to Michaelmas last past; sealed counterparts; given at London 1 Nov. 1379; [f. 199v] witnesses, John Y(u)e, rector of St. Michael Wood Street, William Rykel, William Creswik, Richard Rose.

1043. Sixth Acquittance: This indenture witnesseth that, since on Fri. 29 Mar. 1325 a dissension had arisen between the prior of Holy Trinity and Stephen Ashwy, kt., concerning £16 17s. 8d. which the prior said was in arrears from the tenement of the said Stephen in the parish of St. Mary Aldermanbury which tenement owed 26s. 8d. *p.a.* to Holy Trinity and another tenement formerly of William Boconit(is) son of Sabelina situated between the tenement of the said Stephen, which Walter de Blecchinggeleye held on the east and that of Stephen which John de Burgeyn held on the west, which owed 40s. *p.a.* and which is in Cheap in the parish of All Hallows Honey Lane, the dissension was settled as follows: the prior remitted to Stephen £7 of the £16 17s. 8d. and he paid the remainder to the prior or his attorney the arrears to Christmas last past, he paid in instalments, 17s. 8d. at the next Easter, 60s. at St. John Baptist, 60s. at Michaelmas and 60s. at next Christmas; sealed counterparts; at London, the above date.

C.A.D., i, A 1513.

1044. Seventh Acquittance: this indenture witnesseth that William prior of Holy Trinity has received from Richard abbot and convent of the abbey of St. Egwin at Evesham 65s. 4d. arrears for one year from divers tenements of the said abbey in London [f. 200] viz. 53s. 4d. *p.a.* from their principal tenement called le Abbotesyn once held by Margery Broun in the parish of St. Katherine Cricherch and 10s. *p.a.* from a tenement of the said abbot with a certain alley (*aleia*) called Kelshillisaleye in the same parish once held by the said Margery and 2s. *p.a.* for another tenement once held by Margery in the parish of St. Dunstan East by the Tower; and that all arrears are cleared; sealed counterparts; 25 June 1426 [28 lines blank, ff. 200v–201 blank].

1045. [f. 201v] Memorandum: that 14 May 1441 was born to a certain [blank ? wife] of the lord de Be(u)amont a daughter within the limits of the church of St. Botolph, a church appropriated to the prior and convent of Holy Trinity and the lord came and said that he was a parishioner of that parish and he asked the sub-prior to what extent one of the canons could baptize the child within the monastery of St. Mary Graces and he was

Acquittances of Several Parishes

asked to withdraw as he was infringing the parochial rights in this,[1] there being present at the time Simon Campe, esquire, Ralph Prestbury, doctor of canon law (*decretorum doctore*), Hugh Cardugan, Edward Lymesay, gentleman, John Rouse and many others.

> 1. The text here is almost illegible and in other parts of this entry there are omissions and deletions.

1046. Note: on 9 Feb. 1340 Thomas Heron, prior of Holy Trinity, died, on which day at the request of the sub-prior and convent, John de St. Pol (*de Sancto Paulo*) for the chancellor (*vice cancellarius*) with the agreement of John de Stradford[1] then archbishop of Canterbury announced in parliament[?] (*in communi parliamento*) that the sub-prior and convent should have the custody of the priory in the form contained in the following.

> 1. *Rectius* Stratford, archbishop of Canterbury, 1333–48.

1047. Letters patent of Edward III, for a fine of 20 marks paid by the sub-prior and convent, that they shall have the custody of the priory during the vacancy due to the death of brother Thomas Heron with all the goods etc. together with the rents collected from the time of the vacancy if it continues for a month or less but if the vacancy lasts for more than one month, then they shall pay 20 marks a month to the exchequer and pro rata; the escheator, sheriff and any other bailiff or official is forbidden to interfere in the affairs of the priory during the vacancy; witness Edward duke of Cornwall and earl of Chester, our dearest son, custodian of England, at Kenyngton 19 Feb. 1340.

1048. [f. 202] Note: it is recorded on Roll 6 in the exchequer that the sub-prior and convent gave 20 marks as a fine to have the custody of the priory on the resignation (*per cessionem*) of brother Roger Poley which custody the king granted 5 June 1331 [as above in **1047**]; enrolled on the Originalia Rolls of 5 Ed. III.

1049. Note: in the Great Roll (*in magno rotulo*) of 4 Hy. VI, the sub-prior and convent owe to the king for the custody of the priory for the next vacancy (*in proxima vacacione*) after 5 Feb. 1393, 20 marks per month at the exchequer, which priorship fell vacant 4 Aug. 1407 on the death of Robert Exceter as is contained in the account of Richard Whityngton, former mayor and escheator of the City for the year from 28 Oct. 1406 to 28 Oct. 1407 and was vacant until 22 Sep. when the king received the fealty of William Harynton a canon of the house elected to the priorship and returned the temporalia to him as appears on Roll 11 of 8 Hy. IV;[1] payment due £23 16s. 2½d.

> 1. *C.P.R. 1405–8*, 346.

1050. Note: that the sub-prior and convent were summoned to pay but they replied that Richard Whitington had accounted in his escheator's accounts for £23 16s. 2½d. [f. 202v blank: f. 203 is blank except for the signature 'Stephanus Batman' written twice at the head of the folio, the second time in a (poor) Anglo-Saxon script.]

St. Dunstan Est

1051. [f. 203v]¹ [1197–1212] Grant by Peter prior and convent to Roger de Blakesappilton of land with a stone house and wharf on the Thames which was formerly held by Master James in the parish of St. Dunstan of the soke of the archbishop of Canterbury; rent 1 mark *p.a.*; swore fealty paying the rent without fraud or miskenning; if the grantee wishes to pledge or sell the fee, the canons shall have the first claim; the land is 29 ells in length from the upper part to the street along (*versus*) the Thames and in width from the upper and inner part 11½ ells and from the outer part next to the public street 13 ells, the wharf also has 13 ells in width; gersuma 8 marks in silver and 3s. for pittances; witnesses, Ralph the priest of St. Mary de Hell, John de Ballio, priest, Ralph the priest of St. Dionis, Henry mayor of London, Peter his son.

    1. This folio has a piece 7 ins. by 5 ins. cut out of the bottom left side.

1052. [List of those paying rent]: Roger Blakesappilton; Roger the Weaver (*Telarius*); Reginald de Wudeham; Robert de Walflet; Walter Auberkyn [See also after **1053**] as appears by the following.

1053. [? 1345–6] Recognisance of Walter Auberkyn that he owes a rent of 13s. 4d. *p.a.* to the prior and convent of Holy Trinity from his house which R. de Blakesappilton once held in the parish of St. Dunstan; abutments, the lane which leads to the messuage (*managium*) of Matilda de Sandwich on the west and the tenement of Hamon de Paris on the east, and 19 Ed. III.¹

    1. The cut out portion makes it impossible to read the date in full.

1052 contd. [f. 204]¹ John Maundevill, 30 Ed. III; John Malewayne, 30 Ed. III as appears by an inquisition² taken at the time of John Pechche, mayor of London, 36 Ed. III in which the jurors stated that Malewayne died seised of a tenement worth, if let (*si esset locatus*), 10 marks *p.a.* on which he paid 13s. 4d. *p.a.* to Holy Trinity; Helmingus Leget, 39 Ed. III; William Walworth, 10 Ric. II; William Ascham.

    1. Incorrectly numbered 203.   2. *C.I.P.M.*, xi, 131.

1054. [1170–97] Grant by Stephen prior and convent to Hugh (*de*) Polestede of land next the Thames which William the priest (*presbiter*) held of them for William sold the fee, without their assent, to Hugh, for 19 marks; 2s. given to the prior for recognition (*de recognicione*) and a London sextary of wine to the convent; swore fealty; rent 2s. *p.a.*; to hold as long as the rent is paid; witnesses, Roger de Ginges, brothers Henry and Robert.

    C.A.D., iv, A 7292.

1055. [List of those paying rent]: H. Polested; Richard Blundus; Edmund the Baker; Adam Rokesle, 1 Ed. II who granted the tenement to Peter de Blakeney as appears in his will¹ enrolled 5 Ed. II; Godwin Turk who granted it to Robert Wodhous as in a charter² enrolled 19 Ed. II, which Robert

St. Dunstan in the East

Wodhous granted it to Thomas Broun as in a charter[3] enrolled 11 Ed. III; his widow, 31 Ed. III as appears by the Second Acquittance of divers parishes;[4] the abbot of Evesham.

1. *C. Wills*, i, 223.
2. H.R. 54 (14, 15, 16).
3. H.R. 64 (61).
4. **1039**.

1056. Grant by Peter son of Roger son of William to Richard prior and convent of 4s. *p.a.* of quit rent; 2s. from land with houses and a wharf which Benet Stokfysch holds; abutments, the land of Robert Panifader on the west and the land of John de St. Dunstan on the east and extending from the king's street to the Thames; and 2s. from land with houses which William de Lamee holds of the grantor; abutments, land of Nicholas Bat [f. 204v] on the west and land of John de St. Dunstan on the east in the parish of St. Dunstan; to hold to the canons in free alms, the grantees to pay to the king's socage on Palm Sunday $3\frac{1}{2}$d., and rent to the grantor and his heirs $\frac{1}{2}$d. *p.a.*; the canons gave 40s. to further the grantor's business affairs (*ad negocia mea expedienda*); Fri. 11 Mar. 1250; witnesses, Roger son of Roger, mayor, John Tulsan, Ralph Hardel, sheriffs.

1057. [List of those paying quit rent]: Benet Stoffissh or Trenchemer paid 2s. and he granted the tenement to John of Canterbury, 2 Ed. I which tenement is situated between that of the late William le Monek on the west and that of the late Pentecostes Ferun on the east and extends from the king's street on the north to the Thames on the south; afterwards Clemence widow of the aforesaid William released to John of Canterbury all her right in the tenement as in a charter[1] enrolled 6 Ed. I; Margaret wife of John paid 19 Ed. II as appears in the poundage; Henry Comartin, 1 Ed. III; William Box, 6 Ed. III; Andrew Turk, 31 Ed. III; Gocelin Clyf, 46 Ed. III; Henry Hyrton, 8 Ric. II; Hugh Battisford: William Lamheth paid 2s.; Richard Bonaventure or Hakborne who granted the tenement to William de Combe as in a charter enrolled 8 Ed. I; William Boteler; Thomas Cros, 1 and 5 Ed. II; John of Oxford,[2] 3 Ed. III; Henry Staunton, 32 Ed. III; Adam de Bury.

1. II.R. 11 (47).
2. Inserted above the line 'testamentum suum irrotulatum in festo Sancte Marie Magdalene'. *C. Wills*, i, 460–1.

1058. [f. 205] [1170–97] Grant by Stephen prior and convent to James the Chaplain of that unbuilt land which the house had as a gift of the lady Ro[e]is, wife of Robert Mantel, in Manninelane in the parish of St. Dunstan; rent 5s. 6d. *p.a.*; swore fealty; gersuma 2s.; witnesses, Robert the chaplain, Master Robert the chaplain of St. Olave, John de St. Michael, John the chaplain of St. Clement, Roger the chaplain of St. Edmund.

1059. [List of those paying rent]: James the chaplain, from the 5s. 6d. he paid 18d. *p.a.* to the hospital of St. Katherine which Ralph prior and convent granted to the hospital, also James paid another 18d. out of the rent which prior Peter granted to the hospital, as appears in a chirograph made between the hospital and Holy Trinity, and so James paid the hospital 3s.

St. Dunstan in the East

and Holy Trinity 2s. 6d. and after James there paid 2s. 6d. *p.a.*; his widow; Walter the Goldsmith; Ralph the priest (*presbiter*); Stephen Casuen; John Casuen, then the tenement was divided for Michael Unctor paid 12d., Edmund Combe paid 12d. and John Boys 6d.: after Michael Unctor; William de Wynton; Reginald de Conductu, 19 Ed. II: after Edmund Combe; Hugh Hereford; Reginald de Conductu: after John Boys; Reginald de Conductu who paid the whole sum, 19 Ed. II and 1 Ed. III; John fitz-Symond; Thomas Perle, 34 Ed. III paid 4s. *p.a.* for the two tenements abovesaid as appears in a plea held in the Husting Mon. 25 Jan. 1360.

1060. [1271–2] Grant by William Crouere (*de la Crouere*), citizen, of 8s. *p.a.* of quit rent to Eustace prior and convent in a street by the Tower against (*contra*) Wyvelastone from a certain house with an oven (*cum furno*) and shops adjacent between the tenement with tenter-grounds formerly held by Matthew Bokerel on one side and the tenement of Roger de Graschirch on the other; to hold in free alms; [f. 205v] if by reason of fire or lack of maintenance, the canons cannot collect this rent then they may distrain on all William's rents in the City; the canons gave 72s. to further the grantor's business affairs; sealed; witnesses, Walter Hervy, mayor, Richard de Parys, John de Buttele, sheriffs.

1061. [1197–1212] Grant of Peter prior and convent to Ralph the Usurer (*Fenarius*) and Goda his wife of land in the parish of St. Dunstan which immediately before them was held by Stephen the Dyer (*Tinctor*); rent 6s. *p.a.* to be paid without miskenning; Ralph and Goda swore fealty; gersuma 20s.; witnesses, Henry mayor of London, Matthew the alderman, Ralph Bat, Peter Bat.

See **228.**

1062. [List of those paying rent]: Ralph the Usurer and Goda; Robert Batte; Lyedulfus; William de la Cornere; Christine Box who granted the tenement to Matilda de la Barre as appears in a charter[1] enrolled 20 or 22 Ed. I; Adam Lutekyn, 5 and 19 Ed. II and 1 Ed. III; William Ha(m)sard, 6 Ed. III; Walter S(a)rode, 34 and 49 Ed. III.

1. H.R. 27 (72) probably 26 Ed. I.
See **229.**

[f. 206] [The whole of this page is cancelled by two diagonal lines drawn across it and repeats f. 40.]

1063–8 as **200–5.**

1069 [incomplete] as **206.**

1070. [A fragment] Here lies Ainulf the first founder of the Canons in England and lover of this house (*Hic iacet Anglorum vir primus canonicorum huius fundator Ainulphus et edis amator*).[1]

1. *Note*: Versus in ecclesie Colcestre.

Chronicle

1071. [f. 207 r and v] An index of all the parishes in the cartulary.

1072. [f. 208]¹ *Narrative*: [here summarised]. From the birth of Christ to the time of Edward the Confessor there were in England 165 kings of whom Oswy, Oswald, Ethelburt, Kenelm (*Kenelinus*), Edmund and Edward were martyrs. St. Petroc, king of Wales, Constans, Cedwallus, Sibert, Wynfrid, Etheldred, Edbert and Kynred were buried in the monk's habit. In the reign of Edward the Confessor the principal ruler (*gubernator*) of the city of London was called the portshyreve and his name was Wulfgar. In 1066 Duke Harold was crowned king and reigned from Epiphany [6 Jan.] until the feast of St. Kalixtus [14 Oct.] and was buried at Waltham. In 1067 William the Bastard, duke of Normandy was crowned and he caused England to be described in a book called 'Domusday'. He was buried at Caen. In 1080 William Rufus was crowned: he was buried at Winchester. Henry I was crowned in 1100 and he was buried at Reading. His wife Matilda, daughter of Malcolm, king of the Scots, and St. Margaret founded the church of Holy Trinity. At this time Hugh de Boch[land] was sheriff of London and Leofstanus was reeve (*prepositus*) and afterwards Albericus de Ver was sheriff and Robert de Berquereola reeve. In 1135 Stephen was crowned and he was buried in the abbey of Faversham. In this time Gilbert Beket was sheriff of London and Andrew Buchuint was reeve. In 1154 Henry II was crowned and he lies at Fontevrault. In his reign, Peter son of Walter, John son of Neal, Ernulf Buchel and William son of Isabel, who was buried in Holy Trinity, were sheriffs. In 1189 Richard I was crowned and he lies with his father at Fontevrault. During his reign there began to be two sheriffs in the city of London whose names follow.

1. Unnumbered and written in two columns.

1073. [f. 208v] List of sheriffs:
1 Ric. I elected on 21 Sep., Henry Cornhill, Richard son of Renerus
2 Ric. I, John Herlion, Roger le Duke
3 Ric. I, William de Hauerhull, John Buquoynt
4 Ric. I, Nicholas Duket, Peter Newelyn
5 Ric. I, Roger le Duke, Richard son of Aleyn
6 Ric. I, William son of Isabel, William son of Arnulph
7 Ric. I, Robert Besant, Jokel le Jof(n)e
8 Ric. I, Gerard de Antioche, Robert Durant
9 Ric. I, Roger le Blund, Nicholas Duket
10 Ric. I, Constantine son of Arnulph, Robert le Beel
1 John, Arnald son of Arnulf, Richard son of Bartholomew
2 John, Roger Desert, James son of Bartholomew
3 John, William son of Alice, Simon de Aldermanbury
4 John, Norman Blund, John de Ely
5 John, Walter Broun, William Chamberleyn
6 John, Thomas Heverhull, Hamon Bronde
7 John, John Walraven, Richard of Winchester
8 John, John Holyland, Edmund son of Gerard
9 John, Richard of Winchester, Edmund Hardell

Sheriffs

Henry son of Alwin son of Leofstan was the first mayor who was accustomed to be elected on the day of St. Edward the Confessor[1]
10 John, Peter Buke, Thomas son of Neel
11 John, Peter Jeofne, William de Blount
12 John, Adam Whyteby, Stephen le Graas
13 John, Joce fitzPiers, John Gerland
14 John, Ralph Elylond, Constantine le Jeofne
15 John, Roger son of Alan, mayor, Martin son of Alice, Peter Bat, sheriffs
16 John, Serlo le Mercer, mayor, Salamon Basyngs, Hugh Basyngs, sheriffs
17 John, William Hardell, mayor, John Travers, Andrew Neweland, sheriffs
1 Hy. III, James le Alderman and Solomon le Basyngs [both] mayors, [B]ureis le Seinturer, William de Blund, sheriffs
2 Hy. III, Serlo the Mercer, mayor [? to 6 Henry III], Thomas Bokerell, Ralph Elylond, sheriffs
3 Hy. III, John Vyel, John le Spycer, sheriffs
4 Hy. III, Richard Wymbulden, John Vyel, sheriffs
5 Hy. III, Richard Renger, John le Jeofu, sheriffs
6 Hy. III, Richard Renger, Thomas Lambard, sheriffs.

1. *Margin*: Hic sepelitur infra introitum cappelli in medio sub lanura marmorea.

APPENDIX

1. [f. 1] Anno dominice incarnacionis Millesimo centesimo Nonas Augusti coronacio apud Westmonasterium Henrici primi cognomento Beauclerk, qui fuit tercius natus Willelmi Conquestoris, qui duxit in uxorem Matildam, Regis Scocie Malcolmi filiam, cui Malcolmo nupserat aliquando Margareta filia Edwardi filii Edmundi Regis Anglie dicti ferrei lateris, de qua idem Malcolmus genuit sex filios et duas filias Matildam scilicet et Mariam et Matilda vero, ut dictum est, nupsit primo Henrico Regi Anglie de qua processit Matildam que postea fuit Imperatrix. Maria autem nupsit Eustachio Comiti Boloniensi de qua idem Comes genuit filiam nomine Matildam, que postea fuit desponsata Stephano regi Anglie. Timueruntque populus regem Henricum videntes dei sapienciam esse in eo in faciendum iudicium. Nam ut in cronica legitur, strenue in omnibus operibus suis se habuit Trinitatem creatorem suum omnibus preponens, ut de iure decuit, assidue diligebat ecclesias et monasteria a Danis obruta et destructa reparabat nonnulla a fundamento nova edificabat pauperes alebat Anselmumque ab exilio revocabat et, ut breviter concludam, in lege et timore dei perfectum fidelem se prebuit fidei cultorem. Huius illustris regis fama nobili primitus propalata de sue uxoris Matilde bone regine benevolencia bonitate et virtuosis operibus scribere conor insufficiens quamvis videar et ignarus cum nec bene concipi eius largiflua bonitas valeat aut proferri. Hec namque sancta ac deo devota Anselmi Archiepiscopi decorata doctrinis acceptabile deo impendebat obsequium. Nam missas ceteraque servicia divina devotissime interiori suo auditui commendabat Christi ministris monachis precipue et aliis religiosis vero dei eloquio ignita reverenciam ex animo impendebat infirmorum visitatrix assidua, pauperum relevatrix continua, captivis compaciens, pregnantibus ministratrix, non solum leprosorum consolatrix set humillissima eorum lotrix in omnibus se Christo famulam exhibendo. Nam ut premissa veritatis robore decorentur que vivens regina voluit secreta teneri ut lucerna supra candelabrum posita cunctis lumen prebeat bonitatis in palam duxi ipsa mundo mortua producendo. Inter cetera pietatis opera quondam eam contigit in regie camere loco secreciori pedes lavare benigniter leprosorum quod, cum David frater predicte regine tunc cameram subito ingressus, regina nesciente, perpendens idque abhorrens ipsam quodammodo increpando est taliter allocutus 'Vestram non decet dignitatem tam vilia opera perpetrare: ymmo quod magis est si regie celsitudini innotesceret nunquam ipsum scitote ad vos de cetero ingressurum' cui regina inquit 'o mi frater accede et disce quia ipse est qui fecit nos et non ipsi nos qui in evangelio ait "Quod uni ex minimis meis fecistis" et "infirmus eram et visitastis [*sic*] me" quod si tu infirmos ita visitando volueris confortare, scias te salutem anime tue a domino recepturum'. Hiis itaque regine exortacionibus renovatus accesit et singulos osculabatur omnibus munera tribuendo: qui postea

Appendix

superni iudicis timore pariter et amore percussus sanis regine consiliis usque ad sue vite extrema libentissime acquievit. Regine ergo talibus virtutibus insignite nomen concessit dominus quod est super omne nomen reginarum Anglie ut videlicet ab angligenis omnibus usque ad presens Domina Matilda bona regina vulgariter nuncupetur. Hec namque regina sancti archipresulis Anselmi amore suavissimisque eloquiis adornata beatam et individuam Trinitatem tanto dilectionis fervorisque zelo adamabat ut in ipsius sancte Trinitatis honore in convenienciori honorabiliorique quo posset loco ecclesiam edificare diligencius nitebatur in qua laudes et graciarum actiones indesinenter altissimo redderentur [f. lv] noctibus et diebus que consilio dicti Archipresulis in civitate London' ut tocius regni loco digniori in soka sui propositi exitum feliciter perimplevit quia numquam antea in civitate predicta fuerat ecclesia huiusmodi edificata in honore sanctissime Trinitatis cuius misericordia foveat, protegat, iugiter defendat omnes convenientes et inhabitantes in prelibatis regno et civitate cuius et sit nomen benedictum per infinita secula seculorum AMEN.

Anno igitur ab incarnatione domini millesimo centesimo octavo fundata est ecclesia Sancte Trinitatis infra Algate London' per nobilem reginam Matildam in loco ubi quidam Syredus nomine antiquitus ecclesiam fundare ceperat in honore Sancte Crucis et sancte Marie Magdalene de qua Decanus et capitulum de Waltham percipere solebant xxx s. quos tamen a multis annis antea non habebant. Regina vero ut ecclesiam suam quietam faceret dedit illis in excambium illorum xxx s. unum molendinum Rege Henrico id annuente et hoc ipsum confirmante ut carta sequens verissime comprobabit.

2. Henricus rex Anglie Ricardo Episcopo et Hugoni de Boch[land] et omnibus fidelibus suis francis et anglis tocius Anglie salutem. Sciatis me concessisse quod Matilda regina uxor mea ponat canonicos regulares in ecclesia Sancte Trinitatis in London' sciatisque eciam quod hec eadem ecclesia libera est et absoluta a subieccione ecclesie de Waltham per escambium quod predicta regina inde dedit ecclesie de Waltham meo concessu: T[estibus] episcopo Saresburiensi, Th[oma] de Sancto Johanne et Jordano de Say.
Volo autem atque precipio ut ipsa Sancte Trinitatis ecclesia et omnes res ad eam pertinentes ita sint libere et quiete in omnibus sicut umquam melius fuerunt in tempore ipsius regine et tempore Willelmi Dunelmensis episcopi: T[estibus] eisdem apud Dunestapl.

Margin: Et ista carta scripta est in Rotulo Regis Ricardi anno regni eius viij°.

3. Et sic liberata est ecclesia ista a subieccione ecclesie de Waltham ut verissime patebit per cartam eiusdem capituli subsequentem:
[?1108] Walterus decanus et totum capitulum de Waltham Ricardo episcopo London' et omnibus fidelibus salutem. Sciatis nos clamasse quietam ecclesiam Sancte Trinitatis de London' que pertinebat ad ecclesiam nostram pro escambio quod Matilda Regina nobis dedit per concessum domini Regis Henrici, Valete.

4. Hiis itaque peractis, consilio sepedicti patris Anselmi data est hec dicte

Appendix

Trinitatis ecclesia cuidam Normanno primo tocius regni canonico a quo tota Anglia sancti Augustini regula et habitu canonicali annuente domino perlustratur. Dedit et eadem regina deo ecclesie et Normanno ac eciam servientibus in eadem ecclesia portam de Algate et sokam ad eam pertinentem cum omnibus consuetudinibus suis adeo integre sicut ipsa habuit ac eciam xxv libras blancheas quas ipsa habuit de civitate Exonie ut per cartam sequentem ipsius nobilis regine inde prefato Normanno tunc dicte ecclesie Priori et canonicis suisque successoribus in eadem ecclesia deo servientibus specialiter factam sub tenore qui sequitur verborum evidencius pleniusque poterit apparere:

[f. 2] Matilda dei gratia Anglorum Regina R(icardo) Episcopo London' et omnibus sancte ecclesie fidelibus salutem. Notum sit vobis me, consilio Archiepiscopi Anselmi et concessione et confirmacione domini mei Regis Henrici, dedisse et confirmasse ecclesiam Christi infra muros London' sitam liberam et quietam ab omni subieccione tam ecclesie de Waltham quam omnium ecclesiarum preter ecclesie Sancti Pauli London' et episcopi cum omnibus ad eam pertinentibus ad honorem Dei canonicis in ea regulariter cum Normanno priore deo servientibus in perpetuum pro redempcione animarum nostrarum et parentum nostrorum. Similiter dedi eis portam de Algate cum soca ad eam pertinente que fuit mea dominica et duas partes redditus civitatis Exonie. Et volo et precipio quod iidem canonici bene et in pace et honorifice et libere teneant terras suas et omnia ad ecclesiam suam pertinencia cum omnibus libertatibus et consuetudinibus quas dominus meus Rex Henricus eis per cartam suam confirmavit ita ne eis iniuria vel contumelia fiat Testibus Willemo episcopo Wintoniensi; Rogero episcopo Sarisberiensi; Roberto episcopo Lincolniensi; Randolfo et Bernardo cancellariis; Giffardo Clarebc; Guafrido de Clinton; Willemo de Ponte; Ald(uino); apud Westmonasterium.

5. Hanc donacionem supradictam prefate nobilissime regine predictus rex illustris Henricus non solum confirmat set eciam privilegiis immensis benigne roborat ut sequens carta expressius demonstrabit:

[1109] Henricus Rex Anglie Archiepiscopis, episcopis, abbatibus, vicecomitibus, et omnibus fidelibus suis francis et anglis salutem. Sciatis me concessisse et confirmasse canonicatum regularium canonicorum in ecclesia Christi London' quam uxor mea Matilda regina ibi instituit esse stabilem imperpetuum et liberum ab omni subieccione preter episcopi Sancti Pauli et volo et precipio quod iidem canonici bene et in pace et honorifice et libere teneant terras suas et omnes res ecclesie sue pertinentes cum saca et soca et toll et theam et infongenetheof cum omnibus consuetudinibus suis tam infra civitatem quam extra et ita ne eis iniuria vel contumelia fiat Testibus Rogero episcopo Salesberiensi et Roberto episcopo Lincolniensi apud Westmonasterium.

Hec omnia supranominata idem rex nobilis uberius confirmat per suam cartam scilicet primam de pluribus parochiis prout plenissime patet in eadem.

6. Quia que religioni canonicali ordinis sanctissimi patris nostri beati Augustini dei omnipotentis gloriosi episcopi et confessoris de necessario competunt edicere conveniat, nunc de Normanno ecclesie huius primo priore qui primo in Angliam religionem istam feliciter acquisivit aliqua libet prout Deus dederit inserenda ne quod absit per processum temporis necligencia et indevocione hominum succrescente quid faciendum, sumendum aut relinquendum foret necligencius pretermitteretur. Hic ergo Normannus in Insula que Thanet dicitur in Kancia parte ex orientali, nobili prosapia editus, cum Anselmo in Gallia litterarum habuit excercicium ubi sciencia preditus et ut fructus probitatis sue senectutis tempore [f. 2v] germinaret virtutum radiis ibidem suam iuventutem adornans Angliam repeciit et Colecestream veniens ibidem sacerdotibus quibusdam in ecclesia Sancti Botulphi congregatis devotissime se sociavit. Factum est autem dum ibi moraretur omnes unanimes religionis habitum suscipere intendebant. Ainulfus igitur illius ecclesie tunc presbiter ad se convocavit Normannum et quid super premissis melius faceret iugiter inquisivit cui Normannus respondit 'si religionem proponitis induere est quidam ordo in partibus transmarinis honestus satis et pulcher partibus istis vero penitus est ignotus. Vita scilicet et regula sanctissimi Augustini doctoris gloriosi auctoritate firmata que eciam regula a catholicis regula canonica appellatur quam qui amant et sequuntur viam tenent regiam atque eius sancto ductu redeunt ad patriam. Nunc ergo unum vel duos provideatis providos et discretos ex vobis qui illuc vadent et ordinem ac regulam discant habitumque ibi suscipiant et cum perfecte sciverint reversi inde illi vos doceant.' Placuit Ainulpho et sociis eius consilium quod Normannus dederat et ait Ainulphus 'numquid sapienciorem te ad hoc poterimus invenire?' Et quia tibi deus hec ostendit omnes ad tui oris consilium obediemus, uno tamen inquit Ainulphus 'in ista ecclesia nomine te precedam'. Miserunt ergo eum ad Archiepiscopum Anselmum rogantes quatinus ad aliquam domum dicte religionis ipsum litteratorie destinaret. Videns ergo memoratus Episcopus bonam eorum intencionem eum cum honore suscepit et ad abbatem Montis Eligii litteratorie transmisit suo sub sigillo cuius litere tenor sequitur in hunc modum:

7. Anselmus servus ecclesie Cantuariensis amico suo Johanni priori canonicorum de Monte Sancti Eligii et congregacioni sub illo deo servienti salutem. Clericus iste nacione Anglicus nomine Normannus, de quadam ecclesia in qua noviter sunt congregati clerici qui regulariter vestro more vivere volunt, venit ad vos desiderans vobiscum aliquanto tempore quanto vobis placuerit conversari quatinus vestro ordine et vestris consuetudinibus instrui possit in servicio dei ad suam et aliorum utilitatem: qui quoniam noster familiaris est ne aliquis suspicetur eum alia causa peregrinari rogat literarum nostrarum testimonio notificari et nostra noticia et prece apud vos ad hoc quod desiderat adiuvari. Quamvis ergo de vestra religione nichil nisi sola dileccione meruerim tamen quia de vestra conversacione et benevolencia confido quoniam religiosorum est ad religionem volentes proficere libenter cum oportunitas se exhibet instruere precor ut ei quantum vobis oportunum erit concedatis sicut postulat in vestra conversacione remanere.

8. Normannus itaque Anselmi Archiepiscopi auctoritate roboratus transfretavit comitanter quodam germano suo Bernardo nomine qui Bernardus

Appendix

postea ecclesie Sancti Petri de Dunstaple optinuit prioratum veniensque vir dei Normannus Carnotum ibidem cum omni reverencia susceptus mansit multis diebus, in Belvaco quoque cum regularibus fratribus consuetudines discens ordinis: quomodo in singulis locis fratres se haberent in choro scilicet claustro, refectorio, dormitorio, locis omnibus aliis regulam eciam sancti Augustini et habitus formam scribens que similiter cuilibet canonico forent necessaria regulariter tradens memorie videlicet: tria paria pannorum lineorum, duo lumbaria cum ligulis pertinentibus, duo sudaria linea, una cappa alba pro nocte furrata duo paria linthiaminum ad minus, unum materas spissum, unum coopertorium pro lecto furratum, ij chalones et unum canabacium [f. 3] longum et latum, ij pulvinaria, ij blanketts, iiij superpellicia quorum ij festivalia et ij cotidiana, ij pellicia agnilia, iiij tunice de blanket, ij wardecot quorum j ad minus sit furrat(a), ij cape de worstede cum capuciis furratis, j capa de worstede cum capucio non furrato, ij zone cum knyvet et cultello pro pane (s)cindendo, j bursa, j aguler cum acu et filo, unum par tabularum eburnearum portaticarum cum pectine, i par cirotecarum, j capa pluvialis cum ij capuciis, ij rochete, j almucium, ij cape de burnet quarum una sit furrata, j capilla, ij paria caligarum linearum, i par caligarum lanearum, iiij paria pedalium lanearum, ij paria pinsonum, ij paria sotularum de cordewane, unum par sotularum nocturnalium: unum coclear de argento, unus ciphus de murra, una pecia de argento, unus cultellus pro mensa. Tandem venerabilis vir iste Normannus se in ordine canonicali eruditum stabilitum et ad plenum edoctum conspiciens, valedicens abbati et fratribus ibidem pro eius separanda sancta et honesta societate lugentibus Angliam repeciit Colcestriam veniens, fratres ibidem eius adventu gaudentes ordinem acceptum edocuit beatique Augustini dei confessoris regulam ordinis et consuetudines a transmarinis partibus allatas eis plenarie committebat, qui postea a suo Priore Aignulpho ibi licentiatus et de obediencia benevole absolutus ab eodem prout in littera subsequenti patebit London' petiit anno scilicet dominice incarnacionis millesimo centesimo octavo.

9. Tenor littere subsequentis:
Ainulfus Prior et conventus canonicorum ecclesie Colcestriensis Matilde regine reverende domine sue et Ricardo episcopo London' cunctisque fidelibus Christi salutem. Noverit caritas vestra nos velle et assensu communi annuere ut dominus Normannus frater noster et ecclesie nostre noster hactenus canonicus amodo peticioni ac voluntati prefate domine nostre regine satisfaciat et regimen canonicorum et ecclesie Sancte Trinitatis London' sibi a regina concessum et a Pontifice predicto canonice injunctum absolucione nostra licenter suscipiat et in nomine ac favore domini Jhesu Christi secure teneat. Hac una tantum inter nos et ipsius loci Fratres condicione manente quod licet ecclesia Christi quaquaversum difusa per orbem in omnibus membris suis pro invicem orare non desinat ipsi tamen nosque pariter speciali familiaritate pro invicem orare nosque utrobique invicem consolari debito iure non cessimus. Valeat semper in Christo vestra fraternitas Amen.

10. Predictus ergo vir dei Normannus anno supradicto Christi ecclesiam suscepit regendam videlicet nonas Aprilis dono et concessione Regis Henrici et Matilde uxoris sue et ut dictum est Anselmi archiepiscopi ac Ricardi London' episcopi auctoritate suffultus. Qui Christi ecclesie sic presidens fratres ordinans et in observanciis regularibus eos instruens nobiliter novas construens officinas claustrum idoneum libros quoque plures de novo fieri faciens ecclesieque nova ornamenta et vestimenta preciosa iuxta fratrum numerum, nimia sollicitudine diligentissime ordinans cepit ut vitis paulatim crescere de se ramos pro ordinis edificacione procul emittens ad mare scilicet extendens palmites suas et usque ad flumen propagines eius, fratrem suum videlicet Bernardum mittens ad ecclesiam Sancti Petri de Dunstaple et alium ad Lanston (Launceston) in Cornubiam ad Plympton eciam in Devonia ad ecclesiam similiter Sancte Frideswithe in Oxon' ad ecclesiam Sancte Osithe in Est Sexia in villa Chic(c)he nuncupata videlicet Willelmum Corbuil virum utique valde discretum postea factum archiepiscopum Cantuariensem et cum eo Sywardum quem idem archiepiscopus postea appellavit Simonem ad ecclesiam quoque sancte Marie de Mertona in Southereia aliisque locis multis ut cerni potest per totam Anglie regionem. Igitur Aynulfus et Normannus videntes opus dei per manus illorum prosperari miserunt quemdam canonicum ordinis predicti Senonem nomine ad Pascalem papam rogantes ut ordinem privilegiis insigniret qui papa, ipsum paterne suscipiens, bullas valde speciales concedens, cum reliquiis diversorum sanctorum illum remisit. Set Parisuis [*sic*] obiit redeundo, reliquiis ibidem retentis, et, perdita prima bulla, secunda Colcestriam delata est cuius copia irrotulatur in quanta cum littera A folio xviijº Kalend' secundi.

[f. 3v] In primis itaque domo ista gravi egestate oppressa, quadam contigit die dominica plures huius civitatis utriusque sexus ad processionem, more solito, devotius convenisse qui girando claustrum processionem sequentes et refectorium inspicientes mensas mappis coopertas videntes absque pane, 'pulcher' aiunt, 'est hic apparatus set panis unde veniet?' quibus responsum est multociens deesse tempore reficiendi fratresque in perquirendis necessariis multa gravamina sustinere. Unde mulieres tunc pietate mote inter se statuerunt singulas ipsarum panem unum singulis diebus dominicis ad altare Christi fideliter oblaturas aliis tunc non ibidem presentibus mulieribus panificis consimiliter facere persuadentes. Tot ergo panes die qualibet dominica allati fuerunt ut fratribus et suis hospitibus hic tota septimana sufficerent et habundarent. Ista vero panum oblacio finem attingens generacionis constituencium primorum divina clemencia non cessavit donec tot redditus hec haberet ecclesia quibus in ipsa degentes possent comode sustentari et sicut reddituum accrevit possessio mirabiliter panis decrevit hec oblacio. Et sic domui huic ex fidelium devocione possessionum copia arridebat quod miserabilis fratrum indigencia, divina providencia, exulabat. Tempore quidem dicti Normanni huius ecclesie, ut predicitur, venerabilis primi prioris isti ecclesie concessit Matilda nobilis prefata regina sokam et portam de Algate quam ad fundacionem presentis ecclesie illustris Rex Henricus prelibatus benevole confirmavit ut in carta sua prima de pluribus parochiis evidentissime declaratur.

11. Preterea sciendum est quanta sit ista soka cuius fines tales sunt: a porta

Appendix

de Algate usque ad portam Ballii Turris que nuncupatur Cungata et tota venella vocata Chykenlane versus Berkyngchirche usque ad cimiterium excepta una domo viciniore cimiterio et iterum redditur eadem via usque ad ecclesiam Sancti Olavi et tunc redditur per viculum qui tendit ad ecclesiam de Colemanschurch; deinde versus Fenchurch usque ad domum brasineam ubi nunc habetur signum Columbe; extitit itaque ibi olim viculus per quem ibatur usque ad domum Teol [? Theobald] filii Iwonis aldermanni in Lymstrete qui viculus nunc obstructus est quia suspectus erat pro furibus nocturnis et ideo quia non ibi patet via, redditur iterum per viculum versus capellam Sancti Michaelis et sic usque ad Lymstratam ad domum Ricardi Ca(v)el et deinde itur per vicum iuxta ecclesiam Sancti Andree usque ad ecclesiam Sancti Augustini iuxta murum civitatis. Deinde usque ad portam de Algata. Hanc nobis dedit prefata Matilda bona regina cum porta de Algate quam dictus Prior Normannus de novo a fundamento reedificavit et omnibus diebus vite sue pacifice custodivit cum omnibus consuetudinibus suis tam infra civitatem quam extra. Dedit eciam eadem Regina xx^{li}. ad scalam de exitu civitatis Exonie ut patet per cartam prescriptam. Item terra et soka de Anglica knyghtengilda cui adquirende fuit auxilio precipue erga milites quorum soka erat et prece et pretio vir venerabilis Gaufridus de Clyntona qui, inter cetera bona que fecit huic ecclesie, viam inter ecclesiam et murum civitatis, ut viam illam ad nos includere possumus muro a rege impetravit ut per cartam sequentem verius declaratur verborum subsequentum seriem continentem:

12. [f. 4] [1121–2] Henricus Rex Anglie [*sic*] Ricardo Episcopo London', Alberico de Ver vicecomiti et omnibus baronibus et fidelibus suis Londoniensibus salutem. Sciatis me concessisse Sancte Trinitati et Normanno Priori et canonicis sancte Trinitatis London' ut claudant muro unam viam que erat inter ecclesiam et officinas eorum et murum civitatis London' ex utraque parte usque ad murum predictum civitatis. Et in pace teneant. Et via que solebat ibi esse, sit amodo ante ecclesiam suam ex alia parte. Et hoc concedo eis pro animabus patris mei et matris et predecessorum et successorum meorum et pro salute mea et statu regni mei. Testibus Ranulfo cancellario et Gaufrido de Clyntona et Radulfo Basset apud Norhantonam.

13. Multa dispendia et gravamina sustulit hec ecclesia illius vie causa quia bis vel ter fuit spoliata per viam illam. Due eciam hide terre in Lintona huic ecclesie dono Simonis Mulins collate fuerunt: ecclesia etiam de Totenham dono David piissimi Regis Scotorum: ecclesia eciam de Bixill largitione Willelmi Cantuariensis archiepiscopi cuius frater fuerat hic canonicus ordinatus: necnon ecclesia de Waltamstowe dono Adelicie de Toenio et alia multa que hic non specificantur quia de redditibus in London' perquisitis hic modo restat solummodo pertractandum: nam infra civitatem London' tam empcione quam gratuito dono bonorum Christi fidelium, dictus Normannus ad summam viginti librarum redditus adquisivit quem multum amabant et honorabant homines huius civitatis dei et cuius amore ecclesie huic bona plurima contulerunt. Qui quidem Normannus a prefata nobili regina specialiter ceteris predilectus toto termino vite sue

Appendix

pater confessionum eiusdem bone regine ab eadem eligitur que se totam suo consilio tradidit spiritualiter gubernandam intelligens hunc esse in omnibus servum Christi: ipsius etenim instinctu et persuasione pauperibus ac eciam ecclesiis in elemosinis et ceteris pietatis operibus exhibuit se devotam istamque ecclesiam ditandam disposuerat quod minime contigit vite spacio non longius permansuro. Corpus tamen suum in ista ecclesia volens sepeliri xx libratas terre et suam capellam cum suis reliquiis huic cum corpore concessit ecclesie. Monachi tamen Westmonasterii ipsius egrotacionis desperate tempore, nuncio celeri regem Henricum tunc agentem in Normannia prevenientes regiis consiliariis promissis et datis muneribus inclinatis eidem regi fortiter suggesserunt regine corpus in ecclesia Westmonasterii omnino sepeliri debita racione quia ibidem iidem rex et regina tam regalis unccionis sacramentum quam regni coronam susceperant. Sicque negocio expedito monachorum nuncius tercia die post regine obitum cum eius corpus ad hanc ecclesiam sepeliendum deferretur regiis litteris munitus veniens precipit idem corpus ad Westmonasterium reportari ibidem solempniter sepeliendum quod factum neminis audacia revocavit. Nichil tamen monachis ut speraverant extitit condonatum ipsa sic ibidem honorifice contra tamen sui testamenti voluntatem ultimam tumulata. Terram vero nobis legatam malo consilio consultus penitus denegavit [f. 4v.] benevole nobis, tamen ipsius regine reliquias preciossimas inter quas cassa auro argento et gemis fabricata mirifice habebatur cum ligno dominice crucis et aliis ornamentis palliisque necnon et septra regine aurea dictus illustris Rex concessit, quas quidem reliquias imperator Constantinopolis eidem regi Henrico transmisit per Hugonem de Rymers suum baronem magnificum quas dicte regine idem Rex et eadem Regina huic·ecclesie condonavit [*sic*] cum capsa operis Constantinopolitani et tabula eciam plures diversas reliquias continente prout in Qua(n)ta Petri folio xvij⁰ Kalend[ar] secundo plenius inseruntur. Mortua est igitur domina Matilda laudanda regina que obiit primo die mensis Maij anno gracie millesimo centesimo octavodecimo post a dicto Priore Normanno huius loci susceptum prioratum anno decimo, in sacrario Westmonasterii sepulta; quo loco annis plurimis requiescens, Regis Henrici secundi et Sancti Thome Archiepiscopi tunc Cantuariensis necnon ceterorum regni nobilium consilio, assumpta in parte orientali summi altaris a latere dextro Edithe regine et virginis sanctissimi Regis et Confessoris Edwardi consortis honorifice recondita est non indigne ut feretrum eiusdem clarissimi regis quasi lucerna super candelabrum poneretur in domo domini ut omnes ingredientes lumen queant palam intueri. Cuius venerabilis Matilde bone regine memoriale merito recolendum literis huiusmodi ibidem in tabula titulatur: Hic iacet domina Matilda secunda bona regina Anglorum quondam uxor regis Henrici primi, mater Matilde Imperatricis, filia domini Malcolmi quondam Regis Scocie et Sancte Margarete consortis eiusdem domini Malcolmi que obiit primo die mensis Maij anno gracie M⁰ C⁰ xviij⁰ de cuius bonitate et morum probitate dicere omnia, si volumus, dies non sufficeret. Cuius anime propicietur altissimus. Amen. Anno incarnacionis domini M⁰ C⁰ xxxij⁰ anno scilicet xxiiij⁰ Normanni prioratus presens ecclesia Christi cum omnibus fere suis officinis conbusta est ab igne superveniente de civitate a domo scilicet quondam Gilberti Beket quo igne pars maxima London' tunc erat lamentabiliter devastata. Quo tempore in hac ecclesia dominus ostendebat grande miraculum de quadam cruce quam, cum ignis invaluit cum ceteris bonis dicte ecclesie homines eicere voluissent cum funibus eam trahentes removere non poterant sicque plumbo ecclesie liquescente coacti decesserunt. Crastino vero redeuntes, putantes eam cum ceteris fuisse consumptam, illesam ab incendio invenerunt; tanto igitur miraculo exhilarati gratias altissimo referentes sperando solacio huius adversitatis animati, fiduciam in domino non modicam venture prosperitatis resumpserunt.

Normannus, dei servus, per triennium ante suum exitum eo vel amplius deficere cepit in corpore non valens conventum sequi. Dum sanus vero lautioribus cibis quam sui fratres numquam refici voluit nec veste indui preciosiori, in refectorio semper cum fratribus ad mensam aliud quam fratribus in communi sibi apponi non permisit quod si aliquid esset ei appositum infirmioribus distribuit, cibo contentus generali. In dormitorio quoque cum fratribus requiescens primus ad alios excitandos [f. 5] solebat exurgere. Cameram quoque multum detestabatur habere, dicens quod aliis presidentes cum suis subditis pro suo posse esse deberent: pro causa facili suam eciam presenciam eis aliquando subtrahere qui quidem hic observandum constituit quod nullus successorum suorum priorum monasterii huius cameram habeat set in refectorio et dormitorio cum fratribus nisi maior urgeret necessitas semper interessent. Dum igitur, ut predicitur, viribus corporeis destitueretur, volens se de prioratu exonerari aliumque magistrum videlicet Radulphum sibi succedere hac peticione a fratribus non auditus nec quovismodo obtinens eorum assensum in hac parte, Bernardi fratris sui Prioris de Dunstaple consilio ac aliorum sapientium per consensum fratrum, prefatum Radulphum sub se constituit Suppriorem, Roberto London' episcopo ad ipsorum Normanni et suorum fratrum requisicionem specialem et presentacionem ipsum confirmante, cui committebatur cura tocius huius domus tam infra quam extra ab ipso Normanno Priore existente. Ne omnino depositus pater et huius loci fundator filii sui obedenciarius videretur quem antea suscepisset. Longa igitur egritudine dei servus Normannus fatigatus velut aurum bonum decoctus qualibet die dominica altaris sacramento refectus cuius abstinencia, cibi et potus parcitas ac indumenti asperitas, carnis sue rigiditas, necnon peccatorum timor de facili non dicentur tocius vite sue spacio virgo permanens, corporee infirmitatis camino purgatus ad plenum, ab hac miseria seculari ij Idus Januarii die dominica illucescente aurora migravit ad dominum: hic super pauca fidelis, illic supra multa in gaudio statuendus. Obiit ergo Prior Normannus anno dominice incarnacionis millesimo centesimo quadragesimo septimo in hac ecclesia Christi quam triginta et novem annis nobiliter rexerat ante summum altare in novo sarcofago conditus est et sepultus unde anno millesimo centesimo septuagesimo sexto in partem altaris septentrionalem est translatus ubi integro et incorrupto corpore ad instar dormientis dicitur permanere. Normannus igitur Prior Primus creatus est anno domini $M^0 C^0$ vij^0 viz. Nonas Aprilis et ecclesiam hanc honorifice rexit triginta et novem annis qui obiit ij Idus Januarii anno domini $M^0 C^0 xlvij^0$.

14. Radulphus Prior secundus qui ante supprior, ut predicitur, creatus est

Appendix

xvj⁰ Kalendas Februarii M⁰ C⁰ xlvij⁰ qui prius curam domus huius gesserat valde bene: vir venerabilis etate maturus in divina et humana pagina optime eruditus, hac urbe natus et nutritus, omnibus civibus amabilis et devotus, regi Stephano et eius uxori Matilde regine et curie regie cognitus et dilectus qui curam confessionum dicte regine Matilde ab archiepiscopo Theobaldo suscepit. In huius itaque eleccione quedam capitula secundum institutionem Prioris Normanni imperpetuum observanda decrevimus explanare videlicet ut Prior huius ecclesie nullam iniquam proprietatem habeat, clavem non portet, cameram non habeat, cum fratribus semper pro posse communiter vivat, redditum vel ornamentum ecclesie non det neque vendat nec invadiet, canonicum non recipiat neque hinc in aliam domum mittat nisi per capitulum. Et siquis in aliquem manum male miserit domum hanc amittat nisi misericordia communi omnium [f. 5v] assensu ei fuerit subventum visa eius penitencia post expulsionem. Hec omnia debere observari in hac ecclesia secundum institucionem Normanni Prioris omnes in verbo veritatis iuravimus, prior primo et reliqui in ordine. Stephanus Rex et Regina dictum Radulphum priorem et hanc ecclesiam adeo dilexerunt quod filium suum Baldwinum et filiam suam Matildam quondam uxorem Comitis de Medlint [Meulan, S-et-O.], hunc videlicet Baldwinum ad aquilonarem partem altaris et Matildam ad australem in hac ecclesia fecerunt honorifice sepeliri. Dormicioni vero dicte venerabilis regine Matilde uxoris dicti regis illustris Stephani prefatus Radulfus Prior affuit apud Halyngham, vocatus specialiter ab eo triduo ante suum obitum quia pater extitit suarum confessionum ex licencia et commissione Theobaldi archiepiscopi, qui quidem Radulfus dicte regine ministravit omnia sacramenta que hinc migraturis debentur cuius consilio eadem Regina multas fecit elemosinas et monachorum nobile construxit cenobium apud Feversham ubi tumulata in domino requiescit regi eciam Stephano apud Dovoriam affuit in extremis. Archiepiscopus vero Theobaldus eundem Priorem Radulfum magno honore favoreque non modico preveniebat et huic ecclesie de suis largiens nunquam gravaminis aliquid intulit aut abstulit quicquam quod noceret, qui, anno incarnacionis dominice M⁰ C⁰ lv⁰, filium regis Henrici de Regina Alienora natum, in ista ecclesia baptizavit qui nominabatur Henricus: ac anno sequente euisdem regis filiam natam de dicta regina idem Pontifex hic eciam baptizavit que Matilda vocabatur. Cuius archiepiscopi successor nobilis sanctissimus, dei atleta et gloriosissimus martir Thomas, tocius ecclesie catholice invictissimus propugnator, in magna famuliaritate et dileccione dictum Priorem habuit quem secretorum suorum constituit conscium et patrem suarum confessionum de quo Priore idem sanctus Pontifex cum prope vel in civitate esset London' dorso ad flagella nudato disciplinam secretam sepius recipiebat cuius sanctissimi martiris mors preciosa eidem Priori Radulfo revelabatur quia nocte qua martirium sustulit per sompnium idem Prior in sole figens intuitum vidit in corpore solis episcopum episcopalibus splendidissime decoratum. Tandem dictus Prior Radulfus veniens ad extrema qui antea in adquirendis terris et redditibus aliisque necessariis huic ecclesie multum laboravit, obdormivit in domino cuius sagaci providencia in duplum crevit summa reddituum istius ecclesie. Et sic obiit idem Prior Radulfus pridie Idus Octobris M⁰ C⁰ lxvij⁰ et vixit prior fere viginti annis cuius corpus transposuimus ad latus

Appendix

exterius iuxta sepulcrum Prioris Normanni quorum altissimus sit propicius animabus Amen. Et extitit ista domus sine priore per ij^{os} annos xxxij^{as} septimanas et i diem. Omnia ergo que fiebant per sigillum commune illis diebus fiebant, sub nomine Prioris Edmundi cum nullus talis creatus extiterat ut patet per literam testimonialem Gylberti Lond' episcopi scriptam in quanta cum litera B folio xc^0.

15. Stephanus Prior tercius creatus est xvj^0 Kalendas Junii Anno Domini M^{0}C^{0}lxx^0 depositus est vj^0 Nonas Maii M^{0}C^{0}lxxxxvij^0 et obiit postea xix^0 Kalendas Septembrii millesimo C^0 xcviij^0 et sepultus est.

16. [f. 6] Petrus de Cornubia prior quartus creatus est vij^0 Idus Maij Anno Domini M^{0}C^{0}lxxxxvij^0 et obiit Nonas Julii Anno Domini M^{0}CC^{0}xxj^0 et sepultus est in medio capelle beate Marie virginis quam ipse edificavit. Qui quidem prior precipuus doctor inter omnes doctores Anglicos suo tempore floruit. Per triennium cum quodam iudeo subtili disputans, ipsum convertens, concanonicum suum fecit. De sua disputacione, diversos libros composuit ac eciam Pantheologon: de reparacione lapsus: de duabus corrigiis predestinacionis et reprobationis et plures alios perutiles penes nos et alios habitos in diversis locis ad laudem Trinitatis. Huius eciam tempore Edmundus huius ecclesie canonicus in Hiberniam dirigitur ordinem nostrum ibidem incepturus ubi in tantum profecit quod in episcopum Lymericensem electus est per Johannem regem qui, postea rediens, obiit ij Nonas Novembris et in hac ecclesia in parte aquilonari inter duas columpnas prope presbiterium sepultus est.

[f. 8] IN PAROCHIIS SANCTE TRINITATIS SANCTI MICHELIS MARIE MAGDALENE SANCTE KATHERINE

31. Civitate igitur London' bis igne consumpta ex quo domus hec fundata extitit a primevo vidilicet primo a domo Gilberti Bekette usque ad hanc ecclesiam, ut supradiximus, tempore Normanni primi prioris quem ignem extinxit dominus virtute sue sancte crucis in ecclesia ista predicta existentis ut superius meminimus. Ac eciam tempore Radulfi secundi, a domo Ailwardi iuxta London ston [London Stone in Cannon Street] fere usque ad portam que Algate communiter nuncupatur qui ignis usque ad feretrum sanctissimi confessoris Erkenwaldi in ecclesia Sancti Pauli proveniens domino iubente merito sui venerandi Pontificis prelibati nullius lesionis vestigium ibi reliquit quod grande miraculum merito memorie commendatur. Igitur loco isto in magnam angustiam causa predicta depresso in relevacionem tam civitatis de novo edificande quam huius ecclesie melius imposterum sustentande, unanimi assensu, Prior tunc cum fratribus omnibus censuerunt vendere terram ecclesie huic perquisitam redditu modico inde imperpetuum reservato. Iamque quia mundus unumquemque letatur decipere ac in tantum malum est progressus ut antiquorum facta in tantum contradicendo despicit quod vix aliquis sine magna evidenciarum copia et ex antiquo verissime probatarum nova iustificatione quietum redditum nostrum solui libenter non permittat, idcirco, rentale istud ego Frater Thomas de Axebrigge vocatus filius Johannis de Cornubia huius ecclesie

233

Appendix

canonicus, sacerdos et professus, renovare dispono non secundum tempora priorum set iuxta antiquorum ordinem librorum cum nominibus in eis scriptis et eciam, si potero, tenementa exprimere et inter quorum tenementa modo consistunt ac etiam nomina in eis nunc habitancium ad meorum posterorum informacionem utique meliorem. Nam iuxta dictum sapientis non minor est veritas parere quam parta tueri. In parochiis [as above] que nunc sunt una parochia, o fili gloriose virginis me faciat proficere.

165. Hec est finalis composicio facta inter religiosos viros dominum Ricardum de Wymbisch priorem ecclesie Sancte Trinitatis London' ac eiusdem loci conventum ex parte una et religiosos viros Fratrem Adam priorem fratrum ordinis Sancte Crucis London' et fratres eiusdem loci ex altera, videlicet quod cum dicti prior et fratres Sancte Crucis teneant quoddam tenementum in parochia Sancti Olavi prope Turrim London' per redditum servicium tresdecim solidorum et octo denariorum argenti per annum ut capitalibus dominis feodi usualiter solvendum, infra quod tenementum ecclesia dictorum fratrum constructa extiterit die confectionis presencium et edificata, ac cimiterium extitit, quod quidem tenementum extendit se per viam regiam ex parte boriali a tenemento [f. 33v] Johannis priour usque ad tenementum Constantie de Stratford, et in parte australi a tenemento abbatis de Lileshull usque ad tenementum Rogeri Frowyk, et utraque capita in oriente et occidente extendunt se a vico regio predicto ad tenementum abbatis de Lileshull supradicti, que quidem ecclesia continet die confectionis presencium in longitudine xxvj ulnas ferreas domini Regis et unum quarterium ulne, in latitudine ix ulnas et unum quarterium ulne que nondum extitit dedicata, cimiterium vero eorundem fratrum nondum benedictum continet in longitudine ex parte australi xxv ulnas et ex parte boriali etiam in longitudine xviij ulnas et in latitudine ex parte orientali xvj ulnas et in parte occidentali xiiij ulnas nondum benedictum; quam etiam ecclesiam dicti religiosi Sancte Crucis dedicari ac cimiterium predictum benedici facere intendunt; volunt et concedunt iidem religiosi expresse quod nullum eisdem religiosis Sancte Trinitatis nec successoribus suis eorum de redditu predicto xiijs. viijd. de toto tenemento seu tenementis suis de ipsis et ecclesia sua Sancte Trinitatis predicta tentis et tenendis dicte ecclesie circumquaque adiacentibus tam ex parte orientali et australi quam occidentali generetur preiudicium nec domui sue in aliquo detrimentum, concesserunt eciam dicti prior et fratres Sancte Crucis pro se et successoribus suis dictos tresdecim solidos et octo denarios redditus servicii cum pertinentibus de toto tenemento predicto dictam ecclesiam ut predictum est circumquaque adiacente et benedicto solvere, et dicta tenementa inde fore onerata et secundum consuetudinem civitatis redditu predicto aretro existente pro predicto redditu in omnibus predictis tenementis distringere asportare et retinere quousque dictis priori et conventui Sancte Trinitatis inde fuerit satisfactum. Preterea volunt et concedunt dicti Prior et fratres Sancte Crucis quod nullum faciant obstupacionem nec preclusionem vie nec ingressus aut ingressus [*sic*] dictorum prioris et conventus Sancte Trinitatis quin licite et sine impedimento ubilibet possint ingredi dicta

Appendix

tenementa pro redditu predicto petendo et recipiendo ut domini illius feodi omnibus contraplacitis et contraplacitandis seu impedimentis dictorum prioris et fratrum Sancte Crucis ac successorum suorum omnino imposterum postpositis: quia insuper locus ille in quo dicta ecclesia dictorum religiosorum de Sancta Cruce est constructa ac cimiterium predictum de feodo dictorum religiosorum Sancte Trinitatis existunt per quod, si eandem ecclesiam dedicari ac cimiterium predictum benedici contigerit, potestatem forsan amitterunt in eisdem locis pro redditu suo predicto distringendi, concedunt dicti religiosi ordinis Sancte Crucis quod si quovismodo occasione dedicacionis ecclesie predicte aut benedictionis cimiterii predicti a percepcione dicti redditus seu potestate distringendi pro redditu predicto impediantur quod absit, extunc officiarius domini archidiaconi London' qui pro tempore fuerit cui se sponte submittunt in hac parte, facta fide primitus super premissis, solo iuramento procuratoris dictorum religiosorum Sancte Trinitatis sine omni strepitu iudiciali ad solucionem tresdecim solidorum et octo denariorum huius tociens quotiens aretro fuerint singulis diebus per sentenciam excommunicacionis maioris in eorum priorem, interdicti in eorum ecclesiam compellere possit. In cuius rei testimonium huic scripto indentato in modum cirographi confecto sigillum commune predictorum prioris et conventus Sancte Trinitatis et sigillum commune prioris et fratrum ordinis Sancte Crucis predictorum alternatim sunt appensa: Data London primo die Marcii anno Domini MCCC^{mo} decimo nono.

GENERAL INDEX

Roman numerals refer to pages of the Introduction. Arabic numerals refer not to pages but to entries in the text or, when preceded by 'App.', to entries in the Appendix.

A., chancellor, 976
Abbechirch, *see* St. Mary Abchurch
Abbot, Stephen, 278
'Abbotesyn', inn of the abbot of Evesham, 1044
Abindon (Abyndon, Habyndon)
  Richard, 390
  Simon, 381
  Simon de, sheriff, 940
  Stephen de, 390; sheriff, 925, 927, 1029
Abraham
  Gregory, 258
  John, 258, 1025
Ace, John, 903
Acres
  John, 595
  Sayerus, 595
Acton, William, 865
Adam
  brother of Ralph, clerk, of Stepney, 887
  chamberlain, 202
  chaplain, 202
  clerk, 152
  famulus of Robert Coringham, 143, 145
  priest, 109
  prior of Crutched Friars, 165
Adeliza, queen of England, 875
Adelstanus (Aldstanus), 552
Adhelwold, Robert, 91
Adrian
  alderman [? *rectius* John Adrian], 190
  mercer, 485–6; his widow, 486
Adrian (Adryan)
  John (son of), 127, 467, 501; bailiff of London, 889; draper, 507; mayor, 60, 93, 292, 369, 684, 864, 905, 916, 1008; sheriff, 134, 447, 641
  John, sheriff *1277–8*, 378, 906, 1007
  Thomas son of, 486
Aelwy, *see* Eswy
Agnes, sister of St. Thomas, *see* Becket
Agulun, Robert de, 1021
Agulus, William, 856, 862
Aiguel (Aignel), William, 9th prior of Holy Trinity, 21, 45, 52, 237, 277, 323, 560, 646, 897, 992
Ailnodus, priest & scribe, 967

Ailward (Aluard, Alwardus), 31
  alderman, 1008
  baker, 136, 270
  forger, 963
  priest, 963
  priest of St. Peter ad Vincula, 964
Ailwin (Alwin, Eilwin), 963
  clerk, 960
  relative of Blakstan, 871
  son of Leofstan, 871
  son of Raduinfus, 960
  son of Syredus, 871
Ailwin
  Henry fitz (son of, son of Leofstan), mayor, 41, 76, 206, 223, 228, 270, 273, 426, 551, 663, 687, 824, 866, 1005, 1012, 1015, 1022–4, 1051, 1061, 1073
  Norman fitz, 930
  Peter son of Henry fitz, 223, 1051
Ainulf, priest, xiv, 6, 9, 1070, App. 6, 9
Aketon, *see* Haketon
Alan
  canon of Holy Trinity, 1031
  deacon, 790
  nephew of Herbert, bishop of Avranches, 739
  son of Peter, *see* Peter
Alan
  Ranulf, potter, 955
  Roger (fitz, son of), 76, 206, 687, 729, 824, 1012, 1015; mayor, 335, 1073; sheriff, 1023
Alban, tailor, 666
Albano, Stephen, 944
Alberic (Albricus), *see* Aubrey
Albrinc, Hubert, *see* Hubert, bishop of Avranches
Albus, *see* White
Aldermanbury, 688, 1023
Aldermanbury (Aldermaunebury)
  Gervase de, 335
  Simon de, sheriff, 1073
Aldermarychyrch, *see* St. Mary Aldermary
Aldermen (before 1272), *see* Adrian; Ailward; Balan, Alan; Ballio, John de; Basing, Adam de; Benet, William fitz; Blund, James; Blund, Matthew; Blund, Peter; Durham, Thomas de;

General Index

Edmund; Estmund; Ferrun, Alexander le; Fulc, Gilbert; Geoffrey; Gervase; Godwin; Haverhill, Thomas de; Insula, Walter de; Ivo, Theobald fitz; Joce, junior; Living; Martin son of Alice; Mary, Simon fitz; Matthew; Northampton, John; Peter; Peter, Joce fitz; Reggi, Richard fitz; Renger, Richard; Renger, Roger; Robert son of Bartholomew; Roger, Roger fitz; St. Helens, Henry de; Solio, John de; Sperling, Jordan son of Jordan; Tabur, Hugh; Theobald; Thomas; Walbrok, Richard de; Walter; Walter, Richard fitz; Warde, Edmund; Wilkyn, William; Winchester, Geoffrey de; *see also under names of mayors*
Alderman, deputy, *see* Hanin
Aldgate, gate & soke, xiii–xviii, 4, 11, 31, 33, 44, 47, 66, 323, 871, 875, 995–6, 1004, App. 4, 11; *see also* St. Botolph Aldgate
Aldgate Street (Algatestret), 822, 891, 894, 896, 937
Alditha, 1013
Aldstanus, *see* Adelstanus
Alduino, 4, App. 4
Alexander III, pope, 981
Alexander
  clerk, 270
  deacon, 136
  mercer, 838
  of Gutter Lane, 841
  rector of St. Swithin, 430, 1017
  son of Geoffrey le Coureur & Hodierna his wife, 920, 955
  whittawer, 636
Alfegus, 963
Alfred
  baker, 346
  butcher (le Bochere, etc.), 171–2, 900, 910–11
  mercer, 687–8, 1023; Alice his daughter, 688, 1023
  tiler, 202
Alfric Cheic, 960
Alfwin, *see* Hallen
Algar
  bishop of Coutances, 960
  brother of Gerald, 960
  priest, 612, 672; [? another], 871
  priest of St. Benet, 967
  Secusune, 871
Algate (Alegate)
  Adam de, 930, 946
  Bartholomew de, 882, 886, 923, 930, 933, 938
  John de, 610
  John de, potter, 911, 915, 917
  Jordan de, butcher, 904
  Juliana de, *see* Crepyn, Juliana
  Nicholas de, 15th prior of Holy Trinity, 27, 479, 702, 879, 892, 952, 958, 996, 1032, 1039–40
  Ralph de, 886, 900, 908, 910, 930
  Ralph de, *see* Crepyn, Ralph
  Richard (de), 896, 919
  Terricus de, 882, 886, 930, 933, 938, 946
  Thomas de, *see* Bonsergaunt
  Thomas de, rector of Sheering, 1032
  William de, 62, 882, 886, 900, 906, 908, 930, 933, 938, 946
  William de, son of Stephen de Sharnbrok, 888–9
Alice
  daughter of Henry, 84
  [? Perrers] (the Lady, Alice Regina), 770, *see also* Perers, Alice
Alkelinus, baker, 946
All Hallows Barking (Berkyngchirche) cemetery, 192; church, 11, 191, 968, App. 11; parish, 181–94, 1030, 1040
All Hallows Bread Street, parish, 599–601, 1031
All Hallows Colemanchurch, *see* St. Katherine Coleman
All Hallows Fenchurch *see* St. Gabriel Fenchurch
All Hallows Honey Lane, parish, 539–44, 1030, 1041, 1043
All Hallows Lombard Street (Graschirch), parish, 329–39, 1012–13, 1030
All Hallows London Wall (by the Wall), parish, xvii, 732, 779–86, 1030
All Hallows Staining, parish, 103–8, 993, 1007
All Hallows the Great (ad Fenum, Haywharf), parish, 418, 430–3, 1030
Allyngebery (Alyngbery)
  Adam de, cit. 646; linendraper, 647; sheriff, 665
  Margery, 647
Alman, William, 855
Alphanus Juncarius, 35
Alsius, 960
Alswick (Alsiswick), Herts., 1004
Aluard, *see* Ailward
Aluerma, Adam de, 832
Alulf (Arnulf)
  archdeacon of Seés, 960
  Arnald [? *rectius* Alulf] son of, sheriff, 1073
  Arnulf son of, 443
  Constantine son of, 442–3; sheriff, 1073
  William son of, 231
Alvricus, priest, 624, 963
Alwardus, *see* Ailward
Alwell, John, 634

237

General Index

Alwin, *see* Ailwin
Ancett, William, 285
Anchorites of London, 621
Andrew
   chaplain of St. Augustine by St. Paul's, 634
   goldsmith, 126
   priest, 400
   the old, 687, 1023
Andrew(e)
   James, 498
   John, mayor, *see* Adrian, John
   Richard, 40, 1034
   Robert, junior, 377
   Thomas, 377
Anesty (Anesteye, Anestie)
   Hubert de, 64–5, 1004; Denise his wife, 1004
   John de, & J. his son, 858
   Richard de, 1004
Anger (Aunger), Peter (son of), 129, 530, 785; *see also* Peter, alderman
Anglo-Saxon language, 341, 872
Angodus son of Odo, 993–4
Angulo, John de, 1028
Anselm, 381
   archbishop of Canterbury, xiv, 1, 4, 7–8, 10, App. 1, 4, 7–8, 10
   baker, 84
   priest of St. Nicholas Shambles, 1024
Anstis, John, Garter King of Arms, xi–xii
Antioche, Gerard de, sheriff, 1073
Appilby (Appulby)
   John, 290
   Thomas (de), rector of St. Olave [? Hart Street], 207, 1040
Apprentice, takes name of master, 1036
Aqua, William de, 645
Aquarius, *see* Geoffrey, ewerer
Aras (Araz), *see* Arras
Arches, Court of, *see* Osbert, dean of
Arches, Les, *see* College Street
Arconerus, *see* Turbernus
Arcubus, *see* Wiganus
Ardernne, John, esquire, 591
Argentan, Richard de, king's steward, 1004
Armener, *see* Castell, William de
Armenters (Armentieres), John, sheriff, 73, 391, 767
Armerer, Nicholas, 518
Armiger, *see* Peter; William
Arnold, cook, 839
Arnold, Robert, 107, 179
Arnulf, *see* Alulf
Arnyze, William, 332
Arras (Aras, Araz)
   Gunter de, 185
   Richard de, 635, 993
   Robert de, sheriff, 307, 499, 718, 752
   William de, 43; [*alias* Horermed], 488

Arundell
   [? Edmund], earl of, 80
   Richard, earl of, 1005
Ascham, William, 224, 664, 1052
Ascheford, *see* Asshford
Aschellus (Aschuillus), 871
   custodian of the Tower, 960
Ascheton, John, cit. & fishmonger, 591
Aschewell (Asshewelle), John, attorney, 188, 479, 490
Aschwy, *see* Eswy
Ascomb, Robert, 651
Aspenden (Aspeden), Herts., 722
Asponis, 754
Asse
   Edwin, 776
   Robert, 1011
Assendon
   Katherine, 642
   William de, 642
Asshewelle, *see* Aschewell
Asshford (Ascheford, Asseford)
   John, 822
   William (de), 167–8; his widow, 168
Astle, Thomas, xii
Aswy, *see* Eswy
At Cok, *see* Cok
Athelby, Roger, 100
Attorneys, *see* Aschewell, John; Bury, Christian de; Cornhill, John de; Dauncere, John; Forster, Richard; Frye, Richard de; Gillingham, Alan; Gladewyn, Richard; Good, John; Hethingham, John; Horwode, Alan de; Meldeborne, Gilbert; Morton, John; Newport, Thomas; Symcok, Nicholas
Auberkyn, Walter, 225, 1052–3
Aubrees Watergate, 197
Aubrey (Alberic), of Billingsgate, 234; *see also* Ver
Aubrey (Aubre, Aubrer, Awbrei)
   Andrew, 473, 554, 673
   John, 386, 572, 725; sheriff, 188
Aubyn, Matilda, 939
Audeville, Thomas de, 658, 1012
Augo, John de, 430
Augustine, Saint, xiv, 6, 8, App. 6, 8
Augustine
   mercer, 329, 1009
   son of Wlwardus, 1004
Aumbesbury, Martin de, sheriff, 255
Aumener, Henry, 427
Aunger, *see* Anger
Austin Friars, 775, 1033
Averhull, *see* Haverhill
Avranches, bishop of, *see* Hubert
Awbrei, *see* Aubrey
Ax, Edmund del, *see* Epping, Edmund
Axbridge (Axebrigge, Axbrygge), Thomas

238

General Index

de, brother of Holy Trinity, xi–xiii, xx, 31, 287, 525, 954, 995, App. 31
Axstone, Robert, 405
Aylere, *see* Luke

Baalun, *see* Balan
Bacon (Baconn, Bacun)
  John, 347
  Peter, 1017
  Richard, 390, 1025
  William, 390; [another] & Alice his wife, 958
'Bacunnysyn', tenement called, 1035
Bacwell (Bakwell)
  Cecily de, 127
  Henry, 127
  Thomas (de), 127, 264–5
  Thomas, master goldsmith, 657
  Thomas son of Thomas, 264–6
  William, 264, 268
Baddyng, Robert, 885, 930
Badecoks (Batecoks), *see* Rufus, Geoffrey
Bagger, Brian, 137; *see also* Brian, merchant
Bail, Le, *see* Old Bailey
Bailey, chaplain of the, *see* John; William
Bakehouse, Pistrina Bokerel, 701
Baker (Pistor) *see* Ailward; Alfred; Alkelinus; Anselm; Bernard; Edmund; Fulc; Geoffrey; Gervase; Hugh; Ingolf; Martin; Matthew; Ralph; Robert; Roger; Simon; William; Wulmar; *and* Broun, Richard; Compere, Richard; Danger, Reginald; Kemesyng, John; Weye, Richard atte; Winchester, Simon de; *see also* King's baker
Baker (Bakere)
  Gilbert, *see* Lyrper
  William, 472
Balan (Baalun, Balon)
  Alan, 604
  Alan [alderman] & Juliana his wife, 177; ward of, *see* Queenhithe
Balancer, Ralph le, sheriff, 563
Bald, Alexander, 171
Baldok, Thomas, master of fraternity of St. Anne, 374
Baldwin (Baldewin)
  parmenter, 664
  priest, 185
  son of King Stephen, 14, 973, 977, App. 14
Baldwin (Baldewyn, Baldewyne)
  John, 783
  Richard (son of), 664
  William, cit. & saddler, & Emmota his wife, 1035
Balistarius, *see* John, crossbowman

Ball
  Godwin, 960
  John de, priest of St. Dionis, 223, 859
Ballio
  John de, [? haberdasher], alderman, 171, 312, 634
  John de, priest, 1051
Balls, Ralph, 708
Balnai, Adam de, 960
Balon, *see* Balan
Balsham, Thomas de, & Matilda his widow, 885
Bamme, Adam & his widow, 305
Banissehere, Martin, 185
Barber (Barbour)
  John le, 292
  Richard le, 153, 431–2
  Robert, *alias* Youn, & his widow, 891
  Roger le, 153,
  see also Joce; *and* Shanketon, Richard de
Bardeneye, Walter, *alias* Papworth, 388, 939–40
Bardolf, Robert & Amice his widow, 783
Barentyne, Drew, 440
Baret, Richard, 216
Barford, William, 888
Barher, John, 725
Barking (Berkyng), Essex, abbess & convent, 106, 499, 1007; abbess, *see* Merton, Alice de
Barn, Gervase, *see* Gervase, alderman
Barnet
  Edmund, *see* Hoddesdon
  John, 295
  Thomas, 552
Barra
  Geoffrey de, 748
  Henry de, 885
  Ralph de, 655
Barre, Matilda de la, 229, 1061
Barsham, Richard de, 280; Roesia his daughter, 280–1
Bartholomew
  bishop of Exeter, 740
  clerk, 270
  cook, 787
  parmenter, 39
  son of Philip, 993
Barun, Richard, 792
Bary, *see* Du Bary
Basing (Basyng, Basynges, Rasing, Rasyng)
  Adam de, 501, 730; alderman, 512; mayor, 140, 516, 616, 756, 794; sheriff, 636
  Hugh, sheriff, 1073
  John de, 958
  Nicholas & Isabel his widow, 498
  Robert de, 381, 551; sheriff, 192, 534
  Solomon (de), 183, 467; sheriff, 1073

General Index

Basing, *continued*
  Thomas de, sheriff, 213, 375, 845
  William (de), sheriff, 66, 123, 203, 732, 937, 1066
'Basket, atte', tenement called, 1034
Basket, Richard atte, *see* Weye
Basse (Bas, Baas)
  Algar, 948
  Gilbert le, 501
  John, 923, 1034; Emma his wife, 1034
Basset
  Fulk, bishop of London, 984–6
  Ralph, 12, 651, 998, App. 12
  William (son-in-law of), 609, 848, 938
Bassishaw (Bassyngshawe), 688, 712, 715, 718, 727, 1023
Bath & Glastonbury, bishop of, *see* Jocelin
Batingcourt (Batancort, Batincort, Batencuit), Luke de, bailiff of London, 889; sheriff, 134, 447, 921, 928
Batlismere
  Bartholomew, 80
  Giles & his widow, 80
Batman, Dr. Stephen, xi, 341
Batoneslane [? *rectius* Ratoneslane, near Timberhithe], 604; *see also* Pudding Lane
Batte (Bat)
  Gerard, mayor, 1018; sheriff, 262, 549
  Nicholas, 123, 189, 218, 849, 853, 1017, 1056; mayor, 190, 501, 596, 731; sheriff, 516, 616, 756, 794, 818
  Peter, 1061; sheriff, 1073
  Ralph, 1061
  Robert, 228–9, 404, 1025, 1062
  Roger, 726
Battisford (Battysford), Hugh, 219, 1057
Batun, 960
Batur
  John le, 354
  Peter le, 783
  Thomas le, 354–5
Baudricus, fisherman, 259–60
Baynard (Beynard) Richard, 321, 373
Beadle, *see* Bedell
Beamond, Ralph, 186
Bearbinder Lane (Berbynderyslane), 469, 479–80
Beauchamp (de Belcampo)
  Anselm, 109
  Richard de, earl of Warwick, 825
  Robert, 109
  Thomas, earl of Warwick, 1005
  William, chamberlain, 1005
Beaumont (Beuamont), [John viscount], 1045
Beauvais, France, xiv, 8, App. 8
Beauvais (Belvaco), Philip de, 189
Beawneys, Nicholas & William his son, 249

Becham (Bekham, Bekeham)
  John, 82–3
  Walter de, 289
  William, 1011
Beche, Osbert, 423
Beckenham? (Bekeham) Kent, 1004
Becket (Beket)
  Gilbert, sheriff, 13, 31, 963, 1072
  Thomas, chancellor & archbishop, 14, 1002–3, App. 14; Agnes his sister, 64
Bedell (Bedel, Bidell)
  Adam, 459
  Edmund (le, the), 921, 924, 927
  John le, 394
  Laurence son of Edmund le, 927
  Nicholas the, 346
  Richard, 40
  Thomas le, 888, 925
  see also Hoder, Simon le
Bedford (Bedeford)
  Alexander de, son of Agnes, 443
  John, 63, 193
  Master John, 377
  Robert de, 443
Bedfunt, Walter, 865
Bedyngton, Simon de, sheriff, 211, 368
Beel, Robert le, sheriff, 1073
Begne, Stephen de, 1004
Beifuin, Godfrey, 1004
Bekeham, *see* Beckenham, Kent
Bekeount, *see* Buccuinte
Belch, Walter de, 579
Belebarber, Hugh, 754
Belebouch, William, 104
Belegh, Walter, 583
Belerece, Edeva, 366–7
Belhume (Belhome), William, 783, 878
Bell, melted down, 1038
Belleyetlane (Belyetereslane), *see* Billeter Street
Bellhows, Thomas, 822
Bell-ringer, *see* William
Belmeis
  Richard de (I), bishop of London, xiv, 3–4, 12, 875, App. 3–4, 12
  Richard de (II), archdeacon of Middlesex, 614
  William de (I), archdeacon of London, 962, 966
Belmonte (Blemonte, Blemund), William de, 349, 481, 487, 1004, 1014
Belvaco, *see* Beauvais
Bemptona, Richard de, 136
Bendeng, Peter de, 1004
Benedisse, Roger de, butcher, 262, 264
Benercheruer, *see* Suething
Benet
  abbot of Stratford Langthorne, 385, 574, 627, 1015
  deacon, 152

240

General Index

goldsmith, father of Richard, 250, 362
son of Turkyll, 298, 1011
Benet, William (fitz son of), 316, 494; alderman, 528
Benit, Richard de, cook, 171
Bensted, Robert de, 704
Bentleghe, Adam de, sheriff, 533
Benyngton (Beninton, Benyton)
  Ralph son of Adam de, 923
  Richard de, 335
  Simon de, sheriff, 61, 356
Berbynderyslane, *see* Bearbinder Lane
Berchenerislane, *see* Birchin Lane
Berden, *see* Burden
Berdfeld, John, 712
Bere, John de la, 65
Berengarius, father of Rennerus, 387
Berewards Lane (Berwardyslane), 855
Berkesden (Berkeden), Herts., brothers at, 986; land of, 1004
Berkyng, *see* Barking, Essex
Berkyng
  Juliana de, 679
  Richard de, 330
  William, 65
  William (de), 539, 1004, 1027
  William de, *alias* William the Baker, 759–61; Matilda his wife, 761
Berkyngchirche, *see* All Hallows Barking
Berman, 960
Bermondsey, Surrey, 1005
  priory, later abbey of St. Saviour: abbot, 389, 428; land, 271, 335; monks, 460, 977, 1016; priors, *see also* Hugh *and* Humbert
Bernard
  baker, 271
  clerk, 4, App. 4
  prior of St. Peter Dunstable, 8, 10, 13, 871, App. 8, 10, 13
Bernard (Bernerd)
  Roger, 332
  William, 145, 151
Berners, Agnes, 216
Bernes
  Edmund, 105
  John de, sheriff, 660, 675
Berneval (Breneval), Peter, 877, 804, 955
Berneye (Bernere), Walter de, sheriff, 133, 156, 330
Berquereola, Robert de, reeve of London, 1072
Berskernereslane, *see* Birchin Lane
Bertelot, John, carpenter, 356
Bery, Robert (de), *see* Kelsey, Robert
Besant (Bisant), Robert, sheriff, 687, 1073
Betele, Richard, 642
Beth, Henry atte, 309
Bethleham (Bedlehem), master of, 863

Bethune, Robert de, bishop of Hereford, 973
Betonia
  John de, 425
  William de, 73
Beuamont, *see* Beaumont
Beufront, John, 249
Beverle (Beverlaco)
  John, 783
  Robert de, 993
  Roger de, 826
  Simon de, 103
Bexhill (Bixhill, Bixill), Sussex, 916; church, App. 13
Bexile, Ralph de, 585
Beynard, *see* Baynard
Bidell, *see* Bedell
Bigge, Roger, 886
Bigot
  Hugh le, 960
  R., 960
Bilesherse, 1004
Billericay (Billerika, Billirica), John de, carter, 904, 907, 922, 927, 940; John his son, 922
Billeter Street (Belleyetlane, Belyetereslane), 55, 65
Billingsgate, 232, 255; *see also* Aubrey
Birchin Lane (Berchenerislane, Berskernereslane, *etc.*), 355, 361, 363, 363a
Bisant, *see* Besant
Bishopsgate (Bisshopesgate), gate, 871; street, 787, 849, 858, 861, 863
Bisshopsgate, Nicholas de, & Isabel his wife, 787
Bisshopyston, John, 488
Bixill (Bixhill), *see* Bexhill, Sussex
Black (Black, Niger)
  Edmund, 659
  Thomas, *alias* Jurdan, *see* Jordan
  Walter, 578, *see also* Walter, goldsmith
Black Friars (Friars Preachers), 1033
Blakeney, Peter de, sheriff, 95, 113, 227, 1055
Blakesapelton (Blakesappilton), Roger de, 222–4, 1052; William his son, 224
Blakstan, 871
Blandecute (Blandekete), Richard, *see* Machechrier, Richard
Blanket, John, 636
Blaunchard, Walter, 944
Blecchinggeleye, Walter de, 1043
Blemonte (Blemund), *see* Belmonte
Bloet, Robert, bishop of Lincoln, 4, App. 4
Blokeley, John, 216
Blomvylle, Richard, 46, 83
Blondy, Robert, 908
Bloxham, John de, 607
Blunt (Blond, Blound, Blund)
  Andrew, 482, 561–2, 1018

241

General Index

Blunt, *continued*
  Bartholomew, 497, 655; John his son, *see* John, goldsmith
  Edward, 457; [another], 562
  Edward, sheriff, 129, 499, 530
  Geoffrey, 171, 666
  Henry, & Henry & Richard, his sons, 1023
  Henry, tanner, & his widow, 861
  Hugh, *alias* White (Albo), sheriff, 636
  Hugh & Isabel his daughter, 832
  James, alderman, 754, 759, 761–2
  John, 280; [? another], 991
  John, clerk, 349, 1014
  John le, mayor, 73, 104, 111, 408, 457, 537, 631, 711, 732, 834, 904
  Laurence, 234
  Matthew, alderman, 74, 402, 453
  Norman, draper, sheriff, 551, 658, 1012
  Peter, alderman, 785
  Peter, felter, alderman, 178, 186
  Ralph, 824
  Ralph, sheriff, 37, 94, 437, 474, 599, 664, 1031; Matilda his wife, 1031
  Richard, fishmonger, 227, 283, 689, 1055
  Richard son of Henry, 1023
  Robert, 264, 335, 381, 449
  Robert, butcher, 1025
  Roger, 1073
  Simon, 340, 372, 449, 482, 1020
  Walter, 457; [another], 575
  Walter (le), potter, 578, 582, 812–13, 1018; Matilda his widow, 812
  Walter le, sheriff, 221
  William, 855, 861
  William, sheriff, 1073
Bochland (Bockland), Hugh de, sheriff, 873, 1072, App. 2
Bockyng
  Henry (de), carpenter, 155, 170
  John de, 701
Boconitis, William, son of Sabelina, 1043
Bocton, John (de), cit. & cofferer, 751–2
Bodele (Buddele, Buttele), John de, 173, 195, 293
Bogoys, Katherine, 113
Bohon (Bohun)
  Humphrey de, dapifer, 1002
  Master James de, 836
Bokelerisbury (Bokelesby), *see* Bucklersbury
Bokeount, *see* Buccuinte
Bokerel (Bokerell, Bukerel)
  Andrew, mayor, 262, 273, 549, 618, 650, 690
  Isabel, 670
  Matthew, sheriff, 32, 195, 200, 292, 369, 375, 510, 692, 893, 1008, 1021, 1063
  Peter, 459, 744, 1014
  Stephen, 963

  Stephen, alderman & sheriff, 354–5, 668, 692–3, 701
  Thomas, sheriff, 1073
  William, 670
Bole
  Henry (le), 367; sheriff, 646
  John, 607
  Nicholas, 153
'Bole, Le', house called, 375
Bonaventure, Richard, *alias* Hakborne, 219, 1057
Bond, John (two), 488
Bonech, Geoffrey, 1012
Bonet, Gilbert, 566
Bononia, Nicholas de, 174
Bonsergaunt (Bonseriaunt)
  J., 1034
  Thomas, son of William, *alias* de Algate, 821, 1034
  William, moneyer, 820–1, 901, 903
Bonvalet, William, 704
Borden, *see* Burden
Bordesden, *see* Braughing, Herts.
Bordesdon, Thomas de, 1004
Boreford (Borford)
  John, sheriff, 834
  Robert, 954
  Ros, 63
Borham, John, 290
Bortewold, John, 94; *see also* Dortewold
Borwasch, *see* Burghersh
Bosewarth, Adam, 326
Bosham (Boseham, Bosenham, Bosheham)
  Agnes, 924, 934, 947
  John, 242, 705
  Peter (de), sheriff, 408, 711
Boteler (Botiller, Botoner)
  Agnes (le), 155, 170
  James le, sheriff, 66, 458a, 732; Agnes his widow, 458a
  John, sheriff, 418
  John (le), draper, 478, 496, 506
  John le, [? father & son], 506
  Richard, 350
  William, 1057
Botere, Walter le, 37
Botham, Geoffrey de, 677
Boturwyke, Thomas, 846
Boucher (Bustcher), *see* Pain; *see also* Butcher
Boulogne, honour of, lands of, 1004
Bourne, John, 258
Bourton, Robert de, formerly guardian of the chantry at Layer Marney, 441
Bowelane (parish of St. Michael Paternoster), *see* College Street
Bowier(e), Benet, 246
Bowmaker, *see* Ernald
Bowstryng
  Ralph, 87

General Index

Simon, 87
Box
  Benedicta, 33-4
  Christine, 229, 301, 1062
  Hamo, 33
  Helen, daughter of Martin, 174
  John, 34
  Martin, sheriff, 47, 174
  William, 219, 958, 1057
Boyden, Robert, 309
Boylon, John, 83
Boys
  Geoffrey, 172
  John, *see* Bussh
  Simon, 215
Brabason (Brabeson)
  Adam, 562, 587
  Robert, 588
Braching, Bracking, *see* Braughing, Herts.
Brachyng (Brackyng, Brauhingg)
  Adam de, clerk, 834, 837, 1029
  Theobald de, 1004
Brackele (Bracle), Robert de, 845-6
Braddeman, James & Whattenow, learned in the law, 258
Bradele, Gilbert de, 1004
Bradwell, John, prior of Holy Trinity, xxiii
Braibroke, William, 290
Brakley, Michael de, 382
Brambeleg, *see* Bromley
Bran, Gervase, *see* Gervase, alderman
Brancestre
  Alan, 625
  Thomas, 631
Brand, 225; master, canon of St. Paul's, 620, 624
Brand (Bronde)
  Hamo, 1028; sheriff, 1073
  Ralph, 497
Brandeston, John, 40
Brandon, Thomas, *see* Irland
Brangwayn (Brangweyn)
  Thomas, 767
  William, 541
Brantingham, Thomas, bishop of Exeter, 1005
Braughing (Braching, Bracking, Brackyng), Herts., 811, 973-4, 1004, 1020
  brothers at, 986
  canons' market at, 1005
  Bordesden, 1004
  Gatesbury (Catesbiry), 1004; field (Gatisbifeld), 811
  Kingshohell in, 811
  Wodcroft in, 811
Brawstok, John, 958
Bray
  John, 954
  Nicholas, 298, 313

William, 763, 765-6, 769, 777, 798, 1016; [another], 298
Brazier, *see* Langhorne, John
Bread Street (Bredstret), 575, 594, 599-600, 749, 751, 773, 1031; *see* Thomas
Bread Street ward, 586n
Breklesworth, William, 130
Bremble (Brembyl, Brembir), Nicholas, 441, 446, 730
Breneval, *see* Berneval
Bret, Robert, 657
Breton (Bretonne)
  John le, kt., warden of London, 255, 665
  Thomas le, 1007
Brevetur, John le, 797
Brewer, [William], 224
  see also Estbrok, Richard; Horer, John; Payn, John; Traynell, John
Brewhouses, xx, 11, 363, 382, App. 11; equipment of, 954
Brian, merchant, 148-9, *see also* Bagger, Brian
Brian (Bryan)
  Lord Guy, 80
  John, 682; [another], 725
  John, sheriff, 906
  William, 290
Brictred Cuherd, 960
Bricus, ropemaker, 233
Brid (Bridde, Bryd, Brydde)
  Geoffrey, 996
  German, cit. & fishmonger, 129-31; Alice de Essex his wife, 129; Lucy his wife, 131
  John, 996, *see also* Byrd
Bridge Street (Brygestrete, *etc.*), 283, 286-7, 305, 1010
Bridport (Bryddeport)
  Giles de, bishop of Salisbury, 986, 989
  Thomas de, 111
Brik, Richard de, sacristan, 107
Brikelesworth, John de, sheriff, 441
'Brisstret', [parish of St. Faith], 626
Bristowe (Bristol, Brystowe)
  John, 768
  Simon de, 697
  William de, 42; [another], 66, 615; [another], 151, 224, 697
Brithmar (Brihtmar)
  priest, 624
  son-in-law of Godwin Brothesouche, 394
Brito, Robert, 423
Brockele (Brokle), John, sheriff, 418, 996
Broderer (browderer), *see* Freton, Thomas; Hauekyn
'Brodeselde', xviii, 510-11
Brodhers, Godwin, 963
Brokedych, William de & Walter his son, 759

243

General Index

Brokesheved (Brokeshevede)
  Geoffrey de, 406–7
  Richard & Alice his wife, 49
Brole, William, brother of Holy Trinity, 815
Bromfeld (Brumfeld), Richer de, 84, 86
Bromhil, John de, 252
Bromley (Brambeleg), 962, 1004
  monk's mill in, 1004
Bronde, *see* Brand
'Brook, le', within the walls, 782
Brook, Geoffrey, sheriff, 290
Broom (Brom, Brome), Robert, 808, 896
Broomfield (Brumfeld), ? Essex, 1004
Brother, Arnold le, 783
Brothesouche, Godwin, 394
Broun (Brun, Brunus)
  Adam, 317, 482
  John, 193, 216, 770
  Lucy, 317
  Matthew & his widow, 216
  Richard, baker, 440
  Robert, 815
  Thomas (I), 56, 59, 227, 531, 1039, 1055; Margery (his widow), 56, 59, 61, 227, 531, 1039, 1044, 1055
  Thomas (II), 531, 536; his widow, 531
  Walter le, mercer, 204, 510; sheriff, 663, 993, 1067, 1073
  William, 207
Brounesby, John, 313
Brounlocus, 257
Brounyng (Bruning)
  Adam, sheriff, 154, 798, 1016
  Eymericus, 535
  Walter, 582
Bruhull, Richard de, 751
Brumfeld, *see* Bromfeld; Broomfield
Brumle, Ralph, 170
Brumtune, William de, 825
Brunton (Bruton), Henry, tailor, 130–1; Imania his wife, 131; Emma (? *rectius* Imania) his widow, 130
Brusous, Robert, 304
Bryccheford, Richard, 896
Brygge, Philip atte, 441
Bryght (Brygth), Thomas, 954, 995, 996
Buccel, Ralph, 273
Buccuinte (Bekeount, Bokeount, Bucumte, Buchiunt, *etc.*)
  Andrew, 871, 963, 1072
  Geoffrey, 371–2, 625
  John, sheriff, 76, 963, 1011, 1073; son of Geoffrey, 371–2
  Laurence, 963
  see also Boconitis
Buchel, Ernulf, sheriff, 1072
Buckingham, earl of, *see* Thomas, of Woodstock
Bucklersbury (Bokelerisbury, Bokelesby), 496, 1014

Buctone, Adam de, 883
Bufle, Walter le, 618
Buke, Peter, sheriff, 1073
Bukerel, *see* Bokerel
Bullok
  William, 939
  William, cit. & tapicer, 117
Bunburne, *see* Wimburn
Bungay (Bungey)
  Reyner (Reynger) de, sheriff, 299, 440, 636, 1018
  Simon, currier, 856, 863, 1017
  Thomas (de), cit. & currier, 863–4
Burchayn, Robert, 659
Burden (Berden, Borden, Burdeyn)
  John, 674, 755
  Robert, sheriff, 55, 673
  Walter, 673
  William, 552, 675
Burdeux, William, 42
Bure, William, 111
Bureller (Buriler), *see* Henry; Ralph; William; *and* Myngy, Warin; Oxford, Thomas de; Preest, William; *see also* Burrell
Bures, Peter, 826
Burford
  Robert, 888
  William, father of Robert, 891
Burgage tenure, xviii, 1005
Burgh, Hubert de, justiciar, 1004
Burghersh (Borwasch), Lord Bartholomew, 1036
Burgoyn (Burgeyn, Burgundia)
  John de, 1043
  William de, 168
Burgum (Burgo)
  John, 578
  William de, clerk, 531–2; Margery his wife, 532
Buriler, *see* Bureller
Burrell (Burel, Burell)
  John, 172
  Ralph, 172, 179
  Robert, 199, 350, 488, 1004, 1014
  William, 179
Burser (Bursier)
  Henry le, 489
  Robert, 321–3
  William, 321
  see also Roger
Burton
  Philip, 210
  Robert, 715
  Thomas, 715
Burton [-on-Trent], Staffs., abbot & convent of, 1035
Buruch, Brother Walter, canon of Holy Trinity, 237
Burwell, Ralph, 130

244

General Index

Bury
  Adam de, mayor, 441, 1057
  Christian de, attorney, 57
  John de, butcher, 309
  Roger de, *alias* Roger Rose, 815
  Thomas de, butcher, 305, 308
  Thomas de, guardian of Thomas Bacwell, 265
Burys, John, sheriff, 660
Business, money given said to be for, 195, 197, 218, 369, 505, 1056
Bussh, John, *alias* Boys, 113, 210, 1059
Bussheye, Robert, 896
But, father of Robert, 963
But, Alan, 579
Butcher, *see* Alfred; Edric; Nicholas; Pain; Ralph; Reginald; Robinel; Roger; William; Wulfric; *and* Algate, Jordan de; Benedisse, Roger de; Blund, Robert; Bury, John de, & Thomas de; Joye, Benet; Kyng, Thomas le; Leman, Richard; Swyft, Roger; *see also* Machechrier
Buttele, *see* Bodele
Buurges, Peter de, 423-4; O. his sister, 423
Buxford, William, 896
Byblesword, Hugh de, steward, 527
Bydyk (Bydik), Henry de, 730, 732
Bykir, John, 42
Byrd, John, 954, *see also* Brid
Bys, William, 235
Bysshop, *alias* Knyght, Alexander, 239

Caen, burial of William I at, 1072
Cakyer, John, 853
Caldecote (Kaldecote), ? Herts., mill of, 1004
Calesby, William, 718
Callere, Robert (le), sheriff, 559, 562-3, 711
Camail, Walter, 382
Cambin (Cambyn), *see* Fulbert, Cambin
Cambio, John de, clerk (of Canterbury), 877-8, 881
Cambridge, earl of, *see* Edmund
Cambridge (Cambrygge, Cantebrigg, Cauntbrigge, *etc.*)
  Adam de, 370, 373
  Henry son of Ralph, 745
  John, 585
  Master John, 63, 1033, 1035
  John, cit. & fishmonger, Agnes & Elizabeth his late wives & Katherine his wife, 1035
  Nicholas (de) & Agnes his wife, 677
  Ralph de, 705, 745, 1041
Campe (Caump)
  Estmund, 366
  Simon, esquire, 1045
Candelwykstrete, *see* Cannon Street

Canefeld
  Reginald, 311
  Thomas de, 268
Cannon Street (Candelwykstrete, *etc.*), 213, 298, 374, 380, 386, 405, 407, 410, 424, 427, 458, 460, 1016
Canoun (Canon), Adam, 242, 881, 934
Cans, Robert le, 664
Cant, Cancia, *see* Kent
Cantebrigg, *see* Cambridge
Canter (Kanter)
  Elias le, 596
  Ralph & Alice his daughter, 689-90
  Roger, 689-90; Marsilia his widow, 690
Canterbury, Kent
  archbishops of, *see* Anselm; Becket, Thomas; Corbeil, William de; Stratford, John; Sudbury, Simon; Theobald
  archbishop's soke, 223, 1051
  archdeacon of, *see* Roger
  monks of Christchurch, 527
  prior of Christchurch, 749, 751
Canterbury (Caunterbury)
  Henry de, 56
  John de, 219, 221, 1057; Margaret his wife, 219, 1057; Margery his daughter, 219
  Ralph of, 11th prior of Holy Trinity, 23, 55, 66, 95, 99, 455, 537, 837, 904, 925, 996, 1029, 1059
  see also Cambio, John de
Canvill, Richard de, 976
Capeler (Capelere), Richard (le), 173-4; Sibyl his wife, 173
Capell
  Hamon, 171
  Peter, 171
  Robert, 171
Capella
  Henry de, 1004
  Jordan de, 166
Caponer (Capoeshors), Thomas de, 215
Capper, *see* Alan; Constantine; Gervase; Ralph; Theobald; *and* Capeler, Richard le; Eldyng, Stephen; Freure, Ralph; Wall, John atte
Carbunel, Ralph, 582, *see also* Ralph, coalman
Cardinal's Hat (Cardinalshatt), inn called, 490
Cardugan, Hugh, 1045
Carleton
  Oliver de, 833
  Richard, 138, 332; Katherine his wife, 332
  Simon son of Oliver, 833, 846
Carlisle, bishop of, *see* Chause, Robert de
Carmelites, *see* White Friars
Carpenter
  Adam, 770

General Index

Carpenter, *continued*
  John, 628
  Stephen, 84
  see also Henry; Ralph; Richard; Simon; Stephen palmer; Turold; William; Wurthing; *and* Bertelot, John; Bockyng, Henry
Carswell, John de, 664
Carter, *see* Walter; *see also* Osbert, chapman; *and* Billericay, John de; Gamene, Henry
Carteys, Claricia, 75
Carwe, William, his widow, 718
Castell (Castro)
  Bartholomew de, 669–70, 677, 691; alderman, 684
  Henry de, chaplains of, *see* Reginald; *and* W.
  William de, *alias* le Armener, 836
Castle Hedingham (? Halyngham, Hayngham), Essex, 975, App. 14
Casven (Casewem)
  John, 210, 386, 1059
  Stephen, 210, 386, 1059
Catelon (Katelon, *etc.*), Robert (de), 381, 382
Catesbery, Nicholas de, & Katherine his wife, 1004
Catesbiry, *see* Braughing, Herts., Gatesbury
Cauel, Richard, 11, 663, App. 11
Cauntbrigge, *see* Cambridge
Caus, Robert, 1005
Causton(e)
  John de, 939
  Richard; his widow, 216
  William, 511
  William de, sheriff, 563, 631
Cavendych (Caundych, *etc.*)
  Lettice, 472
  Roger de, 511
  Stephen de, escheator, 469, 625
  Thomas, 531, 1039
  Walter de, 721
Caxton, Robert, 901
Cay (Cayo), John de, sheriff, 551, 1023
Cedwallus, king, 1072
Celario, Hugh de, 270
Celer, Richard atte, 46, 188
Cestre
  Ralph de, 378
  Richard de, 62
Cestrehunt, *see* Cheshunt, Herts.
Cestrehunt, Edward de, whittawer, 701a
Cestute, John de, 35
Cevethenlane, *see* Seething Lane
Chachepoll, Robert le, 273
Chaddesden
  Geoffrey de, parson of Long Whatton, 625–6
  Master Henry de, archdeacon of Leicester, 625–6
  Nicholas de, clerk, 625
Chadisle (Chatisle), Richard, 597, 896
Chalfont, William (de), 94, 98
Chaloner
  Ralph, 204, 993, 1067
  Simon (the), 380, 993
Chaltone, John, 896
Chambere (Chaumbyr, *etc.*)
  Thomas, *see* Convers, Thomas
  William, *see* Convers, William
Chamberlain (de Camera, Camerarius, Chambelyn, Chaumberleyn, *etc.*)
  Geoffrey the, 628–9
  Godfrey the, 628, 1015
  Henry, Parnel his wife & Thomas their son, 722
  John, 200
  Jordan, 545, 682
  Osbert, 618
  Philip, 87, 89, 92, 909
  Ralph son of Robert the, 824
  Robert the, father of Agnes, 442
  Thomas, 722
  Thomas son of Robert the, 634–5
  William, (sheriff), 234, 371, 434, 439, 663
  William brother of Agnes, 442, 444
  William father of Denise, 553, 1019
  William father of Margaret, 594
  William son of Jordan, 545–6, 553, ?593–4
  William son of Robert, 561, 565, 570, 602, 638, 824–5, 1018
Champeneys, Gilbert, 863
Chandler (Chandeler, Chaundeler)
  Alan & his widow, 636
  Arnold le, 252, 326, 330
  Hugh le (two), 839
  Matilda le, 839
  see also Matthew; *and* Chelse, John de; Hatfeld, John, senior
Changour (Chongonur), Adam, 216, 233, 566
Chapeler, Joce *or* Joseph, 107
Chaplains of London, *see* London
Chapman, John, 715
  see also Osbert
Chapsheth (Clapsheth), John, 815
Charleton, Thomas, 536
Charterhouse, prior, 285, 412, 472, 475, 843; tenement, 773
Chartres, France, xiv, 8, App. 8
Chatisle, *see* Chadisle
Chaucer, John, cit. & vintner, 896, 915, 926, 996; Agnes his wife, 915, 926, 996
Chaumbyr, *see* Chambere
Chaumpeneys
  Robert, 326
  William, 552

General Index

Chaundeler, *see* Chandler
Chaundos, Robert, 249
Chause, Robert de, bishop of Carlisle, 986, 988
Cheapside (Chepe, Westchepe), 505, 507, 516–17, 525, 537, 543, 632, 641–2, 655, 657, 707, 1035, 1043
Cheesemaker, *see* Richard
Cheke, John, 142
Chelmesford
    Walter (de) & Agnes his widow, 815
    Walter (? son of Walter), 815–16
Chelse, John de, chandler, 537
Chent, Robert de, 400
Cherenburcer (Cherunburt), Robert son of John, 484, 1022
Chertsey, Surrey, abbot of, 273
Chese, William, 947
Chesewyk (Chesewyke, Cheswyk)
    Gilbert, 285
    Henry de, 346
    Walter de, 259
Cheshunt (Cestrehunt), Herts., nuns of, 856
Chessham, Richard, 405
Chester, bishop of, 824
Chester & Lincoln, earl of, *see* Ranulf
Chesterford, John, 418
Chesthunt, John de, 110
Cheyndeduit, William de, rector of St. Lawrence Pountney, 401
Chichester, bishop of, *see* Hilary; Ralph
Chichestre
    John de, sheriff, 61, 132, 675
    Roger de, 628
Chick Lane (Chikinelane, Chykenlane), 11, 192, App. 11
Chigwell (Chikewell, Chykewelle)
    Hamo de, mayor, 940; sheriff, 925, 927, 1029
    John, 172
    Nicholas, 1033
    Richard, sheriff, 425
    Roger de, 62
    Simon de, 901, 903
Chircheman, John, cit. & grocer, 364, 770, 772, 773
Chissebech, Margaret de *see under* Covert
Chivaler, Richard, 511
Chnotte, *see* Knotte
Chobham, Henry de, 1018
Chose, Roger, 171
Christmas Land (Cristemasselond) [parish of St. Olave Hart Street], 144
Chykenlane, *see* Chick Lane
Chykewelle, *see* Chigwell
Chyld, Peter, 803, 805
Chyngeford (Chynggeford)
    Alexander de, 947
    Alice de, 55

    Richard de, potter, 45–6; Christine his daughter, 46
    Simon son of William de, 880
Chyngelford, William de, 797
Chyvele, William, 815
Cimand
    Nicholas, 871
    Peter, 871
Cincur, Robert, 993
Clakton, John, 56
Clapsheth, *see* Chapsheth
Clapwell, Robert de, & his widow, 465
Clare, Ralph, 839
Clareb, Giffard, 4, App. 4
Claveryng, Richard, 317
Clayhurst (Clayherst) [in Beckenham], Kent, 1004
Clayman (Cleyman), Thomas, 40, 100; Agnes his daughter, 40
Clerk
    Geoffrey, churchwarden of St. Margaret Fish Street Hill, 287
    John le, 388
    Peter *rectius* William, prior, *see below*
    Richard, 941
    Thomas, 896, 909
    William, 19th prior of Holy Trinity (Peter), 421, 591, 995–6, 1044
    William le (husband of Agnes le Potter), 915, 919, 940; his widow, 919
Clerkenwell, Middx.
    hospital of St. John of Jerusalem, 183–4, 461–2; vice-gerent, *see* Richard
    priory of St. Mary, nuns, 326, 447, 529, 632, 664, 670; prioress, *see* Marcy
Clerkenwell, William de, 842
Clevehand (Clevhand), Walter, 186–7; Matilda his wife, 187
Cleyman, *see* Clayman
Clinton, Geoffrey de, 4, 11, 12, 871, 875, 998, App. 4, 11, 12
Cloak, gift of, 968
Clothes & other equipment of an Austin canon, App. 8
Clove, John, 768
Clyf, Gocelin, 1057
Cnihtengild, *see* English Knyghtengild
Cnut, king, 871
Coalman, *see* Ralph
Cobbe
    Alexander, 924
    J., 132
    Nicholas, 924
    Walter, 922
Cobeler, John, 939, 941
Coberd, Thomas, *alias* de Leycestria, 799
Cobham (Cobeham)
    Adam de, *alias* Cobhambery, 46, 83
    Reginald de, 137
    William de, 427

General Index

Coch (Cocher), Robert, 203, 1066
Cock Lane (Cockislane, Colkeslane, Kockeslane), 838, 840, 1021, 1028
Codres, John de, 594
Cofferer (Cofferere)
  John le, 877, 883
  Solomon le, 193
  see also Henry; Bocton, John de
Cofford, Henry de, 815
Cofyn, Peter, 172
Coggeshall (Coggeshale), Essex, abbot of, 943, 947
Coggishale, John, 496
Cok (Coke)
  James, 595
  James, cutler, & Joan his wife, 480
  John, 249
  John, clerk, 1007
  Richard, 482
  Sibyl at, 636
  Thomas, 81
  Walter, 107
Cokelin
  Benet, 860
  Peter son of Benet, *see* Peter, clerk
Cokermuth (Cokirmouth, Cokyrmouth), John, 55, 95–6, 203, 205, 1066, 1068
Cokham (Cokam, Kokham)
  Henry de, sheriff, 692–3, 744, 1014
  Simon de, 449, 451
Coks, Robert, 290
Colchester, Essex, church of St. Botolph at, xiv, 6, 9, 1070, App. 6, 9
Colchester, William de, & Emma his wife, 842
Colchirch, Henry de, 331
Cole, William, 1020
Colebrok, Robert de, 705
Coleman, John, 602–4
Coleman Street, 1012
Coleman(s)church, *see* St. Katherine Coleman
Colemanhawe (Colmanhawe), garden, 66, 80, 111
Colkeslane, *see* Cock Lane
Colle, Richard, 174
College Street (Bowelane, Les Arches), 437
Colne, Essex, 995
Cologne, Guildhall of the men of, 243n
Colshill, Thomas & his widow, 176
Colvyle, John, 121
Colwell (Colewell, Colvell), John, (cit. & mercer), 138, 149, 697–9
Combe (Coumbe)
  Edmund, 210, 1059
  Master John, 488, 491
  John son of John, 491; Joan his wife, 491
  Reginald, 210
  William (de), 221, 1057

Combemartin (Comartin, Commarty)
  Henry, 219, 1057
  William de, 834
Compere, Richard, baker, 241–2
Conductu
  Alan de, 1035
  Reginald de, alderman, 207–8, 210–12, 1040, 1059
  Thomas de, cit. & vintner, 450–1
Cone, Robert, clerk of John de Chichestre, 132–3
Consaldus, 578
Constable, Geoffrey, canon of St. Paul's, 614
Constance, son of King Stephen, 976
Constans, king, 1072
Constantine
  capper, 161, 163
  chaplain, 142
  son of Alulf, *see* Alulf
Constantinople, Emperor of, 13, App. 13
Constantyn (Constentyn)
  John (two), 547
  Richard, 547
  Walter de, 1038
Convers (Conversus)
  Master Andrew, 636
  Roger, 833, 846
  Thomas, *alias* Chaumbyr, 1035–6; Isabel his wife, 1035
  William, son of Thomas, cit. & fishmonger, *alias* Chaumbrer, *alias* Kelshull, 585, 590–1, 1035–6
  see also Stephen
Converts (*conversi* of the Temple), 239
Conyngsby, Theobald de, clerk, 631
Cook, *see* Arnold; Bartholomew; Edward; Edward son of Robert; Elias; John; Philip; Robert; Simon; William; *see also*, Benit, Richard de; Cok; Foliot, Gilbert
Cooper's Row (Wouderovelane), 154
Coote, H. C., xii
Copton(e)
  Agnes daughter of John, *see* Chaucer
  Hamo (de), cit. & moneyer, 896, 911, 925–6, 996; *see also* Hamo
  John, 926, 996
Copyn, Thomas, 891
Corbeil (Corbuil), William de, archbishop of Canterbury, 965, App. 10, 13
Corbet, Roger, 98
Cordiwisse, Sabina daughter of David, 1025
Cordwainer (Cordwaner), *see* Edmund; Gervase, alderman; Michael; Richard; Robert; Walter
Cordwainer Street, 562–3, 566, 572
Coreour, *see* Curreour
Coringham, *see* Coryngham

248

General Index

Corner (Cornur)
  Lawrence, 594
  Peter at, 674
  William (de la, le), cit., 197, 229, 369, 595, 1062
Corney (Corneya), Herts., annual fair & weekly market at, 1005; brothers at, 986; their land, 1004
Corney (Corneya), Henry de, 1004
Cornhill (Cornhull), 347, 350, 472, 475, 489, 1014
Cornhill (Cornhell, Cornhull, Kornelle, etc.)
  David de, 361-3
  Elias son of Richard de, 848
  Henry de, 344, 859, 1073
  Joce de, draper, 316-17
  John de, attorney, 49
  Ralph de, 361, 498
  Robert de, 497, 1010
  Robert de, sheriff, 213, 375, 845; [another] 533, 641
  Roger de, 425
  Stephen de, sheriff, 45, 424-5, 636
  William de, 362-3
  see also Hupcornhille, Edward
Cornmeter (Cornmonger), Hugh (le), 863-4
Cornuto de, monasterio, *see* Hornchurch
Cornwaleys
  John 272, (Cornewayle), 330, 941, 954
  Thomas, 272, 929, 936
Cornwall, duke of, *see* Edward
Cornwall (Cornewayle, Cornub')
  John de, 31
  Peter de, 255
  Peter de, 4th prior of Holy Trinity, xv, 16, 62, 64, 70, 74, 122, 171, 181, 183, 185, 204, 206, 223, 228, 267, 302, 312, 340, 353, 387, 404, 485, 574, 578, 620, 704, 717, 838, 848, 950, 994, 1015, 1020, 1028, 1051, 1061, 1067, 1069
Corold, *see* Turold, shoemaker
Coroner, Richard, 480
Corp, Simon, sheriff, 95
Corrodians, 1005
Corum, Robert, 407
Cory (Corry)
  John, clerk, 212, 952, 958, 1040
  Michael, 461
  William, 883
Coryngham (Coringham, Curryngham)
  Agnes, 149
  Robert, 42, 52, 143, 145, 149, 190, 802, 808, 905; his *famulus*, *see* Adam
  William son of Robert, 145
Costyn, John, 107
Cosyn, William, 888
Cotekyn, John, 321

Coteler (Cotteler)
  James, 347
  Jordan le, 462
  Katherine, 249
  see also Cutler
Cotlond, John, 319
Coton, Robert, cit. & draper, 418
Cotyngham, Richard, 896
Coutances, bishop of, *see* Algar
Coventre(e)
  Henry de, sheriff, 154, 322, 798, 1016
  John, 330
  John de, 764
  Jordan de, warden (? of Holy Trinity), 115, 762-4
  Ralph de, 181
  William de, 46, 83
Coventry, chancellor & archdeacon of, *see* Kylkenny, William de
Covert, John, kt., & Margaret de Chissebech his wife, 212
Craddock Lane (Craddokeslane), 993
Crane, Nicholas, sheriff, 695
Cras (Crasser, Crassus)
  Geoffrey, 848
  Serlo, 629
  Stephen, 566, 571, 613, 930, 1019
  William son of Geoffrey, 848, 1019; *see also* Goodchep
Cray (Crey)
  Edmund de, 37
  German de, 36-7
  John de, 587
  William de, 298
Crepilgate, *see* Cripplegate
Crepyn
  Agnes, 896
  Juliana daughter of Ralph, 896
  Ralph, clerk, *alias* Algate, 198, 722, 896, 905
  Walter son of Ralph, *alias* de Gloucester, 200-1
Cresburt, John de, 497
Cressingham, Thomas, 179
Creswyk (Cresewyk, Cresswyk), William, 117-18, 120, 645, 1037, 1042
Crey, *see* Cray
Crichcote, Ralph de, 962
Cripplegate (Crepilgate), 665, 672
Cristemasse
  Robert, 142, 149
  William, 61-2, 162, 166-7; his widow, 166
Croft, John, 995-6
Croke, John, 200
Cron, William (de la), 196
Cross (Cros, de Cruce)
  Gilbert, 233
  Helen, 958
  John, 323

249

General Index

Cross, *continued*
    John, *alias* St. Edmund, 233, 295
    Nicholas, 943–5
    Thomas, alderman & sheriff, 144, 215, 219, 255, 285–6, 752, 897, 1057
Crossbowman, *see* John
Crouche
    John, 566, 572; Isabel his wife, 566
    Thomas atte, spurrier, 846
Croucheman, Thomas, 901, 903
Crouere, William (de la), 1060
Crowhurst, John, 1032
Crowmer, William, 151; master draper, 427
'Crowne, le', shop called, 525
Croydon (Croydonne)
    John de, 287
    Richard, 246, 249, 251, 254, 272
Crutched Friars (Friars of the Holy Cross), 135, 158, 160, 163–5, 168, 170, 172, 934, 1033; prior, *see* Adam
Cruyland, Richard, 1004
Cucu, Ralph, 335
Cugel, Elfiet, 960
Cuherd, *see* Brictred
Cumin, spice, 213–1018 *passim*
Cumin, John, 740
Cunighope, William de, 666
Cupere (Cupgher)
    Martin, 597
    William, 831
Curcy, Robert de, 960
Curreour (Coreour), Geoffrey & Gunilda his wife, 677; *see also* Alexander son of Geoffrey
Currier *see* Bungay, Somon & Thomas
Curryngham, *see* Coryngham
Curteis (Curteys)
    Bartholomew, 705
    John, 176, 332, 863
    Richard, 251, 303
    Robert le, & Margaret his wife, 704
    Robert son of Robert le, 704–5
Curtilages, 236
Cuspy, Robert, 855
Cust, John, 893
Cutler, *see* Eudes; Peter; Stephen; *and* Cok, James; Hert, William; Sturry, Simon; *see also* Coteler
Cylbryght, John, marshal, 900
Cyprian, master, 241
Cytoler, Robert le, 552

Dacia, Oliva daughter of Robert de, 800
Dacus, David, 394
Dalby, John, 249; chantry priest, 954, 995
Dallying, John, 632
Daners, Richard, 472
Danger
    Reginald, baker, 248–9, 316
    William son of Reginald, 248

Daniel, draper, 1012
Daniel (Danyel)
    Walter, 905, 945
    William, 40, 81, 927, 934, 1034, 1038; [another], 924, 947
Dapifer, *see* Gregory; *and* Bohon, Humphrey de; Martel, William
Darcy, John, 615
Darkyngton, Reginald, cit. & fishmonger, 581
Dartford (Derteford, Dertford, Dortford), Kent, hospital of, 815; nuns of, 51
Daubeney, Stephen, 883
Dauncere, John, attorney, 266, 660
Daunehurst, John de, 418
David, king of Scots, 1, App. 1
David
    son of Ralph, 963
    son of Ralph, vintner, 551
David
    John, 783
    Thomas, 799
Davis, E. Jeffries, xviii–xix
Dawe
    Simon son of William, 878, 881
    William, 878
Dedynton, Nicholas de, 958
Delabare, Geoffrey, 331
Delpare, R., 873
Denicomb, Henry & Alice his widow, 685
Densouth, Richard, 307
Denton, Robert, chaplain, 1035
Denxmars (Denxmas)
    Bartholomew, cit. & ropemaker, 410
    Thomas son of Thomas son of Robert, cit. & ropemaker, 410
Denys, John, 730
Denyver, John, 242
Depam, Roger de, alderman, 673
Depedene, Richard de, & Roysia his daughter, 897
Derby
    Richard de, clerk, 131
    Robert (de), 677, 679
    Thomas de, 664
Derekinus, spicer, 262, 1010
Derekyn (Derekkyng), Richard, 488, 701
Derhant, William, 290
Derman (Dermannus), priest of St. Peter ad Vincula, 964
Derman, Nicholas, 888, 901, 903, 925, 927, 940
Dertford (Derteford), *see* Dartford, Kent
Dertford, Eustace de, 730
Desert, Roger, sheriff, 1073
Despenser, Hugh, 80
Deubeneye, Henry, 905
Deverose, John, 554, 562
Devon, sheriff of, 1004
Dewmars, Robert, 83, 87

General Index

Dieubeye, Walter, 94
Digge *or* Gigge, John, 891
Dilli, Fulk de, 1005
Diringus, 234
Distavelane, Cecily de, 913
Doctor (Medicus), *see* Ernulf; Gregory; Iwodus; Ralph; Roger
Dodding Pond (Doddyngpond, Duddyngespond), 871, 958, 964
Dode, John, cit., 712
Dodenham, William, *see* Thodyngton
Dogett (Doget)
   John, 305, 307; [another], 305
   Walter, sheriff, 264, 268, 506, 588; Alice his widow, 268
Dokesworth, Richard, 348
Dokett, *see* Duket
Dolcell, Simon, mayor, 81
Domesday Book, 1072
Donewich, Richard de, 751
Donkele, Roger, 511
Donyngton
   Hugh de, 440
   John, 472
Dorchester (Dorset), Master Alexander de, 528–9, 707
Dordrecht (Durdraght), Holland, wool carried to, 1040
Dortewold, John, 96; *see also* Bortewold
Dortford, *see* Dartford, Kent
Double (Dowble)
   John, 290
   Richard, 246, 249, 251
'Dove', brewhouse at sign of, 11, App. 11
Dover, Kent, 14, App. 14
Dowgate, 430
Dowry, *see* Legal matters
Draper
   Alan, 264, 267, 314
   Laurence, 316
   see also Daniel; *and* Adrian, John; Blunt, Norman; Boteler, John (le); Cornhill, Joce; Cotton, Robert; Crowmer, William; Gedeney, John; Hyham, John; Nolyf, Thomas; Welles, Thomas; Weston, William; Wyndesores, Godfrey de
Drapers, fraternity of, 427
Drayton, Roger, 454
Drinchepyn, Osbert, 871
Drury, Nigel, sheriff, 904
Druy, Geoffrey, 317
Du Bary, Simon, 62
Dubber, *see* Toltrich, Henry
Dubbur (Dubhour)
   Ailwin, 426
   Solomon le, 1017
Dublin, archbishop of, *see* Loundres, Henry de
Ducarel, A. C., xii

Duddyngespond, *see* Dodding Pond
Dugdale, William, xi
Duke (Duc, Duce, Dux), Roger (le), 222, 242, 606, 618, 856, 862, 1009, 1017; mayor, 304, 744; sheriff, 283, 548, 690, 693; weaver, 224
Duket (Doket, Dokett)
   Humphrey, 424–5
   Mary, 454
   Nicholas, sheriff, 74, 439–40, 442, 453–4, 1018, 1073
   Ranulf, 453
Dullyng, David (de), 89, 92
Dulyngham, Martin & Agnes his wife, 903
Dunmowe, Richard, 815
Dunnus, Ralph, 678
Dunstable, Beds., 2, App. 2
   priory of St. Peter, 10, App. 10; prior, *see* Bernard
Dunstapel, John de, sheriff, 665
Dunston, William, 701a
Durant, Robert, sheriff, 1073
Durdraght, *see* Dordrecht
Durham, bishop of, *see* Rufus, Geoffrey; William
Durham (Dorham, Dunelm, Dureara, Dureyn, *etc.*)
   Henry de & Agnes his wife, 389–90, 1016
   John de, 662
   Margery daughter of Henry de, 390
   Thomas de, 190, 331, 355; alderman, 115, 126, 380–1, 383; sheriff, 571, 1019
   William de, bailiff of London, 899; sheriff, 68, 189, 259, 489, 764, 792
Dyche, Richard atte, 409
Dycton, Robert de, *see* Kyngiston, Robert de
Dyer, *see* Stephen
Dykeman, William, 100
Dykonn, Richard, 127
Dyry, William, 249

Eastcheap, 262, 271, 306, 310, 312, 1011–12
East Smithfield, 871, 921, 937, 945–6, 950, 961–2, 964
Ebbgate (Ebgate, Ebbegate), 394, 398, 1035
Ecclesale
   John, clerk, 1035
   Robert & his widow, 896
Echyngham (Echynghamme)
   James son of Richard, 57
   Richard brother of Simon, 57
   Robert, 56
   Simon de, parson of Hurstmonceaux, 57
Edbert, king, 1072
Edes, Henry, 200
Edesworth, Stephen de, warden of London, 899
Edeua daughter of Walter, 203–4

General Index

Edgar, king of all England, 871
Edith, queen of England, 13, App. 13
Edith, widow, 1004; *see also under* Estmund
Edmonton (Edelmeton), Middx., 991, 1004
Edmund, king & martyr, 1072
Edmund (Ironside), king, App. 1
Edmund, lord, brother of Edward I, 920, 955
Edmund (Eadmund), 1004
    alderman, 809; *see also* Warde, Edmund
    baker, 227, 1055
    bedell, *see* Bedell
    canon of Holy Trinity, 16, App. 16
    cordwainer, 1007
    earl of Cambridge, 1005
    gate-keeper, 931
    mercer, 493, 496
    prior of Holy Trinity, xv, 14, App. 14
    smith, 292
    tailor, 405
Edmund
    Thomas, 585
    William, 585
Edredeshede, *see* Queenhithe
Edric (Edricus)
    butcher, 271
    father of Bartholomew de Algate, 930
    merchant, 887–8
Edulf, hosier, 157–8
Edward, the Confessor, king, xxiii, 13, 871, App. 13
Edward, king & martyr, 1072
Edward I, king 871
Edward II, king, 1005
Edward III, king, 959, 1005, 1047
Edward, duke of Cornwall, *etc.*, 519, 1047
Edward, 963
    cook, 270
    of Essex, *see* Wulmar
    priest, 232
    son of Alfward, 871
    son of Gocelinus, 950
    son of Robert, cook, 137
    son of Simuus, 963
    vintner, 529
Edward, John, 954, 995–6
Edwin
    felter, 199
    son of Oswant, 232
Eilricus, 'rusticus' & Godlune his wife, 964
Eilwin, *see* Ailwin
Eldyng
    Hugh de, 190
    Stephen (de), capper, 163, 191–2
Eleanor, queen (of Henry II), 14, 1002, App. 14
Eleanor, queen (of Henry III), xiii, 982, 986–7
Elias (Helia, Helius)
    canon of Holy Trinity, 968
    cook, 171
    Jew, 708
    mercer, & Matilda his wife, 314
    moneyer, 750–1
    priest, 271
    son of Godard, *see* Godard
Eliot, John, 940
Elsing Spital (Elsyngspitel), prior of, 677, 697
Elsyng, William (de), 677, 679
Ely, Cambs., bishop of, 871
Ely
    John de, sheriff, 1073
    Ralph (de), 565, 1018
    Robert, 585
    Roger de, sheriff, 455, 587, 590, 1035; Agnes his daughter, *see* Rayham
    William, sacristan of St. Paul's, 625
Elylond, Ralph, sheriff, 1073
Elyngham
    John, 290
    Roger de, 100
Empascorat, Picotus, 1004
Enfeld (Enefeld)
    David de, 670
    John de, 511, 702, 1039; [another], 725, 906; [? another], 896
Enfield (Enefeld), Middx., 1004
Engleis, Walter le, sheriff, 378, 906, 1007
English Knyghtengild (Cnihtengild, *etc.*) & soke of, xiii, xv, xvii–xviii, 11, 109, 871, 873, 874, 875, 876, 960, 962, 986, 998, 1005, App. 11
Epping (Eppyng)
    Edmund, *alias* Spyng, *alias* del Ax, 804–5
    Roger, 919
Erith
    John, 745, 749
    Mary, 745
Erkenwald, shrine of, *see* St. Paul's
Ernald
    'horsdrivere', 938–9; his widow, 939
    priest of St. Mary Somerset, 609
    son of Simon, bowmaker, & Margaret his daughter, 380
Ernulf, 423
    doctor, 962
Esby, John, 871
Espayne, *see* Spain
Essex
    bishop on visitation in, 995
    earl of, *see* Mandeville
Essex
    Andrew, 215
    Geoffrey de, goldsmith, 332, 406, 658, 1008; Lettice his wife, 1008
    Henry de, king's constable, 973
    John de, 735
    Richard (de), shopkeeper, 510
    Walter de, 505, 734, *see also* Totham

General Index

see also Wulmar son of Edward of Essex
Est, William, 419–20
Estbrok, Richard, brewer, & Agnes his wife, 117
Estchep
  Edmund son of Thomas de, 264
  Hugh de, 272, 299–300
  Thomas de, 264, 272, 301
Estmund, alderman, 394, 960; Edith his widow, 729
Eston, Robert de, cit., 530
Estreys, Haman le, 197
Estrilda, sister of William nephew of Keneward, 902–3
Estwyk, Thomas de, cit. & fishmonger, 1035
Eswy (Aelwy, Aschwy, Aswy)
  Agnes relict of Adrian, 389, 1016
  Ralph, sheriff, & mayor 307, 571, 636, 1018; [another], 694
  Richard, alderman, 617
  Stephen (de), kt., 305, 307, 695, 1043
  Master Thomas, canon of St. Paul's, 534
  William, sheriff, 476, 505, 756–7, 912, 1021
Ethelburt, king & martyr, 1072
Etheldred, king, 871, 1072
Eu, John (de), 248, 499
Eudes (Eudo)
  cutler, 395
  fishmonger, 582
Euere (Eure, Evere)
  Henry (de), 103, 330
  John (de), 344–5
  Roger (de), 345
  Walter, 748, 1041
  William, ironmonger, 103–5
Eustace, count of Boulogne, App. 1
Eustace, earl, son of King Stephen, 975
Eustace
  bishop of London, *see* Fauconberg, Eustace de
  mercer, 546
  nephew of Fulcred, 963
  8th prior of Holy Trinity, 20, 37, 43, 47, 93, 97, 103, 173, 195, 197, 245, 293, 307, 322, 344, 369, 374, 450, 451, 534, 684, 787, 871, 905, 906, 916, 921, 928, 1008, 1060
  son of David, 476, 840
Eustace, Peter son of, 90–1, 498
Everard (Everand, Everhard)
  Alan, 595
  Thomas, 506, 622
Evesham, Worc., abbot of, 56, 59, 227, 1044, 1055; his inn, *see* 'Abbotesyn'
Evesham, Thomas, 216
Evi, Ralph, 316
Ewelle, Richard de, sheriff, 476, 505, 912, 1021
Ewerer, *see* Geoffrey
Ewhurst (Uherst), Surrey, parson of, *see*

Kelsey, Thomas
Exchequer, 871; plea roll of, 982
Exeter, Devon, xiv, 4, 11, 998, 1004, App. 4, 11
  bishop of, *see* Bartholomew; Brantingham, Thomas; Warelwast, Robert
  treasurer of, *see* Salisbury, John de
Exeter (Excestre), Robert, 17th prior of Holy Trinity, 29, 290, 374, 491, 568, 737, 773, 1048
Exsport, John, 424
Exton (Extone)
  Nicholas, 332, 745
  Thomas, 805
Eylond, John, 659
Eynesford, William de, 1004

Facet (Facetus, Faiciet, Faith, Fayth, Lafait)
  Master Henry, 64, 74, 810, 815
  John son of William, 814
  Ralph la, 273
  William (le), 272–3, 809–10, 813–14, 902
Fairchyld, Geoffrey, 326
Faith, William le, *see* Facet, William
Fanchurch Stret, *see* Fenchurch Street
Faneneri, John, 388
Fanner (Fannere)
  Henry, 450; [another] & his widow, 936
  Robert, 436
Farndon (Frandon)
  Nicholas de, 73; alderman, 631; mayor, 55, 66
  William de, sheriff, 451
Farrier, *see* St. Albans, Adam de
Fastolf, Hugh, 725
Fauconberg (Fawkenberge), Eustace de, bishop of London, 372, 1004
Faukoner, John, 249
Faversham (Feversham), Kent, 1072, App. 14
Feld, Geoffrey at, 783
Felford, Gilbert de, 1008
Felim (?), Peter, 316
Felter (feltrarius, feltriere, feutrier), *see* Edwin; Gilbert; *and* Blunt, Peter
Fencherch, *see* St. Gabriel Fenchurch
Fenchurch Street (Fanchurchstret), 105
Ferbourne, William, 472
Ferebras (Ferbras, Fererbras)
  Gunote, 691
  John, 388
  Stephen, 408
Ferrinier, Gilbert, 350
Ferrun (Ferre, Ferron, Ferun, *etc.*)
  Alexander (le), alderman, 461–2, 467, 1010
  Andrew, 760–1; Wymarca his wife, 761
  John son of Alexander, 462
  Pentecost, 219, 1057

253

General Index

Ferrour, *see* Wylymyn, John
Ferthyng, J., 132
Festigart, Gilbert, 625
Feutrier, *see* Gilbert, felter
Fevre
  Humphrey le, sheriff, 329, 515
  Ralph, sheriff, 307, 501
Fifhyde, John, mercer, 117; sheriff, 188n
Finatat, Alfred, 1015
Fince, Ordgarus, 185
Fingre (Fyngre), Henry de, sheriff, 73, 767
Fink (Fynk, Fynks)
  James, 761
  William, 317
Fipbod, John, *see* Fifhyde, John
Firminus, chaplain, 390
Fish Market, *see* Old Fish Market
Fisherman, *see* Baudricus
Fishmonger, *see* Eudes; Pain; Roger; Stephen; *and* Ascheton, John; Blunt, Richard; Brid, German; Cambridge, John; Convers, William; Darkyngton, Reginald; Estwyk, Thomas de; Kelshull, William; Lambyn, Henry; Long, John; Mockyng, John; Newport, William; Newton, John; Ostage, William; Rufus, Alexander; Triple, John; Upchirch, Hugh; *see also* Stockfishmonger
Fisshbourn, William (de), 272, 274
Fitz Ailwin, *see* Ailwin
Fitz Alulf, *see* Alulf
Fitz . . . etc., *see under patronymic*
Flanders, Guy of [Flandrensis], 494
Flel (Flael)
  Matilda, 103
  Ralph, 206, 366
  William, 1028
Flemyng
  Robert le, 916, 921, 928
  Walter le, (of Bexhill), gate-keeper, 916–17, 921, 928
Flete, Simon, mercer, 525
Flitt (Flytt), Richard de, 688, 723, 1023; Alice his wife, 723, 1023
Flori, William, 208
Flynt, Walter & his widow, 607
Flynthard, Richard, 579
Fokes, William, 539
Folbert, *see* Fulbert
Folde, Robert atte, 370, 373
Foleham, *see* Fulham, Middx.
Foliot
  Gilbert, bishop of London, 14, App. 14
  Gilbert, cook, 136
  Richard, 1019
Folond, Stephen de, 705
Fonte, Geoffrey de, 66, 137
Fontevrault, burial of Henry II at, 1072

Forda
  Robert de la, 856
  Thomas de, sheriff, 535
  Walter de, cit., 436–7; Christine his wife, 437
  William de, 991
Fordam, John, keeper of the privy seal, 1005
Forester(e), Reginald le, 276
Forfot, Sexi, 963
Forger, *see* Ailward
Forges, 471
Fornham, Master Henry de, clerk, 378
Forster (Foster)
  Henry, 712
  Richard, attorney, 290, 480, 491, 613
  Robert, 636
  Stephen & Agnes his wife, 364
  Walter, 472, 475, 705, 1041
Founder, *see* Wodeward, William
Foundur, Margery la, 711
Fourneux, *see* Furneux
Fowest, Thomas de, 705
Fowliner (Fouliner), John, 246–7
Frandon, *see* Farndon
Franks, Simon, 732
Franyer, Ralph, 1018
Fratrer, John le, 77
Fraunces (Franceis, Frances, Frounceis, etc.)
  Adam, 498, 536, 712
  Gylminus, 203
  H., 826
  John, 309
  John, baron of the exchequer, 982
  John le, goldsmith, 489, 1014
  Roger & Alice his widow, 783, 785
  Simon, mayor, 411
Fraxinent, Roger de, 979
Free Warren, grant of, 1005
Freedom, admission to, 177
Frekeberewere, Robert & N. his wife, 813
Frensch, John, 469
Frenyngham, William, 636
Fresh Wharf (Froyssher Werf), 258
Freton, Thomas, broderer, 562
Freure, Ralph, capper, 181–3
Friars, *see* Austin Friars; Black Friars; Crutched Friars; Grey Friars; White Friars
Friars of the Penitence (Jewry), 530
Friars Preachers, *see* Black Friars
Fridaiestrete, John de, 436
Frosher
  Geoffrey, 258; wharf named after, *see* Fresh Wharf
  William, 258
Frowyk
  Geoffrey de, goldsmith, 331, 336, 539–40, 659, 1010

254

General Index

Henry, 659
Henry de, sheriff, 215, 921, 928
John, 715
Laurence, sheriff, 516, 616, 756, 795
Roger, 165, 330
Thomas, 595
Froysh, Richard, 89
Froyssher Werf, *see* Fresh Wharf
Frye, Richard le, attorney, 742
Frytmonger, John, 801
Fulbert (Folbert, Fulberti)
    Cambin & Christine Cambyn his widow, 334
    Michael son of William, 456-7
    William, 456
    William son of William, 456, 810
Fulc (Fulk)
    baker, 346
    of Lime Street, 64
Fulc, Gilbert (fitz, son of), alderman, 39, 86, 150, 161, 167, 310, 371, 734, 811, 818; *see also* Gilbert, alderman
Fulchred, limeburner, 942
Fulcredus, 271, 918-19
Fule Lane, 129
Fuleham, Walter de, 280
Fulham, (Foleham), Middx., 359
Fullere
    Reginald le, 285, 309
    Robert, 249
Fuloc, Edgar, 963
Furbur
    Ernaldus, 456
    William le, 377
Furmage, Robert, 575
Furnell, Henry de, 701a, 1004
Furner, Martin le, 233
Furneux (Fourneux)
    Robert, 305, 309
    William & his widow, 896
Furneys, Isabel, 898
Fuster, Walter le, 785
Fynch, William, 480
Fynchyngfeld, Walter (de), 73, 659
Fysch
    Henry, 755
    John, 805
Fysymon, John, 210; *see also* Symon

Gadesby, Robert de, 957
Galeys (Galeis), *see* Waleys
Game, William, 958
Gamene, Henry, carter, 939-41
Gant, *see* Want
Gardiner (Gardino, Gardyner)
    John, 947, 951
    Ralph de, & Roesia his wife, 310
    Roger (le), 880-1, 923; Alice his wife, 880
    Stacius de, clerk, 134
    Stephen le, & Florence his wife, 921
Garland (Gerlond)
    J., 235
    John, 242; sheriff, 1073
    Thomas, 235
    William, 42
Garton (Garto)
    Hugh de, 55, 498
    John, 511
    Thomas de, 498
Gate
    John, 881
    Peter at, 843
    Richard atte, 252
    see also Porta, Walter de
Gate-keeper, *see* Edmund; Hugh; John; Ralph; *and* Flemyng, Walter le; Long, Richard
Gatton, Robert de, 1004
Gaunt
    Augustine le, 428
    John of, duke of Lancaster, 1005; executors of, 708, 891
Gautrun, Walter, 799, 801
Gavelet, *see* Legal matters
Gaver, John, 562
Gedeney, John, master draper, 427, 480, 745
Gelusdi, Benet, goldsmith, 362
Geoffrey
    alderman, 346
    baker, 676, 678, 856
    chancellor, 875
    chaplain, son of Warin, 676
    clerk, 947
    ewerer, 938
    glover, 157
    minister of the sheriff, 185
    priest, 672
    Brother, rent-collector, 247
    shopkeeper, 1010
    son of Robert, 1004
    son of Stephen, *see* Stephen, Geoffrey son of
    son of Susan, *see* Trentmars, Geoffrey
    tanner, 871; [another], 948
    vintner, 497-8
    young (iuvenis), 171
Gepiswych, *see* Ipswich
Geraldus, 960, 963
Gerard
    master of the hospital of St. Giles, 829
    warden of the queen's wardrobe, 252
Gerard
    Edmund son of, sheriff, 744
    Henry, 562
Gerlond, *see* Garland
German
    clerk, 144
    mercer, 272-3; Rose his daughter, 272
    parmenter, 270, 1020

General Index

Gersuma, *see* Legal matters
Gervase
  alderman, (Barn), 58; (Bran), 82, 94, 97, 190; (cordwainer), 35, 90, 171
  ? baker, 171
  capper, 39, 140, 170
  clerk, 963
  son of Agnes, 963
  see also Aldermanbury; Gracechurch
Geryn, John, 863
Gesors, *see* Gisors
Giffard, Robert, kt., 237
Gigge, *see* Digge
Gilberd, John, 153
Gilbert, 496
  alderman, 50, 62, 204, 1067; *see also* Fulc, Gilbert
  (the Universal), bishop of London, xvii, 779, 966, 969
  canon of Holy Trinity, 970
  chaplain of St. Katherine's hospital, 986
  clerk, 387, 471–2
  cook, *see* Foliot, Gilbert
  felter (feutrier), 236
  moneyer, 859
  priest, 963
  7th prior of Holy Trinity, 19, 68, 124, 129, 134, 470, 530, 535, 716, 769, 802, 880, 890
  son of Benet (? de Hakeneye), 908
  son of Walter the Woolmonger, 472, 1014
  whittawer, 1012
Gilds & fraternities, *see* Drapers; Rectors; Saddlers; Skinners; Tailors; *and under* St. Michael Cornhill
Gill (Gille, Gyll)
  Alan, 239
  John, 748, 751
  Robert, 63, 822
  William, 85
Gillingham (Gilyngham, Gillyngham)
  Alan (de), attorney, 351
  John, 237
Ginges, Roger de, Henry & Robert his brothers, 226, 1054
Gipeswich, *see* Ipswich
Girdler, *see* Henry; *and* Tryp, Nicholas; *see also* Gyrdelere; Seinturer
Giseborne (Gysseborne, Gyseburne)
  Adam de, 374–5, 1008; Marcella his wife, 374, 1008
  Stephen de, 344
Gisors (Gesors, Gysors, *etc*).
  Anketin de, alderman, 55
  Edward, 254
  Francus, 600
  James, 254
  John (de) (I), 189, 756, 1016; alderman, 447, 501; mayor, 533, 641

John (de) (II), 599–600, 1031; his widow; 600
John (de) (III), mayor, 99, 925, 927, 1029
John (IV), 254
Peter de, 447, 454, 552; Joan his daughter, 447
Thomas, 462
Gladewyn, Richard, attorney, 557, 607
Gladwin, Margaret his widow, 812
Glastonbury, Somerset, abbot of, 499; *see also* Bath & Glastonbury
Glastonbury, Eustace, 175
Glazier, *see* William
Gloucester, earl of, 111; *see also* Mandeville, Geoffrey de
Gloucester (Glovernia)
  Richard de, 73, 155, 745
  Walter de, *see* Crepyn
Glover, *see* Geoffrey; Lambert; Walter; *and* Hertford, John de; Stortford, Ralph de; *see also* Want
Goda, usurer, *see* Ralph
Godacus, *see* Murte
Godard
  brother of Walter the alderman, 199
  brother of William the Goldsmith, 672
  merchant, 271
  priest, 963
Godard
  Alan, 642
  Elias son of, 206–7
  Geoffrey, merchant, 488–9
  John & Christine his widow, 552
  Katherine, 642
Godchep, *see* Goodchep
Godesname, Richard, 705
Godesune
  Algar son of Ralph, 963
  Edmund, brother of Ralph, 963
  Ralph, 963
Godfray, William, 925
Godfrey (Godefrey)
  priest, 963
  prior of the hospital of St. Mary without Bishopsgate, 1028
  treasurer, 963
Godhewe (Goodhewe)
  Auger, 797, 801
  Henry, 801
  Henry, father of Auger, 801; Katherine his wife, widow of Moses, *see* Waltham, Moses de
Godhier, *see* John son of
Godistold, Robert, 511
Godlune, *see* Eilricus
Godmund, mercer, 122–3
Godmund, *see* William, son of
Godrun(s)lane, *see* Gutter Lane
Godstow (Godestowe), Oxon., nuns of, 761, 866

256

General Index

Godwin, 963
  alderman, 394
  son of Firminus & his wife, 942
Godwyne (Godewyn)
  Nicholas, skinner, 472–3
  Stephen son of Thomas, 473
  Thomas, 472–3, 475
  see also Philyppere
Godyn, John, 486
Gofair (Gofairer), *see* Waffrer
Goldcorn (Golcorn)
  Joan, 891
  John, 920, 955
Goldsmith, *see* Andrew; Benet; Ingelinerus; John; Leofstan; Nigel; Ralph; Reginald; Richard; Roger; Tewald; Walter; Walter son of James; William; Zachary; *and* Bacwell, Thomas; Essex, Geoffrey de; Fraunces, John le; Frowyk, Geoffrey de; Gelusdi, Benet; Hakeney, William de; Ipswich, Robert de; Kemesyng, John; Lacer, Richard; Scot, Laurence; Travers, Walter; Wendleswurth, Stephen de
Goldsmithery, 1035
Goldyng father of Robert, *see* Waterladere, Robert(le)
Good, John, attorney, 648
Goodchep (Godchep, Goodcheep)
  Hamo & (Isabel) his widow, 246, 249, 251–2
  Henry & Agnes his wife, 1035
  Jordan, sheriff, 47
  Philip, 651
  Roger, 848
  William, *alias* Crassus, 849
Goodlak, Thomas, 552
'Goot, le,' tenement called, 1041
Goraleng, soke of, 609
Gorges, Christine, 330
Gorgurer, Gerard, 730
Gorney (Gourneye), James, *alias* le Shereman, 350–1; & Joan his wife, 351
Gouayr (Goueyre)
  John, 461
  Roger, 476
Gowell, Richard, 664
Goy (Goye)
  Robert, 181
  Walter, 306
Gozo son of Ralph the Vintner, 497
Graas, Stephen le, sheriff, 1073
Gracechurch (Graschirch), *see* Wilemy, John
Gracechurch Street (Graschirchstete), 317, 319, 321, 323, 330, 334
Grapefige, William, sheriff, 512
Grapinell, Henry, 123

Graschirch, *see* All Hallows Lombard Street
Graschurch (Graschirch, Greschirch)
  Gervase de, 1013
  Robert (de) & his wife, 219
  Roger de, 195
Gravesend (Gravisend), John, 151, 745
Gray
  lord de, 203, 1066
  Richard, 184
Gregory
  brother of William Russo, 400
  chaplain, 136
  dapifer, 962
  Master, doctor, 776
Grene
  Boidinus (de, atte), 49, 305, 308, 313; Alice his wife, 313
  Simon atte, 382, 490
Grey, John de, 1005
Grey Friars (Friars Minor), 631, 1033
Greylond, Robert, 922, 947; his widow, 922
Greyner, Baldwin le, 604
Grocer, *see* Chircheman, John; Gyn, Richard; *see also* Pepperer; Spicer
Gross, Charles, xii–xiii
Grove, William, 418
Grun, 529
Guildhall, 996; chapel, 1034; clerk of the chamber, *see* Osberne, Richard; curtilage of, 711; garden, 243
Gulle, Walter, 704
Gunter, 814
Guthlok, Cecilia, 115
Gutter Lane (Godrun(s)lane), 641–2, 646; *see also* Alexander
Gwayt, Ivo (Ives) le, 329–30; Matilda his wife, 329
Gyfford, William, bishop of Winchester, 4, App. 4
Gyldeford, Henry, 301
Gyll, *see* Gill
Gyn, Richard, cit. & grocer, 417–18
Gynnor(e), Thomas, 123
Gypwich, *see* Ipswich
Gyrdelere, John, 518
Gyesburne (Gysseborne), *see* Giseborne
Gysors, *see* Gisors
Gyspo, William, 635

Haberdasher?, *see* Ballio, John de
Habitonne, John de, prior of the hospital of St. Mary without Bishopsgate, 208
Habyndon, *see* Abindon
Hackney, Middx., 921
Haco, deacon, 871, 963, 966
Hadestoke (Haddestok, Hadestok)
  Richard, chaplain, 791–2, 794
  Roger de, 457
  William de, 566–7, 572, 1007

General Index

Hadham (Haddam)
  John, 808
  William de, 799, 808
Hadlee (Hadele, Hadle), John, mayor, 502–3, 588
Hailee (Hayle), John de, 684–5
Hailesdon, John, 518
Hakborne, *see* Bonaventure
Hakeney (Hakeneye)
  Benet de, 173, 175, 179, 221, 905–7; Emma his wife, 905–6, 947; *see also* Gilbert, son of
  Geoffrey de, & Agnes his wife, 1029; *see also* Haneke
  John, *alias* Hauteyn, 345, 947
  Nigel de, 311
  Richard de, 129, 134, 590; [? another], 311
  Robert, 587
  Robert (de), woolmonger, 880, 896, 899, 905
  Warin de, 893–4
  William de, goldsmith, 912
  see also Osbert, chapman
Haket
  Adam, 639
  William, 946
Haketon (Aketon), Robert de, 667, 669
Hakrege, Ralph de, 634
Halden (Haldenus), 185
  William son of, 185
  William de, recorder of London, 441
Hale
  Thomas, canon of Holy Trinity, 915, 996
  William (atte, at), cit. & taverner, 36, 40, 915, 926, 954, 996; Agnes his wife, 36, 40, 46, 83, 436, 996; *see also* Halle
Halewyk, John de, 946
Halimote, *see* Legal matters
Haliwell (Halywell), Middx., priory of St. John, 292, 347, 362, 365, 378, 529, 657, 674, 725, 811, 825, 838, 841, 848, 864, 1018; prioress, *see* Matilda
Halle
  John, 405
  Stephen atte, 482
  William, 243, *see also* Hale
Hallen, Alfwin, 960
Halliwell, David de, 219
Hallyngby (Halyngby), Adam, 631
Halsted (Halstede)
  Asketin, whittawer, 802–4
  John, 98
  Peter de, *alias* de St. Paul, chaplain, 344, 347
  Ralph, 98
Halton, Henry, sheriff, 480, 613
Halyngham, *see* ? Castle Hedingham, Essex

Hamelamstede, William, 386
Hamerton, John, 903, 954
Hamme (Hame), William (de), woolmonger, *alias* Woolchirchehawe, 214–16, 486
Hammes, Richard, 883
Hamo
  butler, 548
  moneyer, 833, 846; *see also* Copton, Hamo
  son of Constantine, 238–9
Hamond, John & his widow, 427
Hamstede, *see* Hanstead, Herts.
Hamundesham, Edmund de, 770
Hanaper, 871
Hanasted, William, 725
Haneke, Geoffrey de, 894; *see also* Hakeney
Hanham, Robert (de), 712
Hanhamsted, Thomas, 386, 572
Hanin (Hanyn), John, deputy alderman, 304, 306, 316
Hansard, William, 229, 1062
Hanstead ? (Hahnstede), Herts., 1004
Haradon (Haryngton), William, 18th prior of Holy Trinity, 30, 243, 398, 480, 581, 727, 749, 898, 954, 996, 1040
Harang, Thomas de, 668
Hardel (Hardell)
  Edmund, sheriff, 1073
  John son of William, 110–12, 235, 237
  Michael, 126
  Ralph, mayor, 32, 146, 355, 476, 832, 893, 912, 983, 1021; sheriff, 218, 327, 720, 1056
  Robert, 115, 204, 347, 430, 450–1, 1017, 1067; sheriff, 262, 549
  Thomas son of William, 110–12; Agnes his wife, 111
  William, 110–13; mayor, 1011
Hardy, Thomas, 642
Hardyngham, Henry & his widow, 345
Harmer, F. E., xiii
Harold, king, 1072
Harpe, John, atte, 179, 748; his widow, 179
Harwe, John (de), 294, 622
Haryng (Hareng), Ralph, 622, 1004
Hastings (Hastyng)
  Ralph de, 1002
  William, 285
Hat, Roger, 400
Hatfeld (Hattefeld)
  Denise, daughter of John, senior, 648
  John, 414
  John, senior, chandler, 317, 648
  Peter, 414
  Richard, 317
  Roger, 214–15
  Simon, 1034

General Index

Thomas, son of John, senior, 648
Hauekyn
—, broderer, 885
John, 132, ?883, 885, 1032; rent collector, 415
Haukeseye (Hakeseye), Geoffrey, 891, 937; his widow, 891
Hauteyn (Hautein, Hawteyn)
John, *see* Hakeney, John
Walter, sheriff, 144, 215, 752, 897
Haverhill (Averhull, Haverhull, Haverill, *etc.*)
Brithmar de, 1024
James de, 280
John, 954
Richard de, 157, 1022
Simon, 878, 1034
Thomas de, sheriff, 183, 442–3, 663, 1011, 1022, 1024, 1028, 1073; Ida his widow, 782–3
William de, king's treasurer, 818
William de, sheriff, 273, 663, 724–5, 1012, 1073
William de, son of Brithmar, & Alice his wife, 1024
Havering, Essex, 1005
Haversand, William, sheriff, 54
Haveryng
John de, 849
William & his widow, 896
Hay, John, 216
Haydon, Essex, 418
Hayngham, *see* Castle Hedingham, Essex
Hayron, John, 679
Haywharf Lane (Heiwharflane), 418
Hearne, Thomas, xi
Hecstan, 931
Heldest, John, 632
Helebuc, Robert, 280
Helia, *see* Elias
Helpiston, John & his widow, 801
Hemenhale, Edmund de, 392
Hende, John, 454
Henewade, Geoffrey de, 958
Henkle, John, 46
Henore, John, 469
Henry I, king, xiii–xv, 1, 2, 4, 5, 10, 12, 780, 874, 875, 960, 979, 998, 1005, 1072, App. 1, 2, 4, 5, 10, 12
Henry II, king, xv, 13, 15, 426, 1002, App. 13, 15
Henry III, king, 1004–5
Henry, son of Henry II, 14, App. 14
Henry
bureller, called Juvenis, 408–9
carpenter, 62, 215
clerk, 904
cofferer, 766; Joan his wife, 766–7, *see also* St. Edmund, John de
girdler, 406

mason, 92–3
mayor, *see* Ailwin, Henry fitz
prior of Wenlock, 796
son of Alfred, 1012
son of Rennerus, 387–8
son of Turgisius, 624
Henteston, Ralph, 130
Herbert, bishop of Avranches, *see* Hubert
Herberti, Matilda, 791
Hercmonnceux, *see* Hurstmonceaux
Herdy, Stephen, 480
Here, Siward, 963
Hereford, bishop of, *see* Bethune, Robert de
Hereford (Herford, Herthford)
—, countess of, 92, 94, 96
Hugh, 210, 1059
Laurence de, 576
Richard, 94, 96
Richard de, & Isabel his wife, 832
Robert de, 234
William de, alderman, 131, 144; sheriff, 274, 557, 784
Hereloc, Roger, 777
Hereward, 963
Palmer, 948
Ruffus, 950
Herghes, Andrew de, parmenter, 1012
Herl, Ralph son of, 333
Herlawe, John, 309
Herlicon (Herlion), John son of, sheriff, 270, 1073
Herliyn, John, 171
Herlowe, William & his widow, 562
Herman, canon of ? Southwark, 895
Herne, Walter in le, 951
Heron (Heroun), *see* Heyron
Herrings, gift of, 232
Hert
Henry, cit., 898
William, cit. & cutler, 480
Hertford, John de, glover, 220–1
Hertwell, Thomas & Alice his wife, 229
Hertyng, William de, 130
Hervy, shoemaker, 932
Hervy (Hervi, Hervey)
John, 105; [another], 921, 934
John son of, 932
Walter, bailiff of London, 899; mayor, 173, 195, 197, 293, 344, 787, 1060; sheriff, 68
William, 502; [another], 768
Hese, Richard (de), 578, 582–3
Heston, Middx., 1004
Hethingham, John, attorney, 648, 996
Heved, Richard, 896
Heyham, John, *see* Hore, John le
Heylisdon, John, 330
Heyron (Heron, Heroun, *etc*).
Ralph de, 1004

259

General Index

Heyron, *continued*
  Thomas, 502
  Thomas, 14th prior of Holy Trinity, 26, 252, 351, 473, 699, 1046
Hilary, bishop of Chichester, 973
Hildresham, Peter de, 537
Hill (Hyll)
  John atte, & his widow, 317
  Robert atte, 216
Hinton (Hynton)
  Henry, 600
  John de, & his widow, 600
  Roger, 188
Hippynke, William, 903
Hirton (Hyrton), Henry, 219, 1057
Hispania, *see* Spain
Hocton (Hoctonis)
  Hugh fitz, constable of the Tower, 213
  Laurence de, 215
Hod, Robert & Katherine his daughter, 552
Hoddesdon (Hoddisdon, Hoddysdon)
  Edmund, cit. & mercer, *alias* Barnet, 482, 735
  John de, 99
  Richard & his widow, 482
  Richard son of Richard, 482
Hodenhoe (Hoddenho), Herts., 1004
Hoder (Hodere)
  Elias le, 370, 373
  John le, cit. & skinner, 239, 1033; Margery his widow & Joan her daughter, 1033
  Peter le, skinner, 772, 783, 785
  Simon le, bedel, 940, 1032
Hodestok, William de, & Joan his daughter, 711
Hog Lane (Hoggestrete), 958
Hoggenlane, *see* Huggin Lane
Hogles, Walter, 281
Hok (Hoke), *see* Hook
Holborn, hospital of St. Giles, 97, 126, 283, 312, 545, 752, 977, 1010; master of, *see* Gerard
Holborn Bridge (Holbourne Brygge), 830
Holborne, Nicholas, 260
Holebagge, Atheliza, 687
Holecuhame, *see* West Ham (?)
Holherst, Walter de, 834
Holy Trinity Aldgate
  arms of, xxiii
  canons, *see* Alan; Edmund; Elias; Gilbert; Ralph; Richer; Robert; Rusus; Walter; Warin; *and* Axbridge, Thomas de; Brole, William; Buruch, Walter; Hale, Thomas; Wymbyssh, Richard
  chaplain of St. Michael, *see* John
  choirboys, 1032
  church, 1, 4, 9, 12–13, 871, 875, 973, App. 1, 4, 9, 12–13
  fabric, 1033
  foundation of priory, 1–35 *passim*, 871, App. 1–16, 31
  garden, 871, 889, 891, 908, 925
  infirmary, 1007
  mill, 871
  parish, xvii, 80, 993, 1020; *see also* St. Katherine Cree; St. Mary Magdalen; St. Michael Aldgate
  priors, list of, 10–30 *passim*
  sacristan, 37, 107, 899
  sub-prior, 372; *see also* Robert; Walter
Holy Trinity the Less, parish, 570–3, 1018, 1030, 1035
Holyland, John, sheriff, 1073
Holyrode Wharf, 870
Hondesdych, *see* Houndesdych
Honilane, Elias de, 552
Honyteil (Honiteil, Huniteil)
  Peter, clerk, 68, 70–1
  Richard, 71
Hoo, William de, 674
Hooham, *see* Howham
Hook (Hok, Hoke)
  Henry at, 83, 901, 954
  Thomas at, 85, 87, 89, 92; his widow, 85
Hore
  John le, *alias* Heyham, 674, 783; Joan his widow, 674
  Walter le, 477, 479; Berta his wife, 479
Horeh, Alfred & Norman his son, 887
Horer, John, brewer, & Alice his wife, 727
Horermed, William, *see* Arras, William de
Horleus, *alias* Pyioun, John, 896
Horn (Hornn)
  Egidia, 321
  John, 319
  John, sheriff, 37, 197, 437, 664, 787
  Martin, 292–4; Alice his wife, 292–3
Hornchurch (de Monasterio Cornuto), Essex, master of, 66
Hornepitesune, Adelardus, 871
Horner
  Geoffrey, 903
  John, 295; [another], 901, 903
Horold, Roger, 878
Horsedriver (horsdrivere), *see* Ernald
Horsham, William, 896
Horton, William de, prior of the hospital of St. Mary without Bishopsgate, 208
Horwode (Horewode, Horerwode, *etc.*)
  Alan de, attorney, 61, 132, 156, 211, 266, 309, 356, 368, 478, 580, 660, 675, 795
  John, 562; [another], 595, 708, 815, 817; Matilda his wife, 817
  Richard, 174
  William, 642

260

General Index

Hosier, *see* Edulf; Walter
Hosteler, Simon, 833, 846, 945
Hotot, Nicholas, 486
Hottere, Robert, 938
Hougate, Thomas, 587
Houndesdych (Hondesdych, Hundesdich)
  Julian, 83
  Laurence, 871
  Richard, 905, 916
  Solomon son of Laurence, 871
  Stephen, 913
Houndsditch, 878, 881, 883, 885
Houses
  built of stone, xx, 223, 430, 453, 484, 493, 707, 1014, 1017, 1022, 1051
  named (including inns, shops, *etc*)., *see* 'Abbotesyn'; 'Bacunnysyn'; 'Basket'; 'Bole'; 'Brodeselde'; Cardinal's Hat; 'Crowne'; Dove; 'Goot'; 'Legge'; 'Oitheram'; Paul's Tavern; 'Petyt'; 'Threleggs'; 'Weuel atte Stone'; Winchester Seld
  tiled roof, 1067
  with an oven, 195
  see also Latrines; Sewers; Stables; Tenter-grounds
Hoveldere, Simon, 91–2
Hovyle, Thomas & Katherine his wife, 242
Howham (Hooham), John, 799, 801
Hubert
  (Herbert, Hubert Albrinc), bishop of Arranches, 739, 1002
  chaplain, 729
  priest, 963
  queen's chamberlain, 1004
  uncle of Roger, *see* Roger, nephew of Hubert
Huggin Lane (Hoggenlane), 646, 660
Hugh
  ? baker, 171
  clerk, 136
  gate-keeper, 933
  mason, 32
  master of the hospital of St. Bartholomew, 829
  Palmer, 612–13
  priest, 612
  prior of Bermondsey, 338
  son of Baldwyn, 1004
  son of Ralph, 871
  son of Wlgar, 871, 963
Huingus, a monk, 970
Hull (Hulla)
  Agnes de, 827
  Benet de, 678
Humbert, prior of Bermondsey, 462
Hume, Aldwin & Alice his wife, 718–19
Huniteil, *see* Honyteil
Huntemanne, Adam, 249
Hunter, Dr. William, xi–xii

Hupcornhille, Edward, 871
Hur, ? prior of Mountjoy, 43
Hurer (Hurere)
  Alan le, 189–91
  John le, 186, 191; Isabel his wife, 191
  Walter le, & his widow, 179
Hurricus, 967
Hurstmonceaux (Hercmonnceux), Sussex, parson of, *see* Echyngham, Simon de
Huscaill, Roger & William his son, 1020
Huscardus, *see* Robert
Hutman, Adam, 168
Hwyte, Robert, 260, 1033
Hyham, John, master draper, 427
Hyll, *see* Hill
Hynelond, William, rector of St. Olave, 175, 177

Ilchester, Richard of, bishop of Winchester, 739–40 742
Ilgirus, 644
Illefoster, James, 494
Ingelinerus, goldsmith, 639
Ingellard, 691
Ingestret, *see* Maiden Lane, near Wood Street
Ingolf (Ingulphus), baker, 154–5
Innocent III, pope, 871
Inns, *see under* Houses
Inquisitions, *see* Legal matters
Insula, Walter de, alderman, 366, 771
Ipswich (Gepiswych, Gipeswich, Gypwich, *etc*,)
  Laurence de, 890
  Nicholas de, clerk, 154; Matilda his widow, 928–9
  Reimund de, moneyer, 729–30; *see also* Reimund
  Robert de, goldsmith, 692–4
Irchestre, Reginald, 628
Ireland, 16, App. 16
Irland (Irlond, Yrlond, *etc*.), Thomas (de), *alias* Brandon, 184, 186, 350; cit. & skinner, 352; sheriff, 441
Ironmonger, *see* Euere, William
Ironmonger Lane (Ysmongerslane), 527–8, 533, 535
Isele (Ysle)
  John, 642
  John, junior, 642
Isle of Thanet, Kent, 6, App. 6
Islelane, Henry, 799
Ives, chaplain of St. Sepulchre, 829
Ivo, Theobald (fitz, son of), 11; App. 11; *see also* Theobald, alderman
Ivory (Iuory, Yvory), William, 298, 313
Iwodus, doctor, 962

James, 942
'lord', 734

261

General Index

James, *continued*
  master, 223, 968, 1051; [?another], 1059
  alderman, 387, 736; mayor, 1073
  chaplain, 209–10; his widow, 210
  clerk, 963
  priest, 993
  son of Bartholomew, sheriff, 1073
Jernemouth, Nicholas de, & his widow, 200
Jerusalem, Richard I in, 871
Jewry, *see also* Friars of the Penitence
Jews, land not to be pledged or sold to, xix, 45–946 *passim*; *see also* Elias; Seymoth; *and* Petevyn, Benet
Joce (Josceus, *etc.*)
  barber, 1007
  junior, (alderman & sheriff), 262, 283, 386, 406, ?442–3, 528, 1010; Felicia his wife, 263, 284, 458, 1010
  son of Peter, alderman, *see* Peter
  son of William, 449
  vintner, *see* Ralph, brother of
  weigher, 401–2, 485; sheriff, 993; Bola his daughter, 401
Joce, Nicholas son of, 355, 507
Jocelin, bishop of Bath & Glastonbury, 1004
Jofne (Jeofne, Jeofer)
  Constantine, sheriff, 1073
  John le, sheriff, 1073
  Jokel, le, sheriff, 1073
  Peter, sheriff, 1073
John, king, 871
John
  chaplain, 891
  chaplain of St. Michael, 471, 700, 1058
  chaplain of St. Clement, 1058
  chaplain of the Bailey, 471
  clerk, 552, 804, 905; [another], 977
  cook, 832
  crossbowman, 842
  deacon, 109
  gate-keeper, 945
  goldsmith, son of Bartholomew Blund, 655–6
  goldsmith, son of James, 335, 338
  junior, 405
  parmenter, 464–5, 1020
  preacher, 83
  priest, 963
  priest of St. Peter Westcheap, 1024
  prior of Launde, 871
  prior of Mont-St.-Eloi, 7, App. 7
  prior of St. Bartholomew, 785
  reeve of Laleham, 447
  son of Bernard, 124, 380
  son of Daniel, 334–6, 635, 771, 1012
  son of Edwin, 963
  son of Geoffrey, 552
  son of Godhier, 137
  son of Nigel, *see* Nigel
  son of Norman, *see* Norman
  son of Peter, 732
  son of Robert, 933
  son of Serlo, *see* Serle, John
  son of Terricus, 539
  son of William the Cook, 682
  spicer, 812; sheriff, 1073
John
  Nicholas, potter, 955
  Richard son of, 355
  Robert son of, sheriff, 332, 539, 856
Jon, Louis & his wife, 995
Jonner, William, 629
Jordan, 529
  priest, 400
  son of Seth, 157
Jordan (Jurdan)
  Thomas, *alias* Black, 137, 457–8
  Thomas & Alice his wife, 292–3
  William, 414
Joseph, priest, 963
Joye (Joie)
  Benet, butcher, 262
  Clement (de), 50–2, 800
  Katherine, 47, 51, 53
  Robert, tiler, 85
  Walter, 262
  William son of Clement, 51–2, 82, 85
Jukell, sheriff, 687; *see also* Jofne, Jokel le
Juliana, abbess of the Poor Clares, 855
Juncarius, *see* Alphanus
Junior (Juvenis, le Juvene, *etc.*), *see* Geoffrey; Henry, bureller; Joce; John; Matilda; Nicholas; Stephen; Thomas; *and* Jofne
Jurdan, *see* Jordan
Jury, *see* Legal matters
Justice, Ralph le, 434–5, 444–5, 553, 566, 589, 1018, 1019; Denise his daughter, 434, 444, 1018, 1019

Kaldecote, *see* Caldecote, Herts.
Kampeden, Robert de, skinner, 820
Kant, *see* Kent
Kanter, *see* Canter
Katel, William, 912
Katelon, *see* Catelon
Katenham, Geoffrey de, 684
Katherine, abbess of the Poor Clares, 956
Kegworth, Simon, 615
Kelles Alley (Kelshillisaleye), 1044
Kelsey (Kelesey, Kelysseye)
  Robert, *alias* (de) Bery, 36, 38; Margaret his wife, 38
  Robert (de), 518, 520, 1038
  Thomas (de), (clerk, parson), 518–21
Kelshull (Kelcyll, Kellhull, Kelshill)
  R. de, 742
  William, cit. & fishmonger, & Agnes his wife, 1035

General Index

William, cit. & fishmonger, *alias* Convers, *see* Convers, William
Kemesyng
  John (de), baker, 427–8; his widow, 427
  John, goldsmith, 427
Kempe, John, bishop of London, 995
Kendal (Kendale)
  Stephen, 632
  Thomas, 575
Keneward (Kenewardus)
  turner, 930, 932, 938
  uncle of William, *see* William
Keneward, John, 933
Kent (Cancia, Kant, *etc.*)
  John (de), 94, 87–8
  Richard de, 56–7, 62
  Thomas, 374
  Thomas de, 212
  Walter de, 216
  William de, 72
  William de, cit. & tailor, 665
Kentish Town, (Kentissetune), Middx., 1004
Kenutus, tanner, 1012
Kersteven, Robert, 409
Ketellus, 234
Keuelinus, king & martyr, 1072
Kilburn (Keleburn, Kylbourne), Middx., nuns of, 437, 848, *see also* Sancto Benedicto, Joan de; prioress of, 114, 295, 863, 865
Kinardisle, Simon de, 454–5; Margery his wife, 455
King's baker, *see* William
King's bench, justice of, *see* Stonor, John de
Kingus, 948
Kirkeby, John, 418
Kisselynbury, Richard, mayor, 410
Knightecote, William, sheriff, 588
Knightrider Lane (Knyghtryderlane), 595
Knights Templar, 828–9
Knollys (Knoll), Robert, 233; kt., 186, 525; Knolles college, *see* Pontefract, Yorks.
Knotte (Chnotte, Knot)
  Ancelinus, 285
  Richard, 285–6, 289
Knut, Peter, 677
Knyght
  Alexander, *see* Bysshop
  Peter, 239
  William, 305
Knyghtengild, *see* English Knyghtengild
Kockeslane *see* Cock Lane
Kokham, *see* Cokham
Kokyr, John, incumbent of St. Botolph Algate, 954
Kolemere, John de, 1018
Konncedieu, Richard, 224
Kornelle, *see* Cornhill

Krauer, John, 901
Kydemynstre, Simon de, 326
Kylinworth, Adam, 309
Kylkenny (Kylkeni, Kylkeny), Master William de, chancellor & archdeacon of Coventry, 818, 981, 1005
Kyneli, Turold de, 258
Kyng (Kyngs)
  Alan, 578–9
  John, 585
  Richard, 172, 188; [another], 307
  Stephen & his widow, 705
  Thomas le, butcher, 834–5, 1029; Alice his wife, 834, 1029
  William, 705
Kyngisson (Kyngeston, Kyngsone), Henry, 575, 584, 586
Kyngiston (Kyngeston, Kynggestonne)
  Henry, *see* Kyngisson
  John, 130, 132–3, 186, 1035
  Robert de [? *alias* Dycton], clerk, 254–5
Kyngsbery, Thomas de, 622
Kynred, king, 1072
Kyronlane, *see* Maiden Lane
Kyssere, Gilbert le, 767
Kytell, John, 285

Lacer (Lac)
  Adam, 776
  Agnes, 590
  John, 590
  Richard, goldsmith, (mayor), 177, 440–1, 613, 694–6, 701–2; Alice his daughter, *see* Marny, Robert; Katherine his daughter, *see* Pole
  Richard, junior, 441
  William le, 701
Lacy, Peter, 566
Lafait, *see* Facet
Lagele, Gunilde, 74, 76
Laleham, Middx., reeve of, *see* John
Lambard, (Lambert)
  Robert, 888
  Robert son of Robert, 888–90; Albreda his wife, 888–9
  Thomas, 629; sheriff, 1073
  William, 913
Lambe, Richard, 863
Lambert, glover, 942–3, 993, 1020
Lambeth (Lamee, Lamheth), William (de), 219, 1056–7
Lamburne, James de, kt., 820
Lambyn
  Edmund, 285
  Henry, fishmonger, 285–6
  John, 285, 289
Lancaster, duke of, *see* Gaunt, John of
Lancastre, Thomas, 745
Lane (in venella)
  Adam, 98–9

Lane, *continued*
  Henry in le, 808, 1038
  Peter (le, atte), 98, 112–13
Langedon, Thomas, 939
Langhorne
  Alice, 595
  John, 595
  John, brazier, 815
Lanham, Ralph de, 824
Lapyn, Roger, 367
Lardener, Robin, master of fraternity of St. Anne, 374
Laston, John de, 447
Latrines, 646
Launceston, Cornwall, 10, App. 10
Launde, Leics., prior of, *see* John
Laurence
  chaplain of St. Alphege, 680
  clerk, 776
  plumber, 426
  son of Pain, 285
Laurence, John, 233
Law, men learned in, *see* Braddeman
Lawe, John, 909
Layer Marney (Leyre Marny), Essex, chantry in church of, 441
Layston (Lefstanechirch), Herts., 1004
Leddrede, William de, & Margery his wife, 927
Ledulf (Lyedulfus), 229, 369, 1062
Lee
  John at, 100–1, 919, 954; Agnes his wife, 101
  Richard atte, 427
Leesnes, *see* Lesnes, Kent
Leflyf (Leflye)
  James, 351
  John, 350–1
Lefsi, 814
Lefstanecher, Richard de, 280
Lefstanechirch, *see* Layston, Herts.
Legal matters
  acquittances, 217, 287, 661, 699, 727, 773, 1038–44
  dowry, 434, 493
  final composition, 165
  final concord, 629
  gavelet, 49–1014 *passim*
  gersuma, xix, 39–1067 *passim*
  halimote, 942
  indentures, 101–1042 *passim*
  inquisitions, 81, 224, 285; post mortem, 674
  jury of twenty-four, 309
  lease for 100 years, 208
  leases, restrictions upon, *see* Jews
  miskenning, 152–1061 *passim*
  mortmain, statute of, xix, 480, 491, 737, 920, 1005
  plea in exchequer, 982
  plea in king's bench, 742
  pleas in the Husting, 34–817 *passim*
  pleas of assize, 290, 480, 491
  pleas of taking naam, 54–1064 *passim*
  quit rents, xvi–xx, 52–1034 *passim*; sale of,
  quitclaims, 208–1029 *passim*
  recognisances, 225–1053 *passim*
  release, 118–962 *passim*
  rents: clove-gillyflower, 197, 215, 255, 292, 378, 425, 447, 1007; cumin or pepper, xix, 90–1018 *passim*; rose, 378; 'schaldflet', called, 991
  shartford, judgment of, 133 & n, 269, 478–9, 721
  socage, bishop's, 489, 811, 848, 1018; king's, 140–1056 *passim*
  wills proved in Husting, 143–1037 *passim*; entered in cartulary, 1031–7
  see also Attorneys; Freedom
Leget, Helmyngus, 224, 305, 412, 1052
'Legge, le', shop called, 525
Leggy (Legg, Legge), Thomas, alderman, 541, 705, 748, 1041
Legh, Walter de, 631
Leicester, archdeacon of, *see* Chaddesden, Henry de
Leighs, Essex, prior of, 224
Leman (Lemman)
  John, 305, 309, 480
  Richard, butcher, & Margery his wife, 309
  William, 309, 323
Lenn, *see* Lynne
Leofstan (Leofstanus, Liovestanus)
  goldsmith, 871, 1005
  reeve of London, 1072
Leowinus (Leofwinus), priest, 807, 963
Lesnes (Leesnes, Lyesnes), Kent, abbot of, 603; brothers at, 986; manor of, 1004
Lesthild, John, 673
Lesuer (Lesu)
  Alice de, 632
  John de, 70
Leuegar, priest, 871; *see also* Peter son of
Leuere, John, apprentice of John de Cantebregg, 1035
Leuesham
  John, 81
  Roger de, 58, 889, 912, 916, 1007
Leuesine, smith, 960
Levelyf, Simon, 258
Lewes (Lewys), Sussex, prior of, 557; tenement of the prior of, 562–3, 1019
Lewes, William (de), 104, 901
Lewisham, Kent, prior of, 215
Leycestre (Leycestria)
  Alexander de, 783
  John, 395
  Roger de, 326

General Index

Thomas de, *see* Coberd
Walter, 367
Walter de, 770
Leyr, William le, 617
Leyre Marny, *see* Layer Marney, Essex
Leyton, Essex, 1004–5
Lichfield, *see* Chester, bishop of
Liesn, John de, 335
Lilleshall, Salop, abbot of, 155, 165
Lime Street (Lymstrete, *etc.*), 11, 122–3, 125, 818, App. 11; *see also* Fulc; Nolicia
Limeburner, *see* Fulchred; Lymbernere
Limerick, bishop of, *see* Edmund, canon
Lincoln, bishop of, *see* Bloet, Robert
Lincoln (Lyncoln, Lyncolne)
    John de, sheriff, 111, 450, 537
    Margery, 907
    Richard de, skinner, 732
    Robert de, 332
    William, 642
Lindraper (Lingedraper, Lyndraper)
    Benet, 280
    John, 839
    Laurence, 950
Linendraper, *see* Allyngebery, Adam de
Linton,? Cambs., App. 13
Linton (Lynton, Lyntona)
    Alexander de, 1022
    Roger (de), 642
Listyngston, Thomas, sheriff's chief clerk, 309
Littlinton, Edward de, whittawer, 718, 720
Living (Lunngus), alderman, 185, 644
    see also Lungus
Locwrichte, William, 400
Lodeby
    Richard de, *alias* More, 849, 851
    Walter de, 849
Lodewyk, Robert, 309
Lofe, *see* Love
Loftie, W. J., xii
Lok, John, 531–2
Lombard Street (Longebordstrete, Lumbardstrete, *etc.*), 363, 367, 373, 472, 490–1
Lomhuth, Richard de, 252
London
    archdeacon of, 965, 990; *see also* Belmeis, William de (I); Mareni, Hugh de; Nicholas
    archdeacon's official, 165, 431, 534
    bishops of, *see* Basset, Fulk; Belmeis, Richard de (I); Fauconberg, Eustace de; Foliot, Gilbert; Gilbert the Universal; Kempe, John; Maurice; Northburgh, Michael; Ste. Mère-Eglise, William de; Sigillio, Robert de; Stratford, Ralph; Sudbury, Simon de; Wyngeham, Henry de; lands, etc.
    of, 877, 1004
    chaplains (in general), 529, 621
    fires in, 31
    Letter-book C & Liber Dunthorn, xii
    sheriff's farm of London & Middlesex, 958
    Tower of, *see* Tower of London
    see also Aldermen; Gilds & fraternities; Guildhall; Halimote; Mayor & commonalty; Reeve; *and under the names of churches, parishes, streets, etc.*
London
    John, sacristan, 107
    John de, 628
    Master Walter de, 430
    see also Robert son of Gervase
London Bridge, 64, 302, 610, 752; estate, 243, 854; wardens & masters, 317, 751n, 855
London Stone, 31, App. 31
London Wall, xiv, 12, 146, 731, 790, 824, 825, 998, 1018, 1024
Londonstone
    John, 233
    William de, 427–8
    see also Ston
Long (Longe, Longus, Lung, Lunge)
    Benet, 298, 314
    Henry le, 1007
    James son of Robert, 326–7
    John, 894
    John, fishmonger, 477, 479
    John le, 515, 901, 904
    Nicholas, 894, 896, 922; his widow, 894
    Ralph, 385–6, 1015
    Richard, 782–3; gate-keeper, 785
    Robert, 314, 316, 1013
    Roger, 325–6
Long Whatton (Longwatton), Leics., parson of, *see* Chaddesden, Geoffrey de
Longebordstrete, *see* Lombard Street
Lorchon, John, 939–40
Lorimer, *see* Morpat, John de
Louekenore, Thomas de, 767
Loundres, Henry de, archbishop of Dublin, 449
Louthe (Lowthe)
    Walter, 642
    William, sheriff, 491
Love (Lofe), Reginald, 186, 188
Lovekyn
    John, 294; mayor, 951
    Matilda, 590
Lovel, Philip, treasurer, 819, 982
Lovett, Thomas, 597
Lucas, Richard, 995
Lucy (Luci)
    Geoffrey son of Richard, 64
    Richard (de), 64, 961, 973, 975, 977–8, 1002, 1004

265

General Index

Ludgate (Luthgate), 832
Luke
  priest, 271
  (le Aylere), stockfishmonger, 254–5
Lumbardstrete, see Lombard Street
Lumbour, Richard, 752
Lunar, William de, 93–4
Lung (Lunge), see Long
Lungus, priest, 963
Lunngus, see Living
Lupus, see Wolf
Lusore (Lusores), Warner de, 995–7, 1005
Lutekyn, Adam, 229, 1062
Luthgate, see Ludgate
Luymudhe, piece of land next Luiam, see West Ham (?)
Lychfeld, Master Thomas de, 646
Lyedulfus, see Ledulf
Lyghtfot, Robert, 642
Lymbernere (Lymbarner, Lymbrennere)
  John le, 323
  Richard, 482
  Walter, 856
Lymesay, Edward, gent., 1045
Lymstrete, see Lime Street
Lynne (Lenn)
  Ralph de, tailor, 610
  Robert de, 447
  William, 216
Lyons (Lyouns), Richard, 566, 568, 572
Lyrper (Lyrpper), Gilbert, alias Baker, 664, 685
Lythum, Richard, 995
Lyttille, John, 751

Mabun, John, 901
Machechrier
  Ralph, 271–2
  Richard, alias Blandecute, son of Sivat, 312–13, 316, 1011; Matilda his daughter, 313–14
  see also Butcher
Maiden Lane (Ingestret), near Wood Street, 661
Maiden Lane (Kyronlane), in Vintry ward, 566
Maidenestan, see Maydston
Maillard, Gilbert, 828
Maionelane, see Mincing Lane
Maitland, William, xi
Makenheved, William, 65
Makesey, Robert, 465
Malcolm, king of Scots, 1072, App. 1, 13
Malgerus, uncle of Gilbert the clerk, 471
Mallyng
  Adam de, 160, 164
  Reginald de, 161, 167
  Richard, 566
Malmesbury, Richard, 995
Maltmetere, Peter & Agnes his wife, 192

Malwyn (Malewayn), John, cit. & merchant, 51, 224, 289, 309, 410–11, 1052; Margery his wife, 410
Man, William, 801
Mandeville (Mandaville, Maundevilla, Maundevyle)
  Geoffrey de, 873
  Geoffrey de, earl of Essex, xv, 960–2, 972, 1004; Rohesa his wife, 962
  Geoffrey de, earl of Essex & Gloucester, 527–8, 701a
  John, 224, 1052
  Ralph de, 79
  Walter de, 1004
  William de, earl of Essex, 527, 701a, 1004
Manekin (Manekyn), Geoffrey, 663
Mangunelane (Manunlane), see Mincing Lane
Manhale
  Robert, 42
  William, 55, 715–16, 896
Manifeld, Robert de, & his widow, 830
Manschipe
  Alexander & his widow, 107
  Roger, 107
Mansel, Henry, 824
Mantel, Lady Roais, wife of Robert, 209, 1058
Marc, William, 1005
March, earl of, 44, 66, 137; see also Mortimer, Roger
March(e)
  Gilbert de la, potter, 144, 810, 813, 815; see also Potter
  John de la, alias le Potter, 48, 55–7; see also Potter
  Thomas de (la), 63, 813, 815, 820
  William de la, 813, 815
Marchall, Marescall, see Marshal
Marchaunt
  John, 511
  Nicholas, 511
Marcy, Agnes de, prioress of Clerkenwell, 665
Marem, John de, 1015
Mareni (Mateni)
  Hugh de, archdeacon of London, 964
  William de, dean of St. Paul's, 965
Maresmay (Mayresmay), Peter, see Roger, Peter fitz
Mareys (Marreys), John, chaplain of Salcott Virley, 441, 482, 622
Margaret, saint, queen of Scots, 1072, App. 1, 13
Marines, Hugh de, 1004
Mark Lane (Martelane, Marthelane), 173, 175, 1007
Markele, Robert, 465, 480
Marlee, see Morlee

General Index

Marny (Marney, Marni)
  Edmund, 130
  John, 627
  Robert, 833, 846
  Robert, kt., 613, 696; Alice (de), his wife, daughter of Richard Lac, 37, 440–1, 613, 696
Marshall (Marchall, Marescall, *etc.*)
  Alexander, 462
  Geoffrey, 336
  Gilbert, 367, 370, 373
  Godewin, 388
  Godfrey, 896
  Hugh, 772
  Ralph, 460, 900–1, 905, 911–13; Matilda his wife, 912
  Richard, 367
  Robert, 480
  Robert le, 664
  Roger, smith, 172
  Simon, 896–7; Roysia his wife, 897
  William, 424
  William son of Alice, 336
  see also Cylbryght, John; Taillefer, William
Martel, William, 824; dapifer, 960, 973, 978
Martelane (Marthelane), *see* Mark Lane
Martelane, Hervy de, 905
Martin
  baker, & Eugenia his wife, 771
  prior of St. Mary Southwark, 1028
  rector of St. Edmund, 360
  smith, 725–6; his widow, 725
  son of Alice, alderman, 442; sheriff, 1073
  son of Benet, 910
  son of William, *see* William, Martin son of
Martin's Lane (lane of St. Martin Orgar), 396–7, 1016
Martrino, Hugh de, 335
Martyn, Henry, 276; Matilda, ? his wife, daughter of Benet son of Luke, 276
Mary, Simon fitz (son of), alderman, 461
Mary Axe Street (Seyntmarystrete), 799, 801, 808
Maryns
  John & his widow, 105
  Thomas (de), chamberlain, 105, 177, 411, 473, 673
Maseliner (Mazeliner), William (le), 498–9; Roisia his wife, 499
Mason, *see* Henry; Hugh; William
Mateni, *see* Mareni
Mathew (Matheu)
  John, 996
  William, 995
Matilda
  empress, 1004, App. 1, 13
  queen (wife of Henry I), xiii–xv, 1, 4, 9, 11, 13, 997, 1001, 1072, App. 1–5, 9–10, 13
  queen (wife of Stephen), xv, 14, 960–1, 972, 974, 976, 978–80, 1004, App. 14
  daughter of Henry II, App. 14
  daughter of King Stephen, 14, 973, 977, App. 14
  Juvenis, 393–4
  prioress of Haliwell, 811
  prioress of St. Helen, 336
Matthew
  alderman, 228, 234–5, 387, 1061
  baker, 353–4
  chandler, 65, 292; Joan his widow, 65
Maune, Walter, 562
Maurice
  Master, 967
  bishop of London, 873
Mawfeld, Geoffrey, 260
May (Maii)
  Adam, coroner, 996
  Hugh, 90
  John, 184
  Ralph, 88–90
  Richard, 35, 50, 250, 933, 1067
  William, 123
Maydour, Robert le, 252
Maydston (Maidenestan), John (de), king's clerk, 235, 237
Makyn, John, 137
Mayn, John, 664
Maynard, John, 607
Mayor & commonalty, 421
Mayresmay (Maresmay), *see* Roger, Peter fitz
Mazerere, William (le), sheriff, 192, 425, 496, 534
Megre, John, 472, 480
Meguzer (Meguser)
  Nicholas le, 800
  Norman le, 800
  William le, 787; *see also* William, whittawer
Meldeborne, Gilbert, attorney, 188
Melford, Master William, 622, 625
Melkere, William (le), 299–301
Meluarad, *see* Monener
Menchunlane, *see* Mincing Lane
Mend, Ralph de, 171
Mendeham (Mandeham)
  Master Benet de, 754
  Roger de, 754–5
Mercer, *see* Adrian; Alexander; Alfred; Augustine; Edmund; Elias; German; Godmund, Paulinus; Robert; Serlo; Wygot; *and* Broun, Walter le; Colwell, John; Fifhyde, John; Flete, Simon; Hoddesdon, Edmund; Refham, Richer; Wodcok, John
Merchant, *see* Brian; Edric; Godard;

Merchant, *continued*
  Simon; *and* Godard, Geoffrey; Malwyn, John
Meremearer
  Adam, 607
  Richard, 607
Mereton, *see* Merton
Mereworth (Merworth)
  Richard, 405
  Simon (de), sheriff, 99, 386; 409
Merk, Henry, 772
Merlan, Richard, 830
Mersch (Merssh)
  Gilbert & his widow, 450
  Ralph, 772
Mersk, Robert, 290
Merton, Surrey, church of St. Mary in, 10, App. 10; canons of, 386, 397, 1022–3
Merton (Mereton)
  Alice de, abbess of Barking, 1007
  John de, 270
Messager (Mesagere)
  Adam le, & Zarilda his wife, 168
  Simon le, 184
Messende (Messendone), *see* Missenden, Bucks.
Michael
  clerk, 238–9
  cordwainer, 1023
  son of John, 1015
  son of Stonphardus, 86
  unctor (? seller of grease), 144, 210, 1059
Micham (Michham), Peter (de), 382–3
Middlesex
  archdeacon of, *see* Belemis, Richard de (II)
  farm of London and, *see* London, sheriff's farm
Middleton (Middilton)
  Henry de, 1035
  John, 239; [another], 566; his widow, 718
Miles, Roger, 715
Milkechirche, *see* St. Leonard Eastcheap
Miller, *see* Simon
Milreth, William, sheriff, 996
Milward, John, 278
Mincing Lane (Maionelane, Mangunelane, Manunlane, Menchunlane, Mynchynlane, *etc.*), 204–5, 207–9, 1040, 1058
Minor (Minour, Minur). John le, sheriff, 213, 510, 716
Minoresses, *see* St. Clare without Aldgate
Miskenning, *see* Legal matters
Missenden (Messende, Messendone), Bucks., abbot & convent of, 488, 489, 637; abbot, *see also* Roger
Mitegolde, Aluena, 790
Mockyng (Mockyngg)
  John (de), cit. & fishmonger, 285, 305, 309
  Nicholas, 285, 305, 309
Modlieuesune, Edric, 960
Moigne (Monek, Moyn, Moygne)
  Arnold, 397
  William (le), woolmonger, 33, 219–21, 1057; Clemence his widow, 1057
Monener *or* Meluarad, Walter, 216
Moneyer, *see* Elias; Gilbert; Hamo; Reimund; Spirlingus; Theodoric; *and* Bonsergaunt, William; Copton, Hamo; Ipswich, Reimund de
Montague (Montagu, Monte Acuto)
  Adam de, 610, 834, 836
  John de, fishmonger, 610, 834, 836
  Richard de, 976
Montibus, James de, 622
Mont-St.-Éloi, France, abbot of, xiv, 6, App. 6; prior of the canons of, *see* John
Mordone
  Gilbert de, 377
  Walter de, sheriff, 816–17
More, Le (la), xix, 782, 785
More (Mora)
  Agnes de la, 877
  Cecily de la, 178
  John, 290
  Jordan de, 858, 1017
  Ralph de, sheriff, 499, 905, 1007
  Richard de, *see* Lodeby, Richard de
  Richard de, painter, 684
  Robert de la, 808
  Thomas de, 849
  Thomas de la, 920, 955
  William, cit. & vintner, 566, 568
Morecok, Richard, 924
Morhaunt, Thomas, 885
Morlee (Marlee), Thomas, clerk, 615, 1033
Morpat, John de, lorimer, 646
Morse, clerk, 70
Mort, David, 628
Mortimer (Mortymer)
  John, 469
  Roger, 842
  Roger, earl of March, 80
Mortmain, *see* Legal matters
Morton
  John, attorney, 795
  John, clerk, 216–17
  William de, 405
Moses, clerk, 270
Motone (Moton)
  John, 541–2
  Robert, 363a
Mouner, John, 277
Mounteux, Robert, 92
Mountford, N. de, 874
Mountjoy, hospital, brothers of, 32, 43–4, 68, 70, 80; prior of, *see* Hur

General Index

Mower, William, 861
Moygne (Moyn), *see* Moigne
Mulins, Simon, App. 13
Mullyng, Adam, 307
Multon
  John, skinner, 685
  Robert de, 460
Munden
  Matilda, 677
  Simon de, 677
Muntpeller (Muntpelleis, Mundepelles), Robert (de), sheriff, 124, 716, 769, 890
Murer, Richard, 137
Murte (Murta)
  Godacus (? Goderic), 624
  Henry son of Epi son of Goderic, 185–6; his mother, 185
Musard, John, 309
Mychel, John, 552, 566
Mylius, Clement, 242, 243
Mynchynlane, *see* Mincing Lane
Myngy, Warin, cit. & bureller, 417–18, 486; Margaret his wife, 417–18
Mynot, Michael, 566

Naam, *see* Legal matters, pleas of taking naam
Naps, Thomas at, 100–1
Nax, William at, 63
Neel, Walter, 566
  see also Nigel
Neubery (Niewbery), John (de), 42, 615
Neve (Neue), William le, 294–5
Nevile (Nevill), Hugh de, 527, 529
New Hospital, *see* St. Mary without Bishopsgate
New Temple, *see* Temple Bar
Newcastle (Novo Castro), Peter de, 575
Newchirch, *see* St. Mary Woolchurch
Newcourt, Richard, xi
Neweland, Andrew, sheriff, 1073; *see also* Newelin, Andrew
Newelin (Neuelim, Neuelyn)
  Andrew, 1023, *see also* Neweland
  John de, 1038
  Peter, sheriff, 1073
Newgate, gate, 824, 830
Newham (Niweham), William de, 'minister' of the Knights Templar, 828
Newport (Neweport)
  Isabel, 595
  Simon de, 933–4; Florietta his wife, 933
  Thomas, attorney, 156
  William, cit. & fishmonger, 587–8
Newton, 1004
Newton (Neweton)
  Geoffrey, 808
  Hugh de, 584
  John, cit. & fishmonger, 581
  Robert, 566

Nicholas
  archdeacon of London, 969–71
  butcher, 271, 312
  chaplain, 529, 750
  clerk, 921
  Master, clerk, 626
  deacon, 270
  junior, 596
  priest, 234
  rector of St. Edmund, 375
  son of Edmund son of Gerard, 744
  son of Joce, *see* Joce
  son of Ralph, 518
Nicholas (Nicolas)
  Stephen, father of Alice Horn, 292
  Stephen son of, 299
  William son of, 271
Nied, William, 362, 363
Niewbery, *see* Neubery
Nigel
  chaplain, 97
  goldsmith, 655
Nigel (Neel, Neal)
  John son of, 273; sheriff, 1072
  Thomas son of, 1073
Ni-(n)ler, Simon & his widow, 347
Nimore, Constantine & Joan his wife, 1028
Noke, Thomas atte, 488, 490
Nolicia, of Lime Street, 115
Nolyf, Thomas, draper, 478
Norable, Isabel, 597
Noreys (Norensis)
  Osbert, 751
  Robert, 993
Norfolk, Gilbert de, 458a
Norham', *see* Northampton
Norhampton (Norhamton, *etc.*)
  Alan, 506
  Henry, 562
  Isabel, 562
  John (de), alderman, 37, 45, 47, 68, 802, 906, 1007; sheriff, 190, 467, 501, 596, 731
  John (de), (clerk), 557, 559–60, 562, 575–6
  William de, 576
Norman
  clerk, 906, 939; *see also* Lorchon
  first prior of Holy Trinity, xiv–xv, 1, 4, 6–10, 12–14, 31, 624, 739, 779, 807, 871, 960, 965, 997, App. 1, 4, 6–10, 12–14, 31
Norman, John (son of), mayor, 88, 329, 405, 515, 571–2; his heirs, 447
Normandy, App. 13
Northampton (Norham'), Northants., 12, 979, 998, App. 12
Northbiry, Richard, 511
Northburgh
  John & his widow, 1063
  Michael, bishop of London, 952

General Index

Northfol, Ralph de, 346
Northman, Geoffrey, bailiff of Southwark, 276
Norton
  Gregory, cit., 903–4
  John, cit., 891–2; Alice his wife, 892
  Robert, 107
  William, 36, 40, 46, 83, 85, 436; alderman, 954
Norwich, bishop of, *see* William
Norwich (Norwic, Norwysch)
  John de, 651
  Walter, 511
  William, 1033
Noth, John, 245–7
Notley (Nuteleg), Essex, 1004
Notte, John, sheriff, 410
Notyngham, John de, 941
Novo Castro, *see* Newcastle
Nuteleg, *see* Notley, Essex
Nycol, Stephen, 863

Oault, Giles, 748
Odiam, Richard, 386
Odo
  chaplain of St. Andrew Hubbard, 241
  clerk, 977
Ofham, John, chantry of, 715
Oily (Oyry), Fulk de, 777
'Oitheram', brewhouse with the sign, 382
Old Bailey (Le Bail, without Luthgate, towards Newgate, *etc.*), 832, 834, 845
Old Change, 636
Old Fish Market (Fishmarket, West Fish Market), 578, 586, 609, 637, 646, 1019
Old Fish Street, 581, 587
Old Fish Street (? lane called West Fish Market), 588
Olivere (Olyver)
  Edmund & his widow, 179
  William, 319, 321, 324, 407
Olney, John, 317
Olyons, Richard, 768
Ordgar, *see* Fince
Orfeur, Sampson, 51, 53; Christine his wife, 53
Organ, John, rector of St. Margaret Lothbury, 735
Orgar
  le Prude, 871, 960
  son of Deremann, 871
Orival, Peter de, baron of the exchequer, 982
Orpedeman
  Henry, 172
  Thomas, 348
Osbern
  nephew of Ranulf, 781
  ? prior of Holy Trinity, xv

Osberne (Osbarn)
  John de, 701
  Richard, cit., 898; clerk of the chamber at Guildhall, 954
Osbert
  chaplain of St. Augustine Papey, 790
  chapman, son of Richard, of Hackney, 921–2
  dean of the Arches, rector of St. Mary Bothaw, 460–2, 860
  woolmonger, 787
Osekyn, Robert, 625
Osmund, vintner, 790
Osney (Osneye), Oxon., abbot of, *see* William; abbot & convent, 424–5
Ostage, William, cit. & fishmonger, Matilda his wife & Juliana his daughter, 479
Ostregate (Oystergate), Stephen de, sheriff, 146, 355, 832
Oswald, king & martyr, 1072
Oswant, *see* Edwin son of; Richard son of
Oswy, king & martyr, 1072
Oteswych (Otiswich)
  Martin de, 759
  Master William de, surgeon, 766–8, 770
Othulphus (Othulfus Viviano), 43
Othwerus, custodian of the Tower, 960
Ottle
  John, 89, 92
  Thomas, 87, 89
Otto, Hugh son of, warden of London, 375, 845; *see also* Hocton
Overe, Roger de, 575
Oxbrygge, Thomas, 805
Oxefot, Godwin, 963
Oxford, 955
  church of St. Frideswithe, 10, App. 10
  countess of, 445–6, 1019
  earls of, 447, 995; *see also* Ver, Aubrey de
  New College (of St. Mary), 33, 44, 80
Oxford
  Henry de, 622, 730
  John de, 566, 1057
  Martin de, *alias* Preaty, 715–16; Matilda his wife, 716
  Stephen de, 242; junior (Iuvenus [*sic*]), 242
  Thomas de, bureller, 213–14, 1008; Alice his wife, 213, 1008
Oyldelarum, Aurifilia daughter of Alan, 329
Oyledebef, Gemma, 268
Oyry, *see* Oily
Oystergate, *see* Ostregate

Padegrys, Robert, 110
Pagan, Gauselinus, 566
Page
  John, 55, 99–101, 469, 927; Agnes his

General Index

wife, 99, 101
Philip, junior, 309
Pageman, Richard, 418
Paien, William, 423
Pain
  butcher, 283; Laurence his son, 285
  fishmonger, 202, 1065
Painter (Pictor), Peter the, 682
  see also More, Richard de
Pake, Andrew, 39
Palmer (Paumer)
  Henry le, 375; [another], 436, 438, 496, 498
  Matthew (le), 436, 752
  Richard, 332, 579
  Roger (le), 595; sheriff, 286, 820; Beatrice his wife, 595
  see also Hereward; Hugh; Roger; Stephen; William
Panchemer, Hugh, 666
Panchier, Robert, 747
Panifader (Panyfader)
  John, 32–3
  Robert, 33, 35, 39–40, 218, 1038, 1056
Pappekertel (Puppekertel), Walter, 'le Tailiator', 574–5
Papworth, Walter, *see* Bardeneye
Parin, Gervasia, 335
Paris (Parys, Pareys)
  Hamo (de), 225, 1053; *see also* Perarys
  Hugh, 418
  John de, 958
  John de, deacon, 270
  Nicholas son of Hugh, 418
  Richard de, sheriff, 173, 195, 293, 344, 718, 863–4, 958, 1060
  Robert de, potter, 811, 813
  Roger de, sheriff, 111, 537
  Simon (de), sheriff, 73, 631, 861
  William de, 335
Parker, William, 193; [? another], 203, 480, 863, 1066
Parmenter, *see* Baldwin; Bartholomew; German; John; Thomas; *and* Herghes, Andrew de
Parnes, John, 290
Parux, Robert le, 680
Pasce, Erchebald, 977
Paschal II, pope, 10, App. 10
Pascharius, 676
Pasfeld, William, 846
Passeto, Adam de, 586; *see also* Plesseto
Pater, Richard le, 912
Paternoster Row (Paternosterstret), 626
Paternosterchirch, *see* St. Michael Paternoster
Patishill, Martin de, dean of St. Paul's, 744
Patrik (Patryk)
  Richard & his widow, 319
  Robert, 751

Paul, parson of St. Clement Eastcheap, 1011
Paulinus, mercer, brother of John Blund, 350, 1014
Paul's Chain (Poulisheyn), 615
Paul's Tavern (Poulestaverne), 309
Paul's Wharf (Pouliswharf), 615
Paxton, Richard, 939, 941
Payable, Roger, 575
Payn
  John, brewer, 679, 924, 927; Margery his wife, 924, 927
  Robert, 642
Pays, John, 364
Pecche (Pechche), John, (mayor), 224, 490, (Pecham), 547, 1052
Pecok, Mathew & his widow, 552
Peerle, *see* Perle
Pekeman, Andrew, 305
Pelham
  Awreda, 414
  John, 664
Penne, John, alderman, 418
Pentecost, *see* Wodemongere
Pepper, 90–1018 *passim*
Pepperer, *see* Wiltshyr, John
Pepyr, Haukynus, 94, 96
Perarys (Perariis), Hamo(n), clerk, 615, 617, *see also* Paris
Percy, Robert, rent-collector of Holy Trinity, 661
Perers, Alice, 891, 896; *see also* Alice
Perle (Peerle), Thomas, 186, 207, 210–11, 1059
Perone, Thomas, 290
Persted, Richard (de), 272, 274
Peryere, Thomas, 615
Pescur, Roger le, 140, 159–60
Pessoner, Roger le, & his widow, 354
Peter, 942
  (Armiger, ? *rectius* Aunger), alderman, 769, 785
  clerk, 442
  clerk, son of Benet Cokelin, 860
  cutler, 181
  priest, 423
  son of Alan, 507, 530
  son of Daniel, 650–2
  son of Leuegarius, 790
  son of Walter, sheriff, 1072
  tiler, 178
Peter (Piers)
  Alan (fitz, son of), 288, 297, 312, 637, 824, 1011–12, 1015, 1022; Sabina his widow, 714
  Joce (fitz, son of), 280; alderman, 826, 831; sheriff, 1073
Petevyn
  Benet, Jew, 707–8
  Henry de, 1005

Petipas, Henry, stockfishmonger, 175
Petrocus, saint, king of Wales, 1072
'Petyt, le', tenement called, 752
Peyntour, William, 813
Phelipper, *see* Philypper
Philip
  chaplain, 812
  cook, 761
  nephew of Warin, 677
Philip, John, rector of St. Margaret Fish Street Hill, 287
Philip Lane (Philipeslane), 676, 680
Philosopher, *see* Robert
Philpot (Philepot, Phillipot, Philpotts), John, 246, 249, 251, 305
Philpott Lane, 251
Philyppere (Phelipper), Godwin, 239, 472, 475
Picard, *see* Pykard
Picot (Pykott)
  John, 347
  Nicholas, 347; sheriff, 904
  Ralph, 977
  Thomas, 347
Pictor, *see* Painter
Piebaker, *see* Pyebakere
Piedefer
  Osbert, father of William, 1025–6
  William, son of Sabina Cordiwisse, 1025–6
Pikeman, Adam, 268–9
Pipehurst (Pypehurst)
  Henry de, 642
  Thomas, 659–60; Joan his wife, 660
Piro, *see* Pyrho
Pisere, William, 903
Pittances, 223, 380, 471, 529, 716–17, 798, 802, 812, 880, 1013, 1028, 1051; of a salmon worth 2s, 950
Plass[ey], Robert, de 383
Plesseto, Adam de, 586; *see also* Passeto
Plesyngton, R. de, 1030
Plommer
  Denise, *see* Virly
  Katherine, 409
Plotte, John, 815
Plumber, *see* Laurence
Plumer, John, 278
Plumstede, John de, 407
Plympton, Devon, 10, App. 10
Podyngden, Gilbert de, 594
Poete, Roger, 191
Pole, John (at, atte), 59, 440–1, 613, 696; Katherine his wife, 440–1, 613, 696
Polested, Hugh, 226–7, 1054–5
Poly (Pole, Poley, Poulay), Roger, 13th prior of Holy Trinity, 25, 54, 308, 438, 520, 532, 580, 1048
Ponde, Roger atte, 951
Pont de l'Arche (Pont Arc'), William, 1001

Ponte
  Robert de, 109
  William de, 4, App. 4
Pontefract (Ponnefrert, Pontefrect), Yorks., Knolles college at, 186, 191, 233
Pontisbury (Pontesbury), Master Thomas de, 783
Poor Clares, *see* St. Clare without Aldgate
Poore, R[ichard], bishop of Salisbury, 1004
Popil, John, 863
Porta
  Walter de, 908
  Walter son of Walter de, 908–9
  see also Gate
Porter (Portar)
  John, 798
  Richard le, & Lucy his wife, 958
  Thomas, 215
  William, 843
  see also Gate-keeper
Portesmuthe, Alice de, 1007
Portsoken, *see* Aldgate; ward sergeant, *see* Simon
Potell
  John, 613
  Richard, 613
Poterell, Richard, 552
Potter (Poter, Pottar, *etc.*)
  Agnes le, *see* Clerk, William le
  Alan le, *see* Suffolk
  Gilbert the, 955; *see also* Marche
  Hamon le, 904
  Humphrey(?) le, 144
  John (le), 877, 904–5, 909, 955; *see also* Marche
  Laurence, 734
  Richard, rector of Stapleford, 59, 83
  Richard le, 144; *see also* Pater
  Walter (le, the), 40, 745, 905; alderman, 344; sheriff, 197, 787, 1008
  William le, clerk, 925, 996
  see also Alan, Ranulf; Algate, John de; Blunt, Walter le; Chyngeford, Richard de; John, Nicholas; Paris, Robert de; Raughton, Robert; Stowe, John de; Totenham, Gilbert de; Weston, Peter de; Wolcomstowe, John de
Potyn, Nicholas, 216
Pouder, John, 382
Poulestaverne, *see* Paul's Tavern
Poulisheyn, *see* Paul's Chain
Pouliswharf, *see* Paul's Wharf
Poundage (Pondagium), 151, 216, 839, 846, 861
Pountfreit (Pomifreyt, Poumfreyt)
  Henry, 330, 480
  Humphrey, 330
Pourte (Pout), Hugh, sheriff, 73, 631
Poynant (Poyaunt), John, 585, 588

General Index

Poyntel, John, 541
Preacher, *see* John
Preaty, Martin, *see* Oxford, Martin de
Preest, William, bureller, 115
Prensse, William, 303
Prentys, John, 414, 511
Prestbury, Ralph, D. Can. L., 1045
Preston
  Henry, 290
  Henry, cit. & ropemaker, & Isabel his wife, 417–18
  John de, sheriff, 640
  Richard (de), cit., 878–9
Prian, John, 1010
Priour, John, 165, App. 165
Prishet, John, 216
Prudhom (Prodehom, Proudhom)
  Henry, 89, 92
  William, 579–80, 588
Prynce, Gilbert, 685
Prys, Master David, 995
Pudding Lane (Redersgate, Retherlane, Roderesgate), 257, 259, 264, 268
Pulloxhill (Pullokeshill), Beds., *see* Travaill, William
Pulsham, John, 572
Pulteney, John, kt., 401
Puppe, Geoffrey, 151
Puppekertel, *see* Pappekertel
Purser, Roger le, 732
Putford, Richard de, & Margaret his wife, 796
Pyebakere, Andrew le, 356
Pyioun, John, *see* Horleus
Pykard (Picard, Pycard)
  Henry, 174, 334, 488; his widow, 174
  John, 174, 334
  Margery, 334, 600
  Richard, sheriff, 190, 467, 501, 596, 731
Pykeneye (Pykenia)
  Arnold, 595
  Ralph, 285
Pykott, *see* Picot
Pyne, John, 486
Pyrho (Piro), William de, 1004, 1020

Queenhithe (Edredeshede, Ripa Regine), 975–7, 979–80; ward, 1015n
Querendun, Geoffrey de, 962
Quernebeter, Stephen (de, le), 916, 921, 928
Queyntel, Richard, 716

Radington, Baldwin, warden of London, 420
Radyng, *see* Reading, Berks.
Radyng, Richard, 771; Isabel his widow, 771–2
Raginaldus cum botis, 948
Ragton, William, *alias* William of the Wardrobe, 907

Ralph, 884
  baker, 417
  bishop of Chichester, chancellor, 1004
  brother of Joce the Vintner, 453
  brother of Walter the Hosier, 157
  bureller, 993
  butcher, *see* Machechrier
  canon of Holy Trinity, 968
  capper, 150, 157, 181–2
  carpenter, 86, 171, 270; *see also* Carpenter
  chaplain, 761, 977, 1009
  chaplain (? of St. Magnus), 280
  clerk, 394
  clerk, of Stepney, 887
  coalman, 843; *see also* Carbunel
  deacon, 152
  dean, 967–8
  doctor, 666
  father of Alice, 689–90
  gate-keeper, 70, 924
  goldsmith, 333, 814; [another], 516
  goldsmith, son of John, 845
  priest, 122, 210, 236, 919, 1059
  priest of St. Dionis, 1051
  priest of St. Magnus, 259
  priest of St. Mary at Hill, 223, 1051
  2nd prior of Holy Trinity, xv–xvi, 13–14, 31, 77, 210, 232, 257, 280, 299, 361, 394, 423, 612, 644, 809, 895, 948, 964, 968, 970, 1059, App. 13–14, 31
  smith, 496, 826; Christine his daughter, 826–7
  son of Algod (Algadus), 871, 963
  son of Andrew, 963
  son of Gervase, 41
  son of Osbert, 404–5
  son of Thomas, 515–18
  tanner, 946
  usurer, 228–9, 1061–2; Goda (Gabliere) his wife, 222, 228–9, 304, 405, 1061–2
  vintner, 497; *see also* David son of
Ramesey, Robert, 289–90
Ramsden (Ramesden, Ramesdon)
  John, 285
  Robert de, 1033
Ranulf (Randulf)
  canon of St. Paul's, 963; dean, 967
  chancellor, 4, 12, 998, App. 4, 12
  earl of Chester & Lincoln, 1004
  monk of Reading, xvii, 779
  priest, 779–81
Ranus, Richard son of, 273
Rasing (Rasyng), *see* Basing, Adam de
Rasyn, William, 597
Ratoneslane, *see* Batoneslane
Rauf, Simon fitz, *see* Simon
Raughton, Robert (de), potter, 909, 940, 1038
Rawlyn (Raulyn), John, 894, 896, 898

General Index

Rayham, Agnes, daughter of Roger de Ely, 1035
Rayne (Reynis), Essex, 995
Re, John at, 722
Reading (Radyng, Rethyng), Berks., 873; abbot of, 779; burial of Henry I at, 1072; monks of, 325; *see also* Ranulf
Rectors, fraternity, register of, 377
Redersgate, *see* Pudding Lane
Reding (Redyng)
  Gilbert de, spurrier, 687
  John, 708
Reeve of London, *see* Berquereola; Leofstan; Wulfgarus
Refham
  John, 506, 513, 536; his widow, 536
  Richer (de), cit. & mercer, 506, 513, 536–7; mayor, 95
Reggi, Richard fitz, 325
Reginald
  butcher, son of Nicholas, 303, 1012
  chaplain of Henry de Castell, 546
  goldsmith, 45, 906
  son of Peter, 836
  tanner, 931–2
Reigate (Reygate)
  Nicholas de, 705, 1041
  Nicholas son of Nicholas de, 705
Reimund (Reimundus), 204, 1067
  moneyer, 730
Reneshale, John, 174
Renger (Reinger, Reniger, Reyner, fitz Reyngarus)
  John son of Richard, 139–40, 151, 159, 162, 169
  Richard, alderman, 280
  Richard (son of William), 76, 91, 139, 161, 167, 222, 242, 270, 314, 413, 430, 552, 571, 606, 618, 692–3, 744, 852, 856–7, 862, 1004, 1017; alderman, 283, 304; mayor, 248, 283, 548, 650, 690, 1014; sheriff, 449, 528, 629, 1073
  Roger, alderman, 306
  William (son of), 161, 241, 424, 427, 461
Rennerus son of Berengarius, 387
Rennes
  Richard de, 109
  William de, 109
Rents, *see* Legal Matters
Reole, *see* Riole
Rerdon, Alexander de, 945
Restwolde, Thomas, 477
Retherhethe
  Robert de, & Agnes his wife, 871
  Stephen de, & Juliana his wife, 927
Retherlane, *see* Pudding Lane
Rethyng, *see* Reading, Berks.
Revell, William, 883
Reyn, Walter, 529
Reynham, Walter de, 590

Reynis, *see* Rayne, Essex
Reynwell, William, 808
Ricarius, 791
Richard I, king, 871, 1072
Richard II, king, 1005, 1030
Richard
  bishop of London, *see* Belmeis, Richard de (I)
  bishop of Salisbury, *see* Poore, Richard
  brother of Archdeacon Nicholas, 970
  carpenter, 769
  chaplain, 887
  chaplain of St. Peter le Poor, 529
  cheesemaker, 855
  clerk, 46, 109
  cordwainer, 676
  goldsmith, 1027
  priest, 335, 400; [another], 624, 963
  priest of St. Christopher, 747
  priest of St. Margaret, 967
  priest of St. Mary Magdalen, Old Fish Street, 609
  priest of the chapel, 609
  5th prior of Holy Trinity, xvi, xix, 17, 39, 50, 58, 84, 86, 91, 126, 142, 150, 161, 167, 218, 238, 248, 250, 263, 290, 304, 306, 310, 316, 318, 320, 327, 331, 336, 380–1, 383, 400, 408, 435, 458, 480–1, 487, 493–4, 529, 533, 539, 547–9, 553, 555, 565, 570–1, 584, 586, 589, 593, 606, 618, 629, 638, 650, 658, 690, 692, 714, 734, 736, 744, 754, 800, 811, 818, 826, 830–1, 852, 857, 882, 884, 886, 900, 908, 910, 923, 930, 933, 938, 940, 946, 990, 1010, 1013–14, 1017–19, 1056
  saddler, 142, 150, 153
  son of Aleya, sheriff, 1073
  son of Baldwin the Tailor, 664
  son of Bartholomew, sheriff, 1073
  son of Benet the Goldsmith, 350, 362
  son of David, 811
  son of Edwin, son of Oswant, 232
  son of Gocelinus, 950
  son of Osbert, 1004
  son of Oswant, 231, 233–4
  son of Ralph, 963
  son of Reginald, 76
  son of Robert, 819; [another], 1004
  son of Ruffus, 614
  son of Walter, *see* Walter
  son of William, *see* Renger, Richard
  son of Wolfinus, 807
  spurrier, 946
  tanner, 880
  vice-gerent of St. John of Jerusalem, 183
  whittawer, 730, 732
Richard, William (fitz, son of), 190, 501; mayor, 154, 512, 798, 858, 1016; sheriff, 329, 515

General Index

Richeer (Richer)
  John, 1033
  Lorissa, 1033
  Mabel, 1033
  Margery, 1033
  Matilda, 1033
  Thomas, chaplain, 1005, 1033
Richer, canon of Holy Trinity, 497
Ridelstrete, Isabel, 832–3
Rider (Ryder), John, clerk, 417–18
Rigero, *see* Warino
Riole, La (Reole, Roial), 440–1, 1042
Ripa Regine, *see* Queenhithe
Rippyle, Robert, 298
Risby, Robert, 883
Rislingbury, Richard, 883
Risyng (Rysyng), William, 16th prior of Holy Trinity, 28, 101, 503, 815, 1042
Roais, the Lady, *see* Mantel
Robert
  archdeacon of Surrey, 740
  baker, 866
  bishop of Exeter, *see* Warelwast
  bishop of Hereford, *see* Bethune
  bishop of Lincoln, *see* Bloet
  bishop of London, *see* Sigillio
  canon of Holy Trinity, 970
  chamberlain, 270, 726
  chaplain, 148, 209, 700, 887, 1058
  chaplain of John de Cantebregg, 1035
  chaplain of St. Olave [? Hart Street], 209, 1058
  clerk, 234; [another], 552
  clerk, of West Ham, 1015
  cook, 137, 678–9; Goetha his wife, 137
  cordwainer, 839
  de St. Alphege, 257
  Huscardus, 895
  mercer, 993
  philosopher, 969, 971
  priest, 257
  [? priest] of St. Nicholas Cole Abbey, 967
  rector of St. Martin Outwich, 762
  saddler, 148, 152–3; Alice his wife, 152
  saddler, 859–60; Cecily his wife, 859
  smith, 248; [another], 1004
  son of Alice, & Matilda his wife, 336–7
  son of Bartholomew, alderman, 482, 1014
  son of But, 963
  son of Gervase, of London, canon of Southwark, 74–5
  son of Hervi, 534
  son of Leofstan, 809, 871
  son of Ralph, 963
  son of Symon, 555–6, 1018
  son of Walter, 615, 618
  sub-prior of Holy Trinity, 931
  ward of Master Alexander de Dorchester, 529

Robilard
  Denise, 268
  Robert, 264, 268
Robin, clerk of Master Alexander de Dorchester, 529
Robinel (Robinellus), butcher, 310–14
Robinel, Denise, 311, 313
Robiry, Hugh, 300
Rocheford (Recheford), Walran de, kt., 718, 722
Rochester, bishop of, 566
Rochester
  Eustace de, 64
  Ralph de, 64
  Richard de, 64
  William de, 64
Rocle, *see* Rokesle
Roderesgate, *see* Pudding Lane
Rodyng, William, 896
Roger, 902
  abbot of Missenden, 489
  archdeacon of Canterbury, 977
  baker, 248
  bishop of Salisbury, 2, 4, App. 2, 4
  bursar, 700–1
  butcher, 304–5, 1010
  chancellor, 960
  chaplain, 637
  chaplain, of St. Edmund 148, 1058
  Master, doctor, 325, 335; Alice his wife, 325
  fishmonger, 1011
  gardener, *see* Gardener
  goldsmith, 657
  nephew of Hubert, 394, 871
  Palmer, 831, 1027; Henry, Nicholas, Ralph & William his sons, 1027
  son of Alan, *see* Alan
  son of Brian, & Matilda his wife, 1004
  son of Renus senior, 750
  son of Richard, 594
  tailor, 848
  tiler, 945
  vicar of St. Mary Abchurch, 431
  weaver, 1051
Roger
  Peter (fitz, ? son of), *alias* Maresmay, 197, 218, 1056; Clemence his widow, 219
  Roger (fitz, son of), alderman & mayor, 189–90, 218, 327, 355, 501, 508, 515–17, 595, 720, 731, 1056
  William fitz, 218
Roial, *see* Riole
Rois, Robert, 595
Rokesle (Rocle, Rokele, *etc.*)
  Adam, 227, 1039, 1055
  Gregory de, 264, 292; alderman, 437; mayor, 37, 45, 192, 307, 378, 437, 451, 499, 534, 664, 783, 906, 921, 928, 1007;

Rokesle, *continued*
   sheriff, 60, 369, 535, 684, 864, 905, 916
   John, 347
   John de, sheriff, 351
   Robert de (la), 35–6, 45; sheriff, 255
Roland, Hugh de, 453
Romeney(Romeneye, Romoney), John, cit. & potter, 235, 901, 903, 915, 919, 954, 995–6, 1038; Agnes his daughter, 903
Romeseye, John de, 441
Romeyn (Romayn), Thomas, 554, 725; mayor, 286, 820, sheriff, 617; Juliana his wife, 554, 725
Rook, Roger, 1033
Ropemaker, *see* Bricus; *see also* Denxmars, Bartholomew & Thomas; Preston, Henry
Ropery, 418
Rosamond (Rosamund), John, 213, 374–6, 1008
Rose
   Richard, 1042
   Roger, *see* Bury, Roger de
Rote, Nicholas, 46, 83
Rothyng
   Geoffrey de, 783
   Richard, 216, 377, 934
   William de, 911
Rouen (Rotomag')
   Nigel de, 734–5
   William de, 735–7
Round, J. H., xii
Rous (Rouse)
   Adam, 364
   Alice, 364
   John, 285, 287; [another], 1045
Rudham, Berthus de, 330
Rufus (Ruffus)
   Alexander, fishmonger, 283, 285
   Awyn, 77, 80, 90
   Geoffrey, *alias* Badecoks, 285
   Geoffrey, chancellor, bishop of Durham, 875
   Hereward, *see* Hereward
   Humphrey, 203–4, 1066–7
   Laurence & his widow, 610
   Nicholas son of Awyn, 77
   Osbert, 1015
   Richard, 614–15
   Roger, 42
   William, 610, 1026
Ruhaued, Robert, 234
Rumbold, Nicholas, 783
Rus (Ruse, Russo)
   Emma la, 791
   John le, 899, 905
   Robert, 65, 374, 490
   William, 400
   William, sacristan of Holy Trinity, 60
   see also Russie

Russel (Russell)
   Alan, 172
   Elias, mayor, 73, 767; sheriff, 646
Russie (Rusy)
   John son of Richard, 905
   Maurice de, 387
   Richard, 905
   see also Rus
Rusus, canon of Holy Trinity, 986
Rye, John atte, 332
Ryffyn, Robert & his widow, 278
Rykel, William, 1042
Rymers, Hugh de, App. 13
Ryot, Roger, 909

Sabern, William, 158
Sabrigtesworth (Sabrygelworth), R(ichard) de, 249, 388
Sacker
   John, 685
   Robert le, 685
Saddler, *see* Richard; Robert; Serlo; Thomas; Walter; *and* Baldwin, William
Sadeler (Sadelere), John, vintner, 121, 321, 323, 405
Saet, Jordan, 717, 782; his sisters, 782
Saham, Thomas & his widow, 881
Sahipp, Nicholas, 309
Saiena, daughter of Albinus, 86
Saikye, John, 418
St. Alban Wood Street, parish, 663–71, 1012, 1030
St. Albans, Herts., abbot of, 757; monks of, 527, 1012; tenement of abbey of, 767
St. Albans
   Adam de, farrier, 537
   Henry de, 545, 618, 1018; [another], 752
   Isabel de, 708–9
   John de, sheriff, 490, 566
   Thomas de, 801
St. Alphege, chaplain, *see* Laurence *and* Walter; parish, 672–83, 1030
St. Alphege, Robert de, *see* Robert
St. Andrew Hubbard (Estchep, *etc.*), chaplain, *see* Odo; parish, 241–56, 447, 1030
St. Andrew Undershaft (at Knap, Cornhill), cemetery, 808; church, 11, 995, App. 11; parish, 807–23, 1030, 1032
St. Anne, fraternity, *see under* St. Michael Cornhill
St. Audoen, parish (824), 1035; *see also* St. Sepulchre
St. Augustine by St. Paul's (iuxta Portam), chaplain, *see* Andrew; parish, 596, 634–40, 1018, 1030
St. Augustine Papey (by the City Wall), chaplain, *see* Osbert; church, xvii, 11,

General Index

789, App. 11; parish, 789–93
St. Bartholomew, hospital, 447, 529, 645, 655; chaplain, *see* Thomas; master, 654, *see also* Hugh
St. Bartholomew, priory, 437, 836; canons, 783, 1012; priors, 364, 525, *see also* John
St. Bartholomew by the Exchange (the Less), parish, 747–53, 1041
St. Bartholomew the Less, parish, 747n; *see also* St. Bartholomew by the Exchange
St. Benet, priest, *see* Algar
St. Benet Fink, parish, 754–8, 1030
St. Benet Gracechurch (Graschirch, *etc.*), parish, 316–28, 992, 1013, 1015, 1030
St. Benet Paul's Wharf (West), parish, 612–19, 1030, 1042
St. Benet Sherehog (Schorhog), parish, 493–500, 1030
St. Botolph Aldgate, cemetery, 891, 1009; chantry in church, 954; church, xv, xvii, 871, 875–6, 903–5, 919–20, 954, 964, 1045; churchwardens, 901; incumbent, *see* Kokyr, John; parish, 323, 869–971 *passim*, 986, 1009, 1029–30; priest, *see* Withulfus; rector, 954
St. Botolph Billingsgate, parish, 257–61, 1030
St. Botolph Bishopsgate, chaplain, *see* William; parish, 811, 848–67, 1017
St. Bride, church, 833
St. Christopher le Stocks (next Cornhill), parish, 744–6, 1030; priest, *see* Richard
St. Clare without Aldgate (Minoresses without Alegate, Poor Clares), abbey (of St. Mary without Aldgate), 954–6; abbesses, 815, 926, *see also* Juliana *and* Katherine; order, 920
St. Clement Danes, *see* Westminster
St. Clement Eastcheap (Candlewick Street), chaplain, *see* John; church, 313; parish, 380–4, 1011, 1030; parson, *see* Paul
St. Clement's Lane (Street), 380, 382
St. Dionis Backchurch (Bacchirch), church, 849, 861; parish, 117–28, 1030; priest, *see* Ball, John de *and* Ralph
St. Dunstan, John de, 218, 1056
St. Dunstan in the East (by the Tower), cemetery, 215; church, 137, 216; parish, 195–230, ? 369, 993, 1008, 1030, 1040, 1044, 1051–69; rector, 200
St. Edmund, chaplain of, *see* Roger
St. Edmund
  Fulk de, 200, 405, 1063
  James de, sheriff, 286, 417–18, 820
  John de, *see* Cros

John de, 767; Joan his wife, 767; *see also* Henry, cofferer
Thomas de, 798–9
St. Edmund King & Martyr (Graschirch, *etc.*), parish, xvii, 358–79, 1008, 1030; rector, 358, *see also* Martin; Nicholas
St. Ethelburga, parish, 787–8, 1030
St. Faith (the Virgin) under St. Paul's, parish, 624–30, 1015, 1019, 1030
St. Gabriel Fenchurch (All Hallows Fenchurch), advowson, 109; church, xvii, 11, 98, 109, App. 11; parish, 109–16, 993, 1030
St. George, John de, chaplain, 142
St. George Botolph Lane (Eastcheap), church, 273; parish, 262–75, 1025, 1030
St. Giles, hospital, *see* Holborn
St. Giles Cripplegate, parish, 684–6, 1030, 1035
St. Gregory, parish, 620–3
St. Helen Bishopsgate, priory, 91–2, 172, 334, 529, 792, 864, 939, 1035; prioress, *see* Matilda; prioress's garden, 813
St. Helens (St. Helen, St. Helena)
  Adam de, 759
  Henry de, alderman, 759, 761, 848
  Michael de, 618
St. Ives, ? Hunts., 1027
St. James Garlickhithe (super Tamisiam, *etc.*), church, 571; parish, 565–9, 1018–19, 1030
St. James Westminster, *see* Westminster
St. John (Sancto Johanne), Thomas de, 2, App. 2
St. John Haliwell, *see* Haliwell, Middx.
St. John of Jerusalem, *see* Clerkenwell
St. John the Baptist, Walbrook, parish, (449), 453–63, 1010, 1030
St. John Zachary, parish, 644–9, 1030
St. Katherine by the Tower, hospital, xiii, xv, 35, 210, 320, 323, 871, 941, 946, 973–94, 1004, 1013, 1059; brother of, *see* Stephen; master, *see* Thomas
St. Katherine Coleman (All Hallows Coleman(s)church), church, 11, 78, App. 11; parish, 68–102, 1030
St. Katherine Cree, parish, xvii, 31–67, 421, 1030, 1032; *see also* Holy Trinity, parish
St. Lawrence Jewry, parish, 704–6, 996, 1030, 1041
St. Lawrence Pountney (by the Thames, Candelwykstrete, the Martyr), cemetery, 396; church, 406; parish, 394–403, 1035; rector, *see* Cheyndeduit, William de; *and* William
St. Lawrence Pountney College, 401, 410
St. Lawrence Pountney Lane (St. Lawrence Street), 410

277

General Index

St. Leonard Eastcheap (Milkechirche), parish, 297–315, 469, 1025, 1030
St. Magnus the Martyr, chaplain, *see* Ralph; parish, 280–2; priest, *see* Ralph
St. Margaret, priest of, *see* Richard
St. Margaret Fish Street Hill (Bridge Street, *etc.*), church, 285; churchwardens, *see* Clerk, Geoffrey, *and* Whaplode, Robert; parish, 283–91, 1010, 1030; rector, *see* Philip, John
St. Margaret Lothbury, parish, 734–8; rector, *see* Organ, John
St. Margaret Moses, Friday Street, church, 596
St. Margaret Pattens, parish, 241–4, 255, 1030
St. Margaret Southwark, *see* Southwark
St. Martin in the Fields, soke of, *see* Westminster
St. Martin le Grand, canon, *see* Tiulfus; dean & chapter, 509; plea respited at, 742
St. Martin Ludgate, parish, 845–7, 1030
St. Martin Orgar (Candelwrichestrate), lane, *see* Martin's Lane; parish, 385–93, 1015, 1030
St. Martin Outwich, parish, 759–74, 1016, 1030; rector, *see* Robert
St. Martin Pomary, parish, 707–10, 1030
St. Martin Vintry (Beremaneschirch, by the Thames), parish, 449–52, 1030
St. Mary Abchurch (Abbechirch), parish, 404–16, 1008, 1022, 1030; rector, *see* Whytby, John; vicar, *see* Roger
St. Mary Aldermanbury, church, 701; churchwardens, 691, 701; parish, 687–703, 993, 1030, 1043
St. Mary Aldermary (Aldermarychyrch), parish, 545–50, 1030
St. Mary at Hill, church, 235, 311; parish, 231–40, 255, 993, 1005, 1009, 1030, 1033; priest, *see* Ralph
St. Mary Axe, parish, (789), 794–806, 1030, 1038
St. Mary Bothaw, church, 425, 460; parish, 213, 423–9, 1030; rector, *see* Osbert
St. Mary Clerkenwell, *see* Clerkenwell
St. Mary Colechurch, parish, 421, 527–38, 1030, 1039
St. Mary Graces, abbey, 258, 1045; abbot, 896, 907, 952, 958; cemetery, 995; garden, 898, 958
St. Mary in Poultry, chapel, 739–40
St. Mary le Bow (de Arcubus), parish, 515–26, 1030
St. Mary Magdalen, parish, xvii, (31), App. 31, *see also* Holy Trinity, parish
St. Mary Magdalen [? Milk Street or ? Old Fish Street], church, 715

St. Mary Magdalen, Old Fish Street (West Fishmarket), parish, 609–11, 616, 1024, 1030; priest, *see* Richard
St. Mary Overy, *see* Southwark
St. Mary Somerset, church, 767; parish, 606–8, 1017, 1030; priest, *see* Ernald
St. Mary Staining (de Staningelane), church, 1012; parish, 650–3
St. Mary Whitechapel, *see* Whitechapel
St. Mary without Aldgate, abbey, *see* St. Clare without Aldgate
St. Mary without Bishopsgate, (New) Hospital, 65, 138, 172, 207–8, 303, 342, 395, 409, 428, 458, 460, 529, 639, 669, 751, 849, 853, 861, 864; priors, *see* Godfrey; Habitone, John de; Horton, William de
St. Mary Woolchurch (Newchirch, Wolchirch), parish, 464–83, 1014, 1021–2, 1030
St. Mary Woolnoth (Wolnoth, Wulnodmaricherch), parish, 474–92, 1014, 1022, 1030
St. Matthew Friday Street, parish, 535, 631–3
St. Michael
  John de, 209, 1058
  Laurence de, 504, 507–8, 512
  William father of Laurence de, 507, 512
St. Michael, chapel [near Lime Street], 11, 55, App. 11
St. Michael Aldgate, chaplain, *see* John; parish, xvii, (31), 1007, 1030, *see also* Holy Trinity, parish
St. Michael Bassishaw, church, 896; parish, 711–28, 1030
St. Michael Cornhill, fraternity of St. Anne in church of, 374, 377; parish, 344–57, 490, 1030; rector, *see* Whythed, Thomas; wardens, 350–1
St. Michael Crooked Lane (Candelwykstrete, *etc.*), parish, 292–6, 447, 1036
St. Michael [? le Querne], church, 642
St. Michael Paternoster (Paternosterchirch), parish, 434–48, 1018–19, 1030, 1042
St. Michael Queenhithe (Ad Ripam), parish, 602–5, 1018, 1030
St. Michael Wood Street (Hoggenlane), parish, 658–62, 1012; rector, *see* Yue, John
St. Mildred (Mildrethe) Bread Street, parish, 593–8, 1018, 1030
St. Mildred (Mildrethe) Poultry, parish, 739–43
St. Nicholas
  Gilbert de, chaplain, 431
  Robert de, *see* Robert, [? priest]
St. Nicholas Cole Abbey (Cold Abbey, ? Old Fish Street, de Westmacekaria),

278

General Index

parish, 418, 578–92, 1015, 1019, 1024, 1030, 1035; priest, *see* Robert
St. Nicholas Olave (St. Olave Bredstret), parish, 574–7, 1018, 1030
St. Nicholas Shambles, priest, *see* Anselm
St. Olave Bread Street (Bredstret), *see* St. Nicholas Olave
St. Olave Broad Street (Bradestrete), church, 775; parish, 775–8
St. Olave Hart Street (by the Tower, *etc.*), cemetery, 186; chaplain, *see* Robert; church, 11, 175, App. 11; parish, 129–80, 993, 1021; ? rectors, *see* Appilby, Thomas *and* Hynelond, William; *see also* Christmas Land
St. Osyth, Essex, 10, App. 10
St. Osyth (Sancta Ositha), John de, 486, 911, 913; his daughter, 911
St. Pancras, Middx., parish, 1004
St. Pancras Soper Lane, cemetery, 503; parish, xviii, 501–14, 1030
St. Paul
John de, 1046
Jordan de, 951
Peter de, *see* Halsted
St. Paul's, xiii, 4, 31, 301, 1002, App. 4, 31; canons, *see* Brand; Constable, Geoffrey; Eswy, Thomas; Ranulf; Soudan, John; chantry in church, 89; deans, *see* Mareni, William de; Patishill, Martin de; Watford, Robert de; dean & chapter, 358, 489, 891, 965; sacristan, *see* Ely, William; shrine of Erkenwald, 31, App. 31; treasurer, *see* Ste.-Mère-Eglise, Peter de
St. Peter ad Vincula (in the bailiwick of the Tower), cemetery, 964; priests, *see* Ailward; Derman
St. Peter Cornhill, parish, 340–3, 1015, 1030, 1041
St. Peter le Poor (Bradestret), chaplain, *see* Richard; church, 775; parish, 529
St. Peter Paul's Wharf, rector & parishioners, 216
St. Peter Westcheap (Wodstret), chaplain, *see* William; parish, 654–7, 848, 1027, 1030; priest, *see* John
St. Saviour, *see* Bermondsey, Surrey
St. Sepulchre, Newgate, chaplain, *see* Ives; parish, 824–44, 1029–30
St. Stephen Coleman Street, parish, 729–33, 1012, 1030
St. Stephen Walbrook, parish, 464–6, 1020, 1030; rector, 518
St. Swithin, parish, 417–22, 492, 1017, 1030; rector, 418, *see also* Alexander
St. Swithin's Lane, 486
St. Thomas Acon, church, 685, 849; hospital, 529, 854; master, 552
St. Thomas the Apostle, parish, 551–64, 1018–19
St. Vedast, parish, 641–3, 1030
Ste.-Mère-Eglise
Peter de, treasurer, of St. Paul's, 620
William de, bishop of London, 620
Salamon, Laurence, 871
Salcott Virley (Salcote Virly), Essex, *see* Mareys, John
Saleda, smith, 241
Salesby
Idonea, 151
John, 701
Robert, 151
Salisbury, bishops of, *see* Bridport, Giles de; Poore, Richard; Roger
Salisbury (Salesbury, Sarum)
Master John de, treasurer of Exeter, 740–1
Paul, 427
Thomas (de), [two], 427
Salle
Edward, 200
Sabina de, 863–4
Simon, 562
Salman, Christine, 625
Saltmonger, *see* William
Samewelle, Reginald de, 437
Samuel, Thomas, 42
Sancta Maria Ecclesia, *see* Ste.-Mère-Eglise
Sancta Ositha, *see* St. Osyth
Sancto Benedicto, Joan de, nun of Kilburn, 437
Sanctona, Geoffrey de, 170, *see also* Shanketon
Sandale, *see* Sendale
Sandon (Sandun by Kyngeston), Surrey, hospital of, 318–19, 1013
Sandwich (Sandwico, *etc.*)
Matilda de, 225, 1053
Ralph de, kt., warden of London, 131, 144, 151, 215, 221, 274, 323, 557, 617, 646, 752, 784, 897, 992
Sannford, Edward, 216
Santon, Geoffrey de, *see* Shanketon
Sare, Edward, 259
Sarode, Walter, 1062
Sartare, Thomas de, 89–90
Sartrino (Sarterino)
Hugh de, 812
Richer de, 136, 942
Roger de, & Agnes his wife, 937
Sarum, *see* Salisbury
Savage
Henry son of Thomas, 59
Thomas, clerk, 59, 1038
Savuner (Soppier), Warin le, 717–18
Sawardus, 963
Sawyer, *see* Winter, William
Say, Jordan de, 2, App. 2

279

General Index

Scabdeburgh, Roger de, cit., & Idonea his daughter, 378
Scalarus, Henry de, & Joan his daughter, 1004
Scaldour
  Osbert, 303
  Reginald, 303
Schaftysbury, John, 365
'Schaldflet', *see* Legal matters, rents
Schardlowe
  John, 651
  Thomas, 651
Scharp, *see* Sharp
Schefhanger, Stephen de, 631
Schelford, *see* Selford
Schene, *see* Sheen, Surrey
Scherehog, *see* Sherehog
Schering, *see* Sheering
Scherman, *see* Gorney
Scherwode, Robert, 377
Schirburne, John de, & Margery his widow, 691
Schonk, John, 590
Schoppe, Robert de, 234
Scorfeyn, John, 562
Scot (Scotte, Scotus)
  John, 363
  Laurence, goldsmith, 628–9
  Robert, 427
Scribe, *see* Ailnodus
Scrip, Robert, 663
Scrope, Stephen, 80
Sebily, Walter, 390
Sées, archdeacon of, *see* Alulf
Seething Lane (Cevethenlane), 188
Segrave
  Hugh de, steward of the household, 1005
  Roger, 1034
Seinturer, Bureis le, sheriff, 1073
Selegeford, ? Herts., 1004
Selegeford, Edward de, 962
Selford (Schelford, Seluorde), Gilbert de, 371–5
Sely
  John, 153; [another], 465, 745
  Thomas, 153
Semar, 960
Semmanus, clerk, 255, 993
Sendale (Sandale, Sendal), John (de), clerk, 66, 71, 73, 75, 77, 80, 137
Sendon, Ralph de, 701a
Seriaunt (Seriant)
  Richard, 319
  Roger le, 530, 535–7
Serle, John (son of Serlo), 346–7, 811, 849
Serlo
  mercer, 346, 395–6, 545, 673, 761, 855, 1028; mayor, 442–3, 449, 527–8, 993, 1073; Isabel his wife, 397
  saddler, 1024

Sevenok, William, alderman, 591
Sewale, Simon, 642
Sewers, 131
Seymoth, Jewess, 708
Seyntmarystrete, *see* Mary Axe Street
Seyton, John, 330
Shambles of Eastcheap, *see* Eastcheap
Shanketon
  Geoffrey de, *alias* Santon, 151, 155, *see also* Sanctona
  Richard de, barber, 151
Sharnbrok
  Stephen de, 888
  William son of Stephen de, *see* Algate
Sharp (Scharp, Sharpp)
  John, woolmonger, 467, 469, 476, 1021; Alice his wife, 467, 469
  Richard, 289, 311
  Richard son of Thomas, 469–70
Sharpe, R. R., xii
Shartford, *see* Legal matters
Shawe, John, 894, 896
Sheen, (Schene), Surrey, prior of, 125
Sheep, gift of, 968
Sheering (Schering), Essex, 1032
Sheppeton (Sippeton), abbey of, abbot of, 48, 55
Shepton, William, 418
Sherehog (Scherehog), Thomas, priest, son of Alwin, 399; *see also* William, priest of Sherehog
Shereman, James le, *see* Gorney
Shipbrok, Roger, 285
Shippe (Shipp), John, 472, 474, 475
Shire, Gregory atte, alderman, 473
Shoemaker, *see* Hervy; Turold; Walter; William; *see also* Cordwainer
Shopkeeper, *see* Geoffrey; *and* Essex, Richard de
Shops, 81–1027 *passim*; named, 525; with solars, 57, 111, 510, 515, 530, 580; stall in Eastcheap, 271
Shoreditch (Shordich), Middx., *see* Pole, John atte of
Shyryve, Roger, 639
Sibeling (Sibilyn, Sybillyng)
  Emma, 472, 515; widow of Thomas, 517
  Margaret, 344; mother of Roger, 752
  Margery (? *rectius* Margaret), 751
  Roger, son of Thomas, 517
  Thomas, 751n; late husband of Emma, 517
Sibert, king, 1072
Sigerus, 270
Sigillio, Robert de, bishop of London, 973, 977–8
Silvester, Master, 109–10
Simon
  alias Syward, App. 10

General Index

archbishop of Canterbury, *see* Sudbury
baker, 1033
carpenter, 725–6
chaloner, *see* Chaloner
cook, 529
merchant, 812
miller, & Adelina his wife, 1005
sergeant of [Portsoken] ward, 904
son of Mary, alderman, *see* Mary
son of (fitz) Rauf, 919
son of Walter, woolmonger, 472
tiler, 955
weaver, 83, 87
Simon
  Edmund son of, 815
  John son of, 123; *see also* Fysymon
Siredus, *see* Syredus
Siward (Syward)
  alias Simon, *see* Simon
  son of Herebricht, 948
Skelton, John, chantry chaplain, 995
Skinner, *see* Godwyne, Nicholas; Hoder, John le & Peter le; Ireland, Thomas; Kampeden, Robert de; Lincoln, Richard de; Multon, John; Tetesbury, John; Wedford, John de; Wodehous, William
Skinners, fraternity of, 454
Skip, John, 1031
Skynner
  Hugh, apprentice, 1032
  John, father of Hugh, 1032
  William, 805
Skyrwyt, Geoffrey, 687
Slory, John, 830, 833, 846
Smalstrete, Adam, 480
Smeltts, Richard, 272
Smith, *see* Edmund; Leuesine; Martin; Ralph; Robert; Saleda; Wulspus; *and* Marshal, Roger
Smithfield, *see* East Smithfield; West Smithfield
Socage, *see* Legal matters
Soke, *see* Aldgate; Canterbury, archbishop's; Goraleng
Solio, John de, alderman, 811, 1013
Soloman, son of Laurence, 886, 910, 946
Somer, William, 794, 928
Sonke, John, 1019
Sonner, John de, 646
Soper's Lane (Sopereslane), xviii, 501, 505, 507–8, 512
Sopper[e], Geoffrey, 283
Soppier, *see* Savuner
Sorcwod, Thomas de, 944
Sotebrok, Hugh, 316
Soudan, John, canon of St. Paul's, 323
Southe, Katherine, 65
Southwark (Suthwerc, Suwerk, *etc.*)
  bailiff, *see* Northman, Geoffrey

houses, garden, meadows & quay, 447
parish of St. Margaret, 276–9; shops, 262, 1010
priory of St. Mary Overy, canons, 181, 215, 239, 430, 432, 441, 539, 541, 670, 739, 740, 772, *see also* Herman: Robert son of Gervase: prior, 431 & n, 432, 621, 741, 1035, *see also* Martin
Spain (Espayne, Hispania)
  Domengo of, 441
  Peter, son of Richard of, 494
  Richard of, 493; Clemence his widow, 493–5
Spaldyng
  John & his widow, 298
  Robert, 298, 313
Spark, Richard, 249
Spelman (Spelman), Stephen, City chamberlain, 420; sheriff, 491
Spencer, John, 321
Sperling (Sperlenc, Sperlyng, Sprakeling)
  Alexander (son of), 235–6
  Hamon, 74, 77, 80
  John, 76–7, 233, 236, 253–5, 1009, 1025–6
  Jordan, 241, 288, 1011
  Jordan son of Jordan, alderman, 241, 270
  Ralph, alderman, 238, 248, 250, 267, 299, 314, 1010, 1013
Spicer, *see* Derekinus; John
Spigurnel, Thomas, 441
Spilman, William, 103
Spinythiot, William, 752
Spirling, moneyer, 206
Spitel Lane (Spitelelane, Spytillane), 904, 954
Sporier, Nicholas, 846
Sprakelingus, priest, 739
Sprot (Sprott)
  Alexander, 995–6
  Hugh, 210
  John, 711
  William, 711
Spurrier, *see* Richard; Stephen; *and* Crouche, Thomas atte; Reding, Gilbert de; *see also* Sporier
Sputyng, William, 545
Spylnia, Stephen, 642
Spyng, Edmund, *see* Epping, Edmund
Squyrry (Squyer), John, 264, 839
Stable, Adam, 502, 708, 891; his widow, 891
Stables, 441
Stacy, Richard, 745
Staford, Master Richard de, 651
Staines (Stanes), Middx., meadow at, 447
Stalke, William, 273
Stamford
  Stephen, 398
  William, 398

General Index

Stammer, William, 830
Stanes (Stanis, Stanys)
  Simon de, 406
  Thomas, sheriff, 274, 557, 657, 784
  William de, 203, 606–7, 1017, 1066
Stanford (Staneford, Staunford)
  David de, 467, 1021
  Eustace son of David de, 467–8, 1021
  Robert de, 278
  William, 137–8, 395, 410, 751
Stanhardus, 88, 933
Stanhoppe, John, 502
Stapilford, Osbern de, 334
Stapleford (Stapilford), rector of, *see* Potter, Richard
Staunton (Staundon)
  Henry, 219, 1057
  Henry de, 395–6; Agnes his daughter, 396; Christine & Wymark his daughters, 395–7
  John son of Peter de, 657
  Peter de, 657, 947
  Richard de, 730
  William (de, le), 447, 595
Stebee, Solomon de, 850–1; Aliena his wife, 851
Stebenheth, *see* Stepney, Middx.
Stebenheth (Stebbeheha, Stebeneth, *etc.*)
  Gilbert de, clerk, 730–1
  John de, 322, 324
  Solomon de, 895; Goditha his wife, 895–6
  Solomon de, son of Goditha, 896
  William de, chaplain, 71
Sted (Stede)
  Edmund, 808
  Huctredus, 41–2, 808; Matilda his daughter, 41
Stennbatur, Richard, 726
Stenton, Sir Frank, xiii
Stephen, king of England, xv, 14, 871, 960–1, 973, 975–80, 982–3, 1001, 1004–5, 1072, App. 14
Stephen
  brother of the hospital of St. Katherine, 984
  clerk of the exchequer, 985
  conversus, 394
  dyer, 228, 1061
  fishmonger, 582
  junior (Iuvenus *sic*), 242
  palmer (carpenter), 86–7, 760–2, 764; Eufemia his wife, 761–2
  3rd prior of Holy Trinity, xv, 15, 76, 79, 136, 148, 152, 157, 199, 202, 209, 226, 234, 236, 241, 271, 346, 453, 456, 471, 197, 609, 614, 666, 676, 678, 680–1, 700, 729, 747, 750, 776, 790, 814, 877, 887, 902, 918, 920, 931, 942, 1054, 1058, App. 15

  son of Andrew, 842
  spurrier, 863
  tanner, 882–6, 900, 908, 910, 946; his widow, 883
Stephen
  Bartholomew, 423
  Geoffrey fitz, 302, 1012
Stepney (Stebenheth), Middx., 887; field of, 905
Stepranc, Ralph, 204, 1067
Stepynght
  Gregory de, 319
  John de, 319
Sterry (Stere, Sterre)
  John, 285, 305, 410
  Peter, 1040
  Robert & his widow, 770
Stertford, *see* Stortford
Stetter, Clement le, 811
Stevens, John, xi
Steward, *see* Byblesword, Hugh de
Steynton, John de, 712
Stocfysch, Benet, *alias* Trenchemer, 218–19, 1056–7
Stockfish Wharf, 219
Stockfishmonger, *see* Luke, Walter son of Luke; *and* Petipas, Henry
Stodey
  John, 446, 552
  William, 450
Stoktone (Stocton), Roger, 345, 374
Stokynbury, John, 939, 941
Ston
  Roger at, 233
  William at, 534; *see also* Londonstone
Stonor, John de, justice of king's bench, 742
Storme, Richard, 382, 480
Stortford (Stertford, Storteford)
  John, glover, 219–21
  Ralph, bishop of London, *see* Stratford
  Ralph de, glover, 272
Stoulard, William, 590
Stow (Stowe)
  John, xi
  John de, 896
  John de, potter, 715, 1038
  Robert, 843
  William, 843
Strangray, Walter, 132
Stratford Langthorne (Stratteford), Essex, abbot & convent of, 385, 612; *see also* Benet, abbot
Stratford-by-Bow (Stratteford), nuns of, 388, 464, 1004, 1020
Stratford (Stratteford)
  Constance de, 165–6, 191
  John, archbishop of Canterbury, 1046
  John de, 135, 166, 191
  Ralph (Stortford), bishop of London, 109

General Index

Strete, Walter, 755
Stroder, William, 229
Sturry (Storrey)
  Simon, 'catteler' [? cutler], 249
  William, 249
Stuuecle, Geoffrey & his widow, 350, 352
Subiria, Reginald de, 377–8
Subseye, Henry, 562
Suche, Alan la, warden of London, 889
Sudbury, Suffolk, college, of 354
Sudbury, Simon de, bishop of London, archbishop of Canterbury, 354, 958, 1005
Sudflete, Walter de, 248
Suething Benercheruer, 361
Suethinus, Huneman, 963
Suffolk (Southfolk, Suthfolchia, *etc.*)
  Alan de, potter, 904, 915, 917, 919; Agnes his daughter, 915; Agnes his wife, 917, 919
  Elias de, 600
  John de, 197, 250–2, 424; Agnes his wife, 197
  Osbert de, sheriff, 124, 716, 769, 890
  Reginald de, 447
  Robert de, cit., 436–7, 450
  William de, 45, 47–9, 52, 144, 346; Christine his daughter, 48
Sumd
  Nicholas, 590, 667
  Richard son of Nicholas, 667–8
Sumer (Sumeri), Ralph (de), 399–402; Emma his daughter, 401–2
Surgeon, *see* Oteswych, William de
Surrey, archdeacon of, *see* Robert
Suthcote, John, 418
Suthflite, Robert de, 380
Suthwerk
  Edward de, 871
  William son of Edward de, 871
Sutton, Henry de, 958
Swanne
  Henry atte, 566
  Thomas atte, & his widow, 347
Swetenote, Richard, 161–2
Swethmanus, 672
Swetyng, Matilda, 958
Swyft (Sweyft), Roger, butcher, 305–6
Symcok, Nicholas, attorney, 491
Symean, Symon, 203, 1066
Symon (Symond), John fitz, 123, 1040, 1059; *see also* Fysymon
Symson, Symon, 96
Syredus (Siredus), xiii–xiv, 1, 963, App. 1
Syward, *see* Siward

Tabur, Hugh, alderman, 714, 719
Tailhast, Richard, 783–4
Taillefer, William, marshal, 829–31
Tailor, *see* Alban; Edmund; Roger; Thomas; *and* Brunton, Henry; Kent, William de; Lynne, Ralph de; *see also* Taylor
Tailors, gild, 772; hall (Taillourshalle), 773
Talbot
  Henry, 153
  John, 446
Taliator (Tailiator, Talliator), *see* Walter; William; *and* Pappekertel, Richard
Tallage, exemption, 832, 998
Talper, Stephen, 903
Tamworth, Nicholas, 595
Tanner (Tannour, Tannur, *etc.*)
  Henry le, 157, 859
  Ralph le, 144
  Dr. Thomas, xi
  William, 901, 905, 913, 921
  see also Geoffrey; Kenutus; Ralph; Reginald; Richard; Stephen; *and* Blunt, Henry
Tanton, Henry de, & Geoffrey his son, 397
Tapicer, *see* Bullok, William
Tapisser, Ralph le, 294
Tathyngbury, William, 285
Tauers, *see* Travers
Taun, Geoffrey, 232
Tauntoft, John, 995
Taverne, Paul le, 309
Taverner, *see* Hale, William atte
Taverns, *see under* Houses
Taylor (Taillour, Tailur, *etc.*)
  Adam (the), 390–1; Denise his wife, 391
  Adam le, 414, 566
  Godmund, 556–7, 560, 563; Helen his wife, 557, 560
  John le, 322
  Nicholas, 954
  Peter & his widow, 907
  Philip, sheriff, 233, 447, 1008
  Walter, 458a
  William le, 558–9, 878, 1018
Temple, 239
Temple Bar (bar of the New Temple), 1082
Tenements, named, *see* Houses
Tenter-grounds, xx, 195, 292, 1060
Terricus, son of Edwin, the Felter, 199; *see also* John son of
Testard, John, clerk, 829
Tetesbury, John, cit. & skinner, 395, 398
Teuler, *see* Tuler
Teuredus, priest, 624
Teveresham
  John, 628
  William, 628
Tewald, goldsmith 78
Thames, river, 197, 218, 220, 222, 226, 871
Thames Street, 229, 398
Theiden
  Roger de, 62

Theiden, *continued*
  Wedde de, weaver, 62–3
Theobald
  alderman, 152; *see also* Ivo, Theobald fitz
  archbishop of Canterbury, 14, 973, 977, 980, App. 14
  capper, 35, 946
Theodoric
  moneyer, 624–5
  son of Deremanus, 963
Thiep, Ighanne, 950
Thirlewell, William, 480
Thodyngton, William, *alias* Dodenham, 712
Tholusan, *see* Tulesan
Thomas
  alderman, 1008
  bishop of Exeter, *see* Brantingham
  chaplain, 906; [another], 961, 976
  chaplain of the hospital of St. Bartholomew, 827
  junior, 863
  master of the hospital of St. Katherine, 992
  Master, of Bread Street, 920
  of Woodstock, earl of Buckingham, 1005
  parmenter, 40
  priest, Alice daughter of, 1024
  priest, *see* Sherehog
  saddler, 148–9, 152; Alice his wife, 152
  son of Adrian, 395
  tailor, 37, 144, 906; [? another], 461
Thomas (Thomas fitz Richard), Thomas (fitz, son of), 1018; alderman, 604; mayor, 124, 129, 530, 535, 716, 769, 785, 890; sheriff, 32, 512
Thormeston, William, de, 1005
Thorneye, William de, sheriff, 351, 713
Thorp, John (de), 677, 682
Thotech, Gilbert de, 991
Thotenhale, Simon de, 1038
Thotenham, *see* Totenham
Thourswey, John, 278
'Threleggs, le', shop called, 525
Thrisse, William, 1004
Throcking (Trockyng), Herts., 1004
Thunderle. Roger de, 455
Tiler, *see* Alfred; Peter; Roger; Simon; *and* Joye, Robert; *see also* Tuler
Tilteye
  Geoffrey son of Maurice, 79
  Maurice, sheriff, 78–80
Tilty (Tiltey), Essex, monks of, 80, 639
Timberhithe (Tymbheth), 604
Tiptoft (Tiptot). Lord, 80
Tiryton, Richard, 651
Tithes, on mill and gardens, 991
Tiulfus, canon of St. Martin [? le Grand], 967

Toki (Toky)
  Richard, 321, 324, 370
  Stephen son of, 271
Tolosan, *see* Tulesan
Toltrich, Henry, dubber, 426–7; his widow, 427
Tonyl, Michael, warden of the Bridge, 751
Toom, Roger, 1024
Toppesfeld (Toppisfeld, Topusfeld)
  John, 815
  Thomas, 833, 846
Torks, John, 289
Torneis (Tornes), Osbert, 609, 644
Torold, *see* Turold
Torold, Roger, 436
Tortington (Tortyngtone), Sussex, garden of the prior of, 427; priory of, 1005
Totenham (Thotenham)
  Gilbert de, potter, 955
  John de, 377; [another], 772
Totham
  Helewisa (?), 506, 513
  Katherine, 506
  William, 504–6, 512–13; Margery his wife, 505; Christine his daughter, 505
Tothill, abbot of, 258
Tottenham (Totenham), Middx., church of, 13, App. 13; brothers at, 986
Totynge, John de, 6th prior of Holy Trinity, 18, 32, 82, 88, 139, 146, 154, 159, 169, 190, 259, 329, 389, 476, 501, 504, 508, 510, 512, 515, 516, 517, 596, 616, 641, 667, 668, 730, 731, 756, 765, 792, 794, 795, 797, 832, 893, 981, 986, 1016, 1021
Tour (Toure, Tours)
  John de, 691, 701
  John de la, 215; *see also* Turri
Tourstrate, *see* Tower Street
Tovy (Tovi)
  Michael, mayor, 189, 213, 501, 756, 818
  Walter, 899
Tower Hill, 958; mill on, 975–6, 980
Tower of London, xiii, 11, 32, 33, 35, 39, 66, 871, 898, 959, 962, App. 11; constable, *see* Hocton, Hugh fitz; 'Cungate', 11, App. 11; custodian, *see* Othwerus; new ditch, 871; vineyard near, 972; wall, 871
Tower Street (Tourstrate), 215
Travaill (Trauill)
  John, 943, 946
  William, of Pulloxhill, 943–4
Travers (Tauers)
  John, alderman & sheriff, 142, 331, 336, 366, 371–2, 545–8, 566, 641, 718–20, 744–5, 1073; Margery his daughter, 547, 549
  Walter, goldsmith, 658
  William, 963

General Index

Trayer, *see* Treyer
Traynell (Traynyll)
  John, brewer, 272
  William, sheriff's officer, 491
Trehur, Adam le, 276–8; Alice his wife, 276–7
Trenchemer, *see* Stocfysch
Trenowthe, John, 472
Trentmars (Trentemarse, Trentemare)
  Edmund son of Walter, 877, 890–1, 899, 904, 913, 921, 928, 936–7, 955
  Geoffrey son of Susan, 930, 933, 936, 938, 950
  Mundekinus, 889
  Osbert, 935–6
  Susan, 181, 183, 936
  Walter, 880, 912, 923, 927, 936, 945
Tresgoz, Mabel de, 700
Tresse, William, 303
Tretheck, William, 647–8
Trey, Ralph, 584
Treyer (Trayer, Tryer)
  Adam le, 870
  Alexander le, 323, 939
  Edmund le, 286
  Ranulf le, 586
  Robert le, 255
Trie, *see* Trye
Triket
  Hugh, 1004
  Ralph, 1004
Triple (Tripyl, Tryple)
  John (de), cit. & fishmonger, 354, 356, 579–80; Katherine his wife, 580
  William, 588
Tristour (Tristur), William, 330, 642
Trockyng, *see* Throcking, Herts.
Trompton (Trumpton, Trumpynton)
  Alice, 799, 909
  John, 799
Tropinell, Robert, 264, 267–8
Trye (Trie)
  Geoffrey & Idoena his widow, 378
  Jeremiah de, 436–7
  Peter de, 435–6, 1019
Tryer *see* Treyer
Tryp, Nicholas, girdler, 289
Tudenham, Walter, 772
Tuler (Teuler), Solomon le, 920, 955
Tulesan (Tholusan, Tolosan, *etc.*)
  John (de), mayor, 189, 259, 467, 489, 517, 764, 792; sheriff, 218, 327, 720, 1056
  Michael (le), 380, 1014
Turbernus Arconerus, 178
Turbertus, 902, 948–9
Turg (Turgis), Maurice, 94, 98
Turgisius, 624, 812, 933
Turgund, servant, 171
Turk
  Andrew, 219, 298, 313, 1057

Godwin, 227, 1055
  Master John, 815
Turnour
  John le, 881
  Keneward, *see* Keneward
  Robert son of John le, 881, 894, 896, 925; his widow, 881, 894
  William & Margaret his widow, 242–3
Turold (Torold)
  carpenter, 726
  shoemaker, (miscalled Corold), 663, 665
Turri (Ture, Turre, *etc.*)
  John son of Jordan, de 200
  Jordan de, clerk, 186, 199–200
  Nicholas de, 93
  Robert de, 164, 178, 186, 190, 200
  Roger de (la), 189, 291
  Master William de, cit., 189–90, 615–16
  see also Tour
Twyer, Robert, 480
Twyford
  John, 498
  Nicholas, 498, 645
Tykyl, Thomas, 85, 87, 89, 92
Tymbheth, *see* Timberhithe
Tynbeter, Richard, 725
Tywe, John, 751

Uggel, William, 1004
Uherst, *see* Ewhurst
Unbarrio, Solomon, 404
Unctor, *see* Michael
Underwode
  Roger, 896
  William, 911, 919; his widow, 911
Upchirch, Hugh, fishmonger, 586–7
Upton
  Stephen, 566
  Stephen de, 566
Usurer, *see* Ralph (& Goda his wife)

Valener, *see* Walerant
Valensi, *see* Waleys
Vannere
  John, 309
  Simon le, 323
  Walter, 309
Vantot, Richard, 502
Vaux (de Vallibus), John, 72
Veisin (Versin, Vicinus), William, 235–6, 993, 1025–6
Venella, *see* Lane
Venour, William, 454
Ver
  Aubrey (Albericus) de, earl of Oxford, & his wife, 969
  Aubrey (Albericus) de, sheriff, 12, 871, 960, 1072, App. 12
  Robert de, 973, 1005

General Index

Verhierde, Geoffrey, 1026
Versin, *see* Veisin
Very, Peter atte, 219
Viel (Viell, Vital, *etc.*)
   John (I), 629; alderman, 584; sheriff, 442–3, 993, 1073
   John (II) son of John (son of), sheriff, 571, 1019
   John (?III), junior, 498; Isabel his daughter, 498
   John (?IV), 597
   William (le), 596–7, 615–16; sheriff, 818
Vileine (Vileyn, Vyleyn)
   Denise la, 584
   Geoffrey, 783, 785
   William (le), 782
Vinea, Roger de, 552
Vineyard, *see* Tower of London
Vintner, *see* David son of Ralph; Edward; Geoffrey; Joce; Osmund; Ralph; *and* Chaucer, John; Conductu, Thomas de; More, William; Sadeler, John; Walworth, John
Vintry (Vyntery), 432, 449
Virly, *alias* Plommer, Denise, 405, 801
Vital, *see* Viel
Viterbo, Italy, 981
Vyndines, Bartholomew, 566
Vyne
   Alice atte, 365
   Isabel atte, 212
   Matilda atte, 370, 373
   Peter atte, 958
Vynent, John, 600
Vyntery, *see* Vintry
Vynur (Vinor), John (le), sheriff, 893, 923

W., chaplain of Henry de Castell, 546
Wade, John, sheriff, 131, 221
Waffrer (Gofair, Gofairer)
   Elias, cit., 417–18
   John (le), 134–5, 748
   Matilda, 748
Wakefeld
   John, 117–18, 188
   William, 421
Wakle, John, 768
Walbrok, Richard de, alderman, 716
Walbrook, 441, 447, 451, 465; ditch of, 785
Walclive, William de, 595
Walcreth, Adam, 595
Waldegrave, Henry de, 575
Walden
   Herman de, 783
   John, 682
   Thomas, 203, 755, 1066
   Walter, 755
Waldeschef (Waldesshef), Walter, 440, 745
Wale, Henry, 777

Walerant (Valener, Walemunt)
   Henry de, sheriff, 146, 355, 832
   William, 428
Waleton (Waketone, Walecune), Gilbert de, 527–8
Waleys (Galeys, Valensi, Walense, *etc.*)
   Augustine le, *alias* de Woxbrigge, 48, 51, 54, 815; Matilda his wife, 54
   Henry (le), 71–3, 447, 631, 641; mayor, 47, 322, 425, 567; sheriff, 60, 292, 369, 684, 864, 905, 916
   John, 527, 529
   Richard, 747–8, 751, 811, 1004
   Robert, 64
   Roger, 977
   Walter le, 631
   William le, 913–16
Walflet, Robert de, 1052
Walkelinus, 963
Walkote, John, 395, 496; his widow, 496
Wall (Walle)
   John atte, capper, 132–3, 175, 188
   William atte, 309
Walraven, John, sheriff, 1073
Walter
   alderman, 199
   canon of Holy Trinity, 968; ? sub-prior, 970
   carter, 91, 281
   chaplain, 202
   chaplain of St. Alphege, 678
   cordwainer, & Avice his wife, 458a
   deacon, 729
   dean of Waltham, 3, App. 3
   glover, 458a, 510
   goldsmith, 210; *alias* Black, 645, 1059
   hosier, 157
   priest, 456
   saddler, 860
   ? shoemaker (*calcearius*), 372
   son of Ailred, 848–9
   son of Baldwin, 461
   son of Edmund son of Gerard, 744
   son of James, goldsmith, 1012
   son of Luke, stockfishmonger, 254–5
   son of Simon, 383, 736
   sub-prior of Holy Trinity, 970
   'Talliator', 1015
   whittawer, 69
   woolmonger, 472
Walter, Richard (fitz, son of) alderman, 84, 501
Waltham, Essex, abbey of Holy Cross, 192, 235, 239, 870; church, 3, 1004, 1072, App. 2, 3, 4; dean, *see* Walter; dean & chapter, xiii, 1, App. 1
Waltham (Wautham)
   Felicia wife of John de, 1035
   Master Henry de, & Nigra his wife, 372
   Hugh de, 347

General Index

Joan de, 33
John de, 82–4, 260, 800
Moses de, 798–801; Katherine his wife, 798, 800–1
Stephen de, 33, 1033
Thomas, 33
William de, & Ellen his wife, 920, 955
William de, chamberlain, 335
Walthamstow (Welcomstowe), Essex, brothers at, 986; church of, 13, App. 13
Walworth
  John, vintner, 235
  William, 224, 664, 1052
Wandegos, Benet, 859
Wandelworth
  Robert, 242
  Stephen, 659
Want (Gant, Wanter, Waunter)
  Godfrey le, 139–41
  Odelina widow of William le, 814–15
  William le, 58–60; *see also* Glover
Warde, Edmund, alderman, 963; *see also* Edmund, alderman
Wardon, William de, 1033
Wardrobe, William of the, *see* Ragton
Ware, Herts., prior of, 124–5, 802
Ware
  Adam de, 719
  John de, 309
  John de, *alias* de Woodford, 482
  Nicholas de, 88–9
  Thomas (de), 488, 490
Warefeld, John, 1033
Warelwast, Robert, bishop of Exeter, 973
Wares, John de, 800
Warin
  brother [? of Holy Trinity], 828
  chaplain (priest), 676–7
  son of Gerold, 962
Warino, Rigero, 270
Warner, John, 367–8
Warwick, earls of, *see* Beauchamp
Wastel
  Laurence, 488
  William, 883, 896, 925, 928; his widow, 883, 928
Wateman, Thomas, 259
Water, John at, 901
Waterden, Richard, rent collector of Holy Trinity, 996
Wateladere
  Geoffrey (le), 938, 949–50, 958
  Robert (le), son of Goldyng, 946–7, 951
Watford (Watteford)
  Robert de, dean of St. Paul's, 620
  William de, 83
Watling Street, 639
Watton, Stephen de, 10th prior of Holy Trinity, 22, 72–3, 109n, 709, 711

Wauch, John, 493
Wax candles, 834, 843
Waye, *see* Weye
Wayte, Stephen le, 1004
Weaver, *see* Roger; Simon; *and* Duke, Roger; Theiden, Wedde de
Webbe, William, 896
Wedde (Weddes), Mabel, 58, 63
Wedford, John de, skinner, 61
Wedon, William, 805
Wedyngdon, Robert, 364
Welcomstowe, *see* Walthamstow, Essex
Welford, Richard de, sheriff, 99
Well, Geoffrey atte, 72
Welles (Wellis, Wellys)
  John de, 46
  Thomas, draper, 364
  William de, 888
Weluby, Margery, 454
Wendene, Stephen (de), clerk, 911–12
Wendleswurth, Stephen de, goldsmith, 1012
Wengrave, John de, mayor, 563
Wenlock, Salop, prior of, 791, 795–6, *see also* Henry
Wenne, John, 450
Wenton
  Richard de, 485
  Robert de, 122
Weseby, Richard de, 830
West Fish Market, *see* Old Fish Market; Old Fish Street
West Ham, Essex, 1015
  ? 'Holecuhame' near Pikeshoc mill, 1015
  ? 'Luymudhe', piece of land next Luiam, 1015
West Smithfield, bar of, 842
Westchepe, *see* Cheapside
Westmelle (Westmeln', Westmyll, *etc.*)
  Agnes, 677
  Giles, 46, 83
  Michael de, & Alice his widow, 684
  Richard de, 946
  Robert, 562
  William, 838
Westmill (Westmelne), Hert 1094
Westminster, Middx., 4, 874, 1005, App. 4
  abbot & convent of, 218, 231, 354, 401, 428, 509, 1035
  chapel, dean of, 332
  chapel of the sick, 970
  church of, 13, App. 13
  hospital of St. James, 529, 1024
  parish of St. Clement Danes, 1028
  plea held at, 982
  soke of St. Martin in the Fields, 641
Westminster, Edward of, baron of the Exchequer, 982
Weston
  John, 235, 350

General Index

Weston, *continued*
  Nicholas de, 407
  Peter (de), cit. & potter, 36, 40, 799, 909, 929, 1038
  William, master draper, 427, 480
Westwode
  Eustace, 922
  John, 735
'Weuel atte Stone', tenement called, 1040; *see also* 'Wyvelastone'
Weyder, Alan (le), 447, 1010
Weye (Waye), Richard atte, baker, *alias* atte Basket, 40, 1038
Whaplode, Robert, churchwarden of St. Margaret Fish Street Hill, 287
Whetele, William, 175
White (Whyte)
  Hugh, *see* Blunt, Hugh
  Nicholas, 490
  Ralph, 270
  William, 431, 485, 692, 1022
White Friars (of Mount Carmel), 1033
Whitechapel, parish of St. Mary, field & garden of, 957; *see also* Hog Lane
Whitingham, Robert, sheriff, 418
Whittawer, *see* Alexander; Gilbert; Richard; Walter; William; *and* Cestrehunt, Edward de; Halsted, Asketin; Littlinton, Edward de; *see also* Meguzer
Whittington, *see* Whytington
Whytby (Whyteby)
  Adam, sheriff, 1073
  John, rector of St. Mary Abchurch, 374
Whyte, *see* White
Whytebred, John, 480
Whythed, Thomas, rector of St. Michael Cornhill, 374
Whytington (Whytendon, Whytinton), Richard, 418–19, 440, 446–7n; escheator, 1049–50; mayor, 418, 1049
Whytsand, Heluisa de, 808
Wicera, 271
Widihale, *see* Wyddial, Herts.
Wifladeston, *see* Wyvelastone
Wiganus de Arcubus, 714–15; his daughter, 715
Wilbertus, 236
Wileby, Thomas de, 993
Wilemy, John, of Gracechurch, 787
Wilford (Wylford), Thomas, 203, 1066
Wilihale, *see* Wirhale
Wilkyn (Wilekin, Wylekyn)
  Thomas son of William, 372
  William, 318, 320, 325, 329, 331; alderman, 1013; woolmonger, 717; Amice (Avice) his daughter, 318, 320, 406, 1013
William I, king, 1005, 1072, App. 1
William II, king, 871, 1005, 1072

William, son of King Stephen, 976
William
  abbot of Osney, 425
  archdeacon of London, *see* Belmeis, William de (I)
  armiger, 423, 902
  baker, 529, 676; *see also* Berkyng, William
  bell-ringer, 812
  bishop of Durham, 2, App. 2
  bishop of Norwich, 973
  brother of Gozo, 497
  bureller, father of Agnes, 903
  butcher, 272
  chaplain of St. Botolph [Bishopsgate], 860
  chaplain of the Bailey, 148
  chaplain of Wood Street [St. Peter Westcheap], 1027
  clerk, 62; [another], 871, 963
  cook, son of Jordan, & John his son, 682
  de Infirmorio, 136
  father of Agnes, 142–3, 151
  father of Amice, 406
  glazier, 840, 1021
  goldsmith, brother of Godard, 672
  king's baker, 255
  mason, 68, 92; Hawise his daughter, 68, 71
  nephew of Keneward, 902–3
  of the Wardrobe, *see* Ragton
  palmer, son of Osmund, 790–1
  preceptor, 828
  priest, 226, ? 948, 1054; [another], 871; [another], 919
  priest of Sherehog, 400
  ? prior of Holy Trinity, xv
  rector of St. Lawrence [? Pountney], 431
  saltmonger, 726
  shoemaker, 920, 955
  son of Alice, sheriff, 1073
  son of Arnulph, sheriff, 1073
  son of Benet, *see* Benet
  son of Godmund the Mercer, 123, 126–7
  son of Haldenus, 185
  son of Isabel, sheriff, 654–5, 759, 1072–3; Denise his wife, 655
  son of Nicholas, 270
  son of Ralph the Justiciar, & Denise his wife, 1018
  son of Ralph the Vintner, 497
  son of Richard, *see* Richard
  son of Roger, 389, 765, 1016
  son of Sabeline, 704, 1012, 1024
  son of the priest, 856
  son of Wido, 962
  son of William, 761
  son of Wolfinus, 807
'Taliator', 1022

General Index

Vicinus, *see* Veisin
whittawer, & his widow, 929
William, Martin (fitz, son of, son of Isabel), sheriff, 283, 548, 759, 761
Wills, *see* Legal matters
Wiltshyr
  John, cit. & pepperer, 417–18; Alice his wife, 418
  Richard, 417–18
Wiluby, *see* Wylughby
Wimburn (Bunburne, Wymborne, *etc.*)
  Gilbert de, 912
  Robert, 454
  Thomas de, 905; alderman, 912; sheriff, 189, 259, 489, 517, 764, 792; 'sockener' of the soke, 880; soke reeve, 945
Wimundus, priest, 963
Winchester
  bishop of, 1001; *see also* Gyffard, William; Ilchester, Richard of
  burial of William II at, 1072
Winchester (Wynchestre, Wynton *etc.*)
  Adrian de, 396–7
  Geoffrey de, alderman, 745, 1016
  John de, 409, 664
  Miles de, 255
  Nicholas de, alderman, 378; sheriff, 322, 451; [? another], 547
  Philip de, 493–4
  Ralph de, 680
  Richard of, sheriff, 1073
  Robert de, 94, 485
  Simon de (de Wirencestre), baker, 245–6
  Thomas son of Adrian de, 395, 407
  Walter de, sheriff, 856
  William de, 210, 1059
Winchester Seld (Wynchestreselde), 437
Windeleshores, Alfred de, 1024
Wine, London sextaries of, 41–1054 *passim*
Winter (Wint')
  Andrew, 69, 71; Amabilla his wife, 71
  Richard, sawyer, 69, 71–2; Amabilla formerly his wife, 71
  William, 404
Wircestre, William de, sheriff, 410
Wirencestre, Simon de, *see under* Winchester
Wirhale (Wilhal, Wilihale, Wyrehall, *etc.*)
  John son of William, 534, 638–9, 641, 645
  Richard de, 436, 446–7, 488; Joan his wife, 447, 639
  Richard son of Richard, 446, 454, 639, 645
  William (de), 501, 530–1, 533, 536
  William brother of John, 641
  William son of William, 642
Wiryng, John, 954
Wiskard, Richard, 944
Withulfus (Witthulfus), priest of St. Botolph [Aldgate], 964, 968

Wizo, son of Leofstan the goldsmith, 871
Wlfred, *see* Wulfred
Wlfric, *see* Wulfric
Wlgar, *see* Wulgar
Wlmer, *see* Wulmar
Wlnardus, *see* Wulnard
Wlpsus, *see* Wulpus
Wlwinus, *see* Wulwin
Woburn (Woburnia, Wuburne)
  John de, 645, 826
  Nicholas de, 645
  Robert de, 64
  Roger de, 842
Wodcok (Wodecok)
  John, 461
  John, cit. & mercer, 518, 525
Wodegate (Wodgate), John, 123, 597
Wodehous (Wodhous, Woudhous)
  Robert, 227, 1055
  Thomas, 350
  William, skinner, 350, 352
Wodekot, Alan de, 476–7
Wodeleye, John de, sheriff, 344
Wodemongere, Pentecost le, 250
Wodeward (Wodward), William, founder, 909, 954, 995–6
Wodirton, Edward, 405
Wolcomstowe (Welcomstowe), John de, potter, 896, 925; Constance his wife, 925
Wolf (Lupus, Wolfe, Wolffe)
  Gilbert, 427
  Martin, 203
  Matilda, le 201
  Ralph, 350
  Walter, 350
Wolfinus Grand, 807–8; his sons, *see* Richard; William
Wolmere, Richard, 246
Wood Street, 650, 661, 663–4
Woodford, John de, *see* Ware
Woodstock, Oxon., 875
Woodstock, Thomas of, earl of Buckingham, *see* Thomas
Wool, in the king's hands, 1040
Woolchurchehawe, *see* Hamme, William
Woolmonger, *see* Osbert; Simon; Walter; *and* Hackney, Robert de; Hamme, William; Moigne, William; Sharp, John; Wilkyn, William
Wordon, William, 132
Wortham, *see* Wrotham
Worthyn, John, 995
Wotton, Nicholas, sheriff, 290
Wouderovelane, *see* Cooper's Row
Woxbrigge, Augustine de, *see* Waleys, Augustine le
Wrestelyngworth, John de, 477–8; Juliana his wife, 478

General Index

Wretyl (Wretele, Writele)
  John, 815
  Robert, 123
  Walter de, 457
Wroth, William de, 395
Wrotham (Wortham, Wroth)
  John, mayor, 285, 309
  John de, & his widow, 235, 382
  Robert de, 213
  William de, 252
Wuburne, *see* Woburn
Wudeham, Reginald de, 1052
Wulfgar, 'portshyreve' of London under Edward the Confessor, 1072
Wulfred (Wlfred), 960
Wulfric (Wlfric), 960
  butcher, 960
Wulgar (Wlgar), 185; *see also* Hugh, son of
Wulmar (Wlmer, Wulonar)
  baker, 115
  son of Edward of Essex, 197, 255
Wulnard (Wlunardus), 850
  'le Douerisshe', 871
Wulpsus (Wlpsus), smith, 960
Wulsun, bridge of, gate of Thames at, 222
Wulwin (Wlwinus), abbot, 960
Wurthing, carpenter, 950
Wyddial (Widihale), Herts., 1004
Wydmere, John, 636
Wygot (Wygod), mercer, 283, 1010
Wyke, William atte, 922
Wyle, William at, & his widow, 839
Wylenhale, John de, 1018
Wylughby (Wiluby), Richard, 833, 846
Wylymyn, Master John, 'ferrour', 334
Wymborne *see* Wimburn
Wymbulden, Richard, sheriff, 1073
Wymbyssh (Wymbisch), Richard (de), 12th prior of Holy Trinity, 24, 57, 165, 187, 205, 265, 722, 742, 1068; canon of Holy Trinity, 237
Wymond (Wymund), Henry, 172, 174; his sister, 172
Wymondyswold (Wymonyswold), William de, 130, 133
Wympler
  Alan & Beatrice his widow, 664–5
  Henry (le), 755
Wymundham, Peter, 418
Wynchestre, *see* Winchester
Wynchestreselde, *see* Winchester Seld

Wyndesor (Wyndlesores)
  Godfrey de, *alias* Draper, 644–5
  Robert de, 642
Wyndrawere (Windraker), Adam le, & Alice his wife, 920, 955
Wynfrid, king, 1072
Wyngeham, Henry de, bishop of London, 986–7
Wynnok, William, 277
Wynton, *see* Winchester
Wyrehall, *see* Wirhale
Wysbech (Wysebech), Peter, chaplain, 117–19
Wysset, William, 155
Wyssingshed, John, 659, 661
Wyte, *see* White
Wythe, Walter le, sheriff, 131
Wyvelastone (Wifladeston, Wyvelaston), land near, 199; street by the Tower against, 1060; street opposite, 195; *see also* Weuel atte Stone

Ydonia, 572
Yford (Yfford)
  William, 735
  William de, 735
Yhope, John, 944
Yngs, William, 229
Yonge
  John, 414–15
  Thomas son of John, 414–15
York, archbishop of, *see* Kempe, John, bishop of London
You
  John, 260
  Robert & his widow, 260
Youn, Robert, *see* Barber
Ypres (Ypre)
  John, 562
  William de, 961, 973, 977–8, 980
Yreis
  Hugh le, 842
  William, 1024
Yrlond, *see* Irland
Ysle, *see* Isele
Ysmongerslane, *see* Ironmonger Lane
Yue, John, rector of St. Michael Wood Street, 1042
Yvory, *see* Ivory
Yweyn, John, 475

Zadelyngstanes, Hugh de & his widow, 645
Zakary, goldsmith, 673
Zakarye, Benet, 562

LONDON RECORD SOCIETY

The London Record Society was founded in December 1964 to publish transcripts, abstracts and lists of the primary sources for the history of London, and generally to stimulate interest in archives relating to London. Membership is open to any individual or institution, the annual subscription is £3·15, which entitles a member to receive one copy of each volume published during the year and to attend and vote at meetings of the Society. Prospective members should apply to the Hon. Secretary, Mr Brian Burch, c/o Leicester University Library, University Road, Leicester.

The following volumes have already been published:
1. *London possessory assizes: a calendar*, edited by Helena M. Chew (1965)
2. *London inhabitants within the Walls, 1695*, with an introduction by D. V. Glass (1966)
3. *London Consistory Court wills, 1492–1547*, edited by Ida Darlington (1967)
4. *Scriveners' Company Common Paper, 1357–1628, with a continuation to 1678*, edited by Francis W. Steer (1968)
5. *London Radicalism, 1830–1843: a selection from the papers of Francis Place*, edited by D. J. Rowe (1970)
6. *The London Eyre of 1244*, edited by Helena M. Chew and Martin Weinbaum (1970)

Price: to members £3·15 each, and to non-members £3·75 each.

The following Occasional Publication is also available:
London and Middlesex Published Records, compiled by J. M. Sims (1970)
Price: free to members, and to non-members £1.

A leaflet describing some of the volumes in preparation may be obtained from the Hon. Secretary.